17-SC

Priest, Politics and Society in Post famine Ireland

Series
Topics in Modern Irish History
General Editor: R. V. Comerford

Published
Priest, Politics and Society in Post-famine Ireland
A Study of County Tipperary, 1850-1891
James O'Shea

Towards a National University: William Delaney S.J.
(1835-1924) and an Era of Initiative in Irish Education
Thomas Morrissey S.J.

In Preparation
The Context of Fenianism: Irish Politics and Society, 1848-1880
R. V. Comerford
The Moulds of Nationalism: A Comparative Study of Irish
Political Movements 1800-1921
H. Van Der Wusten

Priest, Politics and Society in Post-famine Ireland

*A study of County Tipperary 1850*1891*

JAMES O'SHEA

WOLFHOUND PRESS: Dublin

HUMANITIES PRESS: New Jersey

First published by
WOLFHOUND PRESS
68 Mountjoy Square
Dublin 1.

and published in the United States of America by
HUMANITIES PRESS, Inc
Atlantic Highlands,
New Jersey, 07716.

British Library Cataloguing in Publication Data
O'Shea, James
The priest, society and politics
in nineteenth century Ireland.
1. Tipperary, Ireland (county) — History — 19th century
I. Title
941.7081   DA950

ISBN 0-905473-71-X WOLFHOUND PRESS

ISBN 0-391-02974-6 HUMANITIES PRESS

Cover design by Jarlath Hayes.
Typeset by Print Prep (Ireland) Ltd.
Printed in Great Britain.

Contents

MAPS

ILLUSTRATIONS & PORTRAITS

LIST OF TABLES (Pages 306 – 325)

ABBREVIATIONS

A.H.R.	*American Historical Review*
C.	Archdiocese of Cashel and Emly
C.C.	*Clonmel Chronicle*
C.D.A., B.P.	Cashel Diocesan Archives, Bray papers
C.D.A., C.P.	Cashel Diocesan Archives, Croke papers
C.D.A., L.P.	Cashel Diocesan Archives, Leahy papers
C.D.A., S.P.	Cashel Diocesan Archives, Slattery papers
C.E.	*Cork Examiner*
C.G.	*Cashel Gazette*
D.D.A., C.P.	Dublin Diocesan Archives, Cullen papers
D.D.A., McC.	Dublin Diocesan Archives, McCabe papers
D.D.A., W.P.	Dublin Diocesan Archives, Walsh papers
D.U.M.	*Dublin University Magazine*
F.J.	*Freeman's Journal*
H.C.S.A.	Habeus Corpus Suspension Act files, Dublin Castle
I.C.D.	*Irish Catholic Directory*
I.E.R.	*Irish Ecclesiastical Record*
I.H.S.	*Irish Historical Studies*
I.N.L.	Irish National League
I.N.L.L.	Irish National Land League (Land League)
I.P.	*Irish People*
I.T.	*Irish Times*
K.	Diocese of Killaloe
K.P.	Kirby papers, Irish College Rome
L.L.L.	Ladies Land League
L.R.	*Limerick Reporter*
M.T.	*Midland Tribune*
N.L.I.	National Library of Ireland
N.G.	*Nenagh Guardian*
P.L.G.	Poor Law guardian
P.L.U.	Poor Law union
S.C., Irlanda	Archives of Propaganda (Rome), Scritture riferite nei congressi, Irlanda
S.P.O., C.S.O., R.P.	State Paper Office (Dublin Castle) Chief Secretary's Office, registered papers
S.P.O., C.B.S. D.I.C.	State Paper Office, Crime branch special, divisional reports
S.P.O., F.P.	State Paper Office, police and crime records, fenian papers
S.P.O., O.R.	State Paper Office, police crime records, outrage papers
T.A.	*Tipperary Advocate*
T.F.P.	*Tipperary Free Press*
T.L.	*Tipperary Leader*
T.N.	*Tipperary Nationalist*
T.P.	*Tipperary People*
T.S.	*Tipperary Star*
U.I.	*United Ireland*
W.	Diocese of Waterford and Lismore
W.D.A.	Waterford Diocesan Archives

Ireland — counties and provinces — with the dioceses of County Tipperary super-imposed.

Shadowing the Shadows. 'Fac-simile of the instantaneous Photograph taken by Mr. P. O'Brien, M.P., of Father Humphries in the streets of Tipperary, closely attended by his two Shadows in uniform.' See Chapter 4. (*United Ireland* 12.7.1890).

Foreword

Today, the catholics of Ireland are accustomed to large colourful churches equipped with baptismal fonts, confessionals, bright lights, comfortable seats and perhaps the pleasant sound of folk-hymns at mass. Despite a perceptible wind of change among city inhabitants, regular attendance at mass and the sacraments is accepted by most Irish people as the norm. Contact with their ministers of religion is generally confined to a brief encounter at the altar-rails, a few moments in confession, an occasional visit to a sick member of the family or an annual pastoral visit.

Things were very different 130 years ago. Although there was a vigorous programme of church-building in pre-famine years, ecclesiastical decor as we know it was largely absent. It was only in the mid-1850s that baptismal fonts and confessionals were introduced in many places, and seating accommodation was gradually provided throughout the remainder of the century. But the most startling difference lay in the relationship between the priests and their flocks. This was forged not only as a response to religious needs but also to the social, economic and political circumstances peculiar to the nineteenth century.

The relationship was a many-sided and interestingly open one, with frequent and close contact between priest and laity. Religious communication was more often made in the homes of the people than in the chapel at a time when the stations were an important ingredient in formal religious practice. This was partly a hangover from penal days. Socially the priests had a strong affinity with the tenant farming class from which they were largely drawn. This in turn engaged their sympathy with the economic difficulties of the tenants, a sympathy which took the form of political activity. Political involvement, however, was far more comprehensive than agrarian agitation.

The presence of priests on public political platforms was not only a most conspicuous sign of the bond between themselves and their

9

parishoners, it was also an ingredient which significantly contributed to the frankness of the mutual relationship, not always perhaps in the interests of religion. This book hopes to clarify that fascinating relationship and to pinpoint the degree of influence and power wielded by the priest in the society of the period 1850 to 1891. This particular span was chosen because 1850 saw the convening of the great national synod in Thurles, the first for centuries, and from the social point of view witnessed the beginning of post-famine land agitation in the form of the Tenant League. The year 1891 saw the death of Charles Stewart Parnell with the resulting destruction of the popular movement, the National League.

County Tipperary is the location of the study. This is partly due to the availability of well-organised and catalogued archival material for the archdiocese of Cashel and Emly of a type not generally available elsewhere in Ireland. Consequently the book provides analyses and conclusions of a kind not often heretofore possible. As well as this, as will be seen, Tipperary people were politically highly volatile.

Tipperary, a large county of 1,061,731 statute acres, straddles the south-midlands of Ireland and stretches from the border of Galway in the west to the border of Waterford in the south-east. By any standards it was a wealthy county and had a population of comfortable farmers who were able and willing to contribute to the support of their pastors. Seventy-eight per cent of its parishes contained the valuable dry mineral and organic soils.[1] The remainder was of a poorer quality. Much of this, however, was suitable for grazing, though in mountain areas it tended to correlate with smaller farms. The 1851 census classification of 82.9% of its land as arable is reasonably accurate.[2]

As in the rest of Ireland the population of Tipperary suffered a serious decline in the second half of the nineteenth century. In 1851 it stood at 331,567 people, having decreased by over 103,986 since 1841. By 1891 it stood at a mere 173,188 or a little over half the population of mid-century. Indeed the decline was even more drastic in certain areas of the county. On average 94% of the population was Roman Catholic.

The religious needs of these catholics were catered for through the basic administrative unit of their church, the parish. Apart from the amalgamation of Bansha and Kilmoyler parishes in 1852 and the occasional realignment of townlands, the pattern of the county's parochial network was settled by mid-century. Altogether Tipperary had 64 parishes, 35 of which belonged to the archdiocese of Cashel and Emly, 17 to Waterford and Lismore, and 12 to Killaloe. These dioceses straddled the county boundary and sometimes parishes themselves projected into adjoining counties. The catholic parishes of the nineteenth century often had two or more churches or chapels as they were called. These were indicative of the old administrative structure of smaller mainly pre-reformation parishes. Following the reformation the latter became the official administrative units of the protestant church and were henceforth labelled civil parishes. Some catholic parishes of the nineteenth century were composed of as many as three of the older units. These civil parishes are not really relevant to this book except insofar as they formed natural organisational units for various political or semi-political movements. *Pobal Ailbe*, the census of Cashel and Emly, frequently referred to later in the book, has an excellent map showing the superimposition of the older upon the later parishes.

The overall parish network in the county came under the authority of the archbishop of Cashel and Emly, the bishop of Waterford and the bishop of Killaloe. The episcopal seat for Cashel and Emly was Thurles, situated in mid-Tipperary, that for Waterford was the city of Waterford, while the bishop of Killaloe lived in Nenagh in north Tipperary until the mid 1860s when he transferred to Killaloe, Co. Clare; finally in the early 1890s he moved to Ennis, Co. Clare. As regards civil administration, Nenagh was the capital of the North Riding of the county and Clonmel was that of the South Riding.

From 1850 to 1891 the parishes were administered by no less than 575 secular priests, 246 (43%) being in Cashel, 166 (29%) in Killaloe and 163 (28%) in Waterford. Only 247 or 43% of these are known to have been born in Tipperary itself; 148 (26%) came from other counties, mainly Clare, Limerick and Waterford; 180 (31%) could not be traced. Biographical details of these priests may be seen in the 'Directory' of the priests, which was abstracted from volume two of my doctoral thesis 'The priest and politics in county Tipperary 1850 to 1891', pp 250-352. This book has developed from that dissertation, but because volume two contains over 350 pages of tables and appendices it is, unfortunately, impossible to reproduce them all here. Where statistics are given, therefore, or where more detailed information is desired, the reader is referred to the specific table, map or appendix in the thesis, all of which are based on primary sources. This, with the author's permission, may be consulted in the library of University College, Cork, or in the Tipperary County Library, Thurles.

In gathering a rather intimidating amount of material on the clergy of by-gone days I was aided by many kind and generous people, and it is now with great pleasure that I make the acknowlegements so richly merited. I am very much indebted to Dr John B. O'Brien of University College Cork, who guided me in the original study. Professor Joseph Lee of University College Cork read the manuscript of the book and made many helpful suggestions for which I am very grateful. I would also like to thank Dr R.V. Comerford of Maynooth College who made the final recommendations. Considering the nature of my project, the clergy were the first people I turned to for assistance, which was given most willingly. I thank Archbishop Thomas Morris for permission to research the Cashel Diocesan Archives, and I also thank Fr Christopher O'Dwyer, the Archivist, for his unfailing kindness to me. I am indebted to Mgr Augustine O'Donnell, President of St Patrick's College, Thurles, for the almost unlimited use of the wonderful library there, and I owe a special word of appreciation to Dr Maurice Dooley of the same college. My gratitude is due to the secretaries of the bishops of Killaloe and Waterford, Fr Brendan Crowley and Fr Caimin O'Carroll, who were most kind to a travelling scholar. There are three priests to whom I am particularly obliged for unusual forbearance towards a person of irritating tenacity. These are Fr Edmund Ryan, Pallotine College, Thurles, Dom Mark Tierney O.S.B., Glenstal Abbey, and Fr John Silke, Archivist, Irish College, Rome. I wish to thank the brothers of Thurles C.B.S. especially Brothers Dalton, Brennan and Cronin, for the use of their office equipment. My thanks, also, to Fr Thomas Crosse C.C. Tipperary town.

I am most grateful to the staffs of all the libraries I studied in, to those of the National Library, to the staff of the Tipperary County Library, Thurles, to Miss Semple, University College Dublin, Miss Browne, University College Cork, and to Mrs Cremin, Trinity College. Despite unreasonable demands I always received the utmost kindness and co-operation from the staff in the State Paper Office, Dublin Castle. I thank the staff of the British Newspaper Library, London, for supplying me with newspapers not available in Ireland, and I tender thanks to Mr William Corbett, B.A., H.D.E. for giving me books not available in libraries. I am indebted to Mr Gerard O'Grady for providing facilities in the *Tipperary Star* office, Thurles, and likewise Mr Patrick Ryan, Editor of the *Nenagh Guardian*, was equally kind. I must record my obligation to Mr Harry Lloyd of the Land Commission for assisting me with a soil map of Tipperary, and to my colleague Mr Timothy Coffey, B.A., H.D.E. for his aid to this poor classical scholar. My thanks, too, to Mr Arthur Moore, Mooresfort, for allowing me to read the very interesting collection of letters in his possession. I am also indebted to all those who have granted me permission to publish the material in this book, which is identified in the source section. Finally, I record my thanks to my wife, who for years has suffered the uncertain moods of a writer as well as typing the original thesis for me. I dedicate the book to her.

Chapter One

THE PRIEST AND HIS PEOPLE

'Whosoever, unless in case of necessity, of which the clergy in their respective parishes are the judges, buys or sells anything spirituous on a Sunday in a licenced or unlicenced house, is thereby deprived of the use of the sacraments by the withdrawal of faculties from the clergy until the person transgressing presents himself or herself to the bishop of the Diocese'. — Pastoral of Archbishop Patrick Leahy, Cashel and Emly, 11 Nov. 1861, on the Sunday Drinking Law.

The establishment of seminaries and diocesan colleges in Ireland was an important development in the church's efforts to cope with a population which mushroomed between the middle of the eighteenth century and the famine. The supply of students to these colleges and to Irish seminaries in Europe was influenced by several factors which can be readily identified in a study of Tipperary[1], with particular emphasis on the archdiocese of Cashel and Emly. With a few notable exceptions the larger, more populous parishes were the main reservoirs of vocations throughout the nineteenth century, producing the body of priests born from the end of the eighteenth century to the early 1860s, who manned the ecclesiastical network from 1850 to 1891.

But the real key to vocation numbers lay not so much in parish size or population as in soil fertility. By dividing the parishes into first and second grade soil types it emerges that the average number of vocations for the grade 2 parishes was a mere 0.6, while that for the grade 1 parishes was 6.4. The less fertile category contained the large parishes of Newport, Kilcommon, Upperchurch and Ballinahinch, which also had sizeable populations. But the clearest proof of the crucial importance of good land lies in the farming background of the priests. This has been illustrated by contemporary comment and accepted by some, but not all, modern historians.[2] It has been possible to confirm, either from the present clergy or from the general valuation carried out by Sir Richard Griffith in the early 1850s, that the vast majority of Tipperary priests (1850-91), whose birthplaces are known, were the

13

sons of farmers. Precise figures for 135 of these were compiled from Griffith's valuation, and concern 214 holdings, 70 of these being undivided; of the latter 76% were over 50 acres and 40% over 110 acres.[3] These represent the minimum size of farms, and it is probable that several of the families concerned had land in other townlands. In his evidence to the Bessborough Commission the parish priest of Ballinahinch, William J. McKeogh, revealed that he was born on a 30 acre farm, but his father also had an 81 acre farm near Tipperary Town.[4] Admittedly, the birth-range of these Tipperary priests began in the 1760s,[5] and it is possible that the farms recorded by Griffith were larger than the original ones. On the other hand the valuation shows considerable evidence of subdivision, so that the reverse may have been the case; for example, the 275 acre farm where John O'Brien P.P. Holycross was born in 1816 is subdivided between four brothers in Griffith. The inclusion of the 144 sub-divided holdings traced would promote the Tipperary clergy to an even wealthier social background. Not only, however, were these farms extensive, they were also fertile; 82% of all holdings recorded were higher than 10 shillings an acre valuation, and a significant number were £1 and over. County Clare farms accounted for 14 of the 38 under 10 shillings valuation.

Popular tradition, therefore, of the poverty-stricken peasants struggling from dawn to dusk, desperately trying to eke out the fees for their sons in Maynooth, well exemplified by an t-Athair Peadar Ó Laoghaire in *Mo Scéal Féin*,[6] may have been true of parts of the west and south, but was not applicable to Tipperary where the priests were generally the sons of well-off tenant-farmers. Ó Laoghaire, of course, put his finger squarely on the underlying reason for the common social background of the nineteenth-century priesthood. It was largely a matter of finance. Generally speaking, only those blessed with a reasonable income could hope to set out the long road to the priesthood, and in the absence of a significant non-farming middle-class, especially in rural areas, these were mainly sons of the soil. Considering that the average value of livestock on holdings of 16 to 30 acres was only £46 in 1841,[7] and further bearing in mind the miserable pittance earned by labourers,[8] the cost of clerical education was very considerable indeed. It varied at the different stages of the student's career. Pre-seminary education was acquired either at local classical schools or at the larger establishments, which also served as diocesan colleges, where part or all of the course for the priesthood could be pursued. Classical-school fees, ranging from a half-guinea to a guinea per quarter, were light, although the burden might be increased if lodgings were required.[9] Frequently the parish clergy established such small schools for local aspirants and Tipperary was reasonably well catered for in this respect. There were some, for example, in Nenagh, Ballingarry, Castleiney, Templemore, and Thurles.[10] When it opened in 1837,

St Patrick's College, Thurles, served as an exclusive boarding school similar to that in Navan,[11] and it later became the diocesan college for Cashel and Emly.

Such colleges were far more expensive than classical schools. Despite a few burses, most of the students who passed through St Patrick's[12] faced an annual bill of 30 guineas.[13] The 25 alumni of Carlow (the oldest college, opened in 1793) were obliged to pay £25 per year with an additional £25 to cover expenses,[14] and the 76 Tipperary priests educated in St John's College, Waterford, who served in Tipperary 1850-91 also paid heavy bills. One of the interesting aspects revealed by research on St John's was the high fees charged at the beginning of the century, which subsequently decreased for many years. The fee of £30 was reduced to £26 by 1826 and only reached £30 again in the 1870s. The well-kept registers of the college have survived and reveal substantial cumulative expenses;[15] 36% of the 39 seminarians noted paid between £71 and £120, 28% between £121 and £170, and 18% between £171 and £275. Individual amounts ranged from £14 to £275. The low figures represent fees paid by day pupils, and the larger sums resulted from a longer time-span spent in the college. These students suffered anything from 2 to 11 years in the college. Those in the latter category obviously completed their classical education there also, one of them being only 14 years old when entering.

Only the national seminary, Maynooth, was endowed by the state, thereby arousing the anxiety of the bishop of Kildare and Leighlin, who feared that numbers in Carlow might be adversely affected as a result.[16] Maynooth catered for an average of 52% of the Tipperary priesthood. The extent of their expenses depended upon whether they studied there before or after 1845, when the grant was increased from £8928 to £26,360, and the number of free places for Cashel, Killaloe and Waterford dioceses doubled.[17] Prior to 1845, 110 Tipperary priests had been students in the college. All seminarians during this period had to pay expenses, but about 50 per cent of first year students secured free places in the 1820s; the remainder did so as they moved through the college. The 194 Tipperary priests who studied in Maynooth after 1845 were more fortunate. The great majority were given places on the establishment, and every Divinity student received an allowance of £20 which covered the fee. They did, however, have to pay expenses, which, as far back as the 1820s had stood at about £14,[18] although in his evidence in 1826 Dr Crotty quoted the suspiciously high figure of £70 as expenses for first year students.[19]

Still, even if a Maynooth education was not without considerable financial outlay it was far cheaper than local colleges. It was also much less expensive than the continental seminaries, although some of these had excellent burse systems. The Irish College, Paris, where 37 of the priests serving in Tipperary between 1850 and 1891 were educated, had burses that in 1826 provided for about 60 Irish students.[20] This, of course, was entirely inadequate to cater for the church's total requirements. The college had only 3 free places for Cashel in 1839, 4 in 1861, and 5 in 1866.[21] It is likely that over the long period involved many of the 37 were aided by burses. The Irish College, Rome, which had educated only 16 of the Tipperary priests we are examining, had a correspondingly smaller number of burses; and fees in 1840 were 30 guineas per annum plus £25 for expenses, including travel.[22] In 1885 most of the students there were pensioners, that is, fee-paying, and Bishop James Ryan, Killaloe, pointed out that only the better-off students were sent to Rome.[23] This is confirmed by the social background of three priests educated there − all came from farms of over 100 acres. Finally, the Irish College, Salamanca was least important, catering for 4 Tipperary priests. In 1825 the total cost per annum for each Salamanca student amounted to £45, and the college had only 'trifling funds'.[24]

None of the colleges, Irish or continental, depended upon student fees as a main source of income. Had they done so fees would have been enormously increased. St Patrick's College Thurles was financed by annual collections from each parish in the archdiocese. Even this was not sufficient, and in 1849 Archbishop Slattery was forced to reduce the £50 annual salary of some professors, allowing 2 years mission benefit in lieu.[25] A similar shortage of money plagued the colleges in Rome and Paris. In 1864 pensioners' fees yielded a mere £528 out of a total income of £3,141 for Paris.[26] The authorities of both colleges constantly complained of inadequate funds and rising expenses.[27]

Such problems did not directly concern the aspirants, but money was of prime consideration when the question of priestly vocation was discussed in a nineteenth-century household. Of couse it could not automatically purchase a place in the seminaries. The religious convictions of the aspirant were well scrutinised by the local priests, and there is evidence that the very supply of clerical personnel was related to the spiritual atmosphere of a parish. There is, for example, a correlation between levels of mass attendance in the parish and vocation numbers. The average vocation figures for the 51%-70% and 71%-100% attendance groups are significantly higher than for the lower categories.[28] There is one puzzling exception to this, the parish of Ballingarry, which had the lowest attendance rate and the highest number of vocations.

But, neither the length of his purse nor the soundness of his character could guarantee the success of the young man who desired to become a priest. Reasonable intelligence and good health were essential to endure the long training period ahead, with its accompanying discipline.[29] Excluding initial classical education, studies for the priesthood ranged from five to seven years, beginning in Maynooth with Humanity, and progressing through Rhetoric, Logic, Metaphysics, Ethics, Physics, Philosophy and three years' Divinity or Theology.[30] Much depended upon the student's success at the initial examination, for which credit was given by reducing the course by a year or two, but five years was the minimum laid down by the colleges.[31] Tipperary priests conformed to the 5-7 year norm, with 59% of Maynooth alumni falling into that category.[32] Only 8% spent longer than this, suggesting either entry at a young age,[33] lack of progress at studies, or exceptional ability meriting an extra 3 years on the postgraduate Dunboyne Establishment. Most of the students who spent less than 5 years in Maynooth had already completed part of the course in other colleges, and so matriculated into a higher class, usually Physics or even Theology.

This suggests that initial academic requirements were basically the same for entry to all colleges. A working knowledge of Latin was essential because many lectures were delivered in that language. Admission to Humanity class in Maynooth entailed an examination in selections from Cicero, Caesar, Virgil, Sallust, Horace and the Greek text, Xenophon, while extra sections were prescribed if the Rhetoric class was the student's ambition; the list was further extended if he aspired to Logic.[34] 189 or 62% of Maynooth-trained priests in Tipperary 1850-91 had entered these admission classes, 40% of them going into Humanity, 32% into Rhetoric and 28% into Logic, meaning in effect that 60% of entrants had a better than average grasp of the Classics or were lucky in the pieces selected.[35] Deficiencies were repaired during the first few years at Maynooth, and the penalty of expulsion for continued lack of progress was rarely imposed because of the shortage of priests in Ireland in the early years of the century.[36]

There is some evidence, however, that the standard of Latin among students left something to be desired. As late as 1883 the *Irish Ecclesiastical Record* blamed an alleged decline of standards upon the Intermediate examinations.[37] The writer, however, conceded that the poor quality of this Latin might be sufficient to pass the Maynooth entrance examination. But there is no doubt that the standard required for the Propaganda University in Rome (the Irish College was only residential) was much higher. The Vatican authorities were far from pleased with the Latin of Irish priests, and Cardinal Barnabo reminded Archbishop Leahy of the bishops' responsibility to see that the language was taught to their students from an early age.[38] While rector of the Irish College in Rome Dr Paul Cullen (later a famous archbishop of Armagh and then Dublin) insisted that aspirants to that college should have either studied in an Irish seminary or undergone a test by diocesan examiners.[39] All students entering the Irish College, Paris were examined by the superior and professors.[40]

Latin was not the only linguistic problem it seems. In 1857 a set of 'Rules suggested for improving the study of French and English literature and of Sacred Eloquence in Maynooth College' was compiled.[41] The professor of English was instructed to conduct the entrance examination, which consisted of a written translation of passages from a Latin classic, a short original composition on a stated subject, and of questions on English grammar. The compositions were later scrutinised by the president, the vice-president, the dean of the Junior College and the professor of Scripture and Ecclesiastical History. Special classes were held each week for those whose English was inferior. Yet by 1870, as Walter McDonald, one of the students and later professors in Maynooth, admitted, 'English lectures were of the poorest'.[42]

The whole operation was entirely functional and could not neglect the problem of the Irish language, which was spoken in parts of the country, including sections of Tipperary.[43] Classes in the language were not only a feature of Maynooth but also of the Irish College, Paris.[44] In 1841 William Heffernan P.P., Clerihan, asked Archbishop Slattery to send him a curate who could speak Irish and hear confessions in the language.[45] During the Land War some Tipperary tenants were unable to speak English, and Thomas Finn P.P. Newcastle put himself forward as interpreter in the land courts.[46] The decrees of the provincial synod of Cashel, drawn up in September 1853 and published in 1854, placed responsibility upon the bishops to see that their priests were proficient in Irish.[47]

Language was only a means to an end, and the main aim of the seminaries was to impart philosophical and theological principles in preparation for the active ministry. There was no notable difference between the courses at the various colleges, Irish or continental.[48] The theology textbooks preserved in the research library of St Patrick's College, Thurles are largely the same as those found in Carlow, Maynooth or Rome. Their examination systems were also remarkably similar. Maynooth students underwent a public examination for 3 days each year[49] and the most important requirement seems to have been a good memory. The unfortunate Rhetoric students committed the entire treatise to memory.[50] The Roman method was equally unimaginative. One subject formed the basis of each examination and the aspirant was obliged to spend 5 hours writing a long Latin essay, 'carefully reflecting the professor's treatment, opinions, and mode of treatment'.[51] Uniformity was, therefore, all important, and this was very understandable when morality was weighed, measured and labelled with comforting precision.

Such rigidity was typical not only of examination and subject matter, but of overall discipline, and while discipline may have been sometimes lax, as Walter McDonald said, stamina was certainly necessary;[52] Peadar Ó Laoghaire was not exaggerating when he wrote about the debilitating effect that the Maynooth regime had on students there.[53] The seminarians' day was long and well-ordered, beginning at 6 a.m., involving nine hours of study and class work and two hours of spiritual exercises, with silence during study, lectures and meals.[54] Annual reports were made to the respective bishops on the conduct and academic progress of each student. The Roman regime was similar, again with 9 hours classwork, one hour commuting to the university, 3 hours recreation and 2½ hours religious devotions.[55] Unlike his Maynooth counterpart the Roman seminarian did not return home for holidays, mainly on the grounds that this would weaken ecclesiastical discipline[56] (although the 1854 decrees ordered priests to supervise the conduct of students at such times).[57] Instead he remained at the vacation house in Tivoli, where in the midst of recreation 'everything was conducted on a sort of monastic system of complete seclusion from the world'.[58] It may be safely said that discipline was well-maintained under Paul Cullen; Tobias Kirby, his vice-rector and successor, seems to have been even more strict. Apparently six Waterford students wrote to Bishop Foran requesting permission to change from the college because of Kirby's harshness.[59] Foran's successor, Dominick O'Brien, remarked that one Waterford student 'brought up in the worldly and independent spirit of Maynooth' would hardly submit to the regime in Rome.[60] It appears, therefore, that while the rules in Maynooth were strict their observance was not always what it should have been.

The same might be said of the Irish College, Paris, which had a distinctly Irish flavour. Not only was the Irish language on the curriculum, but all the staff were Irishmen, and one of its rectors, Dr McSweeney had been Professor of Theology in Carlow from 1819 to 1825.[61] Although subject to the archbishop of Paris in general matters, internal discipline was very much under the control of the Irish hierarchy, who framed the rules and appointed the staff. Unlike Rome, lectures were delivered in the college and the students rarely attended the Sorbonne.[62] As with Maynooth, the seminarians returned home for vacation[63] (the French Government forbade them to remain in the college during the Summer), and so they retained contact with Irish life during their most impressionable years. The college's long list of rules and penalties, approved by the bishops in 1849, is quite formidable,[64] but disciplinary problems arose during the rectorate of Dr Miley, who refused to implement recommendations drawn up by an investigating commission in 1852.[65] The difficulty seems to have been largely administrative, and also involved a clash of personalities between Miley and some of the staff. The rancour generated did not tend towards good order among the students themselves, and Archbishop Slattery flatly refused to send Cashel students to Paris while Miley remained

Rector. The Vatican agreed to endorse any episcopal decisions against him and he was forced to resign in 1858.[66] Discipline subsequently improved and reports painted an increasingly optimistic picture, although a small number of students were occasionally refused orders either because they had not the necessary 'soundness' of character or had imbibed in the wine-cellar.[67] In 1863 5 out of 87 were excluded from orders and this was considered an excellent situation. The fact that sanctions were executed is an indication that discipline was being enforced.

What, therefore, was the result of this long and tough system of training? Certainly not a liberally educated, nor necessarily a particularly pious priesthood, although this obviously varied with individuals. The relative paucity of purely religious exercises vis-a-vis the academic suggests that monastic as their regimes were, the seminaries were not monasteries. Theology textbooks were not prayerbooks and by their nature were dry, precise, uninspiring works. Historians, therefore, should avoid viewing nineteenth century seminaries either as monasteries or universities. Their role should be seen as their own professors saw it — the function of Maynooth in the words of Dr Higgins was to enable students 'to comprehend the matter that is to be studied', and no more.[68] Lord Beaumont, an unlikely commentator perhaps, defined Maynooth's role as instructing the students 'merely as Roman Catholic priests, and nothing else, it gives them no other education, but that which is suited to Roman Catholic priests. It confines itself narrowly to that sole object'.[69] In short, it aimed at the creation of a body of professional men capable of carrying out the spiritual and administrative duties of parish life.

It must have been with a deep sense of relief that the young priest took up these duties. He could now look forward to a worthwhile life and one with some desirable prospects, not least a comfortable standard of living and eventually a good income, at least on promotion to the level of parish priest. Examination of extant records immediately reveals the substantial nature of parish revenue from the 1830s onwards. This held true even of such infertile parishes as Kilcommon and Ballinahinch. Income for Kilcommon[70] in the first quarter of 1840 amounted to over £81, while for the periods September 1854 to June 1855 and September 1855 to June 1856, receipts in Ballinahinch[71] were £141 and £136 respectively. This was by no means total annual revenue — babies continued to be born and people died during each month of the year! Furthermore, collections may have been held, and probably were, at other periods. In 1852 prior to amalgamation with Bansha, the tiny parish of Kilmoyler had receipts of £120 a year.[72] The two stations at Easter and Christmas in the parish of Thurles grossed an annual average of £200 from 1834 to 1848.[73] The highest collections there were £225 in 1841 and 1844. By 1882 the Sunday and holyday collections in Thurles amounted to £379 per annum.[74]

As already mentioned some of this revenue came from gate collections or stations. But the accounts for Kilcommon reveal more diverse sources such as marriage, baptism and funeral dues. Unquestionably, marriages were the most important of these, which suggests that the revenue quoted for Thurles would be greatly expanded if statistics were available for weddings. Out of the quarterly receipts of £81 for Kilcommon no less than £66 came from marriages. Individual marriage dues ranged from £1-5-0 to £7-18-0. There are examples, however, of much larger figures. In 1850 Redmond Burke P.P. Newport was pleased to tell his Archbishop that he had reaped £20 on one occasion.[75] Much depended upon the social status of the parties getting married. The quarterly total for 'corpse masses' in Kilcommon was only £1-8-9, while baptism brought in £4. It has to be borne in mind that income from stations, and marriages (most of which were celebrated just before Lent) was highly seasonal.

But, it would be a mistake to imagine that the clergy were dependent solely upon the parish for their income. In the mid-nineteenth century at least 40 of Tipperary's 64 parish priests rented farms which yielded pleasant annual profits.[76] More surprising still, 43% of these occupied holdings in excess of 40 statute acres, often extending into different townlands. Farms of 60, 64, 83, 110 and 115 acres were traced. Furthermore, Griffith's valuation shows that many of these farms were the most fertile in the townlands concerned.

There were yet more financial springs tapped by the clergy, which, however, were either less lucrative or were limited to a few parishes. One of the former was the renting of pews in the chapel. In 1871 an individual who had emigrated to London 30 years earlier was annoyed because the family name had been removed from a pew; he offered to continue the annual rent of 10/- to have it restored.[77] A rarer but quite valuable source of income was the salary for chaplaincy of workhouses. The chaplain to the Cashel workhouse received £50 p.a. in 1847 and £90 in 1884,[78] while the Thurles chaplain was paid £62 in 1846 and £85 in 1853, a figure which still stood in 1887.[79] To put their salaries in their proper perspective it may be mentioned that in 1851 the hospital nurse in the Thurles workhouse received an annual income of £20 with full board, the schoolmaster got £30, (if properly qualified), the master's salary was £70, that of the matron £30, while the clerk on the Union received £80.[80]

The result of such an accumulation of income plus various bequests, legacies and gifts, was a relatively well-off priesthood in Tipperary, in comparison with the majority of their flock. When Philip Fitzgerald P.P. Ballingarry died, he bequeathed £1000 to the Archbishop, and left his house to his sister.[81] Michael Pyne P.P. Nenagh donated several thousand pounds for the building of the new church there.[82] Their relative affluence was reflected in generous personal subscriptions to various causes, spiritual, social or political.[83]

Nevertheless a sharp distinction must be drawn between the income of pastors and that of curates who often had to wait considerable periods for promotion. One sample of 40 priests on Table 4 gives some idea of the promotion structure in Co. Tipperary between 1850 and 1891. It is obvious that more than half the curates were promoted between the ages of 41 and 50 but it is equally clear that promotion was not based upon seniority by age but rather upon length of service in the ministry. No less than 67% of the curates listed served between 20 and 29 years by the time they were promoted (most of these served from 20 to 24 years). Thus there were cases of priests who were not promoted until they were in their fifties because they were obliged to serve over 20 years as curates. Many of these were what might be called late vocations. On the other hand it should be pointed out that these criteria were not always adhered to; some late vocations were promoted after a shortened span. The bishops had the final say in the matter of promotion. Indeed, being a relative or a close friend of the bishops or of a senior diocesan ecclesiastic was a distinct advantage as may be seen in the case of John Butler, Thomas Fennelly and John Ryan. Other relevant factors included one's social background or academic achievements. Obviously the bishops considered that such men would have advanced in any walk of life they might have chosen and decided to reward them with promotion at an earlier age than normal.

But the majority had to wait and their income was quite limited. None of the curates had farms, almost always the chaplain to the local workhouse was the parish priest, and he too received the greater portion of the revenue from all other sources. For a long period there was no uniform salary laid down for the curate. Of the £78 reaped by Dr Delaney P.P. Ballyporeen from the 1880 Christmas collection his curate received £10.[84] A salary of £20 seems to have been common around mid-century, and as late as 1867 Rome advised that such a salary was too low and recommended that a provincial synod of Munster should settle the matter of clerical support.[85] The curates themselves were not always happy with their lot. John Ryan C.C. Cashel requested an increase to £52 in 1854,[86] and that same year Archbishop Slattery ordered that 52 guineas p.a. be paid to the curate of Donaskeigh.[87] Some parish priests decided on a fixed salary for their subordinates but the visitation reports for the archdiocese show that in 17 of the 35 parishes recorded curates collections were held each year, usually in September or October.[88] Unfortunately, they do not specify amounts. It was customary, too, in certain parishes to allow the curates a share in some of the fees received for specific services. In 1849 Thomas Gilhooly C.C. Solohead while getting only £15 a year salary, also shared in the corpse masses.[89] As well as requesting a raise, John Ryan sought the continuance of this concession too. In an unusual case the curate of Murroe, in the County Limerick part of the archdiocese, was allowed to say all the requiem masses and keep the proceeds.[90] Fees normally split between the priests of a parish were known as divisible dues, and increasing attention was given to them as a means of raising the curates' salaries. The reply to Archbishop Leahy's request for information in 1868 revealed that in the Diocese of Cloyne baptism and marriage offerings as well as the Christmas and Easter collections were classed as divisible dues.[91] In all cases the parish priest received twice as much as the curate or curates. It seems that traditionally such offerings were not placed in this category in the Archdiocese of Cashel, but that each case was left to the discretion of the parish priest. However, the diocesan synod of 1880 under Dr Croke changed this and legislated that from then on all marriage fees (including certificates of freedom), Christmas and Easter collections, baptism offerings, churchings, and blessing of clay fees, were to be considered as divisible dues, with the parish priest getting two-thirds when he had one curate, half if he had two, and two-fifths if he had three.[92] As in previous years receipts from corpse Masses were divided. Offerings for private intentions, however, belonged to whatever priest received them.

By the 1880s, therefore, the financial position of the Tipperary curate had improved considerably. Yet he was never burdened by financial worries. As well as this he and his pastor enjoyed a very comfortable standard of living. When the parish priest had paid the various expenses, such as rent for his house, wages of housekeeper, servant, workman, sometimes the pension of a retired predecessor, and in a few cases mensal dues, he had sufficient left to keep himself and his coadjutors in a style which was at least equal and generally superior to that of the better-off farmers in the parish. Hopefully not all were as fastidious as Francis O'Brien, curate in Cahir from 1876 to 1878. His wealthy but eccentric pastor, Maurice Mooney, wrote in chagrin to Bishop John Power — 'No wonder he may complain of a cold leg of mutton for dinner at my table, when he lunches on such dainties as roast chicken and brandy at the convent where I supply them with vegetables, potatoes and milk'.[93] The Kilcommon report of 1840 shows that the priest there dined upon such good solid fare as fish, beef, bacon and turkey. Since this was one of the poorer Tipperary parishes the standard of living of its priests may be considered as the very least enjoyed by the other clergy. It was a much more varied and better diet than that enjoyed by priests west of the Shannon in the 1830s, however.[94] It was also infinitely superior to the monotonous and meagre diet of the labouring classes.[95]

The clergy enjoyed such material comfort mainly because of their status as ministers of religion. As mere farmers' sons few of them would have been as well-off when they left the family hearth. It was indeed a big step from peasantry to priesthood. Their ecclesiastical status raised them high on the social scale, and their relatively advanced level of education ensured that they were leaders in a society of functional literacy, and a society which was also predominantly rural and Catholic. The esteem they were held in was symbolised by the presentation of expensive testimonials, usually when they were being transferred from a parish. Patrick Glynn, curate of the poor hilly parish of Templederry, received 'a beautiful chalice, richly chased and embossed, with a magnificent gold watch and chain',[96] while Patrick Ryan got a 'splendid brougham' when leaving Pallasgreen for Galbally in Tipperary.[97]

It would be a distortion, however, to present the Tipperary priests as wealthy, well-fed, pampered clergymen. If they were well-sheltered from the caprices of poverty their entire lives were encompassed by restrictive rules and regulations enshrined in various diocesan statutes. Broadly speaking these centered on zeal for the pastorate, wealth, sexual morality and drink. The code of conduct for the last three was quite explicit. On the question of fees for administering the sacraments, the 1850 Synod stipulated under threat of censure that all traces of avarice and simony should be avoided.[98] This was confirmed by the 1854 Provincial Synod of Thurles, which put the earlier decrees into effect in Cashel and Emly, and was adopted by all Munster dioceses.[99] While the Fifth Precept of the Church implied that ecclesiastical services could be withdrawn if the people failed to maintain the clergy,[100] the 1850 synod decreed that the sacraments were not to be denied to those who could not afford an offering.[101] Offerings at baptisms could be accepted according to diocesan rules and approved practice, but prior agreement on the amount was strictly forbidden.[102] The 1854 Synod also confirmed that offerings at marriages must be brought within reasonable limits, and over-rigorous exaction by priests merited episcopal censure.[103] Dr Croke continued such rules in his statutes, and, to prevent the accumulation of wealth by priests or unseemly squabbles after their deaths, statute 30 urged that superfluous wealth be donated to works of piety or charity while the donor was still living.[104] Partly with the same aim in view the 1850 statutes forbade the leasing of farms exceeding 15 acres, without the consent of the bishop, a rule which took some time to enforce, until the 1875 Maynooth Synod closed its loopholes.[105] Finally, at the Provincial Synod of Thurles in 1881, a new rule was introduced forbidding the custom of testimonials.[106] This applied to all the dioceses of Munster and was strictly enforced. In 1890, for example, the people of Clonmel were frustrated in their desire to make a presentation to their departing curate, William Meagher, who was transferred much against their wishes.[107]

The Synod of Thurles (*Illustrated London News*, 14.9.1850).

The codes on sexual behaviour and drink may be quickly dealt with. A life of celibacy was fundamental to the priesthood, and to prevent this from being endangered, either in spirit or in practice, priests were forbidden by the 1850 Synod to attend public concerts, theatres or dances.[108] They were ordered to wear black or dark clothes and to avoid undue familiarity with women.[109] To ensure that their reputations were above suspicion, and probably to ensure that they did not develop a taste for pretty housekeepers, the priests were allowed to hire only elderly ladies, and these had to be of 'known virtue'.[110] Over-indulgence in liquor was obviously a serious matter and Dr Croke was especially strict on this. His statutes laid down automatic suspension if a priest drank before the main meal without necessity.[111]

Such legislation clearly focussed upon the personal behaviour of the clergy and is directly related to the question of personal spirituality and zeal for the pastorate. The keynote of the 1850 Synod was that the priests should excel in all forms of justice and follow a way of life above the ordinary.[112] They were instructed to cultivate daily prayer and meditation, visit the Blessed Sacrament, recite the Rosary and de-vote time to reading Scripture, the lives of the Saints, and Moral Theo-logy.[113] All these were again stressed by the Synod of 1854.[114] From 1875 Archbishop Croke maintained a tight rein on his priests, and held annual diocesan synods to re-affirm old rules and introduce new ones if necessary. His 1878 statutes laid down automatic suspension, reserved to the bishop, for any priest who absented himself from diocesan con-ferences without permission.[115] Such rules were re-stated 'for the last time' in 1891.[116] The priests, too, were expected to live together in harmony, not always an easy matter. Until the 1870s the great majority of curates resided with their parish priests, who leased their houses from the local landlords, usually at a low rent. During the 1870s the policy of providing permanent parochial houses took root. This enabled Croke to introduce the option of separate maintenance in 1880.[117] Those curates who elected to remain with their pastors were instructed to pay for their board and lodgings. Specific rules were sometimes drawn up for curates who decided to live apart from the parish priest, and one interesting set for the Templemore curates is preserved in the Croke Papers.[118] These rules laid down that eatables in the curates' houses would be in common, but that the host would provide drinkables for the whole table when a guest was present. The senior curate ran the household and had the responsibility of hiring or firing servants. The curates were forbidden to carry on 'horse-traffick-ing' in the presbytery or to oblige parishoners with stabling for their horses.

A high standard of personal conduct and spirituality was seen by the synods from mid-century onwards as a prerequisite to the proper and efficient administration of the parish. It was partly a question of setting good example. The 1850 decrees stated the procedure for the administration of the sacraments, and it was the priests' duty to see that this was carried out. The synod especially mentioned the clergy's duty to care for the sick.[119] It also stressed the obligation of the parish priest to personally say Mass in the parish church on Sundays and holydays; he was forbidden to use a substitute.[120] It was his duty to give a brief exposition of Christian doctrine during Mass. Croke's statutes were equally emphatic and imposed automatic suspension on any priest who failed to preach on three Sundays of the month.[121] He later reiterated the necessity of registering marriages and births, visiting schools, saying daily Mass in villages, having benediction once a month and having fixed times for confessions.[122]

The increasing flow of diocesan rules from 1850, especially during Croke's tenure, suggests that not only was the Church becoming more efficient, but that the priests had not previously measured up to the ideals proposed in the Synod of 1850, or did not always continue to do so in its wake. It would indeed have been something of a miracle had not some black sheep existed among the 575 priests who ministered in Tipperary from 1850 to 1891. But as far as celibacy is concerned, there can be no doubt that most of the priests were intensely loyal to their pledge. The incidence of scandal was negligible. Confidential records, however, do show that a small minority of priests had a drink problem.

The question of clerical avarice is rather more complex, but it can be stated with certainty that the improving post-famine economic climate, coupled with the restrictions of the synods, prevented the type of tension which had characterised certain periods from the beginning of the century. Increasing prosperity among the farmers, by affecting parish income, made it possible for the 1850 legislators to restrict the size of parochial farms, and so ultimately removed what would certainly have been a source of discord in some parishes, where farmers might have been envious of or scandalised by farmer-priests, or where the latter might have shown more interest in their animal rather than their human flocks. Reform, however, did not mean that priests were reluctant to demand dues or that some instances of abuse did not arise. Individual parishioners were quite sensitive to increasing dues and several objected to an increase in the stations from 5/- to 7/6 in the 1870s. Nevertheless, such complaints were thoroughly investigated by the bishops. The case of Michael Fitzgerald C.C. Anacarty, who made a strong altar attack upon a parishoner's inadequate collection contribution in 1873, was heard by a clerical court, but the accused was found not guilty of insulting the individual concerned.[123] It was a practice in some parishes to read a list of defaulters (called the rascally list by the priests) and Thomas Duggan P.P. Murroe was complained to Archbishop Leahy by the local doctor, because of his remarks when reading this list.[124] Duggan informed Leahy that one man paid only £1 instead of his usual £3. The Archbishop did not consider Duggan's action a breach of diocesan rules. However, he did reprimand William Cooney P.P. Caherconlish for altar remarks in a somewhat similar context.[125] The offended parishioner threatened to publish the case or lay it before Cardinal Cullen.[126] He demanded a public apology from Cooney to be dictated by Leahy. The latter refused to suspend Cooney.[127] It should be mentioned, perhaps, that answers to a questionnaire in 1841 showed some divergence of procedure in various dioceses throughout Ireland. It was generally the custom in Killaloe to call the names of those who paid.[128] The list of defaulters was only occasionally read, and then only in the case of non-payment of chapel cess. The same applied to Cashel, but not to Waterford, where none of the lists was read.[129] Attitudes seemed to have changed by the 1870s especially in Cashel under the shrewd Leahy.

The bishops as administrators of large ecclesiastical units, were excellent guardians of the coffers. While they could not be accused of avarice in the canonical sense, they certainly knew how to maximise their income. With a dexterity which would be the envy of any tax-dodger today Archbishop Slattery managed to return a taxable income of £35 out of a gross income of £600.[130] Of the three Archbishops, Leahy seems to have had the keenest financial acumen. When he was unable to attend the dedication of Boher chapel in 1874 he advised the parish priest, Redmond Burke, to conceal his absence until the last moment lest the collection be injured.[131] The Archbishop had by then 12 years experience in collecting for the new cathedral in Thurles. He personally visited every church in the archdiocese in 1864 and 1866, and sat at the altar-rails, where he read out a list of all adults in the parish, who then meekly presented their offerings.[132] Of course this was a special case where the bishop was faced with an enormously expensive project demanding special exertions. It may be said that some of the clergy were also faced with such problems when renovating their churches for example. In such instances they were forced to make an additional levy or cess on their parishioners since their own income would not be sufficient to meet such additional costs.

The bishops, too, were prepared to be quite contrary on the matter of workhouse chaplains' salaries, and were not willing to accept pro-posed rates or any suggestion of a reduction in salary because of a fall in the number of inmates. The Cashel Diocesan Archives contain evidence of several protracted disputes on this issue. In 1849 Dean James McDonnell, acting on Dr Slattery's instructions, informed a Poor Law official that the appointment of chaplain and his salary were matters for the archbishop alone.[133] That same year Slattery dictated the correspondence of Thomas Mahony C.C. Solohead about the chaplaincy of the auxiliary workhouse at Castle Lloyd.[134] In 1841 Slattery had been quite clear in his refusal to allow the celebration of mass in any workhouse until an equitable salary had been agreed.[135] He forced the Poor Law Commissioners to considerably revise their figures upwards. Armed with his archbishop's approval, Dean Patrick Leahy refused £70 salary for the chaplaincy of Cashel workhouse in 1855, arguing that a fall in numbers did not affect the salaries of other officials.[136] It was a question of placing the issue squarely in the realm of ecclesiastical jurisdiction. It was also a tussle between two professional groups, with the unfortunate paupers as the possible victims.

It could be said that whatever degree of avarice did exist stemmed from an over-professional approach, but it must be asked if such professionalism extended to the overall performance of pastoral duties, or were the priests less efficient in their execution than they were in extracting payment for them. They certainly earned their money during the Famine years, when they were appalled at misery, destitution, illness and death. The Cashel Diocesan Archives reveal that through their bishops the priests were a source of financial relief to the destitute. As ministers of religion they were greatly overworked, some like Edmund Cahill C.C. Newport succumbing to the dreaded cholera.[137] A Killaloe curate described his day as beginning at 4 a.m. followed by an arduous tour of his parish until 5 p.m., holding stations and administering the last rites to many who saw death from hunger or disease as imminent.[138] This hectic routine was frequently interrupted by immediate calls from the dying in other localities. The curate's return to his house brought little respite because starving people gathered at his door throughout the evening.

From the priests' point of view the Famine also had an unpleasant religious side-effect, which, however, was confined to the poorer parishes. This was the tormenting problem of proselytism. It was only with the arrival of the Famine that the Bible Societies, active since the 1830s, began to have some success. By November 1847 Rome was seriously concerned about rumours of defections, and Cardinals Fransoni and Barnabo suggested to Slattery that Protestant charity be counteracted by Catholic money and alms.[139] The parishes of Doon, Cappamore and Pallasgrean were the centres of proselytism in the Archdiocese, and all had essentially the same story to tell. The people of Doon, which lay partly in County Tipperary, were especially hard-hit by hunger, fever and clearances, and were, therefore, ripe for offers of money, food, and shelter by the zealous Bible Society ministers. Apart from the religious issue at stake the priests themselves were clearly worried about their own reputation in Rome where an impression existed that they lacked zeal. This was not true of the indefatigable curate of Doon, John O'Dwyer, who with his pastor, Patrick Hickey made an analysis of the situation, and pointed out that despite the efforts of the Society and the money from Exeter Hall the number of 'Cath-breaks', (so-called perverts), was not only quite small, but was confined to the very young, the very old, or a small number who apostasised in a desperate effort to save themselves from a painful death[140]. O'Dwyer estimated that the total number involved from 1849 to 1852 was 36, although Dr Slattery's letter to Rome listed 49 persons. As well as this, the energy of O'Dwyer combined with the impact of a mission (which had been suggested to him by William Maunsell M.P., and later applauded by Rome) succeeded in winning back the majority of the 'perverts' to the catholic fold. In his letter to Rome of July 1853 Slattery could confidently defend himself and his priests, and it seems this made a favourable impression on the authorities.[141]

It proved much easier to wean the poor people of West Tipperary or East Limerick from the clutches of hopeful evangelicals than from that most extensive and deep-rooted of Irish scourges — a fondness for the demon booze. The priests considered the problem from a moral viewpoint and had their own interesting methods of dealing with it. The existence in Thurles of St. Paul's Total Abstinence Society, founded in 1839 and still going strong in 1845, is one example.[142] It was established under the patronage of Archbishop Slattery and its 'guardian' was Father William Barron. Its avowed aim was 'to associate and unite men together in the bonds of christian charity and fraternal affection, and to induce them to live soberly, justly, and Godly'. The Society, which forbade under pain of dismissal the taking of any quantity of drink, was a curious blend of the religious, the benevolent and the abstemious. Anybody whose character was 'sullied by any act of dishonesty or injustice' was forbidden to join, and the members were bound (and had to prove the fact) to approach the sacraments of Penance and the Eucharist at Easter and Christmas. Piety and abstinence were rewarded, however, by receiving a sliding scale of sickness benefit ranging from 6/- to 2/- per week for up to 20 weeks or longer, if unemployed. There was even an old-age pension of 3/- per week for long-standing members and funeral expenses were met by the Society.

But such local efforts, combined with the Mathew crusade of the 40s, were only partly successful, and in the mid-century 'sheebeens' (unlicenced public-houses), abounded in the county. Indeed, the parish priest of Kilcommon saw fit to mention their presence in that area in his 1853 visitation report.[143] It was not until the arrival of Patrick Leahy to the See of Cashel in 1857 that firm and effective steps were taken by the church to curb over-indulgence. The tenacious Archbishop was obsessed by the issue, and his papers contain many reports from bridewells, giving statistics of committals for drunkenness.[144] He even noted details on his private *Ordo*.[145] In his pastoral of November 1861 Leahy revealed that he had worked 'in a special manner' to propagate temperance throughout the diocese.[146] This document showed his concern that Sunday was often the day specially chosen by people to visit the public houses 'and there protracting their carousals all through the day and far into the night'. His answer was an astonishing diocesan rule, called the Sunday Drinking Law, rigidly administered by the priests, which made a reserved sin, normally to the Archbishop himself, of either selling or buying liquor on a Sunday. The law, which had already been in operation for some months, was extended to all parishes by the pastoral of November 1861.

However unpopular it was, there can be no doubt of its success, partly because of the priests' vigilance. The statistics supplied to Leahy on imprisonments for drunkenness show a dramatic decrease from 1861 onwards; the Cashel bridewell figures for Sunday transgressions recorded a decrease from 101 in 1858 to 12 in 1861, and there were no recorded offences from 1862 to 1864. Leahy's successor, Thomas William Croke, saw no reason to abolish this law, and it was incorporated into his 1878 statutes.[147] Croke was also seriously concerned about the abuse of drink at wakes and funerals, and these statutes forbade priests to say mass in houses where drink was supplied.[148] His circular of July 1890 warned them to seek guarantees from the heads of families that such occasions would be drink-free;[149] deception on the part of these people was a reserved sin, a method which the bishops used with rather too much liberality at times. The circular, partly with the same aim in view, ordered that all funerals and marriages should in future be held before noon and 2 p.m. respectively. The 1880s, too, witnessed a resurgence of the total abstinence drive in an effort to combat an increase in drinking partly due to the proliferation of local political meetings, always excellent social opportunities for bravado and beer.[150]

Their efforts to keep their flocks Catholic and sober are, therefore, of some importance in gauging the zeal of the priests for their work. But one even better way of judging their pastoral performance is to examine the state of formal religious practices in Tipperary, both before and after the Famine. Mass-attendance is one good guide to this. The only statistics available were compiled in 1835 with the Protestant (or civil) parish as the basic unit used by the Commissioners.[151] The availability of the census and maps of Cashel and Emly makes it possible to reconstruct the findings on the basis of the larger Catholic parishes.[152] A sample of 28 parishes chosen reveals extensive laxity in pre-Famine Tipperary, with only about 45% of the population attending Mass.[153] There was, however, wide inter-parish variation with a suspiciously low minimum rate of 13% for Ballingarry and a maximum of 90% in Thurles. Nine parishes fell into the 13% − 30% group, 11 from 31% − 50%, 5 from 51% − 70% and 3 from 71% − 100%.[154] Neither is the overall picture quite as gloomy as the statistics initially suggest. Exemption of children under 7 from compulsory attendance is an important consideration. While the Commissioners did not make any age distinctions, it may be safely concluded that the majority of such children, particularly in rural areas, were regular absentees. Since the average number of each household was 7 for 23 of the parishes selected, and 6 for 5 of them in 1841, and assuming that a similar pattern existed in 1835, it would be no exaggeration to suggest that each household contained on average 2 children under 7 years of age. Their exclusion from the total population figures results in a significant increase in Mass-attendance percentages. Unfortunately, house statistics are not available for 1835, and because of an increasing population the use of the 1841 house numbers would result in too great a distortion upwards. However, the population of Anacarty and Ballina showed a decline between 1835 and 1841, and a deduction of children on the basis of the 1841 house numbers results in an increase from 31% to 43% and 48% to 62% respectively. Thus, it may not be unrealistic to conclude that an increase of 14% on the statistics compiled would be a more accurate picture for rural parishes. Apart from the question of young children, emphasis on household representation is also fruitful in showing the spread of Mass-attendance, because the Commissioners' figures may represent individual members from a large number of families rather than a smaller number of complete families. At least two members from the majority of families could conceivably be included in the report. The overall rate has been calculated at 2.7, and since the 1841 house figures were used this is understating the position. It should be noted, too, that the priests in their visitation reports recorded only the heads of families when noting absentees from Easter duty. Of equal interest, the priests informed the Commissioners that Mass-attendance figures were increasing so that considerable improvement must have occurred during the 15 years to the middle of the century.

Nevertheless, the truth cannot be denied. At best only half the people of Tipperary went to Mass in 1835. There were various reasons for this unsatisfactory state. Social and economic factors such as poor roads and stark poverty immediately spring to mind, and several of the visitation reports of the 1840s noted abstention from Easter duty because people were ashamed to appear in chapel. But, did the Church provide a sufficient number of adequate buildings and personnel to cater for a steadily increasing population? Historians are not altogether unanimous about this.[155] The question of church numbers certainly seems to be relevant in a number of Tipperary parishes. The case of Ballingarry is illustrative. This parish had only one church to cater for 9,000 people spread over an area of 18,000 acres. Many Ballingarry people were forced to attend Mass in neighbouring Killenaule and New Bermingham. Doon, with one chapel, a similar area and 5,500 people, recorded the low rate of 25%. It is also noteworthy that urban parishes, with chapels at a more convenient distance, had the highest level of attendances. Nevertheless, 6 of the 9 parishes in the lowest grouping of 13%—30% had two chapels each. On the other hand the number of parishes in the higher groups with one chapel was very low. The truth is that increasing chapel numbers had little enough bearing upon any future growth in Tipperary Mass-attendance, for the very simple reason that they were almost static between 1835 and 1891. Over 70% of Tipperary's churches were built between 1800 and 1849, most of them between 1800 and 1839, many of which are still in use to-day, although they may have been extended.[156] Clearly any revolution in church building occurred before the Famine and not after it. So, overemphasis on chapel numbers as an influence on low Mass-attendance must be avoided. Perhaps, however, the chapels available did not have adequate capacity to house the ever-increasing pre-Famine population. There is no doubt that some of the smaller rural chapels could not accommodate more than 600 people, but, bearing in mind that seating was not spread over the entire chapel area, and considering the existence of spacious galleries, admittedly sometimes for the better-off classes, it can be argued that many chapels could have coped with a much larger attendance rate. Chapels with only one mass, such as Ballingarry or Bansha, had attendance numbers of 1,200 and 1,500, showing that they could house those numbers. Certainly the church of Ballingarry, although renovated, has not increased capacity since then. In answer to the 1841 questionnaire a priest from the archdiocese of Cashel advised that within the previous 'seven or eight years' most of the chapels there had been replaced or 'considerably enlarged', and that many of these had 2 or 3 galleries.[157]

But even if there was congestion in some parishes an increase in mass numbers would have helped to solve the problem. Most chapels might have doubled the number of masses, had the priests celebrated the canonically allowed 2 masses each. Ballingarry had a potential of 6 masses instead of the one offered. The average number of masses was higher for each succeeding attendance group recorded, although not all parishes with a high number of masses showed a correspondingly high rate. Anacarty, with maximum mass celebration, is a pertinent example. Still, it is difficult to avoid the conclusion that some priests were lax in providing facilities for their parishioners. Moreover, it seems that the tradition of mass-going in Ireland was not a particularly strong one, and as products of their environment many priests were not alive to the desirability of breaking this pattern. But, the famine partly solved the problem. It decimated the poor, the very class who contributed least to formal devotional practices in Tipperary, and at the same time solved any real or potential problem of congestion in the churches.[158] In 1852 Patrick Hickey P.P. Doon complained that his new church was only half filled.[159] It is revealing that the 1846–1855 visitation reports for the 28 parishes analysed show that between 1835 and 1855 the number of masses celebrated in 15 remained unchanged, 3 showed a decrease, 5 cannot be checked and only 5 registered an increase.[160]

Despite the certainty that the number of masses could have been greatly increased, there is evidence that the existing distribution of clergy did have some bearing on the matter, in some cases making greater contact with parishioners possible. Both Moyne and Drangan had similar statistics for chapel numbers, population and area, but Moyne with three priests has an attendance rate of 58% while that for Drangan where two priests ministered was only 36%. Again, both Upperchurch and Clonoulty were alike in area and population, but while Upperchurch had the advantage in chapel numbers, Clonoulty with more priests, had a significantly higher attendance rate. Yet the fact remains that the lowest attendance group had as high a clerical numerical strength as the others, and it is equally notable that the ratio between priests and population shows a remarkable similarity of 1 priest to approximately 2,800 people for all groups in 1835. It has been suggested, however, that an increase in post-Famine clerical personnel contributed to an improving situation.[161] As far as Tipperary is concerned this is not true simply because there was no significant increase between 1835 and 1891.[162] Of the four categories groups one and four actually show a slight decline in numbers, while groups two and three remained static, with, however, some compensating internal changes. For the county as a whole there was only an overall increase of 9.4% between 1835 and 1900, and the increase between 1861 and 1900 was a mere 1.8%. Indeed the Waterford section experienced a decrease of 8.1%. In 1854 it was a 'source of great embarrassment and anxiety' to Archbishop Slattery that he had no place in the diocese for a large number of young priests about to emerge from Maynooth.[163] He was prepared to allow them reside with clerical relatives in the diocese on the strict understanding that they were not there in the capacity of curates and had no prior claim to any future vacancies.

Clearly, therefore, the Church was well organised in Tipperary before the Famine. This seems to be in striking contrast to the national situation where apparently the number of priests increased by 24% between 1849 and 1900. Yet the truth is that this statistic conceals very real diocesan differences. A spot check (head count) from the *Irish Catholic Directory* shows, for example, that Armagh, Killaloe, and Limerick dioceses experienced only an insignificant increase between 1847 and 1860, with, in fact, several slight decreases, but thereafter a steady increase. Tuam, Waterford and Cashel showed a general decline in numbers, while Meath recorded a very small increase. There was, however, a consistent and general increase in the dioceses of Dublin and

Cork both having a city core. The increases were invariably in the curate population. Undoubtedly, the matter is more complex, involving non-parochial clergy such as chaplains and regular priests, and more research is required in this area. Historians should be less ready to draw conclusions for the country as a whole without at least testing their assumptions on a number of regions. Of course post-famine demographic changes were vital in increasing priestly efficiency. Using the populations of the 4 groups it can be readily shown that the clerical-lay ratio altered from 1:2,700-2,800 in 1835 to 1:1,500-1,900 in 1861 to 1:1,100-1,300 in 1891. A similar result is obtained by simply dividing total county population by the total number of priests.

The Mass is the centre-piece of formal religious practice, but the 1835 report does not represent the overall state of such practice, much less the total extent of popular piety in Tipperary. Unfortunately there is little material extant for 1835 to provide insight into other devotional practices, but an analysis of 35 parishes from the visitation reports of the famine period, with details of weekly catechism classes, Sunday sermons, monthly communicants, confirmations and an impressive selection of confraternities, does not give the impression of a religion-starved society during those troubled years.[164] The confraternities were important because they provided the nucleus of monthly communicants. While the number of monthly communicants was quite small in the 1840s there was rarely an increase recorded in the 1851 − 1855 statistics in the visitation reports, although the rapidly decreasing population must be taken into account when making this observation. The canonical obligation was communion once a year, and while some of the priests were unhappy at the number of defaulters, most were satisfied. In 1846 P. Larkin P.P. Moyne enthusiastically reported that the people would go to confession every day if given the opportunity.[165] Sometimes, however, the people themselves were not satisfied that sufficient opportunity was, in fact, being given.[166] Nevertheless, the Waterford respondent to the 1841 questionnaire made the interesting reply that the names of those who did not comply with their religious obligations were read from the altar.[167]

It seems that the term devotional revolution used by one historian is perhaps too strong to describe the development of post-famine practices as far as Tipperary is concerned. The real revolution was a demographic and social one, with, as the communion figures suggest, the tenant farmers continuing to be the spiritual and material bulwark of the Church, but becoming in post-famine years the majority in Catholic society, so that an increase in mass-attendance or devotional practice in relation to total population was inevitable irrespective of the priests' missionary zeal or any other contributory factors. This is not to deny, however, the importance of the jolt given to clerical awareness, or of the ecclesiastical discipline introduced by the national synod of 1850, the first comprehensive reform scheme for centuries, which set the pattern for subsequent provincial and diocesan synods. Despite periodic complaints of laxity the church's machinery functioned smoothly from the mid-50s onwards. The 1854 Synod, for example, re-emphasised the value of confraternities,[168] and although the visitation reports show that their distribution did not notably expand up to 1855, membership may have grown. There was a deluge of requests to Rome, many of them through Tobias Kirby in the Irish College, requiring faculties to enrol new members or re-erect demised confraternities.[169] Judging by the increasing number of articles in the *Irish Ecclesiastical Record* interest seems to have reached its peak in the last quarter of the century.[170] James Cantwell Adm. Thurles, better known for his leading political role, devoted several articles to confraternities, which he saw as an antidote to an age of 'such frivolous distractions' as light literature.[171] Cantwell's articles revealed that members of the Holy Family Confraternity were bound to approach the sacraments of penance and the eucharist twice a year, and some members were obliged to do so 8 times a year. By that time, too, the concept of more frequent Communion was beginning to arouse debate among theologians, some of whom feared that it might cause disrespect for the Blessed Sacrament.[172] Clerical reports to Kirby were also optimistic about the number of people going to confession. In 1865 Bishop Dominick O'Brien, Waterford, wrote of his church being 'crowded to suffocation'.[173] William Burke C.C. Kilbarron in north Tipperary, related that he had spent 9 hours in the confessional on Christmas Eve 1884 and 7 on New Years Eve.[174]

It was on this very issue of sacraments that the 1850 Synod made its most revolutionary impact. Traditionally the sacraments of baptism, matrimony, penance and the eucharist had frequently been celebrated in private houses, the latter two as part of the stations system. But the new decrees ordained that this tradition be discontinued. Only infants in danger of death or living in remote areas could henceforth be baptised at home.[175] To ensure that matrimony was performed in the churches, the synod ordered the bishops to legislate that no fees could be charged if the new rule was not observed.[176] It was the duty of the parish priest to ensure that the marriage partners had the rudiments of the faith and received the sacraments of Penance and the Eucharist before the wedding. Both these sacraments were to be celebrated in the church, particularly confessions for women, and the Blessed Sacrament could now be reserved in cathedrals and parish churches.[177] Parish priests were also instructed to have stations in church at least twice a year over and above the ordinary ones.[178]

Some of these decrees, shattering as they did a long tradition, came as a tremendous shock not only to the laity but to many of the clergy too. Several of the bishops, Michael Slattery included, were decidedly reluctant to abolish the old system of stations. Dominick O'Brien, St. John's College, soon to be bishop, lamented that many bishops upheld 'with all their might' the 'longstanding custom (abuse) of stations'.[179] Such bishops also greatly resented the interference of Dr Cullen with what they considered their own prerogatives. A remarkable memorandum from Dr Patrick Leahy, Slattery's secretary and successor, to the Archbishop for the benefit of Bishop Keane of Ross, then in Rome, reveals this outlook very well.[180] He advised that Cullen was 'meditating changes in the general constitution of the Irish Church, which can hardly be effected without confusion . . . a new system, too, is being introduced (I do not say by Dr Cullen) of checking and checkmating and thwarting the bishops in the administration of their dioceses by secret, unseen, underhand means, chiefly by secret representations to Rome'. Leahy urged that the stations should be maintained and advised that Rome was poorly informed about this old tradition. As late as 1855 the Vatican authorities were more than concerned at the delay in implementing the decrees on the stations, and channelled their ire through Slattery as the Metropolitan of Munster.[181] In this capacity the probably reluctant prelate contacted the Munster bishops for assurance that the synodical rules were being implemented.[182]

Bishop Keane's purpose in Rome had been to enlighten the authorities on the custom of stations, and to smooth the passage of Slatterys 1854 provincial synodical decrees; he seems to have largely succeeded. Grudgingly, after an impractical suggestion, soon abandoned, that they would allow a 'travelling chapel', the Cardinals agreed to accept, with some modifications, the 1854 decrees,[183] which were not as strict as those of 1850.[184] Stations in private houses were sanctioned in remote areas at a distance from the chapel, but the custom was finally laid to rest as far as villages and towns were concerned. Slattery was perturbed at the possible reaction of some of his priests to the new decrees and during Lent of 1854 he tried to soften the blow — 'for my part I will only say that I did all in my power to have the business satisfactorily arranged, and though I may not have succeeded to the full extent of my wishes, at all events I did the best I could, and were it not for me probably the state of things would be much worse than it is. God alone knows what I have suffered from anxiety of mind during the past year and that not on my own account only but chiefly on yours'.[185] Having thus sympathised with his clergy, Slattery's pastoral of October 1854, 'to be observed with the most implicit obedience' was read from the altar, (but not published in the newspapers); [186] the laity were formally informed of the retreat of the priests to the sanctuary, and the chapel, soon to acquire baptismal fonts and confessionals, became the focal point of formal religious practices. Thus was weakened one traditional point of contact between priest and people, a development aptly symbolished by the introduction of a distinctive clerical garb and

Roman collar. Yet any interference with this bond by ecclesiastical reform was partly compensated for by the ever-increasing presence of the priests on political platforms, a phenomenon begun by Daniel O'Connell in the 1820s.[187]

'Reasoning with an Irish free and independent.' (*Punch* cartoon, 14.8.1852).

Parochial map of County Tipperary.

Roman Catholic Chapels in County Tipperary.

The Diocese of Waterford.

The Archdiocese of Cashel and Emily (W = belonging to Waterford Diocese).

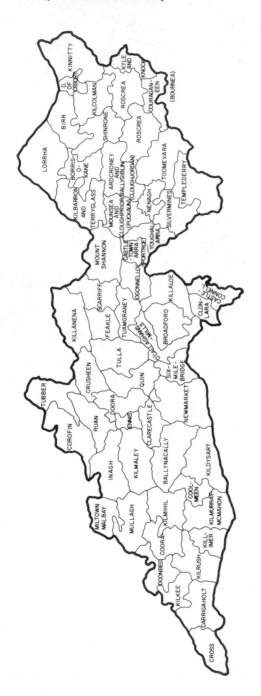

The Diocese of Killaloe.

Chapter Two

CONFLICT ON THE HUSTINGS

"In addition to using the altar as a political platform and the fear of Hell as a scourge, the ignorance of the simple-minded parishoners of many parts of Tipperary was shamefully and criminally abused". — *Irishman* 21 Feb. 1874.

So great had been O'Connell's success in encouraging the priests to become politically active that they came to regard such involvement if not as their birthright, then as an essential part of their duty, and they strongly defended this deviation from purely spiritual matters. Patrick O'Keeffe C.C. Fethard emphasised their dual role, spiritual and temporal, by pointing to the Gospel: 'Our Lord cured the body as well as the soul'.[1] Archbishop Leahy drew attention to the close relationship between religion and politics in Ireland,[2] a definite hangover from the days of the exciting struggle for Catholic Emancipation. Political involvement was also seen as a civil right by such well-known theologians as Dr Patrick Murray (professor of Moral Theology in Maynooth from 1841 to 1849), J.S. Vaughan, and J. O'Reilly, as well as by prelates like Patrick Leahy or ordinary priests such as Michael B. Corry C.C. Nenagh.[3] Murray, who wrote a pamphlet on the subject, pointed out that the priestly character in no way detracted from the priest's status as a citizen, which the state could not interfere with, although the Church could suspend certain civil rights if necessary.[4] He did not consider that clerical abuse of temporal power in the past undermined the clergy's essential political rights, and he denied that such abuse ever existed in the clerical body as a whole.[5] As well as defending their right the priests also justified their activity as a necessity either to combat landlord influence, help their people redress grievances, or indeed to keep them within the limits of constitutionality.[6] In this capacity some priests saw themselves with their bishops as the political leaders of the parishoners.[7]

Murray's statement epitomises how easily they adapted to their political role, and so natural did such involvement become for them, that Maynooth professors, (while discouraging a political atmosphere there by forbidding political discussions or the reading of newspapers by the students),[8] became aware of the need to provide some guidelines for the Divinity students on the scope, quality and limitations of their future political activity. Unlike their colleague Thomas Furlong, who advised total abstention,[9] both Patrick Murray and George Crolly emphasised moderation.[10] Murray devoted a series of lectures to the matter towards the end of the final year, and was particularly concerned about electioneering. Statistics for Tipperary alone show that he was more than justified in this.[11] A grand total of 929 involvements of priests in election campaigns were recorded there from 1850 to 1891; this represented 324 individual priests or 56% of the entire priesthood.[12] Cashel clergy accounted for 52% of these which is 9% higher than their numerical ratio, the Waterford percentage is normal, while Killaloe is 7% below the numerical ratio. The education breakdown generally reflects the normal relationships within the county, but Maynooth-trained priests had a higher and Thurles a lower percentage than usual. Although they were speaking in the context of Repeal, the assertion of Patrick Murray and Henry Neville of Maynooth that those priests who interfered prominently in politics were not Maynooth-trained is entirely untrue, and probably reflects their desire to present the college in the best possible light to the 1854 commissioners.[13]

Extensive involvement does not highlight the degree of intensity of activity. The statistics include such passive participation as the signing of requisitions, and this considerably distorts the overall picture. On a more active level the priests attended, chaired, and spoke at meetings, proposed and seconded candidates, formulated resolutions, held their own separate meetings, were even proposed as candidates, canvassed their parishoners, supplied them with refreshments and transport to the polling booths, where they kept an over-paternal watch on proceedings during the days of the open ballot.[14] One hostile source alleged that the Fethard priests directed the women not to live with their husbands unless they promised to vote Liberal. Such activity often intensely irritated the priests' political opponents, but the question of spiritual influence i.e. that exercised by the priest as a priest, was more controversial, although one suspects those opponents raised the matter for propaganda purposes. Still, this was not always the case. Archbishop Leahy, who frowned upon any pressure 'passing the limits of persuasion', regarded political harangues from the altar as acts of spiritual influence, but precisely similar sentiments outside the church, while reprehensible, were merely the actions of a citizen, irrespective of the speaker's priestly character or its added influence.[15] Leahy forbade altar speeches with more or less success;[16] a similar rule had been applied in various dioceses from the 1830s, although it had lapsed for long periods.[17] When politico-religious issues dominated election campaigns the priests felt entitled to use the altar, and the bishops were not inclined to interfere. Five Tipperary priests were accused of spiritual intimidation at the 1867 election hearing.[18] The enquiry committee, however, sagely decided that while they had 'exercised their influence upon their congregation in a manner calculated to prejudice the free choice of the electors', this did not amount to undue influence as defined by law.[19] Whether it infringed upon ecclesiastical rules is another matter. The most celebrated case was the Galway election of 1872 when a bishop and 19 priests were arraigned by Judge Keogh,[20] a man much disliked by the priests of Tipperary, who reacted strongly to the judge's statements, and, unlike the Dublin priests,[21] attacked the justice of the decision as well as its tone. They were especially annoyed at Keogh's reference to the confessional as a means of intimidation. Apart from resolutions issued by the clergy of Cashel and Emly,[22] 33 priests attended protest meetings in Templemore, Roscrea, and Clonmel.[23] Keogh was burnt in effigy in Clonmel, although the priests were not involved in this.[24]

Such indignation carries the implication that the clergy were opposed to the use of spiritual influence; but the matter was not quite so simple. Even the theologians were divided on it. Patrick Murray was distinctly hostile to the priests in their spiritual capacity trying to influence the electorate. He concluded that a vote in itself was ethically indifferent, even if it promoted the election of an M.P. hostile to religious reforms such as Catholic Emancipation.[25] In short, an elector was not morally responsible for an M.P.'s own malice. Murray particularly disliked such pressure if the voter was threatened with eviction by his landlord because of his choice. George Crolly added that a priest himself might be guilty of sin by forcing an elector to endanger his family in opposing the wishes of an exacting landlord.[26] But, John O'Hanlon, a contemporary of Murray and Crolly at Maynooth, put forward a view common to other theologians[27] that theology was relevant to all political matters. He proposed that a vote could be a spiritual as well as a temporal matter if the effect of electing a particular M.P. was sinful.[28] While holding that such a case would rarely arise in practice, he maintained that an elector would be bound under pain of mortal sin to vote for a candidate favourable to a measure such as Catholic Emancipation, if that candidate was decidedly and undeniably superior to others, and of great importance in carrying the measure. He upheld the priests' right to withold the sacraments in such rare cases. O'Hanlon, however, underlined the importance of a voter's education and intelligence, and held that priests were not justified in dictating to an intelligent well-educated audience, although they were entitled to inform the consciences of ignorant people. This can hardly be reconciled with his statement on the moral dimension, but then he placed most Irish audiences in the ignorant category. He was prepared to concede that the uneducated were entitled to form their political opinions from the educated laity if they so desired.

O'Hanlon's views were more compatible than Murray's or Crolly's with the attitude of most Tipperary priests involved in practical and often heated politics. During the stormy 1852 election when religious issues were at stake,[29] John Mackey P.P. Clonoulty stressed the obligation to vote against the Tories, and regarded the keeping of promises due to alleged landlord intimidation as 'a most culpable breach of moral duties'.[30] The *Dublin University Magazine*, always glad to strike a blow at the priests, reported that the Bishop of Ossory dispensed Carlow voters from such promises.[31] This magazine, however, did not always exaggerate. Even Archbishop Leahy, despite his condemnation of altar speeches warned his congregation that a vote against their religion, country or the public good was a 'grevious sin'.[32] Andrew James Scanlan P.P. Bournea, referring to the splitting of votes, dramatically advised his audience that there was no such thing as one vote for God and one for the Devil, while Joseph Organ C.C. Fethard warned that a vote for the current Government was a vote against conscience.[33] These were not extreme cases of spiritual influence; yet the very allegation of mortal sin implied if not the witholding of the sacraments then the necessity of seeking absolution. There is, however, no evidence to support the allegation of the *Dublin University Magazine* that the priests denied the sacraments to anyone who voted against their wishes.[34]

Altar threats such as that of Patrick Hickey P.P. Doon, implying the hostile intervention of the Almighty, made for the benefit of the superstitutious, were another type of spiritual intimidation. Without mentioning names, Hickey drew attention to the 'scabby people' in the gallery and stated that 'their cattle were sick and their substance melting away, their children would also fall sick, and they would yet meet a death they did not expect.'[35] The individual concerned was murdered soon afterwards, and the police partly blamed Hickey's sermon. Other priests were adept at using apparent religious animosity, often as a back-up to spiritual pressure. Archdeacon Michael Laffan, who had a large capacity for invective from an early age, attacked the Tory leader Benjamin Disraeli as 'the lineal descendant of the scoundrel who betrayed Our Saviour'.[36] This was basically the use of religion as election propaganda, and candidates' politics rather than their religion was the chief issue. John Scanlan P.P. Toomevara reflected this very well in his refence to the absurdity of a Catholic Tory.[37] Indeed, the very fact that a number of Tipperary M.P.s who were Protestants received the support of the priests is sufficient proof of this. It should be said, too, that the type of harangue used by Michael Laffan was well understood, and the Protestant clergymen of Fethard attended his funeral.[38]

Spiritual pressure to influence a voter's choice may have been theologically controversial, but the priests' right as ministers of religion to point out certain election duties was acknowledged. Such duties included the obligation to vote, to abstain from violence or intimidation, to avoid perjury and refuse bribes. Yet, if the priests themselves did not always practise the finer points of theology in the case of intimidation, neither were they particularly immune to the rewards offered by wealthy candidates, although they indulged in some remarkable theological hairsplitting on the matter. Archbishop Leahy warned a cathedral congregation that the retention of bribe money was nothing less than a mortal sin.[39] He placed heavy emphasis on the benefactor's motive, and refused a candidate's offer of a site for the Presentation convent Cashel, because the motive was suspect.[40] Nevertheless, the Archbishop submitted that an elector might legitimately be swayed by a candidate's ability and disposition to support local charities.

Cashel, like some other boroughs, achieved notoriety for corruption, and was disfranchised as a result. During the 1868 election there, money was lavished on the spiritual and on the temporal. One candidate, apart from patronising the shops, laid aside £1225 for general distribution among the people, £200 was donated for a convent site in Fethard, a set of Stations of the Cross to the local church, (at least equal to any in the kingdom, according to Dean Cantwell), £500 to the Christian Brothers' school in Cashel (to be returned if the candidate was defeated) and the construction of a private telegraph line between Cashel and Gooldscross.[41]

Money given after an election was not deemed as bribery by the clergy. Following the County election of 1869 the National Association candidate, Captain Charles White, sent £100 to the Thurles cathedral building fund, £25 to Maurice Mooney P.P. Cahir for distribution among the poor, and £100 to the Bishop of Killaloe for a similar purpose.[42] In 1859 John Ryan P.P. Newinn used this loophole when he informed the candidate, Sir Timothy O'Brien, that the chapel needed a new organ. He received a handsome £300. But Ryan's attitude was distinctly curious, if evolving. Seven years prior to this, when curate in Cashel, he had lodged evidence with a solicitor of the 'enormous amount' of patronage, drink and bribery there.[43] By 1868, however, his advice to 'friars, nuns, monks and bishops' was 'take all you get'.[44] He sprinkled similar advice to the laity with the ethical admonition not to allow such money to influence their votes. His innuendo about bishops drew an immediate retort from Leahy, who suspended him, although the Archbishop admitted being offered the above-mentioned £100 for the new cathedral, which he had apparently initially refused but accepted on seeing Ryan's letter in the paper.[45] This priest further exasperated the Archbishop by recalling Leahy's part (when President of St. Patrick's) in introducing to him a candidate willing to pay £400 towards Cashel charities in 1852, which Ryan then considered an 'indirect bribe'.[46]

In the currency of the last century these were very large sums indeed.

They clearly highlight the candidates' sensitivity to priestly electioneering influence. Some of them considered this decisive, and even Conservative candidates were advised not to neglect it. The Earl of Donoughmore told Robert Jocelyn Otway of Templederry not to commit himself 'until you are very sure of the candid support of at least a portion of the clergy'.[47] Although their comments tended to vary with the circumstances, complaining about absolute clerical power when the priests' side won and questioning it when the opposite happened, contemporary hostile commentators were generally convinced of the potency of clerical electioneering ability.[48] But opponents of the priests were not alone in emphasising it. Patrick Murray, despite his dislike of excessive political involvement, waxed eloquent on the priests ruling 'over the masses of the people with unlimited sway'.[49] He traced this alleged influence to the people's lack of education and degradation over the centuries, and to the priests' role especially during the Famine.[50]

Were such comments justified? Undoubtedly there were individual cases of politically powerful and influential priests. Dr Michael Burke P.P. Clonmel was one, although he once maintained that his recognised influence stemmed from the people themselves.[51] He candidly remarked, however, that his audience would be surprised at the large number of candidates who normally contacted him prior to elections in the borough. During the 1857 election, when the opposition was apparently formidable, Burke, speaking for 2¼ hours at one meeting, correctly forecast of his opponents — 'I will show them that I am not to be conquered'.[52] Revealing the priests' decisive influence in another respect, Francis Clearly P.P. Bournea stated that some voters, especially the old or ill, would not go to the polls at all without the priests' company.[53] Again, evidence of strong priestly influence was the response, 'Fr. McGrath' or 'Fr. Gleeson', by some voters, when asked their choice at the polling booths.[54] Such examples clearly represent a certain pattern, but not all voters in Tipperary were old or ill, and not all priests had the political ability of Dr. Burke. While, therefore, the priestly office influenced some voters, it was basic political talent that swayed most. Neither did the rank of the priest within the Church's hierarchical structure nor his academic achievement necessarily have any notable bearing on it. Patrick Murray was astounded to see ordinary priests who had barely passed their examination becoming, as he saw it, political celebrities.[55]

The truth is that the political power of the priests was anything but absolute. Later chapters will prove more conclusively the unique, very real, sometimes decisive, but nevertheless limited influence exercised by the priests as a whole. Electioneering, which will also be seen in the context of particular political questions, proves this too. Patrick Hickey P.P. was quite unsuccessful in his efforts to change Lord Derby's Doon tenants from voting Conservative.[56] Bribery proved more powerful than clerical influence in Cashel where 'honest' John Lanigan, cousin of John Ryan and Dean Laffan, was soundly defeated. As will be seen later not only did the priests sometimes fail to unite the Liberal electors, but suffered a split in their own ranks, demonstrating the impact of public opinion upon their own political outlook. Despite the view of John O'Hanlon on the ignorance of the Irish electorate, many of the laity were able to distinguish between the priest on the altar and the priestly politician on the platform, and resented anything that savoured of naked or corporate clerical dictation. Some electors voted against the National Association candidate in the by-election of 1865 because a clerical meeting under Leahy recommended him before the laity had deliberated on the matter.[57] This was not the last separate clerical gathering, and in 1866 Leahy, not very convincingly, explained that he had convened the clergy at the request of laymen and priests.[58] In the elections of 1868 and 1869, however, the priests did not meet until the lay section had met first.[59]

This points to the existence of other forces at work in the world of politics at local level. Basically the priests shared their influence with landlords, other educated laymen, newspapers, and what may be called the mob. Tory landlords were the chief opposing pressure group as far as the electors were concerned. Little is known about the election *modus operandi* of the landlords mainly because they did not hold large controversial public meetings as the Liberals or Nationalists did. The diary of John Trant, a landlord in Dovea, near Thurles, even with its brief recordings, shows that they formed an election committee which met privately at least once a week in the run up to the 1852 election, but the diarist did not record details of proceedings.[60] In 1857 the landlord campaign in Clonmel was run by what was known as the Central Conservative Association;[61] occasionally a particular estate was the centre of organisation; for example the Hawarden estate near Dundrum served this purpose in 1866.[62] Unlike their opponents, the Conservatives could not rely upon the extensive support of their clergymen, a situation which had been quite the reverse in the early part of the century.[63] The interest taken by the Rev. Charles Fry, Clonmel, in the 1859 election, and the advice he offered to Lord Naas was kept very private.[64] Land agents and bailiffs were obvious cogs in the landlord machine,[65] and it appears, too, that many electors with some justification regarded the presence of the military on polling day as an effort to impose Conservative views upon them.[66] The landlords were in a strong position to influence the voters, and there is evidence of eviction threats for failure to vote Tory.[67] In his private notes of 1866 in preparation for the election committee hearing, Archbishop Leahy referred to the eviction of many tenants because of breaking their promises to landlords. There is not sufficient evidence to support this, however. Some landlords or agents did inconvenience or damage electors by demanding the rent before the harvest, or by seizing cattle on failure to promptly pay, whereas previously they had allowed a period of grace.[68] Nevertheless, even this was not normal practice in Tipperary. The vast majority of tenants were not afraid to oppose their landlords' wishes, and John Trant noted in his diary his own canvassing of electors 'without effect'.[69]

Apart from such opposing influence, the priests had to share their own platform with Liberal landlords and the educated middle-class, who were particularly important in urban areas, where the electors themselves had a higher standard of education because of the proximity of schools. It would not be accurate to hold that the priests were always the main bulwark of Liberal support, although they were the chief professional group in electioneering and sometimes did initate and practically direct campaigns. Generally speaking, however, elections were guided by the so-called Liberal club, usually a temporary body, which was established by leading laymen with the aid of influential priests. Local J.P.s such as Charles Bianconi or Frederick Lidwell, Town Commissioners, Aldermen and the Mayor of Clonmel were important participants in Tipperary electioneering.[70] The increasing political consciousness of the electorate themselves cannot be ignored either, and many of these people could make up their own minds independently of lay or clerical pressure. Newspapers run by such men as Alderman Hackett of Clonmel, were important instruments in disseminating political opinion, although the literacy level of some electors reduced their effectiveness. The Liberal papers voiced the opinions of the educated middle-classes, and sometimes were instrumental in initiating election campaigns, and carried the first news of an election several months in advance.[71]

Finally, the priests shared their influence with the mobs. Apparently an entire mob could be hired in the 1860s for 2/6 per day.[72] Fortified by drink they intimidated the opponents of those who hired them. They were seen as an essential ingredient of Tipperary electioneering even by the priests, who, however, tried to keep them within reasonable limits, although they were sometimes victims of violence themselves.[73] Fr John Kenyon rarely failed to retain his composure in the face of mob heckling, and denounced the 'stolid perversion of the human intellect, which can be produced by beer or porter'.[74] Nevertheless, some priests supplied 'refreshments' to electors and presumably to their escorts.[75] Bishop Butler of Limerick agreed that this led to abuses and declared his intention of investigating cases where priests offered drink to the crowd.[76] Thus mob violence helped indirectly to limit priestly power by provoking more stringent ecclesiastical control over clerical political action. Following what he called the unprecedented violence of the 1857 by-election, Dr Leahy in a circular to his priests on 3 April

1857, drew their attention to the 1850 and 1854 synodical rules.[77] He introduced a regulation into the Archdiocese binding the minority to the majority clerical decision.[78] The minority, although allowed the right to state their opposition privately and vote against the favoured candidate, were forbidden to act against him. The aim of the rule was to avoid scandal to the laity, and to lessen electioneering tension. Indeed, Bishop Dominick O'Brien, Waterford, who also acted to prevent inter-clerical clashes, remarked that the Irish priests were 'the least fit to meddle in public matters in excited times, for they always lose their temper'.[79] It is arguable, therefore, that the large part played by the mob in some elections modifies the view, modern and contemporary, that the priests exercised more complete control over the minds of the more ignorant portion of society.[80] Every section of society, not least the poorest, could, if circumstances warranted, display an independence of priestly influence, not only in electioneering, but, as later chapters will show, in the formation of political opinions.

Eventually the pressure of all parties on the unfortunate electorate was eased by the Ballot Act of 1872, which not only introduced the secret vote but greatly increased the number of polling stations,[81] thus diluting electoral tension by rendering mob intimidation far less effective.[82] Of course the landlords' influence was drastically undermined too. But, the priests' role was considerably altered also. Yet they were very much in favour of the secret ballot from an early stage, and in 1859 32 priests had been active in the short-lived Tipperary Ballot Association, which was formed by Liberals, lay and clerical.[83] All priests in fact were ex-officio members. Their involvement is important in so far as it reveals that they saw landlord and mob influence, and not their own, as the major coercive forces in electioneering. But it has been argued that the priest still had the use of the pulpit and the confessional when the Ballot Act became law. In pre-ballot discussions Bishop Butler and John McDermott P.P. Co. Sligo were adamant that the confessional would not be used,[84] and considering clerical indignation at Judge Keogh's reference they were probably largely correct. It is indisputable, however, that there was a marked decrease in the electioneering involvement of the priests during the 1870s and 1880s[85] partly due to the secret ballot and partly because of Fenian intimidation or the centralising policy of Parnell. These will be looked at in some detail later.

Chapter 3

THE PRIEST AND THE LAND 1850-1876

"If you say the likeness between child and parent proves against the father of the bastard, why then there is no doubt the persecuting landlord, the slave slasher, is the father of all calamities and ruin which have desolated our poor country". Father William Mullally, *Limerick Reporter* 19 March 1850.

Any hollows in the graph of priestly electioneering either at mid-century or later were well-filled by clerical involvement in other political issues. Since the farming community supplied the Church with person-nel, capital and a devotional nucleus, as well as forming the bulk of the Tipperary electorate, it seems logical to continue with a study of agrarian politics. Contrary to one modern opinion,[1] their farming background sharpened the priests' concern with the land issue, and familiarised them with complex agrarian problems, while the possession of parochial farms gave them some vested interest in reform. So interested was one priest in the matter that he proposed to write a 'catechism' of tenant right, using such diverse sources as the Bible, Bentham, Wade's treatises on Political Economy, and ideas of the Protestant moralist, Paley.[2] The priests' conviction of the necessity for reform was amply demonstrated by their vocal presence on public platforms, intense involvement in agrarian movements, detailed evidence before Govern-ment commissions, and extensive newspaper correspondence. But, as priests, their attitude to reform was always tempered by ethical and theological principles which deserve some scrutiny.[3]

Theology was broadly conservative, tending to preserve the status quo, while at the same time allowing a sufficient degree of accommo-dation for changing agrarian policy. It offered a solution to the apparent moral indefensibility of a native Catholic majority being dominated by a largely Protestant landlord class, whose forefathers had forcibly supplanted the original Catholic owners. The theological rationale hinged upon the state's obligation to make some provision for peace and stability. Ownership rights were deemed 'sanctified by public authority',

and justified by their 'public utility';[4] the initial injustice of the confis-
cations did not negate this obligation. It was an underlying principle
of theology that in aiming at the common good the Government could
not 'take away from the rich in order to give to the poor'.[5] Theologically,
ownership signified the 'right of substance',[6] which automatically con-
ferred the right to make and enjoy profits,[7] which in the landlord's
case were his rents. The theological qualifications on property rights,
however, were vital in a period where the desire for tenurial change, if
not always vocal, was never far from the surface. The most important
qualification concerned the nature of ownership and the assertion that
it did not bestow absolute power of disposal, land being 'naturally
common' in the sense that nature assigned no portion of it to any
particular individual, although this 'natural state of negative communism',
as it was called, in no way prevented exclusive rights of ownership.[8]
Obviously, despite this reference to exclusiveness, the very denial of
absolute ownership allowed sufficient scope to accommodate the
tenants' claims. According to theology the tenant, through contract
and not ownership, enjoyed the *usufruct* i.e. the use and some of the
profit of the land.[9] Freedom by both parties to negotiate such a contract was a fundamental theological tenet, which also coincided with
accepted legal principle.[10] Morally speaking, coercion invalidated a
contract, though fear in itself did not do so; it gave the contracting
party the right to withdraw, however, a choice which offered little
consolation to the tenant in a practical situation.

The restrictive elements of these tenets had some bearing upon the
priests' outlook. They rarely failed to examine the moral basis of
proposed reforms, or to urge moderation if these seemed morally
dubious. In their strict regard for property rights the priests were
horrified at any hint of confiscation. Michael Cleary C.C. Killenaule
summarised their mid-century attitude that the rights of 'even the
rack-renting landlords' would not be infringed.[11] Few references were
made to peasant proprietary prior to 1880, although this policy did not
per se deny ownership. In 1851 Thomas Meagher C.C. Galbally was
prepared to advocate it on a restricted scale, through purchase from
the Incumbered Estates Court.[12] Prior to the 1870 Land Act, Canon
Richard Cahill, Donaskeigh, made a similar proposal, urging that the
Board of Works advance loans at 6%.[13] The fact that Cahill professed
himself satisfied with the purchase clauses[14] of that act shows how
little he, or indeed any other priest, considered peasant proprietary
either a practical aim or even a necessary one. The following decade
told a different story.

The priests' moral emphasis was most evident in their belief that the
end did not justify the means, portrayed by their support only of
constitutional agitation,[15] an outlook which never fundamentally
wavered during the four decades. Philip Fitzgerald C.C. Ballingarry,

still acutely conscious of the uprising there a few years earlier, agreed to support the Tenant League of the '50s only because it was 'beginning to assume a more wholesome and healthy tone', and was 'confined within the letter and the constitution of the law'.[16] Ultra-sensitive on this issue, as most O'Connellite priests were, Dr Michael Burke carefully explained that their principles were not those of 'rebellion, insurrection or communism',[17] a sentiment also re-echoed throughout the Land War decade.[18] The priests were, therefore, faced with the dilemma of condemning outrages, while attacking alleged landlord injustice. As frequently happened when theology failed to accord fully with public opinion, a degree of ambivalence arose, and, for example, William Quirke C.C. Anacarty, while condemning outrages as criminal, proceeded to blame landlords by reasoning that it was not 'human nature to allow oneself to be ground down without retaliating'.[19] This was a stock theme whenever the land issue became contentious.[20]

If, however, the priests' statements were influenced by a cautious theological base, they were in practical politics equally ready to utilise the qualifying tenets already outlined. An examination of their extensive polemics easily confirms this, particularly an 1851 controversy between John Kenyon P.P. Templederry and Dr T.W. Croke C.C. Charleville, Co. Cork (later Archbishop of Cashel), which is the best illustration of conflicting views on the three Fs policy[21] promoted by the Tenant League of Frederick Lucas in the 1850s and that of Isaac Butt in 1869.[22] In what he called his 'profession of political faith' Croke strongly supported the policy. He drew attention to the central theological proposition denying absolute ownership of land, arguing that the natural law only gave a man a life interest in ownership. He developed his thesis on the lines laid down by theologians. This enabled him to defend the tenant's interest in the land. Consequently, he felt justified in advocating compensation for improvements on the basis that these were the tenant's own property, and in concluding that God's law never ordained 'the fruits of industry are to become the spoils of idleness'. He clarified that permanent improvements, affecting what he called the substance of the holding, consisted of such matters as drainage or fencing, rather than purely decorative efforts like hedge-planting. He also based his premise upon the theory that improvements added substantially to a nation's wealth.

Kenyon displaying a distinctly negative attitude dismissed some of Croke's arguments as facile, and could only find a measure of agreement with him on this single point of compensation. But he also brought his characteristic cynicism to bear on this by countering that 'infinite railroads, countless ships, endless exports, interminable ledgers and all the hot and dusty requirements of our go-ahead system of civilisation may be very excellent things, and very beneficial to society, but for my part, I cannot understand why it should be so desperately hard to live'.

Partly dispensing with theology he shrewdly predicted expensive litigious proceedings arising from compensation claims, which he denied were in society's interest. Tipperary Tenant League priests, however, fully supported the underlying morality of Croke's view on this issue, which was a prominent one.[23] Like other priests,[24] William Cahill C.C. Mullinahone was prepared to greatly simplify the problem for his semi-illiterate audience by explaining that an improvement of 10/- an acre resulting from a tenant's labour was the property of that tenant, and that rent increases based on improvements were nothing less than robbery.[25] The curate of Galbally, Thomas Meagher, also a league member, was less banal in his discussion. His highly technical pamphlet drew attention to the similarity between Canon and Justinian Law, and considered the application of the Roman tenurial systems of *Locatio, Emphyteusis* and *Contractus Superficiarius* to Irish circumstances.[26] Meagher demonstrated that compensation for improvements was part of *Emphyteusis* even when such improvements were carried out without the landlord's consent. Compensation was either a cash payment or a rent concession, and in cases of eviction was obligatory both for improvements and disturbance.[27] Having highlighted Justinian Law as more equitable, and praised the Napoleonic Code, which was based on it, he concluded tersely that Irish land law 'is a violation of all principle'.

The priests, therefore, rightly considered compensation as central to the question of tenant right, the name given to the tenant's property in his holding created by capital investment; this was the core of free sale, one of the three Fs. Here, however, there was a clear divergence between theology, which recognised this as a moral right, and the civil law, which did not, although in practice many landlords refrained from interfering in its operation. The few landlords who were hardy enough or shrewd enough either to prohibit the sale of tenant right or to demand a hefty slice of the purchase price, were pilloried by the priests.[28] The Ulster Custom is of some relevance in relation to this issue. Canon Richard Cahill, in anticipation of the 1870 bill, defined the Custom as 'the right to sell the good-will of your farm to the highest bidder, giving the landlord a preference, and if evicted the right of claiming at the hands of the landlord the full value of the good-will, including all improvements made on his farm by the tenant, the landlord deducting any arrears of rent due'.[29] Yet the issue was rarely discussed by the Tipperary priests, and when it was such clerics as Thomas Meagher dismissed it as practically useless as long as rent kept pace with improvements,[30] a view shared by priests on a national level.[31] Like Meagher, Dr Michael O'Neill C.C. Tipperary did not view the Custom as particularly beneficial, although, paradoxically, he considered the failure of the 1870 act to extend it as the basic injustice of that bill.[32] Unlike Canon Cahill,[33] he was also critical of its corresponding compensation clauses, and made the telling observation that any southern tenant would get more for the goodwill of his holding than the maximum proposed on the act's scale.

It is so far clear that it was relatively easy for the priests to offer support on moral grounds for the related questions of free sale and compensation for improvements. The remaining two Fs, fixity of tenure and fair rents, were also amenable to theological principles, although the former perhaps less so. Considering the qualified nature of land ownership, excessive rents could plausibly be portrayed as an abuse of property rights. General clerical comments on rents varied prior to the Land War, but bearing in mind the views of modern economic historians that rents were not generally exorbitant,[34] the priests were the main agents in propagating the belief in a poverty-stricken, underfed, overworked peasantry, ground down by relentless, tyrannical landlords. William Cahill was one of several who proposed that the 1850 rents were rackrents.[35] Thomas Meagher condemned the rents charged by purchasers of incumbered estates, who apparently breached the rather naive understanding that the rents would only be 35% or 40% of the old rental.[36]

On a positive but blatantly biased level, the clergy were prepared to put forward suggestions for a fair (though not necessarily just) rent. Meagher's pamphlet showed that Roman, ecclesiastical and Napoleonic law tied rent to the value of the soil,[37] and interestingly enough this idea was favoured by many priests, and no doubt by tenants. William Cahill pointed to the Scottish computation of rent as ⅓ or ¼ of the produce value.[38] Using Adam Smith and the *Rural Encyclopedia* as his sources, Cahill quoted Smith's view of rent as the surplus remaining after deducting all farming expenses, a fair profit for capital and labour, and a decent maintenance for the tenant's family. The *Encyclopedia* held the comforting theory that a fair rent was what remained after the payment of all costs. Non-Tipperary priests had similar thinking; James Redmond P.P. Arklow, Co. Wicklow, suggested that the corn standard price be used to determine rent by a jury of ratepayers striking an average every 7 years.[39]

Since the priests were convinced that rents were excessive, and had definite views on the computation of a fair rent, their support for the idea of government interference to control valuation was a logical consequence. Such a proposition constituted meddling with property rights, but again the theological *a priori* limitations on ownership rendered it morally plausible.[40] Accordingly, Dr Croke argued that the Government was bound to interfere in what he saw as a situation of absolute ownership, and he fully endorsed the League's request for a valuation commission. In his second letter he proposed the prosecution of landlords who might refuse to accept the appointed rent. With the exception of Kenyon, vocal Tipperary priests concurred with his view.[41] This was, nonetheless, quite a revolutionary view in the 1850s, and James Redmond felt it necessary to deny that legislative valuation was communistic.[42] With his usual precision, Thomas Meagher saw a contradiction in the Government's power to prevent mortgagers charging over 5% for their money against landlords' property, and the latter's freedom to levy excessive rents.[43]

But the principle of state control raised two problems, interference in contract, and the curbing of competition for tenancies. The question of contract was in particular a moral and legal one. Thomas Meagher's view of rent as a continuous contract (like that of labour), subject to revision in times of depression, was one solution.[44] But the legal and theological emphasis on freedom of contract provided a more reasonable answer because it was not too difficult for the priests to depict the Irish tenant as an unwilling partner forced to accept the landlord's terms. This was Croke's approach and that of Thomas Finn C.C. Kilrossanty, Co Waterford, better known as the pastor of Newcastle in South Tipperary during the Land War.[45] Kenyon could not refute this reasoning, but theologically he differed fundamentally from his fellow clergy in his refusal to distinguish between ownership of land and other types of property. Betraying the bias of his urban background, he pointed to the similar predicament of artisans, who were also controlled 'by the laws of nature and the tyranny of circumstances'. Within those limits, he argued, freedom of contract existed. Apart from this, Kenyon disagreed that Government interference with valuation would curb competition, which he saw as a natural element in the law of supply and demand regulating all prices. Cynical as he was and secluded as he may have been in the hills of Templederry, Kenyon's shrewdness in this is undeniable. He again attacked the social exclusiveness of this policy, which did not advocate state control of all prices, urban as well as rural. Croke dismissed Kenyon's natural law as no more than a selfish impulse to make the highest profit, and refused to accept it as a true standard of value. He made no apology for the exclusiveness of the policy, because to him the land question was the most immediate and vital. Far from supporting free competition, William Quirke proposed that one of the league's main duties was to curb the 'reckless and ruinous competition of the land jobber'.[46] William Heffernan P.P. Clerihan had a drastic solution for the so-called grabber, — 'let no father give him his daughter in marriage, let no one attend his funeral, or say the Lord have mercy on his soul'.[47] This was a unique reference in mid-century, and perfectly defined the boycott technique of three decades later, which raised quite a moral storm as will be seen in the next chapter. The views of the league priests were valid in so far as competition pushed the price of land to a very high level; for example it increased it to £3 per acre in certain baronies in Tipperary.[48]

The whole question of rent and competition was intimately related to the more controversial eviction problem. This lay at the centre of the League's third plank, fixity of tenure, which aimed to limit the landlords' power of inflicting what John O'Dwyer called 'legal death'.[49] From the moral point of view a careful definition was required here, and the policy of both leagues seemed to offer precisely that. Therefore, William Mullally defined it as the right to possession on payment of a just rent,[50] a definition repeated by Richard Cahill during the existence of Butt's movement.[51] Willingness to pay such a rent was a vital theological consideration, and some priests were quick to admit the justice and even necessity of evicting lazy or improvident tenants.[52] Thomas Meagher's pamphlet explained the Roman law allowing eviction for dilapidation of property.[53] Generally speaking, however, the priests' public orations tended to depict evictions as capricious and unjust. They were loud in their condemnation of landlords in general, while, with some ambivalence, they exempted the more benevolent ones in their own parishes. John Moloney P.P. Kilcommon, a man not noted for the temperance of his remarks, could only praise Lord Dunally, who was later reviled by the Land War priests.[54] While in 1850 Dr Burke was careful to make clear that he was not the 'blind partisan' of the tenants,[55] he did not hesitate in an open letter to the Earl of Donoughmore in 1853 to publish a list of eviction statistics, townland by townland, mainly because the Earl had presented his emigrating tenants with Protestant bibles.[56]

The profound experience of the Famine and the resulting rise in the eviction rate[57] tended to submerge the more reasoned language of morality or justice and provoked the most intense invective, in which landlords were painted at best as indolent parasites, otherwise as demons incarnate, hellish monsters and 'bloodsucking vampires'.[58] James Redmond claimed that he would use the confessional to question a landlord on his valuation during the Famine, and if it had been unfair would call him a murderer.[59] Archdeacon Fitzgerald, Rathkeale, Co. Limerick, saw the Famine as an artifical one created by landlord greed,[60] a view held by such Tipperary priests as William Mullally, John Moloney and William Cahill. Even the more intellectual clerics were inclined to make similar judgements,[61] which contrasted to the fatalistic view of John Ryan, who portrayed it as a visitation of God's providence and held out the hope of better times in the next world.[62]

Because of their vocation the clergy were especially aware of the gruesome details of famine suffering, and were sensitive to the stunning demographic decline from 1845 to 1850. A glance at *Pobal Ailbe Cashel and Emly, Census of Population 1841-1971* shows that most parishes suffered a population loss of about 30% by 1851. In some parishes whole townlands were severely depopulated, leaving an indelible impression on the priest's mind. Tenant League priests associated famine depopulation not with starvation but mainly with landlord clearances. Patrick Hickey and his curate, John O'Dwyer witnessed a

32% decrease in the population of Doon parish; O'Dwyer saw the eviction of 900 people and 159 houses levelled by desperate landlords since 1847.[63] He was especially incensed because 'most of them are dead . . . those that did not die in sheds died in the poor house . . . others, and these were the most numerous, have I seen burrowing in ditches and pits of old lime-kilns . . . often I crept, ankle deep in water, under those sheelings. . . . I will not speak of 300 adults, who, in one half year, died of starvation under my very own eyes in that parish'. He dwelt specifically upon the clearances in the townlands of Coolnamona, Carrigmore, and Coolbane by two landlords.[64] Other league priests were equally eloquent and specific in pinpointing clearances in their parishes.[65] Despite his fatalism, John Ryan was deeply affected by the famine.[66] He had witnessed an unprecedented influx of over 4,000 starving paupers into the Cashel workhouse,[67] which was reflected by a small 3% decrease in the parish population between 1841 and 1851. The real story emerged in the 1861 census which registered a drastic 40% decrease.

If, therefore, the priests were convinced of the sound morality of land reform and if their conviction was sharpened by such Famine experience, what was their response to the organisations that promoted the land issue — the leagues of Lucas and Butt, and the National Association of the 1860s? Sixty-eight priests or 44% of the county's total (1850-1852) were involved in, or sympathised with the 1850 league,[68] 40 priests or 25% were members of the National Association[69] and only one, Dr Michael O'Neill C.C. Tipperary, was involved in Butt's movement. Maynooth representation was greater than normal, but the figure of 72% for the National Association is significantly higher than the 57% for the Tenant League. This seems to indicate a preference by Maynooth priests for an organisation which was held in higher favour by the hierarchy; Maynooth statistics, however, always defy interpretation because they invariably show a majority over the normal for widely different if not conflicting political issues. The relatively conservative nature of both organisations is underlined by the heavy involvement of parish priests in them, 51% and 60% for the league and association respectively, an unusual reversal of the usual statistics. This is more clearly seen in an age breakdown, with 40% of league priests and 43% of association priests over fifty, a striking contrast with the composition of the Land War organisations.[70] The diocesan figures suggest that the league drew greater support from the Archdiocese of Cashel than the association did.

These statistics indicate a considerable reservoir of clerical sympathy with agrarian reform; how vigorous this was and how vital the priests' role in the organisations remain to be seen. The early league was the only movement from 1850 to 1891 partly inspired by priests, springing as it did from the Callan Tenant Protection Society, whose most important leaders were the local curates, Thomas O'Shea and Matthew Keeffe.[71] The chief national organisers, Lucas, Gray and Greer, were convinced that the proposed network could not survive without the active co-operation of the clergy. Consequently, the Dublin organising committee accurately defined the league as 'limited in its objects, limited in its means, checked and controlled by the supervision of the ministers of religion'.[72] Clearly, this included clergymen of another persuasion too, a fact borne out by the involvement of some northern presbyterian ministers. While the better-off laity were deeply involved in the spread of the league, and sometimes in a leading capacity,[73] there is clear evidence that the organisers were correct in stressing the importance of the priests' role. This role was essentially administrative, and varied from signing requisitions to attendance at major meetings, Dublin-based as well as local, making detailed speeches, and most important, operating the league's machinery.[74] The pattern of involvement closely resembled that in other counties.[75] The ratio of 31 priests to 22 laymen on the county's organising committee is conclusive proof of clerical importance.[76] As the principal branch executives, the priests were also key figures in collecting and contributing to badly needed funds.[77] William Mullally, who announced that he had personally collected £300 and copied 50 petitions since his entry into politics,[78] ventured into neighbouring Donaskeigh to aid Michael McDonnell C.C. to collect there.[79] He boasted of his success in extracting money from his own Anacarty parishioners, although he was not entirely satisfied with the weak efforts of some priests to collect the penny in the pound levy. A special annual collecting committee was appointed in Mullinahone, and William Cahill as well as proposing the withdrawal of league membership from ratepayers who refused to subscribe, also, to his parish priest's chagrin, called for a vote of censure on reluctant collectors.[80]

While the clergy played an important organising role in the Tenant League, their contribution to the National Association was much more confined and was mainly electoral, as will be seen later. On the other hand Dr Michael O'Neill was the president and guiding force of the Tipperary Tenant League under the umbrella of Butt's movement, which itself was launched in Tipperary town with the usual quota of priests present.[81] O'Neill chaired its weekly meetings,[82] engaged in lively public controversies, and travelled to the Dublin meetings of the parent body.[83] So determined was this curate that Leopold Cust, agent of the local landlord, Smith-Barry, threatened him with legal proceedings and closed the town hall in Tipperary to the league.[84]

But, if the vital organising contribution of the clergy, especially in the 1850s may be conceded, the effectiveness of their endeavours must be immediately questioned. The National Association may be dismissed at once because of its severe institutional weakness at local level. It totally lacked a network, a situation deplored by one of its leading advocates, W.J. O'Neill-Daunt, who pointed to the vital necessity of clerical involvement.[85] Butt's league of the late 1860s was a limited affair also, having a very sparse national network, despite his aspirations to build a structure like O'Connell's Catholic Association.[86] Only one branch was established in County Tipperary in the parish of Tipperary. This branch bravely if naively proposed to deal with tenant problems within the Tipperary Poor Law Union, although O'Neill, against some opposition, insisted that the entire county came within its sphere.[87] With very few exceptions, however, the league confined its operations to Tipperary parish during its short existence.

The Tenant League of Lucas was a more substantial local organisation lasting in theory from 1850 to 1858. The proposal of William Morris P.P. Borrisoleigh at the Cashel organising meeting of October 1850 to set up 11 districts of approximately 6 parishes each did not materialise, although 9 districts were established consisting of 25 parishes or 39% of the county's total.[88] These, however, were not uniform, and varied from one to 11 parishes, a clear symptom of weakness, when compared with the much smaller units of Land War organisations. The districts were grouped mainly in the Baronies of Iffa and Offa East, Clanwilliam, the Kilnamanaghs, Middlethird and Slieveardagh, with some patchy representation in Eliogarty and Lower Ormond. Predominantly they stretched across the lower fertile portion of mid-Tipperary, the main east and west blocks being linked by the small Cashel district. In effect, the greater part of Tipperary, north of Clonoulty, and a considerable sector of the south were untouched by the league, although several priests in northern parishes offered co-operation. Furthermore, the movement failed to compensate for this geographical deficiency by sustained and effective action as the alleged watchdog of the farmers, (a title given to it by William Mullally).[89] Cognisant of this role, William Cahill tried to organise committees in the small Mullinahone district to investigate landlord-tenant relations in various townlands, particularly Cloonagoose, where considerable tension seems to have existed.[90] The Tipperary district, with Mullally as secretary, also met on a regular basis for over a year, but the others rapidly collapsed. After 10 weeks the *Tipperary Free Press* complained of apathy in the Clonmel branch.[91] The Borrisoleigh district, despite the efforts of the Parish Priest, William Morris, was little more than a collecting agency, while there is no evidence of activity by the Drangan society.

The inability of the priests to sustain or extend the various movements in Tipperary is clear. Yet, considering the eagerness and efforts of the determined Tenant League nucleus such as Mullally, Quirke, Morris, Cahill and O'Dwyer, it is equally true that the fault did not always lie at the clergy's door. The sporadic nature of priestly land agitation until 1877 had several causes. These consisted of immediate religious and political problems, plus the more fundamental, long-term state of tenant farmer opinion. Since the first two were less important, they may be dealt with quickly. Naturally the religious issues readily aroused the interest of many priests. The main distracting influences during the early 1850s were the controversial Ecclesiastical Titles Bill and the proposed nunneries bills. The ever-present question of the protestant church establishment sometimes reared its head but this was not the subject of agitation at local level.

The Ecclesiastical Titles Bill of 1851 is the more important and was exploited with zest in the 1852 general election campaign. This bill, which declared the ecclesiastical titles used by church dignitaries illegal and prohibited the wearing of canonicals in public, was also more divisive because it came at a crucial time, when the priests of the Tenant League organisation were trying to float their movement. Partly for this reason they viewed the act in a sober and realistic light, and dismissed it for what it was — a dead letter. (Only in Donegal and Galway were tentative enquiries made about putting it into execution, but the righteous indignation of the priests in Donegal plus the difficulty of securing a successful prosecution had a sobering effect upon both the police and the attorney general.)[92] Conscious of the apparent unity between catholic and non-catholic leaguers, several priests genuinely, and justifiably, feared an infusion of sectarianism into politics.[93] Dr Croke and William Cahill argued that Repeal had failed because of sectarianism.[94] Willing to demonstrate his sincerity, Dr Michael Burke, in an uncharacteristic pose, held the hand of the Revd. David Bell, a Northern presbyterian minister, at a Tenant League meeting in Cashel.[95] William Cahill portrayed the bill as a deliberate effort to destroy the league,[96] and priests of his frame of mind were careful where they placed the emphasis when they condemned its author, Lord John Russell. It is interesting that John O'Dwyer attacked him on the land issues, that is upon his alleged defence of the landlords' right to evict,[97] and not for the ecclesiastical legislation.

It was, however, impossible to divert attention from the bill, and extensive protests were made in the form of petitions from 28 parishes (43% of the county's total);[98] there were also several meetings held and the altars rang with indignation.[99] Dr Burke was one of the main protagonists, as he had been during the agitation for Catholic Emancipation. But the *bona fide* league clergy pointedly abstained from attending emotive meetings. The radical West Tipperary group did not sign the requisition convening a major protest meeting in Cashel, which was, however, signed by 74 priests from 29 parishes;[100] these accounted for half the priesthood of Tipperary. Fifty-two of these had signed the land requisition of October 1850 to float the league in the county. This implies that a large body of priests was prepared to support land reform but did not view it in such exclusive terms as the league priests did.

The formation of the Catholic Defence Association[101] in 1851 to oppose the imposition of the Ecclesiastical Titles Bill, was hardly palatable to the leaguers either. While it did not have a network the new body weakened the allegiance of the more lukewarm leaguers, 18 of whom were among its 41 clerical members from Tipperary.[102] The confirmed league priests remained aloof, although they were forced into a working relationship with it when the executives of both bodies cemented a rather shaky alliance in 1851.[103] The league by refusing to make the religious issue one of its planks seemed to score over the association, which promised to seek agrarian reform. This, however, did not make the union any more attractive to league clerics, who were not convinced about the commitment of a semi-religious movement to the land problem. The coalition was, nevertheless, real, as the combined drive of the movements during the 1852 election testified. The two leading exponents of each organisation held a preliminary conference in Thurles to prepare for a public meeting, Dr Burke being chairman, and William Mullally joint-secretary.[104] A committee of 5 laymen and 6 priests from both groups was formed to organise the subsequent public meeting, the requisition for which was signed by about half the priests in the county.[105] This larger meeting was attended by 19 priests, including the hard core of leaguers.[106] The clergy played a major role in organising the county for the election, and the leaguers, though in a minority of 13 to 21 and 4 to 17 on the county election committee and the baronial committee respectively, were involved more or less according to their overall strength in Tipperary.[107]

Naturally, the league priests tended to dwell on the land issue,[108] and 3 of them appended their names to an address from 41 Irish priests and 22 laymen to the electors of Ireland.[109] The association clergy waxed eloquent on the religious question,[110] which really dominated the election not only because some priests were genuinely angered by it, but also because it was a splendid rabble-rousing platform cry.[111] Even the Tipperary district society adopted it as such in its proclamation signed by 13 priests — 'if you vote for Captain Otway, you vote to have your religion enchained, you vote to have your bishops and priests imprisoned and banished'.[112] This was a relatively mild statement compared with the sentiments of association priests.

Since the religious movement received its main impetus from the election campaign it is not surprising that in the autumn of 1852 it collapsed in the aftermath of the election. It was replaced by the insipid Friends of Religious Freedom and Equality, which also lacked a national network.[113] Still, it promoted a series of protests against the proposed convents bills of 1853 and 1854.[114] The 1853 effort, known as A Bill to Facilitate the Recovery of Personal Liberty in Certain Cases, was mooted to investigate suspicions of females forcibly detained in convents. Apart from its basic insinuation, the bill was obnoxious to priests because it intended to give the commissioners appointed the right of forcible entry to convents. The later act proposed by T. Chambers M.P., known as the Nuns Property Disposal Bill, was less offensive, but any state interference in the affairs of the Church was greatly resented by the clergy. Protest meetings were held in Cashel and Birr, and petitions were extensively signed.[115] Nun-hunting speeches were delivered with passion by such priests as Dr Burke, John Ryan, and Dean James McDonnell, who delved back to the time of Henry II. Ryan excelled himself with his particular kind of humour: 'get Chambers's portrait taken and sent to some eminent delph manufacturer to be stamped on the inside of chamber-pots. These chamber-pots will, I am sure, sell at a premium and be used all over the country and thus will Chambers receive daily, hourly, everywhere the reward he so richly deserves.' Archbishop Slattery marshalled his priests against the bill, and detailed instructions were set out for all lay and clerical witnesses who might be called to give evidence.[116] They were ordered to refuse information on the general principle that the civil law must yield if it collided with the moral law. On a national level the *Tablet* of 27 May 1854 contained two full pages of names attached to a protest declaration. These included the signatures of 23 Tipperary priests. The fact that the small core of league priests were involved points to a shift of attitude since 1851 for reasons which will be seen later.

These emotive protests, however, were strictly short term competitors with the league of Lucas, because the measures proposed never became law. The remaining religious and semi-religious questions, the protestant establishment and denominational education, did not turn attention from the land problem until the following decades. Both education and disestablishment were planks in the National Association's platform, although it made land reform a priority after 1865. Naturally, too, National Association candidates, many of them wealthy landlords, such as the Tipperary M.P. Charles Moore, were hardly likely to support radical land reform. There was also the difficulty of pursuing three aims. Indeed, the Meath clergy withdrew from the association in November 1865 on the grounds that its agrarian policy was not sufficiently advanced.[117] Although the priests of Tipperary and Meath were singularly close in political outlook, the split was not so evident in the former, where Archbishop Leahy, who placed more emphasis on religious issues, imposed tight discipline on the priests. But a total of 55 priests were involved in two stormy Thurles meetings in October 1869 where both clergy and laity demanded priority for land over education.[118] Dr Michael O'Neill showed his priorities when he vainly requested John Stuart Mill to stand for the constituency on the naive expectation that Mill as Tipperary's representative would waive his objections to denominational education.[119] But despite his preference for an agrarian policy O'Neill was forced to bow to National Association policy, and acknowledge the importance of education also. Like the education issue, the protestant establishment was a long-standing complaint, but it rarely generated local public meetings simply because its existence was no real threat to the catholic church or faith at local level. It dominated the 1868 election because Gladstone's legislation was pending. Speaking to a Thurles audience, which included 31 priests, John Scanlan P.P. Toomevara, with neat oratorical dexterity considered the land question as 'first in importance but second only in point of time'.[120]

The religious questions were mainly the concern of the bishops, the majority of whom considered them a priority, an attitude which irked the outspoken Archdeacon Fitzgerald, Rathkeale, Co. Limerick.[121] The hierarchy was obsessed with the education question to such an extent that it scarcely trusted any other body, even the National Association, to negotiate the issue. The extensive and significant collection for the Catholic University in 1851 was unquestionably due to the bishops' influence,[122] and the very mediocre Tenant League subscriptions partly reflect an absence of episcopal interest. Out of 15 Tenant League parishes a total of £407 was raised for the university, while only a very small sum was gathered for the league.[123] Only in 3 of these parishes, (Anacarty, Donaskeigh, and Doon), did the league collection exceed that of the university, and this was solely due to the efforts of William Mullally and John O'Dwyer, who unlike most other priests were not influenced by the negative attitude of the bishops. That the bishops could have inspired clerical enthusiasm is evident from the position in Clare where 66 priests under the chairmanship of Bishop Daniel Vaughan, made a large personal contribution to league funds in 1852 and 1853.[124] The league leaders were keenly aware of the desirability of episcopal support. They were certainly conscious of the thinly-veiled hostility of some prelates, and a league meeting in Dublin, attended by William Mullally and John O'Dwyer, issued a memorial to the hierarchy, which contained the revealing assurance that 'we of the league are no body of conspirators, revolutionists or anarchists'.[125] A small number of bishops responded with money but the plea was largely in vain. Although the bishops acknowledged the existence and sometimes the urgency of the land problem their response to agrarian movements between 1850 and 1876 was limited to a few meagre petitions, and certainly was not in proportion to their interest in education.

Yet while episcopal indifference influenced the priests it was the least important hindrance to the promotion of land reform. There were other political considerations of greater import, though again they were not crucial. The league of the 1850s operated under a basic political handicap. Considering the vital importance of parliamentary activity to promote the organisation's policies, borough and county M.P.s in their letters to John Ryan C.C. Cashel, secretary of the league's county organising committee of 1850, showed a surprising degree of ignorance of or disagreement with these policies.[126] This merely reflected the national position. Some of the 41 M.P.s who attended the Dublin land conference (attended by nine Tipperary priests) were decidedly unhappy at the presumption of a non-parliamentary body to dictate to them.[127] Furthermore, the status of the league's leaders,[128] the association of some of these with Young Irelandism, and their policy of independent opposition[129] all militated against a greater degree of support, lay and clerical, for the league. The unprecedented decision to appeal to Rome[130] against a rumoured clerical withdrawal from politics was largely promoted by leaguers, and certainly raised the suspicions of would-be supporters. Twenty-three of the 29 Tipperary priests who signed the memorial were leaguers, and Cardinal Cullen in his detailed report to Rome on the affair associated them with 'violent political discussions', and portrayed them as 'agents of the league even in contempt of their own prelates'. Finally, the defection of Sadleir and Keogh seems to have sapped the already waning enthusiasm of some supporters, also; William Mullally lamented that subscribers in his parish had lost confidence in the party and were refusing to contribute to the league.[131]

In the following decade a different set of political circumstances arose. These centred around fenianism, although the association between fenianism and agrarianism sometimes feared by the priests, did not materialise. However, a definite effort was made to yoke the land issue to the amnesty movement, and James Ryan Administrator of Nenagh sought to sever any connection between the two. He adroitly proposed that agrarian reform was too important to share any other platform.[132] In practice, and no doubt to his relief, the two issues proved incompatible planks, and the fenian element sometimes violently rejected the agrarian one. Such clashes were rare in Tipperary, because amnesty meetings tended to concentrate solely upon the movement's prime objective. Only a Cashel meeting combined both, and the shrewd John Ryan (by then promoted to the pastorate of Newinn), expounded on the urgency of tenurial reform, with the nationalistic threat of 14,000,000 Irishmen 'within a few hours walk of the Canadian frontier, full of money, full of knowledge, and full of angry feelings towards England'.[133] Ryan, however, was only displaying a certain degree of political astuteness, if not simple self-preservation, since his speech was little more than an exercise to harmonise both issues and silence fenian abuse at the meeting.

The by-elections of late 1869 and early 1870, however, witnessed a clash of interests, and again the clergy tried to focus attention upon the land issue. The best example of this is the speech of Canon Richard Cahill, Donaskeigh, at the 1870 nomination in Clonmel, where he expounded on the 1870 Land Act amid prolonged groaning from the fenian section of the audience.[134] Other priests tried to focus attention upon the virtues of landlord candidates; John Ryan proposed Massy

Dawson of Aherlow as a candidate and extolled him as a model land-lord.[135] But the discerning Archbishop Leahy saw Isaac Butt as a more suitable choice, acceptable to the clergy as a promoter of agrarian reform, and possibly to the fenians as the most prominent amnesty leader.[136] Butt's refusal[137] resulted in the choice of Denis Caulfield Heron, a lecturer in Political Economy in the Catholic University, whose closest contact with the land question had been a series of articles, one of which was printed in the *Irish Catholic Directory* of 1865, showing that he stood in high favour with the Church.[138] Eventually the choice of Liberal candidate was academic, and all issues, including land, were eclipsed in the fierce election struggles of '69 and '70, when the Fenian leaders O'Donovan Rossa and Charles Kickham were in the field.

In the final analysis, however, all the political, as well as the religious issues, exercised only a peripheral influence on the weak measure of local support for agrarian reform prior to the Land War. Their impact was momentary, and their absence would have made little difference in the long term. The vital underlying factor was nothing less than sheer tenant apathy. The reality was that the farmers were not particularly motivated by the moral compatibility or otherwise of suggested reforms, nor were they noticeably inspired by Famine ravages. The more politically aware priests did not ignore this apathy and some were more than a little frustrated by it. Despite his endeavours in West Tipperary, William Mullally could only report 'slow but sure progress',[139] while by 1852 John O'Dwyer drew attention to the 'deadly coldness of the people at present'.[140] Bishop Daniel Vaughan, at a Dublin conference of the league, proposed that a number of members travel throughout the country visiting people in their homes, explaining the league's principles.[141] He suggested his own diocese as a beginning and promised support. Only 3 months earlier, however, a fund-raising deputation of the league had been rebuffed in Clonmel by the mayor as well as others, despite being supported by two of the curates, Patrick Meany and Peter O'Connor.[142] Vaughan also suggested that the league's organ, the *Tenant League*, be streamlined and clearly outline the movement's principles. The declining circulation of this is another indication of farmer indifference. William Mullally distributed it to 39 Anacarty families, and John O'Dwyer to 20 in Doon in 1851, while in 1852 Patrick McGrath P.P. promoted it in the parish of Ballylooby.[143] Early in 1852 the Anacarty circulation was reduced to 10 copies.[144] Indeed, an overall reluctance to loosen the purse strings was symptomatic of tenant apathy, and angered William Cahill.[145] His disillusionment was justified because the Cashel meeting of October 1850 had pledged County Tipperary for £600 to league funds, but by 1851 only a fraction had been collected.[146] Following the 1852 election, when the more vigorous Tipperary town branch collapsed, the league was little more

Thomas Feehan, C.C. Rathdowney,
Co. Laois.

Joseph Farrell, C.C. Monasterevan,
Co. Kildare.

James E. Delaney, C.C. Clonegall,
Co. Carlow.

James Cantwell, Administrator, Thurles,
Co. Tipperary.

Mr. Peter E. Gill, Nenagh, Co. Tipperary,
Editor *Tipperary Advocate*.

Eugene Sheehy, P.P., Bruree, Co. Limerick.

(Sources *United Ireland* and *Weekly Freeman*).

than an inactive paper organisation in the county, as was the case on a national level.

Subsequently the sharper political awareness and dynamism of the league priests were characterised by their periodic but ineffective exhortations to reorganise. Both James Bermingham P.P. and his curate Michael Spain failed to root a branch in Borrisokane, but, as late as 1854, they pointed to the land issue as the 'question of all questions', and vainly suggested the establishment of parochial committees, with treasurers and collectors, keeping constant contact with the league's Dublin headquarters.[147] Bermingham made the rather desperate suggestion that a deputation from the hierarchy and Catholic nobility visit Napoleon III, and persuade him to remonstrate with his new ally, the Queen. In December 1854 William Mullally, promoting the league's bill, reminded a Thurles audience that public apathy in the first instance had forced the organisation to adopt the more diluted policy, known as Sharman Crawford's measure.[148] The 1857 election of The O'Donoghue,[149] (a member of the council of the league) as M.P. for Tipperary, may have been a parliamentary triumph for the organisation, but it did little to revive it at local level, and the following year witnessed its final and formal demise.

Despite evident local apathy the decision to dissolve the organisation was deprecated by a Tipperary newspaper, and five Tipperary priests revealed their loyalty by attending the league's general meeting in August.[150] The Tipperary Independent Club[151] also tried to arouse popular enthusiasm after the league's collapse, and at least 17 priests were involved in a meeting to that effect.[152] It was a futile gesture, and until 1877 public apathy continued; the land question remained little more than an election issue. Despite the continuous emphasis by the enthusiastic Dr O'Neill on alleged rent abuses on the Smith-Barry estate in 1869, not one of the tenants there were members of his league.[153] The 1870 act, irrespective of O'Neill's criticism of it, soothed whatever agrarian ruffles that may have existed, and the Smith-Barry tenants themselves made their attitude plain by sabotaging the league through a round-robin,[154] an action which precipitated the curate's bitter retirement from politics, except for a brief period during the Land War. Its demise was a clear sign of tenant indifference, later symbolised by the poor Tipperary representation at the Dublin land conference of October 1876, in spite of the organisers having circularised the Poor Law Guardians of each county.[155] Apathy arose not from lack of priestly interest, but from tenant sensitivity to such social and economic circumstances as improving harvests, high prices and falling eviction rates. The price issue in particular was of crucial importance, as William Mullally well recognised in his reference to the catastrophe of the Famine coming relatively soon after the prosperity of the Napoleonic wars which he himself remembered as a child.[156] His words may have been prophetic as far as the Land War was concerned, but the period of agricultural prosperity from about 1853 to 1876, was fatal to the existence of the Tenant League. Even when prices were low in the autumn of 1850 farmers were partly cushioned by rent abatements of anything up to 25%.[157]

The social problems of evictions and falling population were of less importance to the existence of an active agrarian movement like the Tenant League, although the priests were deeply concerned. A clear divergence of attitude to these emerged between priest and farmer. The truth was that the cottiers, labourers and small farmers generally bore the main brunt of hunger and wholesale clearances, while the better-off farmer actually benefited materially by further land acquisition. It is revealing that the league did not exist in parishes which witnessed evictions worthy of publicity in 1850; for example, in Toomevara, Silvermines, Roscrea or Clonoulty.[158] So, from 1852 to 1876 relative agrarian calm prevailed in Tipperary, and brief periodic downturns, or occasional landlord harshness resulted at best in sporadic though heated localised meetings,[159] and at worst in frequent and savage agrarian outrage,[160] rather than in priestly-led tenant right societies. The untimely combination of drought and deluge producing the sharp downturn of the early and, to a lesser extent, the late 1860s, and the consequent rise in evictions, are prime examples of conditions which provoked serious outrage.[161] Clearly, therefore, despite the overall satisfaction of the tenant farmers with their lot, the land problem always contained the germ of violence, which only required a series of bad harvests combined with a change of tenant outlook to excite widespread discontent and organised resistance.

Chapter Four

THE PRIEST AND THE AGRARIAN REVOLUTION 1877-1891

"Landlords, land-grabbers, grass-grabbers, hay-grabbers, and all those who support the blood-stained are your enemies, and it is your bounden duty to oppose all such persons in every way that the law allows." Father David Humphreys, *Tipperary Leader* 7 Nov. 1884.

The severe downturn beginning in 1877 and extending into the 1880s provided the necessary economic circumstances to spark off a degree of agrarian unrest rarely witnessed previously in Tipperary. Apart from their daily contact with the farmers, the clergy were aware of the depression for several other pertinent reasons. They may very well have felt the economic pinch themselves. Certainly one type of ecclesiastical revenue suffered — Bishop John Power excused the Waterford diocese from sending Peter's Pence in 1879.[1] Bishop James Ryan, Killaloe, did the same as well as unhappily revealing his own commitment to a bond of £16,000 for the erection of a new diocesan college in Ennis.[2] On another level those priests who leased farms were tangibly acquainted with the fall in cattle prices; Thomas Finn P.P. Newcastle revealed to a meeting of tenants his own loss on cattle purchased at £11 a head in 1878.[3] These were fed on hay and oats during the winter, and sold for £12 each the following year. Finn was also alarmed at the difficulty of selling even at reduced prices. He was undoubtedly mirroring the anxiety of most farmers which eventually blossomed into more strident unrest.

It must be stressed that this unrest was not born solely from the agricultural depression. A noticeable rise in social expectations seems to have taken place since the 1850s and 1860s. D.G. Crosse, a large tenant farmer and sub-agent from Nenagh, told the 1887 commissioners about tenant reluctance to reduce expenditure during bad harvests, and he pointed to an increase in drinking as one example of this.[4] Even the aspirations of Tipperary womenfolk heightened, and Arthur Moore's agent, Whittaker, confided to his master that 'they want to dress and live without working for it, hence arises a good deal of the discontent now existing in the country'.[5] The pious contention made years later

71

by a former Land League priest that tenants accepted religion as an adequate compensation for the loss of earthly goods did not reflect the reality of the late nineteenth century.[6]

Nevertheless, the initial response to the downturn in Tipperary was not an explosive one, and it took a succession of bad harvests to enflame public opinion. In some interesting ways this early reaction resembled that of the early 1850s, especially in the establishment of two rather conservative bodies, the Tipperary Independent Club[7] and the Tipperary Farmers' Club.[8] These were similar in certain respects. Both were confined to small sections of the county. The Independent Club, like its namesake of the 1850s, centred around Thurles, while the Farmers' Club operated in Nenagh, although its founder, Peter E. Gill, vainly tried to extend it to the Thurles area.[9] Their agrarian aims also coincided, centring around the three Fs through amendment of the 1870 act.[10] As in the 1850s, membership was confined to the better-off farmers, the annual membership fee ranging from 5/- to £1. But, there were notable differences between the two bodies also. Only 3 priests participated in the Farmers' Club, reflecting the mutual dislike between Gill and the clergy.[11] The Independent Club, on the other hand, was powered by an executive of 10 laymen and 10 clerics, including several ex-Tenant League priests, now senior clergy, such as Dean William Quirke, Thomas Meagher P.P. Newport, and Canon Richard Cahill.[12] These carried over the aspirations of the old league.

Despite common ideals the two clubs were in reality distinct rivals, and Gill had no hesitation in calling the Thurles body 'a hole and corner organisation' and a 'corrupt thing',[13] accusations also levelled at its predecessor of the 1850s. William Quirke was more diplomatic in his hope that both would complement each other.[14] Yet not one priest attended a Thurles meeting of the Farmers' Club held in July 1879.[15] Despite their differences these bodies made some contribution, however unintentional, in preparing the county for the late arrival of the Land League in June 1880. The motto of Daniel O'Connell — 'who would be free must themselves strike the first blow' — adopted by Richard Cahill for the Independent Club, was also the maxim of the Land League, and likewise Dean Quirke strongly urged the formation of tenant societies in every barony to expose 'the ruthless deeds of oppressive landlords'.[16] The clubs and the league co-existed for some time,[17] but as the depression continued the new organisation proved more capable of meeting the crisis, and swallowed them up. The Land League itself was suppressed in 1881, and was succeeded by the Ladies' Land League, which in turn was replaced by the Irish National League in 1882.

The Agrarian Organisations 1880-1890
These three organisations varied considerably in extent.[18] Fifty-nine

Land League branches were established in 1880, while only 43 Ladies Land League units partly filled the vacuum created by its suppression, but a significant 96 Irish National League branches took root, admittedly over a much longer time span. Normally branches did not correspond with the Catholic parishes, but were centred around the chapels, with, therefore, an older parish structure as the basic unit, such small links being a sure sign of strength. For the purpose of greater communication some Land League branches formed a type of district federation. The Slievenamon Land League had 5 affiliated, though autonomous, branches.[19] County boundaries were ignored in the formation of such groups; a district on the Tipperary—Limerick border consisted of 5 Limerick and 6 Tipperary branches.[20] Carrick-on-Suir co-operated with the branches of Carrickbeg and Windgap in Waterford and Kilkenny.[21]

Fifty-two Catholic parishes, or 81% of Tipperary's total had Land League branches, but the Ladies movement was confined to 35 parishes, or 55% of the total. The National League, however, penetrated no less than 63 parishes, or 98% of the total, which as the police noted, compared more than favourably with national statistics,[22] an observation borne out by the larger than average contribution of Tipperary to the central fund.[23] Considering the large portion of the county covered by the Cashel archdiocese, it is not surprising that the organisations were most extensive there, with 58% of the Land League, 65% of the Ladies Land League and 60% of the National League branches concentrated in that diocese. The Land League and National League ratios correlate roughly with Cashel's proportion of the county, but the Ladies Land League is 10% higher. Killaloe, as the next largest section, held 27%, 16% and 25% of the Land League, Ladies Land League, and National League respectively, again showing a correlation for the two male organisations, but interestingly, the ladies body was 10% below the normal ratio. The smaller Waterford portion accounted for 15%, 19% and 15% of the three bodies, showing an exact correlation for the women's league, and 4% lower for the other two organisations. A more accurate pattern of individual diocesan representation emerges when it is realised that 80% of parishes in Cashel diocese contained Land League units, 57% had Ladies Land League branches and every parish had at least one branch of the National League, while 88%, 41% and 94% of Killaloe's parishes were involved. All Waterford parishes had National League branches, 75% of its parishes had Land League units, and 44% had branches of the Ladies' Land League.

But did the pattern of clerical involvement generally coincide with the geographical spread of these movements? Since the branches centred around ecclesiastical units it is logical that a general correlation would have existed. This, however, was true only of the two bigger organisations. The priests remained aloof from the women's movement, which must, therefore, be excluded from the following analysis.[24] Before examining the two main bodies individually, an overall view of priestly participation in both from 1880 to 1890 may be of value. At least 164 priests, or 58% of the Tipperary priesthood were so involved.[25] The parish priest — curate ratio of 38% to 62% is close to the 35% to 65% which was the normal ratio in the Tipperary priest-hood. But, the 63 parish priest executives represented 64% of the pastors' body, while the 101 curate leaguers accounted for only 55% of their group. Education statistics reveal that 56% of the leaguers were Maynooth trained, which is higher than their normal share, but the other groups, except Waterford, correlate with their usual proportion in the county. It may be noted, therefore, that with the exception of the Waterford-trained, a majority of all groups participated. In line with the spread of the organisations, the diocesan breakdown shows that Cashel priests represented 59% of the leaguers, Killaloe 25% and Waterford 16%. The Cashel figure is 12% higher than the normal pro-portion, while Killaloe and Waterford are 4% and 8% lower, respectively. No less than 72% of all Cashel priests were executives, but only 49% and 40% of Killaloe and Waterford were involved. An age analysis[26] shows that the 20-50 year old priests accounted for 64% of the total, which, however, strongly correlates with their normal 63% of the priesthood 1880-1890. Sixty per cent of this group were leaguers, but 71% of the 41-50 sub-group were involved; the latter normally accounted for 23% of the total clerical body. Of the older priests, 82% of the 51-60 year olds were executives, but this group only represented 12% of the total priesthood.

On the level of general clerical activity it is striking that no less than 72% of the Tipperary priesthood attended public meetings during the Land League period of 1880 to 1881, compared with 64% of the priest-hood (1882-1890), who were at meetings during the National League period.[27] Furthermore, statistics for the latter are grossly inflated by 3 Thurles meetings, which accounted for a total of 166 attendances. This points to the vigour of the earlier movement. The situation, how-ever, is totally reversed when one considers the more important degree of solid and continuous activity at executive level. While an admittedly significant minority of 57 priests, or 31% of the total priesthood, were Land League executives in 69% of the branches, a majority (53%) were National Leaguers in 93% of its branches.[28] This included a noticeable transfer by 46% of non-Land Leaguers into the National League, and this may well have been higher. Interestingly the parish priest-curate ratio for both organisations, (32% to 68% for the Land League, 40% to 60% for the National League), correlates closely to their normal ratio in the county for both spans. Nevertheless, in real terms, only 24% of total parish priests were Land Leaguers, while 62% were National Leaguers. On the other hand a more notable 37% of curates were involved in the Land League, but, interestingly, the relative increase to 49% on the National League was not at all as significant as that of the parish priests. On the basis of figures for Tipperary therefore, where involvement was especially strong a modern view that a majority of all priests participated, is incorrect.[29]

The age pattern is frustratingly difficult to disentangle, and the most that can be done without introducing confusion is to pinpoint a few of the clearer trends. Sixty-five per cent of Land Leaguers and 69% of National Leaguers were under 51 years old. This group, however, accounted for 57% and 64% of the total priesthood for the two respective periods. Nevertheless, only 35% of the group were Land Leaguers while a more significant 57% joined the National League. A more detailed breakdown into sub-groups shows that 40% of the 20-30 year olds, 40% of the 31-40 year olds, and only 26% of the 41-50 year olds were in the Land League, while the respective figures for the National League are 31%, 55%, and 72%. The big increase in the National League figure for the 31–40 year olds corresponds with the greater response by parish priests to this movement. This is further reflected by a breakdown of the over 50 year olds, which show huge increases for each sub-group. The conclusion that can be drawn is that while the younger priests were more extensively involved because of their numerical superiority at any given time, there was a far greater transfer of older priests from the ranks of non-Land Leaguers to the National League.

The education statistics are more amenable to analysis, and immediately reveal the usual predominant position of Maynooth-trained clerics, with 58% of Land Leaguers and 57% of National Leaguers falling into this category. Both figures are near the normal ratio of 56% and 51% for the respective periods. But only 33% of the total Maynooth priests were Land Leaguers, while 61% were National Leaguers. This partly arose from the transfer of 57 non-Land Leaguers, 68% of whom were Maynooth-trained. Despite first appearances, therefore, it is clear that Maynooth priests were not any more radical or politicised than their counterparts. Indeed a higher percentage of the Carlow, Rome and Salamanca groups were Land Leaguers, although numberwise they were of little addition to the movement.

A diocesan analysis shows that 47% of Land League and 66% of National League priests were from Cashel and Emly, the former being lower than the normal proportion, and the latter much higher. Only 29% of the Cashel body were Land Leaguers, while 74% joined the later movement. This reflects the transfer of 57 non-Land Leaguers to the National League, 72% of these being from Cashel. The Killaloe and Waterford statistics show an opposite trend; 37% of Land League priests but only 20% of National Leaguers were from Killaloe, and 43% of Killaloe priests were in the Land League, while 38% were in the

National League. The Land League figure exceeds the normal ratio, but that for the National League falls below it. Similarly 16% of Land Leaguers came from the Waterford diocese, and only 14% of National Leaguers did so. Interestingly, however, only 23% of Waterford priests were Land Leaguers, while 31% joined the National League.

Apart from the normal ratios which influenced some of the foregoing statistics, the significant differences between participation in the three leagues require further explanation. Because of extensive priestly abstention, the Ladies' League may be dealt with more easily. As the first organised female political movement in Ireland, it naturally excited the suspicion of priests. Some clergy maintained that they had no objection to the involvement of women in the Land League or National League, but they only viewed them as an extra source of income;[30] they did not at all envisage fiery platform viragos in an exclusively female movement. Consequently, the few priests who had the courage to approve of the league were careful to stress the benevolent society image it pretended. James Cantwell Adm. Thurles, who allowed the members to meet in the presbytery,[31] or perhaps insisted that they meet there, where he could keep a close watch on them, remarked that those who attacked the movement 'might just as well censure the good Sisters of Mercy';[32] Anna Parnell on the same occasion accordingly emphasised the league's aim of relieving tenants evicted for non-payment of rent, an aim which she rigidly adhered to.[33] Their other semi-charitable function of aiding prisoners was reflected in the title of the Doon branch — the Doon Ladies Sustentation Fund.[34] Similarly, their support of the labourers' cause by seeking half-acre plots for houses may legitimately be regarded as a benevolent one.[35] But in their pursuit of these aims the ladies' approach was anything but charitable; it may well have been no more extreme than that of the men, but to nineteenth century clerical eyes it seemed glaringly inconsistent with female propriety.

Predictably, the ladies were especially vociferous on eviction matters. One woman delivered a fiery speech at an eviction scene on Lord Dunally's property, while the Doon branch condemned a bailiff on the Erasmus Smith estate.[36] Apart from a clear hostility towards landlords, they had as strong a political consciousness as their menfolk, displayed, for example, in their vigorous attack on the Tipperary M.P., P.J. Smyth, for his vote on the *Clôture*.[37] They also showed a keen interest in local elections, and 4 branches became involved in an extremely acrimonious dispute over the election of a Poor Law Guardian.[38] The lady leaguers displayed very definite anti-England views as well. One of the Burncourt women referred to the 'slap in the face' given to the government by the election of O'Donovan Rossa in 1869, and warned that they could 'do it again'; the patriotically-titled Sarah Curran branch, Drom, attacked the 'alien government'.[39] The priests may have heartily agreed with some of these sentiments, but they were alarmed at the force and vehemence with which they were delivered by the normally retiring ladies. They had yet another cause for concern in the league's affiliated society, the Children's League, a 'most objectionable organisation', according to the draft of the bishops' 1882 pastoral.[40] Dr Croke, however, was not unduly alarmed, and with characteristic wit pronounced it an educational body.[41] Father Dennehy P.P. Kanturk, Co. Cork saw little educational in its special alphabet.[42] The 'God save Ireland — pay no rent' postscript in the childish hand of a Cashel boy leaguer explains Dennehy's attitude.[43]

Moral anxiety, private prejudice or tradition alone do not fully explain priestly caution towards the Ladies' Land League. The question of coercion had some bearing on it, since close association with it held a certain amount of danger for the priests, following the successful suppression of the Land League. Having solidly denounced the coercion act[44] the ladies movement was itself brought under its umbrella, although this was not at first clear.[45] Few priests had the hardihood, or perhaps the inclination, to criticise the government's action in this. Privately John R. Crowe C.C. Cappawhite advised Anna Parnell to test the legality of police interference, and assured her that if the organisation proved legal he would 'announce from the altar next Sunday to have every female, both the old and the young, the crippled and the blind to attend the league rooms'.[46] An altar sermon by the curate of Kilbride, Co. Meath, on the same lines was discussed in the House of Commons.[47] Other radical non-Tipperary priests took more active steps to protect ladies. Thomas Feehan C.C. Rathdowney, Co. Laois, allowed them to hold their meetings in his house and refused to admit the police.[48] Patrick Phelan C.C. Cullohill, Co. Laois (known as Queen's County) used the same means, barefacedly informing the police that the meeting was a devotional one.[49] Only one lady leaguer was arrested in Tipperary. She served two weeks imprisonment for allegedly sending a notice to a tenant advising him to hold his rent.[50] Four years later the local curate, Patrick Crowe, used the incident to denigrate an agent, George 'Mule' Finch J.P., then involved in a wrangle with tenants.[51] The relatively few arrests pointed to government caution in pursuing an intensely emotive policy, and one which very likely would have thrown clerical support behind the league. Ultimately, it was not the coercion act which ended the league's career, but Parnell himself by severing its financial pipeline.

Few Tipperary priests, therefore, showed any sympathy with the Ladies' Land League, most studiously avoided it, but only three were openly hostile either by verbal threats, dispersing meetings or locking the sacristy door against them. The outlook seems to have differed in Co. Offaly, (then known as King's County), where most of the parish priests were reported as hostile; public opinion reacted accordingly and a dead donkey was dumped in the field of B. Flood P.P. Frankfurt for his threat to 'make a public show' of any female parishioner who dared to join.[52] Public opinion was probably one reason for the confined and muted hostility in Tipperary, but as in so many cases the attitude of Dr Croke was of importance, particularly his well-publicised controversy with Archbishop McCabe of Dublin, whose hard-hitting pastoral ordered his clergy not to tolerate lady leaguers in their sodalities.[53] Despite the advice of other bishops, Croke would retreat no further than admit that he was 'technically wrong' in publicly admonishing his fellow prelate and praising A.M. Sullivan's attack on him.[54] Significantly several branches applauded Croke's stand,[55] and within a short time John Walsh C.C. Ballyneale took it upon himself to publicly declare that the leaguers were 'as virtuous, as moral, and as jealously conservative of feminine propriety as any other women on the face of the globe'.[56] Croke's influence, too, was definitely stamped on the pastoral of June 1882, which omitted all reference to the move-ment, while the private draft described it as 'a danger, objectionable, not only on political, but social grounds'.[57] It did not, however, place the organisation in the category of condemned societies. Croke was at pains to emphasise that the hierarchy had not condemned the league, and he publicly denied that the primate had instructed his clergy to withhold their support.[58]

Unquestionably, however, the bishops had serious reservations about the movement, and while their memorandum of June 1882 to the priests did not contain a specific condemnation, they advised that 'nothing should be countenanced that could draw the women of Ireland from the retirement, which is the safeguard of their modesty'.[59] Roman pressure was at work, too, and the circular enclosed the Vatican admonition on the league. It is noteworthy that the memorandum was confidential, although some priests did not feel bound to keep it so, and some weeks later *United Ireland* published it.[60] This paper had earlier reported that priests in the Dioceses of Armagh, Ossory and Tuam were forbidden to attend meetings of the league.[61] Clearly, some bishops, while not openly condemning the organisation, took private steps to deprive it of clerical support. Even Croke himself, despite his public stand, displayed a certain private ambivalence. He remarked to Kirby that episcopal condemnation might have infused new life into the movement.[62] This, was partly to soothe Rome's ear, but it also reflec-ted his own relief that this unexpected social and political development was finally laid to rest.

Although the priests' attitude to the Ladies' Land League is readily explained, their varying degrees of involvement in the other bodies pre-sumes a more complex reaction. All priests, irrespective of grade, age or education, regarded the Land League with more reserve than the National League. It was suspect in their eyes partly because, unlike the

Tenant League, it began independently of them, with only a dozen clergymen (including Dean William Quirke) on the national organising committee. Furthermore, the important pre-league Westport meeting was directed at a priest, Canon Geoffrey Burke, and was denounced by the popular Archbishop of Tuam, John McHale. Clearly, too, the league's fenian nucleus[63] and apparently suspicious slogan[64] underlined the presence of a section, who lacked both political and social affinity with the priests, in sharp contrast to the Tenant League of 1850s or the clubs of 1878. Nevertheless, some of these factors were also present in the National League, which commanded such extensive clerical support. But, the prior existence of the earlier movement conditioned the clerical mind to the idea of a broadly based extensive agitation. More important, however, the birth of the National League took place in far different circumstances, involving a much closer initial relationship with the priests. From the beginning, too, it was less agrarian in character, more disciplined and tightly controlled by the Parnellite party, which had by then firmly secured the support of the Tipperary priest-hood.[65] Parnell himself shrewdly realised the importance of clerical involvement in a disciplined network, partly indeed to maintain such discipline, which the clergy greatly stressed.[66] With this in mind he requested James Cantwell, Adm. Thurles, to propose the adoption of the league's programme at the Dublin meeting of October 1882, which was attended by a large number of priests, including six from Tipperary.[67] A widespread clerical viewpoint was illustrated by the interesting observation of Canon Patrick Ryan, Galbally, that clerical leaguers were following in the footsteps of O'Connell,[68] a comparison he was hardly likely to make in the case of the Land Leaguers.

Such factors may largely account for the divergent degrees of clerical involvement in the two leagues, but they do not explain extensive over-all involvement in the Land War, including the significant minority support for the Land League. If public opinion, that is tenant farmer opinion, was crucial in silencing the priests in the 1850s, it was equally decisive in evoking clerical support during the 1880s, and in sharpening considerably the underlying sympathy the priests always entertained for their farmer kinsfolk. Despite their initial caution, the clergy made clear their desire to involve themselves on their people's behalf. In some cases, of course, it was no more than lip service, but even that was better than hostility. Arthur Ryan of St. Patrick's College, Thurles, was at pains to point out, not altogether accurately, that the 'hearts of the Irish clergy, young and old have been with the league from the beginning'.[69] Others made the well-worn proposal that religion and nationality were inseparable, and stressed the duty of clerical participation in movements to forward popular aspirations.[70] Undoubtedly, too, the very infrequency of overt disapproval on the priests' part is an accurate pointer to the force of public opinion.

Public opinion was also important in its impact upon the bishops,[71] who in turn influenced their priests. Some bishops were hostile, some favourable and many were neutral; the latter did not hinder clerical involvement. Archbishop Croke genuinely and justifiably feared that clerical indifference or hostility to the Land League would have an adverse effect upon religion in Ireland. Croke, through Tobias Kirby, was very conscious of the possibility of Roman interference to hold the priests aloof from the new movement.[72] Kirby seems to have warned many prelates about Rome's hostility, and this may have accounted for their cautious neutrality. He told Bishop John Power, Waterford, that the authorities viewed the league leaders as 'unprincipled and designing men', who, under the pretext of aiding the farmers, were 'trying to separate the people from the clergy'.[73] Most Irish bishops would not accept such an ill-informed opinion of the movement, and even those who did were not enamoured by the prospect of Roman interference, seeing it as a potential danger to religion by arousing popular scorn. That unwavering antagonist of the league, Dr McCabe of Dublin,[74] seems to have agreed with Croke on this.[75] When the pope's letter did arrive Croke chose to brand it as a 'very milk and waterish' document, which could do little good and some harm.[76] He worked rapidly to influence his fellow-prelates. His impact on the 1882 pastoral was not only evident in the case of the Ladies' Land League, but of the Land League, too. The published version contained several terminological differences from the draft; for example it showed some restraint in the remark — 'in every peaceful and just movement of yours, the clergy shall be with you to guide and, if necessary, restrain you, but you must not expect them to do what, in conscience, they condemn'. The draft is less tactful — 'in every peaceful and just movement of yours your clergy shall be with you, but let it be remembered in their own place, beside and before you, to guide and, if necessary, to restrain you. You must not expect them, Heaven forbid you should, to advocate what in conscience they condemn, or to be led by those whom they, by right, should lead'.

Croke's most ostentatious defence of the Land League was his famous 1881 visitation, which resembled a propaganda crusade on its behalf. The people responded with an enthusiasm that according to James J. Ryan, of St. Patrick's College, was not adequately recorded in the papers.[77] He related how the people of Holycross unharnassed the archbishop's carriage and pulled it themselves. The clergy were not slow to publicise Croke's advocacy of the cause.[78] John Ryan felt sufficiently confident under his shadow to announce that Gladstone had persuaded some 'weak-kneed' cleric to contact Rome, and get 'some document' that would make 'poor Paddy a little tender-hearted and afraid'.[79] Another highly politicised priest, James Ryan C.C. Tipperary, used Croke's support of the movement as a guarantee of the National

League's 'constitutionality and Justice'.[80] Nevertheless, as with public opinion, the archbishop's influence must be seen in its total context, — the abstention of 71% of Cashel priests from the Land League. But, had Croke been hostile that percentage would certainly have been significantly higher.

Episcopal influence in the other two sections of Tipperary is impossible to define. Several anomalies arise. With a long history of involvement in Tipperary agrarian agitation behind him, Bishop Power was sympathetic to both leagues.[81] He assured Kirby of the widespread desire for reform, and dismissed any suggestion of the movement 'seducing the people from the influence of the clergy'.[82] Later Waterford bishops were less friendly, however, and the divisional magistrate noted, with pleasure, the action of John Egan in transferring 'troublesome' priests from their respective parishes.[83] This seems to explain the decrease of Waterford's proportion of total National League priests viz-a-viz the Land League, but the increase in the percentage of the Waterford priestly body as National Leaguers is a contradiction of this. In reality, too, the magistrate was not unduly accurate in his observations on clerical changes in south Tipperary. Most of the clergy listed by him were changed in the normal course of events. All but 4 were labelled 'good' by the policeman, and only one was definitely changed for political reasons. Finally, James Ryan of Killaloe was privately hostile to the Land League, telling a probably bewildered Kirby that the people were 'lashed into fury by mischievous leaders ... we have no one like O'Connell to pour oil on troubled waters'.[84] Ryan, however, wisely preferred to keep his hostility concealed, and did not interfere with his clergy's political freedom of action, which was reflected by their significant minority membership of the Land League.

The widespread involvement of the Tipperary priesthood in the two leagues cannot therefore, be denied; but it must be asked if the influence they wielded was proportionately extensive, and if it was reflected in their role. It can be said at once that clerical influence in the leagues was largely similar to their political power as a whole, — limited by the views of the laity, and in accordance with the political ability of individual priests themselves, or with level of education and political consciousness of their parishioners. In some areas the top echelon of a branch was composed of very politicised priests.[85] There were instances of priests being the prime movers of branches[86] and more often than not branches were initiated in the chapel yard or even received their political baptism in the sacristy.[87] At one stage the church committee in Emly dissolved itself at the close of business and became the executive of the National League.

But despite such intimacy between the clergy and the land organisations, the laity generally filled some of the most vital positions, especially that of secretary, which was held by priests only in a minority of cases.[88]

Quite frequently the priests were simply requested to accept the presidency of branches subsequent to their formation,[89] and refusals were frowned upon as a sign of hostility. Laymen were always involved in establishing branches, and sometimes exclusively so. The Slievenamon Land League, which extended the network to surrounding parishes, sometimes in the face of priestly opposition, was powered by the able lay secretary, Michael Cusack. The League's national organiser, Michael P. Boyton, was indefatigable. He organised it in 22 counties, and ranged from Dunmanway in the south to Carndonagh in the north.[90] Like Cusack, Boyton met with some clerical abuse, and helped to implant a certain independence in the minds of his hearers. As in other political matters lay executives sometimes resented over-domination by priests. The answer of one member to the action of John Fennelly P.P. Anacarty in dissolving the Donohill branch of his own accord is loaded with significance: 'This dictatorial power is well enough in its own sphere if exercised properly, but when put to a use foreign to its purpose resistance is a duty and the sooner it is got rid of the better'.[91] Hence the branch was reconstructed with full lay control. Angered at the postponement of a branch meeting because the president, Fr John A. Power, was absent, a Solohead member argued that the laity were sufficiently intelligent to proceed without the priests and quite sensibly remarked that over-dependence upon any single individual undermined the branch's strength.[92] Edmund Doheny, the parish priest of Donaskeigh did not agree with similar sentiments by two leaguers there, and declared his reluctance to adopt resolutions from branches which had no clerical involvement.[93] The police were aware that some priests deluded themselves in thinking that they controlled branch members; they referred specifically to Drangan, Tipperary and Mullinahone.[94]

The Land League agitation proved important in awakening a lively political consciousness in the laity, and the notable increase in clerical involvement in the National League should not obscure this. By 1886 the diarist, William Scawen Blunt, was struck by the 'absolute equality' between layman and priest in political matters, and he was not wildly exaggerating.[95] Increasing political confidence was evident, not only from laymen taking over the prestigious presidencies of branches,[96] but their active participation in the larger meetings also increased substantially; the intensity of priestly activity accordingly decreased.[97] While priests accounted for 93% of chairmen for the 1880-1881 meetings, they represented only 62% of the 1882-1890 chairmen. However, the increasing incidence of M.P.s chairing meetings largely accounts for this — M.P.s chaired at least 42 meetings during this period. But there was a definite increase in the number of local lay speakers and a corresponding decline in the number of clerical speakers. No less than 255 priests spoke in the meetings from 1880 to 1890, but 162 of these or 64% were concerned with the shorter 1880-1881 Land League period.

All this only proves that the political power of the priest was far from absolute. But, considering the general clerical-lay ratio, the priests' contribution was far in excess of their numbers, and it was of great importance. Clerical involvement was one of the most frequent themes in police files, and they attributed the success of the National League in Tipperary and neighbouring Limerick to such activity.[98] As in the Tenant League, the priests' role was largely administrative and co-ordinative, and it admirably suited their taste as trained ecclesiastical administrators. The highest position of presidency, which was not always merely titular, accounted for 69% of total clerical offices during the Land League period, and 63% during the National League years.[99] Vice-presidency was next in numerical order, but least important, while that of secretaryship and treasurership ranked third and fourth respectively. These positions entailed such obvious tasks as chairing meetings, explaining the leagues' rules,[100] composing resolutions, filling in reports for the Dublin executives,[101] recording receipts, organising larger meetings and securing prominent national speakers. As organisers, the priests were anxious to keep the leagues functioning with maximum membership, and they employed various means to achieve this. Basically, it was important to show the relevance of the movements. Literally thousands of exhortations were issued, some off the altar; the importance of the organisations was stressed,[102] and at least 23 priests condemned apathy.[103] An extensive network over a long period did not signify continued and intensive activity as the un-even distribution of major meetings over the years 1879 to 1890 demonstrates.[104] Agitation varied from area to area, depending upon such factors as landlord-tenant relations, the quality of harvests or the price of produce and cattle. From 1883 onwards there were localised complaints of farmer indifference shown either by a reluctance to pay subscriptions, or by the failure of National League meetings because of insufficient attendance.[105] But the priests kept at least the bones of the organisation intact by their constant attendance at meetings and so preserved the machinery necessary to launch a new offensive at short notice, if this became necessary. The police understood this very well.[106]

It was logical, therefore, that such priests as John Ryan P.P. Newinn, Thomas Finn P.P. Newcastle and even Bishop Nulty of Meath should portray the Land League as a type of trade union,[107] and the necessity for such a trade union was emphasised by pointing to the action of the House of Lords in rejecting the Compensation for Improvements Bill in August 1880, when the Land League was in its infancy in Tipperary.[108] More than anything else, however, the leagues were pre-sented as anti-landlord organisations, and the success of the Land League was held forth as an inducement to continue the struggle despite the concessions of the 1881 land act.[109] Accordingly, James Cantwell emphasised the necessity for the National League to protect tenants evicted during the Land League years,[110] and Archdeacon T.H. Kinnane, among others,[111] saw it as a counterforce to the hated Land Corporation,[112] an organisation dealt with later in this book. Many priests proposed that branches could be used as watch-dogs on the land courts,[113] while Paul Power C.C. Carrick-on-Suir shrewdly envisaged the National League as a practical election machine.[114] The old well-worn Tenant League propaganda on a union of North and South was aired by John R. Crowe C.C. Cappawhite, John Tuohy P.P. Shinrone, and John Ryan.[115] Clerical advice to hold firm in the face of coercion was a very prominent theme as well,[116] and corresponded with their mockery of coercion acts, evasion of police surveillance, or convening of league meetings in their own houses to avoid suppression.[117] The priests took other practical steps to keep the agitation alive. A few like James Ryan C.C. Tipperary and John Cunningham C.C. Silvermines were sceptical of the efficacy of periodic conventions to inspire local organising,[118] but the formidable clerical attendance at these meetings throughout the decade indicates that most priests felt differently. This was the prevailing opinion at an 1884 convention held in St. Patrick's College Thurles, attended by 45 priests.[119] There were no less than 899 priestly attendances at public league meetings from 1879 to 1890, and of these 278 or 31% included speeches, while 85% of the meetings were chaired by priests.[120] In real terms these figures represent 204 individual priests or 67% of the total priesthood.

Finally, in their efforts to maintain public interest, the priests, more than all others, were conscious of the need for a newspaper to preach the gospel of agitation. The paper *Tipperary* provided this, and was far more radical than any of its predecessors, closely resembling its national contemporary *United Ireland* in tone and theme. When it went into liquidation in 1882 the priests played the chief role in the foundation of the *Tipperary Leader*, which purchased the plant of the demised organ. They saw the *Leader* as a necessary counterbalance to the Conservative papers, the *Clonmel Chronicle* or the *Nenagh Guardian*.[121] The Tipperary Newspaper Publishing Company floated the new paper, and Dr Croke who invested in it was at the centre of this to such an extent that he could lay down three essential conditions for the proposed paper: (1) that the directorate be people in whose good sense and character he could have confidence; (2) that the purchase price of the plant should not be largely in excess of what he considered fair; (3) that the subscription list be *bona fide* and all shares taken.[122] He even took the opportunity of a circular to his clergy on behalf of St. Patrick's College to urge support for the paper.[123] Ten priests were provisional directors of the takeover company, and at least 65 were involved in its promotion by canvassing, collecting, and even a special clerical subscription was established.[124] Priestly efforts, however, were unavailing in the face of public apathy, and while the paper did not totally collapse like its namesake of the 1850s, it was necessary to change it to a larger urban area — Clonmel — although not all priests favoured the move.[125] At the time of the takeover the paper showed a deficit of £120, and because the editor was unwilling to hand over the plant James Cantwell was forced to sue for possession and for repayment of £100.[126]

So far it is clear that the role of the priest was a very positive one, which offered encouragement and buoyed sometimes flagging enthusiasm. But, this seems to belie the relative caution reflected in the Land League statistics. The truth is that vigorous promotion of the agitation does not reflect the complete gamut of the priestly outlook. If they had one foot on the agrarian accelerator, the other was placed firmly on the brake. This partly arose from the old dilemma of the need to fire enthusiasm, yet cool passions. Consequently, many priests saw themselves as the proper and natural leaders of the agitation in a watchdog capacity. Michael Duggan C.C. Drom urged his parishioners to join the Land League under the priests' leadership,[127] while Patrick O'Keeffe C.C. Fethard confidently remarked that 'the priests know how to lead, the people know how to follow'.[128] Some clerics, therefore, were alarmed when they were not consulted about meetings.[129] In the best O'Connellite tradition, Bishop John Power advised that perpetrators of outrage should be handed over to the police.[130] One file in Dublin Castle contains at least nine reports on an altar sermon by the somewhat paranoiac pastor of Ballyporeen, Dr Patrick Delaney, who made a list of suspected would-be offenders, whom he threatened to expose.[131] Police investigation, however, showed that Delaney's suspicions were unfounded. The existence of outrage, of course, showed the failure of priestly admonitions on some occasions.

Clearly, the statement of James Lowther M.P. to the House of Commons that clerical action 'calls for recognition at the hands of the Government and all lovers of order',[132] was not without solid foundation. At least 64 priests, several on more than one occasion, dwelt upon the theme of law and order in public speeches.[133] The percentage of parish priests, who stressed the issue, is somewhat higher than their normal representation, apparently supporting the contention of the police that the older priests joined to exert some control on their flocks and younger curates.[134] Apart from the fact that the stock emphasis of chairmen, usually parish priests, was upon the question of law and order, the age statistics do not fully bear out the police report. The over 50 age groups correlated closely with their numerical position in the county, the 41-50 group was 6% higher than usual, the 31-40 year olds correlated exactly, and the under 30 section was 5% lower than normal. It must be concluded that emphasis on constitutional agitation was spread among all age groups in proportion to their usual ratio in Tipperary. The various alma maters had no distinguishing influences upon their attitude, and the proportion of Maynooth priests is precisely correlative with their normal representation.

Such uniformity simply shows that the fundamental morality of their vocation largely shaped the priests' view of outrages. They were, however, also careful to propose more practical objections to agrarian crime. They showed that such crime provided landlords with an excuse for appealing to parliament against radical change, or they portrayed it as a factor alienating foreign sympathy, inviting suppression or simply as a method doomed to failure.[135] As well as these, the district levy known as the 'Blood Tax' (used to finance compensation for the injured or to pay for extra police in the offending locality) was used by the priests as a rather mercenary objection against outrage. Numbered among the innocent rate-payers, they too were requested to meet the call, a situation greatly resented by such priests as Thomas O'Donnell P.P. Doon, who refused to pay 5d fine, or by John Ryan.[136] O'Donnell's curate forfeited his cow rather than pay his small portion of another claim.[137]

Truly, apart from their priestliness the clergy also shared the prejudices of their kinsfolk. As in previous decades, in their wish not to antagonise the farmers, they displayed a certain ambivalence while condemning outrage. Even bishops were not averse to some degree of ambiguity. Despite the general clerical outcry against the Phoenix Park murders,[138] Dr Croke refused to sign an episcopal declaration on the basis that murder was far more rife in England, adding for Archbishop McCabe's benefit, that 'there would be no howl as there is now' had the victims been Irishmen.[139] This is not to say that Croke countenanced outrages.[140] Apart from suggesting, with some proof, that the incidence of outrage was deliberately exaggerated by the authorities,[141] the priests, like their predecessors, coupled their condemnation of crime with various excuses for outrage, specifically seeing them as retaliation against landlord injustice. The remark of Michael Duggan C.C., in the context of New Bermingham evictions, that the patience of the 'young peaceful and religious men' was 'sorely tried',[142] is one of several pertinent examples. There is evidence that the priests were correct in this, since both evictions and outrages increased in 1880. Interestingly, some clerics pointed to the leagues as a safety valve, which reduced the number of outrages. But, always bearing in mind the connection between agitation and eviction, the opposite may very well have been the case; the 1880 figure of 106 outrages for Tipperary is notably higher than the figure of 28 for 1879 when the Land League had not yet been established in the county.[143] The rapid increase in outrages from September 1880, (with an accompanying upsurge in priestly references to the matter), corresponds with the organising period of the league there, suggesting that the statistics might be more relevant by dwelling upon the number of branches being established, rather than upon the number of larger meetings held.

Fr. Matt Ryan, C.C. Hospital, Co. Limerick, and later C.C. Lattin, Co. Tipperary. (*Weekly Freeman*, 9.4.1887).

The Land Act of 1881
The concurrence of Land League organising and outrage, therefore, underlines a period of intense agrarian unrest in 1880, but the priests' increasing emphasis on apathy after 1881 suggests a corresponding amelioration of the tenants' circumstances. This was partly due to the Government's response to the unrest in the shape of the 1881 Land Act, which was based upon the long-sought three Fs. The priests showed an early and keen interest in the act, and Dr Croke warned of serious disturbance if the House of Lords mutilated it.[144] Significantly, he advised that the priests would not over-exert themselves, 'if at all', to allay public anger at any such interference with its clauses. In the same context David Humphreys asserted that the Lords 'would be made swallow a more sweeping measure within a year'.[145] This was a theme used by many priests.[146] When the bill was passed, general clerical consensus saw it as a step in the right direction.[147] To Matt Ryan C.C. it changed 'petty tyrants into mere recipients of a rent charge'.[148] But, most priests insisted that the act required substantial amendments. The bishops viewed it in a similar light, pronouncing its leading principles as 'honest and statesmanlike', while suggesting no less than 17 amendments.[149] Croke did not conceal his annoyance when the Parnellite party voted against the measure by 17 votes to 12.[150] The attitude of the party, however, placed some of the priests in a predicament, but they diplomatically decided to leave local decisions to the Land League branches.[151] Interestingly, at Parnell's Dublin convention in April 1881 (attended by 4 Tipperary priests) James Cantwell supported this view, but drew a different conclusion to his archbishop by confidently announcing that if the party rejected the bill 'Tipperary would not shed a tear'.[152]

Whatever their attitude, some priests were prepared to examine the act in minute detail. The best clerical analysis came from the pens of William Walsh, professor in Maynooth and later archbishop of Dublin[153] and David Humphreys C.C. Clonoulty better known in later years for his part in the Smith-Barry dispute in Tipperary town. Walsh's large pamphlet is much more detailed than Humphreys's 25 page work, but is, as the title suggests, explanatory rather than exploratory. The curate's commentary is far more critical and more valuable as a guide to contemporary clerical thinking. In keeping with its ironic title, 'The Logic of the Land Bill', Humphreys's thesis hinged on the alleged lack of 'logical consistency' in the bill. (He had been Professor of Logic in St. Patrick's College, Thurles.) He upheld the recommendations of the bishops and of the 1881 land convention. Much of his argument centred around the act's vital recognition of dual ownership, and while he applauded such a legal concession[154] he nevertheless saw certain clauses which violated its principle. Unlike Thomas Meagher's earlier point,[155] Humphreys disagreed with the clause on forfeiture through delapidation, on the logical yet biased assumption that waste was as much the tenants' property as improvements were.[156] He felt that this apparent anomaly arose from basing the bill on the English tenurial system by which landlords were responsible for effecting improvements. Humphreys also pointed to the landlord's legal right to minerals such as turf or wood on the tenant's holding as a further contradiction of the dual ownership principle. On the same reasoning he saw the subdivision clause as equally illogical,[157] another interesting divergence from the opinion of Thomas Meagher. Humphreys blandly dismissed the argument that subdivision might mean double compensation in the event of eviction, by the simple assertion that landlords should only have the right to evict in very limited circumstances. He conceded, however, that a clause could be inserted forbidding increased compensation in the case of subdivision within specified limits. In his primary concern with dual-ownership he regarded the pre-emption clause, (by which the landlord had first option of purchasing the interest in a holding), as the most dangerous in the bill. Since it apparently prevented free sale he viewed it as little short of compulsory expropriation of the tenant's interest or tenant right. In his evidence before the Bessborough Commission Thomas Meagher had had no objection to a landlord's pre-emption rights provided he purchased the occupancy for his own use and at the free market price.[158]

Humphreys considered that tenant right entitled the occupier to compensation for disturbance, not precisely because of disturbance, but because the property in the holding was lost.[159] So, he argued that a tenant should be indemnified for the *'damnum emergens'*, (loss arising) that is the loss of subsistence means, and for the *'lucrum cessans'*, (gain ceasing), that is the loss of means to provide for his family. Finally, he felt that landlords were unjustly holding the property of tenants evicted for non-payment of rent, since these were automatically excluded from the act. His complaint was that such tenants could not apply for compensation. He also condemned the exclusion of leaseholders. This was a major bone of contention and one of the few aspects that Walsh criticised in his pamphlet.[160] The Tipperary priest maintained that tenants had been forced to take out leases since 1870 to exclude them from the benefit of that act, and he concluded that such contracts were void.[161] The same attitude was displayed by William Meagher C.C. Clonmel.[162]

Rent

Recognition of dual ownership may have been the most important legal concession of the land act, but its most immediate and practical concern was with the problem of rent, which, in the context of the economic depression, lay at the root of the initial agitation. Reflecting public opinion, the clergy were especially vocal on this issue, particularly prior to the act, and 52 Tipperary priests debated the matter publicly.[163] Interestingly, their sentiments followed the same pattern as those of the 1850s, although on a far more extensive scale. They were concerned at the landlords' legal power,[164] which they claimed was unaffected by the 1870 act, and were as convinced as their predecessors had been that current rents were rackrents, relentlessly grinding the tenants to a state of misery.[165] At least 16 priests produced concrete evidence to support complaints about high rents in their own areas.[166] Patrick Glynn C.C. made a detailed statement about 102 holdings in the rather poor parish of Templederry.[167] Those priests leasing farms had their own story to tell. Two ex-Tipperary priests, Patrick Hurley P.P. Kilcolman, King's Co., and Patrick Horan P.P. Whitegate, Co. Galway, were especially annoyed.[168] Hurley complained that he was forced to pay £70 per annum for 45 acres with a Griffith's valuation of £42. Horan, who had inherited the family farm, in 1848, at a rent of £8 was piqued because it was increased to £10 in 1852, £15 in 1853 and reduced to £14 in 1854, at which level it must have stood in 1883. The most interesting case concerned Dr Patrick Delaney P.P. Ballyporeen, who had a 10 year written battle with his landlord.[169] He flatly refused to pay £50 rent for a farm with a Griffith's valuation of £22. The complaints of these priests mirrored precisely the attitude of the tenants — dissatisfaction at a rent in excess of Griffith's valuation, even if increases in such rent had been rare.

Like their Tenant League predecessors, the Land War priests proceeded to define what they considered a fair rent, but they chose a greater variety of criteria. Pursuing what seemed the most plausible line of argument, some priests linked rents with improvements. David Humphreys defined a fair rent as the commercial rent of a holding less the commercial rent of the tenant's property in it, such property being determined by his improvements.[170] Like James Ryan C.C. Tipperary,[171] Humphreys felt that tenants should be allowed to reclaim rent overpayments for the previous 6 years, the term allowed for the recovery of debts. Daniel Flannery C.C. Nenagh was equally precise in his view of a fair rent, as a moderate interest on money spent by proprietors. Taking £1200 million as the improvement expenditure by landlords in England, with a rental of £55 million, he demonstrated that rent there was 4½% of such expenditure.[172] Assuming that 9/10 of such improvements in Ireland were done by the tenants, Flannery concluded that such rents should *ipso facto* be very low. Thomas Meagher was the most biased computant of a fair rent. On a similar basis to the Nenagh priest, he argued that Irish rents should be 'prairie' rent, (never to increase), that is the 2/6 an acre they had been 150 years earlier.[173] Other clergy were more vague, with statements resembling earlier definitions.[174] James Ryan was less than logical in his assertion that a fair rent was what the tenant could justly afford to pay, and the landlord was justly entitled to receive.[175]

Not one clerical definition of a fair rent favoured the landlords in the slightest; when John Ryan personally engaged a valuator to determine the rents of farms whose leases had expired, the landlord promptly retaliated with a higher counter-valuation.[176] This showed the inherent incompatibility of the term fair rent in a practical situation. Because it was impossible for every priest to engage valuators, whose recommendations would be rejected anyway, the Land League's policy of rent based on Griffith's valuation was a convenient one for the priests.[177] It was also practical since rents often exceeded it.[178] Nevertheless, although the rather mild demands of 1879, voiced for example in the resolutions of the priests from the archdiocese and in the statements of other priests,[179] were probably for less than Griffith's, not all priests considered this adequate when it became the official demand of the Land League. This undoubtedly pointed to an increased radicalism among the clergy under the stimulus of localised dissatisfaction. Daniel Flannery condemned Griffith's valuation on tillage farms in north Tipperary as a rack rent.[180] Even James Ryan, who partly favoured it, offered the comforting advice to tenants to pay their debts first, and several priests including Arthur Ryan, St. Patrick's College, saw it only as a temporary expedient pending further valuation.[181]

Such sustained clamour, combined with miserable harvests, rising outrage incidence, and plain commonsense, prompted landlords to grant abatements even before the Land League was established in Tipperary. It is impossible to judge whether these were in line with Griffith's valuation or not, but by the close of 1880 most Tipperary landlords had conceded reductions.[182] This defused a situation which the land act sought to remedy on a more permanent basis. But, despite their general view that the act deserved support, the priests were loudest in their complaints about the rent section. To begin with, they baldly denounced its administration, questioning both the impartiality of the Commissioners appointed to carry it out, and the integrity of the official valuators. David Humphreys pointed to the administration of the 1870 act as sufficient proof for clerical suspicions, and he identified judges of the civil bill courts with the landlord class.[183] In a more specific reference James Ryan warned against the appointment of the Tipperary county Chairman as one of the judges,[184] and other priests periodically made complaints in the same vein.[185] A few years later Ryan and his fellow clergy produced evidence, when denouncing the sub-commissioners, that the administration of the act was 'one of the most ridiculous public exhibitions that has been seen in the country for a long time'.[186] Dean William Quirke accused the administrators of lacking adequate technical knowledge, and he quoted a letter from a friend involved in its administration, asking Quirke himself for some literature on it.[187] The valuators were denounced equally strongly. Daniel Flannery said they were freemasons, and John Ryan, Newinn, observed that 'in all Ireland or in Europe you could not get a greater set of schemers'.[188]

In their dissatisfaction with judicial rents the priests saw the neglect of the Healy Clauses (forbidding rents on tenants' improvements which had not been compensated for) as an important consideration.[189] David Humphreys was distinctly sceptical of the courts' ability to assess improvements, and so arrive at a fair rent.[190] He felt that tenants should produce figures for improvements with the onus on the land-lords to disprove them, or alternatively landlords should have evidence of their own improvements. Matthew O'Keeffe P.P. Aghaboe, Queen's Co., one of the Tenant League founders, complained that Griffith's valuation was generally the basis of the judicial rent,[191] and Archdeacon T.H. Kinnane was dissatisfied with an official 20% reduction on existing rents.[192] Priests submitted statements of rent changes to prove the alleged inadequacy of decreases.[193] Obviously the economic climate influenced clerical thinking; their complaints were strongest in years of poor harvests or low prices.[194] Thomas Meagher justified his proposal of a 60% reduction all around by showing that the £59 profit of a 44 acre farm in 1883 had dwindled to £16 in 1886.[195] Some priests were astonished at occasional upward adjustments of existing rents by the land courts.[196] Clearly these did not, nor were they prepared to, appreciate the disinterested opinion of Dr Walsh that the act's purpose was to fix a fair rent, not necessarily reduce existing ones.[197] Their scepticism increased further as evidence emerged that judicial rents themselves were sometimes raised on the landlord's submission to the appeal courts. Robert Foran P.P. Ballylooby felt that the appeal machinery unduly influenced the decisions of the sub-commissioners in arriving at judicial rents initially.[198] John O'Halloran C.C. gave several examples of judicial rents being altered in Borrisokane.[199] The clergy were also rightly concerned at the prospect of costly litigation in appeal cases,[200] although some severely overstated costs. Michael Ryan, a Co. Limerick priest, speaking to a Cappamore audience which included 6 Tipperary priests, calculated that every 1/- reduction in rent cost the county 2/6.[201] He put the cost of administering the act at £195,000, with rent reductions of £147,000 to date. He estimated that legal figures might equal this figure and concluded with some liberality that £150,000 rent reductions could only be secured at a cost of £400,000.

Under the circumstances it might reasonably be expected that the priests should have advised the farmers to avoid the courts. Some did so. William Power P.P. Moyne saw the courts as a last resort when private negotiations failed.[202] Robert Foran, who initially favoured them, changed his mind by 1886.[203] But clerical complaints seemed more radical than the attitude of at least those tenants who entered the courts.[204] The landlords, for their part, claimed unjust treatment at the hands of the sub-commissioners. It is clear that their complaints had some foundation, because, despite limited applications, substantial reductions were sometimes made under the act; the Nenagh Sub-Commissioners granted decreases ranging from 8% to 50%, with 11% to 19% as the normal range.[205]

In view, therefore of apparent clerical radicalism, one could be excused for anticipating the priests' support for the No-Rent Manifesto of October 1881. Indeed, some clerical statements prior to the manifesto would tend to strongly reinforce this view, since they showed a certain lack of moral scruples on the witholding of rents.[206] Thomas Meagher and his Newport curates advised the Shower tenants that it was their duty to hold their rents until an abatement was conceded,[207] and the motto of Dr Croke was 'charity begins at home'.[208] The priests never considered that they were advising a breach of contract, because, like the clergy of the 1850s, they did not regard Irish landlord-tenant agreements as morally valid, and frequently pointed to cases of tenants being forced to pay unacceptable rents.[209] According to the very conservative parish priest of Cahir, Maurice Mooney, the relationship entailed 'freedom on one side but serfdom on the other'.[210] Nevertheless, radical as these sentiments seem, they only advocated the witholding of rackrents on the basis of preservation being heaven's first law. Indeed, despite earlier rumblings about a rent strike,[211] the outspoken William Meagher C.C. Clonmel warned that the Land League was not advocating a pay no rent policy, but 'to pay your rents and pay your lawful debts, and to pay them in good time'.[212]

The context of priestly sentiments was, therefore, of some importance. They were prepared only to advise on individual cases in their own parishes. Consequently, while James Cantwell chaired the meeting which promulgated the manifesto,[213] the policy of a national strike against all rents, high and low, was too revolutionary, and a moral pill many priests were unable to swallow. There was no extensive outcry against the measure, but it may have been partly responsible for their quiet withdrawal from the agitation. The usually radical John Ryan considered that the manifesto was incompatible with the Gospel maxim 'evil is not do be done in order that good may follow'.[214] (Ryan seems to have been very strongly influenced in all political matters by the opinions of Dr Croke.) It is worth noting, however, that, with the exception of James Cantwell, even those priests who defended the policy emphasised the temporary nature of the suggested strike. David Humphreys proposed that rent be held until the leaders were released, and then 'a fair rent up to that time and 2% for the period it has been due' be offered.[215] Non-Tipperary priests also justified temporary witholding of rents. 'An Irish Priest' writing in *United Ireland* upheld the justice of deferring the fulfilment of a contract with landlords, because, as he believed, such landlords were responsible for the suspension of the constitution.[216] James E. Delaney C.C. Cloneygall, Co.

Carlow, nicely summed this attitude up by his statement that there was a 'vast difference between the repudiation of lawful debts and the temporary witholding of rents' in a coercion situation.[217] There was, too, an element of cautious ambivalence in the public statements of some priests. Joseph Farrell C.C. Monasterevan, Co. Kildare, referred to the manifesto as 'wise and brave' but a 'tactical error'.[218] But Dr Croke was emphatically opposed to the policy, which he saw as politically inexpedient and morally wrong.[219] His boast to Rome that his 'prompt' pronouncement crushed it had some merit.[220] Yet the weak clerical response to the manifesto, coupled with their withdrawal from the Land League, was as much, if not more, due to the introduction of coercion and the destruction of the league itself. The most decisive influence upon the priests was the attitude of the farmers, who were only mildly interested in the policy. It was obeyed only in pockets of the county,[221] and some tenants probably used it to squeeze further abatements from their landlords.[222] Obviously, the clergy saw no reason for enthusiasm if the farmers themselves were apathetic.

But, if the no-rent manifesto failed to secure their support, the priests were prepared to promote the controversial Plan of Campaign* which involved the systematic witholding of rents that were considered too high. A portion of the witheld rents was laid aside as a defence fund to meet legal costs. On a national level the priests were involved in 15 of the 16 estates traced,[223] while at least 46 priests approved of, or were involved in the Plan in Tipperary.[224] The ratio of parish priests and curates is normal, and the age pattern is not unduly significant, except for the rather high 24% for the 51-60 group, indicating that older priests found it as acceptable as younger ones. The diocesan breakdown reflects the heavy involvement of Cashel priests, the Killaloe percentage correlates exactly with its position in the county, but the Waterford priests were involved on a smaller scale. The Plan's geographical spread largely explains this pattern. Priests were involved in 24 of the 27 Tipperary cases noted,[225] and the small Waterford section was only marginally affected by the agitation. The Cashel portion was slightly lower than its normal position contrasting with the high percentage of Cashel priests involved, and therefore underlining their particular approval of the method.

The priests' involvement in the Plan was a valuable asset to the national promoters, and seemed to guarantee its morality. Their actual role varied, and was of sufficient importance to provoke the arrest and imprisonment of some, although none was from Tipperary.[226] While they were not the originators of the system, they were involved in their

*Note: Although the Plan was formally declared in *United Ireland* in Oct. 1886 an almost similar scheme was advocated in *United Ireland* of Feb. 3 1885, and this has been included for the purpose of analysis.

usual capacity, chairing meetings, speaking, advising, and negotiating with landlords. They were frequently trustees of the tenants' fighting fund or 'war chest'. As administrators, the priests were very concerned about the problem of discipline among the tenants. John Scanlan C.C. Nenagh, referring to the plan of 1885, urged united rather than sporadic action on individual estates.[227] Emphasis upon discipline evoked clerical anger at tenants who broke the common pledge by paying rents.[228] The priests, too, played an important morale-boosting role as propagandists. In this capacity they preached the expediency and effectiveness of the policy. Matt Ryan C.C. Hospital, Co. Limerick, nicknamed 'the general' for his supposedly leading part, boasted of the alleged fright and financial ruin of the landlords,[229] a belief strongly shared by Croke himself.[230] Finally, the priests appealed to the tenants' pride, and John Cunningham C.C. Silvermines, enquired 'is it by whining petition, is it by bowing and scraping like idiots we can hope to obtain largesses from these ghouls?'[231]

It might now profitably be asked why the priests displayed such energy in the Plan of Campaign while they had earlier rejected the formal policy of witholding rents. The answer mainly lies in the changing economic climate from 1885 onwards. The worsening depression of that year inspired relatively extensive tenant participation in the Plan, which inevitably pressurised the clergy into political activity. Furthermore, the policy was neither quite as revolutionary nor as morally untenable as the No-Rent Manifesto. Indeed, the tactics used with clerical approval and connivance in the earlier years of the Land War were remarkably similar to those of the Plan, with tenants meeting to decide on a course of action and offering a reduced rent to the landlord.[232] The chief novel feature of the Plan was the use of the proferred rent, usually less 40%, as a defence fund. The priests, too, were not always totally precise in their operation of the Plan. Canon Daniel Keller, Youghal, Co. Cork, defined it rather vaguely as 'a combination of manifestly oppressed tenants, who, after having exhausted every effort to obtain a just settlement from their landlord, agree to defer payment of their rents, until they receive an assurance that they shall be permitted to retain as much of the fruits of their industry as will allow them to live, if not thrive, on their lands'.[233] In the pre-Plan years the priests had also stressed the necessity of group action, and condemned surreptitious payment of rent in defiance of an agreed concensus.[234] Matt Ryan, for example, pointed with scorn to 'Wyse Lowe's mean crouching serfs',[235] and the Cappawhite National League under Michael Callanan P.P. expelled 3 members for paying their rents.[236] There had been rougher forms of justice (not sanctioned by the priests) meted out to transgressors, which included nocturnal visits, the firing of shots through windows, the burning of haystacks, and even a boycott on the funeral of a tenant's mother.[237]

Canon Daniel Keller, P.P., Youghal, Co. Cork. (*Weekly Freeman*, 26.3.1887).

True to his trust, unmoved by threats of petty persecution,
    The patriot Priest unconquered stands, the victor in the fray,
Despite the knaves who bend and twist each legal institution,
    And whom our race will in the end with measure full repay.
Do what you will the Soggarth still will stand beside his people,
    Their friend, their guide, their counsellor, their champion to the last ;
And God's decree shall echo high o'er altar, tower, and steeple :
    Strive as ye will the tyrant's sway o'er Erin's plains is past.

Ye thought, no doubt, the jail would tend the Levite's gown to tarnish—
    Poor fools ! it lies not in your power to honour give or shame—
Save to the hirelings whom ye daub with Dublin Castle varnish.
    Ye only made the wide world ring with Father Keller's name ;
Thro' every clime his fame now sounds, for those who sought to chain him
    Have gained the cause he advocates recruits in every land,
Whose earnest prayers and sympathy will 'gainst all foes sustain him,
    Whilst history shall with deepest shame his persecutors brand.

The priests were conscious of the various parallels between the Plan and the agitation of these earlier years,[238] and they were prepared to support it on moral grounds. After some initial misgivings, the influential Archbishop of Dublin[239] (as well as the equally influential Archbishop of Cashel)[240] pronounced the Plan sound on the basis that rents were too high; and while hesitant about tenants determining the rent themselves, Walsh concluded, on the dubious moral note, that the landlords had done so long enough. Canon Keller excused the Plan because of the abnormal prevailing circumstances.[241] The blunt Arthur Ryan did not even consider it a question of morality.[242] Unquestionably, the most significant and startling illustration of moral approval for the policy was the priests' immediate hostile reaction against the criticism by Bishop Edward O'Dwyer, Limerick. Taking a bold stand, O'Dwyer confidently announced that the end did not justify the means, and proceeded to make involvement in the Plan a reserved sin.[243] With a tone that might be unthinkable today, David Humphreys strongly questioned his moral logic,[244] and showed further contempt by urging a large attendance at a rally in Limerick city, O'Dwyer's own parish, to defend John Dillon, the bishop's most vocal opponent.[245] Several priests displayed ostentatious approval of Dillon's attacks on the Bishop, by their attendance at other meetings supporting the M.P. Dr Croke, who had private reservations about the public references of both protagonists,[246] entertained Dillon on his visit to Thurles, and a meeting there was chaired by Nicholas Rafferty C.C. Thurles, and attended by Daniel Ryan P.P. Clonoulty, Patrick O'Keeffe C.C. Templemore, Michael O'Sullivan C.C. Upperchurch, and several priests from St Patrick's College.[247] Needless to say, Dillon was loudly praised at the meeting. He was also made a freeman of Clonmel where an address to him was signed by Lawrence Condon C.C., and in Tipperary town he was greeted by several priests, Canon Richard Cahill proposing a vote of confidence in him.[248]

But, if such behaviour signified the confidence of a considerable portion of the clergy in the Plan's morality, it certainly did not reflect Rome's view. From the beginning the Vatican was supplied with a continuous flow of information by Captain John Ross of Bladensburg, a northern Irish convert and unofficial agent of the government in the Vatican in the late 1880s. He was especially interested in David Humphreys.[249] Like many priests, Arthur Ryan refused to accept the reality of English influence in Rome.[250] He was confident that 'this latest appeal to papal authority to bolster up tottering British injustice fails as miserably in logic as it does in reverence'. He was soon disabused by the visit of Monsignor Persico in July 1887,[251] which made Rome's interest in priestly Campaigners quite clear. Persico himself referred to the hundreds of letters he received protesting about priests.[252] He made particular reference to Killaloe priests, 3 or 4 of whom had been complained by Bishop O'Dwyer to the bishop of Killaloe.[253] Colonel Turner D.M., Ennis, later reinforced these complaints, and with the Colonel and his friends in mind the priests greatly resented what Michael B. Corry C.C. Nenagh called the 'impudence' of the 'nasty little crew of Clare upstarts'.[254]

It is indicative of Persico's predicament that people like George Errington, Member of Parliament for Longford and unofficial agent of the government in the Vatican from 1881 to 1885, disliked the envoy's seemingly friendly contact with the so-called 'violent clergy',[255] while the priests themselves saw him more as a *'ligio al governo Inglese.'*[256] The publication in 1888 of the Roman rescript[257] condemning the Plan and boycotting, following the visit, seemed to justify the priests' viewpoint, although Persico, apparently truthfully, denied any influence in the matter.[258] Reaction to the rescript varied, involving laity, episcopacy and priesthood, each influencing the other. The response of the laity is of basic importance. Contemporary evidence is somewhat contradictory. Bishop Pierse Power, Waterford, told Kirby that it was received with 'reverent docility and even thankfulness, except by a few village and professional politicians',[259] while the police advised that it had come on the people 'like a thunderclap'.[260] Some catholics seem to have reacted strangely if we are to believe the quotation of J.S. Flanagan P.P. Adare, Co. Limerick, from one of his alarmed parishioners — 'Ah, Father, we shall have no religion now, the pope has gone over to the English, and superceded Dr Walsh'.[261] The continuation of the Plan in 12 Tipperary estates shows that the rescript was ignored in practice,[262] but the response of the more politicised section, especially the M.P.s, was loudly hostile. Thomas Mayne, a Member for Tipperary with little patience towards hostile clerics, curtly remarked that the drafter of the decree knew no more of Irish politics than the 'man in the moon',[263] and his reference was less caustic than those of others.[264]

Statements like these, coming from popular politicians presented the bishops with an embarrassing dilemma. They did not relish open disobedience to Rome, but they also feared that strong lay sentiments might provoke Vatican condemnation of the entire agrarian movement, resulting perhaps in prohibition of the sacraments and consequent damage to religion. Dr Croke, especially, was acutely aware of this dilemma. This popular prelate was privately angered by the rescript, and even more so by Edward O'Dwyer's immediate approbation of it.[265] Croke had hoped to keep it as quiet as possible by not having it read in chapel.[266] He adopted a cautious but far from obedient attitude, and privately advised, but did not order, his clergy to avoid meetings expressly convened to promote the Plan.[267] He instructed them to condemn it 'wherever the Decree applies'; but, his interpretation of the rescript meant that it did not really apply at all. He left the confessional aspect to the discretion of each individual priest.

Hence the Plan continued uncondemned in the Archdiocese. The civil authorities chafed accordingly, and only refrained from prosecuting him because of his stature, and the certain public and clerical backlash to such a course.[268]

The reaction of the priests was mixed. Few were as audacious as David Humphreys. He retaliated in the public press with three articles totalling 7,000 words, easily the most exhaustive clerical reply to the rescript.[269] Having first questioned the theological ability of Bishop O'Dwyer, he paid the Pope the rather shallow compliment of admitting his right to pronounce authoritatively on moral matters; then he proceeded to contradict the relevance of the rescript. He took his stand on two points. First, he emphasised that the document was not *ex-cathedra*, therefore not infallible, and hence deserved only obedience, but not the assent of faith. The latter would have carried spiritual sanctions. Having tried to undermine the authority of the decree, Humphreys endeavoured to offer an escape from the dilemma it posed. His stand was similar to that of Dr Croke. Taking advantage of the limitations of the Latin idiom, Humphreys asserted that the type of landlord-tenant relationship specified in the circular did not exist to any great extent in Ireland. Hence the Plan condemned did not exist either. Such a statement was remarkable enough, but the Tipperary priest further added that the Pope's ignorance of Irish land tenure was the reason for the alleged *faux-pas*. He was unmoved when the Pope declared the rescript absolute, and calmly concluded that the pontiff was misled by the cardinals of the Holy Inquisition, the authors of the document. Humphreys strongly objected to Rome's views that agrarian contracts in Ireland were fair or that rents were 'extorted' from tenants under the Plan, and lodged with unknown persons.

His views were not original,[270] but other priests were not so outspoken, and certainly experienced dismay when the document was published.[271] They studiously avoided attending heated public meetings specifically critical of Rome's interference in Irish politics. This is not to say that they concealed their dissatisfaction at Rome's action. Some were prepared to pay obedient lip service to the decree, but little more. Patrick O'Donnell C.C. Doon, who was not involved in the Plan, accepted, 'as I am bound to accept', Rome's teaching on it, but continued to praise the 'disinterestedness' of a Campaigner then in prison.[272] A few months after the rescript Robert Power P.P. Ballyneale, speaking on a campaign estate, made it clear that his place was with the people.[273] When John Scanlan C.C. Nenagh had finished reading the bishops' pastoral of 16 Oct. 1890, (which again drew attention to the rescript and upheld the Pope's authority to pronounce on the moral content of politics), he treated his congregation to a political sermon in support of the nearby Ballintotty Plan of Campaign.[274] The date of this pastoral shows that the Roman statement continued to reverberate for some years after its issue; but it was largely ignored or sidetracked by the priests. Their negative response was most strikingly illustrated by continued participation in 10 of the 12 campaign estates mentioned, and these were not all 'militant' clergy as has been recently suggested.[275] John Ross, in this context, shrewdly emphasised the power of public opinion when he observed that the priests were popular 'only so far as they follow the multitude'.[276]

The most conspicuous violation of the rescript was the extraordinary Smith-Barry dispute in Tipperary town, which has been fairly recently dealt with,[277] but merits a brief analysis here because of priestly activity in it. Several previous outbursts on this estate[278] in no way resembled the battle which began in 1889. As Archbishop Walsh stated it was not strictly the Plan of Campaign,[279] but while its initial cause was not dissatisfaction with rents on that particular estate, it was initiated in support of the Ponsonby tenants in Youghal, and its *modus operandi* closely resembled that of the Plan. As well as this when the decision was taken the Tipperary tenants did in fact proceed to seek abatements of 33% to 40%, (some even advocated a total strike), and they taxed themselves at 10% on Griffith's valuation, leaving aside 25% to help eviction victims.[280] Tipperary town became the spearhead of the Plan against the landlords' syndicate, and was seen as such by the clergy.[281] The ostensible head of this syndicate, and the alleged defender of landlord oppression, A.H. Smith-Barry, the proprietor of most of Tipperary town, became the prime target of the tenants.

The influence of Dr Croke at the outset can hardly be disputed; and his name was used by priests as a mark of confidence in the tenants' course.[282] The archbishop's reference to Smith-Barry as an 'aggressive busybody and a virulent partisan' left no doubt about where his sympathies lay.[283] His remark that the tenants might have to consider further action if Smith-Barry refused to dissociate himself from the syndicate may have been vague, but it can only have strengthened the tenants' resolve. Neither was it consistent with his later denial of encouraging the tenants' action in any way.[284] But, the row obviously escalated at a rate the archbishop never anticipated, and when in September 1890 he was asked to mediate by Canon Hegarty of Glanmire, his view of a settlement was decidedly pessimistic.[285] A year later he was of the opinion that the tenants should either offer a 'semblance of opposition' and yield, or fight to the bitter end; neither of which, he complained, they did.[286]

Croke was at a safe distance from the scene of conflict, but Canon Richard Cahill, the ex-Leaguer of the 1850s, and his curate David Humphreys, lived in Tipperary town, and were heavily engaged on the tenants' behalf. The consistency and determination of both, however, greatly differed. At the start Cahill played a leading role, partly because of his status as parish priest and partly because of his long experi-

ence of agrarian agitation. But, like Croke, he little realised the ultimate dimension of the affair. Initially he heartily concurred with the
action, and in a rhetorical flourish reminded his audience that the eyes
of the world were 'rivetted' on Tipperary.[287] Cahill's early leadership
was displayed when he headed a deputation to London with an address
to Smith-Barry, vainly requesting his withdrawal from the syndicate.[288]
John Layne C.C. Boherlahan represented Smith-Barry's Cashel tenantry.
The landlord's indignant refusal was given wide publicity, and drew
condemnation from several directions.[289] The consequences in Tipperary
town were swift and brutal. The witholding of rents provoked wholesale
ejectments.[290] Under the circumstances Cahill's suggestion to seek legal
advice was plainly irrelevant.[291] The subsequent extraordinary project
of constructing business premises on Stafford O'Brien's land at the
edge of the town for evicted traders also involved Cahill,[292] and New
Tipperary, for both priests and people, became the symbol of tenant
resistance on a national level.[293] John Scanlan was stirred to use the
biblical analogy of the Macabees' sacrifice and the historical one of
the burning of Moscow.[294]

As chairman of the Tenants Defence Association,[295] Cahill was
anxious to ensure that sufficient funds were available to finance the
project, which eventually cost £50,000. He expressed his confidence
in its efficacy as an anti-landlord device. According to the police not
all priests from the surrounding parishes shared his opinion,[296], but the
opening of New Tipperary in April 1890 provided the opportunity for
widespread propaganda, and Cahill presided at the occasion, which
was attended by priests, a large number of M.P.s and the lord mayors
of Dublin and Cork.[297] William O'Brien described it as 'a sort of Irish
Mecca to the pilgrims of nationality',[298] and indeed excursions to New
Tipperary were organised from several parts of Ireland.[299]

But, as the struggle intensified and internal divisions appeared among
the tenants, Canon Cahill's enthusiasm cooled, and finally turned sour.
His impact upon the affair was not of notable importance. On the other
hand, Humphreys gradually moved to the forefront, and played a major
part in the campaign. John Ross was not exaggerating when he complained that the curate was the 'centre of the disturbance'. Possessing
an iron will and an unshakeable belief in his stand, Humphreys was the
only priest in Tipperary town who refused to change even when majority
opinion seemed to shift, especially with the disillusionment of the
Parnellite split. He was involved in the minutiae of all plans, being for
example one of the chief organisers of the detailed New Tipperary work
rota. It was he who served notices for possession of New Tipperary
premises on those tenants, who had returned to the old town while
apparently hoping to hold their new stalls also.[300] His implacable
hatred for landlords, stemming from the eviction of his aged father
on the Cloncurry estate in earlier years,[301] overruled any trace of

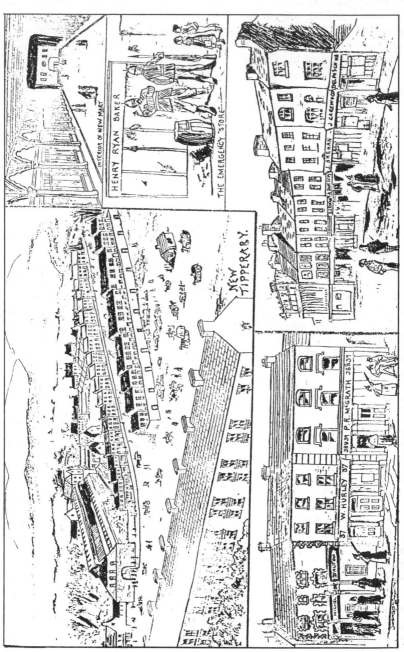

'A Contrast — New Tipperary and Old.' (*United Ireland* 18.4.1890).

scrupulosity in his anti-landlord drive, and he took every opportunity to paint Smith-Barry in the worst possible light. One of his speeches was delivered at the graveside of a 14 year old youth, who had been shot in the leg by the police, but in fact had died as a result of neglect by the doctor.[302] On that emotive occasion Humphreys baldly proposed that Smith-Barry was at least a remote cause of the boy's death. The culpable doctor escaped condemnation. The curate's extreme stand is clear from the terms of reference he put forward as a solution to the whole conflict. He insisted that no settlement would be considered until the landlord paid compensation to the youth's family, to those imprisoned since the beginning of the struggle, to other tenants for the loss of their property, and until he restored the vacant premises to their original condition.[303] He adamantly demanded that past, allegedly high, rents be taken into consideration when settling future rents, and he was equally firm that there could be no settlement until the landlord unconditionally surrendered.[304]

Humphreys was deadly serious in his demands. He was blinded by his own prejudice, and he badly underestimated the resolve and the resources of the landlord. Smith-Barry's determination to continue[305] posed several related problems for the curate. One was financial. Canon Cahill may have been chairman of the Tenants Defence Association, but it was Humphreys who controlled the purse strings, and he constantly badgered the Dublin leaders for funds.[306] He was held responsible by disgruntled traders for local financial transactions.[307] His second problem, deteriorating morale among the tenants themselves, was equally serious. This he tried to counter by depicting the landlord as financially ruined,[308] an obvious untruth. He also endeavoured to obscure the seriousness both of the magistrates' refusal to grant licences for the new shops, and of the injunctions against the weighing machine in the new mart, and he was quite prepared to remove the market for a short time.[309] But, some of the tenants, whose livelihoods were at stake, shared neither his tenacity nor his optimism, and the split became public knowledge. Nevertheless, Humphreys was anxious to conceal its extent,[310] and even when the trickle back to the old town began to increase he blatantly denied that those who had returned were a significant proportion of the total number evicted.[311] He denounced as 'sneaks and snobs' the 30 tenants who requested Croke's interference, and he studiously avoided Canon Cahill's house when the archbishop visited the town.[312] He was further angered when a deputation of 11 travelled to Chester to negotiate with Smith-Barry, and retorted that the 'name of Tipperary would stink the nostrils of every responsible Irishman' if the tenants yielded.[313] This deputation formed the nucleus of a group who requested Croke to remove Humphreys from the town, and threatened to withold the curate's dues if the archbishop refused,[314] an action which irritated such priests as John Scanlan.[315]

It is probable that Croke, a strong-willed and stubborn man himself, admired the obstinate Humphreys. He refused to move him, but when the affair ended in 1895 promptly promoted him to the lucrative pastorate of Killenaule, where he continued abrasive as ever, for the remaining 35 years of his life. It is ironic, perhaps, that this priest who created such a stir during his long pastorate was a very model of good behaviour during his student years in Maynooth.[316]

Evictions
The Tipperary dispute is a clear example of the obvious connection between failure to pay rents and evictions. Since rents were such an integral part of the agrarian debate, the eviction problem was correspondingly important, as Gladstone recognised in his 1881 Land Act. Significantly, the tenants' reponse in the 1880s was much sharper and more intense than at mid-century, a time when evictions were on an enormously larger scale.[317] But, unlike famine clearances, a greater proportion of the larger farmers were victims at this later period, if only because of their numerical superiority. The Kilburry dispute which prompted the introduction of the Land League to Tipperary, resulted from the eviction of the Meagher family for refusal to pay a rent increased from £300 to £500.[318] The expectations of such people were higher than their predecessors; they were more vocal, and it is doubtful indeed if there was any such thing as an acceptable level of evictions during the Land War. The priests responded to the views of this class with whom they had a very close affinity; John Murphy C.C. Mullinahone believed and confidently preached the fallacy that more evictions occurred in the decade 1870 to 1880 than at any other period, although the contrary was true.[319] It is noteworthy that priestly references to the landlord's right to evict lazy tenants were confined to the very early period of the Land War.[320] The best illustration of the power of public opinion to stifle the priests' moral reservations is an 1888 dispute in Kilross in the parish of Lattin. Unusually, almost all the priests involved sympathised with Count Arthur Moore, who evicted an apparently improvident drunken tenant who was a relative of Dr Michael O'Neill P.P., but their sympathy was wisely confined to private correspondence.[321] In deferring to public opinion the priests avidly concentrated upon the human misery of any eviction.[322] Daniel Flannery eloquently summed this up — 'truly Madame Tussaud's Chamber of Horrors won't be complete 'till she has an Irish eviction scene, but no tongue can tell, no brush depict, even partially, all the horrors of an Irish eviction'.[323]

In most cases the clergy were genuinely moved by the plight of victims, and 55 priests, some on more than one occasion, were concerned with evictions.[324] This concern assumed several shapes, and ranged from condemnation of evictions in general to active involvement at eviction scenes. The priests were as regular an eviction fixture as the bailiff. Their role in this varied from the political to the pastoral. Since such occasions were potentially explosive, the clergy acted as peace-makers and prevented violence, as well as offering some comfort to the victims. Patrick O'Donnell C.C. helped to avoid serious bloodshed on Colonel Hare's estate in Doon, when 1,000 Coldstream Guards pre-pared to fire on the crowd.[325] Interestingly, at the beginning of the agitation some priests were actively hostile to the Land League's plan of organised resistance to the process server. Michael Davitt quotes an interesting example of this.[326] Within a short time, however, the power of public opinion prevailed to such an extent that instances arose of priests actually thwarting evictors. Cornelius Egan P.P. Castletownnarra refused to leave the door of a would-be victim,[327] and Robert H. Little, P.P. Six-Mile Bridge, Co. Clare, (an ex-Tipperary priest), was pad-locked and chained to a door, successfully foiling police attempts to remove him.[328]

Normally the priests' role was less dramatic but nonetheless impor-tant. It was not unusual for them to restrain overenthusiastic bailiffs (whom Maurice Power P.P. Emly labelled as 'drunken fools')[329] from damaging furniture,[330] or to ensure that the evictor complied with strict legal procedure. David Humphreys used his considerable legal knowledge on at least one occasion to prevent an agent from 'wheedling' information from the tenants to which he was not legally entitled.[331] As the educated pastors of their flocks the priests, too, invariably acted as mediators, and frequently secured settlements even during the process of eviction.[332] In one case a priest, John Moloney C.C. Lorrha, pre-vented an eviction by personally offering security on the tenant's be-half.[333] Daniel Flannery effected a settlement after a tenant's furniture had been loaded onto fifty carts and possession taken by the landlord.[334]

Unfortunately, even after intensive efforts, including long journeys to Dublin or Cork to plead with landlords,[335] the priests were not al-ways successful in preventing evictions. Failure, however, did not mean that they took no further interest in the fate of those ejected. One remarkable example of community spirit was the gathering of huge crowds to build temporary dwellings for the victims. At least 17 priests showed their solidarity with such action by their active presence on these occasions, or even by initiating such projects.[336] Their role, however, was generally of secondary importance in these matters, sometimes involving little more than offering encouraging advice or performing the symbolic ritual of laying foundation-stones.

Thirty-seven priests had a more active and unusual function, how-ever, at the sale of farm interests following evictions.[337] Such occa-sions, as David Humphreys rightly said, were 'like a powder magazine with fire in the immediate neighbourhood'.[338] At a Clonmel auction of June 1881 several bands played lively airs to a rioting crowd.[339] Even a continuous downpour could not dampen the temper of a Thurles gathering on a similar occasion, when only clerical interference prevented bloodshed.[340] Violence was most likely when emergencymen or employees of the Property Defence Association[341] and the Land Corporation[342] were present. Both organisations had essentially the same objects of defending landlord interests, combatting tenant combinations, aiding financially embarrassed landlords, and providing tenants for evicted farms by purchasing interests with money supplied often by the landlords of the properties concerned. The priests viewed the Land Corporation in particular with distaste,[343] and made every effort to thwart the sales of farms by raising legal technicalities, or even by bidding on holdings on behalf of their parishoners.[344]

Probably the most important post-eviction activity of the priests was fund-raising. At least 75 priests not only collected, but contributed notable sums to aid victims.[345] Some of these were involved in local 'defence' funds, but the majority were members of the Tenants' Defence Association, a national organisation which embraced 44 Tipperary parishes or 69% of the county's total. The 64 priestly members were involved in 40 to these parishes. The association was founded as a direct result of the Smith-Barry dispute, and served as the financial wing of the National League to accumulate badly needed funds and counteract the landlords' syndicate. The priests were acutely conscious of this aim[346] and their close association with the organisation is clear not only from its membership, but also from the fact that its official launching took place in St Patrick's College Thurles, attended by 800 delegates including 16 M.P.s and 66 Tipperary priests.[347] Despite this, the attitude of Dr Croke to the Association is interesting because of his curious ambiguity. Publicly he subscribed £50 and enthusiastically advocated the necessity of the body,[348] while privately he displayed some pique because he was not consulted about its aims.[349] He also doubted the efficacy of the organisation to combat Smith-Barry. But Croke was as sensitive to public opinion as the lower clergy, and in a vexed mood he advised Archbishop Walsh: 'If you and I hold back and do not subscribe, it will languish and probably die ignominiously, and it would be thrown in our face that in a critical moment we had abandoned the people'. This should not obscure the importance of his public letter in motivating the priests and the laity. Despite Croke's reservations, the association's first campaign was eminently successful, raising £60,000, and the relationship between it and evictions was underlined by the £435 contribution of the strife-torn parish of Tipperary, by far the largest parochial figure in Ireland.[350] It is true, of course, that the Parnellite M.P.s were key figures in the Association, and mounted an impressive canvassing campaign; but when their attention was diverted by the crisis of 1890-91, and the organisation collapsed, priestly importance in the drive for eviction funds was immediately evident. Croke personally controlled a large evicted tenants fund, which was almost totally administered by the priests.[351] A conference of clergy chaired by him also raised £358 in personal subscriptions of which the Archbishop gave £100.[352] The priests contributed sums ranging from £1 to £10. Perhaps the climax of clerical participation in eviction fund-raising came with a second Thurles convention attended by 57 Tipperary priests[353] in October 1891.

Boycott
However important finance was and however vital the priests' role in this and other anti-eviction activities, boycott proved by far the most popular, most effective and most controversial weapon used. There are numerous examples of victims appearing before league branches to 'apologise' for their independent spirit.[354] While ostracisation was by no means unknown in earlier decades, it was Parnell who advocated extensive and systematic use of the method. Interestingly enough the neologist of the word was a priest, John O'Malley P.P. Neale, Co Mayo. Considering the dubious morality of the policy it is a little surprising that so many of the clergy supported its use. At least 69 Tipperary priests were involved in disputes or debates on boycotting, while 45 of these supported the more controversial ostracisation of individuals as distinct from boycotting farms from which tenants had been evicted.[355] The parish priest-curate ratio and age analysis of the latter suggest that a representiative cross-section of clergy considered the policy morally defensible, although it was hardly compatible with the virtue of christian charity. This is not to say, however, that priests were unaware of the moral implications of boycott. In 1906 and 1907 three well-known theologians reviewed its use during the Land War and failed to agree fully on its morality.[356] The main points that emerged may be summarised as follows: (1) Boycotting was ordinarily wrong, but legitimate in self-defence; (2) It was a sin against legal justice if it interfered with freedom of contracts of exchange, for example acquiring the necessities of life; (3) It usurped the function of church or state; (4) combination increased the social pressure of boycott; (5) social intercourse should not be denied; (6) leaving the victim 'severely alone' did not necessarily mean complete social isolation.

In 1888 an ex-professor of Theology, (Nicholas Murphy P.P. Kilmanagh, Co Kilkenny), assured the public that this policy of leaving 'obnoxious persons, severely alone was similar to the Catholic doctrine of fraternal correction.[357] This sparked off a debate between Murphy, an 'Anglo-Irish Priest' and a 'German Parish Priest'.[358] The writings of St. Matthew, St. Ligouri, and Gury Ballerini, were called upon. Gury, one of the seminary textbooks, held that 'fraternal correction also in its manner of correction should be combined with true charity. It should be paternal towards inferiors, benignant among equals and reverential towards superiors'.

But, the more complex theological arguments of the question were somewhat irrelevant to the hard-pressed parish clergy, whose statements were made more radical by their political involvement, and indeed by the strong pressure of public opinion, — the religious habit was not necessarily a protection against boycott threats. Patrick Scully P.P. Keash, Co Sligo rented a farm from an evicting landlord, was boycotted and succumbed.[359] Dr Croke frankly admitted that it took all his 'personal influence' to prevent the Sisters of Mercy in Tipperary town from being boycotted for paying their rent, and he revealed that the Christian Brothers were also 'in a bit of a fix'.[360] The priests in succumbing to popular pressure were at pains to propose a general moral justification for the use of boycotting, which, however, differed from the complicated analysis of the professors. The good Saint Paul, who might not have appreciated the application of his teaching in this context, was much quoted by the Tipperary priests.[361] John Scanlan and Thomas Hackett C.C. Loughmore drew attention to his second epistle to the Thessalonians and its message: 'If any man obey not our word by this epistle, note that man and do not keep company with him that he may be ashamed'.[362] David Humphreys also denied that boycotting was contrary to scripture, and proposed that it was not only admissible but a moral duty in a country where the majority were crushed by laws biased in favour of the minority.[363]

The publication of the Roman decree in 1888 condemning boycotting as well as the Plan only concentrated the debate even more on the moral dimension. Humphreys in his three articles used essentially the same reasoning for both, and generously conceded that the policy should be condemned in the non-existent cases of a *locatores-conductores* relationship between landlord and tenant. Otherwise he ignored the landlords' right in property, and morally excused boycotting as a weapon against the allegedly immoral action of taking over the tenant right of another person.[364] The priests' apparent confidence in the moral compatibility of boycotting was partly reflected by their continued support of the policy following the rescript.[365] The laity, too, did not seem over-concerned by the Vatican condemnation. Boycotting, however, had drastically decreased two years earlier and clerical references to it declined accordingly. 32% of all such references were made during the years 1880-1881, 41% in 1884 and 1885, and only 25% from 1886 to 1891. This means in effect that the need for boycotting had almost vanished by 1886 because of its effectiveness, especially in ending the problems of 'grabbing' which had been prevalent as regards the taking of grass in 1884 and 1885.

While the priests may have defended the essential morality of boycotting, their approval was not absolute and unqualified. They certainly advised leniency in specific cases and called for a 'judicious system of boycotting'.[366] They stressed the importance of giving the accused a fair hearing, and asked leaguers to forgive those who had 'repented'.[367] Such priests also discountenanced boycotting which degenerated into tyranny or private spleen.[368] The Smith-Barry affair is a case in point. Three of the priests there — Canon Cahill, Walter Cantwell and Michael Power — much to the chagrin of David Humphreys, preached strong altar-sermons against 'persecution', 'victimisation' and 'brainless bribed busybodies coming into Tipperary to intimidate'.[369] These priests had originally supported the policy of boycotting.

Nevertheless, the clergy were essentially uncompromising, and justified their stand on the morally dubious but popular maxim that 'desperate evils' required 'desperate remedies'.[370] Since grabbing was the most desperate evil in the priests' and tenants' eyes, the grabber bore the main brunt of boycotting, and was easily the most frequent target of clerical barbs. John Hackett, curate in Loughmore, described such individuals as 'erect two-legged reptiles',[371] and John Egan P.P. Burgessbeg agreed that leniency towards such 'vile miscreants' might accord with Christian charity, but was 'love's labour lost'.[372] Grabbing was placed squarely in the moral realm. The citing of the Tenth Commandment by Patrick O'Keeffe C.C. Fethard was reinforced by Matt Ryan's serious assertion that the grabber was in a state of mortal sin.[373] This was by no means an unusual view. To further emphasise it both Michael Callanan P.P. Cappawhite and John Condon C.C. Golden took the unusual step of returning the Easter dues of certain grass-grabbers.[374]

By far the most despised category of so-called grabbers was the emergencymen, who occupied farms at low rents. An especially withering altar attack on one of these was delivered by John R. Crowe C.C. in Cappawhite chapel a few months after the Roman rescript.[375] Having roundly castigated his captive audience for associating with the emergencyman's workmen or allowing their children to play together, Crowe appealed to their sense of shame in a most dramatic way: 'I have known children to leave the school, and the school to be closed up, because one child of an emergencyman entered it . . . shame on you! Have you no manhood'. The introduction of boycott into the schoolroom was certainly distasteful but it was only an occasional occurrence.[376] Even more extreme, and slightly more frequent, was the ostracisation of emergencymen or grabbers in the chapel, an action rarely supported by the priests. This usually took the form of the congregation moving to another part of the building, leaving the victims in conspicuous isolation. An ex-executive of the Loughmore National League, who took an evicted farm was held up to public execration; both himself and his daughter were showered with eggs entering the chapel as well as suffering the humiliation of being ostracised inside.[377] The priests had little sympathy with this man; at an earlier date 16 of them had joined a protest meeting in Loughmore where clerical speeches were the most declamatory. Unlike Limerick or Kerry, Tipperary bishops did not interfere in such rows. The midnight sawing of a grabber's pew in Knockea chapel, Co Limerick, precipitated an interdict from Bishop Edward O'Dwyer, which prohibited priests from hearing confessions, attending at the graveside or 'churching' women after confinement.[378] The Bishop of Kerry closed the chapel of Cullen because the congregation persisted in leaving when a grabber entered.[379]

Chapel incidents were only extreme manifestations of a more total social ostracisation. Every effort was made to make life as miserable as possible for the grabber, and despite theological principles this included deprivation of life's necessities. Consequently, and contrary to official National League policy,[380] other non-agricultural members of society who disobeyed the boycott were themselves victimised, although association with grabbers was not always the cause of such victimisation. The most common targets were shopkeepers who suffered for supplying not only emergencymen but also police in times of coercion, or more dubiously for refusing to join the leagues.[381] These shopkeepers did not always undergo total boycott, but certainly experienced some decline in trade. Undoubtedly, the most intensive and systematic boycott of shopkeepers was staged during the Smith-Barry saga in Tipperary town. John Ross of Bladensburg quite correctly told Balfour that David Humphreys was 'practically the boycotting agent' there.[382] When the trickle back to the old section of the town began to increase, Humphreys warned would-be shoppers 'to beware of fresh paint lest they get their clothes soiled'.[383] Thurles, too, had a well-deserved reputation for boycotting, and shopkeepers there were victimised for supporting a bailiff in the local elections. Tradesmen refused to repair their windows, the children of the Christian Brothers School refused to associate with their children, the porter van-men were warned to avoid them, and the people of Stradavoher boycotted a milk-supplier who gave them milk.[384] This was in 1889. In 1885 Ryan's Hotel was almost ruined by the simple expedient of shopkeepers refusing to buy from commercial travellers who stayed there.[385] As early as 1882 the House of Commons had been told that boycotting was so intimidatory in Thurles and Holycross that a special force of police was required to protect victims.[386]

Of the remaining non-agricultural targets the police ranked high on the list,[387] both for the protection they afforded to grabbers, their role at evictions, and for their task of enforcing the coercion acts at proclaimed meetings. An interesting if unique case was the boycotting of the Nenagh police sports in July 1891, an event which traditionally enjoyed local participation. The priests fully supported this boycott and emphasised its political dimension. Michael B. Corry and John Scanlan, placing it in the context of coercion, remarked that Balfour wished to make 'political capital' out of the sports.[388] The so-called Mitchelstown Massacre[389], when the police opened fire on a crowd killing some, generated intense indignation in Tipperary, and provoked an anti-police reaction by some shopkeepers.[390] Galbally people were especially incensed because a parishioner died in the affair; but, maintaining that his parish was a 'den of vipers, cut-throats and calumniators,' Canon Patrick Ryan refused to yield to the pressure of public opinion to sack a local schoolmistress because she was married to a policeman. [391] Ryan was denounced by placard. David Humphreys would have been willing to oblige had he been in the good Canon's shoes. His dislike of policemen was acute and Humphreyan ridicule was poured on their heads in liberal quantities.[392] The local Resident Magistrate was no more than 'an overgrown policeman' to him,[393] and he went so far as to visit all the publicans in the town to warn them against supplying the police with drink.[394] He boasted that the butchers were refusing to supply them with meat.[395] Humphreys was not afraid to show open contempt for the coercion act which prohibited boycotting. He confidently announced: 'The Crimes Act cannot compel you to speak to any person you meet on the road, it cannot compel you to work for anyone or to buy from anyone, or to sell to anyone'.[396] This attitude was common to other priests also.[397] Neither were the clergy afraid to manifest sympathy for those imprisoned on boycotting charges, and they did not fear to attend such courtcases,[398] a practice which prompted one irritated magistrate to sarcastically invite them to a seat on the bench.[399] It was logical, perhaps, that they should have the courage of their convictions by enduring imprisonment for advocating boycotting. This indeed was the case, although Tipperary priests were not involved.[400] Such instances invariably engaged the attention of the House of Commons.[401]

The Abolition of Landlordism

The prevalence of boycotting among the various social groups should not obscure the fact that the primary, even if not always the direct target of boycotting was the landlords. Apart from direct references to landlords most of the priests' statements supporting the boycotting of particular categories were made in the context of landlord-tenant disputes. As David Humphreys said, grass-grabbing kept landlordism alive by keeping money in the landlords' pockets.[402] The total thrust of the Land War, with all its organisations and tactics, was concentrated against the small wealthy land-owning class. The result was nothing less than an agrarian and social cataclysm with related political side-effects particularly at local level.

Of these the agrarian was the most fundamental and total. What began as a demand for the three Fs rapidly evolved to sound the deathknell of landlordism itself. The clergy were as convinced as the farmers. At least 42 Tipperary priests publicly called for its abolition and the introduction of a peasant proprietary.[403] The parish priests were as inclined towards the new policy as the curates, and the various age groups show a normal pattern, with the exception of the 31-40 year olds who were extra-enthusiastic.

The statistics recorded, however, conceal the complexity of clerical attitudes to this policy, especially in the initial stages, when the total implications of the agitation were not immediately apparent. Yet in some ways the demand for peasant proprietary was inevitable insofar as it was a natural outgrowth. The repeated criticism of landlords, either individually or as a body, in which the priests heartily joined,[404] must eventually have focused attention on the system itself. Furthermore the priests' dictum that the land existed for the benefit of the tenants as well as for the good of landlords[405] was a philosophical and psychological step towards the Land League slogan 'the land for the people'. As early as 1869 Dr Michael O'Neill had said that 'God created the land for the people, not for the millions and not for the monopoly of a few landlords'.[406] Such priests as John Cunningham C.C. Silvermines deplored the fact that Ireland was, as he put it, 'the fattening park of John Bull'.[407] The priests proposed that it was no sin to wish to live in Ireland. Thomas Walsh C.C. Clogheen was quite clear about priorities in a situation of maximum agricultural cultivation, which he and his colleagues mistakenly believed would come in the wake of peasant proprietary.[408] He put the tenant first, the landlord next and society third.

So, while they demanded the three Fs, the priests did not find it too difficult to adapt to changing public opinion which was rapidly becoming impatient with what had been a radical policy in the 1850s. Several priests hastened to repudiate the three Fs.[409] Michael Gleeson P.P. Templederry portrayed fixity of tenure as 'fixity of tyranny',[410] and Eugene Sheehy P.P. Bruree, Co Limerick more logically argued that the dual ownership conceded by Gladstone was an anachronism in Ireland because of the incompatibility between landlord and tenant interests.[411] Still, in the very early years of the Land War the priests did not envisage a sudden tenurial revolution. Many of them saw the three Fs as a practical transition stage towards ultimate ownership.[412]

Even when landlordism was seen by them as 'the root of all evil', and peasant proprietary as the 'panacea of all ills',[413] they were careful to provide a clearly defined interpretation of the Land League's slogan. As the revolution swept through the country they dreaded the possibility of popular confiscation. Archbishop Croke, despite his approval of the Land League, admitted his feeling that initially it had harboured 'unsound and delusive doctrines', which he hastened to add had disappeared because of clerical influence.[414] Such priests as Dean William Quirke stoutly maintained, as much in hope perhaps as in conviction, that their aim was not confiscation, while Archdeacon Kinnane denied, as Croke did, that the league advocated 'Communism or Nihilism or

Socialism'.[415] Certainly some priests seemed to have been nervous of Parnell's contact with the French Communard, Henri de Rochfort, although Croke and the Tipperary clergy were not so naive. Nevertheless, some priests were prompted to refer to the French Revolution, and the *Irish Ecclesiastical Record* of 1881 devoted 68 pages to its principles and their compatibility with current Catholic theology.[416] The conclusion reached was predictable enough — that the Revolution weakened religion and clerical influence, that the rights of man as a definition was vague and indefinite, and that levelling was impossible in practice, since men were only equal in their nature, hence an aristocracy of wealth and privilege must exist.

The leading role of Michael Davitt in the Land League was sufficient to raise clerical suspicion of its slogan. Davitt's theory of land nationalisation was well known and disliked by the priests. It was not, however, entirely incompatible with theology, being based on the principle of the non-absolute nature of land ownership. But the conclusions drawn were utterly polarised. Davitt's theory was purely socialistic, while theological principles were concerned solely with the duties and the rights of ownership. Some priests also had practical as well as theoretical objections to nationalisation. Relying on his not inconsiderable knowledge of human nature, David Humphreys felt that men would only cultivate the land for their own benefit,[417] not for the public good — a conclusion proved sound by events in Russia decades later. In deference to Davitt's popularity, however, Humphreys praised him as a person, [418] a distinction made by other priests also.[419] Thomas McDonnell Adm. Clonmel stressed that a celebration there in Davitt's honour did not signify approval of his theory, and remarked that 'any other observations capable of being misunderstood might have been the ebullition of Irish oratory'.[420] Davitt was under no misapprehension about the priests' opposition to nationalisation, and he could not always resist an indirect thrust at them. At a Cashel meeting he dwelt upon the hostility of European priests to socialistic movements and their consequent isolation from the people.[421] Rather pointedly he expressed satisfaction at the Irish priests' role in the agrarian agitation. It was a back-handed compliment, and the apparent equation of Irish and continental movements must have grated sharply on sensitive clerical ears.

All the evidence, therefore, indicates that a House of Commons statement by one M.P. on clerical warnings against communism and socialism was entirely accurate.[422] Proprietary was *per se* the very antithesis of these doctrines. It may be said, too, that despite their harsh anti-landlord statements some priests saw a place for landlords as private owners in an Ireland of universal peasant proprietary.[423] Not only that, but their denial of confiscation was accompanied by an emphasis on just compensation for the landlords.[424] In this they were motivated by basic moral principles of justice which underlay their vocation. They were, one might say, playing the issue by the book (of theology). Yet their concept of justice was flavoured in no small way by their peasant sympathies, and they were no more ready to advocate purchase at apparently unfavourable terms than the tenants were to accept. There was much priestly debate on the details of this. The 15 years' purchase considered fair by James Ryan C.C. Tipperary did not meet the approval of David Humphreys, who proposed 10 years as sufficient.[425] Humphreys argued that falling prices had reduced the purchase considerably. In view of a continuing decline he, and other priests,[426] advised farmers to wait. Like several contemporary economists, Thomas Meagher looked to the continent for examples.[427] He drew attention to the 16½ years' purchase under the 1850 Prussian scheme. In practice, however, he negotiated for 12 years on behalf of his parishioners.[428] Meagher always bore in mind the type of tenure and its rent basis. In judging Ashbourne's 1885 Act he proposed 10 years purchase on the judicial rents rather than the 19 years purchase he considered fair for pre-1881 years, since the latter was based on a different tenure system, which involved the purchase of both occupancy and ownership.[429] But the calculations of the equally logical David Humphreys ignored the statutory change in tenure.[430] He applied Meagher's principle to pre-1881 rents also, although naturally he was careful to argue that such rents could not be used to calculate purchase terms because they included the tenants' interest, which as we have seen was central to his criticism of the 1881 act.

The loan conditions of this bill did not satisfy him either. He proposed an amendment which would offer the full purchase money at a moderate interest, not exceeding 2½%.[431] The suggestion was a sound one. The 1885 act conceded the full purchase money at a reasonable interest and repayment period, and for this reason was greeted with more satisfaction by the priests.[432] Nevertheless, Thomas Meagher mooted 7 amendments to this act, some of which are worth noting because of their incompatibility with the tenants' outlook or with the views of his fellow priests on peasant proprietary.[433] His argument that a maximum loan of £1000 rather than the £5000 offered would create smaller farms, and hence 'universal happiness', was idealistic but impractical. It betrayed his unusual bias in favour of the landless class, but ran contrary to the principles of the 1880 land conference which did not envisage peasant proprietary as a division of the country into small parcels of land.[434] Meagher's conclusion that small farms were the policy of Henry VIII, or that Tacitus and Pliny attributed Rome's fall to large farms,[435] may have shown his own avid interest in the matter but was hardly likely to convince his ambitious parishioners.

Balfour's Act of 1891 was not so favourably received by priests for practical and political reasons which seem contradictory. 'Bloody Balfour' was intensely disliked by the priests as the author of stringent coercion. Any conciliation measures coming from him were viewed with distinct suspicion. Michael B. Corry, possibly reflecting one strand of political thought, saw the bill as an attempt to kill Home Rule with kindness.[436] As well as this, both Corry and David Humphreys felt that it was biased in the landlords' favour,[437] which was not an entirely correct diagnosis either. Other priests were influenced by more parochial and practical experience. John Moran C.C. Ballyneale drew attention to the inability of Lord Waterford's tenants to pay under the terms of previous acts.[438] None of the priests mentioned the tenants' dislike of land stock rather than cash as the system of repayment.

Whatever the priests' technical or political objections, these acts provided the vital statutory precedents that finally ended centuries of landlordism in the early 1900s. But the destruction of the agrarian system also severely dented the political influence of the landlords. This was not so apparent at the level of parliamentary politics, where landlord power had already been greatly weakened by mid-century. Only one Tory candidate was elected for Tipperary after 1850, and this was on a legal technicality and against the wishes of the vast majority of the electorate.[439] The assault on landlord power at local level in the municipal and Poor Law Guardian elections was, however, a very different matter. While the priests did not entirely neglect these in earlier decades, it was not until the Land War that they became a priority. It may be said that this was not due to clerical initiative, but rather to party strategy which was executed through the National League branches.[440] As chairmen of the branches, the priests were intimately involved in the promotion of this policy. James Cantwell Adm., always well informed on party policy, propagated the view that landlords used the management of Poor Law boardrooms and Grand Juries for 'party purposes and political dodges'.[441] As with parliamentary elections the altar was used to influence the direction of Poor Law contests, and a political sermon by Patrick Brennan C.C. resulted in an army officer marching his men out of Birr chapel.[442] The intense opposition of David Hearn P.P. Newcastle to some Poor Law candidates prompted complaints to his bishop, which revealed also the opposition of Hearn's predecessor Thomas 'Fiery' Finn, because one of them voted for Count de La Poer as chairman of the Clonmel guardians.[443] These individuals feared that Hearn would 'probably curse us', and they threw light on this priest's method of canvassing when he allegedly used 'terrorism, intimidation and . . . malediction on any person who would vote for me'. As in parliamentary elections, too, it was not unusual for priests to propose Poor Law or municipal candidates.[444] In the scramble to return Parnellite candidates for municipal boroughs the debates became strongly heated, and apart from opposition to landlord nominees, deep divisions were sown in local ranks where the rump of Liberalism remained. The outgoing Mayor of Clonmel, E.C. Hackett, member of an erstwhile popular Liberal family and proprietor of the *Tipperary Free Press*, was strongly criticised for opposing the nationalist candidate for the Mayoralty in 1884.[445]

Not only were the priests concerned with the selection and election of candidates, but they took it upon themselves to monitor their subsequent performance. This was especially true of Poor Law guardians whom the clergy sometimes reprimanded for lax attendance at the boardroom. Patrick Crowe C.C. Burgessbeg accused one Parnellite guardian of abstaining from an important vote through fear of the 'ghost of landlordism'.[446] Even the most apolitical duties of guardians were viewed from a distinctly political, that is, anti-landlord perspective. One might imagine that the election of coroners or dispensary doctors would have been exempt from this. But, in the last quarter of the century, politics penetrated almost every nook of Irish life including medical appointments, and since priests were invariably the chairmen of the dispensary committees,[447] they were in a strong position to influence such proceedings. John Power C.C. Solohead branded the Tipperary guardians' vote against the 'nationalist' candidate for the post of union medical officer as one for 'Orangism'.[448]

Inevitably the intense, sustained, many-pronged anti-landlord campaign of the 1880s eroded, but did not fully extinguish, the social influence of the landlords, too. The priests' leadership in this and their insulting rhetoric played a major role in the demise of deference. Apart from hurling insults at landlords in general as 'harpies and vultures', 'incarnate demons', 'jaundice-eyed jackdaws', 'local snobocracy', 'loathsome' descendants from the 'slums of England',[449] the priests were not in the least afraid to launch personal attacks on individuals. A series of diatribes by Matt Ryan against a minister-cum-landlord, the Rev T. Pennefather (Rev Mr Featherhead according to Ryan)[450] were only surpassed by the less than delicate reference of John Ryan to the amorous exploits of the unfortunate Lord Leitrim, 'his bastard children and the women that gave them birth'.[451]

Such comments were both a direct contribution to and a symptom of a sense of personal independence. The priests were quite conscious of the spirit of deference, and wished to dispel it, although this might have rebounded on their own privileged position. If this occurred to them they did not refer to it but concentrated upon the landlords. John Cahill C.C. Cashel advised his hearers not to 'put your hand to your hat' for the 'felonious aristocrats',[452] while John Cunningham reprimanded his parishioners for 'bowing and scraping'.[453] Few, however, stated the issue with more irony than the inimitable John Kenyon, who died a decade prior to the Land War: 'It is pitiable to see crowds in Dublin . . . opening their eyes and mouths in wonder at my Lord Eglinton and Winton, because he advances through the streets in all the trappings of state. . . . Let us take off his spurs, and pluck out one by one his feathers ... conduct him as nature found him to the top of Keeper Hill on a frosty morning in November. ... They would tell you they often saw a finer man bathing in the sea at Lahinch or Kilkee'.[454]

The most conspicuous feature of the social revolution was the ban on foxhunting, a sport which John Tuohy P.P. Shinrone saw as a 'sign of supercilious ascendancy'.[455] It was indeed the traditional hallmark of the aristocracy and large farmers, and an attack on it would have been almost unthinkable in earlier years. During the Land War and particularly in the mid-'80s the ban was operated or discussed in 45% of Tipperary's parishes, and received the support of at least 32 priests.[456] As the leading antagonist of the landlords David Humphreys was by far its most ardent supporter. Apart from using it, as some tenants did, as a means of revenge upon landlords, Humphreys repeatedly concentrated upon its social implications. He saw it as an excellent means of making British public opinion aware of the landlords' crumbling social status.[457] His extreme stand may be gauged from his conclusion 'hunting or no hunting is landlordism or no landlordism'. Humphreys was in favour of an indiscriminate ban, unlike some priests who argued that only rack-renting landlords be penalised.[458] Others feared that a total ban might injure the prospects of ordinary employees connected with hunting, such as grooms, smiths or harness-makers.[459] The question of general employment at local level and the landlords' role in its creation also made certain priests have second thoughts about an absolute measure. Archdeacon Daniel Ryan was discomfited by the banning of a local landlord who was also a large employer in Fethard.[460]

Nevertheless, the priests who were committed to the policy were prepared to apply it ruthlessly. They condemned areas where the ban was not in operation,[461] and advocated not alone legal[462] but stronger measures to enforce it. Michael Duggan C.C. Gurtnahoe promised physical resistance to landlords who ignored it and his pastor, Patrick Kennedy, advised his parishioners to poison their land.[463] They offered definite leadership in this; both Kennedy and William O'Connor P.P. Drangan poisoned their own farms, as did some of the Drangan farmers.[464] It is difficult to assess the success of these methods, but instances arose of clubs dissolving because hounds were poisoned — the Tipperary Hunt Club in Clonmel sold its pack because of this.[465] Some clubs were replaced by National League harriers.[466] Yet the relative success or failure of the ban was not its most important facet. Its real value lay in its spirit, symbolising a new era of tenant independence on the agrarian political and social levels.

That the priests of Tipperary were extensively involved in achieving this revolution is now hopefully clear. It is certain that at least 79% of them participated in the events of these extraordinary years, 1879 to 1891. The ratio between parish priests and curates correlates exactly with their normal relationship in the county,[467] showing an equal commitment by both young and old. A diocesan breakdown also closely correlates with the norm, but 88% of the Cashel priesthood were involved, which is significantly higher than the 76% and 66% of Killaloe and Waterford priests respectively. Yet it should not go unnoticed that these figures constitute a majority of all three sections. An education analysis is quite interesting, showing a precise correlation between Maynooth, Paris and Thurles priests, while the others are not noticeably divergent from the usual proportions. On closer examination, it is seen that a majority of all alumni were participants on the Land War. While Maynooth priests formed the backbone of these due to their numerical superiority, all Carlow, Louvain, Salamanca and Versailles priests were active, although numerically they were not of importance. Only Waterford is relatively low at 63%.

Of the 237 Land War participants 36 were intensely involved, i.e. in over 50% of the various facets recorded, although all aspects obviously did not carry equal political weight. 78% of these 36 were Cashel priests, a far higher proportion than their normal position, suggesting that they were a very highly politicised group indeed under the leadership of Thomas William Croke. The education analysis is also revealing, with Maynooth's 69% significantly higher than the usual 50% proportion. The continental seminaries, however, were equally well represented, but the other Irish colleges seem to have produced less politicised priests.

The overall pattern of the priests' involvement is a logical one because of the close interlinking of the various features of the land struggle. Priests who were members of the leagues tended to dwell either upon apathy or conversely upon the necessity for constitutional rather than violent agitation. Again it is logical that many of the priests involved in rent or eviction disputes should have attacked landlords or called for the abolition of landlordism, while some approved of boycotting or the Plan of Campaign as modes of attack. It is also clear that rents and evictions were the major themes of the agitation, both influenced by economic circumstances, all making an impact upon public opinion. The priests in turn responded to this public opinion with varying shades of enthusiasm. It might be suggested that the highly politicised priests such as James Cantwell, David Humphreys or Daniel Flannery, who headed the list, would have held leading and energetic political positions irrespective of the parish they ministered in. This is not necessarily true, however; they, too, needed the stimulation of a restless and disturbed public opinion. Indeed, it is highly significant that the voice of James Cantwell, (one of the few priests whose sketch appeared in *United Ireland*), was rarely heard when he moved from the central and politically active parish of Thurles to the more remote parish of Ballingarry, where satisfactory landlord-tenant relations existed.

Chapter Five

THE PRIEST AND THE LABOURERS

"The labourer who is now a pariah on his native land, who is the very worm of the earth, whose whole existence is a perpetual lent, whose home is a wretched hovel, . . . whose wages are a mere pittance, whose clothes are the vilest of rags, whose wife and children are the victims of starvation . . ." – Father James K. Frost. *Tipperary Advocate* 26 March 1881.

Any study of agrarian politics would be incomplete without reference to that forgotten class, the agricultural and urban labourers. There is much evidence to suggest that their serious social plight was sadly neglected for most of the period being discussed, only receiving the attention it deserved during the Land War. If society chose to ignore these people it must also be stated that, (despite the exhortation of the 1850 synod, which made the underprivileged the special care of the parish priest),[1] the priests' efforts before 1880 to initiate or promote some kind of organised social plan were demonstratively weak, in sharp contrast to their interest in the farmers' affairs.

To begin with, the labourers' plight was not part of the Tenant League policy in the 1850s, and few League priests pursued the issue with any degree of enthusiasm. This is not to say that labourers remained entirely aloof from league meetings,[2] but there was no place for them on the platform. Dr Michael Burke felt that the league should contain tenants, merchants and shopkeepers.[3] His exclusion of the labourers was not so much a deliberate consideration as a simple pointer to the lack of thought given to the idea at that time. Yet Bishop Daniel Vaughan, then living in Nenagh, was more enlightened than most, and did propose that labourers be brought into the movement to make it more representative and to ensure its success.[4] His suggestion to widen the league's base was probably considered idealistic and impractical, and never received support either from priests or laity. But while the notion of formal organisation was dismissed, the priests were not unaware of the labourers' dreadful state. The famine and immediate post-famine influx into workhouses could not be

119

ignored, and Thomas Meagher, at that time curate in Galbally, was appalled by conditions in these institutions, and revolted by the system which separated husband and wife.[5] Still, the Poor Law was as much disliked for its burden on the farmers in the form of rates, or for the alleged creation of a labour shortage,[6] as for its demoralisation of the poor. Furthermore, while the priests, as chaplains, had first-hand knowledge of workhouse conditions, their concern did not prevent a determination to exact generous salaries.

The more broadly based Land War organisations, the Land League and National League, evoked a far greater response to the labourers' problem. 66 priests or 22% of the total priesthood 1879-1891 showed an interest, although not more than a few dozen were noticeably active or effective.[7] While the parish priests' proportion is higher than normal, no less than 72% of these priests were under 50 years old and 51% were under 40, both notably higher than usual. There is no incompatibility in this since 27% of the parish priests involved were under 50 years of age. A comparison with the relevant statistics for the agrarian leagues suggests a greater degree of caution among the body of older priests for labourer reform. The diocesan breakdown shows a much higher percentage of Cashel priests than normal, possibly due to Dr Croke's sympathy for the labourers' plight although he did not speak frequently on the issue.[8]

The comparatively weak clerical response to the question had several related causes. One obvious influence was the lack of social affinity between priests and labouers, plus the clergy's reluctance to arouse the antagonism of their kinsfolk. It was partly a question of the priests' social background exerting a stronger influence than their pastoral motivation or even their role as social leaders. They were anything but social innovators. A wide difference in social backgrounds was further compounded by the inability of the poor to make a significant contribution to Church revenue, and indeed the more indigent may have been a drain on clercial resources in the form of charity, especially during periods of economic depression. After all the begging activity of their wives was one source of labourers' income.[9] Furthermore, despite the gospel message, and despite a movement within the church in Victorian times to identify with the working classes,[10] the priests were not provided with any coherent policy towards the plight of the poor until 1891. *Rerum Novarum* offered a comprehensive, authoritative, if not exactly pragmatic statement of policy to supplement general principles of justice. But Pope Leo's concern with European Socialistic doctrines was not entirely relevant in Ireland. Admittedly, as has been seen, the priests did refer to this matter, but only in a peripheral way, and it was only in the early part of the present century that they became quite hysterical about the phantom of Socialism. Nevertheless, albeit from the political (Fenian and later Parnellite), as much as the socialistic point of view, the priests were distinctly suspicious of formal labour organisations. They were certainly aware of the identity of P.F. Johnson, one of the 'Reds of Duhallow', who spoke at a Thurles labour meeting in 1873.[11] This was called by the Irish Labourers Association, a movement which failed to take root in Tipperary. Clerical response to invitations from the organisers was confined to the approval of Archbishop Croke and the apologies of his Administrator for being unable to attend.[12] Even during the more radical years of the Land War the priests continued to view the labour movements with a jaundiced eye, and efforts to establish an organisation met with very limited success indeed.[13] The priests of Thurles showed 'decided' opposition to the setting up of a branch of the Labour League there.[14]

The clergy much preferred to keep the labourers under the umbrella of the agrarian leagues, where their own influence was most powerful. Prompted by their parish priest, the labourers of Drangan and Cloneen condemned the 'so-called' South of Ireland Labour League of 1884, and proposed the National League as the most appropriate organisation to forward their interests.[15] William Power P.P. Moyne reflected the priests' attitude nicely in his declaration that social classes were in accordance with the will of God, but that each class should be well cared for and exist in harmony with the other.[16] It was perfect Catholic philosophy. Power obviously feared a clash between farmer and labourer; it is interesting that Marx himself envisaged such a conflict as the second stage of an Irish proletarian revolution, with opposition to the clergy as one of its essential ingredients.[17] But the famine depopulation defused rising tension between farmer and labourer. The post-Famine increase in labourers' wages also helped to avoid class strife, although these were still pitifully inadequate compared with the income and living standards of the priests themselves,[18] or with the relative prosperity of Tipperary farmers, who could afford to send their sons to expensive seminaries.

Archbishop Slattery, through his parish priests, made a fascinating and detailed record of labourers' diet and wages for each parish in the Archdiocese in 1854.[19] Potatoes were the staple diet of this class, with Indian meal substituted in times of scarcity. Milk and vegetables were also available in most parishes, but meat was seldom consumed, and in the great majority of cases there was rarely any difference between the Sunday and weekday meals. Such meagre and often uncertain fare resulted from the reluctance of farmers to supply meals and from the low wages received. Slattery's dossier shows a certain variation in this respect, but one shilling a day was the general rule. As time passed wages gradually improved and in 1893 labourers in the Cashel Union could earn up to 3/6 per day in peak seasons.

Nevertheless, their work was seasonal and their normal working day was from 6 a.m. to 6 p.m. Furthermore, as the priests knew, their plight became quite desperate in times of economic recession. At such periods the danger of class conflict was far from academic. This was particularly true of the Land War decade when labourer expectations had risen proportionately with those of the farming community during the preceding years. One source revealed that by 1893 labourers demanded butter 'and often eggs' for breakfast, 'meat for dinner 4 or 5 days a week', and sometimes tea for supper.[20] Such rising expectations, combined with the severe downturn and its accompanying unemployment, provoked a degree of tension between both classes which strongly resembled the strained landlord-tenant relations. The anomaly did not, and could not, escape shrewd realistic priests. Patrick O'Donnell C.C. Doon informed his audience that the labourer was no longer the 'ignorant toiler' of previous decades.[21] It was certainly a more realistic observation than the fatalistic conclusion of John Shelley C.C. Emly that the labourer's only consolation was to teach his children the faith and be comforted by the thought of 'a happy home beyond the grave'.[22] Still, Shelley's fatalism was accompanied by a comparison between the allegedly contented French labourers (witnessed by him as a boy) and the 'mechanically made poor in Ireland'. A reliance on divine providence was not part of the priests' outlook in the agrarian campaign, nor was it of much use in improving relations between the labourers and farmers.

Neither was mere recognition of the problem sufficient to reduce the possibility of class strife. It did not require any degree of acute perception to see that the solution lay in the amelioration of labourer conditions, but it is not always clear where the emphasis of the priests lay in this respect. It seems that the rising tension plus the initiative of leading national politicians heightened clerical awareness, and they then proceeded to tackle the problems on their own merits rather than as a solution to class conflict. It was easy enough to define the danger areas — unemployment with its natural corollary, emigration, and most conspicuous, inadequate and insanitary housing conditions. Such issues, however, were not open to an immediate solution, and the priests were often forced to employ or become involved in short term charitable measures. These took the form of vital gratuitous relief in the clearly desperate circumstances of the years 1879 and 1880. On a national level 1404 priests were involved in the 840 relief committees of the Mansion House and Marlborough funds.[23] The Tipperary clergy rallied in the face of impending starvation and organised independent local relief groups in various parishes which arranged fuel funds and distributed food.[24] These funds existed in urban areas like Tipperary Town or Nenagh, and in the poorer parishes such as Templederry and Youghalarra.

Despite their activity the priests regarded this system of handouts as degrading and demoralising; Thomas O'Donnell, parish priest in the poor parish of Doon, was unwilling to 'play the role of beggar' by seeking aid from the two national funds.[25] The clergy, however, viewed outdoor relief through employment in a more favourable light. There are many instances of priests approaching Poor Law Guardians requesting the provision of public works.[26] But they felt that the ultimate solution lay with the farmers in the form of constant employment.[27] This presented a thorny dilemma because of the evident clash of interests involved, with the priest caught in the middle. Thomas Meagher expressed this dilemma to the Bessborough commission in 1880 by revealing the bitterness of indigent labourers against the priest 'if he does not denounce this or that from the altar'.[28]

A contemporary witness put a finger on one element of the situation when he pointed out that the farmers aimed to 'exact as much, and the labourers to do as little work as possible'.[29] This may or may not have been overstating the case but it is certain that the labourers were as eager to maximise their income as the farmers were theirs, and when the Tipperary town curates, James Hanly and James Ryan secured employment for labourers they quickly attached themselves to other farmers at higher wages when Spring arrived.[30] But the matter was not quite so simple and the clergy's difficulty was magnified by an increasing reliance by farmers on machinery.[31] The tenants were not motivated by the morality of giving employment, and any scruples they might have had were offset by the alternative of a cheaper source of labour. The result was a localised increase in unemployment, and in a labour surplus,[32] which provoked several farmer-labourer clashes.[33]

Such clashes gave rise to genuine fears among clerics, including Dr Croke and David Humphreys, of an uprising against farmers and landlords by labourers.[34] They hastened to warn labourers against violence. John T. Ryan C.C. Templemore advised them that the curse of God would blight their cause if they resorted to force.[35] Patrick O'Keefe C.C. Fethard took his own preventive action. He mounted a campaign against drink among them and 44 labourers signed one of his pledges.[36] These efforts were of very limited value only, and the priests sensibly focused their attention upon the farmers, however embarrassing this might have been to themselves.

Part of their strategy consisted of appeals to the farmers' sense of justice, by no means a glaring virtue among that class. One obvious injustice concerned exorbitant conacre charges sometimes running at the rate of 15/- for a quarter acre of unmanured ground.[37] A few priests voiced their concern at this but it was not a common public theme.[38] Edmund Foran C.C. Dungarvan Co. Waterford took a cynical view of farmer inconsistency and related to his bishop the case of a farmer whose rent per acre to his subtenants was four times his own rent to the landlord.[39]

This particular approach contained little that was attractive to the farmers' shrewd business sense. But the priests knew the mentality of their kinsfolk intimately, and hastened to produce arguments that appealed to naked self-interest. Using what was a common argument at the time they tried to convince them that the causes of both classes were identical,[40] and stressed that labourers by joining the Land League had furthered farmer aspirations. James Ryan and other priests added to this point by portraying the labourers as a 'powerful reserve force' in the continuing struggle.[41] Patrick O'Donnell asserted, perhaps with some truth, that they had often at personal risk defended farmers, especially at eviction times.[42] The labourers themselves were not slow to learn such themes or to state them with less delicacy. At a later date O'Donnell was interrupted by a labourer, who shouted that they had borne the brunt of the struggle, while 'the farmers were hiding down in the dykes for fear they would be shot in their big bellies'.[43]

In their plea to the farmers' self-interest, the priests also aired an argument on the function of employment as a check on emigration[44] and a preservation of the labour-force. One wonders, however, if this was their only motive in raising this. Not all emigrants were labourers, and emigration while removing the needy might also have been a drain on Church resources. One landlord inferred as much and earned a stinging reply from Michael B. Corry. Judging, too, from the clerical references made to the moral dangers awaiting emigrants in America or Australia, this also seems to have been an important facet of clerical thinking.[45] Dean William Quirke drew his evidence from letters received from ex-parishioners,[46] and Dr Croke was treated to a long letter from a P. O'Connell M.D, in Chicago, which drew the archbishop's attention to the Irish there as a 'dirty shiftless rabble' involved in 'dirty politics, . . . with a fondness for vile whiskey, wakes and funerals'.[47]

Whatever their priority concerning emigration it is clear that the priests' appeal to the farmers fell on deaf ears. Increasing use of machinery points to this. Indeed, the acceleration of emigration rates (particularly in Tipperary which was very high on the list)[48] during and immediately following the famine, had already solved the problem of an over-supply in the labour market, and helped to ease the tension which the famine as a whole had reduced. Emigration had also eased the burden on the rates, a consideration not ignored by the farmers. The nett result was that all through the second half of the century the farmers were not over-perturbed by the exodus to foreign parts. The clergy, of course, as well as being idealists were also realists as far as the question of employment was concerned. Despite their exhortations, therefore, they were conscious of the fact that the very agrarian progress they lauded was not necessarily beneficial to the labouring class. So, they could not lay too much blame on the farmers for what was basically an economic issue. The very evident luxury of the landlords' lifestyle, however, convinced the priests that this class could alleviate chronic unemployment among the labourers. Consequently they held the owners up as scapegoats, and in doing so were not shackled by ties of kinship or religion.

Landlords were certainly prime targets of priestly references to the related issues of emigration and unemployment.[49] Several priests attacked their concentration upon dairying and beef, but conveniently ignored the same course by farmers.[50] They were also linked with the official policy of state-aided emigration,[51] and Canon Patrick Ryan announced that 'transportation and banishment were the hallmarks of English policy since the time of Cromwell'.[52] Comparisons between the vastly different life-styles of landlord and labourer were eloquently made, and were understandable, although a similar analogy could have been proposed for any other country. John Shelley C.C., using his experience as chaplain in Tipperary workhouse, retold labourers' stories of struggling from dawn to dusk to keep landlords in luxury, and further illustrated his point by drawing attention to a specific landlord who showed more concern for his pheasants than for his peasants.[53] Patrick Glynn C.C. Templederry had little pity for landlords who sacked their labourers because of the fall-off in rents from the farmers, and accused them of having squandered their income 'in the halls of Baden and Paris'.[54] David Humphreys reflected a similar outlook, maintaining that landlords should pay the labourers wages from the profits of their own estates,[55] while Canon Thomas O'Donnell suggested that a portion of 'unjust' rents be used for alleviating the poor.[56] This anti-landlord spirit was merely an extension of the agrarian conflict. Undoubtedly landlord culpability was exaggerated, while that of the farmers was toned down. Indeed, the contributions of landlords to relief funds, and their provision of special employment during the severe winter of 1879-1880, show that they were not indifferent to labourer distress.[57]

Serious unemployment and emigration constituted only one dimension of this distress which was always immediate and nothing less than desperate in times of economic depression. Its most conspicuous and permanent symptom, however, was the housing problem, which made a deep impression on the priests as they travelled through their parishes.[58] Maurice Flynn C.C. Clonmel rightly stated that the priests above all others were most keenly aware of the labourers' insanitary living conditions.[59] Patrick O'Keeffe wrote that they lived in cabins 'scarcely fit for savage men, are fed miserably and clad in rags'.[60] The clergy had no hesitation in strongly favouring the political outlook of the 1880s which advocated reform, particularly since the housing problem, unlike that of employment, could be properly solved through legislation. They advocated special legislation to deal with the matter rather than an appendix or suffix to the 1881 land act.[61] David Humphreys and his colleagues, therefore, condemned the act as totally inadequate in this respect.[62] It only briefly mentioned the labourers' problem, but subsequent labourer acts were more comprehensive, although they did not always meet with the priests' approval. Details of the Labourers acts of 1883, 1885, 1886 and 1891 may be read in A.D. Bolton's work.[63]

There can be little doubt that the priests' contact with filthy cabins, which prompted their strong support for the principle of special legislation, produced a crucial difference in their attitude to the housing situation. They placed far more weight on the morality of this issue although it may be said that morality played no part in the legislators' minds. The aim of the acts was to provide good housing conditions for able-bodied labourers in areas where their services were required.[64] From the priests' point of view, however, the question lent itself to a moral slant; Cornelius Egan P.P. Castletownarra was indignant at the hesitation of the Local Government Board in granting a provisional order for the erection of one particular cottage because labour was not required in that locality.[65]

The priests' moral emphasis ranged from the wider concept of social justice to the narrower plane of sexual morality in the community and in the family.[66] On the level of justice, and prior to the official decision of half acre plots, such priests as Maurice Flynn C.C. Clonmel considered that a full acre was necessary for the adequate support of a family.[67] As regards community morality John O'Brien P.P. Holycross concluded that new cottages and half-acre plots would remove the young from 'the bad example and evil tongues of crowded lanes and villages'.[68] Thomas Doyle P.P. Ramsgate Co. Wexford was more concerned about the moral dangers to young women in urban areas.[69] The more realistic Daniel Flannery had no objection to labourers living in the town of Nenagh, however, provided that employment could be found for them.[70] Interestingly, too, the labourers themselves were not so concerned with this type of morality. H.H. Townsend, Smith-Barry's agent, was convinced that most of Tipperary town's labourers would be unwilling to move into rural areas.[71] The question of family morality was of prime concern to the priests also. Apart from the obvious inadequacies of existing hovels, David Humphreys was not convinced that the cottages under the first Local Government scheme satisfied the demands of morality. He personally attended the Tipperary boardroom to protest about the size of cottages built at Bohercrowe.[72] These had two rooms and a kitchen. Humphreys argued that the 'lowest requirements of morality' demanded at least 3 rooms, one for the parents and one each for the male and female children, with a kitchen and perhaps a loft. The labourers themselves were dissatisfied with these first cottages; whether this was from the point of view of morality or simple comfort is debatable.[73] At any rate cottages under later schemes had two extra loft bedrooms.

Armed with their moral convictions the priests had then to face harsh reality in the form of landlord or tenant opposition. As in the quest for employment they sought first to convince by concentrating upon the selfish instincts of the farmers. Both John Scanlan and Canon Alexander Scully contended that cottages would save farmers the cost of transporting labourers or of providing lodgings in their own houses.[74] With remarkable naivety John O'Brien P.P. Holycross and Maurice Mooney P.P. Cahir, portrayed the occupiers of comfortable cottages as 'the watchful guardians of property and the determined foes of night-walkers and pilferers'.[75] James Ryan was less prone to delusion but in the same vein felt that better housing conditions would ease the tension between farmers and labourers.[76]

Appeals to self-interest, justice or morality were not altogether successful in softening the farmers. Captain Slack, the divisional magistrate, reported that the half acre policy was 'a terrible blow' to them,[77] and H.H. Townsend felt that most farmers 'inwardly' opposed the scheme, but were outwardly afraid to do so because they feared unpopularity.[78] One angry Kilsheelan labourer announced that they 'would not give you the sweepings of the dirt off their floor, let alone a half-acre of land'.[79] The priests could not excuse their kinsfolk for reluctance to fulfil what was little less than a moral and social obligation, and, unlike the employment question, they were prepared to threaten, bully, ridicule, and even blackmail them. Although it was repugnant to the national political leaders, one system employed to draw shame on farmers was to publish lists of those who refused to make sites available.[80] In Tipperary town Canon Cahill read out a list of 13 tenants who were unwilling to give the half-acres as conacre until the guardians were in a position to take them up as sites.[81] The list was published with Cahill's additional warning of withholding league support from such farmers if they fell foul of landlords. Interestingly, similar social pressure was generated by publishing lists of those who gave sites. Patrick O'Donnell remarked with much satisfaction that the children of Doon convent planned to write a roll of honour in gold letters of consenting farmers.[82] Like Archdeacon Kinnane[83] he determined to publish the list. David Humphreys, however unwilling he had been to threaten the farmers on the question of employment, bluntly informed both farmers and landlords 'who oppose us that they shall give the cottages' and 'NO THANKS'.[84] His equally irascible friend, John Scanlan, lumped all dissenters into one category 'whose patriotism is synonomous with the love of the belly'.[85] Scanlan was more than sceptical of the excuses raised at a farmers' meeting in Nenagh, even of the legitimate plea[86] that compliance with the 1883 act was in some cases a breach of lease. It is not difficult to guess what his opinion would have been of the excuse, offered to Canon Alexander Scully, Clerihan, that the farmers feared trespass by labourers' goats and fowl.[87]

John Cunningham C.C. Silvermines was equally unsympathetic to farmer protestations. He regarded refusals, without sufficient reason, as a legitimate cause for expulsion from the National League, and he called upon all branches to investigate such cases and take appropriate action.[88] The determined Thomas Meagher would deny tenant right and even fixity of tenure to recalcitrant farmers.[89] Another politicised priest, Matt Ryan, not only disregarded tenant pleas, but suggested that 10 years' purchase on the valuation of the plots was a reasonable price because of 'antecedent ill-treatment' of labourers by farmers and landlords.[90] The strong-willed James Cantwell agreed with A.M. Sullivan that he would not wish to see the landlords replaced by a selfish or ungrateful class of peasant proprietors.[91]

Such statements are remarkable indeed, and in striking contrast to the general train of clerical thought regarding their farmer kinsfolk. They did not, however, forget to level criticism at the landlords, too, on the housing issue. Nevertheless, they were not afforded the usual scope for anti-landlord fulminations, as this class, if only because of their weak numerical status, were not the major obstacles to labour reform. The Poor Law Union minute books offer insight into the number of objections lodged,[92] although it is not clear if landlords coerced some of the tenants to object. James Ryan felt that they did.[93] He was keenly aware of the regulation that three objections could temporarily veto progress in any single area, and worried that landlords might 'entrench' themselves behind the 'red-tapeism' of the Board of Works. He warned farmers against becoming 'the miserable, sneaking dupes of Ireland's hereditary oppressors'. More practically Ryan urged the attendance of elected guardians at board meetings to counteract ex-officio (landlord) members who might prove hostile to the scheme. Lord Dunally, who owned over 21,000 acres in north Tipperary, became the most conspicuous clerical target. In the presence of several priests he explained to a local government inspector at Nenagh that he had only seven labourers, and saw no need to build any more cottages on his estate, especially as his tenants were emigrating each year. John Cunningham was incensed because Dunally successfully prevented the erection of 3 cottages, which had been sanctioned and recommended by the Inspector.[94] His ire was increased when the appeal judge, Sir W. Lawson, ordered both parties to pay their costs, thereby burdening the local ratepayers with an extra £150.[95] Despite the deterrent nature of such proceedings, Cunningham nerved the 42 ratepayers in question to pursue their cause.[96] Matt Ryan also made the landlords the main object of his attack, and David Humphreys, commenting upon the 33 cottages completed in Birdhill, condemned whatever element of landlord opposition that had existed.[97] But, despite such criticism it is significant and contradictory that the priests preferred cottages under landlord rather than farmer control. Thomas Meagher revealed this attitude to the Bessborough Commissioners in his statement — 'I would allow no slavery if I could'.[98]

But, if the priests fought on two fronts, they also encountered a third and possibly more trying and frustrating obstacle — officialdom, in the guise of local government employees and their servants, the Poor Law guardians. The latter were responsible for the acts' administration at local level, and, of course, included both landlords and farmers. In this sense a combination of organised vested interests arose. It is indicative of the priests' importance in the campaign that they were frequently involved with officials and guardians, and not always in an atmosphere of harmony. Friction arose because of the complexity of the acts, the degree of in-built red-tape, and sometimes the caution of guardians and their reluctance to prosecute farmers for non-compliance with the legal provisions.

The 1883 act was particularly complex, and the guardians themselves experienced difficulty interpreting it. The Birr guardians postponed a board meeting to study it with greater care.[99] Some priests, with varying degrees of success, managed to explain it to their unlettered flocks,[100] but they were exasperated by its intricacy and the ease in baulking its operation. After lengthy discussion Michael Duggan C.C. Gurtnahoe declared it 'unworkable in its present form'.[101] Rather despairingly he agreed to give any new feasible scheme a fair trial. William Doherty C.C. Cashel argued that the procedure might be simplified by legislation to facilitate compulsory requisition of land by guardians.[102]

Despite the priests' realisation of the act's complexity, they showed little patience at the guardians' dilemma. This sprang from their own status as relatively independent ecclesiastical administrators, who built and repaired churches with considerable zest, untrammeled by the shackles of bumbledom. Consequently, clerical complaints were rife.[103] The Birr guardians were censured by Patrick Hurley P.P. for lack of progress.[104] John O'Brien was not pleased at the pace of the Thurles guardians and complained that ratepayers were paying interest on money lying idle because sites purchased were not being developed.[105] In 1887 not a single cottage had been built in that union.[106] David Humphreys tried to persuade the Tipperary guardians to take up plots even though they had not complied with the 1885 act's financial stipulations.[107]

In their efforts to move tardy bureaucracy the priests resorted to several direct methods, including visits to Poor Law guardian meetings. They pestered the guardians of the Nenagh Union. At one board meeting John Scanlan, Patrick Crowe, Patrick Glynn, Thomas Meagher and Daniel Flannery strongly disputed the clerk's determined stand that applications were late for the current year.[108] Scanlan, who had representation papers for 42 cottages, was particularly annoyed, and reminded the board members that they were merely the representatives of the ratepayers. The complete Nenagh union scheme for 1885 was declared defective by the Local Government Board because of a legal technicality.[109]

Attendance at the important sworn enquiries, convened by inspectors of the board also proved contentious. A Nenagh meeting attended by Meagher, Scanlan, Humphreys, and Cunningham, was much more acrimonious than a Tipperary town enquiry attended by the local curates, James Ryan and James Hanly.[110] Having been successfully objected to by another witness, Humphreys was quickly silenced by the inspector, when he tried to explain the difference between Land Commission houses and those under the 1883 act. Cunningham, too, was forbidden to express any opinion, and Scanlan vainly claimed the right, not the privilege, to be heard. Clearly, the clash between priest and officialdom resulted in a dinting of clerical pride by people free from local pressure.

But, the guardians were to some extent amenable to such local pressure and the priests employed other methods of persuasion; they availed of National League policy of using local branches as levers of influence,[111] and accepted the more dubious tendency of promoting the interests of labourers who were league members. A letter of John Hennessy C.C. Hollyford to the Tipperary guardians suggesting that leaguers get preference was deemed of sufficient importance to be read in the House of Commons.[112] More significantly, at least one priest upheld the superiority of the local league branch to the board of guardians on the question of selection. Rather antithetically, Patrick O'Donnell argued that the league was free from undue influence, and more legitimately he held that it was the more representative body with a better knowledge of applicants' characters.[113] On another level O'Donnell and his league colleagues felt that the official involvement of league branches in choosing applicants would in effect be the recognition of local self-government by communes. The bias in favour of league labourer members, however, did not augur well for impartiality under such a system. This outlook certainly antagonised boards of guardians, who resented any interference in their prerogatives.

Despite such abrasive tactics the clergy were also prepared to use more rational arguments. The guardians' fear of further increasing the rates, which were never easy to collect, was one facet of their thinking, and the priests sought to reassure them on this issue. Both John Scanlan and Matt Ryan maintained that the existing insanitary hovels of the poor, by contributing to fever and other illnesses, were a burden on the rates in the form of coroners', doctors' and workhouse staff remuneration.[114] The priests also tried to understate the financial impact of the proposed new cottages on the rates. It is an interesting insight into their role in society that they had the hardihood and confidence to dispute the estimates of the guardians and officials, the supposed experts in the matter of costing. Although he later changed his mind, John Scanlan strongly disagreed with the Nenagh board's

estimate of £100 per cottage and £5.12.0 to £5.17.6 annual rent.[115]
He boldly proposed a costing of £70 with a weekly rent of between
11d and 1/5. Patrick Glynn's detailed costings substantially agreed
with Scanlan's figure.[116] He denounced the guardians for publishing
their estimates, which he feared would make farmers apprehensive.
H.H. Townsend, who had built many cottages, revealed that £70
might be realistic when materials were close at hand, but with pigsty,
privy and ashpit £90 would be more accurate.[117] In reality the cost
per cottage in Cashel Union was £107, although the Guardians had
only estimated it at £80.[118] Other results varied from £77 to £100.[119]

It must now be clear that even if the clerical promoters of labourers
reform were a small minority, they were also a powerful, vocal, know-
ledgeable and determined force. There was in fact a degree of rivalry
among them in the cottage campaign. Thomas Meagher, who gave two
sites and wrote a pamphlet on the question,[120] boasted that he was
one of the first, if not the first, to take action under the 1883 act; he
revealed that 140 out of the 640 labourers in his parish were being
considered for cottages.[121] He was irritated by John Scanlan's accusation that he had temporarily waived his claim on behalf of 30 families
because of guardian resistance.[122] Scanlan, himself, who appropriately
delivered an oration on the site of the first cottage in Ireland (under
the 1883 act) in Kilgriffith, Silvermines,[123] claimed a major role in
persuading the Nenagh Poor Law guardians to obtain loans.[124]

These were by no means idle boasts. The evidence points to a considerable clerical impact upon the implementation of the labourers'
cottages acts. This may be gauged in two areas — the acquisition of
sites and the progress of cottage schemes. Because of their familiarity
with every district in their parishes, the priests played an important
role in canvassing for sites, and by confronting individuals personally,
and perhaps creating a certain degree of embarrassment, they extracted
promises from reluctant farmers. Their effectiveness can be tangibly
assessed in this. Patrick O'Donnell visited no less than 40 of the 60
farmers who had promised plots, although only 28 agreed to give
possession.[125] He then proceeded to visit 21 others and secured possession of 18.[126] Archdeacon Kinnane was promised 40 sites in Fethard
and Killusty, but some pledges were not honoured there either.[127]
Canon Richard Cahill was the co-ordinator of canvassing in Lattin,
where deputations toured the 4 electoral divisions. Lattin and Glen-
bane divisions did not yield satisfactory results to the regret of the
Canon and his curate, Matt Ryan.[128] The unloved pastor of Ballinahinch, William J. McKeogh, revealed one cause of his unpopularity,
when he ignored the indignant reluctance of a farmer and proceeded
to choose a site himself.[129]

The priests' precise influence on the number of cottages constructed
is less easy to define, but that they did make an impact is beyond

doubt. This is particularly clear from statistics for the Tipperary and Nenagh Unions, which recorded a high number of cottages completed by 1893.[130] Not only did these two unions experience the most extensive clerical involvement, but they contained strong nucleii of highly politicised and determined priests. Similarly, with the exception of Cashel and Thurles, the low building rate in other unions corresponded with a low clerical participation rate. Cashel and Thurles however offer an interesting contrast. The former with a relatively low level of priestly activity achieved an even better building rate than Nenagh, while Thurles with a reasonably high rate of involvement completed only 60 houses by 1893. These exceptions indicate that priestly influence was not always of vital importance. There were other factors present, such as union area and population. It is true that both Nenagh and Tipperary were the largest unions in the county, although, tantalisingly, Thurles with its poor performance was almost as extensive. This obviously points to the influence of the interested laity, which, judging by the glaring discrepancies between the numbers of houses applied for and the numbers built, could work in contrary directions. On the other hand the clergy all aimed at progress. Guardian diligence was one of the key factors, generosity or stinginess on the farmers' part cannot be discounted. National League influence if exercised, was powerful, although the league was primarily the tool of the tenants. Labour militancy, too, played a part. Relatively speaking labour organisation was weak in Thurles and strong in Nenagh, while the combined force of labourer and clerical campaigning may account for the predominant position of the Tipperary union.

The priests were mainly concerned with the problems of the agricultural labourers but they could not ignore the plight of those living in the six major towns of Tipperary. While the problems of the two groups were parallel, urban circumstances introduced another element into the question. The priests were again concerned with the twin issues of employment and housing, but their emphasis was slightly different. Furthermore, the question of existing rents was an element largely absent from discussions about the agricultural labourers. Urban rents inspired the formation of the House League, an ineffective organisation confined to the three larger towns of Tipperary, Nenagh and Thurles, and the two villages of Golden and Newport.[131] As in other counties,[132] priestly participation in the league was weak, and existed only in Tipperary town and Newport. Walter Cantwell, brother of James, was president in the former,[133] and the politicised Thomas Meagher and his two curates were the dominant figures in the village of Newport. The priests' abstention did not stem from the type of suspicion they entertained for the Labour League, but from the tight control exercised over it by the middle landlords, the very people against whom the movement was directed. The second irony was that these middlemen, who as National Leaguers were most vociferous in demanding abatements for themselves, were less than enthusiastic about reducing the rents of their own less fortunate tenants. One of these, a strong National Leaguer, considered any attempt to change the system of house tenure as absurd. Apparently, too, patriotism and profit were not incompatible – the league became involved in a row with John O'Leary's sister, who owned house property in Tipperary town.[134]

Apart from being excluded from control by a politicised and educated urban middle-class, it is unlikely that priests in general attached major importance to the rent issue. They were more concerned with housing and employment. But, unlike the case of the agricultural labourers, they seemed to place less emphasis on the question of urban housing. This was mainly because they did not differentiate between urban and rural housing. In short a cottage was a cottage irrespective of location. James Cantwell was one of the few priests who did draw some distinction. In 1883 he insisted that urban labourers were 'worse fed, worse housed, and in a more pitiable state' than their rural counterparts;[135] a local newspaper on the same date reported that the town of Thurles was as 'remarkable for its unsightly houses as its magnificent religious structures'.[136] On a practical level in 1880 Cantwell had invited the agent of Lord Dunsandle, the town's owner, to inspect the back-street hovels there.[137] Cantwell later referred to a medical officer's report that 84 Thurles houses checked by him were unfit to house animals.[138] Finally, when the housing schemes were launched the urban-based priests approached the town commissioners, as they had the Poor Law guardians, and felt a similar anxiety at slow progress.[139]

The priests, however, placed considerable emphasis on urban employment which was a more complex matter than in rural areas, where farm-work predominated. The urban priests were concerned with the dual issues of local trade and the related question of home manufacturing. This was evident in Clonmel, Nenagh, Thurles and Tipperary. Attention was focused on these issues at national level by the Parnellite leaders, and the priests, despite their predominantly rural background, responded with at least as much enthusiasm, and in some cases more, than the laity. There was little rural bias in the 1882 declaration of John Scanlan that dependence upon agriculture alone retarded real national prosperity.[140] He agreed with the economic maxim 'the greatest happiness of the greatest number'. Scanlan and four other priests attended an exhibition of Irish goods in Nenagh, which was poorly supported by the laity.[141] His fellow curate, Daniel Flannery, was also at the exhibition, and was sufficiently impressed by it and by a Dublin exhibition which he had visited to take positive action. He was primarily responsible for establishing a small factory in Nenagh, which manufactured straw containers for wine bottles.[142] His parish priest, Michael Pyne, and the other curates were members of the initial committee that floated the factory, which apparently received orders for a large number of containers.[143] It was a small venture which seems to have faded into obscurity later, but it serves to demonstrate clerical willingness to become involved in local industrial development in an agricultural society. The priests in other towns did not show the same initiative, however, but Dean William Quirke, who strongly supported home manufacture,[144] helped to promote a Clonmel exhibition of Irish goods, which was floated by establishing a limited liability company.[145] The Clonmel curates helped, but not in a leading capacity, partly because the merchants were the definite leaders in the business life of that town, as indeed they should have been.

Clerical concern with the Irish manufacture movement automatically turned their attention to the very real problems of the local trades and artisans, and in their support of a buy Irish campaign they were prepared to advocate a boycott of shops that stocked English goods.[146] James Cantwell was especially concerned with the nail-makers and the boot and shoe-makers. He complained that only 7 remained of the 30 nail-makers, who had flourished in Thurles 15 years earlier, and he branded as unpatriotic the natural tendency of carpenters, slaters, builders and shoemakers themselves to purchase cheaper imported nails.[147] Accordingly he recommended the boycotting of shops selling foreign nails and 'affording a livelihood to wife-beaters, and drunkards and English smithies'. He might have added that the Land League, of which he was a prominent member, manufactured its huts with foreign nails.[148] His relationship with the Thurles boot and shoemakers, who were also feeling the keen edge of competition from cheaper factory boots, was an interesting one. He not only helped to form a society of these artisans, whose first meeting he chaired in Thurles Christian Brothers School,[149] but he became its first president, thus nicely fulfilling Pope Leo's advice that workingmen's associations be under 'the sheltering care of religion'.[150]

Unlike the pope, Cantwell was not concerned with labourer association as an alternative to socialism. Also, when the Thurles priest professed himself a believer in trade unions he spoke in the context of a union of independent traders, which radically differed from the type of general workers union disliked by the clergy in later years. Yet he was not hostile to such organisations either. During a dispute on the Great Southern and Western Railway in Thurles, he denounced the threat to bring from England an alternative workforce of 'nobody's children and nobody's people'.[151] Cantwell, however, did not become actively involved in the cause of urban employees as James Hanly and James Ryan did in Tipperary town. Both curates helped the members of the Operative Bakers Friendly Society to canvass their employers for a cessation of night work.[152]

Such involvement in trade unionism, it is true, was a rare occurrence.

When James Ryan died in 1885 it ceased. The Tipperary United Trade Union containing 18 different trades, formed soon after his death, did not evoke clerical support.[153] Generally speaking, therefore, while the urban priests were certainly aware of urban problems, and responded in four large towns, the main clerical concern lay with the agricultural labourers. But in both cases the priests made only a very limited impact on creating employment. Hard-headed business economics were as dominant in the country as in the town, and the moral dimension introduced by the priests was of little practical effect. Yet, while concern for the condition of the poor was a prime priestly function, their portfolio did not necessarily stretch to the level of employment. Housing, however, was an entirely different matter, quite definitely intruding into the *bona fide* clerical mission. Their overall contribution was greatest in this area. Nevertheless, considering the relevance of the labourer issue to the message in the Gospel, one might expect an earlier, if not entirely priestly-dominated, reaction and stirring of the social conscience to eradicate a glaring social scandal. Instead their response was almost solely to the political initiative of the national leaders, and shows how very much they were the product of an environment in which serious social issues not concerned with the farming community were never regarded as a priority. Still, this was one of the few areas where a section of the clergy acted against the wishes, concealed or otherwise, of their own kith and kin, the tenant farmers. It was primarily a question of moral conscience triumphing over the powerful influence of farmer opinion. On the other hand moral reservations were generally in other issues, either muted, stifled, evaded or shelved in the face of a resolute public opinion.

Chapter Six

THE PRIEST AND REPUBLICANISM

"Bless every man who has anything to give,
Long may the Lord Lieutenant lordly live,
And if in time to come, Old Nick should revel
Poor Ireland's Viceroy, then bless the Devil".
The Tribune 26 Jan. 1856.

There were, of course, other purely political issues where a conflict between the priests' moral emphasis and farmer opinion did not occur, and in such cases the priests' stand appeared unequivocally stronger. Republican-separatism was one of these, and in this area the influence of episcopal control was a prominent feature. These influences produced what was mainly a fundamental antipathy to the Irish brand of republicanism, accompanied, for reasons which will be seen, by varying degrees of ambivalence. Nevertheless, whenever republicanism became a potent organised force the ambivalence weakened and more clearcut hostility emerged. It is interesting that clerical antagonism, while resolute, was not as vocal in the 1860s as in the 1880s, when the I.R.B. infiltrated the G.A.A., suggesting, perhaps, that the priests considered the threat of organised fenianism as most serious in these later years, although there seems to have been no danger of a rising at that time.

It is very clear from the columns of the fenian paper, the *Irish People*, however, that the separatists of the 1860s saw the clergy as a major, if not the major, obstacle to the spread of Fenianism. The articulate but insulting letters and editorials of this paper, comparing current clerics unfavourably with their predecessors of penal days, urged obedience to the priests in spiritual matters only.[1] Not surprisingly, priests like John Power P.P. Powertown interpreted such statements as symptoms of anti-clericalism; they also fiercely resented fenian desires to drive them from politics, or, as they saw it, to usurp their influence over their flocks.[2] Power saw the burning in effigy of Daniel Collins P.P. Skibbereen, Co. Cork, by the fenians as another manifestation of anti-clericalism.[3] Yet the number of priests who threatened those who sold or read the paper represented only a tiny minority,[4] which suggests that many priests did not see fenianism as essentially anti-clerical, and did not equate it with continental doctrine.

The fact that extreme clerical hostility was minimal does not imply either tacit support or even neutrality on the part of the silent majority. Indeed, the number who approved of the movement either in Tipperary or on a national level was insignificant. The *Irish People* rarely praised priests, but its Killenaule and Bansha correspondents were pleased at the neutrality of their clergy.[5] Neutrality, however, was far removed from sympathy. The Killenaule priests rarely interfered in politics; the parish priest, Martin Laffan, effectively retired from politics following his frequent activity in the Tenant League. By no stretch of the imagination could the conservative pastor of Bansha, John Cooney, be seen as a fenian sympathiser, and his curates abstained from politics in those years. Only the Ballingarry curate, John O'Connor, was unashamedly pro-fenian, although he did not air his views in Tipperary. But when collecting for the Thurles cathedral building fund in the more congenial American atmosphere, he waxed eloquent in his praise of fenianism, and assured a receptive audience that the sword was the only means to achieve Irish independence.[6] His lectures not only drew the fire of some American bishops,[7] but also excited the ire of his fellow collector, Thomas Francis Meagher C.C. Mullinahone, who kept Archbishop Leahy up to date on O'Connor's apparent neglect of collecting, preferring instead to deliver political orations.[8] For obvious reasons the latter got an *exeat* in 1870 and received a testimonial from Ballingarry nationalists, (as the separists called themselves), praising him 'as the first on the roll of Ireland's patriot priests'.[9] His reply comforted them with a forecast of a revolution and assured them that 'love of country ranked next to love of God'.[10] One other priest, Thomas J. Mackey, who, as a student in St Patrick's College Thurles, reputedly sympathised with the fenians, also got an *exeat* to America in 1888, when the nationalists in Gurtnahoe, where he was curate, were not unmindful of his outlook in those earlier years.[11] Only two Cashel priests, Paul Heney, and his curate, Gerald Barry, were active immediately prior to the rising. They ministered in Kilteely, which lay in the Co Limerick section of the diocese. Detailed police reports supplemented by those of informers, depicted Barry as harbouring weapons, hearing fenians' confessions, carousing with them and preaching that the fenian oath was not sinful.[12] Barry escaped arrest, but on the resident magistrate's report, Archbishop Leahy immediately transferred him to the parish of Cappawhite in Co Tipperary where he died in 1872. It is significant that Barry, like Mackey and O'Connor, seems to have found ecclesiastical discipline a burden. He had left All Hallows seminary, Dublin, before his ordination and he was accepted

County of Limerick

Newpallas 25th April 1867   Confidential

I most respectfully beg
leave to report for the information of
My Officers that I have received information that Father Barry the Catholic
Curate at Kilteely is a Sworn Fenian
and that he was Sworn by a Miss
Walsh who lives in the Town of Tipperary
and at Same time She Made him a
Present of a revolver – I believe She is
Sister to the Man who fired at H.C.
Quade – previous to the Rising he
kept a large quantity of ball Cartridge
and Some pikes in his bedroom –
There was also a large number of
pikes hid under the Alter in the
Chapel of Kilteely – but whether they
have been removed Since the out
break My informant Can't Say –
A great Number of the pike handles
used by the insurgents were Made
in the out Offices of the Parish Priests
house, Superintended by Father
Barry, Michael Hogan, Son to the
National School Master at Kilteely
who is at present Studying in Milesy
for the Priesthood – and a Labourer
Named John Hogan at present on his
Keeping for Carrying arms at Kilteely
on the 7th March last – Father Barry
Swore in a boy Named John Ryan
Much against Ryans will – when

Submitted,
Fenianism

Instructions as
as to Sub

E. Trant Wood
25/4/67

Report further
25/4/67 R271

to Sub Inspector,
E. Trant Wood
27/4/67

Part of a police dossier on Father Paul Heney, P.P., Kilteely, Co. Limerick, and his curate Gerald Barry. 1867 Police report. (S.P.O. C.S.O. R.P. 1867. 8399).

into the Cashel diocese by Dr Slattery.

The great body of the priesthood, however, was more amenable to episcopal strictures. By raising serious moral objections to the fenian movement the bishops[13] crushed whatever open sympathy some priests might have had, and no doubt made it difficult, but obviously not impossible, for laymen to join. So, while few priests strongly denounced Fenianism and less joined the movement, the majority, despite Government fears, opposed it either through the confessional or by private remonstrances on the instructions of their bishops. At a conference of the Cashel clergy in March 1864 Archbishop Leahy made fenian membership a reserved sin, which could only be absolved by himself,[14] a serious step considering that the 1854 synod of Cashel advised that the number of sins reserved for episcopal absolution be severely restricted.[15] Despite Leahy's practical advice to his priests to treat the fenians 'gently', he, nevertheless, at a second conference showed his resolve by reading the papal bulls on secret societies.[16] The Archbishop's determination and instruction almost certainly resulted in the muted but active hostility of Tipperary priests. Episcopal influence was more coercive or preventive and less formative than the more positive forces of clerical education or social background, a combination of which would have ensured an anti-fenian spirit by the majority of priests anyway.

Of these, the priests' training is easiest to deal with. The relevant theology was clearcut and covered two aspects, the morality of revolution and of secret societies. Church teaching on revolution and obedience to temporal authority was very old; most textbooks were based upon the scriptures, St Thomas Aquinas and papal pronouncements.[17] In brief, obedience to lawful authority was considered absolute, but insurrection was morally permissable against tyranny which was general, affected 'many' citizens, atrocious, that is practically intolerable, and, finally, manifest. The more pragmatic rule that rebellion should have a reasonable chance of success was a further addition. Doubt on any of these four issues rendered revolution not only 'wicked' but an 'atrocious crime' in the eyes of the Church. Even in a very repressive situation without hope of amelioration, papal encyclicals urged 'patience and prayer',[18] although Leo XIII did not oppose bloodless revolutions to achieve independence.[19] In view of such doctrine it would have been very difficult, but not impossible, for any priest to theologically justify a rebellion in Ireland either in the 1860s or even in the years of most stringent coercion during the Land War. But, add to this the status of fenianism as a secret society, and the priests were allowed little room for manoeuvre.

Ever-jealous of her prerogatives, the semi-religious flavour of oath-bound secret societies seemed to detract from the Church's authority, and the first official missiles were launched against the Freemasons by Clement XII in 1738, and continued by his various successors.[20]

The *Apostolicae Sedis* of Pius IX laid down excommunication not only against the members of secret societies, but also against those 'who favour in any manner those sects or who do not denounce the leaders and chiefs'. Such teaching applied whether a society was oath-bound or not. Theology textbooks gave explicit confessional instructions on the matter. Gury drew several distinctions:[21] a member of a secret society unaware of the Church's teaching, who repented on being enlightened by the priest, did not incur excommunication, and absolution was permitted. If such an individual, however, refused to repent, excommunication was likely, and absolution refused. If a member was aware of the church's teaching and continued to transgress, not only was excommunication imposed, but any future request for absolution had to be referred to the bishop. Interestingly, Gury advised against the priest revealing such tenets to a penitent, who might plunge deeper into sin by rejecting them. During the Land War several priests, referring specifically to fenianism, requested clarification from the theologian of the *Irish Ecclesiastical Record*. The replies, which referred to the encyclical of June 1870 condemning fenianism, were very much in line with Gury, and emphasised that the teaching of *Apostolicae Sedis* on the obligation under pain of excommunication to reveal the leaders of a secret society to the ecclesiastical authorities, was still in force in Ireland in 1886.[22]

This leaves no doubt that the theology of revolution and secret societies was far from academic. One wonders, too, how heavily they were emphasised during the formative seminary years. It might be expected that Maynooth professors would have paid particular attention to them. After all, one of the primary reasons for government sanction of the college in 1795 was the fear of continental-trained priests imbibing seditious principles;[23] in 1852 Lord Derby, the Prime Minister, made it clear that one of the aims behind the increased grant of 1845 was to foster a loyal priesthood.[24] Both Rome and the Irish hierarchy were at pains to stress Maynooth's role of producing loyal priests; an 1835 Maynooth address to the Viceroy outlined the college's duty to train 'learned and zealous pastors, who might teach the people the great duties of piety to God, allegiance to the sovereign ...'[25] Unquestionably, the professors of the first quarter of the nineteenth century were almost obsessed with principles of law and order. This was only partly due to their consciousness of Maynooth's alleged role, but the real influence on them was their own personal experience of the French Revolution.[26] The two leading theologians, Dr Delahogue and Dr Anglade, who had spent the larger part of their teaching lives in France, held their Maynooth chairs until 1820 and 1828 respectively,[27] in which time 51 Tipperary priests passed through their hands.[28] It seems, too, that the influence of these French professors lingered long after their deaths, when their own students succeeded them as

Professors of Moral Theology, and their textbooks remained in use for many years.[29] Henry Neville, Professor of Moral Theology in the college from 1852 to 1867, held that French theology tinctured Maynooth teaching until a short time before 1879.[30]

The evidence of the 1854 Maynooth enquiry provides most information about the degrees of emphasis laid on the question of allegiance there, but because of Maynooth's status as an endowed college such evidence should be accepted with some caution. The witnesses would have been at pains to present the college in the best possible light. Most of them, however, did not indicate any severe stress upon the matter. Indeed, Thomas Furlong neatly remarked that frequent emphasis might 'imply a doubt of its manifest obligation'.[31] Patrick Murray, an ex-student of Delahogue, considered it a subject 'of the first importance', although he confined himself solely to the theological, avoiding all reference to current political affairs. It seems that the students were also reminded of their future obligation as priests to instruct their parishioners accordingly. Dr Whitehead, the President, concluded, however, that the moral catechetical instruction was sufficient to cover this.[32] He cited the concise points of Butler's Catechism based on sections of Saint Paul and Saint Peter.

The role of Maynooth as a nursery of so-called loyal priests was further underlined by the oath of allegiance peculiar to that college alone. This was taken by both staff and students, and each student received a certificate testifying that he had taken it.[33] The oath contained a pledge not to join any secret society, and anti-government sentiments were liable to be punished by the expulsion of the offender.[34] There is some clash of evidence on the seminarians' attitude to the oath. Several ex-Maynooth priests, who had become protestant ministers, told the commissioners that many students either disliked it or merely pretended to take it.[35] Staff members, however, had a different tale to tell. Jeremiah O'Donovan, one of the 1826 witnesses, was quite indignant at the suggestion that Maynooth-trained priests would break the oath, and emphasised that the students were favourable to the link with England.[36] Nevertheless, he made it clear that obedience to the oath was qualified by the nature of the government in power, and that students took it 'in its strict constitutional meaning' that is loyalty to a government not manifestly tyrannical.[37] Concerned at the pope's power over priests, the commissioners of 1826 and 1854 asked for, and were repeatedly given the assurance that he had no power to instruct a breach of the oath, and that any such instruction would not be obeyed.[38] Patrick Lavelle, later one of the most outspoken defenders of fenianism when he was parish priest of Partry,[39] was one of the witnesses who soothed the commissioners' fears!

It is difficult to decide which witnesses were exaggerating, but it would be a mistake to dismiss too casually the evidence of the 'pervert' priests. It is revealing that in practice some of the Maynooth students were not immune to current political happenings. The insurrections of 1798, 1848 and 1867 generated intense excitement among them. It is highly ironic that of the three, the 1798 rebellion made most impact, when the French influence was probably strongest. The protestant witnesses of 1826 commented upon the 'pleasure' with which the students discussed the rising, and also mentioned their favourable attitude to Emmet's attempt.[40] Interestingly, this was the only instance when the evidence of catholic and protestant coincided. But the facts were undeniable: when the president had revealed his intention of making the students swear on the matter no less than 17 or 18 of them retired, having taken the United Irishmen's oath.[41] Dr Healy, Maynooth's historian, frankly admitted that 'a good many' of the students were Young Irelanders in 1848, and read the *Nation* whenever possible.[42] Even Dr Murray was momentarily sympathetic. Again, in 1867, despite prohibition of newspapers, the students were keenly aware of the rising.[43] The involvement of some of the college's tradesmen was not unknown to them either.[44]

But if the evidence suggests that neither theological tenets nor the oath of allegiance impressed a section of the students, could not this be put down to the natural immaturity and instability of youth? Perhaps clerical training had a delayed impact, resulting in a greater anti-fenian spirit by Maynooth priests on mission? On the surface this appears to have been the case. The *Irish People* certainly thought so.[45] One historian feels that this was due to fenian suspicion of priests educated at the state's expense.[46] He reveals that fenians in some areas, such as Cork, stopped going to Maynooth confessors. The truth is, however, that Maynooth priests seemed more hostile because of their numerical superiority. 63% of the very hostile Tipperary priests and 65% of those outside the county were Maynooth-trained.[47] Since Maynooth priests usually accounted for about 55% of the total Tipperary priesthood, it may be argued that there was some extra bias by them against fenianism. Yet, since 64% of priests supporting the fenian amnesty movement were Maynooth alumni, it could equally be held that they were more sympathetic than others to fenian prisoners.[48] The problem is that for the great majority of themes dealt with in this book the statistics for Maynooth-trained clergy were higher than their normal ratio in the county. A glance at some of the personalities involved does little to clarify the issue. On a national level, John McHale, the main episcopal sympathiser with separatism, was a product of Maynooth, while Paul Cullen its chief opponent, was educated in Rome. The two Tipperary pro-fenian priests, John O'Conner and Gerald Barry were educated in Maynooth and all Hallows, Dublin respectively. Of the three Tipperary priests who were strongly sympathetic to the Young Irelanders in 1848, John Kenyon and James

Bermingham were Maynooth, and William Morris was Carlow trained. All that can be safely concluded is that the oath of allegiance and possible emphasis on anti-rebellion doctrine had only a very marginal effect upon Maynooth priests, who were just as prepared as any others to boycott the special object of their allegiance, the Prince of Wales, in 1885.[49]

While it may be difficult to gauge the impact of Maynooth on priestly anti-fenianism, there can be no doubt that the clergy, wherever trained, drew heavily on their theology to refute the movement; the moral dimension was strongly underlined by the exclusion of fenians from the 1865 papal jubilee indulgence.[50] They tended to use the complete range of theological arguments. Some historians hold that its status as a secret society was not of prime consideration, while others feel that the aim of separation plus the means to secure it were the important issues.[51]

It would be wrong to underrate the priests' dislike of fenianism as a secret society. Their interest in the matter for confessional purposes as late as the 1880s is a good pointer to this. It is quite probable that James Cantwell's refusal to allow Kickham's body into Thurles cathedral stemmed from his mistaken belief that the dead man had not received absolution for being a sworn member of the fenian society before his death.[52] A recent biography has rightly mentioned that it was not a fully established custom at that time to leave corpses in chapel overnight.[53] Yet it was not against canon law and one wonders why Cantwell would not, as he said, take responsibility for allowing the body in. His real motive will never be known for certain, but the fenians were intensely annoyed that the priest would have left the corpse in the van at the railway station since it was far too late to take it to Mullinahone. Until that time Cantwell had been well liked by all political sections, but henceforth the fenians held a grudge against him. A year and a half after Kickham's death he was publicly snubbed when a committee which was established to organise a reception for Michael Davitt's visit to Tipperary, deliberately refrained from sending him an invitation, specifically because of his earlier action.[54] Considering Cantwell's leading role in the land struggle this was a humiliating insult, and was seen as such.

The priests' hostility to fenianism as a secret society was inevitable, largely because they could hardly avoid the question on mission. The same was not as true of other theological points with the important exception of the success factor, which they emphasised more than anything else.[55] This tenet no doubt introduced an element of opportunism, if not cynicism, into the theology of revolution, but its pragmatism strongly reinforced the moral or theological implications in the priests' minds. They were acutely conscious of the inability of a badly armed faction to wage successful war against stronger and better equipped English forces. They were also sceptical about fenian hopes of an

armed raid from America.[56] The most striking example of clerical
antipathy on such grounds was that of John Kenyon, who, despite
an earlier and militant theological defence of revolution,[57] was so
opposed to the rising that he very reluctantly granted temporary
shelter to the fugitive James Stephens.[58] He may also have been piqued
because Stephens had not selected him to give the oration at the
funeral of Terence McManus, but his hostility was hardly in keeping
with his own theological interpretation of the success factor. Even the
pro-fenian Patrick Lavelle warned against a 'premature and therefore
fruitless attempt, no matter how provoked or otherwise justified,
at a violent uprising'.[59]

Apart from the certainty of failure, the priests knew that the movement was riddled with informers, who supplied detailed information
and plans to the Government. Tipperary priests did not unduly dwell
on this aspect, but Fr John Gleeson, writing many years later, recalled
his own youthful rebuke of a Nenagh informer.[60] Thus, despite their
opposition to fenianism, the priests felt an instinctive dislike of informers.
All the same there was some element of ambiguity in their outlook.
While several took positive action against informers,[61] others threatened
to reveal the identity of fenian leaders to the authorities and some
priests warned the police about impending attacks or rumours of such.[62]
In this light the accusations of 'felon-setting' against priests by the *Irish
People* were not completely without foundation.[63] Apart from the
question of supplying information directly, the paper held that altar
sermons were often the first notice the police received of the society's
existence in a parish. Such a view was not totally unreasonable because
the confessional may have highlighted the arrival of fenianism more
quickly than any other source. Subsequent general references from the
altar would not be a breach of the confessional. So, the assertion of
the *Irish Ecclesiastical Record* that informers were invariably drawn
from lay ranks was largely but not fully accurate.[64]

It might also be said in their vindication that the priests were prepared to sacrifice a few leading individual fenians to prevent possible
extensive bloodshed later. They were motivated, too, not only by the
pragmatism of their theological principles but by bitter historic pre-
cedent. The singular lesson of the past was that revolution could not
succeed in Ireland. Because 1798 was the first republican rebellion
there was less unanimity in clerical attitudes towards it. A large number
of priests opposed it, but some were members of the United Irishmen,
and suffered death, imprisonment or transportation as a result.[65]
Tipperary produced its quota of victims. This created some tradition
of clerical involvement in republicanism; John Murphy C.C. Boula-
vogue, Co. Wexford was immortalised in story and verse as a rebel
leader. Yet, along with this tradition lay one not only of failure but
of retribution on priest as well as people, a factor which may or may

not have carried some weight when the second link of the republican chain was forged in 1848. Fifty mid-century Tipperary priests were born between 1763 and 1799,[66] and some of them obviously clearly remembered the event and its grisly aftermath. Michael Burke P.P. Ardfinnan was 35 years old in 1798, Dean James McDonnell was 31, Andrew James Scanlan P.P. Couraganeen and William Laffan P.P. Holycross were 18, and so on down to those who were only children. A considerable number of 1848 priests were also born within a decade of the United Irishmen's rising, and no doubt heard its story from their parents, possibly indeed with a nationalistic flavour. No amount of sentiment, however, could conceal the reality of the effort.

There was another and perhaps more potent prohibitive influence on the priests in 1848 than the failure of 1798. This was the realisation that organised constitutional agitation could be devastatingly effective. The O'Connellite movement, which witnessed the first mass-involvement of priests in politics, amply demonstrates this. It was also of prime importance that O'Connell's system of passive resistance harmonised perfectly with catholic theology, and therefore admirably suited clerical political philosophy. Consequently, the name of O'Connell was still reverently on the priests' lips as late as The Land War, and his methods were held up as a paragon of perfection and sound morality.[67] Obviously his influence was far more powerful in 1848. The dictum of Philip Fitzgerald P.P. Ballingarry that the achievement of liberty was not worth the shedding of blood was undiluted O'Connellism.[68] Dr. Michael Burke, a leading O'Connellite priest, was firmly convinced that 'none but the principles and teachings of O'Connell will ever lead to the regeneration of Ireland',[69] a view totally shared by his friends Archdeacon Michael Laffan and John Ryan.[70]

Political methods, however, were not the only factors which gave the priests food for thought. They watched carefully the 1848 up-heavals in Europe. Initially they viewed the revolution in France favourably, and were aware that the insurgents did not molest the staff of the Irish College Paris, or interfere with its property.[71] Smith O'Brien, Meagher and O'Gorman were enthusiastically received at the college, and the Parisian priests openly encouraged the revolutionaries.[72] Early in May William Morris P.P. Borrisoleigh had the distinction of being mentioned in the *Bulletin de la Republique* Paris, for his con-gratulatory address, signed on behalf of his parishoners, assuring the French revolutionaries of the approbation of the Irish priests and people.[73]

Neither Morris nor most of the other Irish priests understood the social and political complexities of the revolution in Paris. But, the Communard revolution at the end of May, when the archbishop of Paris and several priests were butchered, changed their temper. Morris played no part in the Ballingarry affair, and the ardour of Young

Ireland clergy in general visibly cooled. These were younger priests who, according to Philip Fitzgerald, had joined the movement 'through want of experience' or 'misdirected zeal'.[74] In the event, only the senile Edmund Prendergast P.P. Ballingarry gave some short-lived semblance of support to the insurgents.[75] A few other priests who were sympathetic were subdued by their bishops. Bishop Kennedy of Killaloe checked the activity of James Bermingham P.P. Borrisokane.[76] Perhaps the most surprising clerical absentee from the rising was John Kenyon. His leading role in the Young Ireland movement has been written about and may be briefly summarised here.[77] His short but fiery political career was characterised by scathing attacks on constitutional agitation and on Daniel O'Connell, even when the latter was dead but unburied. In the midst of a serious famine he theologically justified revolution, emphasising that the probability of success was not incompatible with danger, death or even defeat. Consistent with his views he whipped a Templederry audience to a frenzy, leaving no doubt that the day of rebellion was fast approaching. Yet he quickly succumbed to his bishop after suspension, and refused to entertain the rising because it lacked a hope of success.[78] In a very real sense, of course, his *volte face* was no more than basic realism, but in another it is difficult to understand, especially when, even after suspension, he was in Dublin actively making preparations for a rising, although at precisely that time he was negotiating with Archbishop Slattery for a reconciliation with Bishop Kennedy.[79]

When convinced of the folly of revolution some priests were not merely content to abstain or remain neutral. They actively opposed the 1848 uprising with considerable success.[80] Philip Fitzgerald, later stridently anti-fenian, recorded his own impression of the affair and included extracts from the diary of Thomas O'Carroll C.C. Clonoulty.[81] It was hardly a coincidence that this pamphlet was published in 1868, portraying as it did the priests' precise attitude to revolution and to fenianism. Briefly, Fitzgerald, with an ambivalence that characterised the priests' attitude to rebellion, conceded that a plausible excuse for a rising existed, but argued that the means available were totally inadequate; this ambivalence was further underlined by his dual condemnation of government and rebels.[82] A similar ambiguity was displayed by John Moloney P.P. Kilcommon in his reception of some of the fugitives there. He admitted that 'one more rash individual' tried to raise his parishoners.[83] Nevertheless, a few years later he proceeded to denounce the government for driving 'the true and noble-minded' Young Irelanders into insurrection, and concluded that the lord lieutenant 'like Lord Castlereagh' had 'cut the nation's throat and may yet cut his own'.[84] This priest's angry sentiments were born of the famine, and no doubt the antipathy of many others to England was sharpened by the sorry sights they daily witnessed, but heartrending as these were they did not drive the priests into support for the 1848 insurrection.

Therefore the tradition of clerical involvement in rebellion was broken in 1848, and was replaced by one of opposition. The rapid failure of the rising seemed to justify this, and was exploited by the priests from 1850 onwards, when they sternly set their faces against revolt. In 1854 John Ryan C.C. Cashel pointed with scorn to the 'cabbage-garden catherine-dance of Ballingarry, which made Irishmen the sad mockery and laughing-stock of the world'.[85] The hysterical discharge in 1852 of Andrew James Scanlan,[86] the O'Connellite pastor of Couraganeen, who according to himself 'wrote with a pen of steel and I have but one step to go to dip it in the flame', was not a call for revolution. It was an outburst against the Ecclesiastical Titles Bill and was little more than a windy threat. His real attitude to violence was revealed by his opposition to the candidature on The O'Donoghue in the 1857 election because of the latter's undeserved Young Ireland label; in this Scanlan promised Lawrence Waldron, the other candidate, the support of the O'Connellite priests.[87] While Dr Burke was even more enraged at the religious measure he immediately rejected violence as a solution, contrasting the unarmed and untrained Irish peasantry with the well-disciplined English army.[88] Indeed, Burke had earlier rejected violence, even if Ireland had sufficient means to wage a successful war.[89] His opposition to the Tenant League partly arose from the Young Ireland connections of some of its leaders, such as Charles Gavan Duffy on a national level, or Maurice Leyne, the editor of the *Tipperary Leader*. Non-Tipperary priests of the 1850s were also influenced by the failure of the rising.[90] Dr Croke, an ardent Young Irelander, in his controversy with Kenyon, wrote that an armed revolution was 'now happily unthought of', and would be impossible for 50 years, not perhaps a bad guess. Nevertheless, displaying what was to be a characteristic ambivalence, Croke, in a letter to Duffy shortly afterwards, proposed that Ireland's opportunity was fast approaching with the supposed possibility of an invasion of England by the French.[91]

The memory of the 1848 rebellion was very much alive in the 1860s, when no less than 131 serving Tipperary priests had been ordained before 1848, while yet another 66 were either teenagers or students at the time of the Young Ireland outbreak.[92] It is significant also that all the Tipperary clerics who publicly denounced fenianism were priests before 1848. Even in the 1880s when the spectre of fenianism arose once more, the Ballingarry fiasco was used as a deterrent by priests, who were only young children when it occurred. David Humphreys and Daniel Flannery, both only 5 years old in 1848, highlighted its failure.[93] But Humphreys' reference to the 'cabbage-garden revolt' was used as a contemptuous comparison with the cooling enthusiasm of the Smith Barry campaigners. Flannery endeavoured to show that revolution hindered agrarian reform, by portraying the rising as a stumbling-block to the implementation of the Devon Commission recommendations. Archbishop Croke, too, in the presence of a Ballingarry audience in 1881, recalled the folly of 1848 'as it would be foolish to commence now', but he hastened to praise the patriotism of Ballingarry as the site chosen for the rising.[94]

Contempt there may have been, therefore, for the Ballingarry episode, but it is interesting that such contempt was sometimes used as a tactic, and if circumstances required it, the priests were ready to introduce a note of ambiguity into their statements. Dr Croke is a prime example, and a few other clerics have already been cited. But so ambivalent was the general clerical attitude to revolution that it deserves further comment. If, for example, the priests used the failure of past insurrections as a warning against current republicanism, with equal facility they waxed eloquent in their praise of past patriots. The Land War is the best vantage point from which to study this aspect, since by then the fenian rising was past history.

It is not too cynical to say that the more ancient the patriots the more hearty priestly retrospective benediction was. At a Clonmel lecture in 1886 Eugene Sheehy P.P. Bruree Co. Limerick was lavish in his extolling of the town's defence against Cromwell, and concluded that the blood of patriots supplied a nation's most indestructible element.[95] Perhaps the greatest ambivalence was displayed by his bishop, Edward O'Dwyer, who, according to one of his priests was 'rather weak in his patriotism'.[96] Far from objecting to an 1889 Limerick meeting commemorating Patrick Sarsfield, O'Dwyer said that such demonstrations kept patriotism alive and set 'lofty patterns' for the people to imitate.[97] One of his priests, William Higgins Adm., chaired the demonstration, and another, T. Lee C.C., announced that 'the spirit of nationality which nerved the arms of their forefathers was not dead'.[98] Matt Ryan eulogised Sarsfield's exploits, too, but stressed that unlike Sarsfield, he was but a 'kind of lieutenant in the church of Christ'.[99] The maligned men of 1867 received their quota of retrospective praise. These included such men as Mitchel, Davitt, Kickham, Stephens and two Tipperary rebels, Thomas F. Bourke and John Francis Meagher.

Kickham, one of the most determined defenders of fenianism against the clergy in the 1860s, was in later years admired by them for his integrity and spirit of self-sacrifice. The Clonmel curates, Thomas McDonnell, John Everard and Maurice Flynn, attended a meeting there in 1878 to raise a testimonial to him.[100] There was, however, an element of bitterness surrounding his burial in Mullinahone. The very radical *Tipperary People* announced that the church there was 'barricaded as if against one of those who could surpass murderers, robbers and hangmen. . . .'.[101] The ailing parish priest, Thomas Hickey, was ill in Dublin, and, whether by accident or design, the local curates could not be located for some time.[102] Nevertheless, the funeral seems to have been attended by William Corcoran C.C. Killenaule and William Jones, President of St. Patrick's College Thurles.[103] Dr Croke, who had been extremely embarrassed by James Cantwell's exclusion of the body from the cathedral,[104] approved of the project to erect a monument over Kickham's grave in 1886, and even promised financial aid.[105] With his permission the succeeding pastor of Mullinahone, Philip Ryan, had given a site for a memorial in the church-yard in 1883.[106] Likewise, the clerical attitude to the fund for the impoverished James Stephens is an equally good example of retrospective sympathy. The priests chaired the National League meetings, which voiced indignation at Stephens' expulsion by the French Government, and David Humphreys was an ex-officio member of the Tipperary Town Stephens Committee.[107] The most remarkable comments upon the affair were made in 1885 by Thomas McDonnell Adm. Clonmel. With the 'gleaming sabres' of the Volunteers as the background to his speech, he asserted that the Irish people would prefer to honour James Stephens than the Prince of Wales, and for good measure he remarked that the 'ruffians who banished Stephens are the very same who murdered the Archbishop of Paris'.[108] Considering that he had been 36 years old in 1867, McDonnell's unawareness of the irony of this remark is rather peculiar. Croke, too, sent £5 to the fund and praised Stephens' patriotism, with the important qualification, however, that he was 'a deluded lover of his country'.[109] Such local '67 men as John Francis Meagher of Carrick-on-Suir and Thomas Francis Burke were praised by priests like Paul Power C.C. Carrick-on-Suir, Richard J. Casey, an ex-Tipperary priest, and by Archdeacon Daniel Ryan.[110] Various excuses were offered for their physical force philosophy, their patriotism was praised, and Ryan drew comparisons with such long dead heroes as Brian Boru and Hugh O'Neill. The priests' attitude to the Manchester Martyrs also displays a certain degree of retrospective patriotism. David Humphreys, John Shelley, Edmund Hanly and Maurice Power subscribed towards the erection of a 14 foot memorial-cross at Emly.[111] T.H. Kinnane felt that the sacrifice of the trio plus the Clerkenwell explosions had extracted concessions from England.[112]

One final example of apparent approbation of past republicans lay in the priests' unashamed support for such men who ran as parliamentary candidates for Tipperary in later years. P.J. Smyth, 'Nicaragua' of 1848, who engineered Mitchel's release from Van Diemen's land and canvassed for him in Tipperary in the 1870s, was elected in 1880 with clerical support. Thomas J. Condon and John O'Connor, both ex-fenians, were also returned with priestly approval. During the 1885 election campaign, Condon declared that he was no 'shilly-shally, milk and water politician', but one who followed in the footsteps of Mitchel. As late as 1890 O'Connor, referred to as the 'stalwart Cork rebel' by John Kelly C.C. Bansha,[113] startled the House of Commons by saying 'I could not help being a fenian. I cannot fix the hour of the day when I began to hate England, when I began to hate the English people, the English Government, and everything that bore the name of England'.[114]

Yet, ambivalent though the priests undoubtedly were in their attitude to such ex-rebels, their praise carried a certain degree of circumspection; for example, despite their euology of Kickham, they made it clear that their admiration was for his personal character and self-sacrificing spirit and not for his political principles. This was emphasised by Thomas McDonnell despite his later nationalistic utterances. Neither did the clergy's presence at his funeral signify any liking for Kickham's politics. This is more clearly seen by the marked absence of priests from demonstrations to celebrate his anniversary, when such nationalistic topics as the alleged coming of a rising were aired.[115] Similarly, while they were prepared to subscribe to crosses for the Manchester Martyrs, the priests never attended any of the annual commemoration demonstrations, where faith in the pike was invariably renewed.[116] They did, however, attend the assizes following the arrests of fenians at one such Emly meeting.[117] Dr Croke was cautious in his reference to James Stephens, and when he sent a second £5 to the Stephens fund of 1890, he refused to be closely identified with the National Club, which paid Stephens his £113 annuity.[118] Again, on closer examination, it is clear that the priests' support of ex-fenian candidates did not signify approval of republicanism. They were well aware that P.J. Smyth, despite his high-sounding patriotic verbiage,[119] was infinitely more conservative in his politics by 1880, and was not even as radical as they wished him to be. John Ryan, who proposed Smyth, later stressed that he had not supported either him or John Dillon as members of any club or coterie, meaning, of course, fenianism.[120] Despite the references of Thomas J. Condon or John O'Connor, it was evident to the priests that both were firmly harnassed to Parnell's constitutional machine. The clearest illustration, however, of clerical hostility to current republicanism, while simultaneously praising the patriots of earlier years was their reaction to some of the Land War organisations, such as the Land League itself, the Labourers' League, the Young Ireland Society, and, most significant of all, the Gaelic Athletic Association. All these will be examined in greater detail later, but a quotation from the speech of John Scanlan on the G.A.A. beautifully summarises the ambivalence of the priests to republicanism — 'I have mentioned the men of 1865 and 1867, and I ask you to give a cheer for their names. I admire those men, I know they were honest and true. Can I say the same of those who, with the experience of that movement (G.A.A.) would lead the youth of Ireland into the way of ruin and restore again the golden age of informers?'[121]

In view of their unrelenting opposition to the politics of separation, why did the priests feel it necessary to resort to such ambivalence? Was it a genuine conflict of emotions experienced as Irishmen, or was it the instinctive reaction of the politician to the vagaries of public opinion? It was a combination of both, but the weight of evidence suggests that the latter was fundamental. In other words the rhetorical flourishes and sympathetic sentiments, which periodically softened the priests' hostility were largely provoked by a shift in the public opinion of the farming community. The great majority of farmers rejected fenianism, but they were at times jolted by such factors as fenian intimidation, or by emotive issues like the execution of the Manchester Martyrs and the harsh treatment of political prisoners. The priests accommodated such temporary aberrations by a corresponding shift in their own public attitude. In short, they shared the cautious ambivalence of their own kinsfolk. Even the bishops, as products of a middle-class environment, were sensitive to such public opinion. And so while theology was an important factor in crystallising and reinforcing their instinctive antipathy to revolution, the very forces of social background and public opinion, which bred this instinct, sometimes made the clergy assume an attitude, which strictly speaking was not altogether consistent with basic theological tenets.

There was no social affinity between priests and fenians, who were predominantly urban labourers or artisans, with a small sprinkling of agricultural labourers and an even smaller number of farmers or famers' sons.[122] Some clerical references to the social status of fenians positively smacked of class-distinction, even if they were uttered in the heat of the moment. John Mawe, a Kerry parish priest, contrasted the fenians of the 60s with the Young Irelanders, who were 'decent men compared to the present dregs of society';[123] interestingly Lord Mayo was conscious of this aspect too, he traced the progressively declining social status of revolutionary leaders from 1798 to 1866.[124] Clerical attitudes did not change up to 1891 when Patrick Ryan P.P. Galbally referred to Parnell's I.R.B. supporters as 'pothouse men, porter men and bludgeon men'.[125] Apart from a consciousness of social distinction, the priests possibly feared a socialistic policy of confiscation by the lower orders, although social aims were subordinate to the political as far as the ostensible aims of the movement were concerned. This was not a theme of the Tipperary priests, but in later years Thomas Meagher, writing on land division, proposed that every man without land in Ireland is 'a rebel at heart'.[126] This implication that a more equitable land distribution would create a loyal society was definitely not a facet of the tenants' outlook, and Meagher's view was also the exception among the priests themselves. It is certain, too, that the farmers feared damage to their property by the fenians. One 'highly respected' parish priest in Tipperary revealed that in their anxiety even small farmers desired the implementation of the Peace Preservation Act.[127] 130 of his Templederry tenants requested Robert Jocelyn Otway to seek arms for their protection.[128] Nevertheless, the Fenians respected private property during the rising, if only because the affair was so miserably short. This was not only to their credit at the trials, but it also helps to explain the shift in public opinion during the amnesty campaign, and consequently the clergy's change of emphasis.

The graph of general tenant indifference or silent hostility to Irish republican ideology, or to a disrupting revolution is relatively easy to trace. The priests' political path was closely parallel to it. In 1848 the Young Ireland leaders had to depend upon a half-starved group of colliers from Ballingarry and the surrounding areas. Improving harvests from the 1850s made farmers reluctant even to support the constitutional Tenant League. The failure of the *Tribune* (edited by Luby, later editor of the *Irish People*) to arouse a revolutionary whimper in the mid-1850s is clear testimony of widespread apathy. This newspaper is relevant to Tipperary because one of its founders was John Kenyon, although he did not initiate the project.[129] Since he was involved, and since none of his letters appeared in the paper, it is possible that he wrote some of its editorials, which were usually divided into several sections, each perhaps belonging to different writers. The paper, too, contained some references which particularly concerned Kenyon.

It began its career with an article to mollify the priests, requesting toleration between lay and clerical views of republicanism, continued with a guarantee that religion would flourish in an Irish republic, and concluded its short span with the unpalatable suggestion that priests should remain outside politics, and that nationalism should have a secular rather than a religious base.[130] There was no such progression in the philosophy of the *Irish People* which began immediately with the demand that the priests remain in the sanctuary. Perhaps the experience of the *Tribune* contributed to the bluntness of the fenian organ. Reflecting the views of all nationalists, including Kenyon, the *Tribune* portrayed an Irish republic as the panacea of all ills.[131] It argued that the Crimean war made nationalism a question of practical politics, and like Kenyon held that revolution was possible with the aid of foreign intervention.[132] While Andrew James Scanlan the pastor of Couraganeen (Bournea) in North Tipperary, also saw the Crimea as Ireland's opportunity, his basic outlook differed profoundly from Kenyon's. He merely envisaged the voluntary granting of repeal by the English Government; and this he felt would inspire Irishmen to fight on England's side in the Crimea.[133] Nothing could be more contrary to the separatists outlook than this.

The Crimean negotiations ended any hope of concessions and the immediate collapse of the *Tribune* showed the tenuous nature of its frustrated existence. The silence of the priests during its tenure merely mirrored the indifference of the public, and contrasted with their attacks on the *Irish People*. In this atmosphere of apathy the I.R.B. or fenian Society was established in 1858. Its very secrecy makes it difficult to gauge the extent of the organisation in Tipperary in the late '50s or early '60s, but it was probably confined mainly to urban areas and villages, where unemployment was greatest. The emotive execution of the McCormack brothers through perjured evidence in 1858 aroused far greater popular interest than the infant society.[134] While the political implications of the McCormack affair mainly concerned the under-representation of Catholics on juries, the very nationalistic speech of John Kenyon at the protest meeting following the hanging, (attended by 20 priests),[135] makes it relevant to this discussion. Inevitably, Kenyon expounded on the nationalist theme of republicanism as the cure for all ills, including an unfair jury system. At the same time he realistically acknowledged that revolution was not opportune, pessimistically adding 'you are a sheep without a shepherd'. It must be stated, however, that the 48 clerical signatories to the initial requisition for a meeting, or the 11 priestly members of the McCormack Committee,[136] did not see the affair in terms of nationalism, although one priest refused to attend, probably because he feared a violent sequel to the affair. An invitation to William Smith O'Brien to attend is interesting but was perhaps as much based on his popularity as on his Young Ireland past.[137] Despite the widespread publicity given to the meeting and the newspaper heat generated by Kenyon's statement, the whole affair was quickly submerged in a general pool of apathy, and was of little apparent benefit to the fenian movement.

The 1860s were the real years of organised Fenianism, but there is little evidence that it took root among the farmers. The sudden spate of outrages in the early 1860s was not necessarily a symptom of nationalism, but of agrarian unrest. Indeed, efforts to revive interest in the less radical constitutional nationalism, repeal or home rule, were not received with any notable public enthusiasm.[138] The small degree of support given by the priests to a repeal petition of the O'Donoghue in 1860 shows at least their differentiation between repeal and separation.[139] It is true, of course, that a section of the clergy had supported the O'Donoghue in the 1857 election, when he was identified with a romantic Young Irelandism.[140] But despite this label the O'Donoghue made it perfectly clear that should Young Irelandism signify a philosophy of violence he was more fit to represent 'Bedlam' than Tipperary.[141] A banquet of 1862 to honour him as the so-called champion of na-

John Martin, John Mitchel and John Kenyon, P.P., Templederry. Photograph taken in Paris in 1866.

tionality was well supported by the priests, 37 of whom were members of the organising committee, clearly implying that they understood nationality in its constitutional rather than republican sense.[142] John Kenyon was different. He emphasised that The O'Donoghue should be honoured strictly as a nationalist, and took it upon himself to suggest a list of toasts in the following order — Ireland a nation, the martyrs of Ireland, the heroes of Ireland, the artists of Ireland, the wrongs of Ireland, the rights of Ireland and the hopes of Ireland.[143] The O'Donoghue's absence from his own banquet clearly demonstrates his fear of being even remotely associated with republicanism.

The assumption that the priests supported him strictly as a repealer is amply borne out by their conspicuous absence from two nationalist meetings the following year at Slievenamon[144] and Ormond Stile.[145] While these were not fenian inspired, members of the movement were present. Kickham chaired the Slievenamon meeting which rejected parliamentary methods, although it agreed upon co-operation with non-parliamentary bodies such as tenant-rights societies. It also pledged to grasp the fitting opportunity for revolt. The private report of the affair commented upon a 'novel theme' there in the form of anti-clerical references. This bias would soon be anything but novel.

The Ormond Stile meeting was advertised to promote self-government, but the tenor of the speeches was more extreme than that associated with repeal; so the term self-government was rather ambiguous, and probably deliberately so. Members of the Brotherhood of St Patrick, which had an 'ephemeral existence' in Nenagh were present.[146] Although a separate organisation, this was a front for the fenian society, and attracted the attention of the Vatican authorities, who were assured by Dr Leahy that it was not anti-religion, but (amazingly) was anti-Italian, and so was opposed by the bishops.[147] Most of the clergy objected to and boycotted the Ormond Stile meeting. Only Peter Murphy, Kenyon's curate, approved of it, and Patrick Horan C.C. Toomevara was reluctantly present. Neither was a fenian supporter. Still, Horan succumbed sufficiently to the separist bias of the meeting to agree that parliamentary agitation was demoralising, and advised his audience to 'use the means of our salvation . . . when within reach'. This was no more than the response of a politician. Horan felt safe in his platform oratory, and certainly did not envisage the rising of a few years hence. His later active membership of John Martin's and The O'Donoghue's National League, which was established to counteract the fenian society and was roundly ridiculed by the latter, is sufficient proof of his real attitude to Irish republicanism.

The paucity of semi-republican meetings in the first half of the decade, and the marked absence of priests from the few that were held, is one indication of a weak nationalistic spirit among the farmers. The McManus funeral of 1861 may have been indicative of a reservoir

of potential support for fenianism, but the demonstration was predominantly Dublin based, and it is unlikely that the farmers were
involved. The affair did not have any public repercussions in Tipperary.
The limited extent of fenianism in the county in the mid-'60s is itself
a sure guide to farming opinion. While it is true that 29 parishes, or
45% of Tipperary's total, contained supposedly active fenianism, this
was confined to small pockets in each parish.[148] The resident magistrate, Charles De Gernon, rightly considered that certain reports of
illegal drilling were exaggerated, although he admitted that a spirit
of disaffection existed in some localities.[149] Considering tenant appre-
hension, this was undoubtedly mainly limited to labourers, and the
request of one magistrate for prompt government action to hold
tenant loyalty was largely alarmist.[150] The rising, badly organised,
poorly supported, and hampered by wintry weather, was confined
to a few localities.[151] Only a small percentage of fenian prisoners
were farmers, and many of these pleaded that they had been pressed
into service.[152] Others fled to avoid a similar fate and more simply
refused to join marching fenian bands.[153] Such weak farmer participation in the rising was precisely reflected in clerical ranks by the few
priests who were actively sympathetic.

But, because of its rapid collapse, the rising does not facilitate
an in-depth appreciation of farmer opinion. Since the bulk of the
electorate was farmers, an examination of the elections during the '60s
and '70s is a more comprehensive guide to this, and consequently
to the overall outlook of the priests.

Before doing this perhaps a brief outline of these elections may
help to avoid confusion. Three elections took place prior to the rising.
There was a county by-election in 1865, a general election that same
year and a county by-election in 1866. There were seven elections
between the rising and 1877 — a general election in 1868, a county
by-election in 1869, a county by-election in 1870, a general election
in 1874, two county by-elections in 1875 and a county by-election
in 1877.

In the by-election of 1865 the National Association candidate
Charles Moore, a Tipperary landlord, defeated the nationalist, Peter
E. Gill. Later that year in the general election Moore and the sitting
members John B. Dillon (erstwhile Young Irelander), both National
Association candidates, were successful and Gill was again defeated.
When Dillon died in 1866, Captain Charles White, son of Lord Anally,
beat the conservative candidate, Lawrence Waldron, in the ensuing
by-election. Gill did not contest this election although he made several
speeches. In the general election of 1868 Charles Moore and Charles
White, the sitting members, were again returned. Gill also spoke during
this campaign although he did not contest the election. When Moore
died in 1869 Denis Caulfield Heron LL.D, Q.C., ex-professor of Juris-

Poster for a public meeting, 1863.

prudence, was defeated by the imprisoned fenian leader, Jeremiah O'Donovan Rossa. Because of his status Rossa was disqualified and in the resulting by-election of 1870 Heron again stood and narrowly defeated the well-known fenian Charles Kickham. Heron did not contest the general election of 1874 and the Hon. Wilfred Frederick Ormond O'Callaghan, son of Viscount Lismore, joined White who was at that stage a Lieutenant-Colonel in the Scots Fusiliers. White and O'Callaghan defeated the nationalists Gill, John Mitchel and George Roe. White resigned the following year and this time Mitchel was returned unopposed. He was however disqualified because he had broken parole from Van Diemen's land, but in the second by-election of 1875 he was again re-elected. However, on petition the Conservative candidate, Stephen Moore, was given the seat. O'Callaghan, the sitting Liberal member, died in 1877 and in the by-election of that year Edmund Dwyer Gray, proprietor of the *Freeman's Journal*, defeated the nationalist candidate, John Sarsfield Casey. Some of these elections are again looked at in the chapter dealing with the Irish party.

The three pre-rising elections do not reveal any clerical onslaught on fenianism. But solid support for the National Association candidates clearly underlines a firm clerical belief in parliamentary and constitutional methods.[154] The association was seen as a possible counterforce to the fenian movement, and, like the National League, was disliked by that society.[155] The somewhat ambiguous political philosophy of the so-called nationalist candidate, Peter E. Gill, makes analysis of public opinion more difficult. As a repealer he strongly supported Martin's National League, and was one of the chief organisers of the Ormond Stile meeting. As a separatist it was he who originally suggested that O'Donovan Rossa stand for Tipperary,[156] although William O'Brien wrongly disputes his role in this.[157] His act of concealing the fugitive James Stephens in his house for two months earned it the nickname 'the rebel's den'.

The result of his political manouvres was to draw on him the opposition of both priests and fenians. The fenians ridiculed him as a pseudo-nationalist[158] bringing discredit upon republicanism by his platform antics and secret alliance with the Conservatives. The latter, in their desire to split the Liberal vote, provided him with election finance.[159] Gill's denial of this some years later shows him as a man of doubtful veracity.[160] The priests automatically disliked him as an opponent of the National Association candidate, of course, although some were not particularly concerned about him, sharing fenian views of his mediocrity. Others, however, tended to discuss him in the context of fenianism, but this was mainly for propaganda purposes.[161] Generally speaking the clergy did not see him as a threat, and ignored the question of fenianism in the pre-rising elections. John Kenyon was the only priest to support Gill as a separatist, and he earned the opprobium of one Nenagh curate who referred to him as 'renegade priest cut off by his bishop'.[162] Kenyon was well used to criticism. He travelled to the nomination of candidates in Clonmel, poured scorn on the National Association, and ridiculed parliamentary representation by advising his parishoners to remain at home planting cabbages on polling day.[163] He did not regard co-operation with the Conservatives as a breach of nationalistic ethics.

Because Kenyon was regarded as an eccentric and a maverick his stand was not as important as might otherwise have been the case. Gill was generally forced to rely upon support from the labouring classes. An undercurrent of nationalism was evident among these in 1865, and the National Association promoters, lay and clerical, found it difficult to speak amid the storm of heckling on nomination day.[164] Yet, mob vociferation was not always an accurate indication of labourer political outlook; Gill himself was abused by a section of the crowd, and indeed was almost lynched in 1866, when Kenyon, too, suffered a severe heckling.[165] As Kenyon pointed out and as has already been seen, bribery and drink were important facets in the election behaviour of the labouring classes. But if the significance of labourer support for Gill is doubtful the votes of a minority of electors for him despite the opposition of the clergy require scrutiny.

In the 1865 election he secured 30% of the poll i.e. 909 votes against his oponent's 2134.[166] The figures are open to several interpretations. There was an obvious personal vote for Gill. He ran his newspaper, the *Tipperary Advocate*, in the town of Nenagh, and many of the farmers in the district liked him and his wry sense of humour. This was reflected in his good showing for this area. Indeed, he defeated Charles Moore in the Barony of Upper Ormond, a very sharp contrast to the poor results of the *bona fide* fenian candidates there in later contests. It may be confidently said that an extremely small number of the votes cast in his favour in North Tipperary represented legitimate republican interest. On the other hand the relatively low poll for the National Association candidate had two identifiable causes. The independent action of the clergy in initiating the election campaign was resented as a sign of dictation, and a protest was registered by abstaining from voting.[167] But of greater relevance, it was also a very definite symptom of electorate apathy towards constitutional methods, which seemed to be achieving little or nothing at the time. John Power P.P. Powerstown in a letter to the National Association admitted as much, but he hastened to repudiate revolution as an alternative.[168] Later still at a Dublin meeting of the association William Quirke revealed that the priests themselves shared this apathy.[169] This only reinforces the theory that the clergy were profoundly influenced by tenant farmer political opinion. Clearly, too, it was only a negative reaction by priests and people, and while it tended dangerously towards a political vacuum it did not automatically mean a turning to revolution or republicanism. Nevertheless, the *Irish People*, despite its derision of Gill, chose to interpret the election result as a groundswell in favour of physical force nationlism.[170] It is also true that John B. Dillon, a prominent National Association leader, was disturbed because of fenian sympathies among the young men at that time.[171] He did not, however, qualify if these were electors.

The seven post-rising elections from 1868 to 1877, while requiring careful interpretation, are a much more satisfactory source for judging clerical attitudes towards fenianism in the context of public opinion. These elections afforded the only real point of contact between priests and fenians before the Land War. The Ballot Act and extension of the polling places, however, lessened this contact in 1875 and 1877. A study of the elections does not bear out the contention of some historians that the lower (that is parish) clergy were moving closer to fenianism from 1865 onwards.[172] The activity of both parish priests and curates was invariably on the side of the constitutional candidates. Large numbers of priests flocked to meetings, canvassed, issued resolutions of support, and ferried voters to the polls.[173] Priestly exertions at the booths were particularly intense,[174] and in the 1870 contest no less than 40 priests superintended voters in Nenagh.[175] The extent of clerical anti-fenianism may be judged from the petition lodged (in vain) on Kickham's behalf, accusing 25 priests of, among other things, spiritual intimidation.[176] Strenuous clerical efforts to combat this petition were partly a manifestation of this anti-fenian spirit, too. They attended special meetings in Clonmel and Cashel, and at least 45 priests contributed to a 'defence' fund for the National Association candidate, Denis Caulfield Heron.[177]

While such clerical activity was an integral part of nineteenth century electioneering, the accompanying consciousness of the priests that they were combatting fenianism distinguishes these elections from all others. It was no coincidence that the first toast of a Clonmel banquet, preceding the 1868 election, professed loyalty to the queen, and was followed by one to the lord lieutenant.[178] At the banquet, John Power, defending the priests' political involvement, stressed their role of preventing people 'from becoming the dupes of the wild schemes or insane projects of revolutionary adventurers'. Power, like other priests, was also worried that fenian ripples might endanger expected government concessions on education and the church establishment. Their protestations of loyalty, therefore, were also an implied assurance of support for Gladstone.[179] A few weeks after Power's statement, John Ryan, in a letter to the *Freeman's Journal*, drew attention to the fenian opposition to parliament.[180] Ironically, one of Ryan's later anti-landlord speeches[181] was incorrectly interpreted in Rome as a sign of clerical leanings towards fenianism, and was partly responsible for the 1870 decree which condemned the society by name.[182] This typically ambivalent speech was no more than an election stratagem to gain the ear of the fenian audience during the 1869 by-election, when Ryan actually proposed the National Association candidate. The *Irishman* shrewdly saw it as such, and referred to it as 'an unworthy trick'.[183] A modern writer feels that the fenian candidate, Jeremiah O'Donovan Rossa, was returned with the aid of the priests, especially the younger ones.[184] Nothing could be further from the truth. All the priests, with the possible exception of John O'Connor, opposed him; his canvassing was done by laymen, particularly Peter Gill and Daniel O'Connell, Toomevara. The latter, a farmer of 120 acres, had been a fenian instructor in 1865; when arrested he had documents in his possession including a letter composed by himself for *The Irish People* attacking the clergy.[185]

During the election campaign in 1875, John Mitchel admitted that some priests slammed the door in his face as he canvassed.[186] In 1874 others called him a communist and referred to his supporters as anti-catholics or Garibaldians,[187] just as Kickham's followers had been labelled 'infidels'.[188] Thomas Crosse of Garnacanty, near Tipperary town, (one of the nominators of Mitchel and his partner, George Roe), attacked the priests, especially Patrick Canty P.P. Kilcommon who, apparently, 'complimented himself and his brother priests on the triumph they had won over the nationalists'.[189] Clerical anti-fenianism was strengthened after the second by-election of 1875 when it became clear that the Conservative candidate, who had lodged a petition against Mitchel, would gain the seat on the latter's disqualification. The priests were, however, faced with an embarrassing problem. They were appalled by the prospect of a Conservative M.P. for the county, but any attack on Stephen Moore, the individual in question, might be interpreted as an approval of Mitchel and what he stood for. A Clonmel meeting, therefore, chaired by Roger Power P.P., with Patrick F. Flynn C.C. as secretary, hastened to announce that their opposition to Moore's petition did not 'by any means endorse the political programme, which had for its object the disfranchisement of Tipperary county or any other Irish constituency'.[190] In other words the priests and middle-class laity were opposed to Mitchel's deliberate attempt at downgrading parliamentary methods. Mitchel had publicly declared his intention of not sitting for Tipperary if elected, thereby effectively disfranchising it.[191] He intended to pursue the same policy in other counties.

The 1877 election provides an excellent insight into priestly dislike of fenianism, and shows a more vigorous public confidence in constitutional agitation than had been evident for many years. Edmund Dwyer Gray, proprietor of the *Freemans Journal*, was chosen as a candidate with sufficient popularity to prevent the county from falling into fenian hands again. Unlike Mitchel, the fenian candidate John Sarsfield Casey, nicknamed 'the Galtee Boy', was willing to take his seat in parliament, possibly reflecting fenian wishes to recapture electoral sympathy.[192] This concession did nothing to soften the priests' hostility. Bishop James Ryan, Killaloe, succinctly summed up their attitude: 'Our priests look upon it as a struggle between ourselves and the faithless, demoralised fenians, and will leave nothing undone to secure victory'.[193] Dr Croke, too, saw it as a trial of strength with the fenians.[194] William J. McKeogh attacked the 'vexatious opposition' of the fenians in the South Riding of the county, where Casey received most support.[195] The Nenagh priests denounced Casey;[196] their pastor, Dr Patrick O'Mailley, had always resolutely opposed fenian candidates, even when other priests silently succumbed to public opinion.[197] Maurice Mooney refused support to a nationalist deputation in Cahir and Thomas Hickey P.P. objected to the Mullinahone band playing for Casey, while the first political speech of John Murphy, his curate, regarded Gray's victory as 'the greatest triumph for half a century'.[198]

Such consistent clerical opposition to fenian candidates is a good indication of opinion among the electorate, mainly composed of tenant farmers. The pattern of election results shows just how closely the views of priests and electors coincided. But before attempting to interpret these, some distorting influences must be examined. The most important of these was intimidation, which included heckling of priests by pro-fenian audiences,[199] nocturnal visits to electors,[200] and physical assaults on priests leading their voters to the polls. The escorting of Liberal electors to the booths by the military in 1869 and 1870 was a remarkable sight,[201] because this honour was usually reserved for the Conservatives in Irish electioneering. But such protection was not very effective during some of the elections in question. A Mullinahone priest could only look on helplessly and furiously note in his diary the names of saboteurs of his hired cars.[202] Skirmishes en route to the booths and in their proximity were rife, with scant regard shown either for the person or the property of the priest.[203] James O'Connell C.C. Golden and his party were ambushed near Tipperary town and O'Connell was subjected to jeering and hooting, while William O'Keane C.C. Bansha was actually pursued by the crowd.[204] The priests seem to have fared worst in Thurles, where one resident magistrate could scarcely believe the attacks he witnessed.[205] A local newspaper admitted that priests near the courthouse, especially Patrick J. Morris P.P. Borrisoleigh, 'were the objects of special attack' by both men and women.[206] William Wall P.P. Clonoulty, his curate, James O'Carroll, and John Tuohy C.C. Drom were 'mobbed in the street and knocked down'.[207]

Such tactics although partly promoted by liberal quantities of whiskey, were also concrete and determined approval of the philosophy earlier propounded by the *Irish People* that the priests should not meddle in political matters, or otherwise bear the consequences of their interference. Furthermore, although intimidation was by no means rare in any election during the second half of the nineteenth century, a willingness to attack the priests was unusual, and pointed to a ruthlessness which voters themselves would hesitate to ignore. Contemporary reports made this very clear. One magistrate noted farmer unease when Rossa's candidature was first announced.[208] The *Irishman* truthfully wrote that it was to the men 'who have no votes that Ireland owes this victory';[209] the *Times* remarked that priestly influence 'avails little unless it happens to coincide with popular feeling'.[210] If fenian intimidation secured some votes, it also effectively silenced the priests, or forced them to adopt an ambivalent attitude, thus lessening their own influence with the voters.[211] Audience hostility forced Canon Richard Cahill to praise fenian prisoners as 'various good and patriotic men', who 'began to lose faith in parliamentary action'; he refused, however, to condone the rising.[212] Much greater ambivalence was wrung from Tipperary town priests in 1870, when, under the misapprehension that Kickham had won, Thomas F. Meagher[213] and Michael Croke 'went with the current as it flowed in Clanwilliam', and congratulated the people on their supposed victory.[214] As the truth emerged they quickly repented and issued an altar condemnation of the petition against the Liberal victor.[215]

We need not rely solely upon the existence of clerical ambivalence or upon contemporary comment for the effectiveness of intimidation. The pattern of election results are a better guide, although it is not possible to pinpoint precisely the degree of distortion caused by violence or threats. There are, however, some prominent signposts to this. There was a significant difference, for example, between the performance of the fenian candidates in the northern and southern sections of the county. In the extreme north, where fenianism was weak,[216] and priestly influence correspondingly strong, Heron reaped his greatest harvest. In 1869 he defeated Rossa by 609 votes to 34 in the Nenagh polling district, while in 1870 he gained 842 votes to Kickham's 104, getting his greatest number of votes in the Barony of Lower Ormond — 429 votes to 27.[217] This barony, which was furthest north, was untouched by Fenianism. In south Tipperary, on the other hand, the Barony of Clanwilliam, with Tipperary town as its voting centre, was the main bulwark of the fenian candidates. Some influence of intimidation was evident there in 1869, when only 500 out of a total electorate of 1463 voted, and of these 493 opted for Rossa.[218] The pattern was repeated in 1870, when Kickham got 560 votes to Heron's 21.[219] Rossa also won well in the low Clonmel poll,[220] but in the higher poll of 1870, due to more intense police protection, Kickham was defeated by 213 votes to 153. A precisely similar trend, for the same reason, was evident in Thurles, where Rossa won by 415 votes to 140, but Kickham's margin of 473 votes to 437 was considerably smaller. The breakdown for the Cashel centre is illuminating also. Only 274 out of 1,000 voted, and Rossa won by 10 votes;[221] it is not without some significance that all but two of Heron's votes came from the wealthy Barony of Middlethird, where the parishes of the influential dean and archdeacon of the Cashel archdiocese lay. Rossa secured his votes from the Barony of Slieveardagh, which included such parishes as Mullinahone, Ballingarry and Killenaule, all fenian strongholds. Kickham's record in Cashel was much better than Rossa's, with a poll of 376 to 171 votes. This was due to Kickham's popularity in his native parish of Mullinahone and those adjoining.

The extension of the franchise and the introduction of the secret ballot greatly reduced the impact of intimidation. The 1877 election, therefore, provides a more satisfactory picture of the strength of separatism among the electorate. The most noticeable result was the vastly increased Liberal vote, which may also reflect a greater confidence in constitutional procedure. A comparison between the 1857 and 1877 election results highlights this.[222] It is significant that Gray's poll exceeded that of Mitchel's 1875 figure in all but 4 of the 27 polling places, — Cahir, Cappawhite, Cloughjordan and Tipperary. Bearing in mind that the 1875 election was not contested, thus allowing a high margin of sympathy votes for Mitchel, it is also true that the margins were not greatly different in these 4 areas. Tipperary, the traditional bastion of fenianism, was the most significant with 591 votes to 472. This surely underlines the influence of intimidation, which reduced the Liberal vote to such puny proportions there in the earlier elections. On the other hand, Gray's margin was not notably greater than Mitchel's in some of the other polling districts.

While any attempt by the historian to use election results as a gauge of republican feeling among the electorate must obviously take account of considerable distortion due to intimidation, there were other relevant influences; for example, the stature of Rossa, Kickham and Mitchel earned some personal votes, which were not necessarily an approval of their politics. Casey's involvement on behalf of the Buckley tenants in Mitchelstown no doubt earned him some votes, too.[223] Rossa's slender victory may be seen as a manifestation of electoral sympathy with amnesty, and as a protest at the government's refusal to release the prisoners. It is also a fact that his late entry into the arena caught his opponents, lay and clerical, by complete surprise; even the sub-sheriff believed that it was only an election trick to secure support for Gill.[224] The resident magistrate saw it as 'mere mockery' to put Heron to expense,[225] an opinion shared even by the pro-fenian priest, Patrick Lavelle, who had secured a promise from Heron to pay £500 to the prisoners fund if Rossa withdrew.[226] Under the circumstances the priests proved unequal to the 'herculean task'[227] of canvassing suddenly thrust upon them. It can be argued, of course, that the fenians had as little time to prepare, but their energy and ruthlessness were decisive. In the light of such factors the importance of the 1869 election should not be overemphasised as an indication of electoral sympathy with fenian philosophy. It might be borne in mind as well that Rossa's poll was not significantly greater than Gill's 1865 total, and represented only 11.8% of the electorate. It should also be viewed in the light of Kickham's defeat in 1870. The very considerable vote for Mitchel in 1875 cannot be regarded as a vote for separatism either, and must ultimately be balanced against the 1877 election, which saw a huge swing of 41% towards the Home Rule candidate.[228]

But, allowing for distortion in the voting pattern, it is evident and logical that some portion of the Tipperary electorate consistently supported Irish republican ideology. The statistics suggest that it stood at about 1,000 votes, and may have advanced a few per cent by 1877, altogether insufficient to sway the priests. Nevertheless, some did react to the evident electoral sympathy for Mitchel in 1875.[229] The Lorrha priests spoke on his behalf, and favourable speeches were made by the usually hostile Maurice Mooney and Philip Fitzgerald.[230] Still, the reaction of most priests to the swing was basically negative. They may have pretended sympathy, but they abstained from active interference, and neither canvassed for Mitchel nor attended his victory celebrations, which were mainly promoted by the urban labouring and artisan classes.[231] Their real attitude was one of caution, and when by 1877 electoral support for constitutional politics was strong, they responded with enthusiasm.

If the elections are important as a guide to republican opinion among the electorate, and the priest' response to this, they are also an essential framework for studying the amnesty movement and its impact on public opinion. Historians give amnesty undue importance mainly because they tend to examine it in isolation, and they also mistakenly regard the priests' involvement in it as a sign of clerical rapprochement with fenianism. Looking at it from a negative angle, seventy per cent of the Tipperary priests remained aloof from meetings held in Thurles, Emly, Clonmel, Nenagh, Cashel, Barnane, Tipperary and Newport.[232] There is no evidence, for example, that the Thurles priests attended the meeting there, where the more educated laymen, especially fenian town commissioners, were the chief organisers. Only two priests were present in Newport, where fenianism also flourished, and only two attended the Clonmel gathering. Neither were all of these priests who stayed away simply neutral. The Drom clergy tried to dissuade their parishoners from attending at Barnane, one of the areas where the rising flared in 1867.[233] The Bansha priests were not friendly towards the Tipperary town meeting, although a parish contingent went there,[234] and the resident magistrate had the 'greatest confidence' in the priests of the Tipperary district, who 'with one or two exceptions . . . . were thoroughly loyal'.[235]

Nevertheless, the minority of 36 Tipperary priests, who were present at the meetings, is too large to ignore. Interestingly, curates and priests under 50 years old accounted for 72% and 74% respectively of this minority, a sharp contrast to the anti-fenian National Association, where the parish priests formed 60% of clerical membership, and 53% of those involved were over 50. This points to the reluctance of the older priests to display sympathy on any level towards the fenians. But, it does not prove sympathy on the part of younger clergy with republicanism. Neither is there any doubt that some priests attended mainly as watchdogs to ensure that meetings conformed to amnesty regulations, and did not become republican platforms; for example, James Ryan P.P. Nenagh tried to prevent the voluble Peter Gill from speaking at the Nenagh meeting. However, clerical presence on the platform seemed to imply some form of sympathy with fenianism and savoured, therefore, of ambivalence. The action of James O'Connell C.C. in leading a green-sashed contingent from Golden to Tipperary Town was in marked contrast with an ambush made on him some weeks later when leading a party of Liberal voters to the polls.[236] Again, considering his earlier private hostility to fenianism,[237] the act of Thomas Francis Meagher in chairing the Tipperary meeting was a little strange. Unlike some bishops, Dr Leahy was forced to adopt a certain degree of ambivalence by allowing the Templemore priests to finish Mass early to facilitate the Barnane meeting.[238] Some of the clergy who spoke at that meeting were also obviously sensitive to the views of their fenian audience, and carefully blended condemnation of revolution and expressions of faith in constitutional agitation with sympathy for the prisoners. But hostile murmurs from the Barnane audience indicated that they were not enamoured by the paradoxical reference of Maurice Power C.C. to the 'afflicted' but 'unwise' fenians. Dean William Quirke's wide-ranging Cashel speech is one of the clearest examples of clerical amnesty rhetoric. He coupled his ambivalent, semi-biblical theory that 'the blood of Irish patriots will be the prolific seed of Irish disaffection', with the conclusion that Government clemency would convert the Irish people into the 'bulwark' of the Crown, a view shared by George Corbett P.P. Kilbarron. While Quirke admitted his efforts in 1867, 'in public and in private', to dissuade the rebels, he also vouched for the characters of local fenians.

Their personal acquaintance with republican parishioners made priests very much aware of family problems arising from imprisonments; this is an important factor in explaining apparent clerical sympathy. Even those priests most hostile to fenianism stressed this humanitarian aspect long before the amnesty movement. The best evidence of clerical concern for fenians' families is preserved in the Dublin Castle files.[239] Of these the Habeas Corpus Suspension Act records are the most informative, and contain numerous memorials signed by priests opposed to separatism.[240] Even Dr Leahy's name is among these.[241] Theobold Mathew C.C. Tipperary, by no means a political priest, impressed a magistrate with his plea on behalf of a fenian involved in the Ballyhurst rising. The magistrate, in supporting the plea, advised the under-secretary that the 'Government, the country and the wretched insurgents themselves owe much to this young clergyman'.[242] This clearly showed the important distinction made by the priests between sympathy for the man and for his politics. Finally, non-Tipperary priests had a further non-political argument against imprisonments, viz. the creation of an immediate labour shortage;[243] this was not discussed by Tipperary priests, although the problem seems to have arisen, but only in a very localised way. A police report of March 1867 mentioned that Kilcommon farmers were behind in their work because of the arrest of labourers.[244]

While their vocation dictated that the priests should emphasise the humanitarian and even the temporal welfare of their flocks, they did not neglect the political plank of the amnesty platform either, and their attitude in this displayed varying degrees of ambiguity. Such priests as Richard Rafter P.P. Emly and Andrew Walsh C.C. Clonmel foreshadowed modern thought when they looked on the fenians as political prisoners, and objected to their incarceration with criminals, arguing that the action of the fenians in 1867 was not criminal but patriotic and self-sacrificing.[245] Daniel Ryan's distinction between crime and illegality was an over-fine ambiguity. He contended that the fenians were guilty only of a special type of illegality.[246] Even Dean Quirke took a similar approach in his Cashel speech, although he did not deny that some punishment was merited. The altar speech of John Hackett in Lisvernane was glaringly ambivalent.[247] He upheld the duty of Irishmen to fight for their country, and felt that American aid would have ensured a different result. Defending clerical abstention on the basis that the rising lacked hope of success, Hackett advised that the time was fast approaching for another effort. Yet, he fundamentally changed what was a republican speech by ending with a profession of faith in Gladstone. Gerald Barry was, as might be expected, less ambivalent. Reflecting fenian thought, he held that amnesty was of greater importance than all other issues, including that of the land;[248] but William J. McKeogh, with his usual dexterity, combined both by threatening England with the wrath of 14,000,000 Irishmen on the Canadian borders, unless the land question was settled satisfactorily.[249]

Clerical ambivalence was also evident in their rationalising about the rising. Both McKeogh and John McGrath C.C. depicted the fenians as

being forced into rebellion by emigration and extermination.[250]
William Quirke explained the rising as disillusionment with the failure
of constitutional agitation to secure reform, a clear misjudgement of
the basic temper of Irish republicanism, which was not over-concerned
with issues peripheral to the central aim of separation. Nevertheless,
by treating fenianism as a symptom of agrarian discontent, the priests
were shrewdly using amnesty fervour as a stick with which to beat the
government, while at the same time their anglophobic sentiments
were a sop to republican feeling. Even the strongly anti-fenian cleric,
James Ryan of Nenagh, used this device.[251] While careful to emphasise
that a brighter dawn was looming, he was prepared to state that the
rising had demonstrated to the government the impolicy of 'one-sided
legislation', which required a 'garrison of 30,000 to enforce it'. Such
statements provoked an English newspaper to remark that clerical
conservatism was not English but ecclesiastical.[252] Partly true indeed,
but it would have been more accurate to have viewed it as a middle-
class tenant farming conservatism as well. That the farmers were influenced by amnesty fever is beyond doubt, and the priests responded
accordingly. There was a parallel ambivalence in the outlook of both,
which did not escape the notice of Patrick Kennedy C.C. Cashel.[253]
Just as men of substance as well as priests signed memorials for the
release of prisoners, the statements of lay amnesty speakers were
as cautious as those of the clergy,[254] if not more so.

In the final analysis, clerical involvement in the amnesty movement is not too surprising. It had after all a humanitarian base, was
prompted by constitutional members of parliament led by Butt, and
the dismal failure of 1867 had removed the threat of a further uprising, as priests like John Scanlan P.P. Toomevara well recognised.[255]
The view of one writer that priestly involvement in amnesty was the
most 'extraordinary' feature of fenianism is too strong.[256] The importance of the amnesty movement itself has also been somewhat
overestimated; for example the view that sympathy with fenian prisoners kept republicanism alive[257] is only true to a limited extent. This
is not to deny the immediate but temporary public fervour aroused by
the movement. Comparatively speaking the execution of the Manchester
'Martyrs' is of greater significance since it was commemorated annually,
and the spirit of republicanism loudly and publicly proclaimed. Because
public demonstrations were forbidden immediately following the
executions, it is difficult to gauge clerical reaction at that time in
Tipperary. The hostile[258] Martin Cleary, administrator in Nenagh,
was totally opposed to a proposed demonstration there.[259] Neither
did any of the Nenagh clergy offer Mass for them, although the
following year, when Cleary had left the parish, Roderick Kennedy
C.C. did.[260] Nevertheless, evidence for other counties suggests that
the priests were influenced by, and shared, the angry public reaction

to the executions. An t-Athair Peadar Ó Laoghaire describes the feelings of the clergy at an ecclesiastical chapter in Kanturk as 'amazed and angry'.[261]

But, this anger was shortlived, and, as the post-rising elections show, did not convert the priests or the middle-class laity to republicanism. It took a severe economic downturn in the late '70s to give public opinion a massive jolt. Accompanying coercion generated intense hostility against England. Such hostility might have been a fertile breeding ground for tenant republicanism, although a simultaneous policy of land reform toned it down considerably, and fenianism especially in the early '80s was weak and disorganised in Tipperary.[262] Some priests, in line with public outlook, reacted strongly to coercion, openly ridiculing English law in Ireland, denouncing magistrates, pouring scorn on the police and mocking the military.[263] John R. Crowe C.C. Cappawhite said that he had 'no more respect for the law of England than I have for the dirt off my shoe',[264] and James Cantwell insultingly labelled soldiers as 'a class of men that were fed on porter and herrings'.[265] There were also priests who reacted partly in nationalistic terms.[266] Thomas Jones C.C. Kilcommon compared stringent law to the 'state persecution' of Tone, Fitzgerald, Smith O'Brien and the constitutional O'Connell.[267] A controversy between Arthur Ryan, St Patrick's College, Thurles, and an English M.P., Edwin de Lisle, arose from the latter's call for the suspension of the Habeas Corpus Act.[268] Ryan refuted de Lisle's quotation from Papal encyclicals that tyrannical rulers should be endured with patience. He retorted that papal references did not exempt tyrants from temporal penalties, and he rejected O'Connell's maxim that liberty was not worth the shedding of blood. Rather academically Ryan argued that bishops and priests blessed any rebellion against tyranny, provided that the rebellion had a hope of success. He concluded that the priests did not consider acquiescence to the English government a moral obligation, but rather a 'dire necessity'. While mirroring a genuine anger with coercion, Ryan's view was not too far removed from that of his ambivalent archbishop, who declared in his 'political confession' that he was a separatist in the abstract but not in practice.[269] This consistent ambivalence of the priests was also evident in the reference of John Shelley to his own 'rebellious spirit' towards England, which, he hastened to add, was not practicable to impart to his flocks.[270] Such a view was not confined to Tipperary priests alone.[271] Apart from clerical and lay anger at coercion, nationalistic rhetoric fulfilled the old role of threatening the Government and hopefully hastening agrarian reform. The assertion of James Cantwell to a Dublin audience that Tipperary would 'take the field in the morning' if the means were there, was certainly aimed in that direction.[272] For precisely this reason, too, Thomas Jones C.C. Kilcommon, while maintaining that physical force was not desirable, warned that it might be used if constitutional agitation failed to achieve reform.[273]

This intriguing stand was also a measure of the priests' political agility when faced with the heterogeneous political composition of the Land League. The clergy were keenly aware that its platform held both republicans and those who believed in constitutional agitation only. The nucleus of the new organisation was a fenian one; its founder, Michael Davitt, was a member of the I.R.B. supreme council, although by then his policy was separation by constitutional means. Michael Boyton, the main organiser of the league in Tipperary, was also a 1867 fenian. The dynamic secretary of the Slievenamon Land League, Michael Cusack, had fled to America after the rising and learned how to manufacture explosives at the O'Donovan Rossa school in Greenpoint, near New York.[274] Such slogans as 'remember Mitchel' were popular embellishments on Land League flags, and symbolised its fenian content at local level. But even if some priests in these circumstances were prepared to play the republican tune on the league's platform none would dance to it. Indeed, the great majority were suspicious of the fenian section, and any nationalistic remarks must be seen against their overwhelming emphasis on constitutional agitation and their channelling of anglophobia into the safer demands for Home Rule.[275] Certain clerics achieved a nice blend of the constitutional and the extreme by stressing that the league had achieved what Emmet and Tone had dreamed of.[276] James Ryan and Nicholas Rafferty argued that the platform of the less radical National League was sufficiently broad to cater for moderate and 'advanced' politicians; but Rafferty stressed that their aim was not revolution or separation.[277] Others were privately less ambivalent. James J. Ryan, St Patrick's College, obviously concerned about the possibility of a fenian hold over it, inserted the pertinent question in his theology textbook: 'Is the Land League connected with the fenians'. The eccentric pastor of Cahir, Maurice Mooney, in the safety of private correspondence to Tobias Kirby, complained in terms suitable for Rome's ear that 'the ruinous element of the Carbonari secret society, fenianism, is creeping among us'.[278] Michael Bugler P.P. Birr was one of the few Tipperary priests to publicly voice his opposition to fenian involvement in the Land League. He refused to chair the first Birr meeting unless Matthew Harris absented himself. Harris reluctantly deferred to his wishes.[279] Murmurs from a Templemore audience were less deferential when in 1880 the parish prist, Thomas O'Connor, reminded them that he was 'head of the Church' in Templemore, and quoted a long forgotten reference of Archbishop Slattery (probably in 1848), about those 'anxious to be looked upon as patriots' by drawing the poor into rebellion.[280] Other priests were careful to stress the purely agrarian role of the Land League; Michael Callanan P.P. Cappawhite questioned the benefit of nationality, if the people were not rooted in the soil,[281] an axiom which ran directly counter to Irish republican philosophy. Tipperary priests did not take the view of a Cork priest that the Land League had actually weakened the I.R.B. by depriving it of recruits.[282]

The anxiety of those priests who feared a nationalistic backlash from the league was relieved when its aggressive spirit was mainly channeled into agrarian reform, or at worst into local outrages. They had far greater reservations, however, about another organisation, the Gaelic Athletic Association, which had a weaker connection in those days with the farming community. This in itself allowed them a larger degree of freedom to criticise. The G.A.A. is of crucial importance in proving the constancy of clerical antipathy to revolution and separatism. They played little part in its inauguration, although the founders solicited their approval through a circular.[283] Both Dr Croke and the priests were patrons by invitation only. Four curates were patrons of the North Tipperary G.A.A., which included all the clubs in that part of the county.[284] There was little clerical involvement as executives although patrons were entitled to attend conventions as delegates.[285] In 1887 130 clubs reputedly existed in Tipperary,[286] but the extent of priestly participation at club level is difficult to trace.

The priests' objection to the G.A.A. did not spring from its sporting activities, but from its connections with the I.R.B. The association was rapidly becoming a fenian front,[287] which meant that for the first time since the '60s fenianism began to acquire an organised network. The nationalistic mottos on flags or the patriotic titles of clubs — the Lacken '67s or the Allen Larkin and O'Brien club — were the mildest indication of its fenian connection;[288] increasing I.R.B. control at the centre and at local level was the most significant.[289] It was ironic that the fenian executive of the G.A.A. actually proposed a policy of non-interference in politics, a tactic whose sole aim was to sever any connection the sporting organisation had with the National League.[290] The priests easily divined this motive, and were decidedly sensitive to extensive fenian infiltration of the association.[291] Clerical objections were unequivocal. Such priests as John Scanlan argued that Home Rule would be retarded if English public opinion saw the rising generation of Irishmen 'inculcated with ideas of separation' by an I.R.B.-controlled Gaelic Athletic Association.[292] Scanlan also said that the I.R.B. was trying to crush the National League through the G.A.A., a statement which clearly appealed to the farming community,[293] and which was not entirely inaccurate. John Cunningham put the priests' greatest fear — that the I.R.B. would take 'the youth of Ireland . . . out of the hands of the priesthood and mould them according to their own views'.[294] A Cloyne priest anticipated Cunningham's remarks and proceeded to condemn 'the insane and wicked programme' to free Ireland 'by means accursed by heaven and condemned by every honest

man'.[295] Both John Scanlan and this priest dwelt upon the old theme
of informers,[296] and in this they were certainly correct, because the
government had full details of I.R.B. involvement in the G.A.A. Canon
Keller, Youghal, had certain evidence of this, and warned Croke about
a directive from Dublin Castle, which welcomed fenian control both
as a means to weaken the National League and to crush the I.R.B.
quickly and effectively.[297]

Ire at the fenian connection did not at all signify a desire by the
priests to confine the G.A.A. entirely to sport. They were quite prepared to justify its role in politics provided such politics were constitutional. John Cunningham's argument that because nine-tenths of Irish
nationalists were National Leaguers, nine-tenths of the G.A.A. should
be too, sums up clerical outlook.[298] Dr Croke himself while not coun-
tenancing the exclusion of those who played foreign games, saw the
G.A.A. as a symbol of Irish culture and of a new Irish spirit, though
certainly not one of republicanism.[299] By 1887 clerical and fenian views
of the association were utterly polarised, and both sides were equally
determined to assert their control over it.[300] Inevitably an open and
serious confrontation took place. The national convention of 1887
in Thurles provided the necessary contact point.[301] The assembly
literally erupted when John Scanlan, leading a group of tough priests,[302]
objected to the chairmanship of the fenian organiser, Patrick Neville
Fitzgerald,[303] whose brief for the convention was to secure the election
of a completely fenian executive.[304] The priests were verbally abused
and physically jostled,[305] the usual result of direct confrontation with
the fenians. They departed in dudgeon from the convention, followed
by a third of the delegates, and Scanlan chaired several meetings culminating in a gathering at Hayes's Hotel.

Dr Croke felt that the priests' stand was ineffective,[306] and he was
correct insofar as the new executive was fenian, but the furore raised
forced an open split, and made the crisis public, bringing it to grass-
roots level. Subsequently the clergy, especially six North Tipperary
curates led by John Scanlan, spearheaded a vigorous anti-executive
campaign,[307] which was hardly answered by the fenians, who wished
to keep their infiltration as quiet as possible.[308] The priests' stand
also sparked off a chain reaction of club withdrawals from allegiance
to the executive.[309] This was probably also accelerated by the dis-
sociation of the influential Croke 'from that branch of the G.A.A.
which exercised such a sinister influence' at the convention.[310] Apart
from their efforts to isolate the executive, the clergy favoured positive
action by a proposal to establish a new association, which the Cloyne
priest suggested should be called the Gaelic National Athletic Association. The six Tipperary curates then proceeded to consolidate an anti-
I.R.B. front. They convened a meeting of all north Tipperary clubs in
Nenagh on November 10th 1887.[311] At least 20 priests attended this

convention, which repudiated allegiance to the executive, greeted the return of Maurice Davin to reconstruct the movement, and refused to keep it outside politics. Anti-fenian references by the priests at this meeting resulted in an exchange of letters between John Scanlan and the old fenian warrior, John O'Leary, who made the stock-accusation of felon-setting.[312] This priestly-dominated convention was quickly followed by one in south Tipperary, representing 21 clubs.[313] Curiously, the priests were absent from this, possibly reflecting the stronger fenian spirit of the south, although the meeting unreservedly condemned the previous attack on the priests in Thurles. It also repudiated the executive headed by the fenian, Edmond Bennet. In what John Scanlan called the last act of the comedy,[314] Bennet convened the controversial executive in Limerick Junction, County Tipperary, to refute clerical charges, and he accused the priests of trying to impose their will upon the majority,[315] a highly ironic statement considering fenian designs.

Despite the deep chasm that separated both sides, no new organisation as envisaged by the priests emerged. Instead, efforts were made to heal the rift, which in effect meant either a compromise or the surrender of one side. The likelihood of the priests compromising was virtually nil, and the negotiations conducted by Dr Croke resulted in the ousting of the fenians from control.[316] Croke's method of removing the fenian sting was decentralisation, a proposal which for some time hampered the negotiations.[317] The archbishop envisaged autonomous county management, disputes being referred to a central court or council of appeal. This was the centre-piece of five suggestions made by him, and eventually accepted by the reconstruction committee, which included Maurice Davin on the one hand, and R.J. Frewen, the Aherlow fenian, on the other.[318] The ensuing conciliation convention in Thurles, with probably a deliberately low clerical attendance, elected Davin as president; Bennet's nominees were withdrawn.[319] While Croke, in a letter which studiously avoided all reference to politics, expressed his pleasure at this 'very satisfactory result',[320] the convention barely papered over the cracks, and left the I.R.B. distinctly disgruntled. P.N. Fitzgerald, who had an altercation with James Clancy C.C., accused the convention of being rigged, and an editorial in the *Gael* chose Eugene Sheehy P.P. Bruree County Limerick, later elected to the Central Council, as its target. The fenian case had some merit, since of the two deputations from Limerick, the convention accepted that headed by Sheehy, who, however, pointed out that the meeting which chose the rival delegation had excluded clubs with priests involved. Far, therefore, from settling the debate the convention only whetted fenian determination to regain dominance. The police authorities accurately forecast I.R.B. plans to do just this,[321] and the 1889 convention, which was a less turbulent imitation of the 1887 one, saw those plans materialise.[322] Again, there was a secession, resulting in a rival

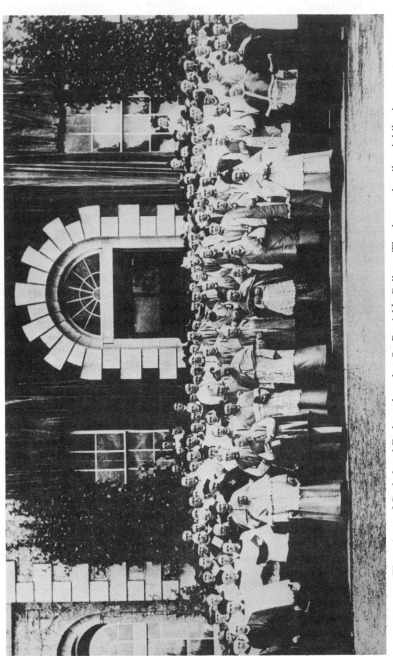

The priests of Cashel and Emly gathered at St. Patrick's College, Thurles on the silver jubilee in 1895 of Archbishop Croke. Beside Dr Croke are Archbishop Walsh of Dublin, Cardinal Logue of Armagh and Archbishop McEvilly of Tuam. Photo reproduced courtesy of Archbishop Thomas Morris.

meeting, this time presided over by Eugene Sheehy, who seems to have succeeded John Scanlan as the main clerical antagonist of the I.R.B. P.N. Fitzgerald once more succeeded in having a fenian executive elected. The bone of contention at this convention was apparently non-political, but the split that occurred was purely on political lines.

Because of the failure to heal the rift to their satisfaction, the priests continued to view the G.A.A. with a jaundiced eye. While drunkeness or neglect of Sunday duties due to sports were the ostensible reasons,[323] the political issue was the crucial one.[324] So stratified did divisions within the association become, and so involved were the clergy that the police categorised clubs as either under fenian control, clerical control, or neutral. An 1890 report showed 30 clubs in Tipperary, of which 14 were under clerical auspices with the fenians controlling half the remainder.[325] A further breakdown revealed that 10 clerical and 5 I.R.B. clubs were in north Tipperary, while in the more nationalistic south 4 were clerical and 3 Fenian. Altogether 895 club members were in the clerical section, while 656 were under fenian control. Priestly influence seems to have been stronger in Wexford with 29 clubs to 4 in their favour, but the startling statistic for Carlow showed 21 fenian clubs, none under priestly influence and 4 unattached, while 29 fenian clubs, no clerical and 1 unattached was the position in Laois. The Wicklow and Kilkenny fenians guided 10 out of 13, and 19 out of 30 respectively.

The priests' antipathy to the G.A.A. in 1890 received a further powerful stimulus with the Parnell crisis. The association became predominantly Parnellite,[326] partly in response to the leader's call to the 'hillside men'. Some of the Parnell leadership committees were controlled by the I.R.B.[327] It was typical of the man that he made such an appeal to the very people he had weakened by building up an effective popular constitutional agitation. The irony of the situation did not escape the priests. David Humphreys saw it as a blatant contradiction.[328] It is true, of course, and one police report hinted as much, that some priests may have been simply using the fenian bogey to further discredit Parnell;[329] this was the first reference made by Humphreys, for example, to the I.R.B. Nevertheless, many priests undoubtedly were 'very fully alive to the possibility of the I.R.B. becoming formidable in the future', and becoming Parnell's lever.[330] Their anxiety about secret societies, whether political or agrarian, certainly intensified at this time, and the altars once more rang with warnings.[331] Dr Patrick Delaney P.P. Ballyporeen 'strenuously denounced' them 'Sunday after Sunday' and compiled a list of 217 people, allegedly sworn in, which he forwarded to a neighbouring parish priest.[332] Apart from serious warnings, the priests resorted to the old tactic of ridicule and portrayed contemporary fenians as 'featherbed hillside men'.[333] This was partly an extension of their anti-Parnellite tactics. It is clear, too, that the crisis produced yet another acrimonious point of contact between priests and fenians, in which weapons as well as words were used. The most severe violence took place in Thurles,[334] which was an area of strong fenian sympathies.[335]

If the Parnellite crisis heightened clerical dislike of fenianism and the Gaelic Athletic Association, it also drew their attention, though on a far more limited scale, towards what in some areas was another I.R.B. front, the Young Ireland Society.[336] This was confined to a few towns in Tipperary, such as Thurles, Carrick-on-Suir and Newport.[337] The Carrick branch was the only one which was anti-fenian and anti-Parnell. The Newport branch, known as the Charles J. Kickham branch, was organised by P.J. Hoctor, showing the interconnection between the I.R.B., G.A.A. and Young Ireland Society, it was originally known as the Newport Literary Institute. Priestly sensitivity to such young men's literary clubs was not new, and always increased when republicanism reared its head, especially in the 1860s; the establishment of the Nenagh Roman Catholic Young Men's Society in 1863 resulted in a controversy between Martin Cleary Adm. and a local fenian named Finnerty, whose aim was the conversion of the Society into a Nationalist club.[338] Finnerty proceeded to enrol young men who attacked the priests' lack of sympathy with fenianism. A similar but more publicised row occurred in Tralee in 1864 when the priests raised strong objections to a normally harmless toast at a soirée.[339]

When fenianism was dormant the priests did not object to such societies, and were generally their spiritual directors, as in the Tralee case. Likewise, some priests occasionally attended the Dublin meetings of the Young Ireland Society,[340] which, be it said, had non-separatist members such as John Dillon, Timothy Harrington, and William O'Brien, all followers of Parnell, whatever the sympathies of their youth had been. Priests did not raise any objections to the nationalistic themes discussed at some of the gatherings; lectures were given on such diverse subjects as the Irish harp and Wolfe Tone; the superiority of nationalism over all other concerns was also a theme.[341] James Cantwell seems to have had good relations with the Thurles Society, and welcomed a lecture by Michael Davitt there.[342] Richard J. Casey C.C., an ex-Tipperary priest, actually presided at meetings in Waterford, and he strongly denied that they were in the least objectionable.[343] Nevertheless, the Parnellite crisis quickly revealed the fenian side of the Society, whose branches generally sided with the leader.[344] A few incidents are on record for Tipperary. A member of the Newport society stormed out of the chapel when Edmund O'Keane denounced it off the altar,[345] and the Nenagh clergy apparently tried to 'smash' the Young Men's Institute, which was something akin to the Society.[346]

It must now be clear that despite bouts of ambivalence or nationalistic rhetoric, the priests at all stages strongly eschewed current Irish republicanism. Their priestly vocation imbued them with an essentially passive outlook, which, however, did not prevent them uttering anti-Government sentiments, especially during the 1880s. This was as far as they were prepared to go. But they were never really tested in a situation where all classes in the community became convinced and active separatists. Their middle-class outlook did not relish the prospect of an upheaval in society by revolution. In this they were reflecting the attitude of their lay kinsfolk, whose main concern was economic and agricultural prosperity. The farmers were quite content with the political *status quo* as long as their rising expectations were being satisfied, and when these expectations became frustrated, it was the landlords rather than the Government who became the immediate target. The tenants were the most realistic of people, and if they were sufficiently shrewd to see that peasant proprietary was not the panacea for all ills, and was attractive only at the right price, they were equally capable of realising that an Irish republic would not improve their lot either. Consequently, they were never really imbued with a strong nationalistic sense. They were eventually converted to Home Rule by strong charismatic leaders, but Home Rule by constitutional means did not threaten a disruption of society. So, apart from the basic passivity of their theology, it was bred in the priests to dislike revolution.

O'Donovan Rossa, M.P. for Tipperary (*Irishman*, 4.12.1869).

Chapter Seven

THE PRIEST AND THE IRISH MEMBERS OF PARLIAMENT
1850-1876

"Such members of the Brigade as have remained true to their colours are called upon just now to vindicate their honour and their honesty by openly disavowing any participation in the misdeeds of others". Father William Cahill, *Tablet* 5 Feb. 1853.

Having decisively rejected an appeal to arms for securing either reform or independence, the priests placed their faith in the parliamentary system buttressed by local constitutional agitation. But, from the days of O'Connell until the rise of Parnell in 1877 they were not unanimous about the precise *modus operandi* Irish members should use in Westminster. In this, however, they only mirrored the conflicting opinions of the day, since divisions in middle-class political philosophy were invariably reflected in clerical ranks. Because the term Irish Catholic Tory was almost a contradiction, the root of the disunity lay in the choice between co-operation of the Irish members with the British Liberal Party, if not integration into that party, or a policy of some type of opposition in the House, which presupposed the existence of an Irish party, however loosely bound. Such a policy was a live but generally controversial issue from the foundation of the Tenant League in 1850 to the collapse of the Tipperary Independent Club in 1859; lip-service was paid to it in the mid-1860s, but it was then submerged in the atmosphere of co-operation with the Liberals, only to re-appear with the formation of the Home Rule Party in 1874, and very gradually gather strength under the obstructionists.

The policy of an Irish party pursuing a course of independent opposition was born from the uneasy liaison of the Tenant League and the Catholic Defence Association in 1851.[1] Appropriately this marriage was celebrated at local level by a Cashel banquet honouring the Tipperary M.P.s where such C.D.A. priests as Michael Burke and Archdeacon Michael Laffan mingled with leaguers like John O'Dwyer, William Mullally and William Cahill.[2] Quite deliberately Nicholas V. Maher, one of Tipperary's members, had at first been omitted from the invitation list because of frequent absences from parliament,[3] an incident which underlined a new emphasis upon the need for Irish M.P.s who took their work more seriously. By that stage both sides had reached the conclusion that an independent Irish party was the most logical and effective way to achieve their respective aims. Early in 1852 the parliamentary committee of the association decided to open an account in the Hibernian Bank to provide funds to help return members supporting its principles.[4] From early in 1850 priests concerned with the land question were conscious of the desirability of such a party, and John Moloney, the outspoken pastor of Kilcommon, roundly castigated the Tipperary M.Ps. as 'ravens croaking for place and pension', who were afraid to attend land meetings.[5] Thomas Croke's first letter to Kenyon some months prior to the alliance speculated on a party financed by the league. As a Young Irelander Croke was well aware of earlier failures to consolidate such a party,[6] and was therefore sceptical not only of the league's ability to pay members, but of finding what he called 'incorruptible and hardworking' candidates. Prophetically he was not sanguine about the durability of a proposed party, or its amenability to the discipline of a leader, if such an individual could be found. It was, however, the religious issue, the Ecclesiastical Titles Bill, not the agrarian, which gave most impetus to the policy; hence in the early 1850s it became identified more with the religious than the agrarian, although this was to change.

The Ecclesiastical Titles Bill automatically drew the fire of a number of Irish M.P.s who became known as the Papal Brigade or Pope's Brass Band. On a non-parliamentary level the Catholic Defence Association was established with the avowed object of opposition to the measure, especially by supporting parliamentary candidates who favoured such strong opposition.[7] The local political implications are important here, therefore, since the act provoked a spontaneous repugnance against its authors in the Russell Ministry. This was well illustrated by the call of Dr Burke on Richard Lalor Shiel to resign as Tuscan Ambassador under that Ministry.[8] Both Burke and his fellow pastor, John Baldwin, urged a course of opposition, and threatened Tipperary M.P.s with dismissal, unless they pursued this policy.[9] But it is significant that Burke advocated opposition to Russell's ministry only — and with the important addendum — 'until at all events they will atone for the late insult to Irish and English Catholics'. Representing the tradition of co-operation with the Liberals, he was consistent in his outlook and later accused the leaguers of being divided on the question themselves.[10] Obviously the problem of definition was crucial, because from 1852 the league's official policy, never rescinded, was total opposition to all governments that refused to make Sharman Crawford's measure a cabinet question. But, because the government never did this, a serious divergence of opinion appeared between

C.D.A. and Tenant League, whose individual aims were totally different anyway, even if their methods briefly coincided. The split was faithfully reflected in clerical ranks.

The heat generated by the 1852 general election momentarily obscured this. Both league and association priests organised the campaign in apparent harmony, although their energies were mainly concentrated against the traditional enemy, the Tories. Ironically, this partly diverted their fire away from the authors of the Ecclesiastical Titles Bill, but not from the religious issue itself. Since, however, both Whigs and Tories supported the bill, the way seemed clear for a policy of opposition to any government, whatever its brand of politics. Thus, the clergy of the Emly portion of the archdiocese met, and issued a resolution of hostility to any County Limerick M.P., who refused to pledge 'in express and unequivocal terms' opposition to any government that refused to deal with the religious and land issues.[11] It seems, however, that the priests of the adjoining Limerick diocese were not as enthusiastic about the policy as their Tipperary brethren.[12]

In Tipperary county and Clonmel and Cashel boroughs the four so-called opposition candidates were successful, and the political atmosphere was considerably defused by the defeat of the Tories. Of greater consequence, the Ecclesiastical Titles Bill was seen as a dead letter, and so the main driving force of independent opposition at parliamentary level was gone. James Sadleir, brother of John, (one of the leading parliamentary opponents of the bill), replaced Nicholas V. Maher, who retired in chagrin, unable or unwilling to meet an apparently early call for election expenses. It is possible, and John O'Dwyer believed so, that pressure from the Tipperary Joint Stock Bank, owned by the Sadleirs, forced Maher to retire.[13] The change of candidates had been agreed at a pre-election meeting in Thurles attended by 24 priests.[14] Not all league priests were happy about Sadleir's election, despite his brother's leading role in Parliament. They were suspicious of the sincerity of his opposition pledge, again underlining the mutual suspicion between the league and the association. John O'Dwyer's parish priest, Patrick Hickey, proposed John Ball, nicknamed 'Racket Ball' because of his propensity to change sides, in Sadleir's stead, but Archdeacon Laffan countered by successfully proposing James. One angry correspondent claimed that the voice of the priests, presumably the leaguers, was ignored at the selection meeting.[15]

The quick defection of John Sadleir and two of his colleagues, Keogh and Flaherty, by taking office in the new ministry, confirmed the suspicions of the league priests, and possibly embarrassed some C.D.A. members. Nevertheless, not all were shocked, and the episode serves to clarify the divergence of opinion which had all along existed. Neither Cecil Lawless, Member for Clonmel, who had proposed the continuance of independent opposition at a post-election land conference in Dublin,[16] nor the local Liberal newspaper were unduly worried.[17] Representing one side of current opinion they sincerely felt that the Aberdeen ministry would 'govern in a spirit of impartiality', and argued that it was premature to judge the Sadleirites until the Government's policy was fully known. This was by no means unreasonable. As well as this there were priests, especially O'Connellite ones like John Mackey P.P. Clonoulty, who were conscious that some of Aberdeen's followers had aided the cause of catholic emancipation in earlier days.[18] All this showed the very tenuous nature of support for an independent opposition party among an influential sector of the priesthood and the electorate. Furthermore, not all league priests were as hard-line as they had seemed prior to the election. Thomas Meagher, one of the signatories of the Emly resolutions, did not agree that the league should send deputations to oppose Keogh, Flaherty and Sadleir in the by-elections following the defection.[19] He feared such a course might split the liberal vote and allow a conservative to slip in, which is what did happen. But he also opposed what he prophetically called obstruction in Parliament, and suggested that the correct definition of the independent opposition pledge was that 'tenant right members were to support every good measure brought forward by any government, and in addition urge on them the adoption of Sharman Crawford's Bill, but at the same time not refusing an instalment, as that might come within the character of a good measure'. Accordingly, he considered that William Keogh's election pledge was a rash one, and he denied that the defectors had violated any pledges, a view not entirely shared by his archbishop. Like Cecil Lawless, Meagher argued that the government would pursue a fair policy towards Ireland, and he underlined the usefulness of a government position to influence such land legislation as Napier's bill.

Despite a softening among some leaguers, a small nucleus of clerics responded sharply to the defection. William Cahill was, however, cautious about concentrated clerical action fearing that it might be interpreted as priestly dictation, but he urged that the defectors be immediately branded as traitors lest the Brigade become demoralised and collapse.[20] This view was shared by other priests.[21] Cahill, too, advised a deputation to Carlow, Athlone and Galway to oppose the defectors in the by-elections. The Council of the league, having circularised its members, met, and after some debate, involving Tipperary priests, decided on this course.[22] In fact the motion was proposed by Martin Laffan P.P. Killenaule, who as a leaguer was more acutely embarrassed because at the nomination of James he had introduced John as 'the soul, the nucleus' of the Irish Brigade.[23]

It soon became clear that the hard line taken by such league priests continued to command solid support among another section of the electorate, even though the potent, emotive C.D.A. base had withered with the collapse of the religious issue. The enthusiasm for the policy generated during the 1852 election outlived its religious basis. After all not only had the electors been conditioned by numerous persuasive speeches, but many of them had braved very real landlord threats, and returned independent Members 'on the faith of the priests' sponsorship', as one 'honest elector of Tipperary' pointed out.[24] His letter, which received widespread publicity in the national as well as local newspapers, revealed current rumours that some Tipperary priests 'were in a hold at the bank', or were trying to secure places for their friends. It gives a valuable insight into the tenor of feeling in parts of the county, which the priests could not ignore. By that stage, too, it became clear that the government had no intention of making Crawford's proposals a cabinet question, and so removed one strong excuse against clerical action. 60 priests of the archdiocese, meeting in Thurles on 5 April 1853 under the chairmanship of the leaguer Thomas Mullaney P.P. Drom, issued resolutions demanding an explanation from the two county members of their adherence to the government, or how their sitting on the ministerial side of the House was consistent with their pledges.[25] These priests were the first to use the title Independent Opposition Party. The signatories represented 40% of the total priesthood of the county, and a majority of the Cashel clergy. Not all of these, of course, were convinced oppositionists; some were yielding to public opinion or were disgusted at the breaking of pledges. A brief look at the 26 Cashel priests who did not sign gives some indication of clerical dislike for the policy. Some of these refused to sign simply because they never showed any interest in politics, but others certainly refused on principle. These included the leaguers, Thomas Meagher and Edward Collins C.C. Bansha. The remainder were predictable absentees, being ex-C.D.A. clerics. The split also reflected some differences of opinion between parish priests and their curates; this was evident in Clonoulty and Templemore where the curates signed but the parish priests did not. Neither the Waterford nor Killaloe sections pronounced on the matter, although Bishop Vaughan and his Clare clergy issued similar resolutions on the same day.[26] One of these, Jeremiah Vaughan P.P. Ruan, wrote a separate letter voicing his suspicions that the Clare Members 'would return to the vomit'.[27] He deplored the fact that 'not having horses we should plough with asses'. This was representative of other non-Tipperary views.[28]

The replies of Sadleir and his cousin Scully denied actual adherence to the government, argued that it should be given a fair trial, and bluntly refused to sit on the Conservative side of the House.[29] Interestingly, these M.P.s received the support of Sharman Crawford himself, who agreed with all the principles in Scully's letter.[30] Crawford, too, touched a sensitive nerve, anticipated by William Cahill, when he accused the clergy of assuming 'political authority as a separate body', although he ignored, deliberately or otherwise, their meeting as a response to electoral opinion. His letter drew two long broadsides, totalling 5,000 words, from Dean James McDonnell, writing under the impressive pseudonym, A.G. Thornside D.D. Rockview.[31] The dean neatly turned the charge of clerical dictation by accusing Crawford of double standards in approving of clerical influence when employed against landlords, but condemning its use against the M.P.s; he concluded: 'We have the power to endorse the bond, but no right to enquire after the absconding debtor.' On the more central issue, McDonnell denied that the pledge was unconstitutional, having been examined by some of Ireland's leading lawyers. He further accused Crawford of distorting the original pledge of general opposition to one of general support, and, facing one point of controversy in many people's minds, he argued that general opposition conceded freedom of conscience on particular issues. The two men were at cross purposes, since Crawford was almost certainly referring to the 1852 policy of the league, which centred around his own bill. But McDonnell's viewpoint did not imply factious opposition, and clearly shows the perceptible and realistic retreat of leaguers from this more uncompromising 1852 pledge. McDonnell's curate, the fiery John Ryan, who was to be the first Tipperary priest to publicly applaud Parnell's policy of obstruction,[32] certainly did not agree with his superior, and some months later publicly defended Crawford against Frederick Lucas,[33] a controversy which is another illustration of the divisive effect of the pledge upon the league itself.

Nevertheless, the hard core leaguers such as Lucas, Duffy and Gray, supported by the small group of convinced Independent Opposition priests, continued to press the policy, which introduced a distinctly bitter tone into electioneering politics for the remainder of the '50s. This applied equally to the boroughs as to the county. Some league priests deeply distrusted Cecil Lawless, who had been nicknamed 'Artful Cecil' by the Young Irelanders in the 1840s. John O'Dwyer hoped that the borough of Clonmel would expel him,[34] a wish which materialised when Lawless died within a month. The Clonmel by-election of 1853 immediately attracted the attention of the leaguers, who saw it as a crucial one for the future of their policy. Their feeling was that a victory in the Sadleirs' native county would be of particular value, hopefully providing a psychological boost for convinced oppo-sitionists, and giving wavering ones food for thought. Much to Dr Burke's chagrin, Lucas, Gray, Duffy and Moore descended on Clonmel, and vainly tried to force the pledge on the candidate John O'Connell, the Liberator's son.[35] The prominent league priests, Thomas O'Shea and William Mullally, accompanied them, but in view of Burke's anta-gonism kept a relatively low profile. John Baldwin P.P. St Marys Clonmel and his curate, Patrick Meany, were sympathetic to the depu-tation's cause, but could not compete with the influence of Burke who was aided by the formidable Archdeacon Laffan and his curates, James Hogan and Joseph Organ. Still, league pressure, in the form of a threat to put forward either John Gray or The O'Donoghue, O'Connell's relative, secured a rather pale pledge from the reluctant candidate, which was witnessed in writing by Baldwin and Meany: 'I declare on the understanding that I am not called upon to pledge myself to what is known as the policy of 1851, I am ready to act with any and every party offering independent opposition to bad measures from any government'.[36] Procured under duress, this lukewarm promise only sharpened O'Connell's hostility to the Independent Opposition Party, and barely concealed the decisive failure of the deputation to impose the policy upon the unreceptive borough.

It was unfortunate for the leaguers that Clonmel happened to be the constituency falling vacant. The dice was heavily loaded against them from the start. Considering his avowed hostility to the policy, Dr Burke's undoubted influence was a major factor. But, the longstanding instinctive hostility of John O'Connell both to the league, which he had earlier seen as a threat to the Repeal Association,[37] and to its Young Ireland composition,[38] made friction inevitable. O'Connell, always quick to court the clergy,[39] had already quarrelled with Gray and then with Lucas at the 1851 religious meeting in Dublin.[40] Provoked by Lucas, O'Connell, speaking on the policy of independent opposition, which was then in vogue among all factions, piously agreed 'to be wrong, if wrong it be, with the bishops and clergy and people'. Appropriately, following his return in Clonmel, he announced that he would 'look but to Sharman Crawford whenever I can agree with him', but promised 'deadly opposition to the Ecclesiastical Titles Bill and other religious issues'.[41] Burke, a fanatical O'Connellite, was enraged that the youngest son of the great Daniel should be obliged to take any pledge, and any proposal to sit with the Tory opposition was anathema to him: 'Would you insist that an Irish virgin should sit amongst and consort with a parcel of strumpets'.[42]

Not only was the O'Connellite dimension of some importance in this election, but it also reveals one fundamental reason why the Independent Opposition Party failed to excite the imagination of many priests and people. This was the problem of leadership. Quite clearly such party leaders as Lucas, Duffy or Moore could not adequately fill the Liberator's shoes. Thomas Meagher, when denying that Lucas had the right to discipline the Irish members, referred to him as the 'public prosecutor of our Irish catholic members'.[43] A series of letters by Dr Burke and John Ryan during the Clonmel election illustrates clear contempt for the unfortunate M.P. Ryan's three letters, oozing with personal abuse, ridiculed Lucas's Quaker antecedents, and contained little practical comment.[44] The Cashel priest attacked his opponent as 'a monster from the foul and leprous outpourings of whose putrid heart bursting upon an astonished and scandalised world through his envenomed pen, and upon his blasphemous paper . . . I tracked you through all our popular movements by the slime and filth you left after you, and at the fitting time, when I vigorously set my heel upon your serpent head, and tore off the mask what could I or the public expect but a hiss'. The letters were more severe than either the rather jocose editorial which provoked them, or than any of the *Tablet's* sometimes cutting articles. Bishops and priests, irrespective of their politics, were genuinely scandalised at Ryan's vituperation. The mild Slattery, contacted by other bishops, was intensely embarrassed and annoyed.[45] He sought and was given an assurance that such public comments would cease.[46] He did not, however, suspend the sharp-tongued priest. Burke's letter to Gray was less disparaging, being content to withdraw subscriptions from the *Freeman's* on the basis that it issued 'fabrications',[47] a theme also pursued by Ryan in Clonmel.[48]

Ironically, it may very well be that the abuse encountered by the league deputation in Clonmel actually made their defeat less significant insofar as it aroused the sympathy of a large number of Tipperary priests. This was evident in two ways. Subsequent collections[49] for both O'Connell and Lucas show that a far larger number of Tipperary priests subscribed to the Lucas Testimonial; for example, 33 of them personally contributed £31-10-0. A small number of O'Connellite priests were the main collectors of the O'Connell tribute, which, however, amounted to a more substantial sum. Dr Burke collected £51 of which £15 was his own contribution, Dr O'Connor, Templemore, raised £40 and John Ryan 15 guineas.

Of greater importance, the publicity given to the controversy strengthened the resolve of the priestly leaguers to support the policy of independent opposition. It prompted John O'Dwyer to seek to extract his precise political philosophy from John O'Connell.[50] Unwilling to accept O'Connell's first reply that his principles were those of his father, the frustrated curate was silenced by the M.P.'s curt but truthful second answer that he never entered into controversies with priests. Most significant, however, was the reaction of a section of the Tipperary priesthood, who met in Thurles in February 1854 and pointedly congratulated the deputation for their stand against 'corruption and place-taking and the immoral doctrine of pledge-breaking'.[51] The decision to establish the *Tipperary Leader*, under the editorship of the Young Irelander, Maurice Leyne, as an organ to promote the policy, was the meeting's unqualified vote of no confidence in the Clonmel Liberal paper, The *Tipperary Free Press*. Despite extensive clerical efforts to save it the new paper succumbed in February 1856 following two successful libel suits against it.[52] A more enduring reaction to the Clonmel row was the foundation of the Tipperary Independent Club which kept alive and organised local belief in independent opposition throughout most of the remainder of the decade. After some delay this was set up in April 1855 at a meeting of 25 priests and some 'influential laymen' in the Franciscan Friary in Thurles.[53] It functioned as an election machine whose purpose was to ensure the return of pledged M.P.s for the county; of its 19 rules the central one was the ineligibility of those not in favour of the basic tenet of independent opposition. Interestingly, the spirit in mid-Tipperary contrasted with the tone of despair beginning to creep into the Dublin executive of the league in the previous year because of the dwindling number of Independent Opposition M.P.s.[54] This pessimism seems to have penetrated such unlikely places as the walls of Maynooth, where it was felt that an election was as much 'a scramble for places generally speaking . . . as it is for power between big parties'.[55]

The Tenant League priests were among the top echelon of the Tipperary Independent Club. The managing committee contained 23 priests out of a total of 34, and altogether the priests accounted for 29 of the 40 executive positions. The club survived until 1859 and collapsed with the party it supported. It signified the swing from agrarian to parliamentary politics by practically replacing the league at local level, although it had no branches. Like the league it was not representative, having only one Killaloe and 3 Waterford priests, and reflected the outlook only of a section of the Cashel clergy, albeit a politically influential section. As in the league's case, too, it seems to have embraced only the better-off farmers, some of whom were related to certain priests. The stiff annual membership fee of 10/- also points to this.

The hope of Frederick Lucas that Dr Slattery would give his official benediction to the proposed club[56] was quickly dashed when the archbishop disclaimed any connection with it.[57] Slattery's action, while depriving the club of his imprimatur, and possibly a wider degree of support, was not a hostile act. It was the action of a man holding a politically neutral stance, who, however, was also increasingly worried by the whole debate. Since the clergy were as deeply split on the issue as the laity, Slattery was afraid that his interference might aggravate the row. So, he aimed to defuse the situation, not only by remaining neutral, but by putting some restraints on public disputes between priests. He privately contacted his parish priests on this point, fearing that Rome might admonish him for what he termed his over-indulgence in failing to impose discipline on his priests.[58] Concerned about disedification to the 'simple laity', the archbishop threatened personal intervention if the parish priests failed to act.

Indeed, the tenor of the debate aroused general episcopal anxiety, and rumours of restrictions on clerical political involvement, far from easing political tension at local level, increased it enormously. This was an over-reaction, but like the attitude of the Catholic Defence Association clergy to the Ecclesiastical Titles Bill, the league-oppositionist clergy and laity did not realise that the 1854 synodical decrees, framed to circumscribe priestly political activity, would have little practical effect outside Dublin. The suspension of the Callan curates by Bishop Walsh[59] did nothing to soften their fears that a general episcopal policy was involved, and at a Callan meeting in November 1854 Frederick Lucas made the extraordinary decision of appealing directly to Rome, an act which underlined his conviction of the vital role played by priests in political matters.[60] A county meeting in Thurles organised by the Independent Club shortly afterwards assumes a greater significance in the light of that decision.[61] Of the 62 priests who signed the requisition calling the meeting, 24 actually attended, most of whom were supporters of the independent opposition policy. The speeches of such priests as William Cahill, Thomas Mullaney, and Martin Laffan clearly linked the question of clerical political involvement with the survival of the party. William Mullally was the most uncompromising speaker. Paying scant attention to either Dr Cullen or Bishop Walsh of Ossory, he shouted to his huge audience: 'The man who would reproach me as a political agitator, I say he is a heathen, I say he is a vile thing, in whose bowels some corruption has rotted away every particle of humanity'.

In spite of such fiery sentiments and an impressive clerical attendance, not all Opposition priests considered the drastic step of an appeal to Rome as either necessary or prudent. 25 of the 62 requisitionists above refused to sign the priests' memorial to Rome; 6 of the 24 priests at the meeting were unwilling to support the move; 7 of the Lucas Testimonial subscribers did not sign, and 9 of the club members felt that the appeal was too extreme. Nevertheless, 29 priests or 19% of the total Tipperary clergy signed.[62] They represented 27% of the county's parishes. An age breakdown shows a normal pattern and does not reveal any extra caution among older priests. Indeed, the number of parish priests exceeded by 7% their usual proportion in Tipperary. While it is true, that the memorialists were a reasonably small minority, they contained the most politically active nucleus, who were especially sensitive to any threat of silencing them. It should be realised also that such a protest to Rome was an unprecedented step and only a hardy or politically dedicated priest would risk being associated with it. Judged by national standards, Tipperary priests were certainly militant since the total signatures represented only 5.5% of the Irish priesthood; the Tipperary section accounted for 22% of the signatories. The predominance of Cashel clergy again suggests their particular sensitivity to the Sadleirite defection, and further shows the connection between the appeal and the independent opposition debate. The high number of Meath signatures reflects the popularity of the policy's champion, Frederick Lucas, as M.P. for that county. Interestingly, the tradition of parliamentary opposition seems to have remained there as it did in County Tipperary.[63]

The memorial itself emphasised independent opposition, and probably presumed a knowledge of Irish political affairs by Rome which was unrealistic, despite Cullen's liaison with them. It neatly connected alleged episcopal sanctions and the party by plainly stating that the defection was 'connived at' and 'approved of' by several 'Whig' bishops. With some calculation the memorial pointed out that the 'godless colleges', Bequests Act, and the Veto had been favoured by the so-called Whig episcopal school, and in a more explicit vein still, earmarked Bishop Walsh as one 'of known Whig propensities'. It did not omit a thrust at Archbishop Cullen, who was regarded with particular suspicion by the lay leaguers, and consequently by the clerical memorialists, who categorised him as one who had 'not become a non-politician, but a Whig politician'. The archbishop's retaliation may be briefly summarised here, since it was of some relevance to Tipperary. Relying upon his detailed knowledge of Roman affairs, Cullen sent a long report in Italian giving his side of the story, as well as documenting every detail of the whole affair.[64] This was certainly a more professional approach than a document attacking church dignitaries. He informed the cardinal prefect of Propaganda that the priests' memorial was composed in the Diocese of Cashel, but 'it seems without the knowledge of the archbishop'.[65] Cullen painted a very anti-Roman portrait of Lucas and Duffy in particular, depicting them as promoting a revolution against religion by trying to undermine the bishops' authority to discipline their priests.[66] Playing the memorialists at their own game, he referred to the 'pernicious maxims' in Duffy's paper, the *Nation*, which, he confided, paraded such '48 rebels as Kossuth and Mazzini for the admiration of the people. He did not neglect to point out Duffy's contribution to the Ballingarry uprising.

This eloquent file shows Cullen's knowledge of almost every move against him by his opponents, and his ability to parry their thrusts. He also kept in touch with Slattery about the 'vile conspiracy', and sent him a copy of the relevant Dublin provincial rules.[67] The harrassed archbishop of Cashel hardly needed any reminders; he had already scotched plans by William Mullally and Martin Laffan to send John O'Dwyer, secretary of the Independent Club, to Rome with the memorial. His reply to their joint-letter was immediate and final, and offered the unpalatable alternative of leaving his diocese if O'Dwyer persisted with his plan.[68] As in the case of the Independent Club, Slattery was annoyed at any effort to identify him with the idea. Nevertheless, despite his decisive action, his overall attitude fundamentally differed from Cullen's. He sent his file to Patrick Leahy, then in Dublin, for his opinion. Leahy regarded Mullally's letter as an insult to Slattery, but, interestingly, his real complaint was at the slovenly manner of organising the mission.[69] He considered that the priests' cause was just, and seemed disappointed that Cullen's 'triumph will be in the end complete', an opinion later amply borne out. The divergence of views between the two Cashel clerics and Cullen can only be understood in the wider context of ecclesiastical discipline. They greatly resented his interference in the ecclesiastical affairs of other dioceses.[70] Contacted by Rome soon after this for his own views on the question of synodical regulations,[71] then being discussed there, Slattery's reply was totally different from Cullen's.[72] As well as quoting from an 1848 31 page letter from himself to Rome defending the priests' role in politics, Slattery dwelt upon the root of the dissension, independent opposition, and gave an account of the clerical split, explaining that the majority were opposed to the breaking of 'solemn' pledges, however rash such pledges had been. While not condoning the violent language used by the oppositionist priests, Slattery, accurately reflecting his own stand, warned that Vatican action against them would seem 'to directly favour one side, and that not the popular one'. He upheld interference only through the bishops, within the framework of the Dublin synodical regulations, and suggested that the bishops might order priests to preserve unity in public and abstain from controversy, a suggestion probably inspired by Leahy. Clearly, apart from politics, the Archbishop of Cashel feared an over-energetic ultramontanism.

Despite Slattery's advice, and despite his earlier remonstrances to priests, the 'Roman Mission' momentarily served to deepen the split in the county. Almost at the very time he was corresponding with Rome, a public controversy was raging between John O'Dwyer and John Mackey P.P. Clonoulty about the venture, in which O'Dwyer drew attention to the longstanding personal friendship between Sadleir's relations, the Scullys, and Mackey himself.[73] This controversy, however, marked the end of public priestly polemics on the matter. Furthermore, the failure of the mission, the death of Lucas, the withdrawal of Duffy, Gray's changing attitude, and the collapse of the *Tipperary Leader* did not augur well for the survival of the opposition policy or the Tipperary Independent Club in the mid-'50s. But, these severe setbacks were partly offset by the collapse of the Tipperary Joint Stock Bank (Sadleir's Bank) in 1856 due to John Sadleir's enormous frauds in which several priests lost money. As well as this, within a year John O'Connell's resignation and assumption of the position of Hanaper Clerk, with Dr Burke's confident approval, was a further boost to the club and seemed a vindication of its views.

Both these events sparked off a series of elections which showed that the policy of independent opposition was as contentious as ever, but that the old problems highlighted in the 1853 Clonmel election remained unsolved. There was still an absence of convinced oppositionist candidates. Patrick J. Murray, the 1857 candidate for Clonmel, announced that 'the age of parties is past', and his subsequent *volte face* failed to secure his return.[74] This election also showed that the parochial but realistic tradition of viewing an M.P. chiefly as a local benefactor was very strong. Dr Burke stressed the ability of John Bagwell, Murray's Protestant opponent and the owner of Clonmel, to improve the town and provide a proper market there. This was a stand taken by other priests, especially older ones.[75] The astute Burke also tried to take the wind from his opponent's sails by arguing that Bagwell's wealth was a guarantee of his parliamentary integrity by placing him above the temptations of office.[76] When Bagwell briefly took office by following in John Sadleir's footsteps as a Junior Lord of the Treasury, the parish priest dismissed the matter by cynically remarking that some men were born to have greatness thrust upon them.[77]

One of the problems with such wealthy landlord-type candidates was their reluctance to follow a leader, and as in the early '50s this question of leadership recurred again and again. Neither did priestly attitudes undergo any radical change. The leadership of George Henry Moore in 1857 was no more acceptable to a section of the clergy than Lucas's had been in 1853. A long address by Dr Burke to the electors amply illustrates this.[78] Having condemned the whole idea of an Irish party as detrimental to Ireland's interests by supposedly arousing the hostility of the House of Commons Burke declared that he could not see why men of equal ability should bind themselves to Moore's leadership. John Ryan also held him up to contempt as 'the little whipster from Mayo',[79] although his denunciation was not as savage as his earlier one of Lucas. John Meagher P.P. Toomevara, smarting from the physical bruises of an election combat, saw him as the 'little Connacht rat-catcher'.[80]

The question of leadership was, however, only one dimension of the O'Connellite legacy. The parallel Young Ireland issue, which had complicated the Clonmel election of 1853, assumed much wider proportions in the county by-election of 1857, when the clerical body split, with the O'Connellite priests ranged against those of the Independent Club oppositionists. The club was clearly identified with Young Irelandism since some of its members were ex-Young Irelanders, and Patrick Hickey P.P. visited Dromoland House the previous year in a vain effort to secure the candidacy of William Smith O'Brien.[81] The club's eventual choice of the flamboyant O'Donoghue, who professed himself a follower of Duffy rather than of his famous grand uncle, Daniel O'Connell, substantiated their preference for a Young Ireland candidate. When the vacancy arose, the split became apparent; the O'Connellite pastor of Templemore, Thomas O'Connor, immediately issued a requisition for a county meeting to choose a candidate, and so tried to checkmate any move by the club.[82] The requisition was signed by 29 priests from 15 parishes. Not surprisingly the club priests refused to sign, and even less surprising, The O'Donoghue's opponent, Lawrence Waldron, a wealthy landowner of over 1,000 acres in the county, proved acceptable to this older section of O'Connellite clergy. This emerged from a stormy meeting of priests, (39 named but 'many more' present), in St Patrick's College, which failed to reach agreement.[83] One of those present, John Meagher P.P. Toomevara, at a later date wrote that he would have supported The O'Donoghue, but for the 'Young Ireland go-ahead young and old vagabonds'.[84] Andrew James Scanlan, another O'Connellite priest, looking to the general election, promised Waldron the 'votes of and influence of all the good and tried of the old school, who received their holy and wholesome principles from the heart and the lips of our ever to be revered and lamented Liberator'.[85] The split was further highlighted at a disorderly public meeting in Thurles, where Dr Burke, away from his own stronghold, was refused the chair, and both Dr Blake P.P. Roscrea and John Ryan, Waldron's proposer and seconder, were shouted down.[86] As a result of this meeting 22 priests issued a public declaration of support for Waldron, and again these were largely from the more elderly section. The Tipperary bishops also supported him.

It is worth noting that the O'Connellite — Young Ireland split of 1857 embraced much more than a mere bitter legacy of the past. It was also strongly tied to the central question of independent opposition. The club's anxiety to secure Smith O'Brien stemmed not only from his popularity as a vote catcher, but from an awareness that he had favoured the formation of an Irish party in the '40s. Although O'Brien refused the invitation he took it upon himself to issue an address to the electors in which he referred to Dr Burke as a 'prominent champion of the Whigs'.[87] This touches upon the opposite view of O'Connellite priests. Burke's address rightly or wrongly recalled that O'Connell's policy favoured keeping the Whigs in power. In this light the politics of the candidates assume a deeper significance than has been suggested.[88] The O'Donoghue professed acceptance of the total policy of independent opposition, was supported strictly on this ticket, and seems to have honoured his pledge to the priests' satisfaction.[89] Waldron, on the other hand, confidently refused to enter parliament as the nominee of any party or 'pledged to the leadership of any individual'.[90]

His confidence was unfounded and despite the support of the influential senior clergy he was roundly defeated by 3,394 to 2,474 votes.[91] Obviously neither he nor his supporters realised the attraction a policy of independent opposition still held for a considerable section of the electorate. Nor was the significance of the result lost upon the local Liberal newspaper, which, although previously hostile, readily admitted that the desire for a unified Irish party had been the decisive factor.[92] The election had several short-term repercussions for the policy at local level, which were seen in the general election soon afterwards. In the first place Waldron's public political statements were less decisively hostile to independent opposition. He entered the contest under the revealing label 'independent Liberal', a small enough concession to public opinion. But, having endured a tough interrogation by none other than Dr Burke's curate, William Shanahan, and William Mullally at a Thurles meeting convened by the Independent Club, he advanced a short step, declaring his willingness to 'augment' and support an Irish party.[93] Under further pressure he agreed to be bound by majority opinion among the Irish members, and — 'if the majority of the Irish members agree to elect a leader I'll follow him'. Even if there was little possibility of this happening, he had conceded a very vital principle, although Shanahan was rightly extremely sceptical of his sincerity. The meeting reached a similar conclusion by rejecting Waldron, as a 'dangerous politician and an enemy of our policy'; it stressed, however, that independent opposition did not mean indiscriminate opposition or blind obedience to any individual. Nevertheless, it upheld the belief in the Independent Opposition Party 'initiated by the Catholic Defence Association in 1851 and constructed by the Tenant League conference September 1852'.

The second and most notable reaction to the by-election result, and the most severe setback to Waldron, was the declaration by 60 priests, some of them his erstwhile supporters, asking him to step down.[94] Clerical solidarity was partly assured by Archbishop Leahy's determination to prevent further public scandal by inter-clerical rows.[95] But this does not diminish the significance of asking Waldron and not The O'Donoghue or the other candidate, Major Massy, to resign. Yet Massey himself was not entirely satisfactory to the club oppositionists, who allowed him to resign over a disagreement on the relatively minor matter of election expense ratios.[96] When assured of election Waldron quickly cast off any pretence of accepting the concept of an Irish party, and he refused to 'follow any leader'.[97] Dr Burke at the same meeting would not even discuss the question of independent opposition. The interesting situation existed, therefore, of electoral opinion, lay and clerical, being thwarted by lack of suitable candidates. In short, the body-politic in Tipperary was more radical than its parliamentary servants in 1857.

Ironically, too, in 1858 the small Independent Opposition Party began to move into support for the minority Conservative government in return for promises of reform. This less rigid stand was ignored by the opposition priests of Tipperary, who decided to honour The O'Donoghue with a banquet for his fidelity to their policy. 46 priests signed the requisition calling the banquet,[98] but since Dr Burke was a signatory, these cannot be taken as an accurate gauge of clerical support for the policy. Some months earlier at a banquet for the anti-oppositionist M.P. for Clonmel, Burke had rejoiced at the 'broad and expanded course of

Liberalism to which political events of the day are tending'[99]. He had the good grace to absent himself from The O'Donoghue's celebration, which was attended by 21 priests, a more reliable guide to support.[100] Not surprisingly, Lawrence Waldron also remained away, and drew the hostility of the club's secretary, who sourly commented upon 'the magic letters D.L.' (Deputy Lieutenant) which the M.P. had recently acquired in contravention of the pledge's spirit.[101]

The banquet was a strong signal that, irrespective of the parliamentary situation, local oppositionists were determined to keep the policy alive. The priests were very much the leaders in this endeavour. It came as a shock, therefore, when prior to the 1859 general election the policy received a fatal blow at local level from clerical quarters. The influence of Dr Leahy in this was decisive. Episcopal determination to achieve priestly unity resulted in simultaneous declarations of support for the O'Donoghue and Waldron as election partners by the clergy of Waterford, Cashel and Emly.[102] This formidable public gesture of solidarity by 106 priests or 70% of the county's total was all the more significant because it included the great majority of club priests. Since the clergy were the backbone of the body the address was nothing less than an act of political sabotage, and was seen as such by the baffled lay members of the club, who were forced to accept Waldron and his vague pledge of opposition.[103] It is not necessarily true that the club's collapse was inevitable anyway with the decline of the party. Divergence of opinion at local and parliamentary levels had been a sign to the contrary.

But, the final irony of the drama was Dr Leahy's post-electoral conversion to the need for an Irish party and some degree of opposition. In June 1859 he issued a declaration, signed by 100 priests, outlining desirable Irish reforms and urging the members to hold themselves independent of every government, Whig or Tory, or mixed, that failed to promote the measures listed, and to strive for the return of a government favourable to Ireland.[104] In fairness to the archbishop, however, this was addressed not to Independent Opposition M.P.s but to Irish Liberals. It foreshadowed the outlook of Isaac Butt by disavowing factious or obstructive opposition, recommending 'only such fair and legitimate line of action as is warranted by parliamentary usage of parties, directed, however, not to the end of serving party purposes, but to that of securing justice for a whole people'. This was compatible with the retreat from the original pledge of independent opposition. Within it, however, may be seen Leahy's distrust of hard line oppositionists.

Ostensibly the declaration was inspired by the success of the Conservatives in securing a majority in Ireland for the first time since 1832, and by divisions among Irish M.P.s. But the simultaneous issuing of a pastoral shows that the archbishop had a deeper motive.[105] He was concerned about the danger just then to the papal temporalities in which the English Government showed a not particularly friendly interest. This was not an election issue in Ireland, although it has been suggested that the Conservative victory there pointed to a belief among the Irish bishops that a government upholding Conservative principles would be less hostile to the pope's temporal possessions than a Liberal one containing Palmerston, Russell and Gladstone.[106] This is not easy to accept. It certainly was not true as far as Tipperary is concerned, where the electorate never showed any liking for Tory candidates nor the clergy any willingness to promote their interests. Leahy's address also reflected traditional distrust of the Conservatives.

The Papal question assumed important proportions in Tipperary six months after the address, and the approbation of Palmerston's Government for the Risorgimento's aims aroused intense anger culminating in recruitment for the Papal Brigade of St. Patrick formed to fight on the Pope's behalf. Collections were made to defray its costs, and priests contributed large amounts.[107] Cashel priests donated £140 in an exclusively clerical collection.[108] Requiem masses were celebrated for Brigadiers killed in action. A total of 45 priests attended two such masses.[109] Apart from this, very large numbers of priests participated in angry protest meetings during 1859 and 1860.[110] While the meetings were held in chapels to give them extra weight and emphasise the religious dimension, they had a distinctly relevant political theme which denounced the government for its sympathy with the pope's enemies. Dr Burke, who chaired a Clonmel meeting, was forced to include Palmerston as well as Russell in his denunciation although he balanced his statement by including Derby and Disraeli. At the same venue Andrew Walsh C.C. argued that Irish public opinion should be reflected in the House of Commons. This could be most effectively done by a unified Irish party, but the united voice of the clergy, which had in many ways killed support for independent opposition at local level, now failed to impress M.P.s, and the intense spate of anti-government sentiments by the priests did not inspire a united party with a policy of opposition.

Yet the memory of the 1850s never fully faded from the public mind in Tipperary. As late as the Land War when Parnell was consolidating his party a more radical priesthood, some with experience of the 1850s, recalled those years as examples either of enlightened priests and politicians or selfish seekers of office. Dean William Quirke referred to the 'immortal Lucas and the pure-minded Duffy', while the biblical John Tuohy P.P. Shinrone concentrated upon Sadleir and Keogh: 'Those Whigs and hacks, worshipped and bowed down before the gold of the Treasury, standing with gaping hungry mouths and hands clutching and extended in gloating expectation of the droppings of office'.[111]

It took the success of Parnell, however, to inspire analogies with the 1850s. Prior to this during the 1860s and much of the 1870s the Irish M.P.s were not a cohesive force in the House, ineffective in opposition and accused of Whiggery when they identified with the Liberals. Of course, the accusation in itself is significant, and an occasional whimper in Tipperary drew attention to the absence of an Irish party.[112] The National Association, stretching from 1864 to 1873 aimed at the reconstruction of a party to achieve its ends.[113] Almost immediately, however, the association began to move towards an alliance with the Liberals, which strengthened considerably prior to the Church Act of 1869. It weakened in the early '70s and finally ruptured with Gladstone's 1873 university legislation, which demonstrated the incompatibility of English Liberalism and Irish Catholicism. Gladstone's 1874 publication on the Vatican Decrees was the clearest illustration of this, but by that time the association had broken up.

It is striking that the opposition rules of the National Association were basically opposed to this policy of co-operation. They were not, however, considered of central importance by leading members, and were introduced mainly to assuage independent oppositionist members. Briefly, rules 3 and 4 proposed a policy of complete parliamentary independence, a pledge to vote for the association's aims, and to oppose any government which failed to make tenant compensation a cabinet measure. This points to the lingering presence of ex-Tenant Leaguers, the main exponents of independent opposition in the 1850s. But the wording of the rules is important, and the term parliamentary opposition rather than independent opposition was deliberately chosen to signify a less intransigent policy than that of the early 1850s. While some were aware of the difference,[114] not all made the distinction in Tipperary, where 14 ex-Tenant League priests constituted 35% of the county's National Association clerics.[115] This divergence between the county and the association, reminiscent of local radicalism during the 1850s, became clear during the two elections in 1865. The ex-Leaguers, Richard Cahill P.P. Donaskeigh and John Power P.P. Powerstown, stressed the importance of opposition.[116] In a letter to the association's executive Power admitted the paucity of independent M.P.s, but stressed the influence of even a few determined members.[117] He used the term independent opposition. A meeting of priests in Thurles issued a resolution proposed by Dean Patrick Laffan, brother of the anti-oppositionist archdeacon of the 1850s, and seconded by Richard Cahill that 'the only true course of policy open to the friends of Ireland to adopt is to return to parliament a body of representatives, who will not attach themselves to either Whigs or Tories, but hold themselves independent of both, and to oppose any and every party that will not concede to this country those measures for which the National Association has been established'.[118]

This may have been an effort by local leaders to divert support from fenianism by the construction of a vigorous and effective parliamentary alternative, but it was clearly more extreme than the official rule of the association and strongly resembled the pledge of 1852. Similarly, strong sentiments were also aired on the matter at a lively meeting, again in Thurles, during the 1866 by-election, which was attended by 18 priests, 4 of whom were ex-leaguers.[119] Not everybody was satisfied with the attitude of the association's candidate, Charles White, to parliamentary independence. He declared himself an 'independent Liberal', the precise tag adopted by Lawrence Waldron in 1857, and an accurate enough description. This was, however, compatible with his status as the association's candidate in the climate of Liberal co-operation, and it satisfied the Tipperary bishops who were keenly aware of the association's policy. They circularised their clergy and secured the signatures of at least 99 priests in support of White.[120] Taken in conjunction with the diocesan rule binding the minority, this effectively stifled clerical reservations, and the question of opposition did not assume any serious importance in these elections.

The protestations of loyalty by the candidates to association aims, or their wealthy status, were the chief criteria which evoked clerical support. Both Charles Moore and Charles White, (candidates in 1865 and 1866), were extremely rich landlords. John Kenyon was especially cynical about lay and clerical efforts to 'bleed' White.[121] His attitude was not too unjustified. The Moores were particularly generous to the Church, and in the context of the election Cardinal Cullen remarked to Leahy that 'Mr Moore could well afford to spend a few thousand pounds, he is worth nearly a million in ready money'.[122] Still, as administrators-in-chief, bishops always had a shrewd grasp of financial realities, and in the absence of a party machine or paid members, it was only common sense to secure a wealthy candidate, all the better if he was a good Catholic. Furthermore, in 1866 the priests were also forced to concentrate their energies against the Conservative candidate, none other than Lawrence Waldron, who had changed his political colours, and caused acute embarrassment to some of his erstwhile clerical supporters.[123] Naturally, too, the presence of a wealthy candidate, who had earlier as a Liberal secured a significant number of votes, tended to unify the priests and relegate the question of an opposition party.

Consequently, and for the first time, the attitude in Clonmel was in harmony with the apparent outlook of the county. There had not been any change of outlook in the borough, of course, but now it was compatible with National Association policy. So, Dr Burke was an ardent supporter of the association, and in accordance with rules 3 and 4 paid lip service to parliamentary opposition. At yet another banquet in honour of his protege, Bagwell, Burke agreed that neither English parties were promoting Irish interests.[124] He stressed, however, that members would not be sent to parliament with their hands tied, a view which coincided with Cullen's and with that of Peter Paul Mac-Swiney, chairman of the association meeting of June 1865, which sanctioned the new rules on parliamentary opposition. Bagwell himself confidently told the banquet audience that he had always held the policies of the National Association, and continued to wax eloquent on the merits of the 'great Liberal Party of England under Palmerston'.

The tightening of the association's alliance with this party as the decade advanced further pushed the question of opposition into the background. The expectation of Gladstonian sweets proved a powerful attraction that swayed even the most convinced Oppositionist cleric. John Power's shift of outlook is clear proof of this. Power not only succeeded Dr Burke in Clonmel, but in adapting to current political thought, radiated Burke's attitude and even plagiarised his stock vocabulary. At the inevitable 1868 banquet to honour Bagwell, Power expounded on this M.P.'s independence of 'the temptations and seductive influence of place and office', and depicted him as a 'firm supporter of what is called the Gladstone policy'.[125] While the Liberal alliance was a practical and worthwhile step, and Power's changed attitude realistic and sensible, his wholehearted applause of Bagwell cannot have been anything but hypocritical, and the shade of Dr Burke must indeed have smiled. In view of Power's earlier stand his assertion that Bagwell would oppose Gladstone for failing to deliver on land, education or religious issues can hardly have been sincere. But then that is the nature of politics.

The proposal of John Crotty, Power's successor in Powerstown, to establish a county Liberal club, rather than an independent club,[126] is a further pointer to the emphatic shift in Tipperary by 1868. The county election pattern in 1868 was similar to the previous one, with White and Moore, the sitting National Association members, receiving the support of Leahy and 49 of his priests.[127] Subsequently the policy of co-operation with the Liberals was strongly boosted by Gladstone's Church act, and Butt's Tenant League endorsed it in anticipation of the proposed land bill. Dr Michael O'Neill, in his speech at the league's inauguration, reflected this view,[128] but rapidly changed his mind when the act was published. He urged that Irish M.P.s 'put aside all consideration of self' and 'stand together independently' in their demands.[129] This priest did not consider rules 3 and 4 as dead letters, and interpreted them literally, that is opposition if the Government failed to legislate satisfactorily on any of the three aims of the association.

But the act's failure was not immediately responsible for the split with the Liberals, although it offered Butt the excuse of forming the Home Government Association. The parliamentary reprecussions of this only became evident with the 1874 election, which produced 59 Home Rulers, even if only about one-third of these formed any type of distinct body. There was, however, no party pledge, but a general resolve to take counsel with each other on various questions. The two Tipperary M.P.s returned on the Home Rule ticket did not pledge themselves to any party, and were Liberal at heart. Still, the return of this amorphous group spelled the death-knell of what might be called Irish Liberalism. Even more important, it produced the determined nucleus of obstructionists pursuing what was in effect a policy of indiscriminate independent opposition, which was proposed only by the hardy few during the troubled years of the early '50s. This group was to triumph within a few years under Parnell as a tightly-knit disciplined party. It is the story of this triumph, the significant contribution made to it by the Tipperary priesthood, and its ultimate tragedy that concerns the next chapter.

John Mitchel (*Irishman*, 27.2.1875).

Chapter Eight

THE PRIEST AND THE PARNELLITE PARTY 1877-1891

'The faults in Parnell are but like the specks that may be seen in the sun by a microscope'.
Father Patrick O'Keeffe. *Tipperary Leader* 11/4/1883.

If the seeds of agrarian discontent were sown in 1877, it was also by coincidence an important year in the history of Parnellism. It was then that Biggar and Parnell systematised the more sporadic obstruction of earlier years, which hastened the destruction of Butt's party, and provoked the public power struggle between Parnell and the ageing leader.[1] in 1877, too, the hitherto hostile Edmund Dwyer Gray, proprietor of the *Freeman's Journal* and newly elected M.P. for Tipperary, threw in his lot with the small Parnellite nucleus.[2] Since Tipperary, apart from Meath, had inherited the strongest tradition of independent opposition from the 1850s, it is not surprising that at least one clerical voice of approval for obstruction was raised there in 1877. It is surprising, however, that this belonged to that once fierce opponent of Frederick Lucas, John Ryan P.P. Newinn. He drew attention to the 'gallant band of seven and the all-powerful mode of parliamentary agitation'.[3] It is impossible to say how representative Ryan's views were at that time, but subsequent events clearly underline the powerful reservoir of support by the Tipperary priests for the construction of a new party. Taking all factors into consideration, at least 133 priests showed unreserved approval.[4] The percentage of parish priests was higher than normal, but not significantly so. A diocesan analysis, however, reveals the very high Cashel proportion, pointing to the influence of Dr Croke, and probably to the tradition of the 1850s. The Waterford percentage is normal, but the Killaloe figure falls far below its 29% share of the county.

Even Clonmel, the borough traditionally opposed to an independent Irish party, showed a more positive reaction to the policy of having such a party than heretofore. Admittedly this was lay-inspired; the priests, who were not as politicised as their predecessors, remained neutral. A section of the electorate there was dissatisfied at the failure of their M.P., Arthur Moore (son of Charles, late member for the county) to vote with the party on a tenant right measure.[5] Nevertheless, opinion in the borough had not swung sufficiently in favour of Parnell to prevent Moore's re-election in 1880, when his catholicity and benevolence proved the decisive factors.[6] In May 1881 Moore's support for the government on the Land Act division was in accordance with the views of the hierarchy and of many priests, but 203 Clonmel electors were quick to complain about his course.[7] By 1884, however, Parnell's tightening grip on the constituencies enabled William O'Brien, in the presence of Thomas McDonnell Adm. and his curate, to sarcastically contrast Moore's amiability and religious devotion with his alleged weaknesses as an M.P.[8] Parnell refused to support his candidature for the 1885 election,[9] and the creation of four county constituencies one of which absorbed the borough of Clonmel tolled his political death-knell in Tipperary.[10]

The Clonmel case is a prime example of Parnell's early difficulty in overcoming the more parochial tradition of supporting the wealthy landlord-type candidates, who were not amenable to party discipline. This extraordinary leader, however, imposed his discipline on the county within a few years, although not without some initial difficulty, also, since the tradition of independent opposition there never embraced the entire electorate. Nevertheless, the foundation of the Tipperary Independent Club in 1879, with its aim of returning 'faithful, independent and incorruptible' M.P.s., was of significance and points to a favourable political atmosphere there.[11] It was more than a little reminiscent of its namesake of the 1850s, being situated in Thurles, and arousing a similar degree of controversy because of its alleged unrepresentativeness. But despite the club's existence Parnell's leadership and policy of centralised party structure were not totally accepted by the priests in the Spring of 1880. The general election of that year was complicated by the candidature of P.J. Smyth, a Repealer popular with the republican sector. Smyth, however, abhorred the notion of a party pledge, although he had been a prominent Young Irelander. At the election selection-meeting William Doherty C.C. Cashel proposed that only candidates who undertook 'to give up individual views' and work within the Parnellite party be selected.[12] Dean Quirke did not press the issue, and, on Smyth's blank refusal, requested only general co-operation with the party. Smyth eventually made the rather vague promise to 'work loyally and earnestly with any party and every party for the good of Ireland'. This was hardly compatible with the theory or practice of centralisation, but Quirke assented to it, and at a subsequent meeting, attended by 24 priests, Canon Richard Cahill also considered it satisfactory.[13] Both had been staunch oppositionists in the '50s, but neither emerge from the 1880 election as convinced

Parnellites, since they must have been aware of Smyth's breach with the Home Rule Party in the mid-'70s, and his rebuff by the Westmeath clergy because of this.[14] Their acceptance of Smyth was only a partial setback for Parnell (who was present at the second Thurles meeting) because the adoption of John Dillon was more than adequate compensation, and the two priests did not directly oppose his policy. Matt Ryan, however, took a more cautious line at this meeting when he enquired 'Do you want to make Parnell dictator of all Ireland'. Prophetic insight, perhaps, but understandable.

At first sight, therefore, Smyth's election might suggest lukewarmness on the priests' part for Parnell's policy; but the reservations of a few must be judged against the almost immediate clerical reaction against Smyth's failure to support Parnell for the sessional chairmanship of the Party. The influential Croke quickly made Smyth aware of his own surprise, advising that Parnell, not Shaw, had the country's confidence.[15] Croke revealed that 'some of the priests have already waited on me expressing their surprise and displeasure at your action in this case. They say it is not a good beginning'. But when Smyth threatened to resign as a result of this letter,[16] the priests prevailed upon him to reconsider, showing a reluctance to exert what may be called Parnellite ruthlessness.[17] When, however, he formally seceded from the Parnellite party on January 14th 1881,[18] the priests and Land League branches under their chairmanship commenced a trenchant three year campaign for his resignation.[19]

This leaves no doubt that at least by the end of 1880 the Tipperary clergy were firmly converted to the policy of having a strong Irish party under Parnell's leadership. Dean Quirke, despite his earlier irresolution, was prominent in the anti-Smyth campaign, adapting to the majority view of his fellow priests. He reduced the issue to its essentials, a choice between Parnell and Smyth, and this time did not leave his own preference in doubt.[20] He chaired a meeting of Land League delegates to demand Smyth's resignation.[21] What better place to hold this than in the presbytery, Thurles, with at least 14 priests present? Clerical sentiments in the presbytery varied in intensity. Quirke dwelt upon the salient theme of party discipline and requested a promise of fidelity to Parnell, while John O'Brien P.P. Holycross curtly demanded Smyth's resignation. Daniel Flannery, having travelled 20 miles from Nenagh, was appropriately indignant. Revealing that the priests in Nenagh had held a special meeting to voice their disapproval, Flannery put forward the argument that Smyth's course weakened the party by showing it as a divided one, unrepresentative of public opnion. His views were upheld in the strong speech of James Cantwell. The final resolution of the meeting called on Smyth to resign and provoked a recalcitrant reply which centred on this very issue of unrepresentativeness. If Smyth did not see the Parnellite Party as representative, he likewise refused to recognise the Thurles meeting, rightly holding that those present were all members of the Land League,[22] an organisation which he heartily despised.[23] In an earlier letter, angrily answered by James Cantwell and his curate, Thomas O'Dwyer, he took no pains to conceal his disapproval of the party's opposition to a government that intended to legislate for Ireland, and he ridiculed the emphasis placed on where a member sat in the House of Commons.[24]

If this initial clerical attack seemed confined, as Smyth contended, his vote with the government on the *Cloture* provoked a representative condemnation by 114 Cashel and 29 Waterford priests in April 1882.[25] This was a marked escalation of the controversy. Smyth's reply[26] highlighted an apparent anomaly in the politics of some signatories, who, he rightly claimed, had recently sought positions through him for their friends.[27] He agreed to resign only if the priests themselves retired from politics, where he alleged they injured religion by causing scandal. Determined to leave the unfortunate individual no room for manoeuvre by scuttling his basic argument, James Cantwell promoted a requisition for his resignation, which was signed at the chapel gates throughout the county. The improverished Smyth, however, desperately needing a government position, reverted to his stock argument that only leaguers had signed.[28]   Abandoning any semblance of restraint he ridiculed the new National League: 'That a packed jury of even 700 dolts could have been scraped together from Ireland, England and Scotland to affirm the conglomeration of absurdities calling itself a programme is a sufficiently lamentable circumstance'.[29] The conflict only ended on his appointment to the Secretaryship of the Loan Fund Office in 1884, although his final attack on the party, the pledge, and the priests, extended beyond the grave through his biased posthumous pamphlet, *The priest in politics*.[30]

This controversy was remarkably similar to the John O'Connell saga of 1854. Both were individualistic, obstinate men bedevilled by poverty and forced to accept office as a result. Both also intensely opposed party pledges and disliked contemporary agrarian organisations. They belonged, however, to opposing political traditions, O'Connellism and Young Irelandism. But the profound difference between the two affairs was the powerful clerical drive against Smyth in contrast with the weaker more confined criticism of O'Connell. The Smyth row was also much more than a parallel with the past; it was a milestone on the road of mass clerical conversion to the centralised party system, without indeed their realising the full practical meaning of this. The Tipperary priests' hostility to Smyth almost marks them as more Parnellite than their flocks at a time when the Irish church had not made its so-called rapprochement with the party.

This is just as evident from their overall electoral stand, which was of the utmost significance in facilitating Parnell's control of the constituencies. Clerical opposition, for example, would have tilted the scales against Parnell's nominee, Thomas Mayne, when Dillon resigned in 1883. But, on the contrary, his nomination papers were signed by the senior ecclesiastics of the county, Dean William Quirke and Archdeacon T.H. Kinnane.[31] He was supported by Croke and his priests specifically as Parnell's candidate at a time, too, when Roman rumblings about the leader were in the air, and when, as James Cantwell broadly hinted, he required support 'now more than ever'.[32]

Mayne was returned unopposed. Even more tangible proof of clerical transcendence of local political boundaries and a closer identification with the new vogue of party machine than the laity is provided by the by-election of 1885 necessitated by Smyth's resignation. After some initial behind-the-scene manoeuvrings,[33] two candidates emerged. Parnell's nominee was John O'Connor from Cork, and he was opposed by a Cashel Town Commissioner, Patrick O'Ryan. Not only was the county convention, chaired by Dean Quirke, held in St Patrick's College and attended by 22 priests, but the local candidate had to rely on laymen, while his Cork opponent was proposed by James Cantwell.[34] All the clerical speeches, specifically those of Canon Patrick Ryan, Galbally, and David Humphreys, were in favour of Parnell's man. Yet, O'Ryan, to the satisfaction of a local paper,[35] was selected by a slight majority, and Dean Quirke, the tactful chairman, approved of the decision. The most significant sequel in this contest was not, perhaps, the unprecedented cancellation of the convention's decision by Parnell (with Croke's approval) or his direct intervention in chairing a second convention, but the vastly increased number of priests, fifty-nine, who attended this latter gathering.[36] John T. Ryan C.C. Templemore, in putting a proposal to rescind the decision of the earlier convention objected to an argument that only a Tipperaryman merited election. Dean Quirke, a personal friend of O'Ryan, agreed that the original choice had been a mistake, and moved O'Connor's adoption. Putting the issue into a national context, Quirke suggested that the selection of O'Ryan had been interpreted by political opponents as a revolt against Parnell. This view was shared by most other priests. David Humphreys was convinced that a rejection of O'Connor the second time would have constituted a 'deadly blow' to the party and to Parnell's political existence.[37]

The importance of such statements lay in their essential justification of Parnell's right to overrule a local democratic political decision, because it was allegedly detrimental to the Party. Facing this obvious charge squarely both Humphreys and John T. Ryan denied that either Parnell or Croke had indulged in dictation. The archbishop, well aware of the revolutionary nature of Parnell's procedure, openly abetted it, although in a typically equivocal statement he denied that he had recommended O'Connor to the convention, while at the same time he

John O'Connor, M.P. for Tipperary.

Thomas Mayne, M.P. for Tipperary.

go to bed to niyt a nu
you vill be sorry
for their is a breack
out to night or last
night Limerich
Newcastle

A Warning - fragment relating to the Rising in Kilkeely (S.P.O. C.S.O.R.P. 1867 8399).

expressed approval of the decision to summon a second convention.[38] Daniel Ryan P.P. Clonoulty was less subtle in defending Parnell: 'As Caesar said of old, Parnell might say, "I came, I saw, I conquered"; ... without attempting to play the dictator, as he never does, his words were law to the convention'.[39] Even two years earlier Thomas Fennelly C.C., future archbishop of Cashel, had maintained that no man had a better right to interfere than the architect of the party.[40]

While not a lover of clerical politicians, Parnell's genius lay in his ability to persuade such politically experienced priests as these to euphemise what was in reality little less than dictation. In the light of lay disunity, the Tipperary priests' cohesive approval of a central-ised party was his ace, and he played it well. His manipulation of the clergy was not a clumsy act, but contained a tactful as well as sensible respect for their traditional electioneering involvement, seen for example, by his care to visit the local clergy during his canvass of 1885. He met groups of priests in Clonmel and Tipperary town.[41] His awareness of the priests' importance in educating the laity on the necessity of a centralised party is well illustrated by their ex-officio membership of county conventions, a concession considered undemocratic by Michael Davitt.[42] It was, however, a very temporary concession, and certain guidelines laid down by Archbishop Walsh on the clerical role in these conventions[43] were rendered unnecessary by the rapid decline of this system; this heralded the real power of the central party machine to choose and impose its own candidates on constituencies. There was an equally rapid decline in priestly electioneering involvement after 1886 signifying the increasingly independent stature of the party from then on.[44] Henry Harrison was elected in 1890 with minimum consulta-tion, except Parnell's recommendation to an agreeable Croke; Nicholas Rafferty Adm. Thurles and Arthur Ryan, President of St Patrick's College, signed his nomination papers.[45]

This evolution was meekly accepted by the priests, and resentment only surfaced during the heated days of the Parnellite crisis, when they suddenly became openly conscious of their relegation from political power. But from December 1885 until the crisis of 1890 Tipperary returned four loyal Parnellites who dutifully signed a party pledge,[46] and all were elected unobtrusively except for the general election of 1885, which was contested by the Conservatives, to the usual chagrin of the priests.[47] The overwhelming victory of the four Parnellites was thoroughly relished by Croke, who was annoyed at the Con-servative tactics of putting the party to expense.[48] In a letter to Tobias Kirby he could not resist the boast that his own political stand of the previous six years had been vindicated, and he added for Vatican ears: 'It now comes to pass that the man who was so bitterly assailed by the famous Roman circular is now the recognised leader of the Irish bishops, priests and people'.[49]

The archbishop was hardly overstating the case in the Winter of 1885, when Parnell probably stood at the pinnacle of his power, with almost universal lay and clerical support behind him. Croke was well entitled to his personal satisfaction. He had demonstrated a political acumen and foresight denied to most other bishops, and had backed the right horse as far back as 1879.[50] He may have supported a loser as a young curate of the 1850s, but he realised that the calibre of Parnell and the political ferment of the 1880s held the ingredients of success despite early difficulties. Croke was indeed a powerful examplar, and undoubtedly many priests placed their bets accordingly. There is, however, no better prescription for success than success, and they viewed positive gains, agrarian or otherwise, as the fruit not only of the land movements, but of energetic Parnellite parliamentary activity.[51] Their frequent eulogistic references betray an intense pride in the party — 'that daring legion of dashing Irish heroes', who were 'a bright constellation around their great patriotic chief and leader'.[52]

The priests were also able to identify more easily with the party, because of its wider social composition; as Thomas Finn said, 'they did not want the sons of the aristocracy to represent them or misrepresent them'.[53] Nicholas Rafferty fully concurred with this more democratic base, too, holding that monied members were not in sympathy with popular aspirations. This was indeed a notable break with a traditional view. Considering this and the less affluent status of at least some Parnellite members,[54] extensively priestly support for a salary scheme for M.P.s, (as distinct from the usual periodic testimonials), was logical. At least 22 priests voiced public approval of the idea.[55] Even if it constituted the least desirable motive, a salary obviously helped to foster some degree of loyalty to the party; James Cantwell considered it an important asset in cementing a united party. By no means a naive politician, however, he proposed certain safeguards to ensure that only 'staunch' members benefited from what was called the parliamentary fund. He suggested a type of monitoring system by local committees, who would report to a national committee on members' parliamentary conduct. While, perhaps, a disciplinary aid to party leaders, this would have detracted from centralisation by introducing a local dimension. It was never adopted. Cantwell also recommended the imposition of a small annual levy on each elector. Interestingly, his archbishop, who applauded individual parliamentary funds for specific persons on the surmise that they would broaden the choice of candidates,[56] was not entirely in favour of the proposed scheme.[57] Croke questioned the calibre of candidates, who might be attracted by a permanent salary — 'every local spouter, every parish patriot, the busybody and big man of every Land League branch'. This clearly contradicted the views of his youth. Neither was it quite compatible with his acceptance of Parnell's right to choose his own candidates, since it essentially questioned the leader's ability to make the best choice. His point was not well founded, and he quickly conformed when the idea became party policy; he then declared that M.P.s deserved salaries as much as doctors, priests or lawyers.[58] Six months later he forwarded £340 to the parliamentary fund, all of it with the exception of £10, coming from himself and his priests.[59] Such contributions were yet another facet of clerical example to the laity in the drive to build and maintain the party. The very size of some other subscriptions at an ecclesiastical conference in Tipperary, where £170 was immediately put on the plate, demonstrated the priests' belief in such a party.[60]

If the priests' response to the Parnellite party was significant, their approval of home rule, closely linked with its growth, was no less remarkable. They experienced what was nothing short of a conversion to home rule, even though there had been a tradition which demanded some form of self-government by constitutional means. But this tradition was exceedingly patchy between the late 1840s and the early 1870s. In the '40s the charismatic O'Connell aroused mass enthusiasm for Repeal, a vague enough policy not too unlike home rule, although considered by some as a more complete form of self-government. But the rigid Parnellite discipline proved more effective than the near hysteria aroused by O'Connell, which wilted in the face of English force, Irish famine and internal party discord. By 1850 the tottering Loyal National Repeal Association creaked along under the aegis of John O'Connell,[61] with a dwindling minority of priests corresponding, subscribing and gathering useless petitions.[62] From a practical point of view John O'Connell's plan[63] for the appointment of repeal district clerks was quite irrelevant, since falling funds closed his headquarters, Conciliation Hall, within a year.[64] Academic as the plan was, however, it serves to illustrate O'Connell's emphasis on priestly importance to the movement; for example, clerical approval of an applicant was considered necessary, and a priest's complaint would be sufficient reason for dismissal. While they were a link in the home government chain, the priests did not promote Repeal in the face of popular apathy. Dr Burke was one of the few clerics who dwelt upon the subject, and in 1850 prophetically asserted that only a strong leader could achieve repeal.[65] His speech a few years later was even more realistic, when he agreed that the question was in abeyance, although he again harped on the leadership issue.[66] Non-Tipperary priests were equally pessimistic, and Tenant League adherents in particular saw the land question as more relevant.[67]

Unlike the land problem, repeal was not even a minor electioneering platform plank during the 1850s. It was only resurrected in the following decade by the National League of John Martin and The O'Donoghue as a counter to fenianism. The league had no local network, failed to stimulate public opinion and hence found very little clerical support in Tipperary. Perhaps, despite the opposite intention of Martin and The O'Donoghue, the priests feared that promotion of constitutional nationalism might further fan the flames of fenianism, which they strongly opposed. Significantly, when the danger of organised republicanism had passed with the failure of 1867, the Limerick clergy under Dean O'Brien issued their famous repeal declaration, following the celebration of mass for the Manchester Martyrs.[68] No less than 1600 priests eventually signed the document,[69] which was confined to the clergy alone, but only 13 Tipperary names were published; these included the National League priests, Patrick Horan and William Shanahan.[70] The declaration seems to have been inspired by clerical desire to demonstrate their own nationalistic sentiments in the context of the martyrs, but it was in no way intended to boost republican sentiment. Apart from Dean O'Brien's specific warning on this point,[71] the statement of John Ryan urging support for the manifesto, because 'it commenced at the right end and in the right way',[72] is an accurate reflection of the Tipperary clergy's outlook, and another reminder of where Ryan's sympathies did not lie. It is even more noteworthy that the priests did not see it as the basis for a new repeal movement, nor did it imply active clerical support for the National League, although a disappointed John Martin logically anticipated this.[73] The manifesto must be clearly seen in the current political context of co-operation with Gladstone, pending his legislation on education, Church Establishment and land. Dean O'Brien was conscious of this, and cannot have been unaware that hostile newspapers and commentators[74] used the declaration as an illustration that Irishmen, lay and clerical, would not be satisfied with such concessions as disestablishment. Hence the virtual silence of the priests on repeal in the election at the end of the year. When the question was raised at all it was more as a threat than a policy; for example John Scanlan P.P. Toomevara warned that failure to legislate satisfactorily on the land question would provoke a demand for repeal.[75]

It might seem that the Limerick declaration was little more than a useless, if not hypocritical exercise, a mere empty reiteration of past principles, without any intention of concrete action. But it was of some import, revealing not only a potential reservoir of clerical support for repeal, but restating the theme and receiving publicity at a time when the policy was out of favour, and so serving as a forerunner to the Home Government Association founded two years later. Nevertheless, even the significance of this should not be overemphasised, since the declaration did not inspire extensive priestly membership of the association, which remained little more than a Dublin pressure group. Records for 1870 show a small membership of 12 priests for the country as a whole,[76] although O'Neill Daunt, one of the leaders, told Archbishop Leahy that 20 to 30 had joined, hardly indeed a notable difference.[77] Daunt's letters lamented the aloofness of the priests from the movement[78] and warned that the separation of Irish Catholicity from nationalism might result in a redirecting against the clergy of traditional Irish distrust of England. Only one Tipperary priest, John Ryan, was recorded as a member, but he was not on the Council. Clerical adherence increased very gradually. There were 50 priests present at the 1873 home rule conference.[79] That same year, too, John Gore Jones R.M. mentioned the existence of clerical approval of home rule in some parts of Tipperary.[80] Attendance at Dublin meetings, or general police reports, however, do not give precise information on the degree of clerical support for the policy at local level. Elections are of some value in this, and indicate considerable clerical approval in some counties, often under pressure from public opinion, which sometimes provoked clashes among the priests themselves. The Kerry and Galway contests of 1872 are the best examples. Unfortunately, there were no elections in Tipperary between 1870 and 1874, making it difficult to judge accurately initial clerical reaction to the Home Government Association. There were 25 priests involved in the 1874 election; they helped to return home rulers, although the quality of the candidates' conviction is very doubtful indeed.[81] One of these, the Honourable Wilfrid O'Callaghan, son of Lord Lismore, was a member of the Home Rule League, but his pledge was decidedly vague; the other, Charles White, ex-National Association M.P. was equally vague, and showed little interest in home rule; he never became a member of the home rule party. This is not to underrate the revolutionary importance of this election in the long term by launching this amorphous party, which gave birth to Parnellism. Nevertheless, the return of the anti-home ruler, John Mitchel, on two occasions the following year, shows that the policy had not firmly gripped either the clerical or the popular imagination in Tipperary. Considering his leading role in later years in forwarding the policy, it is ironic indeed to find John Dillon issue a warning against any 'quasi-home ruler', who might decide to oppose Mitchel.[82]

There were several easily-defined reasons for the lack of enthusiasm among the priests. The bishops in general were hostile from the beginning, and probably influenced some clerics. Despite the best efforts of O'Neill Daunt, Dr Leahy was decidedly unfriendly, although he made it clear that the priests were free agents in choosing their stand.[83] But Daunt drew the archbishop's attention to the plea for anonymity by one clerical member 'lest he be made a martyr'.[84] Leahy's objections to the Home Government Association may very well have been shared by some priests. To begin with, he positively distrusted the leaders, whatever their shade of politics. Despite his own adherence to the Liberal camp in Irish politics, he objected to some prominent Home Rulers for displaying what he called the 'spirit of Liberalism which is the calamity of the Catholic Church all the world over'.[85] Indeed some years prior to this Daunt had sent Leahy a circular from the Association advising that the movement disclaimed any desire to promote 'the ascendancy of any form of religion in Ireland'.[86] This was probably no more than a statement of the non-sectarian nature of the movement, but it can hardly have appealed to the bishops. Allied to this Leahy pointed to the Orange membership of the association and advised that the other bishops shared his views.[87] On a more political level, Leahy, like Cullen, may also have feared a liaison between home rulers and fenians, which in fact never materialised. The turbulent election of 1870 in Tipperary involving Kickham immediately prior to the foundation of the Home Government Association, possibly made some priests wary of joining, lest they might promote republicanism. The apparent connection between the fenians and home rulers was manifested by a home rule meeting of January 1872 in Tipperary Town under republican auspices.[88] It was studiously avoided by the priests. Yet, the widening rift between the fenians and home rulers[89] was hardly unknown to the clergy.

The most serious obstacle to priestly involvement in the movement was neither the fenian nor Orange connections, but the education question, which attracted clerical attention especially in 1872, when meetings were held in four Tipperary towns attended by 27 priests.[90] In his correspondence with Dr Leahy, O'Neill Daunt readily admitted that many priests would remain aloof until this matter was settled,[91] and a local newspaper felt that Gladstone's failure to produce an acceptable university bill would induce Tipperary priests to join.[92] John Ryan partly reflected this mood when he wrote that home rule would solve all issues including the education one.[93] Butt's increasing realisation of clerical importance prompted him to include education in the association's platform. This introduces an element of confusion when trying to diagnose clerical response to home rule.[94] But, it is clear from the speech of Cornelius J. Flavin, Clonmel, that his financial contribution to a testimonial for Butt was prompted by the latter's university bill rather than his promotion of home rule. It is more difficult to decipher sentiments on the hustings. In the 1874 election it is not quite clear whether the priests supported the candidates on the strength of their education or home rule declarations. Both issues seem to have been given an equal weighting by the priests in the election for the borough of Clonmel. Hostility to John Bagwell, the sitting member, may have stemmed from his opposition to each.[95] Two home rule candidates emerged, Alderman Hackett, proprietor of the *Tipperary Free Press*, and Arthur Moore. The newly-consecrated

John Power stepped in and supported the ultra-catholic Moore, who was not even present in Clonmel.[96] The bishop and priests well knew that Moore was a far more sincere advocate of denominational education than of home rule.

While the 1874 election saw the return of a large body of Irish M.P.s with varying degrees of enthusiasm for the policy, the league itself fell into decline, and the policy faded into the background at local level. The subsequent conflict within the party and the struggle for leadership until 1879 further eclipsed the issue, but the triumph of the obstructionists not only resulted in the growth of a new disciplined party but one which, as Parnell said, emphasised home rule as strongly as the party pledge.[97] This signalled a formal transfer from the already redundant league to the party. The very success of the latter and the dominance of Parnell gave the policy a new vitality in the 1880s, which was strongly reflected at local level. While only 29 priests sporadically referred to repeal or home rule in the 28 years from 1850 to 1877,[98] at least 51 did so from 1878 to 1891.[99] Further comparison reveals a greater percentage of older priests for the earlier period, reflecting, perhaps, the lingering influence of O'Connell, while a more balanced age pattern of the Land War underlines Parnell's success in attracting the support of all age groups.

But, Parnell was aided by an important combination of factors denied to O'Connell. The key lay in the combination. Apart from a certain degree of political groundwork laid by Butt, the society of the late 1870s and the 1880s differed fundamentally from that of the 1840s. The majority of Land War tenants not only possessed larger farms, but, with a correspondingly higher level of expectations and an increasing degree of politicisation, their reaction to the circumstances of the time was sharper. This reaction took two forms, anti-landlordism which fostered an anti-English outlook, and, secondly, a more direct dislike of England resulting from coercion, which penetrated every nook of the county with the arrest of local Land League leaders, as well as the imprisonment of well-known popular political figures at national level. Since the tenants did not have a tradition of republicanism or revolution, the home government ideal suited them admirably as an expression of their anti-English feelings. As the class with the franchise, they were important to Parnell's promotion of the policy; the very existence of a home rule party depended upon a convinced electorate.

As usual, tenant reaction was accurately reflected in the timing of the priests' statements. Although Home Rule was only gathering momentum in the early 1880s, intense agrarian frustration from 1880 to 1882 provoked 22% of total clerical references to it. The priests also closely linked coercion and home rule.[100] Consequently, they denounced the union as a source of 'disastrous results', depicted the

Home Rule as seen by the *Weekly Freeman.* 29.10.1887.

government as an alien one incapable of ruling Ireland, and portrayed home rule as a panacea for all ills, social, political or economic. Such ills included unemployment, eviction, emigration, poverty, both personal and national, and low agricultural output. The Newport National League under Thomas Meagher flatly rejected the shrewd observation of the North Tipperary Grand Jury in Nenagh, that home rule would not prevent periodic depressions.[101]

The priests were capable of more demonstrative antipathy to English rule. This was most evident in their attitude to the crown, supposedly the central symbol of loyalty in a home rule situation. While there had been an understandable difference of opinion between the bishops about an address to the queen during the famine period,[102] by mid-century she was the toast of every banquet in Tipperary. But her 1887 jubilee was deliberately snubbed by the priests. Moreover there was a marked contrast between the pregnant silence of Tipperary priests and Vatican wishes. The pope advised an Irish compliment to her, both as a woman and as a symbol of authority.[103]

The priests, however, had reacted in a stronger fashion when the Prince of Wales decided to visit Ireland two years earlier. At least 20 of them wholeheartedly supported a proposed boycott of the royal visitor.[104] Clerics of all ages were involved, and although 75% were under 50 years old, 20% were between 51 and 60, considerably higher than the usual proportion. Interestingly, too, 85% were Maynooth alumni, a far higher percentage than usual, suggesting that the Oath of Allegiance did not inculcate unbounded respect for the sovereign. Privately Dr Croke favoured the presentation of addresses, but feared that it might be interpreted as an approval of government policy.[105] The shrewd prelate was, of course, sensitive to public opinion, and, in what was probably a circular to his clergy, advised that 'the charity of their silence' only should be extended to the prince.[106] Many priests were unwilling to be so charitable, and, influenced by the public outlook, denounced His Royal Highness with relish. Lawrence Condon C.C. Clonmel called 'shame on the Irishman who would wish to see English royalty defiling our shores, especially when it plants its unholy presence in the person of the moral Prince of Wales.'[107] Some people, however, wished to get a glimpse of the distinguished visitor, and David Humphreys lamented that they had 'paid homage to the scion of bastardy and herald of Irish misfortunes'.[108]

It is worth noting that several priests including Humphreys, expressed willingness to greet the prince if he came as king of Ireland to open a native parliament.[109] The hearty welcome afforded to the visit of English home rulers by 46 Tipperary priests in 1887 and 1889 suggests that this was not empty rhetoric.[110] Thomas Fennelly Adm. Thurles, chairing one meeting, praised the 'honest Englishmen', who had come to 'consolidate and strengthen the tie of affection between

Ireland and England'. Perhaps the most telling statement was made by Nicholas Rafferty, his curate, who, drawing upon his experience on the English mission, did not deny the kindness or courtesy of Englishmen. Still, he concluded that he had 'scarcely ever met an Englishman yet, who, either from prejudice or ignorance, could enter into the justice of our demands'.

Such moderate sentiments, however, were rare in the hostile atmosphere of the Land War, which sharpened or generated ill-will against England. While this atmosphere eminently suited the promotion of home rule, the real credit for planting the policy in the public mind must rest with Parnell's skilful manipulation of the situation. With the collapse of the Land League the less agrarian, party-controlled, National League became the local machine to forward the policy. James Cantwell, in moving the adoption of the league's programme at its inception in Dublin, stressed its political aim.[111] This was reflected at local level, where the priests waxed eloquent on the home rule theme at the setting up of branches, or at larger league gatherings.[112] Parnell can also claim some of the credit for the support eventually rendered by many of the bishops to the policy in 1886. The most vital factor of all in the conversion of the clergy was his success in creating a disciplined party. The main debate of the P.J. Smyth controversy may have centred on party discipline, but Smyth's avowed hostility to home rule was a significant adjunct,[113] which in 1876 had drawn the fire of priests from Westmeath, his previous constituency.[114] It need hardly be said that subsequent Tipperary M.P.s were not only staunch Parnellites, but avid home rulers also. Naturally, too, the striking and able performance of the Parnellites in Westminster, which provoked such clerical eulogies, also demonstrated the capability of Irishmen to govern themselves. Many of the 92 clerical references to Home Rule made during the Land War embodied the vision of Parnell ruling under the green flag in College Green. Parnell, with his own dislike of the alleged English sense of superiority, inspired the priests with a sense of self-confidence in the Irish race. John Ryan P.P. Ballingarry pointed to such capable 'Irishmen' as Wellington, Wolseley, Marshal McMahon, president of France, and Marshal O'Donnell, prime minister of Spain.[115] There was little trace of an inferiority complex in the priests' attitude that the Irish were intellectually and culturally the superior race, with the logical conclusion that the current relationship of the two races was anomalous. John Cahill C.C. Mullinahone remarked that Ireland was a civilised nation before 'the Saxon emerged from his barbarian serfdom'.[116] James Cantwell announced that Ireland was subject to a power 'that has not half the pretensions to learning or culture'.[117]

It seems that Parnell touched the nerve of the priests, themselves the leaders of their catholic flocks, and no doubt strongly conscious of their own relatively advanced education in this era of limited literacy.

On a wider level they would have considered themselves at least equal to the great majority of Englishmen. This type of pride was the essence of nationalism, and their role in its dissemination was of some importance at a time when Brittania ruled more than the waves. Considering their own vocation it is more than likely that the priests regarded the Irish as morally superior to their masters; the discovery of a homosexual ring among senior officials in Dublin Castle fortified their views. Their disgust was duly registered by contributions to defend William O'Brien, editor of *United Ireland*, who was sued for publicising the affair. 32 Tipperary priests or 18% of the total subscribed.[118] James Cantwell associated the moral with the political in his conviction that the money was not only spent in the cause of morality, but of 'discrediting the government of the enemy that rules this country in the name of law and order'.[119]

Their vision of Parnell in 'our own dear House in College Green'[120] at the head of the much praised party, presupposed that the priests harboured a special esteem for the leader personally. This was so. At least 84 of them recorded their approval either in eugolistic or monetary terms.[121] The slightly higher percentage of priests over 50 years old reflects Parnell's success in wooing the older, more conservative clergy, and the significant Maynooth proportion suggests that Maynooth priests may have been more politically aware than others in this respect. A diocesan breakdown is of some significance mainly because of the low Killaloe representation. For some inexplicable reason it seems that Parnell's stock was not high in the northern section of the county, especially when one considers the more prominent position of Killaloe clergy in the later anti-Parnellite drive.[122] This, however, detracts little from the considerable groundswell of goodwill for Parnell among the Tipperary priesthood. Comparisons with O'Connell were inevitable, and curiously enough the priests saw the Chief in a more impressive light than the Liberator. John Egan P.P. Burgessbeg was typical:- 'Never, do I maintain, did O'Connell, with all his commanding influence, succeed in making the Irish a united people'.[123] Daniel Ryan P.P. Clonoulty placed him in the imperial company of Caesar,[124] while the biblical John Tuohy P.P. Shinrone saw him as a Moses leading his people to the promised land of home rule.[125] He was their 'immortal chief', their 'great and matchless leader', whose name would be 'written in letters of gold in the annals of Irish history'. Public criticism of Parnell would simply not be tolerated in Tipperary. Croke, himself, was so incensed by an article in the *Tablet* condemning Parnell's interview with the French Communard, Henri de Rochefort, that he cancelled all further orders for the paper.[126]

The most ostentatious manifestation of clerical Parnellism, however, lay not in acclamatory flourishes, but in their enthusiastic promotion of the Parnell Testimonial of 1883 to clear the mortgage on his property,

Avondale. This stands in sharp contrast to their failure to support Butt's testimonial. At least 74 priests were involved, and their contributions ranged from one to five pounds.[127] Both Croke and John Power of Waterford were members of the national committee to promote the affair, and personally contributed £50 and £10 respectively.[128] 18 priests, the majority from Cashel and Emly, were on this body.[129] The parish priests were often treasurers of the fund, although they did not always initiate it; William Power P.P. responded to the wishes of his parishoners, and became treasurer in Moyne.[130] The clergy's personal motives for supporting the testimonial are easy to define. Daniel Flannery saw it as an opportunity, especially for tenants, to repay a debt of gratitude to Parnell for his promotion of the land question.[131] The memory of Parnell's imprisonment inspired the generosity of others.[132] Efforts to identify him with crime, particularly the Phoenix Park murders, aroused priestly anger, and stimulated their interest in the testimonial as a protest.[133] The ever-eloquent John Ryan, when sending his £5, summed up their sense of outrage: 'The beastly bellowings of a British House of Commons might be roused as in O'Connell's day by such an infamous trick but the love and respect and confidence of all right-minded men in Mr Parnell is only increased by such diabolical plans to remove public odium from the real culprits'.[134]

Such enthusiasm was also prompted by Croke's leading role in the testimonial campaign.[135] George Errington, Catholic M.P. for Longford and a rabid anti-Parnellite, was one of the chief links in Anglo-Vatican communications, and he spared no effort to enlighten Rome on Croke's part, or to portray him as a supporter of a crime-ridden Parnellite movement.[136] Vatican anxiety to secure diplomatic relations with England partly resulted in Croke being summoned to Rome. The archbishop obviously considered that a possible danger to religion resulting from clerical aloofness from the movement, outweighed the disapproval of his Italian superiors. Public reaction[137] to the hostile Roman circular, *De Parnellio,*[138] of mid-May 1883 certainly vindicated Croke's astuteness. Lay appreciation of the archbishop, the 'unchanged and unchangeable', was as warm as it was antagonistic towards the circular.[139] Croke himself was cautious in his replies to demonstrations. Speaking from the cathedral pulpit after his return from Rome, he confined himself to the safe theme of 'misrepresentations' about himself there.[140] He explained that papal anxiety about the Irish popular movement was partly in the context of European circumstances, especially of France and Italy. Anxious to soothe troubled waters, he discountenanced all disrespectful comments about the pope, and reminded his congregation that Roman mandates merited the obedience of bishops and priests. His cautioning of his priests resulted in a muted clerical reaction to the circular in the county.

Privately, however, they were dismayed; William Burke C.C. Kilbarron revealed his own feeling to his old mentor, Tobias Kirby, when he referred to public astonishment that 'His Holiness would stoop so low as to condemn in particular the Parnell testimonial'.[141] The shock felt by all sections of the priesthood may be gauged from the observation of James Hasson, President of St Columb's College, Derry, that 'very venerable and prudent ecclesiastics' considered the circular a mistake.[142] Strong public criticism was only aired anonymously, and one Tipperary priest, writing on the 'acute pain' caused by the document, suggested that 'circumstances might arise when resistance (to Rome) became an obligation'.[143] The priests felt more comfortable in public condemnation of Errington, although few reached the vituperative level of a non-Tipperary cleric, R.J. Kelsh P.P. Killucan, who assailed the M.P. as 'the lying lick-spittle of the West Briton government, the mean, mongrel, crossbred, quarter-Celt, three-quarter Saxon'.[144]

Clerical participation in several pro-Croke demonstrations was the most obvious indirect manifestation of disapproval of the circular from Rome. On his arrival in Thurles at the end of May 1883 the priests led large contingents to greet him.[145] There were at least 28 priests and representatives from 16 parishes awaiting him there. Despite this, however, and despite their major role in collecting the testimonial, only a relatively small number attended the banquet when the cheque was formally presented to Parnell. This partly stemmed from limited availability of places at the function, but episcopal reserve following the circular also had some bearing on it. Croke forbade James Cantwell to speak there, although he allowed his priests to attend.[146] 6 of them, including Dean Quirke, did so, and David Humphreys sat at Parnell's table.[147] Only 7 other counties had priestly representatives, and, as in the case of the Roman petition of 1854, Tipperary with a possible 11 ranked next to Meath, who had 18.[148] The considerable size of the amount collected, £38,000, may well have been due to the Roman document, perhaps representing, as Michael Davitt put it, a translation of Peter's Pence into Parnell's pounds.[149] It made no such impact in Tipperary for the very important reason that, under Croke's example, the collection there had largely been gathered before the Vatican pronouncement.[150] In fact, immediately prior to the circular, Tipperary's contribution exceeded the combined total of all other counties.[151]

It seems reasonable to state, therefore that the priests' record of support for Parnell, his party and his policies, often contrary to the explicit wishes of the Vatican, is quite remarkable. Only against a background of such unstinting approval can their dismay, disappointment, and ultimate bitterness at the aftermath of the divorce court proceedings be properly understood. It was an unbearable slap in the face for them when the Moses of the 1880s became the 'Herod' and even the 'Lucifer' of the 1890s.

Their immediate reaction was one of sheer disbelief, reinforced by Parnell's triumph over the *Times'* Commission of 1888. This had been a victory which they savoured with intense relish, having played their own part as channels through which money flowed for the leader's defence.[152] When, therefore, news of the divorce suit broke at the close of 1889, a strong editorial in a local newspaper could only comment 'assuredly Piggotism is not yet dead'.[153] Like most priests, Michael B. Corry saw it as merely another attempt to destroy Parnell, and was confident of its failure.[154] Priests and National League branches hastened to publish resolutions and statements of confidence in his innocence.[155] Later on, Robert Foran P.P. Ballylooby offered this as the basic reason for the clerical delay in condemning Parnell.[156]

After initial confusion and hesitation the priests moved against the leader, and they did so on an extensive scale. At least 117 of them, or 60% of the total priesthood of 1890 - 1891, were involved.[157] Most of the statistics compiled reflect the normal pattern for Tipperary, although the Killaloe percentage is high. More interestingly, the Maynooth figure is only slightly above the normal ratio, reflecting a reluctance, perhaps, to abandon their earlier very strong adhesion to his leadership. The ratio between parish priests and curates is normal, indicating equal hostility by both groups, although in actual fact 65% of total pastors and 58% of total curates were anti-Parnellite. The relative instability of the curates' body, however, explains this; several of those registered for 1890 would have moved to another county at the end of the year before the crisis arose. To complement this, 11 curates entered the county in 1891, and may not have had the opportunity to speak on the issue, or, perhaps, did not wish to introduce dissension into their new parishes. Apart from this, there were always priests who refused to become embroiled in political discussions. It is certain that not all of the 78 priests who maintained a low profile were Parnellite, but it is impossible to hazard a guess at priestly support for Parnell in Tipperary in 1890 and 1891. Only 4 priests spoke of him without hostility, and another, John Layne C.C. Bansha, was privately friendly.[158] The most outspoken Parnellite priest was Robert Power P.P. Ballyneale, who candidly declared that he 'did not give a fig for the opinions of the bishops of Ireland', and pointed to Elizabethan days as proof of episcopal political fallibility.[159] The real significance of Power's case lay in the rejection of his views by a majority of his parishioners, who proceeded to establish the anti-Parnellite Irish National Federation despite his hostility.[160] The other three priests, Dr Lawrence Hayes P.P. Bansha, William Kelly C.C. Powerstown, and Cornelius Egan P.P. Mounsea, were not as outspoken in their Parnellism, but did not join the federation, preferring to remain neutral.[161] This small minority of Parnellite priests reflected the pattern at national level. Some of the more prominent non-Tipperary Parnellite priests were Nicholas Murphy P.P. Kilmanagh, Co Kilkenny, Lawrence Ryan C.C. Frankfurt, Co Offaly, Kit Mullen P.P. Moynalty, Co Meath, J.R. Collins P.P. Co Donegal, Frank O'Connor C.C. Ballymartle, Co Cork and Walter Hurley C.C. Delgany, Co Wicklow.[162]

The sheer size of the anti-Parnellite majority suggests a deep degree of intransigence on the priests' part. Their resoluteness was manifested in various ways. A total opposition to Parnellite candidates at election times, which will be looked at later, was only one dimension of their general intolerance of all Parnellites; for example, while Dean T.H. Kinnane professed anxiety about disunity among his parishoners, and forbade anti-Parnellites to denounce their opponents, he continued to castigate some Parnellites as 'the scum of the earth'.[163] Clearly, the priests' definition of unity meant conformity to their own outlook. A second example of their resolve was their reaction to the Boulogne conference between Parnell, John Dillon and William O'Brien.[164] David Humphreys, realising the influence of O'Brien and Dillon at local level, dreaded the possibility of a compromise between them and Parnell. Humphreys informed Dillon that the negotiations at Boulogne boosted Parnell's influence in the wake of his defeat in the Kilkenny by-election, and made the anti-Parnellite campaign more difficult.[165] In another letter to William O'Brien, he reiterated his feelings, and, depicting Parnell as a ruthless, selfish, ambitious man willing to sacrifice all to keep the leadership, he advised bluntly 'hunt him out of public life'.[166] He further warned O'Brien of clerical solidarity against Parnell's leadership. His anxiety and opinions were similar to those of other priests including his friend, Canon Keller and of Croke himself.[167] The latter's motto to O'Brien, his former pupil, was 'no surrender'. The tormented archbishop was prepared to condemn O'Brien, if necessary, on the premise that if he failed to oppose Parnell he was for him, 'and should be reckoned with as such.'[168] The breakdown of the negotiations and the subsequent anti-Parnellism of O'Brien and Dillon were greeted with relief by the priests, although these two politicians were unhappy at the new surge of clerical political activity, which contributed much to the influence of the peevish Timothy Healy.

Irreconcilable anti-Parnellism suggests that there was a planned drive by the clergy, and this was partly true; five meetings in December 1890 and January 1891 attracted 62 priests, and four of these meetings were chaired by clerics.[169] Archbishop Croke, earlier the bastion of Parnellism, now became the clerical leader of anti-Parnellite feeling in Tipperary. If his famous visitation of 1881 resembled a crusade on behalf of the Land League, his 1891 visitation was nothing less than an anti-Parnellite campaign in which he nerved the arm of the priests and laity, who flocked to hear him.[170] Initially, and Lawrence Hayes mentioned this when he made his stand, Croke had offered freedom of action to his priests, and professed an impartial friendship towards them irrespective of their course.[171] But, he did, however, make the inconsistent addendum that support for Parnell was impossible as far as the priests were concerned. Within a few months, his attitude hardened considerably, and he seconded Dr Walsh's proposal that clerical obedience to the bishops' address of December 1890 be made mandatory.[172] Until then obedience was expected, but not obligatory. It would seem that the bishops were not so confident that all priests would toe the line. The intrepid Croke was now prepared to make them do so, and did not flinch from providing a militant clerical front. He circularised his priests to organise their parishes *'pro aris et focis'* and requested their presence at a Thurles meeting where 'we shall prove that we have a heart to feel and a head to guide us in this matter, aye and an arm to strike as well if necessary in defence of honour, religion and country'.[173] In his private correspondence with Archbishop Walsh, Croke made it plain that 'the blackthorn will be mercilessly applied' to defend a particular anti-Parnellite demonstration.[174] He stiffened the resolve of the anxious pastor of Murroe, Michael Ryan, in the face of an approaching Parnellite meeting, by pointing to himself as a fighting man who would in similar circumstances 'draw the sword'[175] a tactic which Ryan successfully employed.[176]

Such bellicosity was hardly compatible with the priests' vocation as peacemakers. It should be seen, however, in the context of nineteenth century convention. To be fair, too, it was not always merely a symptom of their bitterness, but was also a practical and unavoidable means of self-defence against a very often violent Parnellism. Nevertheless, a tremendously aggressive clericalism in turn was frequently responsible for provoking this violence. Severe fracas took place in such urban centres as Tipperary Town, Nenagh and Thurles. After an hour-long melée in Tipperary, Matt Ryan, David Humphreys and Canon Patrick Ryan, Galbally, succeeded in ejecting a Parnellite faction from a meeting chaired by Canon Cahill.[177] This affair produced much ill-will because of the insults hurled by Canon Ryan, who denounced his opponents, one of whom was a Town Commissioner's son, as the scruff of Tipperary. He later satirised Parnellites as having 'an orange kidney, a black heart and a blue gizzard'.[178] In Nenagh the police reported that similar bad feeling had sundered lifelong friendships.[179] The poster of John Scanlan announcing a meeting was torn from the shop windows, and a constable remarked that 'the people openly say they won't have the interference and wire-pulling of the priests'.[180] Scanlan was so unpopular that a boycott of his collection was contemplated. Several violent clashes took place in Thurles,[181] the seat of the popular archbishop, who denied that he had castigated the people for their stand.[182] Anti-clericalism was so rife there that the administrator, Nicholas Rafferty, felt that the priests might have to retire from politics. This was a rare enough view, and the priests greatly resented the Parnellite cry of clerical dictation.[183] Croke in particular disliked the alleged remark by Parnell about knocking the bottom out of the priests.[184]

Parnellism was strong in such urban areas, as it was in Roscrea, Clonmel, Borrisoleigh and Cahir, as well as in the more rural parishes of Bansha, Golden and Holycross.[185] Parnell leadership committees existed in many of these and formed a convinced organised nucleus. It is difficult, however, to measure the precise strength of the Parnellites in these areas. The priests tried to understate it. David Humphreys maintained that the degree of support for Parnell was grossly exaggerated by the *Freeman's Journal.*[186] He based his opinion on the situation in Tipperary town, where he said the Parnellite minority centred around the 'Dalton family clique'. The violence of Parnellites, influenced by the I.R.B., should not disguise the very real influence of the priests in the county as a whole. One special branch constable reported that the majority of Borrisokane parishioners were anti-Parnellite, 'and will follow their priests anywhere'.[187] He remarked that the majority in Moyne and Templetuohy also responded to the priests' call.[188] This was the case in many other parishes, too.

The emotional intensity aroused on both sides and the increasing depth of the rift are a sad chapter in Irish history. What now remains to be examined are the fundamentals which produced such violent symptoms. These, put forward by the anti-Parnellites, and vehemently refuted by the other side, rested upon three issues, the political, the moral and the agrarian, each closely interacting on the others. Ostensibly and understandably, the priests seemed to attach most importance to the moral dimension,[189] where they had extra authority. The bishops' address,[190] which stressed the moral, was a tame statement indeed in comparison with some of the scurrility indulged in by the priests. It is difficult to divine how much of this was mere platform oratory to swing public opinion against Parnell, and how much was the expression of a genuine feeling of distaste for a serious breach of the sexual code. Apart from a cutting reference to the spending of the 1883 testimonial money for debauchery purposes, David Humphreys used the love affair as a psychological wedge by concentrating upon the outrage done to the supposedly aggrieved husband, Captain William O'Shea, whose wife had suffered 'the grossest insult and injury, which man can inflict upon a woman'.[191] Combining the martial with the marital, James Costigan C.C. Birr tried to identify his audience with the Captain by arguing that many men would prefer to lose their lives than their wives in such a manner,[192] a view shared by Archdeacon Ryan.[193] The so-called fire-escape incident,[194] and Parnell's alleged 'acrobatic performances',[195] were eagerly seized upon by the priests to heap ridicule on his head.[196] The fact that he was, as they put it, unrepentant, also increased their ire,[197] which was further inflamed by his marriage to Katharine in June 1891.

Following this the theological artillery was drawn up in earnest. Michael B. Corry disagreed that Parnell's protestant status exempted him from condemnation, and he pointed to the protestant tenet of indissolubility, concluding that the registry office contract could only be regarded with 'abhorrence and loathing'.[198] Indeed, Dr Jellet, the protestant dean of St Patrick's, Dublin, supported such a view in a sermon which was as hard-hitting as those of some priests.[199] Interestingly, one of the non-Tipperary priests, Nicholas Murphy, who was an ex-professor of moral theology, in a private letter to Timothy Harrington, highlighted the theological viewpoint that protestant marriages were not sacraments, but contracts only.[200] David Humphreys, no mean theologian, dispensed with sophistication, and bluntly upheld the church's right to denounce 'fallen women as the most dangerous pests to society', adding, 'we will tolerate no attempt to make vice respectable, to screen adultery under the so-called privilege of ladies. An adultress will always be an adultress in Ireland and no process of white washing in the registry office or any other office will make her anything else'.[201] Humphreys, noted for keeping an eye on the welfare of 'fallen women', was the terror of the prostitutes who solicited the custom of the garrison in Tipperary town.

There was a second and wider moral perspective aired by the priests, that of public morality, which may have been only a tactic to arouse more widespread opposition to Parnell. One priest, Fr Murphy, Tullamore, King's Co., who claimed to represent the views of his fellow clerics, told his congregation that the leadership was a question of 'social and moral purity'.[202] James Halpin C.C. Roscrea argued that demoralisation among Irishmen was too great a price to pay for the victories of the past.[203] Michael Breen C.C. Shinrone appealed to the superstitious instinct when he warned that God's curse would light upon any freedom achieved under Parnell's leadership.[204] Although it was not a theme in Tipperary, some priests probably feared that their political opinions would be stifled in a home rule situation under a man they had so viciously attacked.[205] An anonymous priest, obviously always an opponent of the whole movement of the 1880s, had wider reservations still, and felt that the only difference in the morality of Parnell and a possible successor was one of degree.[206] He was referring specifically to 'that spoiled serpent', William O'Brien, and to the assertion of John Dillon that he would prefer to take his politics from the sultan of Turkey than from the pope.

The sheer weight of moral outrage pouring from the priests suggests that morality was the principal base of their anti-Parnellism. The high percentage of priests over 40 who spoke on the matter indicates that it particularly influenced the older men. There is no denying the depth of the disgust felt by some of these Victorian clergymen, nor is there any doubt that their campaign was fought with the potent weapons of morality. But nineteenth century platform oratory always tended to be extreme, and the virulence of the anti-Parnellite attacks tends to mask a deeper motivation, which triggered off the whole conflict.

The vital key to this is seen in the timing of public clerical criticism. Not a single public reference to morality was made by Tipperary priests before the publication of Gladstone's letter to John Morley, which, for the first time made it clear that English support for home rule would never be forthcoming while Parnell remained leader of the party. Had they been so morally outraged against Parnell they would surely have dispensed earlier with the initial timidity that vanished on publication of the letter. It may be interesting to realise that prior to this the priests did not expect Parnell to disappear completely from the political scene. Reviewing the issue at a later date, Robert Foran P.P. Ballylooby felt that Parnell might have continued to play an important role as an ordinary M.P. had he resigned.[207] William Meagher C.C. Clonmel, like other priests, went a stage further, and drew the conclusion that his later return to the leadership would have received the blessing of bishops and priests.[208] The logical but unsound ethical implication was that time would erase the moral blot. The disappointment of John Scanlan at Parnell's refusal to accept an 'honourable' retirement was hardly based on moral principles.[209] Parnellites were quick to highlight delayed emphasis on the moral as an act of crass hypocrisy. Dr Croke was especially stung by a *Freeman's* editorial on the timing of the bishops' address, and he denied that he had ever condoned Parnell's morality as a private matter.[210] The few Tipperary Parnellite priests did not dwell upon this, but Frank O'Connor, curate in Ballymartle, Co. Cork, denounced the hypocrisy of these M.P.s, who seceded from the party, particularly of Healy, who on three occasions upheld Parnell's leadership after the divorce court verdict.[211] All the Parnellite priests insisted that private morality should be divorced from politics, and cited cases of immorality among the royal family at various times.[212]

Despite statements to the contrary, therefore, the evidence suggests that political success would have been an acceptable antidote to the unpalatable moral pill. But, the very real danger to home rule galvanised the priests into action, and the moral fuel was used to power the the political debate. An extract from the long, strong rebuke of Bishop Patrick O'Donnell, Raphoe, in referring to the 1886 Galway election best illustrates this: 'He put Ireland under the feet of Mrs O'Shea more effectively than he put Galway under the Captain's'.[213] It took the bishop until Christmas Eve 1890 to make this remark, and it is significant that all clerical opinions on the Galway election were only aired four years after the event,[214] again underlining the primacy of the political issue. The priests were prepared to remain silent while Parnell seemed likely to achieve home rule. This is not to say, however, that they realised the real reason for foisting the unwanted Captain on Galway.

After Gladstone's letter to Morley some of the Parnellite priests saw the choice as one between Parnell and Gladstone, and, like Nicholas Murphy, felt that independence gained 'by cutting the throat of Ireland's greatest benefactor' would not be worth attaining.[215] Such an obviously untenable argument was a serious chink in the armour of Parnell's defenders, and was exploited ruthlessly by their opponents. David Humphreys urged that the country should not be sacrificed 'through false sentimentality'.[216] He contradicted the theses of Parnell's controversial manifesto, and upheld the party's ability to maintain an independent stand in Parliament and attain home rule without Parnell. To support his point, Humphreys drew attention to the leader's prolonged absence from the House, revealing that he had attended only 5 times since 1882.

This was a familiar clerical theme,[217] and introduces the second and equally important dimension of the political question – the unity and therefore the very existence of the party they had supported so strongly. Both issues were closely linked, of course, and in retrospect some priests actually praised the party for its loyalty to Parnell prior to the publication of the fatal letter.[218] Following this the priests clearly expected a unanimous rejection of his leadership by the members; a majority did reject him, and Humphreys stressed obedience to majority decision as a cardinal principle of party discipline.[219] Lack of unanimity, however, evoked hitherto suppressed clerical reservations on the wisdom of having allowed such an acquisition of power and independence of grass roots by the party. The logic was that the party should reflect the opinion of constituents, which in this case, as far as the priests were concerned, was the necessity for Parnell to resign. In an obvious reference to the demise of the convention system, James Halpin C.C. Roscrea attacked the imposing of M.P.s on constituents by 'parcel post', and 'to complete the matter, absolutely no control'.[220] Halpin was reflecting the attitude particularly of bishops, who had not relished the increasing relegation of the Church to junior political partner since the rapprochement of 1885.[221] In his advocacy of decentralisation, Halpin proposed that future M.P.s address their constituents regularly. He suggested the establishment of a committee representing laity and clergy to scrutinise an M.P.'s credentials, including his moral ones, and to note his parliamentary progress. It was a reminder that the priests still saw their role in politics as natural and important. The fact remains, however, that they did not speak against Parnell's centralising process until the crisis shattered the party's equilibrium. At that stage they were powerless to prevent the split, and Dr Michael Bugler P.P. Birr took the occasion of a requiem mass to make the beautifully inappropriate remark that Lucifer drew angels with him.[222] The Tipperary clergy regrouped behind the anti-Parnellite M.P.s, who founded what they called the Irish Parliamentary Party; the involvement of 21 Tipperary priests in the National Committee set up to promote this party was a sure sign of their deep anxiety.[223]

They had good cause for concern, because in contrast to the proportions at national level, two of the four Tipperary Members were fallen angels. These were Henry Harrison, Parnell's biographer, and John O'Connor. James Halpin seethed because of Harrison's failure to reply to a letter from his parish priest, Edmund O'Leary, demanding an explanation of his stand.[224] Halpin's own letter to Harrison seeking 'an account of your stewardship' expressed the feelings of other clerics.[225] But they were powerless until the general election of 1892, when neither Harrison nor O'Connor was re-elected for the county. There were no by-elections in Tipperary during the crisis, but the municipal elections provide some foretaste of later clerical action, and highlight the priests' desire to starve the Parnellites of political power at local level. The Thurles priests nominated two anti-Parnellite Poor Law guardians to oppose the sitting Parnellites there, and provoked some resentment in the town by their interference.[226] The Clonmel curates helped to return all anti-Parnellites as guardians,[227] and Paul Power played a leading role in the success of anti-Parnellites in the elections of town commissioners in Carrick-on-Suir, although he failed to prevent the election of Parnellite guardians.[228]

The non-Tipperary parliamentary by-elections, however, offer the best dress rehearsal of the general election. Historians disagree about the weight of influence wielded by the priests at these elections, but it would be difficult to exaggerate the energy of their involvement. Undoubtedly, many electors had already made up their minds to vote anti-Parnellite irrespective of clerical pressure. Nevertheless, the priests organised the converted and provided a united phalanx against Parnellite efforts. Coming so soon after the divorce, the Kilkenny election gives an indication of Parnell's political standing at that stage. Displaying a mixture of anxiety, nervousness and confidence, Bishop Abraham Brownrigg of Ossory was convinced that victory would come not from politics, morality or the Irish Party, but 'purely and entirely' from the influence, 'family, personal and ministerial, of the priesthood of Ossory'.[229] Traditional after-Mass meetings and canvassing were the main strategy used by the priests.[230] The pattern was similar in Carlow; one newspaper reported upon the 'extraordinary efforts' of the clergy there.[231] Most of them read from the altar the bishops' resolutions of 25 June condemning Parnell.[232] In one such sermon, Edward Kavanagh C.C. reduced the entire affair to a conflict between Parnell and the clergy of Ireland.[233] Accordingly, he advised Parnellite members of the Sacred Heart and other religious societies either to withdraw or discountenance Parnell and his followers. Tipperary priests observed these two elections with intense interest. In fact, David Humphreys travelled to Kilkenny as an electioneering agent.[234] He congratulated the Carlow electors, and predicted that Parnell would not return any candidate outside 'dirty Dublin' in the general election.[235] Michael B. Corry also saw the defeat of Parnell's 'Rusty Kettle' (Andrew J. Kettle) as a sign of future victory.[236]

While the moral and political formed the essential basis of the priests' attack, the agrarian element became increasingly important. It was also a practical and effective lever. If support for Parnell was strongest among the non-farming classes of artisans and labourers,[237] there can be little doubt that the anti-Parnellism of the farmers was at least partly due to the agrarian dimension. References to the so-called destruction of the Land League by the Kilmainham treaty were the least important aspect stressed by the priests.[238] Emphasis on landlord intransigence resulting from the crisis is of much greater significance as a psychological weapon, since it apparently could be substantiated. Michael B. Corry pointed to the troubled Benedine and Bawn estate near Nenagh as an example of this.[239] Archdeacon Daniel Ryan warned the farmers that landlords would became 'stiff and unreasonable' due to the split in their ranks; his proof lay in the changed attitude of a Fethard landlord.[240]

Apart from an alleged change of heart by landlords, the priests were also seriously concerned about possible demoralisation among tenants engaged in rent disputes. Humphreys was frantic at the detrimental influence of the crisis upon the already weakening resolve of the Smith-Barry tenants.[241] He was livid at Parnell's declaration against the struggle and at the action of local Parnellites in persuading the tenants to return to their holdings. Tenants, however, suffered much more than the psychological shock of seeing the Irish party in tatters; the freezing of the Paris fund[242] was even more relevant to their position, and aroused intense hostility among the priests.[243] Humphreys's frequent reassurances to tenants that their 'public exchequer' was healthy[244] were seriously undermined. He bombarded the leaders in Dublin with letters demanding funds for the campaign;[245] his vital role in securing finance explains the private anxiety, which belied the confidence of his public statements. J.F.X. O'Brien was exasperated by the persistence of the Tipperary priest, and Alfred Webb was shocked at the tone of one letter from Humphreys to O'Brien.[246] In these circumstances Humphreys considered that the freezing of the fund was 'a more atrocious and a more disastrous betrayal of the Irish tenantry and of the Irish nation than that of Keogh and Sadleir'.[247]

John Layne C.C. Golden, a secret sympathiser with Parnell, was one of the few priests who did not condemn Parnell's action. Anxious to conclude a longstanding rent dispute in the Cloughleigh estate in the parish, where the tenants were Parnellite, Layne contacted the Parnellite, Timothy Harrington, in an effort to secure funds.[248] He enclosed a letter from the anti-Parnellite, David Sheehy, which absolutely refused to condone any one estate benefiting from the fund to the exclusion of others. Significantly, this dispute reveals that the financial tide had ebbed prior to the crisis, when Layne's parish priest, Michael McDonnell, had bitterly criticised the trickle from the National League as 'perfectly scandalous'.[249]

Nevertheless, the blocking of the Paris fund, and, equally important, the adverse effect of the crisis upon the American cash flow, were of fundamental importance. But, the impact on the less vital local collections was much more apparent to those priests less involved in financial outlay than Humphreys. As with the Sadleirite defection, it is quite certain that some money-conscious farmers availed themselves of the opportunity to withhold assistance.[250] Still, John O'Brien P.P. explaining the small collection in Holycross, was convinced that local farmers were genuinely shocked and disheartened.[251] He considered that the tenants were the real victims of the crisis. In Carrick-on-Suir, Philip Power was forced to canvass the farmers because of the slender sum yielded by the original collection.[252] Matt Ryan was less tactful in Lattin where he published a list of defaulters;[253] a kind of agrarian 'rascally list'! In several areas the Tenants' Defence Association split, with the Parnellites refusing to contribute.[254] The Tipperary town collection was boycotted by them, although David Humphreys expressed satisfaction at the £200 raised.[255] Their concern at the financial position was also highlighted by the attendance of 57 priests at the 1891 fund-raising convention in Thurles, which had more than a whiff of anti-Parnellism about it.[256]

Conscious as the priests were of dwindling funds, the most painful result the crisis to them was the destruction of the Irish National League. Despite this, they were the most forceful and active agents in supplanting it as a Parnellite machine controlling the funds. They did not cease involvement in it until it became obvious that Parnellite control could not be shaken. Bishop Thomas J. McRedmond, Killaloe, favoured clerical withdrawal irrespective of the Boulogne conference results, and Timothy Harrington's reorganising circular was decisively rejected by the Tipperary priests.[257] Accordingly, the reorganisation proceeded with laymen replacing the clergy as local executives.[258] The league, however, was not only weakened memberwise, but had far fewer branches.[259]

It now represented local organised Parnellism, and so made the foundation of a rival body imperative. The Irish National Federation was, therefore, floated on March 10th 1891, when 1500 delegates, many of them priests, assembled in Dublin under Justin McCarthy M.P., who became president of the organisation.[260] It spread rapidly throughout Tipperary, although it failed to take root in a minority of parishes until the autumn of 1891, mainly because of Parnellite opposition or sheer public apathy; other parishes did not have any branches at all for similar reasons. 62 branches were eventually established in 53 parishes, 83% of Tipperary's total.[261] The overall parochial spread was somewhat similar to that of the Land League, although federation units were smaller. It was less extensive than the old National League, probably because of its shorter span of existence or perhaps signifying a withdrawal from politics by less politicised parishes, which had been drawn into the National League. Whatever the weaknesses of the Federation, widespread clerical involvement was its most notable feature. Not only did they attend the larger meetings to launch the movement and help raise badly-needed finance,[262] but their participation in the network was very extensive. 90 priests, or 56% of the total clerical body, were involved,[263] which was a higher percentage than that of either the Land League or the National League, despite the wider network of the latter. This is a sure illustration of the deep hostility the priests felt towards Parnell. For propaganda purposes, the agrarian character of the federation was aired,[264] but in their hearts they saw it in its true light, an anti-Parnellite machine, which had been initially floated by the national committee that lay behind the Irish Parliamentary Party. Edmund O'Leary, although conceding its agrarian role, stressed that it was 'a creature of the people' and not 'the servant of the insolent dictator'.[265] Michael B. Corry particularly emphasised its anti-Parnellite role, arguing that it was not merely a facsimile of the National League.[266] Michael Barry C.C. Gurtnahoe viewed it as an election instrument to oust Parnellite M.P.s;[267] reflecting a common theme at inaugural branch meetings, John Tuohy P.P. Shinrone appropriately saw its fight as one for 'faith, morality and freedom'.[268]

This was the rallying-cry of the priests, but apparently it did not include freedom of the press. They were no more willing to condone freedom of a Parnellite press than agrarian or political freedom under Parnell. Most Tipperary newspapers were anti-Parnellite; the only Parnellite paper, the *Tipperary News*, owned by the Clonmel Parnell Leadership Committee, conspicuously lacked clerical subscribers.[269] Michael McGrath P.P. Drangan, by no means virulently anti-Parnellite, quickly disclaimed any connection with it when he received a copy through his letter-box.[270] The most extensive clerical antagonism, however, was aroused by the *Freeman's Journal*, which, ironically, had been lukewarm towards Parnell in the 1870s, but later became strongly Parnellite and continued so even after the publication of Gladstone's letter. There had been sporadic clerical criticism of the paper in earlier years,[271] but these were tame compared with the denunciations of the early 1890s.[272] The priests' wrath was aroused by alleged distorted reporting.[273] Its policy of relegating the moral issue was obnoxious to Archdeacon Daniel Ryan, who denounced 'some ignorant little scribe' for 'lecturing' Dr Croke on morality.[274] The dramatic action of Dean Kinnane in burning the paper at a public meeting savoured of the medieval, but clearly illustrates clerical antagonism.[275] Croke, one of the paper's important shareholders,[276] was equally hostile.[277] Nevertheless, he opposed an episcopal broadside, doubting its utility and fearing that it might provoke a Parnellite cry on the freedom of the press.[278] He was also the refuge of Edmund Dwyer Gray, who, anxious about falling sales and a possible Roman condemnation, eventually, on the pretext of Parnell's marriage,[279] brought the paper into anti-Parnellite ranks.[280] He promised the Archbishop to express regret at the strong anti-clerical language earlier used by the paper.[281] A requisition signed by Croke and Walsh called an extraordinary general meeting of shareholders, and within a month the Parnellite directors resigned.[282]

This was an actual and a psychological triumph, and was interpreted by Michael Corry as a sign of approaching victory.[283] He was, however, both cynical of the paper's conversion and quite unforgiving — 'whatever the future policty of the *Freeman's* and whatever change its directorate might be contemplating, the people would never forget the fact that they had lost confidence in its teachings'.[284] He seemed to favour a continuation of the boycott which had been in operation for some time with clerical approval. The priests also visited newsagents to promote the sale of the newly-established *National Press*, another dimension of the boycott.[285] Altar sermons in support of this paper underlined the moral side of clerical thought.[286] The weight of contemporary comment and the worry of Dwyer Gray indicate that the new paper began to damage the *Freeman's* circulation. The existence of two rival daily newspapers intensified the level of propaganda between league and federation, and the increased bitterness was hardly blunted by the editorship of Tim Healy. Ironically, the blowing up of the *Press* offices hastened amalgamation with the *Freeman's Journal*.[287]

This unfortunate incident signified that Parnell's death in no way eased the conflict. The historian might be forgiven for supposing that the death of the chief protagonist would have restored some degree of tranquility. After all the Parnellites were not adulterers. But, if anything, the antagonism sharpened, with Parnellites denouncing the priests as their dead leader's most conspicious tormentors,[288] and the anti-Parnellites pointing to divine influence in the death of this relatively young man; as the *Nationalist* solemnly announced, 'the awful chastening hand of God has visibly touched our land, and the situation in more than one respect is heavily laden with the gravest essentials'.[289] What had happened was that the controversy had by then outgrown the personal issue, the split had crystallised almost into two opposing ideologies, and the priests played a very major part in its perpetuation. They continued to view Parnellism as a potent force, a symbol of immorality, anti-clericalism and political dictatorship. They neither attended his funeral nor voiced regret at his passing. Michael B. Corry remarked that his death twelve months earlier would have resulted in mourning a great national loss, but 'the events of the last twelve months forbade them to do more than observe the charity of silence over him'.[290] Both Corry and his fellow curate, John Scanlan, cast sentiment aside with a vengeance, and however desirable, they felt that party unity might be too dearly purchased.[291] The irreconcilable Scanlan promised stern opposition to the re-election of most Parnellite M.P.s. This, too, was the prevailing mood of a federation meeting in Templemore, attended by 11 priests, where Thomas Hackett C.C. Loughmore labelled such M.P.s as 'Elthamite-Brightonite-Bedlamite'.[292] The parish priest, Canon William Meagher, was gratified at the defeat of John Redmond in the Cork by-election. David Humphreys made it plain that Parnell's death had not softened his bitterness, when he travelled to Cork as an anti-Parnellite campaigner in the Winter of 1891.[293]

It may be confidently said, therefore, that few events in the period from the middle of the nineteenth century aroused such a degree of clerical rancour on such an extensive scale as the crisis of 1890-1891. The priests, in many respects politically redundant by that stage because of party centralisation and the growth of the party machine, received a new lease of political life. It has been suggested that they reached a climax of political influence in 1852 when they were driven by animosity towards the Ecclesiastical Titles Bill. This tends to equate political power with extensive platform activity and virulence, and if it is so then the priests were as powerful in 1891 as they were in 1851. They paid a high price, however, for their temporary political resurgence. This was an anti-clerical legacy, which survived, especially in urban centres, long after Parnell's death, and is well portrayed in Joyce's dinner scene.[294] There was some justification for this legacy; but the historian must consider severe criticism directed towards the priests in a balanced perspective. The clergy certainly did not initiate anti-Parnellism. This began in committee room 15. Furthermore their anti-Parnellite sentiments were not significantly stronger than their previous Parnellism. As the most vocal sector of society it was inevitable that their voices should be louder than others. This had always been the case — as landlords, fenians and police had complained on many occasions from mid-century onwards. But, let there be no mistake, this practised eloquence was important in crushing Parnell after the decision of committee room 15; it played no small part in fanning existing flames, contributing to what Yeats called the 'hysterica passio', which 'dragged this quarry down.'

Charles Stewart Parnell

Chapter Nine

THE PRIEST – A POLITICAL PORTRAIT

"The political power of the priesthood rests upon the people's respect for their [the priests'] spiritual functions". *Irish People 19/11/1864*

What has emerged from this investigation is the existence of a relatively well-educated peasant priesthood in a society of little more than functional literacy. This priesthood had by mid-century, or certainly soon afterwards, largely come to grips with various spiritual and ecclesiastical problems. Aided by synodical guidelines these priests imposed a large measure of Catholic discipline upon society, as well as making frequent examinations of their own consciences. Following the dramatic upheaval of the famine, which profoundly changed the church in Ireland, they found themselves in a society dominated by their own kith and kin, the tenant farmers, who were the bastions of this church spiritually and financially. Not only could the clergy identify with this class on a social and spiritual level, but their respective politics were, as might be expected, comfortingly compatible. It was precisely because of this affinity that the priests found themselves sucked into the stormy vortex of popular politics, so that extensive clerical activity became one of the most conspicuous and controversial phenomena of such politics. It reflected their conviction that in the prevailing political and social circumstances their ministry, while primarily spiritual, also embraced the temporal. No less than 77% of the total priesthood played some public part in politics from 1850 to 1891.

Although they justified such activity by spiritual references, the priests' seminary training and theological knowledge, though important, were by no means the most significant influences in determining their political attitudes and priorities. Their farming background and the outlook of the farmers were of fundamental importance, while the power of the bishops to control clerical political activity cannot be ignored either. It seems reasonable to suggest that while social background was essentially the formative, and public opinion the motive, force, which dictated their political path, theology was a guiding influence within the broad confines of that path. The bishops's influence was essentially preventive although rarely used in this manner.

But the primacy of any one influence, and the precise combination of all, depended upon the nature of the question at stake, which in turn also partly determined the limits of the priests' power. While purely political questions absorbed less of their time than agrarian matters, they reveal an interesting interaction of influences. As regards separatism, episcopal and the moral influences emerge as very powerful factors indeed which added an edge to the priests' hostility. Such an edge was not present in the apathetic or self-interested attitude of the laity. Nevertheless, it is vital to analyse clerical anti-fenianism against the largely labourer-artisan background of the fenians, the clergy's own farming origins and the indifference of the farmers towards the republican ideology. Interestingly, however, general apathy allowed more scope for clerical political initiative in other non-agrarian matters also. In politico-religious issues such as the Ecclesiastical Titles Bill or the proposed nunneries bills, the priests, inspired by theological training, ethical principles and episcopal precepts, could and did take the initiative. Nowhere, however, was this more apparent than in their conversion to home rule, and more especially in their early adherence to Parnell and his party, when they clearly moved ahead of their parishioners. Unmistakeable proof of this lies in their hostile reaction to P.J. Smyth, and more significantly in their support of the Parnellite candidate at the divided 1883 convention. Moral considerations, however, while evident, were not of notable importance in constitutional politics, although, again, they made priestly anti-Parnellism more acute than that of the laity, and gives the impression that the priests saw themselves almost as the moral guardians of Tipperary's political future. But the influence of Archbishop Croke on the thinking of his priests regarding the necessity for an Irish party cannot be over-stressed.

While their ability to create political activity on such issues among an apathetic laity must be conceded, it is important to realise that their course was in no way fundamentally antithetical to the political outlook of the farmers, whose political interests were mainly geared towards agrarian matters, and were essentially moulded by self-interest. This is evident, for example, from tenant reaction against the very threat to any decline in their living standard and their lack of sympathy, if not downright hostility, towards the labourer problem. Unlike the case in purely political affairs, local ferment was a vital ingredient in the priests' power in agrarian questions. Invariably, however, on such occasions they tended to follow rather than lead — their social background and sensitivity to public opinion being the deciding factors. Only in the campaign for the labourers' cottages did the priests, and then a small minority of them, strongly oppose the stinginess of their kinsfolk. For this minority the moral consciousness inherent in their pastoral vocation overcame not only an inbred social prejudice, but a reluctance to clash with the self-interest of the farmers.

Such a stand, however, was the exception rather than the rule, either in agrarian or non-agrarian politics. Furthermore, a willingness to lend their support in the cottages and employment problems did not extend into the realm of political ideology, and the priests roundly rejected the republicanism of the labouring classes, which was alien to the political tradition of their kinsfolk. It is notable that the farmers never embraced separatism to any significant extent either in 1848 or 1867, and were not numbered among the so-called Parnellite 'hill-side men' of 1891. As the possessors of some property, however limited, they had all to lose and nothing to gain in a revolution situation. This was clear from their call for the introduction of the Peace Preservation Act prior to the rising. Their relief that property was not molested was partly manifested by their subsequent support of amnesty for fenian prisoners, but this most certainly did not signify an approbation of, much less a desire to embrace, separatist ideology. Certainly, the analysis of the election results after the amnesty campaign refutes the suggestion of a notable republican conviction among the middle-class electorate.

It is significant that the priests' course was largely parallel. Despite some clerical involvement in the ranks of the Young Irelanders, and despite the oratorical flourishes of such men as John Kenyon, not one priest was seriously involved in the Ballingarry rising. The priests, too, like the laity, ignored the call to arms of the *Tribune* during the Crimean War, and while the Tipperary Independent Club of the '50s was strongly identified with Young Irelandism the movement by that time was a spent force. All that remained was an aura of vague romantic nationalism, which helped The O'Donoghue to victory in 1858. But, The O'Donoghue was quick to point out that contemporary Young Irelandism did not mean republicanism, and priestly plans to honour him as a nationalist must be seen in this light. The clergy largely equated his patriotism with the independent stand adopted by him in parliament.

Only a tiny minority of priests showed sympathy with the fenians of the 1860s, none was involved in the rising and none was arrested for conspiracy. Later, the more radical priests of the 1880s were as antipathetic to current republicanism as their predecessors has been. Their frequent anti-English statements against lawful authority, including the government, magistracy, police and military, might suggest otherwise to the historian, but these were little more than angry sentiments provoked by coercion, and were not symptomatic of a clerical republican spirit. Their attitude to the I.R.B. was one of consistent and avowed hostility. They were suspicious of the fenian element in the Land League, and their involvement in it was partly to ensure that it maintained its agrarian character. Similarly, the priests viewed the Labour League with a jaundiced eye because of its identification with the I.R.B., and they, therefore, largely abstained from it, at the same time rightly recognising its political ineffectiveness. Such, too, was the case with the Young Ireland Society.

The priests' unambiguous and active hostility to the G.A.A. — I.R.B. connection, however, is the clearest proof of their rejection of republicanism. The case of John Scanlan is the best illustration of this. He was a prominent anti-coercionist, a strong supporter of boycotting the Prince of Wales, and the principal advocate of boycotting the Nenagh police sports. Furthermore, he claimed to be, and was, one of the leading champions of the labourers' cause, but his most conspicuous role was in the clerical drive against the fenian infiltration of the G.A.A. Clearly, Scanlan's support of the labourers' social aims did not in the least imply approval of their politics.

Social background, however, not only engendered in the priests this basic anti-republicanism, but produced an ambivalence which was sometimes characteristic of the farmers too; for example, they responded to the apparent shift of sympathy among the farmers especially during the amnesty drive. But this was little more than a tactic rather than a genuine symptom of conflicting emotions, and was also prompted by the wish to mollify the republican sector in their parishes and soften possible anti-clericalism, although when the threat of armed revolution became a reality the priests were less willing to resort to ambiguity.

Clerical ambivalence assumed two shapes, praise for patriots and separatists of earlier periods, and sympathy for the plight of current political prisoners. During the amnesty campaign they paid lip service to the prisoners' patriotism, lauded their ideals and spirit of self-sacrifice, and highlighted the sufferings of their families. But, immediate and short-lived nationalistic fervour is no substitute for a long-standing republican conviction and, like the farmers, the priests opposed republican election candidates following the amnesty movement. Even when the electorate gave John Mitchel a significant sympathy vote, the clergy largely abstained from the election, their silence betraying their dislike of his candidature on the one hand, and on the other revealing a disinclination to loudly oppose the wishes of their kinsfolk, however unpalatable these wishes were to the priests themselves.

Praise for revolutionaries of past years was a stock part of the priests' political vocabulary from 1848 onwards. Their later commendation of Young Irelanders was in sharp contrast to the active opposition they had offered to the Ballingarry affair, just as their sentiments of sympathy with the men of 1867 were inconsistent with their anti-fenianism of 1864 onwards. Such ambivalence did not end with the amnesty campaign, and some Land War priests offered financial support for monuments in honour of the men earlier condemned. It is patent, however, that a monument to Charles Kickham in a local churchyard may have been a sop to disorganised republicanism but it did not signify a belief in the politics of the man whose body had been refused admittance to Thurles cathedral for reasons which are not fully clear.

Clearly, while the priests' course was parallel to that of the farmers, their anti-republicanism was sharper. The editors of the *Irish People* were quick to recognise this, and the priests, not the farmers or urban middle-class, became their main targets. The priests' own instinctive middle-class conservatism was powerfully buttressed by episcopal strictures and an emphatic church doctrine, which emerged as one of the most apparent influences in the contemporary debate. Archbishop Leahy's imposition of spiritual sanctions on fenians was one of the few instances of episcopal authority being wielded in a totally preventive manner in Tipperary politics. It undoubtedly quelled any public, if not private, sympathy, that a section of his priests might have entertained towards the society and its aims. Motivated by his own episcopal role and moral commitment, Leahy brought textbook theology into sharp focus for his priests. Seminary textbooks, indeed, strongly reflected the church's traditional consciousness of respect for lawful authority and condemnation of revolution, with other sections depicting secret societies as contrary to ecclesiastical law of the Church. Fenianism came under clerical attack on all three scores.

This rejection of the republican philosophy by the priests implied a reliance upon constitutional politics. First of all it signified clerical confidence in the ability of Irish M.P.s to secure reform through parliamentary pressure, and secondly to ultimately govern Ireland under repeal or home rule. The three principal influences again combined in determining the clergy's attitude to these vital issues at different times from 1850 to 1891. As with republicanism, social background and the public opinion of the farming class were fundamental. The impact of clerical training, however, was of least importance since constitutional politics rarely proved morally contentious, but the epicopal attitude, specifically that of Dr Croke, was vitally important in stimulating the priests to place such policies before a public who were probably less informed about the question of an Irish party than they were about the more popular issue of home rule.

Repeal gripped the public mind in the '40s, and under the aegis of Daniel O'Connell the priests responded to this enthusiasm, becoming vitally important members of the movement. Popular zeal, however, died with the creator of the policy, and the famine effectively buried it. Having responded to the earlier mood of the country, the priests equally clearly reflected this post-famine outlook and made little effort to dispel it. After 1850 they rarely mentioned self-government, and when they did it was more as a threat than a genuine political conviction. The remnant of the Young Ireland party, i.e. the Tipperary Independent Club and its priests, regarded the policy as inexpedient, inappropriate and impractical.

The advent of fenianism did not turn the priests' minds to home rule as an alternative. They felt it necessary, however, to record their own nationalistic sentiments, thereby hoping to refute any suggestion that they were less patriotic than the fenians. This was attempted through the Limerick declaration of 1868, a truly clerical initiative. But, ironically, herein lay its main defect, to wit, it was not bolstered by a strong groundswell of support from those with political muscle, the electorate. Significantly, however, the priests did not desire a lay reaction; their statement was little more than lip-service to nationalism, and did not motivate them to join John Martin's National League with its sole aim of repeal. Whatever degree of nationalism the priests harboured was relegated and stifled lest it perhaps contribute to the more violent nationalism of the fenians, as well as endangering promises of Gladstonian reform on land, education and disestablishment. Had the tenant farmers reacted to the declaration, the story might well have been otherwise, but, in the event, clerical priorities were undisturbed, and having favourably greeted the disestablishment act of 1869 they awaited the agrarian legislation of the following year.

The 1870 land act did not fulfil their expectations, but while the response to its failure was political, not agrarian, it was primarily a parliamentary rather than a local one. This is evident from Butt's failure to arouse extensive support for the Home Government Association, which was reflected by the small number of priests in the movement, and the continuous complaints of O'Neill Daunt to Archbishop Leahy. Interestingly, however, the electorate did show a preference for candidates who professed home rule, and the priests responded with statements of approbation, although their precise affiliation was clouded by the presence of other issues on the hustings, especially that of education.

Priorities, however, became more clearcut during the Land War. The economic downturn fostered the climate both for a vigorous agrarian agitation and an accompanying political one. But, local ferment alone was insufficient. A powerful national co-ordinating figure was essential, and this role Parnell admirably filled. He succeeded in harnessing the political to the agrarian with the result that references to home rule became increasingly frequent on agrarian platforms throughout Tipperary. Suddenly the priests, who had only sporadically referred to the self-government issue during the three preceding decades, were its chief propagators.

This conversion was caused by several pertinent factors absent in earlier years. The two principal ones were the increasing anglophobia among farmers due to the imprisonment of local leaders under the coercion of the early 1880s, and secondly the emergence of the Parnellite party. The priests saw home rule, through this party, as a safe political outlet for hostile tenant energies. But, because of Parnell, this constitutional alternative to possible republicanism among the tenants was more credible than at any stage from mid-century onwards, and this was of the utmost importance to the priests. They had every confidence in the political vision they held forth of Parnell as Irish prime minister in College Green, surrounded by the efficient band, who had given such an excellent account of their capabilities at Westminster.

The formation of such an Irish party was by no means a new concept in constitutional politics, but, as with home rule, the circumstances favouring it were absent until the 1880s. Generally from mid-century the course of most Irish M.P.s in the popular interest was one of cooperation with the English Liberal Party, and until the mid-1870s Tipperary members were labelled Liberal. Nevertheless, when any aspect of Liberal policy seemed anti-Irish or anti-catholic, the priests and the electorate were prepared to urge opposition to it. Such opposition obviously presupposed some element of unity among Irish M.P.s. But the precise measure of opposition and the precise degree of discipline demanded proved extremely divisive at both parliamentary and local levels. Inspired by that controversial piece of legislation, the Ecclesiastical Titles Bill, the general consensus in 1851 and 1852 favoured a policy of strong opposition. Nevertheless, many of the priests merely saw this policy as a temporary expedient, and lacked any serious conviction in its long-term desirability; for them, too, it was a tactic to be used with careful discrimination. Ironically, however, extreme clerical sentiments in its favour during the emotive 1852 election campaign made a more lasting impression upon the laity than upon a majority of the priests themselves; this makes an interesting contrast to the situation in the early 1880s on this particular issue.

This was well illustrated when the so-called Sadleirite defection aroused an angry response from the electorate, which in turn prompted the priests to publicly demand an explanation of their parliamentary course from the Tipperary M.P.s. Yet, subsequent election results show that this anger quickly evaporated among a large section of the laity, and these supported purely Liberal candidates such as Lawrence Waldron whose professions of opposition were wrenched from him and were patently insincere. A majority of priests shared the views of these electors. Still, the desire of another sector of lay opinion for an independent Irish party proved consistent from 1850 to 1859, and was spearheaded by the Independent Club priests.

The politics of the 1850s provide a classic example of a split in Liberal ranks being paralleled among the priesthood, and serves to illustrate the closeness of the political bond between the two. In short, the priests' clerical character did not result in a united front by them. The chief unifying ingredient, a strong parliamentary and national leader, was missing, and there is no doubt that they were as amenable to the influence of such a leader as the laity were. The events of the O'Connell era sustain this. The Liberator's less powerful successors, Gray, Lucas, Duffy or Moore, proved ineffective, and the identification of some of these with Young Irelandism possibly deepened a division that otherwise would have healed more rapidly in the Liberal tradition. The collapse of the Tipperary Independent Club in 1859 and the reappearance of Liberal Clubs during the 1860s symbolised the restoration of Liberalism. Isaac Butt's effort to shake this tradition was not unsuccessful, but it took that masterly parliamentary tactician, Charles Stewart Parnell, to arouse, with clerical help, a genuine confidence in a strong united Irish party. With his success the term Liberal totally vanished from Tipperary political parlance, and that of Nationalist, previously reserved for republicans, became synonymous with Parnellite.

The response of the Tipperary priests to Parnell was remarkably swift, and in this they showed themselves as more politically aware and astute than the laity. Yet it must be stressed that it was only a question of degree, and was not in any fundamental sense opposed to the broad political outlook of their kinsfolk. Again, their anti-Parnellism in the early 1890s may have been sharper and more vocal than that of the farmers, but it was not incompatible with their attitude. While the clergy used the agrarian propaganda lever, the farmers were well aware of the situation from the newspapers and especially from the campaigns of anti-Parnellite M.P.s, and would probably have been largely hostile to Parnell irrespective of priestly invective; the hostility of Ballyneale National Leaguers to the Parnellism of Robert Power P.P. is a most revealing example of independent farmer anti-Parnellism.

But, while the priests' political outlook largely coincided with that of their middle-class kinsfolk, unmistakable evidence of their training, plus episcopal influence, which made them such sharp catalysts, also emerge as contributory factors. The question of moral principles, however, was least important in constitutional politics. It was not relevant to the home rule issue, and surfaced mainly during election campaigns, when as ministers of religion the priests felt bound to point out electors' duties, particularly when religious issues such as the Ecclesiastical Titles Bill were involved. In this it indirectly influenced clerical thinking on the necessity of an Irish party to safeguard catholic religious interests. It had no bearing, however, on the more technical issue of parliamentary procedure, except insofar as some priests saw the breaking of pledges as having a definite moral dimension. As well as this the Parnellite crisis brought into sharp focus the relevance of private morality to public political leadership, and it was the priests' moral commitment which rendered their anti-Parnellism sharper than that of the farmers.

The influence of the bishops, however, had a more considerable bearing upon the priests' action in constitutional politics, and indeed in their overall political involvement. Since the bishops held the power of promotion, transfer and suspension, the clergy were naturally sensitive to their views. The efficacy of episcopal control is only too evident from the tame political activity of the Dublin priests during Cullen's tenure or from the muted response of the Limerick clergy from 1886, when Edward O'Dwyer succeeded George Butler as bishop. Such tight control, however, was rarely exercised in Tipperary, particularly in the substantial Cashel and Emly sector.

Still, there was an interesting difference of approach by the three Archbishops to clerical political involvement. Michael Slattery, almost continually in ill-health from mid-century, was decidedly lax in regulating the quality of his priests' political behaviour. The period of his tenure from 1850 to 1857 witnessed a series of desedifying public political inter-clerical disputes, plus a priests' memorial to Rome on the question of their political activity, which was mainly promoted in his Archdiocese, with one of his priests chosen as the emissary to the Vatican. The decision to make this appeal, and its contents, showed little respect for episcopal authority, and scant understanding of the Roman mind. This sharply contrasted to the report of Cardinal Cullen, which pursued a train of thought appreciated at Vatican level. Of further significance, the memorial followed Slattery's private remonstrance to his priests on their public squabbles. But, Slattery's successor, Patrick Leahy, who was a younger and more energetic individual, eliminated public political quarrels among his priests by introducing a rule subjecting the minority to majority clerical opinion on political questions. He did not, however, limit the scope of their involvement. Of the three Archbishops, Thomas William Croke, the Corkman who succeeded Leahy in 1875, stands out as the most prominent political figure in the church not only in Tipperary, but on a national level, until the arrival of William J. Walsh to the See of Dublin in 1885. Unlike his two predecessors, Croke offered positive, energetic leadership.

Such leadership had a profound influence upon the stand taken by his priests, and was particularly evident from their response to the ideal of a strong Irish party, and, therefore, in their conversion to home rule. Croke's astute espousal of Parnell was partly a resurrection of his longstanding conviction of the need for such a party, which he had demonstrated as a Young Ireland curate in the late 1840s and early 1850s. But, having faced the disapproval of Rome for his consistent and outspoken approval of Parnell, especially in the matter of testimonial, Croke's disappointment and anger at the divorce revelations and their political consequences was translated into action when he marshalled his clerical forces into a solid anti-Parnellite phalanx. Consequently, while he was strongly responsible for the fervour of their earlier Parnellism, Croke was equally influential in the spread of anti-Parnellism among the priests. More concerned with the problems of education and religious issues, his predecessors never harboured any deep interest in the question of an Irish party, and certainly did not influence their priests in its favour. Privately Dr Slattery disliked any extreme manifestation of parliamentary opposition, but he discountenanced the breaking of what he considered solemn pledges, however rashly tendered on the hustings. Leahy, however, showed less sympathy, associating the policy with the Young Ireland faction, and his subjection of minority to majority decision effectively deprived the Independent Club of its priestly backbone, thereby destroying its already slender chance of survival as an organisation of more radical outlook than the Irish parliamentary body of the time.

While, therefore, constitutional politics and republicanism demonstrate the interaction of the major influences of background, moral considerations and episcopal control on clerical political thought, it must be recalled that the priests' main priority lay in their promotion of agrarian reform, with social background and tenant opinion emerging as the dominant motivating influences. Whatever the tone of contemporary criticism about the prejudices of a peasant priesthood, its theme was certainly not unfounded. But, clerical sensitivity to the demands of the class that supplied most of the church's personnel and much of its income is hardly surprising. It is notable that the priests rarely openly dissented from the broad agrarian aims of their kinsfolk, generally articulated their sentiments, and showed a distinct bias in the tenants' favour. Their definitions of a fair rent both in the 1850s and in the 1880s were decidedly weighted against the landlords' interests. Immediately prior to the 1881 land act they concurred when the farmers considered Griffith's valuation an acceptable rent basis, but later, in line with shifting opinion, they voiced their disenchantment with judicial rents, and produced exaggerated calculations to prove that the alleged enormous administrative and legal costs of the act outweighed the rent reductions conceded. The priests were equally partial in their treatment of the closely related question of improvements, which was especially dear to the tenants' hearts. Clerical bias was not only evident from the unfavourable comparisons they drew between improving landlords in England and their non-improving counterparts in Ireland, but also from the generous rent cuts they proposed on the basis of improvement expenditure by tenants.

When the rent issue began to recede in importance, and peasant proprietary was accepted as the ultimate solution to the land question, the priests clearly mirrored the desire of their kinsfolk to own their holdings, only, however, if the conditions were economically advantageous. But the sympathy between the two was most evident from their reaction to evictions. The changing tone of public opinion towards evictions from mid-century effectively reduced priestly emphasis on certain moral implications; for example, although the priests denounced evictions in the strongest terms in the 1850s, they were equally insistent that lazy or improvident tenants deserved their fate, if they fell behind with their rent. The relative stabilisation of rural society in post-Famine decades, with the emergence of the stronger farmers as a large sector, effected a change of clerical attitude, or at least introduced an element of discretion on the part of priests who might have moral misgivings. The social expectations of such farmers produced a determination to hold the family hearth irrespective of rent arrears, whether due to incompetence or not. Consequently the moral scruples of a small minority of priests were quickly stifled at the beginning of the Land War, and they rapidly responded to the loud clamour against evictions in the 1880s. The priests were involved in every stage of the eviction process, partly perhaps because of the humanitarianism of their vocation, although presence at the sale of interests and bidding on the victim's behalf was more a symptom of social affinity than of priestly duty.

This dominance of social background was also evident from the distinct lack of sympathy displayed by priests towards landlord's difficulties, which they graphically depicted as the result of idleness, luxury and extravagance. The undoubted splendour of many landlord residences and lifestyle understandably influenced their outlook. Landlords were portrayed as the agents of all calamities, including the famine and its aftermath, a catastrophe which continued to inspire priestly anti-landlord fulminations as late as the Land War. The vigour of clerical denunciations and ridicule, either on the hustings or on agrarian platforms, greatly contributed to the demise of deference towards landlords in general. Indeed, during the Land War the priests displayed a conscious determination to end this traditional social phenomenon. They were, perhaps, only seeking to elevate the status and dignity of the class from which they sprang, and were betraying a pride both in their Irish catholic nationality and in their own social origins.

Clearly, therefore, the priests' promotion of agrarian objectives, which often constituted a breach of contract, is a strong testimony of the supremacy of public opinion over clerical training. But, of equal importance, they not only did not suspend their moral judgement, but on the contrary used theological tenets to justify their stand. They casually dismissed existing contracts as null and void, because, arguably, these lacked the necessary condition of freedom by both contracting parties. Tenants, therefore, were depicted as being forced by the threat of evictions to accept unfavourable tenurial terms. The priests buttressed this fundamental argument with that powerful and convincing weapon, natural justice, and, to take one example, logically proposed that improvements by tenants automatically merited corresponding compensation. In this light the three Fs, although considered radical in the 1850s, were morally justifiable.

But, the functional nature of the priests' theology, despite an apparent rigidity, and its subordination to social pressure in political matters, was nowhere more evident than in clerical promotion and justification of some morally dubious tactics during the Land War, specifically the plan of campaign and boycotting, both condemned by Rome. The plan of campaign involved a type of boycott and a definite breach of contract, but the priests morally justified it on the somewhat shaky basis that a fair rent was proffered. The crucial point, however, is that the campaigners arbitrarily fixed the rent whether the landlord liked it or not, and so the priests condoned a situation which they had earlier condemned when the landlord was the offending party. Boycotting was a much more contentious tactic morally, open to serious abuse. It almost amounted to persecution when used on a systematic and extensive level. But, despite some mild reservations, the priests proceeded to defend both its theory and practice by liberal quotations from scripture. Apparently, its popularity and effectiveness rather than its morality were the prime considerations in priestly support.

It would, however, be a distortion to portray the priests as the subservient religious arm of the tenantry, willingly giving their benediction to every aim and tactic proposed by the land movements. Their positive theological promotion of agrarian agitation was accompanied by a distinct reluctance to pass certain limits, which were dictated by theological principles and their own moral commitment. They emphasised the fundamental importance of property rights, however battered these rights became from a landlord's point of view. The clergy's initial suspicion of the Land League was partly based upon moral reservations about the danger of confiscation. This, too, inspired their opposition to Davitt's land nationalisation theory, which they rightly identified with socialism. Similarly, while they realised that peasant proprietary was not socialistic, they stressed the necessity to grant landlords adequate compensation. But, although this principle was important, their criterion of adequate compensation was not dictated by any theological yardstick, and was distinctly influenced by their social prejudices. Finally, the most significant impact of theology lay in the invariable consistency it gave to priestly antipathy towards violence. While they were forced into ambivalence by offering excuses for outrages, the priests could not, and did not, condone violence. There is no evidence either that they themselves ever participated in the perpetration of outrages.

Nevertheless, the rarity of the priests' moral objections to agrarian agitation is noteworthy. Their social background engendered in them an instinctive dislike of the landowning class, which enabled them to attack landlords at will. It was a natural dimension of the Irish class structure, but not the only one. Agrarian politics were also complicated by the plight of the labourers, who occupied the third and lowest rung of the social ladder, and, as in the case of republicanism, presented the priests with a dilemma. Tension between farmers and labourers lay at the root of this dilemma, although the famine prevented what might conceivably have developed into a more serious class conflict with the priests caught in the middle. Relations, however, again became strained during the 1880s. It was primarily a question of self-interest. Apart from a lack of social affinity with the labourers, the farmers also exploited them as a labour force, and with the advent of machinery cast them aside at their convenience. Such tension between the two classes resulted in a certain degree of conflict between the social bias of the priests and their moral commitment.

As clergymen they were obviously obliged to minister to the needs of all their parishoners, and their scriptural justification of political involvement on the farmers' behalf applied even more validly to the labourers, who badly needed a temporal boost. But, the slowness and limited extent of clerical involvement in labourer reform underline an unwillingness by many priests to ruffle the harmony between themselves and their kinsfolk. The clergy of the 1850s, for all their concern with famine, emigration, starvation and clearances, did not highlight the plight of the labourers on any notable scale because it was not part of the policy of the Tenant League, a body composed mainly of the wealthier type farmers. The intense activity by a small number of Land War priests, however, signifies a rare challenge to the selfishness of their kinsfolk. These priests were certainly motivated by strong moral principles, but even their action was initially a political response to party policy which itself was partly due to the influence of Michael Davitt.

While social background and public opinion, therefore, emerge as the dominant forces in agrarian politics, with theological principles and clerical training in a more subordinate though conspicuous role, the priests' promotion of the land question automatically presupposes at least the neutrality of their bishops. Generally speaking this was the case. Daniel Vaughan, however, was the only Tipperary bishop in the 1850s, who made a positive effort to forward agrarian reforms, while in the 1860s Archbishop Leahy made periodic ineffective statements about it. Again, Dr Croke emerges as the dominant episcopal figure, and, as in the political questions, threw his weight behind the land movement at an early stage, and at a time when the priests viewed it with a certain degree of alarm. While the majority of the clergy still remained aloof, the Archbishop's stand almost certainly prompted the involvement of many who did join. Later his public controversy with Dr McCabe ensured at least priestly neutrality towards the Ladies Land League, and his espousal of the National League accelerated an already willing clerical support.

On the other hand, Croke's prompt and resolute opposition to the no-rent-manifesto was probably the most important factor in determining the priests' silence on this tactic. But his attitude to the question of boycotting and the Plan of Campaign made continuation of clerical involvement in them possible, despite Vatican condemnation. Croke's stand in this illustrates the role of the bishop as a buffer between the priest and Roman dictates on political matters. Interestingly, Dr Slattery, too, for all his apparent mildness, showed a distinct disapproval of such interference. But, while Croke was convinced that the Vatican authorities did not understand Irish politics, or were nudged in a hostile direction by English diplomacy, Slattery was concerned about the so-called Romanisation of the Irish Church, and he viewed Roman concern with political matters as an extension of Cullen's ultramontanism and an erosion of episcopal authority. Far from being a buffer, however, a bishop might also act as a willing conducting agent of Vatican admonitions, which, indeed, would be more compatible with his episcopal function. Leahy, for example, welcomed, indeed invited, Rome's formal condemnation of the fenian Society, while Bishop Pierse Power supported and promulgated the 1888 decree against the Plan of Campaign and boycotting in the diocese of Waterford.

The interaction of the major influences on the Tipperary priests, therefore, seems clear, but the dominance of any one in determining their own political stand does not necessarily point to its effectiveness in realising their particular political wishes. It seems fair to suggest that the force of public opinion limited the practical power of the priests in this matter. This is evident from their failure to impose their moral standards upon their flocks, so that a proliferation of devotional practices did not necessarily indicate a deeper ethical consciousness on the part of the laity. In the labourers' case the gap between the number of cottages sought and that erected shows that priestly pleas based on moral grounds made little impression on those farmers who raised objections to the erection of cottages on their land. Again, self-interest rather than moral scruples dictated tenant apathy towards land nationalisation. The plain fact was that the farmers as would-be proprietors had no stomach for such a policy.

Their abstention from fenian ranks was also rooted in self-interest, not morality. They had no wish to lose their property by risking imprisonment. Neither is there any substantial evidence that the failure of the no-rent manifesto was due to moral objections raised by Dr

Croke or a number of priests. The collapse of the Land League, the introduction of coercion and the ameliorating influence of the 1881 land act made such a policy impractical, and the farmers were not convinced of its necessity. On the level of constitutional politics the moral tirade against Parnell obscures the basic reason for ousting him, namely, the political campaign mounted by the Irish party because of the danger to home rule. Had home rule not been threatened, and had the party remained behind Parnell, the probability of a silent withdrawal of clerical support on moral grounds cannot be ruled out, but the diluted nature of the priests' political influence in 1890 would have rendered such a withdrawal largely irrelevant to the continuing success of the Parnellite party.

While causes other than morality must be attributed to the farmers' stand on all the above issues, it is even more significant that the priests failed to prevent actions, which were against the teaching of the church. The fact that fenian candidates secured votes shows that some electors did not see any moral incompatibility in voting for members of an organisation specifically condemned as contrary to church doctrine. The strength of fenianism among the non-electorate also underlines clerical inability to impose their moral viewpoint on a large section of their parishoners. Finally, it is clear that agrarian outrages waxed and waned not in accordance with the intensity of clerical admonitions, but with the prevailing mood of the tenants.

If, however, the priests' moral emphasis was ineffective in the face of a resolute public opinion, the same may be said of episcopal pronouncements. It is true to say, too, that while the bishops had the power to determine the degree of the priests' political involvement or to dictate their stand on specific issues, they themselves were not indifferent to public opinion. One can only speculate if Leahy would have invited Roman condemnation of fenianism had that movement contained a strong middle-class base. Anti-clericalism among the labourers was one matter, its prevalence among the majority of catholic parishoners quite another. Certainly, Dr Croke considered that the danger to religion from an adverse public reaction to Roman pronouncements outweighed the displeasure of the authorities there. His stand, too, demonstrates the power of public opinion in the traditional sense, and was a response to the intense agrarian activity of the time. He was portrayed in a more prominent light than the priests, of course, because of his status, but is it not significant that he was relatively silent prior to the Land War?

It can only be concluded, therefore, that the priests' political activity in the second half of the nineteenth century, however extensive, did not mean absolute or dictatorial influence, and the rural Irish society of the time was not, as some contemporaries suggest, a priest-ridden one either in terms of morality or politics. But, failure to change the mainstream of public opinion does not mean that the priests' political contribution was either minimal or ineffective. On the contrary, their education level, status as clergymen and middle-class background ensured that their role was a leading one. Contemporaries were quite conscious of it. Election candidates were particularly sensitive to it, and an equal awareness was displayed by national leaders. Daniel O'Connell was the first to divine its importance, the Tenant League leaders strongly emphasised it, and the correspondence of O'Neill Daunt shows that he considered priestly involvement as absolutely vital to the dissemination of support for home rule. That Butt himself came to a similar conclusion is clear from his incorporation of education reform into the home rule platform. Parnell, too, despite his dislike of clerical politicians, could not afford to ignore this tradition, and he used it to a degree unknown since the days of O'Connell.

The priests' role was wide-ranging and diversified. As the spiritual leaders of large units their administrative expertise was invaluable, and was exploited in all the local agrarian and political bodies from 1850 to 1891. In this capacity they served as chairmen, secretaries, platform orators, correspondents and organisers. In matters of finance for such organisations the priests were almost indispensable. Depending for their own livelihood and the maintenance of their ecclesiastical establishments on a system of voluntary contributions, they had considerable experience in extracting and raising money from the public, a talent they did not hesitate to apply for secular use too. Furthermore, their intimate knowledge of their parishes made them canvassers *par excellance.* As the most articulate sector of society the priests also served an important role as mediators between landlord and tenant, and no deputation to the 'big house' was complete without at least one priest.

But, while the priests' role as administrators and mediators was of basic importance, their political contribution was more far-reaching. As the prime expositors of agrarian legislation as well as the most eloquent critics of such measures, they unquestionably advanced thought upon agrarian reform at local level. This was further supplemented by their clear articulation of tenant demands, which, coupled with frequent anti-landlord diatribes, gradually conditioned the tenants' amenability to social change. Admittedly, the determined Tenant League priests failed to secure extensive or sustained support for the three Fs in the 1850s, but the late '70s provided a climate of opinion, which not only imbibed this hitherto radical policy, but dismissed it as inadequate and favoured a peasant proprietary. Ironically, therefore, the cumulative impact of the priests' statements contributed to an evolution in public opinion, the rapidity of which they had not anticipated, although they quickly responded to the new demand, and articulated it on the tenants' behalf.

The necessity of local ferment to the priests' influence in the land question obviously implies their inability to create political activity in this sphere, even if they did clarify, sharpen and advance goals. The same, however, did not necessarily hold true for non-agrarian matters. This interesting distinction arose because, while agrarian agitation was primarily the result of farmers' self-interest, purely political affairs were often promoted by the advanced politicisation of the priests themselves. In short, tenant apathy allowed the clergy to display their own political initiative and create political activity. Admitting their effectiveness in inciting oppostion to the Ecclesiastical Titles Act, the priests' most significant display of advanced politicisation lay in their stand on the policy of a strong Irish party. The powerful vocal minority of Independent Opposition priests of the '50s proved themselves more politicised than a majority of the laity, and the frequency of public controversy by the priests on the question strongly contributed to the debate and ensured that the tradition of such a party was never entirely forgotten, and was recalled on Land War platforms.

It was, indeed, during the Land War, and on this very issue, that the priests, this time a majority of their body, showed their greatest contribution to politicisation. While it must be conceded that the agrarian discontent facilitated the creation of purely political activity, the priests' early espousal of Parnell's party-building policy demonstrated a remarkable degree of political initiative. This is evident not only from the P.J. Smyth controversy, with the presbytery in Thurles as the focal point of clerical dissatisfaction, but more particularly from the proceedings of the 1883 convention, when the priests supported a candidate foisted on the constituency by Parnell in opposition to the local contender. Of greatest significance, this local nominee was supported by a majority of the lay delegates who represented a large number of National League branches.

Considering the absence of this tradition of party centralisation, the priests' stand was quite an extraordinary and sudden transcendence of local political horizons. It was an act of faith unique in the political history of Tipperary. The priests, because of their more advanced level of education, were disposed to take a wider view of politics than the rural laity. Under the inspiration of Croke they were sufficiently shrewd to realise that Parnell had the stature and the ability to create a strong party. As politicians they also had their own preferences in the methods for promoting, not only political aims such as home rule, but also agrarian reform. They distrusted the fenian connection and the radicalism of the Land League; so, the simultaneous emergence of the Parnellite nucleus offered a safer, less revolutionary channel for tenant grievances and social change. In short, by 1880 the priests saw Parnell's astute involvement in the league as preferable to the leadership of such men as Michael Davitt. This becomes much more apparent from their vastly increased participation in the political, centrally controlled National League. Parnell's genius lay in his ability to bridge political divides; he quickly realised the priests' relevance as a vital link in the politicisation of the rural laity, and his success in manipulating them was remarkable.

But the supreme irony of the priests' support for Parnell's centralisation policy and the creation of the party machine lay in their own subsequent political redundance, directly stemming from the success of this policy. True, they continued their valuable involvement in the National League, and helped to focus public awarement on such vital issues as home rule. The more active participation of Parnellite M.P.s in local meetings, however, reduced the clergy's role in the creation of a home rule political climate. Still, this did not seriously interfere with their influence. But, much more striking, their influence in the promotion of election candidates literally vanished. The abolition of even the convention system deprived them of the last crumbs of involvement in this most important of political functions, their traditional stronghold.

In their initial acceptance of Parnell's course the priests hardly anticipated such an outcome, but as the party machine gathered strength, they were either powerless or unwilling to reassert local influence. Their statements during the divorce crisis, however, revealed what seemed to have been a hitherto suppressed dissatisfaction with this position, while the crack in the machine facilitated and signalled their return to active parliamentary politics. This return took the form of a savage backlash against Parnell from the Winter of 1890. Nevertheless, it must be emphasised that they did not create this backlash, which received its initial impetus from a majority of the Party itself. But, the level and energy of the priests' campaign, and the viciousness of their denunciations undoubtedly strongly contributed to a public anti-Parnellite climate. They certainly sharpened the hostility of the farmers by emphasising the agrarian dimension of the debate and depicting Parnell as a selfish, ungrateful adulterer, who froze one of the main financial pipelines of the agrarian movement. The clergy, therefore, showed themselves as practiced politicians by their blend of the political, moral and agrarian in the generating of anti-Parnellism.

It can only be concluded that priestly involvement from 1850 to 1891 was not only a unique feature of politics but an eminently practical and important one. In hindsight it is difficult to imagine nineteenth century politics without the priests, as indeed it would have been inconceivable to many people of the time. Their confinement to the sanctuary would not, perhaps, have changed the ultimate direction of politics, but issues would certainly have been less clearly defined and articulated, and much of the colour they introduced to public platforms lost. It is more than probable, also, that political activity, particularly agrarian, would have been of a more violent nature. Despite clerical inability to prevent outbreaks of violence, their continual exhortations and use of the confessional in dissuading would-be perpetrators must have been effective in many cases, and at least engendered a degree of caution into the momentum of the agrarian revolution, irresistible as that was. There was, of course, an existing lay political leadership that functioned with the priests, and in their absence would inevitably have played a greater role. As it was, urban politicians such as town commissioners and aldermen played a leading role especially in Clonmel, Nenagh, Thurles and Tipperary, and several urban priests prior to the Land War took little part in politics, and then only in a subsidiary way. There were, however, some important exceptions where the inbred political ability of the priests in question assured them of important and prominent political involvement. Both Dr Michael Burke and Dr John Power of Clonmel stand out as men with a strong taste for politics as well as wielding considerable influence.

Tipperary was predominantly rural, however, and it was in rural Tipperary that the priests made their greatest political contribution. The ecclesiastical structure provided a superb ready-made political or agrarian network, and the clerical administrators an efficient political body. The Poor Law guardians were the lay political nucleii in rural areas, but generally speaking they lacked both the education and administrative expertise of either urban politicians or the priests. Their horizons were also more limited. It is difficult to envisage them as an adequate alternative to that unique, now extinct, species — the priest in politics.

Footnotes

FOREWORD

1. See J. O'Shea, 'The priest and politics in County Tipperary, 1850-1891' (Ph.D., N.U.I., 1979), table 10, p.18.
2. *Census of Ireland 1851,* part 1, Vol. 11, Munster, pp298, 336.
3. O'Shea, op cit., fig. 1, p.197.

1. THE PRIEST AND HIS PEOPLE

1. See O'Shea, op. cit., table 7, p.14.
2. *Eighth report of the commissioners of Irish education, inquiry and appendix to the eighth report,* p.537. H.C. 1826-1827 (509). xiii. *Reports from the select committee on the state of Ireland,* p.125. H.C. 1825 (129) viii. *Papers presented to the House of Commons relating to the Royal College of St Patrick's, Maynooth,* pp13, 14, 18. H.C. 1812-1813 (204) vi. A. de Tocqueville, *Journeys to England and Ireland,* ed. J. P. Mayer (New York, 1968), p.169. K. H. Connell, *Irish peasant society* (Oxford 1968), pp122-6. J. A. Murphy, 'Priests and people in modern Irish history' in *Christus Rex,* 23, no. 4 (1969), pp250-81. F. S. L. Lyons, *Ireland since the famine* (Glasgow, 1974), pp20-21. Emmet Larkin, 'Church, state and nation in modern Ireland' in *American Historical Review,* lxxx, no. 5 (Dec. 1975), p.1253. E. D. Steele, *Irish land and British politics: tenant right and nationality 1865-1870* (Cambridge, 1974), p.26. E. R. Norman, *The Catholic church and Ireland in the age of rebellion* (London, 1965), p.14.
3. O'Shea, op. cit., table II, pp19-24. Table 2 below.
4. *Report of Her Majesty's commission of inquiry into the working of the Landlord and Tenant (Ireland) Act 1870 and the acts amending the same,* iii, *minutes of evidence,* part ii, pp1175-1176 (C 2779-1), H.C. 1881, xviii.
5. O'Shea, op. cit., table 12, p.25.
6. Peter O'Leary, *My story,* translated by Cyril T. O Céirin (Cork, 1970), pp29, 67.
7. L.M. Cullen, *An economic history of Ireland since 1660 (London,* 1972), p.112.
8. P.121.
9. *Irish educ. enquiry,* pp57, 424, H.C. 1826-7, xiii; O'Leary, *My story,* pp64-7.
10. C.D.A., Canon Fogarty's notebook, no. 16. *Second Report of Commissioners, Public Instruction Ireland,* pp44c, 46c, 47c, H.C. 1835 (47), xxxiv.
11. *Irish educ. report,* p.145, H.C. 1826-7, xiii.
12. O'Shea, op. cit., table 13, pp26-27 for a breakdown of attendances at various seminaries.
13. *Irish Catholic Directory,* p.364. See William Jones, president, to Tobias Kirby, 24 Oct. 1884 (K.P.) on burses established by Archbishop Croke.
14. *Irish educ. enquiry,* pp52, 422, H.C. 1826-7, xiii. *State of Ireland,* p.200, H.C. 1825, viii.
15. O'Shea, op. cit., table 14, p.28.
16. Rev. M. Comerford, *Collections relating to the diocese of Kildare and Leighlin,* (Dublin and London, 1883), p.167.
17. John Healy, *Maynooth College, its Centenary History, 1795-1895* (Dublin, 1895), pp233, 414, 442, 730. Emmet Larkin, 'Economic Growth, Capital Investment and the Roman Catholic Church', in *American Historical Review, lxxii, (1966-67), p.859.*
18. *Irish educ. enquiry,* p.58, H.C. 1826-7, xiii.
19. Ibid., pp10, 57.
20. Ibid., p.56; Healy, op. cit., p.418.

21. Dr McSweeney (President) to Archbishop Slattery, 10 Aug. 1839 (C.D.A., S.P.); J. Lynch (President) to Archbishop Leahy, 1861, and Document of 1 Jan. 1866. (C.D.A., L.P.).
22. *Irish Catholic Directory 1840*, p.365; Peadar Mac Suibhne, *Paul Cullen and His Contemporaries*, vol 2, (Naas, 1965), pp6, 7, 8.
23. Ryan to Kirby, 7 Oct. 1885 (K.P.).
24. *State of Ireland*, p.202, H.C. 1825, viii; *Irish educ. enquiry*, p.52, H.C. 1826-7, xiii.
25. C.D.A., S.P., 1849/71; this also shows the parochial contributions.
26. Annual report of the college, 1 June 1865. (C.D.A., L.P.).
27. Dr Miley to Leahy, 14 Sept. 1857, Report, 1 June 1864, Dr McCabe to Leahy 29 Jan. 1868 (C.D.A., L.P.); Dr Michael Verdon to Croke 25 Nov. 1882 (C.D.A., C.P.); an account book for the Irish College, Rome (C.D.A., C.P., 1885/37).
28. As in note 1 above.
29. See O'Leary, *My Story*, pp69-71.
30. *Irish educ. enquiry*, p.10, H.C. 1826-7, xiii; *Report of her majesty's commission appointed to inquire into the management and government of the college of Maynooth*, part 1, report and appendix, p.57, (1896), H.C. 1854-5, xxii-I; O'Leary, *My Story*, p.69.
31. *State of Ireland*, p.201, H.C. 1825, viii; 'The Irish College at Rome' in *Irish Monthly*, ii (1874), pp545, 552; 'The Irish College, Paris', in *I.E.R.*, ii (1866), p.261.
32. O'Shea, op. cit. Table 15, p.29.
33. See *Irish educ. enquiry*, p.56, H.C. 1826-7, xiii, on age limits; see also, *A return of the names, ages and numbers of students attending the college of Maynooth on 31st day of August 1844 . . . and the names and numbers of those who have entered each year from that time till the 31st day of August 1861*, pp577-89, H.C. 1862 (450), xliii.
34. *Irish educ. enquiry*, p.57, H.C. 1826-7, xiii; *Management of Maynooth*, part 1, pp46, 81, 122, (1896), H.C. 1854-5, xxii-I.
35. O'Shea, op. cit., table 16, p.30. See Walter McDonald, *Reminiscences of a Maynooth professor*, ed. Denis Gwynn (London, 1925), p.30 on the importance of some element of luck.
36. *Irish educ. enquiry*, p.62, H.C. 1826-7, xiii.
37. *I.E.R.* 1883 p.679.
38. Barnabo to Leahy, 29 Sept 1868, (C.D.A., L.P.).
39. MacSuibhne, *Paul Cullen*, ii, p.7.
40. MS booklet 6 Oct 1852 (C.D.A., S.P., 1852/53).
41. C.D.A., L.P., 1857/1.
42. McDonald, *op. cit.*, p.32.
43. *Census of Ireland 1881*, Part I, Vol ii, province of Munster, p.852.
44. *Irish educ. enquiry*, p.12, H.C. 1826-7, xiii; Report for Irish College, Paris, 19 May 1863 (C.D.A., L.P.).
45. Heffernan to Slattery, 25 Mar. 1841. (C.D.A., S.P.).
46. *T.L.*, 11 Nov. 1882.
47. *Acta et decreta concilii provinciae Casseliensis in Hibernia* (Dublin, 1854), p.80.
48. *Management of Maynooth*, part 2, p.63 (1896), H.C. 1854-5, xxii; *State of Ireland*, pp200, 287, H.C. 1825, viii; *Irish educ. enquiry*, p.278, H.C. 1826-7, xiii; letter of Rev John Silke, archivist, Irish College, Rome to author, 21 Feb. 1976.
49. *Irish educ. enquiry*, p.12, H.C. 1826-7, xiii.
50. Ibid., p.10.
51. *Irish Monthly*, 1874, p.553.
52. McDonald, op. cit., p.35.
53. O'Leary, op. cit., pp69-71.
54. *Irish educ. enquiry*, p.14, H.C. 1826-7, xiii; *Management of Maynooth*, part 2, pp35-6, (1896), H.C. 1854-5, xxii; McDonald, op. cit., pp32, 48.
55. *Irish Monthly*, 1874, p.548.

56. Terence Cunningham, 'Church Reorganisation' in P. J. Corish (ed.), *A History of Irish Catholicism*, v (Dublin, 1970), pp10-11.
57. *Acta et Decreta* (1854), p.75.
58. *Irish Monthly*, 1874, p.550.
59. E. W. Russell to Cullen, 28 Sept. 1844. (Cullen papers, Irish College, Rome).
60. O'Brien to Kirby, 18 July 1855 (K.P.).
61. *Irish educ. enquiry*, p.277, H.C. 1826-7, xiii.
62. Patrick Boyle, *The Irish College, Paris, 1578-1901*, pp71, 85.
63. Miley to Leahy, 31 May 1858 (C.D.A., L.P.).
64. 'Reglement general du seminaire des Irlandais à Paris', (N.L.I. Microfilm p.5524), (translated in O'Shea, op. cit., appendix 3 pp220-222).
65. C.D.A., S.P., 1852/53; also Austin O'Loughlin, vice-rector, to Slattery, 13 June 1853 (C.D.A., S.P.); Miley to Leahy, 14 Sept. 1857, and 15 Oct. 1857, (C.D.A., L.P.).
66. Leahy to Cullen, 13 June 1858; Miley to Leahy, 16 June 1858; and Cardinal Barnabo to Leahy, 16 July 1858 (C.D.A., L.P.).
67. Dr Lynch to Leahy, 20 July 1860; and reports, 19 May 1863, 1 June 1864, 1 June 1865, 1 June 1866, 15 June 1867, 10 June 1869, (C.D.A., L.P.).
68. *Irish educ. enquiry*, p.277, H.C. 1826-7, xiii.
69. *Hansard 3*, CXXI, p.877 (21 May 1852).
70. Return of money received in the parish of Kilcommon to 20 March 1840. (C.D.A., S.P.). Table 4 below.
71. C.D.A., S.P., 1885/15, 1856/10.
72. James Howley, P.P. V.G. to Slattery, 8 Mar. 1852. (C.D.A., S.P.).
73. Thurles Parish Dues Book, 1834-1848 (breakdown by townland), (C.D.A., S.P.).
74. C.D.A., C.P., 1882/11.
75. Burke to Slattery, 24 Jan. 1850 (C.D.A., S.P.).
76. O'Shea, op. cit., table 18, pp42-43.
77. T. Quin, London, to Leahy 6 Jan. and 11 Mar. 1871. (C.D.A., L.P.).
78. Cashel P.L.U. minute book, July 1847-Jan. 1848, p.88, 1883-1884, p.263.
79. Thurles P.L.U. minute book, 1846-1847, p.173, June-Dec. 1853, p 135, Dec. 1887-June 1888, p.37.
80. Thurles P.L.U. minute book, 1851, 14, 21 June 1851, 19 July 1851, 8 Nov. 1851.
81. C.D.A., L.P., 1868/89; see also will of William Shanahan. (W.D.A.).
82. Rev. John Gleeson, *History of Ely O'Carroll territory* (Dublin, 1915), p.227.
83. P.106. See also priests' subscriptions to the Ursuline Convent, Thurles (C.D.A., L.P. 1858/59), priests' subscriptions to the pope's collection (C.D.A., C.P., 1880/83).
84. Delaney to Cornelius O'Brien (his landlord), 21 Jan 1880 (W.D.A.)
85. Cardinal Barnabo to Leahy, 28 May 1867 (C.D.A., L.P.).
86. Ryan to Slattery, 24 July 1854 (C.D.A., S.P.).
87. Slattery to James Howley P.P., 24 July 1854 (C.D.A., S.P.).
88. O'Shea, op. cit. table 5, pp9-12. Table 7 below.
89. T. Mahony P.P. to Slattery, 14 Aug. 1849 (C.D.A., S.P.).
90. Thomas Duggan P.P. to Leahy, 5 Feb. 1871 (C.D.A., L.P.).
91. Bishop Keane to Leahy, 10 Nov. 1868 (C.D.A., L.P.).
92. Circular from Croke to his priests, 25 Dec. 1880 (C.D.A., C.P.).
93. Fragment of a letter from Mooney (W.D.A.).
94. de Tocqueville, op. cit., p.163.
95. P.8.
96. *T.A.*, 1 Dec. 1883.
97. *T.P.*, 6 May 1881.
98. *Decreta synodi plenariae episcoporum Hiberniae habitae, anno 1850*, p.11.
99. *Acta et decreta* (1854) pp67, 70.
100. 'The fifth precept of the church', in *I.E.R.*, 1886, p.161.
101. *Decreta* (1850), p.11.
102. Ibid., pp12-13.

103. *Acta et decreta* (1854), p.75.
104. *Statuta synodalia pro unitis dioecesibus Casselensis et Imlacensis.* (Dublin, 1878), p.20.
105. John Ahern, 'The Plenary Synod of Thurles', in *I.E.R.*, (June 1952). p.7; Larkin, 'Economic growth', p.863.
106. Private circular from Croke to his clergy, 28 Oct. 1881. (C.D.A., C.P.).
107. *Nationalist*, 23 July 1890.
108. *Decreta* (1850), p.19.
109. Ibid., p.20.
110. Ibid.
111. *Statuta* (1878), p.26.
112. *Decreta* (1850), p.18.
113. Ibid., pp21-22.
114. *Acta et decreta* (1854), pp79-80.
115. *Statuta* (1878), p.27.
116. Notes by Croke in Dr Leahy's conference book. (C.D.A., L.P., 1859/42).
117. Croke's circular to his clergy, 25 Dec 1880. (C.D.A., C.P.)
118. Letter signed by the three curates to Canon Meagher 24 Jan. 1891, Croke to Meagher 28 Jan. 1891, and the three curates to Meagher, 30 Jan. 1891. (C.D.A., C.P.).
119. *Decreta* (1850), p.23.
120. Ibid.
121. *Statuta* (1878), p.27.
122. C.D.A., L.P., 1859/42.
123. Daniel K. Lanigan P.P. to Leahy, 22 Dec. 1873 (C.D.A., L.P.).
124. Duggan to Leahy 9 Dec. 1870; Dr James Heffernan to Leahy 29 Jan. 1871 (C.D.A., L.P.).
125. Leahy to Cooney, 6 Jan. 1873. (C.D.A., L.P.).
126. R. H. Shine to Leahy 13 Dec. 1872, and 12 Jan. 1873 (C.D.A., L.P.).
127. Leahy to Shine, 28 Jan. 1873 (C.D.A., L.P.).
128. *Irish Catholic Directory*, 1842, p.306.
129. Ibid., pp301, 314.
130. C.D.A., S.P., 1854/2.
131. Leahy to Burke 13 June 1874 (C.D.A., L.P.).
132. Rev. Christopher O'Dwyer, 'Paying for a cathedral' in *Cuimhneachán chois t-Siúire*, (Thurles, 1979) p.27.
133. McDonnell to R.M. Lynch, 29 Oct. 1849 (C.D.A., S.P.).
134. Mahony's reply to the Poor Law commissioners on the back of his letter to Slattery 20 July 1849, also Mahony to Slattery 24 July 1849 (C.D.A., S.P.).
135. Slattery to Matthew Moore, chief clerk, Poor Law commissioners 6 July 1841, do. to Poor Law Commissioners 1 Aug. 1841, 25 Nov. 1841, and Moore to Slattery 6 July 1841, 19 July 1841 (C.D.A., S.P.).
136. William Stanley, secretary, Poor Law commissioners to Leahy, 28 Nov., 14 Dec. 1855, 25 Jan. 1856, 1 and 11 Mar. 1856; Leahy to Stanley, 22 Dec. 1855, 21 Feb. 1856, 5 Mar. 1856.
137. Mark Tierney, 'The calendar to Archbishop Slattery's papers', p.18.
138. *Tablet*, 19 June 1847.
139. Cardinal Fransoni to Slattery 27 Nov. 1847, Monsignor Barnabo to Slattery, 24 Sept. 1848 (C.D.A., S.P.).
140. O'Dwyer to Slattery, 24 Aug. 1853; Hickey to Slattery, 27 Aug. 1853 (C.D.A., S.P.).
141. Slattery to Fransoni, 19 July 1853; William Keane, Bishop of Ross, to Slattery from Rome 17 Jan. 1854 (C.D.A., S.P.).
142. Rev. William Barron, 'Rules and regulations of St. Paul's Total Abstinence Society', (Thurles, 1845) (C.D.A., S.P., 1845/50).
143. C.D.A., S.P., 1853/14.
144. List of those committed to New Birmingham bridewell for drunkenness 1857-61

(C.D.A., L.P., 1861/20). For statistics on Cashel bridewell supplied by the keeper, Denis O'Kearney, see C.D.A., L.P. 1865/1, 1865/3, 1868/7, 1868/30, 1868/32, 1869/10.

145. Entry in copy of *Ordo* opposite p.38 (C.D.A., L.P., 1864/52).
146. Pastoral letter, 11 Nov. 1861 (C.D.A., L.P.).
147. *Statuta* (1878), p.25.
148. Ibid., p.21.
149. Circular to the clergy 7 July 1890 (C.D.A., C.P.).
150. See p.123; and *T.L.*, 14 Nov. 1884, 5 Dec. 1884.
151. *Reports from Commissioners Public Instruction Ireland, First Report*, H.C., 1835 (45) (46), xxxiii.I. 892; see also D.W. Miller, 'Irish Catholicism and the great famine' in *Journal of Social History*, ix, no 1 (Sept. 1975), p.84.
152. *Pobal Ailbe: Cashel and Emly, Census of Population 1841-1971*, (Thurles, 1975; with accompanying atlas).
153. O'Shea, op. cit., table 1, pp1-3. Table 6 below.
154. Ibid., table 2, p.4.
155. Seán Connolly, 'Catholicism and social discipline in pre-famine Ireland' (D. Phil thesis, New University of Ulster, 1977), pp205-207, 224; Larkin, 'Economic growth', (1966-7) pp864-5; Connell *op. cit.* p152, n5.
156. O'Shea *op. cit.*, table 3, pp5-6.
157. *I.C.D.*, 1842, p.301.
158. *Pobal Ailbe*, p.1., summary.
159. Visitation report, 13-14 Sept. 1852 (C.D.A., S.P.).
160. As in n.88.
161. E. Larkin, 'The devotional revolution in Ireland, 1850-1875' in *American Historical Review*, lxxvii, no. 3, June 1972, pp627, 644, 651, Larkin, 'Economic growth', p.865; Miller, 'Catholicism and the famine', p.83; Connell, *op. cit.*, p.160.
162. O'Shea, *op. cit.*, table 4, pp7-8.
163. C.D.A, S.P., 1854/6, (probably an address to his clergy on various topics).
164. O'Shea, *op. cit.*, table 5, pp9-12. Table 7 below.
165. Visitation report of P. Larkin P.P., 9-10 June 1846 (C.D.A., S.P.).
166. Mrs. G. Ryan to Slattery, 4 Mar. 1852 (C.D.A., S.P.).
167. *Irish Catholic Directory*, 1842, p.314.
168. *Acta* (1854), p.65.
169. E.g.: Maurice Mooney C.C. to Kirby, 26 Oct. 1860; Robert Power P.P. to Kirby, 26 Oct. 1860 seeking faculties for three Carrick-on-Suir priests; see also Kirby to Croke 26 June 1883 (all K.P.).
170. D. O'Loan, 'The Confraternity of the scapular of Our Lady of Mount Carmel' in *I.E.R.* 1890, pp845-58; D. O'Loan, 'Various confraternities and conditions to be observed in erecting them' in *I.E.R.*, 1891, pp67-74.
171. J. Cantwell, 'Confraternities, their object and use' in *I.E.R.*, 1882, pp560 and ff., 627-632.
172. C.J.M. 'Frequent communion' in *I.E.R.* 1886, pp229-238, 520-529; A. Murphy, 'Frequent communion', *I.E.R. 1886*, pp417-427; J. J. Roche, 'Frequent communion', *I.E.R.* 1887, pp57-62.
173. O'Brien to Kirby, 10 May 1865 (K.P.).
174. Burke to Kirby, 15 Jan. 1884 (K.P.).
175. *Decreta* (1850), pp11-12.
176. Ibid., p.18.
177. Ibid., pp13, 16.
178. Ibid., p.16.
179. O'Brien to Kirby, 20 Sept. 1853 (K.P.).
180. C.D.A., L.P., 1854/2.
181. Cardinal Fransoni to Slattery, 28 Nov. 1855 (C.D.A., S.P.).
182. Slattery to Bishop Ryan of Limerick, 9 Dec. 1855; reply of Robert Cussen P.P. Bruff, Co. Limerick on Ryan's behalf, 14 Dec. 1855; Slattery to Bishop Keane of

Ross, 11 Dec. 1855; same to Bishop Fallon of Kilmacduagh, 12 Dec. 1855; Dominick O'Brien of Waterford to Slattery, 14 Dec. 1855; Daniel Vaughan, Killaloe, to same, 16 Dec. 1855; Bishop O'Donnell of Kerry, to same, 16 Dec. 1855; T. Murphy, Cloyne to same, 17 Dec. 1855 (C.D.A., S.P.).

183. Keane to Slattery, 21 Dec. 1853, 17 Jan., 4 May, 12 May, 19 May; Cardinal Fransoni to Slattery 12 May 1854, and 17 May 1854 (C.D.A., S.P.).

184. *Acta* (1854), pp61, 64, 71, 72.

185. C.D.A. S.P., 1854/6.

186. C.D.A. S.P., 1854/41.

187. See Oliver MacDonagh, 'The Politicisation of the Irish Catholic bishops, 1800-1850' in *Historical Journal* xviii, no. 1 (1975), pp37, 38, 42; Murphy, 'Priests and people', p248; Larkin, 'Church, state and nation' (1975), p.1248.

2. CONFLICT ON THE HUSTINGS

1. *T.L.*, 15 Apr. 1885.

2. Sermon, 21 Mar. 1874 (C.D.A., L.P.).

3. J.S. Vaughan, 'Priests and politics' in *I.E.R.*, 1891, pp32, 34-35; J. O'Reilly, *The Relation of the church to society* (London, 1892), p.93 (this was a reproduction of his essays published in the *Irish Monthly*, vol 4, 1876). See also Leahy's MS notes (C.D.A. L.P.), 1866/51), and *M.T.*, 25 Apr. 1891 (ref. of Michael B. Corry C.C.).

4. P. Murray, *Essays, Chiefly Theological*, iv, (Dublin, 1853), pp270-271.

5. Ibid., pp274, 277.

6. C.D.A. L.P., 1866/51; *Tablet* 11 Dec. 1852, (ref. of Patrick Quaid P.P., O'Callaghan's Mills, Co Clare).

7. *Tablet*, 18 Feb 1854 (letter of John Walsh C.C., Kilmacow, Co Waterford).

8. *Irish educ. enquiry*, pp.42, 94, 356, H.C. 1826-7, xiii; *Management of Maynooth*, p.273, (1896-1), H.C. 1854-5, xxii.

9. Ibid., p.92.

10. Ibid., pp37, 85-86.

11. For an excellent article on electioneering see J.H. Whyte, 'Influence of the catholic clergy in elections in nineteenth century Ireland', in *English Historical Review*, lxxv (Apr. 1960) pp239-59.

12. O'Shea, op. cit., tables 17 and 17A, pp31-41.

13. *Management of Maynooth*, pp57, 86 (1896), H.C. 1854-5, xxii.

14. E.g., *N.G.*, 28 July 1852.

15. C.D.A., L.P., 1866/51.

16. *Minutes of Evidence taken before the Select Committee on the Tipperary Election Petition*, pp36-37, H.C. 1867 (211), viii.

17. Bishop Kennedy, Killaloe, to Slattery, 18 Feb. 1848 (C.D.A. S.P.): Cardinal Fransoni to Archbishop Crolly, 15 Oct. 1844 (C.D.A., S.P.).; Peadar MacSuibhne, *Paul Cullen and his contemporaries*, vol iii, p.316.

18. *Tipp. election petition*, pp.84-6, 88, 95, H.C. 1867, viii.

19. *T.F.P.*, 9 Apr. 1867.

20. Norman, *Cath. ch. & Ire.*, pp422-429; Whyte, 'Catholic clergy in elections', p.247.

21. Norman, *op. cit.*, p.425.

22. *T.F.P.* 7 June 1872.

23. *T.F.P.* 11, 18 June, 2 July 1872; Resident magistrate's report, June 1872 (S.P.O., C.S.O., R.P., 1872/9349).

24. S.P.O., C.S.O., R.P., 1872/13392.

25. *Management of Maynooth*, pp83-4 (1896-I), H.C. 1854-5, xxii.

26. Ibid., pp35-36.

27. Statement of Dean R.B. O'Brien in 'The Irish Election' in *Dublin University Magazine*, xi, (July-Dec. 1852), p.251; P. Finlay, 'The church and civil society' in *Irish Monthly*, xxv, (1897), pp591-2, 594-5; *Report of the Select Committee on*

Parliamentary and Municipal Elections with the proceedings of the Committee, Minutes of Evidence and Appendix, p.484, H.C. 1868-9 (352), viii-I; *Management of Maynooth*, pp65-6, H.C. 1854-5, xxii; Vaughan, 'Priest and politics' (1891), p.32.

28. *Management of Maynooth*, p.13, H.C. 1854-5, xxii.
29. Pp62-63, 180.
30. *L.R.*, 11 June 1852.
31. *D.U.M.*, 1852, p.251.
32. *Tipp. election petition*, p.39, H.C. 1867, viii.
33. *N.G.* 10 July 1852; police report, 18 July 1852 (N.L.I., MS 11037(29).
34. *D.U.M.*, 1852, p.251, see also Rev Massy Dawson, *The Secret History of Romanism* (1853), pp470-472.
35. Detective report, 15 Aug. 1859. (N.L.I., Larcom papers, MS 7636).
36. *T.F.P.*, 14 Apr. 1852.
37. *T.F.P.*, 16 Oct. 1866.
38. *I.C.D.*, 1862, p.300.
39. *Tipp. election petition*, p.39, H.C. 1867, viii.
40. *Reports of commissioners appointed under the act of the 15th and 16th Victoria Cap. 57, for the purposes of making inquiry into the existence of corrupt practices at the last election for Cashel, together with the minutes of evidence*, p.321 (C9), H.C. 1870, xxxii.
41. *T.F.P.*, 23 Nov. 1868; *Cashel election enquiry*, pp159, 162, 204, 205, 324, 326, H.C. 1870, xxxii; J. L. Whittle, 'Irish elections and the influence of the priests' in *Frazer's Magazine*, new series, i, (Jan.-June 1870), p.54; H.J. Hanham, *Politics in the time of Disraeli and Gladstone*, (London, 1959), p.180.
42. *T.F.P.*, 5, 12, 22 Jan. 1869.
43. His letter in *L.R.*, 16 July 1852.
44. His letter in *F.J.*, 29 Oct. 1868.
45. Letter in *F.J.*, 3 Nov. 1868; Fogarty's notebook no. 3. (C.D.A.); *Cashel election enquiry*, pp162, 322, 324, 374, H.C. 1870, xxxii.
46. Ibid., pp160, 320, 324.
47. Earl of Donoughmore to R. J. Otway, 9 July 1865 (N.L.I., Otway papers, MS 13008).
48. *D.U.M.*, 1852, p.254; 'Ultramontane Policy in Ireland' in *D.U.M.*, 1874, p.120; Whittle, op. cit., p.47; J. L Jones, *Political issues of the nineteenth century with important statistics* (London, 1886), pp10-11.
49. Murray, *Essays*, pp285-6.
50. Ibid., pp287-289, 291-293; see also M. O'Connor 'Sogarth Aroon', in *I.E.R.*, (1869), pp550-54, 564-8; Vaughan, 'Priests and politics' (1891), p.30.
51. *T.F.P.*, 29 Nov. 1853.
52. *N.G.*, 14 Feb. 1857.
53. *Tipp. election petition*, p.85, H.C. 1867, viii.
54. *N.G.*, 26 Feb. 1870.
55. *Management of Maynooth*, p.86 (1896-1), H.C. 1854-5, xxii.
56. Detective Report, 18 Aug. 1859 (N.L.I., Larcom papers MS 7636).
57. *T.F.P.*, 28 Feb. 1865.
58. *Tipp. election petition*, p.40, H.C. 1867, viii.
59. *T.F.P.*, 27, 29 Oct. 1868.
60. Diary of John Trant, June 1852-July 1852 (N.L.I., MS 2567).
61. *T.F.P.*, 19 Aug. 1857.
62. *T.F.P.*, 23 Oct. 1866.
63. *State of Ireland*, pp 79, 319, H.C. 1825, viii.
64. Fry to Lord Naas, 3 May, 1859 (N.L.I., Naas papers, MS 11036).
65. *T.F.P.*, 16 Oct. 1866, (letter from the conducting agent of the Conservative candidate).
66. *Committee on elections*, pp289 and ff., 294, 331, 479, H.C. 1868-9, viii.
67. *N.G.*, 10 July 1852; *T.F.P.*, 24 July 1852 (statements of John Scanlan C.C.

Cloughjordan, and Archdeacon Laffan); also articles in *T.F.P.*, 24 July 1852; *N.G.*,
17 July 1852; see *Committee on elections*, pp208-210, 329-330, 337, 489, H.C.
1868-9, viii.

68. *L.R.*, 27 Aug. 1852, 14 Sept. 1852, 2 July 1853; police report, 15 Aug. 1852,
(N.L.I., MS 11037).
69. N.L.I. MS 2567 (entry 21 July 1852).
70. E.g. *T.F.P.*, 14 July, 12, 29 Nov. 1853, 26 Aug. 1856, 3, 6 Mar. 1857, 28 Sept. 1866;
F.J., 27 Oct. 1868.
71. E.g. *T.F.P.*, 13 Nov. 1868 quoted extracts from *Hansard* to illustrate the politics of
one candidate.
72. *Committee on elections*, p.209, H.C. 1868-9, viii.
73. Ibid., pp264, 313, 495; *T.F.P.* 10 Feb. 1857; *L.R.* 13 Mar., 3 Apr. 1857; *N.G.*, 14
Mar. 1857.
74. *T.F.P.*, 16 Oct. 1866; see also *Cashel election enquiry*, p.326, H.C. 1870, xxxii.
75. *Committee on elections*, p.266, H.C. 1868-9, viii.
76. *Ibid.*, pp477, 482.
77. *L.R.*, 7 Apr. 1857.
78. *Tipp. election petition*, pp37-8, H.C. 1867, viii.
79. O'Brien to Kirby, 7 May 1859 (K.P.).
80. Gerald Fitzgibbon, *Ireland in 1868; The battlefield for English party strife* (London,
1868), pp 51-2; A. K. Hanrahan, 'Irish Electioneering 1850-72' (M.A. thesis,
U.C.D., 1965), p.34.
81. Details in *N.G.*, 31 Jan. 1874 and *T.F.P.*, 15 May 1877.
82. *T.F.P.*, 12 Mar. 1875; Bishop James Ryan of Killaloe to Kirby, 18 Mar. 1874,
(K.P.).
83. *T.F.P.*, 8, 25 Mar. 1859.
84. *Committee on elections*, pp333, 478, H.C. 1868-9, viii.
85. As in note 12 above.

3.   THE PRIEST AND THE LAND 1850-1876

1. Connell, *Irish peasant society*, p.132.
2. Statement of John Moloney P.P., Kilcommon in *Tablet*, 24 Mar. 1850 and *L.R.*, 16
Apr. 1850.
3. Theology of the early twentieth century is also included because it is identical to that
of the nineteenth century.
4. J. Kelleher, 'The right to rent and the unearned increment' in *Irish Theological
Quarterly*, v, (1910), pp 427-8; *Catholic Encyclopedia, xii, (London, 1911), p.466;*
Bailly, Theologia Dogmatica et Moralis ad Usum seminariorum, vii, (Parisiis,
1830), p.91.
5. *Catholic Encyclopedia*, xii, p.466.
6. Ibid., p.462.
7. Kelleher *loc. cit.*, p.419.
8. Ibid., pp147, 425; J.E. Canavan, 'Property and the church' in *Studies, xxiv*, (Sept.
1935), pp393, 401, 404. (He quoted from medieval scholastic theologians and the
Scriptures).
9. *Catholic Encyclopedia*, xii, p.462.
10. P. J. P. Gury, *Compendium Theologiae Moralis* (Ratisbone, 1874), pp344-346;
Catholic Encyclopedia, iv, p.332; W. R. Anson, *Principles of English law of
contract* (London, 1886), p.10.
11. *Tablet*, 2 Mar. 1850; *T.F.P.*, 27 Feb. 1850.
12. His letter in *Tablet*, 8 Feb. 1851.
13. *T.F.P.*, 8 Oct. 1869.
14. *T.F.P.*, 25 Feb. 1870; *N.G.*, 23 Feb. 1870. Statement of Michael O'Neill C.C.
Tipperary in *T.F.P.*, 1 Oct. 1869.

15. *T.F.P.*, 27 Feb. 1850; *L.R.*, 19 Mar. 1850; *Tablet*, 23 Mar. 1850; *T.F.P.*, 23 Mar. 1850; *Tablet*, 20 Apr. 1850; *L.R.* 16 Apr. 1850.
16. *T.F.P.*, 6 Feb. 1850.
17. *T.F.P.*, 19 Oct. 1850.
18. Pp112-113.
19. *L.R.*, 19 Mar. 1850.
20. Priests' statements in *T.F.P.*, 5 Oct., 19 Nov. 1869; newscutting in S.P.O., C.S.O., R.P. 1870/1889.
21. Croke's letters in *C.E.*, 26 Feb., 19 Mar. 1851; Kenyon's letter in *C.E.*, 10 Mar. 1851.
22. See David Thornley, *Isaac Butt and Home Rule* (London, 1964), pp69-70 on the aims of Butt's movement.
23. *T.F.P.*, 6, 27 Feb., 1 June, 19 Oct. 1850, 15 Feb. 1859; *Tablet*, 23 Mar. 1850; *L.R.*, 19 Mar. 1850, 21 Mar. 1851 (statements of William Cahill C.C., Mullinahone, William Quirke C.C., John Baldwin P.P., Clonmel, John O'Dwyer C.C., William F. Mullally P.P., John Power P.P., Powerstown).
24. *T.F.P.*, 27 Feb. 1850; *Tablet* 2 Mar. 1850, 2 Dec. 1851 (statements of John Ryan C.C. and Daniel K. Lanigan P.P., Kilcommon).
25. *Tablet*, 25 Jan. 1851.
26. Rev Thomas Meagher, *The Roman law of landlord and tenant with suggestions for its application to Irish tenure* (Dublin, 1854).
27. Ibid., pp14-15, 27, 29.
28. Report by Patrick Glynn C.C., Templederry to the Land League executive, (N.L.I., I.N.L.L. Papers, MS. 17712); Edmund O'Leary P.P., Toomevara to Kirby, 2 Mar. 1874 (K.P.).
29. *T.F.P.*, 8 Oct. 1869.
30. Meagher, op. cit., pp40-41, also his letter in *Tablet*, 8 Feb. 1851.
31. *Tablet*, 20 Apr. 1850 (letter of James Redmond P.P., Arklow, Co Wicklow, to Thomas O'Shea C.C., Callan, Co Kilkenny).
32. His letter in *T.F.P.*, 25 Feb. 1870.
33. Cahill's statement in *T.F.P.*, 25 Feb. 1870; *N.G.*, 23 Feb. 1870.
34. Steele, *Irish Land*, p.9; Cullen, *Econ. Hist.*, pp138-9; J. Donnelly Jnr., *The land and people of nineteenth century Cork* (London, 1975), p.189, J. Lee, *The modernisation of Irish society* (Dublin, 1973), p.38; B.L. Solow, *The land question and the Irish economy 1870-1903* (Massachusetts, 1971), pp76-77. W. E. Vaughan, 'A Study of landlord and tenant relations in Ireland between the famine and the Land War, 1850-1878' (Ph.D. thesis, Trinity College, 1973), p.38.
35. *Tablet*, 2 Mar. 1850; statements of other priests in *Tablet* 23 Mar. 1850 and *T.F.P.*, 1 June 1850.
36. His letter in *Tablet*, 8 Feb. 1851.
37. Meagher, op. cit., pp21-5, 32.
38. *L.R.*, 8 Oct. 1850; *T.F.P.*, 19 Oct. 1850; *Tablet*, 19 Oct. 1850.
39. His letter in *Tablet*, 20 Apr. 1850.
40. Kelleher, 'The right to rent', (1910), p.419.
41. Their statements in *Tablet*, 2 Mar., 20 Apr. 1850, *L.R.* 16 Apr. 1850, 21 Mar. 1851.
42. His letter in *Tablet*, 19 Oct. 1850.
43. Letter in *Tablet*, 8 Feb. 1851.
44. Meagher, op. cit., pp25-6.
45. Finn's letter in *Tablet*, 27 Mar. 1852.
46. *L.R.*, 23 Mar. 1850; *T.F.P.*, 23 Mar. 1850; *Tablet*, 2 Dec. 1854.
47. *T.F.P.*, 1 June 1850.
48. *L.R.*, 19 Nov. 1852.
49. *L.R.*, 16 Apr. 1850.
50. *L.R.*, 21 Mar. 1851.
51. *T.F.P.*, 25 Feb. 1870; *N.G.* 23 Feb. 1870.

52. Priests' statements in *T.F.P.*, 6 Feb. 1850, 19 Mar. 1872; *N.G.*, 25 Feb. 1865; *T.A.*, 23 Mar. 1872; Pastoral of Dr Leahy, 10 July 1862 (C.D.A.).
53. Meagher, op. cit., p.19.
54. *Tablet*, 20 Apr. 1850, *L.R.* 16 Apr. 1850.
55. *T.F.P.*, 1 June 1850.
56. *T.F.P.*, 21 May 1853, *N.G.*, 25 May 1853.
57. O'Shea, *op. cit.*, table 19, pp44-45.
58. Priests' statements in *L.R.*, 19 Mar. 1850, *T.F.P.*, 23 Mar. 1850, *L.R.*, 16 Apr. 1850, 21 Mar. 1851.
59. Letter in *Tablet*, 18 May 1850.
60. *Tablet*, 30 Nov. 1850.
61. Rev. J. O'Rourke, *The history of the great Irish famine of 1847* (3rd ed., Dublin, 1902), pp31, 40, 47, 106, 119-120, 244 and ff, 295, 327-328, 353, 387.
62. *T.F.P.*, 27 Feb. 1850.
63. *L.R.*, 16 Apr. 1850, 21 Jan. 1851.
64. See *Pobal Ailbe*, p.36.
65. *T.F.P.*, 23 Mar. 1850, *Tablet*, 23 Mar. 1850, 19 Oct. 1850.
66. *Tablet*, 2 Mar. 1850; see also Ryan to Slattery, 26 Jan. 1847 (C.D.A., S.P.).
67. *Pobal Ailbe*, pp88, 90.
68. O'Shea, op. cit., table 20, pp46-48.
69. Names traced in *N.G.*, 18 Feb. 1865, 25 Feb. 1865, *T.F.P.*, 14 July 1865, 18 July 1865, 20 Oct. 1865, 25 Sept. 1866, *T.A.*, 6 Oct. 1866, *L.R.*, 21 July 1865.
70. Pp72-73.
71. *T.F.P.*, 20 Oct. 1849.
72. *Tablet*, 1 Mar. 1851.
73. See *T.F.P.*, 27 Feb. 1850, 15 Jan. 1851, *Tablet* 2 Mar. 1850, *L.R.*, 26 Feb. 1850.
74. O'Shea, *op. cit.*, tables 20, 22, 23, 24, pp46-48, 51-54.
75. See e.g. *Tablet*, 11, 25 May, 8, 22 June, 3 Aug., 28 Sept., 12, 26 Oct., 2, 9, 23, 30 Nov. and 21 Dec. 1850.
76. Details in *T.F.P.*, 2 Oct. 1850, *Tablet*, 5, 12, Oct. 1850.
77. O'Shea, op. cit., table 24, pp53-54.
78. *F.J.*, 30 Jan. 1856.
79. *Tablet*, 12 July, 25 Oct. 1851.
80. *T.F.P.*, 31 July 1850, *Tablet*, 30 Nov. 1850.
81. *T.F.P.*, 1 Oct. 1869.
82. *T.F.P.*, 15, 22 Oct., 5, 12, 19 Nov., 3, 24 Dec. 1869, 7, 21 Jan. 1870.
83. *F.J.*, 15 Dec. 1869.
84. *T.F.P.*, 5 Nov. 1869.
85. Daunt to Leahy (N.L.I., W. J. O'Neill Daunt Papers, MS 8046).
86. Butt's speech in *T.F.P.*, 1 Oct. 1869.
87. *T.F.P.*, 5 Nov. 1869.
88. O'Shea, op. cit., table 22, p.51, and Ibid., fig. 8 p.206.
89. Letter in *Tablet*, 25 Oct. 1851.
90. *Tablet*, 17 Aug. 1850.
91. *T.F.P.*, 10 July 1850.
92. These cases are preserved in a large file (S.P.O. C.S.O., R.P. 1859/2632); see also *Hansard* 3 cxxxvi, pp944-6 and cxxxvii, pp169-174.
93. *T.F.P.*, 14 May, 24 Sept. 1851; *Tablet*, 27 Sept. 1851; *L.R.*, 21 Mar. 1851 (statements of William Quirke, John O'Dwyer, and Patrick Meany, C.C., Clonmel).
94. Croke's letter to Kenyon *C.E.*, 26 Feb. 1851; Cahill's statement in *T.F.P.*, 19 Oct 1850, *L.R.*, 18 Oct. 1850.
95. As in note 94 for Cahill.
96. *Tablet*, 25 Jan. 1851.
97. *L.R.*, 21 Mar. 1851.
98. *T.F.P.*, 21, 31, May 1851; *Tablet*, 17, 24 May 1851.
99. *T.F.P.*, 19 Feb., 14 May, 24 Sept. 1851, 3 July 1852; *Tablet* 27 Sept. 1851; *N.G.* 24

Sept. 1851; Election Papers, (N.L.I., MS 11037).

100. *T.F.P.*, 21 May 1851.
101. *Tablet*, 31 May 1851, *F.J.*, 20 Aug. 1851.
102. Names extracted from *T.F.P.*, 18 Oct. 1851, *Tablet*, 19 July, 9 Aug., 18, 25 Oct. 1851.
103. *Tablet*, 23 Aug. 1851; J. H. Whyte, *The independent Irish party 1850-1859* (Oxford, 1958), p.32.
104. *T.F.P.*, 28 Jan. 1852.
105. *T.F.P.*, 20 Mar., 7 Apr. 1852.
106. *T.F.P.*, 14 Apr. 1852, *N.G.*, 17 Apr. 1852.
107. *T.F.P.*, 23 June 1852.
108. *T.F.P.*, 14 Apr., 24 July 1852; *L.R.*, 17 Aug. 1852, (statements of William Cahill, Martin Laffan P.P., Killenaule, and address of Archdeacon Fitzgerald, Rathkeale).
109. *Tablet*, 24 Apr. 1852.
110. *T.F.P.*, 14 Apr., 26, 30 June 1852; *L.R.* 11 June 1852 (statements of Patrick Leahy, John Mackey P.P. Clonoulty, and Dr Burke).
111. *T.F.P.*, 3 July 1852; *N.G.*, 10, 24 July 1852; *D.U.M.*, 1852, p.25; Election Papers, (N.L.I., MS 11037), letter 10 July 1852 from W. B. Septon (S.P.O. O.P., Tipperary): (priests involved were John Ryan C.C, James Bowles C.C, John Meagher P.P., John Scanlan C.C., Andrew J. Scanlan P.P. and Archdeacon Laffan).
112. *L.R.*, 18 June 1852.
113. *F.J.*, 20 Oct 1852, *Tablet*, 30 Oct. 1852, Whyte, *Indep. Irish party*, p.88.
114. *Tablet*, 4, 11, 18 June 1853; *I.C.D.* 1854, p.166.
115. *T.F.P.*, 15 June 1853, 19 April 1854; *L.R.*, 28 Mar., 21, 25 Apr. 1854; *Tablet*, 25 Mar. 1854.
116. Slattery's circular to the clergy of Cashel and Emly 22 Mar. 1854 (C.D.A. S.P.); printed document 27 Apr. 1854 entitled 'Declaration and instruction of the catholic bishops of Great Britain and Ireland the proposed committee of enquiry into religious communities' (C.D.A., L.P.).
117. Norman, *Cath. ch. & Ire.*, pp160-61, 170.
118. *T.F.P.*, 8, 22 Oct. 1869; *N.G.*, 9 Oct. 1869; *L.R.*, 22 Oct. 1869.
119. *T.F.P.*, 15 Oct. 1869, *N.G.*, 16 Oct. 1869; Mill's refusal in *T.F.P.*, 22 Oct. 1869.
120. *T.F.P.*, 27 Oct. 1868; *N.G.*, 28 Oct. 1868; *T.A.*, 31 Oct. 1868, *F.J.*, 27 Oct. 1868.
121. His strong letter in *L.R.*, 4 May 1852.
122. The collection was published showing amounts for each parish and may be consulted in 'Pamphlets, University Education 1844-1852', vol. iii, Oireachtas Library, Dublin.
123. Comparison in O'Shea, op. cit., table 24, pp53-4.
124. *Tablet*, 17 Jan. 1852, 23 Apr. 1853.
125. *Tablet*, 14 Feb. 1852.
126. *T.F.P.*, 9 Oct. 1850.
127. *T.F.P.*, 11 Sept. 1852; *N.G.*, 11 Sept. 1852; *F.J.*, 9 Sept. 1852.
128. Pp128, 190.
129. Pp184, 188, 190-91.
130. Pp187-88.
131. Letter in *Tablet*, 9 Apr. 1853.
132. *T.A.*, 25 Sept. 1869.
133. *T.F.P.*, 5 Oct. 1868.
134. *T.F.P.*, 25 Feb. 1870; *N.G.*, 23 Feb. 1870.
135. Letter in *L.R.*, 24 Aug. 1869.
136. Leahy to Thomas Ryan, Dublin, 10 Oct. 1869 (C.D.A., L.P.). (Ryan was a member of Butt's league). See also John O'Connor C.C., Ballingarry to E. Pigott (N.L.I., Butt Papers, MS 8706) and J. B. Kennedy, Limerick Farmers' Club, to Butt 9 Sept. 1869 (N.L.I., MS 10415).
137. *N.G.*, 9 Oct. 1869, *T.F.P.*, 19 Oct. 1869.
138. *I.C.D.*, 1865, pp329-333; *F.J.*, 8 Oct. 1869; *T.F.P.*, 26 Oct., 2 Nov. 1869; *N.G.*, 30

Oct. 1869.
139. *Tablet*, 5 Apr. 1851.
140. *F.J.*, 15 Jan. 1852.
141. *Tablet*, 17 Jan. 1852; *F.J.*, 14 Jan. 1852.
142. *T.F.P.*, 27 Sept. 1851; *Tablet*, 11 Oct. 1851.
143. *Tablet*, 16 Aug. 1851, 13 March 1852.
144. *Tablet*, 21 Feb. 1852.
145. *T.F.P.*, 15 Jan. 1851.
146. *T.F.P.*, 8 Jan. 1851 (letter).
147. Their letters in *Tablet*, 15 Apr. 1854 and *F.J.*, 26 Apr. 1854.
148. *Tablet*, 2 Dec. 1854.
149. Pp190-91.
150. *T.F.P.*, 13 Aug. 1858; *F.J.*, 18, 19 Aug. 1858.
151. Pp185-86.
152. *T.F.P.*, 25 Jan. 1859.
153. *T.F.P.*, 5 Nov., 3, 24 Dec. 1869, 7 Jan. 1870.
154. Reference by David Humphreys C.C. Tipperary in *T.P.*, 24 Sept. 1891.
155. *T.A.*, 7 Oct. 1876; *F.J.*, 25 Oct. 1876; Thurles P.L.U. minute book, May-Nov. 1876 (Tipperary County Library), p.344.
156. *Tablet*, 2 Dec. 1854.
157. *Tablet*, 14 Sept., 12 Oct., 21 Dec. 1850.
158. *L.R.*, 15 Feb. 1850; *Tablet*, 27 July, 14 Aug. 1850; *N.G.*, 17, 24 Aug. 1850.
159. E.g. *T.F.P.*, 19 Mar. 1872, *T.A.*, 23 Mar. 1872, 8 Jan. 1876; *N.G.*, 1, 5 Jan. 1876; *L.R.*, 4 Jan. 1876; letters from Edward Galway, land agent, to Leahy complaining of altar attacks, dated 11, 15, 29, 30 Dec. 1871 (C.D.A., L.P.).
160. See e.g. *N.G.*, 2, 30 Apr., 7, 21 May 1862, 14 Mar., 6 June, 15 Aug. 1868, 28 Apr. 1869; *T.F.P.*, 16 Feb. 1869, Dr Leahy to Kirby, 19 Jan. 1866 (K.P.); see also S.P.O., C.S.O., R.P. 1864/15189.
161. The O'Carroll Diary, pp107, 153-4, (C.D.A.); Cullen, *Econ. Hist.*, p.137; Solow *Land and economy*, p.97; see also James S. Donnelly Jr, 'The Irish Agricultural Depression of 1859-64' in *Irish Economic and Social History*, iii, (1976), pp33-54.

4.   THE PRIEST AND THE AGRARIAN REVOLUTION 1877-1891

1. Power to Kirby, 3 July 1879 and 1 Mar. 1880 (K.P.).
2. Ryan to Kirby, 18 Sept. 1879 and 19 May 1880 (K.P.).
3. *C.C.*, 27 Sept. 1879.
4. *Report of the royal commission on the Land Law (Ireland) Act 1885, vol II, minutes of evidence and appendices*, p.856 (C4969), H.C. 1887, xxvi.
5. Whittaker to Moore, 19 Feb. 1889 (Mooresfort papers).
6. Rev. J. Guinan, *Priest and People in Doon* (Dublin and Cork, 1925), p.63.
7. *T.F.P.*, 14 May 1878; *L.R.*, 14 June 1878.
8. *T.A.*, 26 Jan., 26 Apr., 31 May, 28 June 1879, 12 July 1879; *T.F.P.*, 1, 4 July 1879.
9. *L.R.*, 4 July 1879.
10. *T.F.P.*, 30 Jan. 1879.
11. P.185.
12. *T.F.P.*, 14 May 1878.
13. *T.A.*, 16 Aug. 1879.
14. Letter in *T.A.*, 26 July 1879.
15. *L.R.*, 4 July 1879.
16. *T.F.P.*, 24 Jan. 1879.
17. *T.F.P.*, 10 Sept. 1880; *T.A.*, 11 Sept. 1880; *Tablet*, 11 Sept. 1880.
18. O'Shea, op. cit., tables 30-32, pp72-85 and ibid., figs. 9-11, pp207-209.
19. Michael Cusack to Thomas Brennan, Sec. of the Land League (N.L.I., MS 8291).
20. *T.P.*, 7 Oct. 1881.

21. *U.I.*, 23 Sept. 1882.
22. S.P.O., I.N.L. Special Commission documents 1888, Police Reports, rept. 3684/83, 14 June 1883; S.P.O., I.N.L. proceedings 1885-1890, Special branch reports, 13 Jan. 1887, 21 Apr. 1887, 31 Mar. 1890 C.S.O. 8081/1886; I.N.L. Proceedings 1883-1884, Rept. C.S.O. 1986, C.S.O. Rept. 17093/1884, C.S.O. Rept. 1039 15 Jan. 1885.
23. *U.I.*, 24 Mar. 1883.
24. O'Shea, op. cit., table 33, p.86.
25. Ibid., table 34, pp87-89.
26. Ibid., table 36, p.93.
27. Ibid., table 29, pp62-71.
28. Ibid., tables 37 and 38, pp94-98.
29. Larkin, 'Church state and nation', pp1264-5.
30. *T.L.*, 6 Feb. 1885. (Robert Prout C.C. Upperchurch).
31. *F.J.*, 11 Feb. 1881.
32. *T.A.*, 26 Mar. 1881; see also *T.P.*, 25 Nov. 1881 (John R. Crowe C.C.).
33. See John Power C.C. Solohead to Anna Parnell, 7 Nov. 1881, and 11 Nov. 1881 (N.L.I., I.N.L.L. papers, MS 17701). Her notes on these show her reluctance to part with money for other purposes.
34. *Tipperary*, 14 Jan. 1882.
35. *Tipperary*, 4 Jan. 1882; *T.P.*, 17 Feb. 1882.
36. *N.G.*, 29 Mar. 1882; *T.P.*, 10 Feb. 1882.
37. *T.P.*, 14 Apr. 1882; *T.A.*, 8 Apr. 1882.
38. *T.P.*, 5 May 1882.
39. *T.L.*, 11 Oct. 1882; *Tipperary*, 28 Jan. 1882.
40. P.80.
41. Letter in *N.G.*, 7 Dec. 1881.
42. *N.G.*, 7 Dec. 1881; for the text of the alphabet see N.D. Palmer, *The Irish Land League Crisis* (Yale, 1940), p.290.
43. P. J. Kennedy to Anna Parnell, 15 Nov. 1881 (N.L.I., I.N.L.L. papers, MS 17701).
44. *T.P.*, 4 Mar. 1881, 21 Oct. 1881; *T.A.*, 1 Apr. 1882; *N.G.*, 29 Mar. 1882; *F.J.*, 11 May, 8 June 1882.
45. *Tablet*, 24 Dec. 1881; Inspector general's instructions to the police (S.P.O., C.S.O., R.P., 1882/11806).
46. Crowe to Anna Parnell, 7 Nov. 1881 (N.L.I., I.N.L.L. papers, MS 17701(3)).
47. *Hansard 3*, cclxvi, p.1938.
48. S.P.O., C.S.O., R.P. 1882/1195. (This file gives the membership of the Rathdowney Ladies Land League.)
49. Ibid.
50. *N.G.*, 20 May 1882.
51. Letter in *T.A.*, 6 Mar. 1886.
52. *N.G.*, 22 Mar. 1882.
53. *F.J.*, 12, 17 Mar. 1881; *N.G.*, 19 Mar. 1881; Croke to Kirby 28 Mar. 1881 (K.P.); McCabe to Croke, 19 Mar. 1881 and Croke's reply 20 Mar. 1881 (C.D.A., C.P.).
54. Croke to McCabe, 8 Apr. 1881 (C.D.A., C.P.); Croke to Kirby, 13 Apr. 1881.
55. *T.P.*, 25 Mar. 1881; Tierney, *Croke*, p.114.
56. *F.J.*, 2 May 1881.
57. Pastoral in *F.J.*, 12 June 1882, *Tipperary*, 14 June 1882; draft in C.D.A., C.P. 1881/15.
58. Letter in *T.A.*, 15 July 1882.
59. Memorandum, 10 June 1882 (C.D.A., C.P.).
60. *U.I.*, 22 July 1882.
61. Ibid.
62. Croke to Kirby, 6 Sept. 1882 (K.P.).
63. Pp170-71.
64. Pp112-13.

65. Pp119-202.
66. Priests' statements in *U.I.*, 3 May 1884, 30 Aug. 1884; *T.A.*, 7 Mar. 1885, 1 June 1889; *T.L.*, 23 May 1884, 8 Apr. 1885.
67. *U.I.*, 21 Oct. 1884.
68. *T.P.*, 5 Oct. 1883.
69. Letter in *Tablet*, 13 Nov. 1880.
70. *T.L.*, 22 Nov. 1882, *T.P.*, 15 Jan. 1889 (Patrick O'Keeffe C.C., Fethard and Matt Ryan C.C., Solohead).
71. See Emmet Larkin, *The Roman Catholic Church and the Creation of the Modern Irish State*, (Dublin, 1975), p.24, W.S. Blunt, *The Land War in Ireland*, (London, 1912), pp46-47; Larkin 'Church, state and nation', p.1265.
72. Croke to Kirby, 8, 19 Dec. 1880 (K.P.).
73. Kirby to Power, 11 May 1880 (W.D.A.).
74. C. J. Woods, 'The Politics of Cardinal McCabe, Archbishop of Dublin, 1879-1885', in *Dublin Historical Record* xxvi, no. 3 (June 1973), p.102.
75. Croke to Kirby, 8 Dec. 1880 (K.P.).
76. Croke to Kirby, 15 Jan. 1881 (K.P.); see also *F.J.*, 10 Jan. 1881 for the pope's letter which was appended to a pastoral from McCabe.
77. Ryan to Kirby, May 1881 (K.P.); see Tierney, *Croke*, pp121-3.
78. *T.A.*, 4 June 1881; Killoscully Rept., 22 May 1881 (S.P.O. Special Commission, 1888 police reports).
79. *T.A.*, 29 Apr. 1881, Bansha Rept. 3 Apr. 1881 (S.P.O., Special Commission 1888, police reports).
80. *T.P.*, 8 Dec 1882; *T.L.*, 6 Dec. 1882.
81. N.L.I., William O'Brien Papers, MS 5930; Power to Parnell, 20 Sept. 1882; (N.L.I., William O'Brien papers, MS 5930); *T.L.*, 12 Sept. 1884.
82. Power to Kirby, 18 June 1880 (K.P.).
83. Confidential report, 1 Apr. 1890 (S.P.O., Crime Branch Special Reports).
84. Ryan to Kirby, 21 Oct. 1881 (K.P.).
85. E.g. Ballycahill, Cashel, Castleiney, Dorrha, Holycross, Inch, Killenaule, Lattin, Lorrha, Loughmore, Moycarkey, Moneygall, Newport, Shinrone and Youghalarra.
86. Summary of National League Returns for Southern Division (S.P.O., I.N.L. proceedings 1883-4).
87. E.g. Ardcroney, Drombane, Kilfeacle, Knockavella, Moyne, Templetuohy.
88. O'Shea, op. cit., tables 30-32, pp72-85.
89. See *T.P.*, 28 Jan. 1881; *N.G.*, 17 Nov. 1880, O'Leary, op. cit., p.118; Canon J. Guinan, *The Soggarth Aroon* (Dublin, 1925), pp126, 139.
90. Boyton to Croke, 16 Jan. 1886 (C.D.A., C.P.). See S.P.O., I.N.L.L. Proceedings, Carton 2 for his activities.
91. Letter from a 'Donohil Boy' in *T.P.*, 28 Jan. 1881.
92. *T.P.*, 14 Oct. 1881.
93. *Nationalist*, 30 Aug., 6, 10 Sept., 6 Dec. 1890; *T.P.*, 21 Nov. 1890.
94. Capt. Slack's Report, 5 Nov. 1889 (S.P.O., D.I.C. reports, see South East division, 10792).
95. Blunt, *The land war*, p.279.
96. E.g. Anacarty, Ardfinan, Ballina, Ballycahill, Ballylooby, Birdhill, Borrisokane, Burncourt, Cahir, Carrick-on-Suir, Clerihan, Cloughjordan etc.
97. O'Shea, op. cit., table 29, p.71.
98. Police report, 14 June 1883 (S.P.O., Special Commission 1888, report 3684/83); official reports, 1 Oct. to 31 Dec. 1883. (S.P.O., I.N.L. proceedings, 1883-4).
99. O'Shea, op. cit., tables 30-32, pp72-85.
100. E.g. *T.A.*, 4 Dec. 1880, 1 Mar. 1884; *T.L.*, 12 Apr. 1884.
101. Report by Patrick Glynn C.C., Templederry giving individual details on over 100 tenants (N.L.I., I.N.L.L. Papers, MS 17712); Report of Patrick Lonergan C.C., Kilsheelan (ibid., MS 17706).
102. See e.g. *T.F.P.*, 8 June, 3, 7 Dec. 1880; *C.C.*, 15, 22 Dec. 1880; *T.A.*, 20, 27 Nov., 4

Dec. 1880, 1, 8 Jan., 2 Apr. 1881; *N.G.*, 5 Jan. 1881; *T.P.*, 22 Apr. 1881, and most of the reports in the Samuel Lee Anderson Papers (N.L.I., MS 11289).

103. O'Shea, op. cit., table 42, p.106.

104. Ibid., table 29, pp62-71.

105. *T.A.*, 13 Jan. 1883, 10 Jan., 25 July 1885, 18 May 1889; *U.I.*, 6 Jan. 1883, 1 Jan. 1887, 3 Nov. 1888; *T.L.*, 3 Oct. 1883; *T.P.*, 8 Feb., 25 Apr. 1884, 17 Apr, 2 Oct. 1885, 15 July 1887; *T.N.*, 11 May, 2 Nov. 1889; *Nationalist*, 15 Mar. 1890; police report, 6 July 1885. (S.P.O., I.N.L. proceedings 1885-90, 1885/14184); police reports 5 Feb. 1890 and July 1890 (S.P.O., Crime branch special, D.I.C.S., South Eastern division 5203/1102.

106. Police report, 30 June 1885. (S.P.O., I.N.L. proceedings 1885/14184).

107. Clonmel report, 24 Oct. 1880. (N.L.I., MS 11289); *F.J.*, 12 Feb. 1881; *T.P.*, 29 July 1881.

108. Clonmel report, 11 Aug. 1880; Mullinahone report, 8 Aug. 1880. (N.L.I., MS 11289): *T.F.P.*, 13 Aug. 1880, 14 Sept. 1880, *T.A.*, 21 Aug. 1880.

109. Priests' statements quoted in Clonmel report, 24 Oct. 1880. Cloneen report, 1 Aug. 1880. (N.L.I., MS 11289); *C.C.*, 15 Dec. 1880; *T.P.*, 8 Dec. 1882; *T.L.*, 6 Dec. 1882, 25 Jan. 1883, 2 Aug. 1884; *T.A.*, 22 Dec. 1883.

110. *U.I.*, 21 Oct. 1882.

111. *T.L.*, 25 Nov. 1882, 31 Oct. 1884. (Robert Prout C.C., Upperchurch and John Cahill C.C., Cashel).

112. *T.L.*, 11 Nov. 1882.

113. Statements in *T.P.*, 29 July 1881; *T.A.*, 20 Aug., 10 Sept. 1881; *N.G.*, 5 Jan., 7 Sept. 1881; *U.I.*, 24 Sept. 1881; *F.J.*, 16 Sept. 1881; Kiloscully report 22 May 1881. (C.S.O., special commission 1880, police reports).

114. *Nationalist*, 10 Sept. 1890.

115. *T.P.*, 7 Jan. 1881, *N.G.*, 9 Feb. 1881. Bansha report, 3 Apr. 1881. (S.P.O. special commission 1888, police reports).

116. O'Shea, op. cit., table 43, p.107.

117. *T.P.*, 14 Apr., 12 Dec. 1884, 23 Nov. 1888; *T.L.*, 24 Oct. 1884, 19 Dec. 1884, 27 Feb. 1885, 6 Mar. 1885, 14 Mar. 1885; *F.J.*, 7 Nov. 1887; *T.A.*, 12 Nov. 1887; 30 Nov. 1889; *U.I.*, 19 Oct. 1889; *T.N.*, 28 Dec. 1889; *Nationalist*, 15 Nov. 1890; *Hansard*, ccvc, p.278.

118. *T.L.*, 26 Jan. 1884, 26 Apr.; *T.P.*, 25 Apr. 1884.

119. *T.L.*, 26 Apr. 1884; *T.P.*, 25 Apr. 1884.

120. O'Shea, op. cit., table 29, pp62-71.

121. E.g., *T.L.*, 29 Nov. 1882, 24 Jan. 1883. (John Ryan and William Power P.P., Moyne).

122. *Tipperary*, 26 July 1882.

123. *T.L.*, 25 Oct. 1882.

124. *Tipperary*, 26 July 1882; *T.L.*, 8, 15, 29 Nov., 20, 27 Dec. 1882, 7 Mar., 19 Sept., 6, 10 Oct., 10 Dec. 1883, 5 Apr. 1884.

125. Names in *T.L.*, 19 Sept. 1883, 29 Sept. 1883.

126. *T.L.*, 29 Sept. 1883.

127. Templemore Report, 10 Oct. 1880. (N.L.I., MS 11289).

128. *T.F.P.*, 7 Dec. 1880.

129. Clonmel Report, 11 Aug. 1880. (N.L.I., MS 11289); *T.F.P.*, 17 Aug. 1880. (William Meagher C.C., Clonmel and James Cantwell).

130. His letter in *T.F.P.*, 26 Oct. 1880.

131. S.P.O., C.S.O., R.P., 1879/10444.

132. *Hansard 3*, ccxlvii, pp432-434.

133. O'Shea, op. cit., table 45, pp110-111.

134. Report of Captain Slack. 6 July 1885 (S.P.O., I.N.L. proceedings 1885-90, 1885/14184).

135. Statements, e.g. in *T.F.P.*, 24 Jan. 1879, *T.L.*, 24 Jan., 3 Oct. 1883, 17 May 1884; *T.A.*, 13 Feb. 1886; *F.J.* 29 Sept. 1886; Kiloscully report, 27 May 1881, Ballingarry

266 *Notes*

report, 4 Oct. 1885 (S.P.O., special commission, 1888, police reports).
136. *T.L.*, 16 Feb. 1882, Ryan's letter in *T.L.*, 8 Aug. 1884.
137. *U.I.*, 8 Nov. 1884.
138. Priests' statements in *N.G.*, 11 May 1882; *F.J.*, 11 May, 9 June 1882.
139. Croke to McCabe, 17 May 1882 (D.D.A., McCabe papers).
140. His sermon in *T.L.*, 11 Oct. 1882; see also *F.J.*, 21 Mar. 1882; Croke to Kirby, 15 July 1885 (K.P.).
141. *T.A.*, 5 Mar. 1881, 22 Jan. 1881 (Patrick Brennan C.C., Birr, and William J. McKeogh P.P., Ballinahinch).
142. *T.L.*, 19 Dec. 1884.
143. *Return showing for each month of the years 1879 and 1880 the number of Land League meetings held and agrarian crimes reported to the Inspector General of the Royal Irish Constabulary in each county throughout Ireland,* p.6, H.C. 1881 (5), lxxvii.
144. *U.I.*, 20 Aug. 1881.
145. *T.P.*, 5 Aug. 1881.
146. E.g. *C.C.*, 12, 15 Dec. 1880, *T.A.*, 1 Jan. 1881; *T.P.*, 22 Apr. 1881.
147. *N.G.*, 7 Sept. 1881, 18 Apr. 1882; *T.P.*, 23 Sept. 1881; *T.A.*, 1 Oct. 1881; *U.I.*, 24 Sept. 1881, 22 Oct. 1881.
148. His letter in *T.P.*, 23 Mar. 1883.
149. *F.J.*, 28 Apr. 1881, *T.A.*, 30 Apr. 1881.
150. *F.J.*, 7 May 1881, 12 May 1881; *T.A.*, 7, 14 May 1881.
151. E.g., *T.P.*, 22 Apr. 1881 (Humphreys).
152. *T.P.*, 22 Apr. 1881; *T.A.*, 23 Apr. 1881.
153. David Humphreys, *The Logic of the Land Bill* (Dublin, 1881) (Pamphlet no. 2 in Pamphlets — Land — cxvii, Oireachtas Library); W. J. Walsh, *A plain exposition of the Irish land act of 1881* (Dublin, 1881). There are several editions of Walsh's pamphlet under pseudonyms.
154. His Dublin speech in *T.P.*, 22 Apr. 1881.
155. P.58.
156. Humphreys, op. cit. p.4.
157. Ibid., pp5, 7.
158. Bessborough Comm., ii, part I, p.82.
159. Humphreys, op. cit. p.14.
160. Walsh, p.18.
161. Humphreys, op. cit. p16-17.
162. *T.P.*, 29 July 1881.
163. O'Shea, op. cit., table 46, pp112-4.
164. E.g., *T.F.P.*, 24 Jan. 1879; Templemore Report, 10 Oct. 1880. (N.L.I., MS 11289). Kiloscully Report, 22 May 1881. (S.P.O. Special Commission 1888). (Richard Cahill, Thomas Hackett C.C., Loughmore, James O'Brien C.C., Ballinahinch).
165. O'Shea, op. cit., table 46, pp112-114
166. Ibid.
167. N.L.I., ms 17712.
168. Letters in *F.J.*, 3 Mar. 1881, *Nation*, 23 June 1883, *T.A.*, 30 July, 4 Aug. 1883.
169. Unsorted file in W.D.A.
170. Pamphlet, pp8, 13.
171. Tipperary report, 31 Oct. 1880 (N.L.I., MS 11289).
172. *T.A.*, 8 Jan. 1887.
173. *1881 land act commission*, p.444, H.C. 1887, xxvi; Newport Report, 30 Aug. 1885. (S.P.O. Special Commission, 1888, police reports).
174. E.g., Kiloscully report, 22 May 1881. (S.P.O., Special Commission 1888, police reports); *T.F.P.*, 24 Jan. 1879.
175. *T.L.*, 22 Aug. 1883.
176. *T.F.P.*, 18 July 1879.
177. O'Shea, op. cit., table 46, pp112-114.

178. *T.A.*, 11 Feb. 1888, and evidence of Maurice Mooney P.P., Cahir in *Bessborough Comm.*, iii, part II, p.952.
179. O'Shea, op. cit., table 46.
180. *T.A.*, 8 Jan. 1881.
181. *Tablet*, 27 Nov. 1880; *C.C.*, 15 Dec. 1880; *T.L.*, 13 Dec. 1882.
182. *T.F.P.*, 5, 9 Sept. 1879; *N.G.*, 17 Dec. 1879; *T.A.*, 14 May 1881.
183. Pamphlet pp21-22.
184. *T.P.*, 22 Apr. 1881.
185. *T.A.*, 28 May, 4 June 1881; *T.L.*, 8 Nov. 1882, 22 Feb., 2 Aug. 1884.
186. *T.L.*, 18 Nov. 1882, 22 Aug. 1883; *N.G.*, 21 Feb. 1885; *T.A.*, 22 Dec. 1883; *U.I.*, 21 Oct. 1882.
187. *T.P.*, 23 Sept. 1881.
188. *T.L.*, 26 Apr. 1881; *N.G.*, 21 Feb. 1885.
189. *T.L.*, 8 Nov. 1882, 24 Jan., 25 Apr., 3 Oct. 1883, 26 Apr. 1884; *N.G.*, 23 Jan. 1884; Anacarty report, 26 Apr. 1885. (S.P.O., Special Commission, 1888, police reports).
190. Pamphlet, p.9.
191. Letter in *T.P.*, 18 Nov. 1881.
192. *T.A.*, 4 June 1881.
193. *U.I.*, 4 Aug. 1883; *T.L.*, 16 Mar. 1885; *T.P.*, 13 Feb. 1885.
194. See statements in *T.L.*, 5 Dec. 1884, 30 Oct. 1885; *T.A.*, 26 Jan. 1884, 5 Sept. 1885, 12 Nov. 1887; Birr Report, 12 Dec. 1886. (S.P.O., Spec. Comm. 1888, police reports).
195. *1881 land act report*, p.445, H.C. 1887, xxvi.
196. Letter of John R. Crowe in *U.I.*, 29 Nov. 1883.
197. Walsh's pamphlet, p.37.
198. *T.L.*, 1 Nov. 1882.
199. Letter in *T.A.*, 8 Apr. 1882.
200. *T.L.*, 26 Apr. 1884. (William Quirke and John Ryan).
201. *T.P.*, 7 Sept. 1883.
202. *Tipperary*, 1 Feb. 1882.
203. Larkin, *R.C. Church* (1975), p.367.
204. For statistics see *Return of proceedings under the Land Law (Ireland) Act, 1881 up to 31st day of July 1883; return showing for each county in Ireland the number of originating notices to have rents fixed lodged with the Irish Land Commissioners . . . to 30th April 1883*, p.2, H.C. 1883 (352), lvii.
205. *T.A.*, 17 Feb. 1883.
206. *T.A.*, 30 Apr. 1881, *U.I.*, 13 Aug. 1881.
207. *T.A.*, 14 May 1881.
208. *F.J.*, 31 May 1880, 16 May 1881.
209. *T.A.*, 8 Jan. 1881; *T.P.*, 7 Jan. 1881, 29 Apr. 1881 (Daniel Flannery, Richard Cahill, Michael McDonnell P.P., Golden). See also Lawrence J. Hayes P.P., Bansha to Arthur Moore, 8 Aug. 1890 (Mooresfort papers).
210. Bessborough Comm., iii, pt. 2, p.955.
211. *T.F.P.*, 24 Aug. 1880; *T.A.*, 29 Jan. 1881.
212. Clonmel Report, 24 Oct. 1880 (N.L.I., MS 11289).
213. *F.J.*, 19 Oct. 1881; *T.A.*, 22 Oct. 1881, *Tablet*, 22 Oct. 1881.
214. Letter in *F.J.*, 29 Oct. 1881.
215. Letter in Ibid.
216. Letter in *U.I.*, 26 Nov. 1881.
217. Letter in *F.J.*, 29 Oct. 1881.
218. *F.J.*, 25 Oct. 1881.
219. Letters in *T.A.*, 22 Oct. 1881, *T.P.*, 18 Nov. 1881.
220. Croke to the Vatican, 8 Feb. 1882 (C.D.A., C.P.).
221. Examples in *N.G.*, 5 Nov. 1881, *Tipperary*, 9 Nov., 3 Dec. 1881, *U.I.*, 26 Nov., 24 Dec. 1881.
222. See *U.I.*, 26 Nov., 3 Dec. 1881.

223. O'Shea, op. cit., table 47, p.115.
224. Ibid., tables 48-49, pp116-9.
225. Ibid., table 49, pp117-9.
226. Ibid., table 50, pp120-1.
227. *T.A.*, 25 July 1885.
228. *T.A.*, 9, 16, 23, 30 Jan., 6 Feb. 1886, 1, 8 Jan. 1887; *T.P.*, 19 Oct. 1888.
229. *T.P.*, 3 June 1887.
230. Croke to Walsh, 27 Dec. 1887 (D.D.A., W.P.).
231. *T.A.*, 8 Jan. 1887.
232. O'Shea, op. cit., table 46, pp112-4.
233. Canon D. Keller, *The Struggle for Life on the Ponsonby Estate*, (London, 1887), p.14.
234. *T.P.*, 22 Apr., 7 Oct. 1881; *T.A.*, 1 Oct. 1881; Kiloscully report, 22 May 1881 (S.P.O., Special Commission 1888, police reports F-K).
235. *T.P.*, 8 Dec. 1882.
236. *T.P.*, 22 Apr. 1881.
237. *N.G.*, 29 Oct., 15 Nov., 15 Dec. 1880; *T.F.P.*, 27 Feb. 1880; *L.R.*, 17 Dec. 1880; Report on Cahir Land League, 31 Dec. 1880 (N.L.I., I.N.L.L. paper MS 19706).
238. E.g. letter of Nicholas Murphy P.P., Kilmanagh in *Tablet*, 19 Mar. 1887.
239. P.J. Walsh, *William J. Walsh, Archbishop of Dublin* (London, 1928), pp237-9.
240. Ibid., pp245-6.
241. Keller, op cit., p.13.
242. Letter in *Tablet*, 25 Dec. 1886.
243. Letters in *F.J.*, 20 Dec. 1887, 19 May 1890; *L.R.*, 26 Aug. 1890; *T.P.*, 26 Sept. 1890; Humphreys to John Dillon, 21 Aug. 1890 (original at Glenstal Abbey).
244. *C.E.*, 3 June 1890; *T.P.*, 6, 20 June 1890.
245. *T.P.*, 26 Sept. 1890; *F.J.*, 25 Sept. 1890; Humphreys to Dillon as in n. 243.
246. Croke to M. Godre (of *l'Univers* (Paris)), 18 July 1890 (C.D.A., C.P.). Croke to Kirby, 30 July 1890 (K.P.).
247. *Nationalist*, 23 Aug., 3 Sept. 1890; *N.G.*, 27 Aug., 3 Sept. 1890; *T.P.*, 5 Sept. 1890; *U.I.*, 6 Sept. 1890.
248. *T.P.*, 26 Sept. 1890; *F.J.*, 25 Sept. 1890.
249. See Ross to Balfour, 10 Sept. 1890 on his contact with Rome. (British Library, Balfour papers, Add. MSS 49821). See also confidential report from Ross to the Vatican, 21 Dec. 1886 (S.C. Irlanda 1886, vol. 42, ff. 458-68).
250. Letter in *Tablet*, 19 Mar. 1887.
251. *T.P.*, 7 Sept. 1887.
252. *W. J. Walsh*, p.306; see S.C. Irlanda vol. 53, ff. 389-489 for letters.
253. Walsh to Persico, 25 Dec. 1887 (D.D.A., W.P.).
254. Letters in *T.A.*, 31 Aug. 1889.
255. Errington to Smith, 30 Aug. 1887. (Rome, St. Paul's outside the Walls, Abbot Smith papers).
256. Blunt, op. cit., p.435.
257. Rescript, 20 Apr. 1888 (C.D.A., C.P.); *W. J. Walsh*, pp331-2.
258. Tierney, *Croke*, p.224.
259. Power to Kirby, 14 Jan. 1889. (W.D.A.)
260. Police report, 7 June 1888 (S.P.O., C.B.S. 1882-1895).
261. Flanagan to Emly, undated (N.L.I., Monsell papers, MS 20683).
262. O'Shea, op. cit., table 49, pp117-9.
263. Clonmel Report, 27 May 1888 (S.P.O., I.N.L. proceedings 1879-1888).
264. Ibid., *T.P.*, 25 Aug. 1888; *N.G.*, 30 May 1888.
265. Croke to Walsh, 14 June, 10, 14 July, 22 Nov. 1888 (D.D.A., W.P.).
266. Croke to Walsh, 10 May 1888 (D.D.A., W.P.).
267. Circular, June 1888 (C.D.A., C.P.).
268. L.P. Curtis Jnr., *Coercion and conciliation in Ireland 1880-1892: a study in Conservative Unionism* (New Jersey, 1963), p.234.

269. *U.I.*, 7, 14, 21 July 1888.
270. See *U.I.*, 9 June 1888 (letter from E. O'Brien P.P., Coleraine).
271. Police report, 7 June 1888 (S.P.O., D.I.Cs., 512W/8199).
272. Letter in *T.P.*, 19 Sept. 1891.
273. Ballyneale Report, 30 Sept. 1888 (I.N.L. proceedings, 1879-88, 91622c).
274. *L.R.*, 28 Oct. 1890, *M.T.*, 1 Nov. 1890.
275. Curtis, *op. cit.*, p.274.
276. Ross to Balfour, 8 July 1888 and 19 Mar. 1889 (British Library, Balfour papers, Add MSS 49821).
277. D. G. Marnane, 'Tipperary Town and the Smith-Barry Estate 1885-1895' (M.A. thesis, U.C.D., 1975).
278. *T.A.*, 5 Mar. 1881; *T.P.*, 25 Mar. 1881, 15 Apr. 1881; *N.G.*, 16 Sept., 7, 14 Oct. 1885; *T.P.*, 30 Apr., 18, 25 June, 3 July, 13 Aug. 1886.
279. Walsh to Manning, 24 Oct. 1889 (Manning papers).
280. *U.I.*, 17 Aug. 1889.
281. *T.A.*, 10 Aug. 1889; *T.N.*, 28 Dec. 1889, *Nationalist*, 12 Nov. 1890 (Michael Power C.C., Tipperary, John O'Brien P.P., Holycross, Michael Power C.C., Gammonsfield); See also James J. Ryan to Kirby, 21 Dec. 1889 (K.P.).
282. *U.I.*, 13 July 1889; *T.N.*, 21 Sept. 1889; *T.P.*, 20 Sept. 1889 (The priests of Cloyne and Nicholas Rafferty C.C., Thurles).
283. Letter of Canon Richard Chaill in *F.J.*, 28 June 1889.
284. *National Press*, 10 Apr. 1891.
285. *F.J.*, 22 Sept. 1890.
286. Croke to Canon Cahill, 25 Sept. 1891 (C.D.A., C.P.).
287. Cahill's statements in *U.I.*, 6, 13 July, 24, 31 Aug. 1889; *T.P.*, 31 May, 28 June 1889; *T.A.*, 24 Aug. 1889 *T.N.*, 3 July 1889.
288. *T.N.*, 3 July 1889; *T.P.*, 5 July 1889.
289. *T.P.*, 12 July 1889; *T.A.*, 13 July 1889; *U.I.*, 13 July 1889; Thurles P.L.U. minute book, Dec. 1888 - July 1889, pp440-41.
290. *T.P.*, 10 Jan., 28 Mar., 8 May 1890; *N.G.*, 1, 8, 25 Jan., 26 Feb. 1890.
291. *U.I.*, 27 July 1889.
292. *T.P.*, 22, 29 Nov. 1889, 18 Apr., 26 Sept. 1890; *F.J.*, 9 Sept. 1889; *U.I.*, 7 Sept. 1889.
293. Statements in *T.P.*, 1 Aug. 1891; *T.N.*, 28 Dec. 1889, 1 Feb. 1890, *U.I.*, 22 Sept. 1890.
294. *M.T.*, 25 Oct. 1890.
295. P.106.
296. Police report, 7 Feb. 1890 (S.P.O., D.I.Cs., 520W/11384).
297. *F.J.*, 14 Apr. 1890; U.I., 19 Apr. 1890; *T.P.*, 18 Apr. 1890.
298. *U.I.*, 17 May 1890.
299. *N.G.*, May 1890.
300. *N.G.*, 4 Nov. 1891.
301. See *T.P.*, 5 Aug. 1881, 21, 28 Apr. 1882, 26 Nov. 1886; *T.L.*, 2 May 1883; *L.R.*, 3 July 1888.
302. *T.P.*, 20 Sept. 1889.
303. *T.P.*, 23 May 1890; *N.G.*, 5 July 1890.
304. *T.P.*, 6 June 1890.
305. Smith-Barry to Croke, 8 May 1890, 15 May 1890 (C.D.A., C.P.).
306. J. F. X. O'Brien papers, especially MS 13431 (N.L.I.).
307. See *N.G.*, 20 June, 9 Sept. 1891; *C.C.*, 20 June 1891.
308. *T.P.*, 9 May, 8 Aug., 21 Nov. 1890.
309. *T.P.*, 2 Jan., 31 July, 14 Aug. 1891, *Nationalist*, 14 Nov. 1891.
310. *T.P.*, 17 Oct. 1890.
311. *T.P.*, 21 Aug. 1891.
312. Police Reports, 4, 6 Apr. 1891 (S.P.O., police and crime records, police reports 1890-94); *T.P.*, 3, 24 Apr. 1891; *L.R.*, 5 May 1891; *National Press*, 7 Apr. 1891.

313. *T.P.*, 29 May 1891, 5 June 1891.
314. *Nationalist*, 17 Oct. 1891; police report, Oct. 1891 (S.P.O., Crime branch special, 4145/5).
315. *M.T.*, 24 Oct. 1891.
316. The Maynooth reports on various students are preserved in C.D.A.
317. For some reports of post-1881 evictions see: H.C. 1882 (145), lv, p.3; H.C. 1882 (199), lv, p.3; H.C. 1887 (c5095), lxviii, p.3; H.C. 1888 (c-5498), lxxxiii, p.3; H.C. 1889 (c5642), lxi, p.4; H.C. 1890-91 (c6248), lxiv, p.3, H.C. 1890-91 (c6447), lxiv, p.3.
318. *T.F.P.*, 8 June 1880; *Tablet*, 12 June 1880; *L.R.*, 8 June 1880; *C.C.*, 9 June 1880.
319. Mullinahone report, 8 Aug. 1880. (N.L.I., MS 11289).
320. *T.F.P.*, 18 July 1879-21 Sept. 1880. (Archdeacon T. H. Kinnane and Maurice Mooney).
321. The correspondence is preserved in the unsorted collection of Mr Arthur Moore, Mooresfort. (See O'Shea, op. cit., appendix 6, pp225-226 for a summary of the letters dealing with the dispute).
322. *T.A.*, 12 Feb. 1881; *T.P.*, 16 Nov. 1888; *T.N.*, 10 Aug. 1889 (John O'Halloran C.C., Borrisokane, Thomas Dunne C.C., Emly, Thomas Walsh C.C., Ballyneale).
323. *T.A.*, *18 Jan. 1881;* see also his speech in *T.A.*, 7 Feb. 1885.
324. O'Shea, op. cit., table 51, pp122-124.
325. *T.P.*, 8 Aug. 1890.
326. Michael Davitt, *The Fall of Feudalism in Ireland* (London, 1905), p.214.
327. *T.A.*, 10 Apr. 1886.
328. *T.P.*, 15 Jan. 1887.
329. *T.N.*, 15 June 1889.
330. *T.P.*, 21 Oct. 1881, 16 Nov. 1888.
331. Letter in *Tipperary*, 14 June 1882.
332. O'Shea, op. cit., table 51, pp122-124.
333. *T.A.*, 7 May 1881.
334. *T.A.*, 11 Oct. 1884.
335. *T.L.*, 6 June 1883; letter in *T.P.*, 22 June 1883.
336. As in n. 332.
337. Do.
338. *T.P.*, 22 Apr. 1881.
339. *N.G.*, 1 June 1881.
340. Letter from a resident of St Patrick's College, Thurles, undated (N.L.I., F. S. Burke papers, MS 10700).
341. See Palmer, op. cit., pp228-30.
342. See Curtis, *Coercian and conciliation,* p.240; *N.G.*, 5 Aug. 1882; *T.A.*, 12 Oct. 1889.
343. *T.L.*, 22, 25 Nov. 1882 and much of David Humphreys' writings and statements.
344. As in n332.
345. O'Shea, op. cit., table 52, pp125-128.
346. *T.N.*, 7, 28 Dec. 1889, 1 Feb. 1890, *Nationalist*, 1 Nov. 1890, 26 Nov. 1890; *U.I.*, 22 Nov. 1890.
347. *T.A.*, 2 Nov. 1889; *U.I.*, 2 Nov. 1889.
348. Letter in *T.P.*, 22 Nov. 1889; N.G. 18 Nov. 1889.
349. Croke to Walsh, 31 Aug. 1889 (D.D.A., W.P.).
350. Letter of Canon Cahill in *T.N.*, 18 Dec. 1889.
351. Document, 20 May 1891, giving a breakdown of money distributed by Croke through the priest (C.D.A, C.P.); letter from T. M. Healy M.P., T. J. Condon M.P. and John Deasy M.P. to Croke (C.D.A., M.P.).
352. *Nationalist*, 6 May 1891; *C.C.*, 6 May 1891.
353. *Nationalist*, 7 Oct. 1891.
354. See e.g.: *N.G.*, 14 Oct. 1885, 11 Sept. 1889, 19 Oct. 1889, 28 Sept. 1891; *T.L.*, 6 Feb. 1884; *T.A.*, 8 Aug., 12 Sept. 17 Oct. 1885; *T.N.*, 19 June 1889; *Nationalist*, 8

Mar. 1890; *T.P.*, 25 July, 21 Nov. 1890.
355. O'Shea, op. cit., tables 53-54, pp129-134.
356. T. J. Slater, *S.J.*, 'The ethical aspect of boycotting' in *Irish Theological Quarterly*, ii (1907), pp242-247; F. Marshal, 'The ethical aspect of boycotting', Ibid., i, (1906), pp435-446; W. McDonald, 'The ethical aspect of boycotting', ibid., pp333-347.
357. Letter in *Tablet*, 7 Jan. 1888.
358. *Tablet*, 14, 21 Jan. 1888.
359. *U.I.*, 29 Nov. 1890.
360. Croke to Walsh, 27 Dec. 1889; *N.G.*, 18, 21 Dec. 1889. (D.D.A., W.P.).
361. *T.A.*, 4 June 1881; *T.P.*, 14 Jan. 1881.
362. *L.R.*, 28 Oct. 1890; *M.T.*, 1 Nov. 1890; *T.A.*, 4 June 1881.
363. *T.P.*, 15 Jan. 1886.
364. *U.I.*, 7 July 1888.
365. O'Shea, op. cit., table 53, pp129-133.
366. *T.A.*, 4 June 1881; *T.P.*, 25 Dec. 1885; Police report, Ballingarry 4 Oct 1885 (S.P.O., Spec. Comm., 1888, police reports B). (John T. Ryan, John Ryan and William J. McKeogh).
367. *T.N.*, 4 Sept., 23 Nov. 1889; *Nationalist* 30 Aug., 6, 31 Dec. 1890; *N.G.*, 4 May 1889; Ballingarry, 4 Oct. 1885, Holycross 5 July 1885. (S.P.O., Spec. Comm. 1888, police reports). (James Cantwell, Thomas Hackett and Thomas Fennelly, Thurles, Michael McDonnell P.P., Edmund Doheny, William Kelly C.C., John Ryan P.P., Newinn, Patrick O'Keeffe C.C.).
368. *T.L.*, 13 Feb. 1882.
369. *N.G.*, 17 Sept. 1890, 4 Feb. 1891; *F.J.*, 18 Sept. 1890; *Nationalist*, 13 Sept. 1890, 4 Feb. 1891;
370. E.g., *N.G.*, 7 Sept. 1881. (James Howard).
371. *T.L.*, 18 Apr. 1885.
372. *T.A.*, 30 May 1885.
373. *T.P.*, 14 Jan. 1881; police report, Fethard. 12 Apr. 1885. (S.P.O., Spec. Comm. 1888, police reports).
374. *T.P.*, 17 Oct. 1884, 17 Apr. 1885.
375. Police Report 916816, 9 Sept. 1888. (S.P.O., I.N.L. proceedings, 1879-88 Carton 3).
376. See *T.L.*, 1 Apr. 1885 for a case in the parish of Golden.
377. *N.G.*, 22 July 1885; background in *T.L.*, 18 Apr. 1885 and Loughmore police report, 26 Apr. 1885 (S.P.O., Spec. Comm., 1888).
378. *N.G.*, 22 June 1889; *T.N.*, 19, 29 June 1889.
379. *N.G.*, 9 May 1888.
380. Reprimands from the Dublin executive in *T.A.*, 14 Nov. 1885; Letters 22 Apr., 12 June 1886. (N.L.I., Harrington papers MS 8933).
381. O'Shea, op. cit., table 53, pp129-133.
382. Ross to Balfour, 18 June 1890, British Museum, Balfour Papers, Add. MSS 49821.
383. For Humphreys's statements and evidence of boycotting in Tipperary town see *T.P.*, 23 May, 6 June 1890, 17 Apr., 19 June, 10, 31 July 1891; *N.G.*, 9, 12 Apr. 1890, 7 Jan. 1891; *Nationalist*, 18, 28 June 1890; N.L.I. J.F.X. O'Brien papers, MSS 13431(2) and 13432(5).
384. *T.N.*, 13 Mar. 1889.
385. *U.I.*, 15 Aug. 1885; *N.G.*, 14 Oct. 1885.
386. *Hansard*, cclxxv, pp202-203.
387. O'Shea, op. cit., table 53, pp129-133.
388. *M.T.*, 25 July, 1 Aug. 1891.
389. See: Donnelly, p.345; C. Cruise O'Brien, *Parnell and his party 1880-1890*, (Oxford, 1957), p.212; Blunt, *Land War*, pp306, 311, 323; William O'Brien, *Evening memories* (Dublin, 1920), pp279-285.
390. *F.J.*, 19 Sept. 1887 (Clonmel).
391. *T.A.*, 17 Sept. 1887; Croke to Walsh, 15 Aug. 1887 (D.D.A., W.P.).

392. Letter in *Nationalist*, 1 Feb. 1891; see also *T.P.*, 9, 23 May 1890, 6, 20 June, 4, 11, 25 July, 1, 8, 22 Aug., 17 Oct., 21 Nov. 1890, 2 Jan. 1891.
393. Letter in *T.P.*, 15 Sept. 1882.
394. Police report, 29 Mar. 1890 (S.P.O., Crime branch special, 501/34 Carton 1).
395. *Nationalist*, 5 Nov. 1890.
396. *N.G.*, 5 Nov. 1884.
397. E.g., *T.P.*, 20 Nov. 1885.
398. *T.N.*, 29 May 1889.
399. *T.P.*, 20 Sept. 1889.
400. O'Shea, op. cit., table 50, pp120-121.
401. E.g. *Hansard 3*, cclxi, pp963-6, 970, 972, 975, 979, 981-2, 994-9, 1001-1003; ibid. cccxiii, pp225, 682, 1412; Ibid., cccxxxii, pp91-92; ibid., cccxxxiv, pp1234-1238, and cccxxxix, pp913, 1134; ibid. cccxlvi, pp210-212.
402. *T.L.*, 26 Apr. 1884, 21 Feb. 1885; *N.G.*, 21 Feb. 1885.
403. O'Shea, op. cit., table 55, pp135-6.
404. O'Shea, op. cit., table 56, p.137.
405. *T.P.*, 7 Jan., 29 April 1881, 12 Oct. 1888; *T.F.P.*, 24 Jan. 1879; *T.A.*, 8 Jan. 1887; Cahir Report, 19 Sept. 1880, Cloneen Report, 1 Aug. 1880, Mullinahone Report, 8 Aug. 1880. (N.L.I., MS 11289).
406. *T.F.P.*, 12 Nov. 1869.
407. *T.P.*, 21 Feb. 1885.
408. *T.F.P.*, 24 Jan. 1879.
409. *T.L.*, 26 Apr. 1881; *F.J.*, 2 May 1881.
410. *T.A.*, 18 Dec. 1880.
411. Police report, Clonmel. 29 Nov. 1886 (S.P.O., Spec. Comm. 1888).
412. *T.A.*, 20 Nov. 1880; *T.F.P.*, 14, 24 Sept., 7 Dec. 1880; *Tablet*, 11 Sept. 1880; Clonmel Reports 11 Aug. and 24 Oct. 1880 (N.L.I., MS 11289).
413. O'Shea, op. cit., table 55, pp135-136.
414. *F.J.*, 30 May 1881; Croke to Kirby, 19 Dec. 1880. (K.P.).
415. *T.F.P.*, 8 June 1880, 26 Oct. 1880; Clonmel Report, 24 Oct. 1880. (N.L.I., MS 11289).
416. W.H. 'The principles of '89' in *I.E.R.* 1881, pp125-42, 200-214, 269-84, 340-49, 701-13.
417. Letter in *T.L.*, 25 Oct. 1882.
418. *T.L.*, 11 Nov. 1884.
419. *T.L.*, 11 Jan. 17 May, 19 Dec., 1884.
420. *T.L.*, 11 Jan. 1884; *U.I.*, 12 Jan. 1884.
421. *T.L.*, 12 Sept. 1883.
422. *Hansard 3*, cclxi, p.987.
423. *L.R.*, 5 Dec. 1879; *T.F.P.*, 28 Sept., 7, 31 Dec. 1880; *C.C.*, 29 Sept. 1880; *T.A.*, 1 Jan., 5 Mar. 1881; *T.P.*, 7 Jan. 1881.
424. *T.A.*, 18 Dec. 1880; *N.G.*, 7 Sept. 1881; *T.F.P.*, 14 Feb., 24 Sept. 1880; *T.L.*, 17 May 1884, 27 Feb. 1885; *U.I.*, 12 Jan. 1884.
425. *T.L.*, 21 Dec. 1883, 1 Feb. 1884.
426. *T.L.*, 1 Feb., 26 Apr. 1884.
427. *T.L.*, 1 Feb. 1884.
428. *1881 land act report*, pp442-6, H.C. 1887, xxvi.
429. *T.P.*, 22 Apr. 1887 (resolutions of the Newport National League branch drafted by him).
430. Pamphlet, p.18.
431. *T.L.*, 26 Apr. 1884.
432. *T.A.*, 5 Sept. 1885; *T.L.*, 20 June 1884 (James Howard and John Casey).
433. As in n429.
434. *The land conference, Thursday, April 29th 1880* (Dublin, 1880), p.2.
435. Bessborough Comm., ii, part 1 — *pp79, 81, 82; 1881 land act report*, pp 445-6, H.C. 1887, xxvi.

436. *M.T.*, 25 Apr. 1891.
437. *L.R.*, 6 May 1890.
438. *Nationalist*, 26 Nov. 1890.
439. P.161.
440. *T.P.*, 4 Mar. 1881; *T.A.*, 26 Feb., 1, 18 Mar. 12 Apr. 1884; *T.L.*, 1, 6 Mar., 12 Apr. 1884, 16 Mar. 1885; *U.I.*, 8 Mar. 1884.
441. Thurles Report, 14 Nov. 1880 (N.L.I., MS 11289).
442. *T.A.*, 2 Apr. 1881.
443. John Condon, P.L.G. to Pierse Power, 12 Mar. 1889, and Edward Nugent, P.L.G. to Power, 13 Mar. 1889 (W.D.A.).
444. *N.G.*, 8 Mar. 1884, 22 Oct. 1887.
445. *T.L.*, 2 Aug., 3, 10, 17, 24 Oct. 1884.
446. *T.A.*, 17 July 1886.
447. See Thurles P.L.U. minute book, Dec. 1888-July 1889, pp237, 318, 334, 446, and minute book Jan.-July 1890, pp286, 318, showing priests as chairmen in 5 of the 6 dispensary districts of the Thurles Union.
448. *T.P.*, 22 Oct. 1886.
449. As in n 403 and 404.
450. Letters in *T.P.*, 9 Mar., 23 Mar. 1883.
451. Clonmel report, 24 Oct. 1880 (N.L.I., MS 11289).
452. Police report, Holycross, 5 July 1885 (S.P.O., Spec. Comm., 1888).
453. *T.A.*, 8 Jan. 1887.
454. Gleeson, *Ely O'Carroll*, pp202-203.
455. *T.A.*, 19 Jan. 1889.
456. O'Shea, op. cit., table 57, pp138-139.
457. Letters in *U.I.*, 4 Nov. 1882, 27 Oct. 1883; his other statements in *T.L.*, 1 Feb., 26 Apr., 28 Nov. 1884; *T.P.*, 15 May 1885.
458. *U.I.*, 4 Nov. 1882; *T.L.*, 26 Apr. 1884, 16 Mar. 1885.
459. Controversy in *U.I.*, 6, 13, 20 Dec. 1884.
460. *Nationalist*, 13 Dec. 1890.
461. *T.L.*, 1 Feb., 26 Apr., 31 Oct. 1884; *Hansard 3*, ccxciii, p.1214.
462. *T.L.*, 3 Oct. 1884 (James Callanan C.C., Newinn).
463. *T.L.*, 22 Jan. 1885.
464. *T.L.*, 14 Oct. 1884 (list published).
465. *N.G.*, 9 Jan. 1886.
466. *T.P.*, 16 Oct. 1885 (Golden).
467. O'Shea, op. cit., table 58, pp140-146.

5. THE LABOURERS

1. *Decreta* (1850), p.23.
2. See e.g. *L.R.*, 16 Apr. 1850 (Kilcommon meeting), also Report of M. J. Ffrench R,M. (S.P.O., C.S.O., R.P., 1858/16837).
3. *T.F.P.*, 1 June 1850.
4. *F.J.*, 14 Jan. 1852; *Tablet*, 17 Jan. 1853.
5. His letter in *Tablet*, 8 Feb. 1851.
6. *Tablet*, 10 May 1851. (Callan); *T.F.P.*, 6 Feb. 1850. (Philip Fitzgerald).
7. O'Shea, op. cit., table 59, pp147-148.
8. See e.g. his statement in *U.I.*, 20 Aug. 1881.
9. The Royal commission on labour (Devonshire Commission), *The agricultural labourer*, iv, Ireland, part ii, p.63, H.C. 1893/4, xxxvii.
10. K.S. Inglis, *Churches and the working classes in Victorian England* (London, 1963), pp309-310.
11. *T.A.*, 20 Sept. 1873.
12. *T.F.P.*, 16 Sept. 1873.
13. O'Shea, op. cit., table 61, pp151-152, and fig. 12, p.210.

14. S.E. Div. Reports, 5 Sept. 1891. (S.P.O., Crime branch special, 5215/4416); see *Nationalist*, 18 Feb. 1891; *C.C.*, 7 Nov. 1891; *Insuppressible*, 3 Jan. 1891.

15. *T.L.*, 17 Oct. 1884.

16. *T.L.*, 1 Nov. 1882.

17. Nicholas Mansergh, *The Irish Question 1840-1921* (London, 1965), pp83-110, esp. p.99.

18. See O'Shea, op. cit., appendix 8, p.228.

19. C.D.A., S.P., 1854/52.

20. As n9 above.

21. *T.L.*, 20 Jan. 1883.

22. *T.P.*, 7 Jan. 1881.

23. Palmer, *Land league*, p.92; see also *The Irish Crisis of 1879-1880: Proceedings of the Dublin Mansion House Relief Committee 1880* (Dublin, 1881), which shows that labourers and cottiers were most afflicted.

24. See: *C.C.*, 13 Feb. 1879; *N.G.*, 17 Dec. 1879, 14, 18 Feb., 3 Apr. 1880; *T.F.P.*, 24 Feb., 2 Mar. 1880; Cahir Report (N.L.I., MS 11289) (Maurice Mooney); Thurles P.L.U. minute book Jan.-July 1880, p.25.

25. *T.F.P.*, 2 Mar. 1880.

26. Thurles P.L.U. minute book, Jan.-July 1880, p.89; *T.F.P.*, 2, 16 Mar. 1880; *N.G.*, 21, 25 Feb. 1880.

27. *T.A.*, 8 Jan. 1881; *T.P.*, 7 Oct. 1881.

28. *Bessborough Comm.*, p.80.

29. *Agric. labourer*, Ireland, p.66, H.C. 1893-4, xxxvii.

30. *T.P.*, 13, 27 Jan. 10 Feb. 1882; see also *U.I.*, 6 Oct. 1883 for the angry statement of Archdeacon Kinnane.

31. As in n28.

32. *Report from the Select Committee on Agricultural Labourers (Ireland), together with the Proceedings of the Committee and Minutes of Evidence* (London, 1884), p.36.

33. Timothy Harrington to T. Ryan (N.L.I., Harrington letter Book, MS 8933) John Power C.C., Oola to Anna Parnell, 11 Nov. 1891. (N.L.I., I.N.L.L. Papers, ms 17701 (4)); *T.L.*, 24 Jan. 1883; *N.G.*, 12 Oct. 1881; *Tablet*, 9 July 1881.

34. *U.I.*, 20 Aug., 30 Sept. 1881; *T.P.*, 29 Sept. 1881, 13 Oct. 1882.

35. *Tipperary*, 1 July 1882.

36. Letter in *T.L.*, 22 Nov. 1882; see also *T.L.*, 11 Nov. 1882.

37. *T.L.*, 13 June 1884.

38. *T.L.*, 20 Jan. 1883; *U.I.*, 20 June 1885; *T.P.*, 29 Jan. 1886.

39. Foran to Power, 18 June 1880 (W.D.A.).

40. *C.C.*, 15 Dec. 1880; *T.L.*, 1 Nov. 1882; *N.G.*, 29 Nov. 1884.

41. *Tipperary*, 8 Apr. 1882; *T.P.*, 7 Jan. 1881; *T.A.*, 10 Sept. 1881, 21 Feb. 1885; *T.L.*, 22 Nov. 1882, 3 Oct. 1883, 1 Feb., 31 Oct. 1884; *N.G.*, 1 July 1882, 13 Mar. 1886; *M.T.*, 25 Oct. 1889; *U.I.*, 1 July 1882, 27 Oct. 1883, 4 Jan. 1884; *F.J.*, 1 July 1882.

42. *T.L.*, 20 Jan. 1883.

43. *T.P.*, 23 Jan. 1885; *T.L.*, 22 Jan. 1885.

44. For an analysis of the social background of emigrants see O. MacDonagh, 'The Irish Famine Emigration to the United States' in *Perspectives in American History*, x. (1976), pp421-2, 425, 426.

45. For some insight into clerical thinking on emigration from mid-century see: *Tablet*, 2 Dec. 1854; *T.F.P.*, 19 Oct. 1850; *L.R.*, 19 Mar. 1851; *T.L.*, 24 Jan. 1883; *U.I.*, 27 Oct. 1883; *T.A.*, 2 Feb. 1884; *T.P.*, 7 Sept. 1883, 21 Dec. 1888.

46. *U.I.*, 5 July 1884.

47. O'Donnell to Croke, 11 June 1887 (C.D.A., C.P.).

48. *Census of Ireland 1891*, part 1, vol. 2, province of Munster, p.858 gives statistics for the years 1851 to 1891.

49. *T.A.*, 8 Jan., 26 Mar. 1881.

50. *T.A.*, 2 Feb., 21 June 1884; *T.P.*, 7 Sept. 1883.
51. *T.A.*, 23 Apr. 1881, 10 Nov. 1883; *T.L.*, 7 July 1883; *T.P.*, 22 Apr. 1881; *N.G.*, 23 Jan. 1884; *U.I.*, 26 Jan. 1884.
52. *T.L.*, 14 Mar. 1884.
53. *T.P.*, 7 Jan. 1881.
54. *T.A.*, 8 Jan. 1881.
55. *R.P.*, 29 Sept. 1881; *U.I.*, 30 Sept. 1881.
56. *T.F.P.*, 2 Mar. 1880.
57. See e.g.: *C.C.*, 13 Dec. 1879; *N.G.*, 17 Dec. 1879; 21 Jan., 14, 25 Feb. 1880; *T.F.P.*, 24 Feb., 2 Mar. 1880.
58. *T.P.*, 7 Jan. 1881; *T.A.*, 8, 29 Jan., 26 Mar. 1881, 1 Aug. 1885; *Tipperary*, 1 July 1882; *F.J.*, 9 Aug. 1882, Thurles Report, 14 Nov. 1880 (N.L.I., MS 11289) (John Shelley, James K. Frost, William Power, Edmund O'Leary, Patrick Glynn, John T. Ryan, John Walsh, John Slattery).
59. *C.C.*, 15 Dec. 1880.
60. Letter in *T.L.*, 22 Nov. 1882.
61. *N.G.*, 18 Apr. 1882 (resolution of the Cashel and Emly priests).
62. Pamphlet, pp23-24; *T.A.*, 30 Apr., 1 Oct. 1881; *F.J.*, 16 Sept. 1881.
63. See A.D. Bolton, *The Labourers (Ireland) Acts 1883-1906* (Dublin, 2 vols, 1908 and 1910).
64. *Agric. labourers* pp38, 41, H.C. 1884.
65. Letter in *T.A.*, 26 June 1886.
66. *T.A.*, 6 Oct. 1883, 26 June 1886; *T.P.*, 7 Sept. 1883, 5 Oct. 1883; *T.L.*, 22 Jan. 1885.
67. *C.C.*, 15 Dec. 1880.
68. *T.L.*, 3 Oct. 1883.
69. Letter in *F.J.*, 30 Dec. 1887.
70. *T.A.*, 12 Dec. 1885.
71. *Agric. labourers*, p.29, H.C. 1884.
72. *T.P.*, 29 Jan. 1886.
73. *Agric. labourer*, Ireland, p.65, H.C. 1893-4, xxxvii.
74. *N.G.*, 27 Oct. 1883; *T.L.*, 24 Nov. 1884.
75. *T.L.*, 22 Nov. 1882, 3 Oct. 1883.
76. *T.P.*, 7 Sept. 1883.
77. South eastern divisional report, 6 July 1885 (S.P.O., I.N.L.L. proceedings, 1885/14184).
78. *Agric. labourers*, pp33-4, H.C. 1884.
79. *T.L.*, 13 June 1884.
80. *T.L.*, 5 Dec. 1884. (Drangan).
81. *N.G.*, 24 Mar. 1886.
82. *T.L.*, 20 Dec. 1882.
83. *T.L.*, 31 Oct. 1884.
84. *T.L.*, 1 Feb. 1884.
85. *T.A.*, 20 Oct. 1883, 27 Oct. 1883; *N.G.*, 27 Oct. 1883 (letters).
86. For some objections see Clonmel P.L.U. minute book, Oct. 1886 — Mar. 1887, p.427.
87. *T.L.*, 24 Nov. 1884.
88. *N.G.*, 23 Jan. 1884; *T.L.*, 25 Jan. 1884; *T.A.*, 26 Jan. 1884.
89. *T.P.*, 5 Aug. 1881, Bessborough Comm., p.80.
90. *T.L.*, 31 Oct. 1884.
91. *T.L.*, 12 Sept. 1884.
92. See Cashel P.L.U. minute book no. 182, 1886-1887, pp488, 491 for a breadown.
93. *T.L.*, 3 Oct. 1883; *T.P.*, 5 Oct. 1883.
94. Letter in *T.A.*, 14 June 1884.
95. Letter in *T.A.*, 21 June 1884.
96. *N.G.*, 29 Nov. 1884; *T.L.*, 12 Dec. 1884.
97. *T.P.*, 18 Sept. 1885; *T.L.*, 7 Nov. 1884.

98. Bessborough Comm. p.81.
99. *U.I.*, 6 Oct. 1883.
100. See, e.g.: *T.P.*, 7, 28 Sept. 1883; *T.L.*, 22 Aug., 26 Sept. 1883, 3, 10, 17 Oct. 1883; *U.I.*, 6 Oct. 1883.
101. *T.L.*, 5 Dec. 1884.
102. *T.L.*, 31 Oct. 1884.
103. *Nationalist,* 11 Apr. 1891; *T.N.*, 12 Oct. 1889.
104. *T.A.*, 2 Feb. 1884.
105. *U.I.*, 22 Dec. 1888; *T.P.*, 21 Dec. 1888.
106. O'Shea, op. cit., table 63, p.154.
107. *T.A.*, 29 Jan. 1886.
108. *T.A.*, 20 Oct. 1883; *T.L.*, 20 Oct. 1883; see also *N.G.*, 7 Nov. 1883, *T.A.*, 6 Oct. 1883, Clonmel P.L.U. minute book, May-Nov. 1887, p.198.
109. *T.A.*, 14 Feb. 1885.
110. *T.A.*, 23 Feb. 1884; *T.L.*, 28 Mar. 1884; see also *N.G.*, 24 Mar. 1886.
111. See *T.P.*, 17 Oct. 1884; *T.L.*, 24 Oct. 1884; *T.A.*, 1 Aug. 1885.
112. *Hansard 3*, cccii, p.1527.
113. Letter in *T.P.*, 10 Dec. 1886 (signed also by the lay secretary and treasurer of the Doon National League branch).
114. Scanlan's letter in *N.G.*, 27 Oct. 1883; Ryan's statement in *T.A.*, 18 Sept. 1885.
115. Ibid.
116. Letter in *T.A.*, 20 Oct. 1883.
117. *Agric. labourers,* p.35, H.C. 1884.
118. Cashel P.L.U. minute book no. 76, 1883-4, p.420; *Agric. labourer,* Ireland, p.64, H.C. 1893-4, xxxvii.
119. Clonmel P.L.U. minute book, Oct. 1883-Apr. 1884, p.56.
120. Rev. T. Meagher, *Land tenure and the lamentable conditions of the rural poor,* 1878, (unfortunately not known to be extant); see also P.J. Lee, *A history of the parish of Newport* (Thurles, 1934), p.42.
121. Letter in *N.G.*, 31 Oct. 1883.
122. Letters in ibid. and *T.A.*, 3 Nov. 1883.
123. *T.A.*, 21 Feb. 1885; *N.G.*, 25 Feb. 1885.
124. *N.G.*, 25 Aug. 1888.
125. *T.L.*, 20 Jan. 1883.
126. *T.L.*, 31 Jan. 1883; *U.I.*, 3 Feb. 1883.
127. *T.L.*, 31 Oct., 19 Dec. 1884, 30 Jan., 27 Feb. 1885.
128. *T.P.*, 9 Feb. 1883; T.A., 10 Feb. 1883.
129. *N.G.*, 27 Mar. 1886.
130. O'Shea, op. cit., table 63, p.154 and fig. 16, p.214.
131. Ibid., table 64, p.155.
132. See *T.A.*, 20 Feb. 1886; *N.G.*, 3 Sept. 1887.
133. Cantwell's statements in *T.P.*, 5 Mar. 1886, 13 Aug. 1886, 25 Feb. 1887; *N.G.*, 22 May 1886.
134. *N.G.*, 5 June 1886; *T.P.*, 17 Dec. 1886.
135. *T.L.*, 17 Oct. 1883.
136. Ibid.
137. Letter in *C.C.*, 1 Feb. 1880.
138. Letter in *T.L.*, 27 Dec. 1884.
139. E.g. *T.L.*, 17 Oct. 1883, *U.I.*, 6 Oct. 1883.
140. *T.A.*, 18 Feb. 1882; see also *T.P.*, 7 Sept. 1883 (John R. Crowe C.C.).
141. Ibid.
142. *T.A.*, 28 Oct. 1882.
143. *T.A.*, 25 Nov., 9 Dec. 1882.
144. Dublin statement in *T.P.*, 23 Sept. 1881.
145. *T.P.*, 1 Feb. 1882; *Tipperary,* 18 Feb. 1882.
146. *T.A.*, 27 Aug. 1881; *T.P.*, 15 May 1885; *T.L.*, 17 May 1884; *U.I.*, 17 May 1884, Police Report, Holycross, 5 July 1885. (S.P.O., Spec. Comm., 1888).

147. Letter in *U.I.*, 1 Oct. 1881.
148. Letters from nailers in *U.I.*, 20 May 1882, 10 June 1886.
149. *Tipperary*, 9 Nov. 1881.
150. Pope Leo xiii, 'Quod Apostolici Muneris', (1878), in *Select letters and addresses on social questions* (London, 1950), p.65.
151. Police report, Ballingarry, 4 Oct. 1885 (S.P.O.. Spec. Comm., 1888).
152. *Tipperary*, 3 Dec. 1881.
153. *T.P.*, 26 June 1885.

6. THE PRIEST AND IRISH REPUBLICANISM

1. E.g.: *I.P.*, 14 May, 4, 14 June, 5, 19 Nov., 17 Dec. 1864, 6 May, 16 Sept. 1865.
2. *T.F.P.*, 18 July 1865; see also O'Leary op. cit., pp81-83.
3. See *I.P.*, 24, 31 Dec. 1864, 7, 28 Jan. 11, 18 Mar., 1 Apr. 1865.
4. See *I.P.*, 2 Apr. 1864, 22 Oct. 1864, 17, 24, 31 Dec. 1864, 14, 21 Jan., 4, 11, 25 Feb., 1, 8, 15 Apr., 6 May, 13, 20 May 1865, 10 June 1865, 1 July 1865, 19 Aug. 1865, 16 Sept. 1865 (5 Tipperary and 15 non-Tipperary priests, and a few others not named).
5. Letters in *I.P.*, 18 Mar. 1865, 19 Aug. 1865.
6. *N.G.*, 10 June 1868.
7. Archbishop McCloskey, New York, to Leahy, 21 Aug. 1867; David W. Bacon, Bishop of Portland, to Leahy 20 Sept. 1867 (C.D.A., L.P.); O'Connor's replies in C.D.A. L.P., 27 Aug. 1867, 28 Oct. 1867.
8. Meagher to Leahy, 20 Sept. 1867 and 5 Feb. 1868 (C.D.A., L.P.) (See p.000 below).
9. *Irishman*, 5 Feb. 1870.
10. Ibid.
11. *T.L.*, 17 Jan. 1884; note by Croke, 6 Jan. 1888 (C.D.A., C.P.).
12. See S.P.O., C.S.O., R.P. 1867 3780, 4314, 8399; N.L.I., Mayo papers, MS 11189(13).
13. See *I.P.*, 7 May, 22 Oct., 24 Dec. 1864; *T.F.P.*, 12 Mar. 1867, *I.C.D.*, 1863, pp268-269; C.D.A. L.P., pastoral letter of Bishop McNally of Clother, 4 Feb. 1861 and Archbishop Leahy's pastoral, 12 Mar. 1867 (C.D.A., L.P.).
14. The diary of Fr O'Carroll, Clonoulty, Mar. 1864 (C.D.A.).
15. *Acta et decreta*, (1854), p.70.
16. O'Carroll diary, Apr. 1864 (C.D.A.).
17. George Crolly, *Disputationes Theologiae de Justitia et Jure*, iii (Dublin, 177 ed.), pp56, 175-179, 183; O'Reilly *Church and society* (1892), pp240, 242, 247, 328-9, 332-3; T. B. Scannell, 'The politics of St. Thomas Aquinas in *I.E.R.*, 1887, p.70; W. Blackstone, *Commentaries on the Laws of England* (London, 1800), pp238, 244. (Crolly, O'Reilly and Blackstone were used in the seminaries).
18. Leo XIII, 'Inscrutabili' (1878) in *Select Letters*, pp17, 21.
19. 'Libertas praestantissimum', ibid., p.93.
20. See *Catholic Encyclopaedia*, iv, pp71-73 for an excellent summary of papal pronouncements from 1738 to 1884.
21. Gury, *Compendium theologiae moralis* (Ratisbon, 1874), p.897.
22. 'The obligation of denouncing the heads of secret societies', in *I.E.R.*, 1886, pp167-8; 'Secret societies and the confessional', in *I.E.R.*, 1887, pp547-8.
23. T.B. Cronin, 'The spiritual trenches of Maynooth' in *Catholic Bulletin*, 1915, p.669; Denis Meehan, *Window of Maynooth* (Dublin, 1949), p.14.
24. *Hansard 3*, cxx, p.880.
25. M.R. O'Connell, 'The political background to the establishment of Maynooth College' in *I.E.R.*, Jan.-June 1965, pp330-31; J. Gunn, 'Reminiscences of Maynooth' in *I.E.R.*, 1884, p.167; *Irish educ. enquiry*, p.144, H.C. 1826-7, xxiii; Healy, *Maynooth*, p.192.
26. Healy, *Maynooth*, pp194, 360.
27. Delahogue lectured in the Sorbonne for 40 years and his theology textbooks are

preserved in St Patrick's College, Thurles; see 'Maynooth one hundred years ago' in *I.E.R.*, July-Dec. 1940, p.18.

28. O'Shea, op. cit., table 13, pp26-27.
29. See Healy, *Maynooth*, pp192, 708-9 for lists of professors.
30. Henry Neville, 'Theology past and present at Maynooth' in *Dublin Review*, 1879, p.454.
31. See *Management of Maynooth*, pp31, 56, 92, 273, 353, 382, (1896-1), H.C. 1854-5, xxii, for his statements and those of his colleagues.
32. Ibid., p.218.
33. *Irish educ. enquiry*, p.111, H.C. 1826-7, xiii.
34. Ibid., pp31, 61.
35. Ibid., pp330-331; *Management of Maynooth*, pp186, 330, (1896-1), H.C. 1854-5, xxii.
36. Ibid., p.142.
37. Ibid., p.139.
38. Ibid., pp149, 153, 156, 158; *Management of Maynooth*, pp272, 361, 381, H.C. 1854-5, xxii.
39. See some of his pro-fenian statements in every edition of the *Irish People* (New York) from Oct. 1866 to May 1868; his letter in *I.P.*, 12 Mar. 1864; Patrick Lavelle, *Patriotism vindicated, a reply to Archbishop Manning*, esp. pp1-2, 4-6, 11-15 (this pamphlet is preserved in S.P.O., Fenian Papers, F2906); see also Lavelle to the Vatican, 25 Jan. 1864 (C.D.A., L.P.).
40. *Irish educ. enquiries*, pp330-331, 355-6, H.C. 1826-7, xxiii.
41. Ibid., p.95.
42. Healy *Maynooth*, pp450, 458.
43. O'Leary, *My story*, p.83.
44. S.P.O., C.S.O., R.P. 1867/11488.
45. See, e.g., *I.P.*, 24 Apr. 1864, 18 Mar., 8 July, 19 Aug. 1865.
46. T. Ó Fiaich, 'The clergy and fenianism, 1860-1870', in *I.E.R.*, 1968, p.101.
47. O'Shea, op. cit., tables 65 and 66, pp156-9.
48. Pp165-66.
49. P.213.
50. *I.P.*, 6 May 1865.
51. T.W. Moody, 'The fenian movement in Irish history', in *The Fenian Movement* (Cork, 1968), p.108; Larkin, 'Church, state and nation', pp1261-1262; E.R.R. Green, 'The beginnings of fenianism' in *The fenian movement*, p.17.
52. P.139.
53. R.V. Comerford, *Charles J. Kickham: a study in Irish nationalism and literature* (Dublin, 1979), p.174.
54. *T.A.*, 5 Jan. 1884.
55. As in n47.
56. *I.P.*, 7 May 1864 (Joseph Flanagan C.C., Cabinteely, Co. Dublin).
57. P.146.
58. See D.F. Gleeson, 'Fr. John Kenyon and Young Ireland' in *Studies* xxxv, no. 137 (Mar. 1946), p.108; Gleeson, *Ely O'Carroll* p.211; O'Fiaich, *loc. cit.*, p.108.
59. Lavelle, *Patriotism*, p.11.
60. Gleeson, *Ely O'Carroll*, p.212.
61. O'Leary, *My story*, p.83; S.P.O., C.S.O., R.P. 1867 12514 and 13503.
62. *I.P.*, 20 May 1865 (letter); Resident magistrate's report, 19 July 1866 (N.L.I., Larcom papers, MS 7590); Report 11 Mar. 1867 (S.P.O., C.S.O., R.P., 1867/4222).
63. *I.P.*, 2 Apr. 1864, 6 Aug. 1864 (letters).
64. Rev. M. O'Connor, 'Sogarth Aroon' in *I.E.R.*, 1869, p.550.
65. Richard Hayes, 'Priests in the independence movement of 1798' in *I.E.R.*, 1945, pp258-270; see also Frank McDermot, *Tone and His Times* (Tralee, 1969), pp201-202, 230, 252, 258.
66. Details in O'Shea, op. cit., table 12, p.25.

67. E.g. *T.F.P.*, 24 Jan. 1879, *T.L.*, 3 Oct. 1883; Mullinahone report, 8 Aug. 1880 (N.L.I., MS 11289); police report, Holycross, 5 July 1885 (S.P.O., Special Commission, 1888).
68. Rev. P. Fitzgerald, *A narrative of the proceedings of the confederates of 1848* (Dublin, 1868), p.44.
69. *T.F.P.*, 1 June 1850; *Tablet*, 19 Oct. 1850.
70. *T.F.P.*, 23 Nov. 1853, 3 Jan. 1855.
71. Boyle, op. cit., p.87.
72. Denis Gwynn, 'The priets and Young Ireland in 1848' in *I.E.R.*, July-Dec. 1948, p.597; Denis Gwynn, 'Fr Kenyon and Young Ireland', part 2, *I.E.R.*, Jan.-June 1949, p.510.
73. *United Irishman*, 13 May 1848.
74. Fitzgerald, op. cit., p.89.
75. Gwynn, 'Priests and Young Ireland', p.595.
76. Their correspondence in *United Irishman*, 29 Apr. 1848.
77. Gwynn, 'Fr Kenyon', esp. pp226, 232, 234-42, 508-12, 518,21, 526-8; C.G. Duffy, *Young Ireland*, part 2, (Dublin, 1883), pp225, 240; L. Fogarty, *Fr John Kenyon, a patriot priest of 1848* (Dublin, n.d.); Gleeson, *Fr Kenyon and Young Ireland'*, pp102-3, 106; T. F. O'Sullivan, *The Young Irelanders* (Tralee, 1944), p.578; Rev. J. Clancy, 'A Study of Fr Kenyon', in *Molua*, 1946; see also Kenyon's statements in *United Irishman*, 12 Feb., 22 Apr., 26 Dec. 1848.
78. Clancy, *loc. cit.*, p.20 is incorrect in his conclusions about Kenyon's suspension.
79. Kenyon to Slattery, 16 May 1848 (C.D.A., S.P.).
80. See editorials in *Tablet*, 29 July and 5 Aug. 1848.
81. See n68.
82. Fitzgerald, op. cit., pp43-44, 59-60, 90, 119.
83. Letter in *Tablet*, 19 Aug. 1848.
84. *L.R.*, 16 Apr. 1850.
85. Letter in *T.F.P.*, 3 Jan. 1855.
86. *L.R.*, 16 May 1852.
87. *T.F.P.*, 6 Mar. 1857; *L.R.*, 7 Apr. 1857.
88. *T.F.P.*, 21 Feb. 1853.
89. *T.F.P.*, 7 June 1851.
90. *Tablet*, 16 Nov. 1850 (James Redmond P.P., Arklow, Co Wicklow).
91. Letter in *L.R.*, 17 Feb. 1852.
92. These may be traced in O'Shea, op. cit., appendix 12, pp250-345.
93. *T.A.*, 20 Nov. 1880; *T.P.*, 29 May 1891.
94. *F.J.*, 16 May 1881.
95. Police report, Clonmel, 29 Nov. 1886. (S.P.O., Spec. Comm. 1888).
96. Blunt, *Land War* (1912), p.130 see also Timothy Harrington's comment in *U.I.*, 7 June 1890.
97. *T.A.*, 17 Aug. 1889.
98. *T.A.*, 24 Aug. 1889; *U.I.*, 24 Aug. 1889.
99. *L.R.*, 20 Jan. 1888.
100. *T.F.P.*, 22 Nov. 1878.
101. *T.P.*, 1 Sept. 1882.
102. Canon Fogarty's notebook no. 10 (C.D.A.); *Nation*, 2 Sept. 1882.
103. *U.I.*, 2 Sept. 1882.
104. Letter in *T.A.*, 9 Sept. 1882.
105. Letter in *T.A.*, 21 Aug. 1886.
106. *T.L.*, 29 Aug. 1883.
107. *T.P.*, 17 Apr. 1885; *T.A.*, 25 Apr. 2, 16 May 1885; *T.L.* 1, 22 Apr 1885; *U.I.*, 21 Mar. 1885.
108. *T.L.*, 15 Apr. 1885.
109. Letter in *F.J.*, 2 Jan. 1887; see Stephens to Croke, Jan. 1887 (C.D.A., C.P.).
110. *T.N.*, 21 Dec. 1889, 8, 22 Jan. 1890; *Nationalist*, 26 Feb., 5, 22 Mar. 1890; see also Leon Ó Broin, *Fenian fever* (London), 1971), pp158, 174, 179, and Norman, *Cath.*

Ch. & Irl. pp125-126 on Burke.
111. *T.P.*, 10 Dec. 1886.
112. *T.A.*, 4 June 1881; *T.L.*, 17 May 1884.
113. Police report, Bansha, 8 Feb. 1885 (S.P.O., Spec. Comm., 1888).
114. *Hansard 3*, cccxli, pp1712-3.
115. E.g., *T.L.*, 29 Aug. 1883, 5 Sept. 1884.
116. E.g.: *T.F.P.*, 20 Nov. 1880; *T.L.*, 29 Nov. 1882; *T.P.*, 26 Nov. 1886, 2 Dec. 1887, 29 Nov. 1888; *T.N.*, 14 Dec. 1889.
117. *T.N.*, 11, 15 Jan. 1890.
118. John Clancy to Croke, 14, 16 Nov. 1890 (C.D.A., C.P.).
119. See: *T.F.P.*, 6 Apr. 1880, 20 Nov. 1880; *T.A.*, 20 Mar. 1880.
120. *T.F.P.*, 26 Mar., 20 Apr. 1880.
121. *F.J.*, 21 Nov. 1887; *T.A.*, 26 Nov. 1887.
122. Emil Strauss, *Irish Nationalism and British democracy* (London, 1951), p.145, Ó Broin, *Fenian Fever* p.9; Ó Broin, *Revolutionary underground. The story of the Irish Republican Brotherhood, 1858-1924* (Dublin, 1976), p.22; see also S.P.O., C.S.O., R.P. 1865 3544.
123. *I.P.*, 16 Sept. 1865.
124. *Hansard 3*, cxc, pp1355-1356.
125. *Nationalist*, 21 Mar. 1891.
126. *1881 land act commission*, p.444, H.C. 1887, xxvi.
127. S.P.O., R.P. 1865 10377 and 3665; Charles de Gernon R.M. to Thomas Larcom, 23 Nov. 1866, and Stephen Moore, Barne, Clonmel, to Larcom (N.L.I., Larcom papers, MS 7590).
128. N.L.I., Mayo papers, MS 11189(5).
129. Article on Kenyon in *Tipperary*, 14 June 1882.
130. *Tribune*, 3 Nov., 29 Dec. 1855, 12 Jan. 1856.
131. *Tribune*, 3, 17 Nov., 8, 22 Dec. 1855, 26 Jan. 1856.
132. *Tribune*, 3, 24 Nov., 22, 29 Dec. 1855.
133. Letter in *L.R.*, 10 Mar. 1854.
134. The County Library in Thurles has a volume of newscuttings and manuscripts on the affair; see also S.P.O., C.S.O., R.P., 1858 17060.
135. *N.G.*, 1 Sept. 1858; *T.F.P.*, 27 Aug. 1858; *L.R.*, 31 Aug. 1858; *L.R.*, 31 Aug. 1858; John Gore Jones R.M.to Larcom, 31 Aug. 1858 (N.L.I., Larcom papers, MS 7636).
136. *T.F.P.*, 27 July, 3, 20, 24 Aug. 1858; *L.R.*, 30 July, 24 Aug. 1858.
137. N.L.I., William Smith O'Brien papers, MS 446.
138. Pp208-09.
139. *T.F.P.*, 7 Dec. 1860, 5 Feb. 1861.
140. P.190.
141. *T.F.P.*, 3 Mar. 1857.
142. See *T.F.P.*, 26 Feb. 1862, 14, 25, 28 Mar. 1862, 1, 11, 14 Apr. 1862; *T.A.*, 15 Mar. 1862.
143. *T.A.*, 5 Apr. 1862.
144. *T.A.*, 22 Aug. 1863; *T.F.P.*, 18 Aug. 1863; N.L.I., Mayo papers, MS 11188(4); N.L.I. microfilm p.4050, p.c17.
145. *T.A.*, 3, 10 Oct. 1863; *N.G.*, 3, 7 Oct. 1863; *T.F.P.*, 6 Oct. 1863; S.P.O., C.S.O., R.P., 1863 8563.
146. Gleeson, *Ely O'Carroll*, pp203-204.
147. Barnabo to Leahy 13 July 1865 and Leahy to Barnabo July 1865 (C.D.A., L.P.).
148. O'Shea, op. cit., tables 68 and 69, pp161-162, and fig. 13, p.211.
149. S.P.O., C.S.O., R.P., 1865/9146.
150. S.P.O., C.S.O., R.P., 1867/4172.
151. As in n148.
152. S.P.O., C.S.O., R.P., 1867/10766.
153. Whittaker to Moore, 13 Mar. 1867 (Mooresfort papers); S.P.O., C.S.O., R.P., 1873/12696.
154. Pp59, 195-96.

155. *T.P.*, 8, 14 Apr. 1865 (letters).
156. N.L.I., J.F.X. O'Brien papers, MS 13465(1).
157. William O'Brien, *Recollections* (London, 1905), p.109.
158. *I.P.*, 4 Mar., 19 Aug. 1865.
159. Document, 20 Feb. 1865 (C.D.A., L.P.); N.L.I. Otway papers, MS 13008.
160. *T.A.*, 10 May 1884.
161. E.g. *T.F.P.*, 18 July 1865. (John Power).
162. *N.G.*, 26 July, 1865.
163. *T.F.P.*, 18 July 1865; *N.G.*, 19 July 1865; *T.A.*, 27 Oct. 1866.
164. *T.A.*, 4 Mar. 1865; *I.P.*, 4 Mar., 22, 29 July 1865; *T.F.P.*, 18 July 1865.
165. *T.F.P.*, 3 Mar. 1865, 16 Oct. 1866.
166. Results in *T.F.P.*, 3 Mar. 1865; *T.A.*, 4 Mar. 1865.
167. *T.F.P.*, 28 Feb. 1865.
168. *T.F.P.*, 20 Oct. 1865.
169. *F.J.*, 13 May 1868.
170. *I.P.*, 4, 11 Mar. 1865.
171. *N.G.*, 26 July 1865.
172. Ó Fiaich, loc. cit., p.90, Norman, op. cit., p.115.
173. See *T.F.P.*, 29 Oct., 2, 9, 16, 23 Nov. 1869, 25 Feb. 1870; *L.R.*, 2, 5, 26 Nov. 1869; *N.G.*, 27 Nov. 1869, 23 Feb. 1870; *T.A.*, 26 Feb. 1870.
174. *Irishman*, 5 Mar. 1870.
175. *N.G.*, 26 Feb. 1870; *T.A.*, 5 Mar. 1870.
176. See *N.G.*, 11, 28 May, 1 June 1870; *T.F.P.*, 31 May 1870; *T.A.*, 9 July 1870.
177. *T.F.P.*, 8, 29 Apr., 13 May 1870.
178. *T.F.P.*, 16 Oct. 1868.
179. E.g. *T.F.P.*, 17 Nov. 1868. (Power).
180. *F.J.*, 29 Oct. 1868.
181. *T.F.P.*, 23 Nov. 1869; *N.G.*, 24 Nov. 1869.
182. Ó Fiaich, op. cit., p.95, Ó Broin, *Fenian fever*, p.136; Norman op. cit., p.130.
183. *Irishman*, 27 Nov. 1869.
184. Ó Broin, *Fenian fever*, p.233.
185. N.L.I., J.F.X. O'Brien papers, MS 13465(1); *N.G.*, 16 Sept. 1865.
186. Blunt, *Land war*, p.329.
187. *Irishman*, 21 Feb. 1874.
188. *T.A.*, 5 Mar. 1870.
189. *Irishman*, 28 Feb. 1874.
190. *T.F.P.*, 13 Apr. 1875; *N.G.*, 14 Apr. 1875.
191. *T.F.P.*, 12 Apr. 1875; *N.G.*, 13 Mar. 1875.
192. *N.G.*, 21 Apr. 1877; *T.F.P.*, 11 May 1877.
193. Ryan to Croke, 9 May 1877 (C.D.A., C.P.).
194. Croke to Cullen, 28 Apr. 1877 (D.D.A., Cullen papers).
195. *N.G.*, 5 May 1877; *T.F.P.*, 11 May 1877.
196. *N.G.*, 12 May 1877; *T.A.*, 11 May 1877.
197. *T.A.*, 6 Mar. 1875; *L.R.*, 2 Mar. 1875; *N.G.*, 3 Mar. 1875.
198. *T.F.P.*, 15 May 1877; *Irishman*, 26 May 1877.
199. E.g.: *T.F.P.*, 23 Nov. 1869, 25 Feb. 1870; special supplement of *N.G.*, 24 Nov. 1869, 23 Feb. 1870; *Irishman*, 27 Nov. 1869.
200. *L.R.*, 26 Nov. 1869; *F.J.*, 25 Nov. 1869; *Times*, 1 Mar. 1870.
201. *N.G.*, 2 Mar. 1870; S.P.O., C.S.O., R.P., 1869/17565 and 1870/4183.
202. S.P.O., C.S.O., R.P., 1869/18242.
203. E.g. *N.G.*, 19, 26 Feb. 1870; *T.F.P.*, 1 Mar. 1870, *F.J.*, 25 Nov. 1869; *L.R.*, 26 Nov. 1869; *Times*, 27 Nov. 1869; *T.A.*, 26 Feb. 1870; 1 Mar. 1870; S.P.O., C.S.O., R.P., 1870/4183.
204. *Irishman*, 4 Dec. 1869; *N.G.*, 27 Nov. 1869; *T.F.P.*, 26 Nov. 1869.
205. S.P.O., C.S.O., R.P., 1870/4183.
206. *T.A.*, 5 Mar. 1870.
207. *T.A.*, 1 Mar. 1870; *T.F.P.*, 1 Mar. 1870.

208. S.P.O., C.S.O., R.P., 1869/17473.
209. *Irishman*, 4 Dec. 1869.
210. *Times*, 27 Nov. 1869.
211. E.g. Police report, 20 Nov. 1869 (S.P.O., C.S.O., R.P., 1869/18149).
212. *T.F.P.*, 23 Nov. 1869, 25 Feb. 1870; *N.G.*, 24 Nov. 1869, 23 Feb. 1870, *Irishman*, 27 Nov. 1869, *T.A.*, 26 Feb. 1870.
213. P.137, see also Police reports 27 Feb. and 1 Mar. 1870. (S.P.O., C.S.O. R.P., 1870/4183).
214. *T.A.*, 8 Mar. 1870.
215. *T.F.P.*, 8 Mar. 1870.
216. As in n148.
217. *L.R.*, 26 Nov. 1869; *T.A.*, 1, 5 Mar. 1870.
218. *L.R.*, 26 Nov. 1869; *N.G.*, 27 Nov. 1869, *T.F.P.*, 26 Nov. 1869.
219. *T.A.*, 5 Mar. 1870.
220. *N.G.*, 27 Nov. 1869 (129 votes to 45).
221. *L.R.*, 26 Nov. 1869; S.P.O., C.S.O., R.P., 1869/18242.
222. Such a comparison for the 27 polling stations may be seen in *T.F.P.*, 15 May 1877.
223. E.g., N.L.I., Butt Papers, MS 8698(4); Donnelly *19th Century Cork*, p.197.
224. Letter, 17 Nov. 1869 (S.P.O., C.S.O., R.P., 1869/17565).
225. Letter from John Gore Jones, 22 Nov. 1869. (S.P.O., C.S.O., R.P., 1869/17873).
226. N.L.I., J.F.X. O'Brien papers MS 13465(1).
227. Letter in *T.F.P.*, 7 Dec. 1869.
228. O'Shea, op. cit., table 70, p.163. Table 1 below.
229. *L.R.*, 12 Feb. 1875; *Tablet*, 13, 20 Feb. 1875; *Irishman*, 27 Feb. 1875.
230. *T.A.*, 13 Feb., 13 Mar. 1875; *Irishman*, 13 Feb., 13 Mar. 1875.
231. E.g. *T.F.P.*, 19 Feb. 1875 (Clonmel).
232. Details of these meetings in *T.A.*, 21 Aug., 25 Sept., 9 Oct. 1869, *L.R.*, 24, 28 Sept., 12, 15 Oct. 1869, *N.G.*, 6, 13 Oct., 1869, *T.F.P.*, 5, 26 Oct. 1869, and S.P.O., Fenian papers 'F' papers nos. 7622R, 4869R, 4807R, 4815R, 4819R.
233. *N.G.*, 6 Oct. 1869.
234. S.P.O., F.P., 'F' papers, 4819R.
235. S.P.O., F.P., 'F' papers, 4869R.
236. P.162.
237. See n.213.
238. Letter from Andrew Carden, 4 Oct. 1869. (S.P.O. 'F' papers, 7622R).
239. Memorials in S.P.O., C.S.O., R.P., 1867/3431, 8545, 15985, 12169, and F.P., 'F' papers, 2374R.
240. E.g., S.P.O., Habeas Corpus Suspension Act, vol. ii, pp130B, 133, 146B, 167, 321, 340, 505.
241. Ibid., p.146B.
242. Charles de Gernon to Larcom, 17 Mar. 1867. (N.L.I., Larcom papers, MS 7590).
243. Letter of George Sheehan P.P., Bantry, Co Cork cited in *Hansard*, 1866, clxxxiii, pp460-61.
244. S.P.O., C.S.O., R.P., 1867, 10841.
245. *L.R.*, 28 Sept. 1869; *T.A.*, 25 Sept. 1869.
246. *T.F.P.*, 5 Oct. 1869.
247. Police report, 10 Oct. 1869. (S.P.O., 'F' papers, 4869R).
248. *T.F.P.*, 26 Oct. 1869.
249. *T.F.P.*, 5 Oct. 1869.
250. *L.R.*, 28 Sept. 1869; *T.A.*, 9 Oct. 1869.
251. *N.G.*, 13 Oct. 1869.
252. *Express*, 3 Jan. 1868. (newscutting in N.L.I. Larcom papers, MS 7729).
253. *T.F.P.*, 5 Oct. 1869.
254. See e.g. newscutting in S.P.O., C.S.O., R.P., 1870/8812, for a totally lay Inchicore amnesty meeting.
255. *N.G.*, 13 Oct. 1869.
256. MacDonagh, 'Irish catholic bishops', p.53.

257. Lyons, *Ir. since the famine,* p.134.
258. E.g. *N.G.,* 9, 16 Mar. 1867.
259. *N.G.,* 11 Dec. 1867.
260. *N.G.,* 25 Nov. 1868.
261. O'Leary, *My story,* p.84.
262. See detective report, 4 Oct. 1882. (S.P.O., C.B.S., B134). Croke to Kirby, 13 June 1884. (K.P.).
263. *T.A.,* 16 Apr. 1887, *Nationalist,* 2 Apr. 1881. (Denis Sheehan C.C. and letter of David Humphreys).
264. Police report, 9 Sept. 1888. (S.P.O., I.N.L.L. — I.N.L. proceedings 1879-1888).
265. *T.A.,* 2 Apr. 1881.
266. *T.A.,* 17 Feb. 1881, 22 Oct. 1881; *T.N.,* 5 June 1889.
267. *T.A.,* 18 Dec. 1880.
268. Letters in *Tablet,* 25 Dec. 1886, 12, 19 Mar. 1887.
269. Croke to Bishop Vaughan, Salford, 24 Jan. 1885. (C.D.A., C.P.).
270. *T.P.,* 7 Jan. 1881.
271. *T.P.,* 18 Mar. 1881; *Hansard 3,* cclxix, p.456.
272. *T.P.,* 14 Oct. 1881.
273. *T.A.,* 21 Aug. 1880.
274. S.P.O., P.&C. Police reports 1883. Rept. No. 492W/2636.
275. Pp85-86, 211.
276. *T.P.,* 7 Jan. 1881; *T.A.,* 8 Jan. 1881; *T.F.P.,* 30 Nov. 1880; *T.L.,* 14 Mar., 5 Dec. 1884, 15 Apr. 1885; Police report, Anacarty, 26 Apr. 1885. (S.P.O., Spec. Comm. 1888).
277. *T.L.,* 6 Dec. 1882, 7 Mar. 1883.
278. Mooney to Kirby, 2 Dec. 1882. (K.P.).
279. *T.F.P.,* 8 Oct. 1880.
280. N.L.I., MS 11289, Templemore report, 10 Oct. 1880. (N.L.I., MS 11289).
281. *T.A.,* 21 Aug. 1880.
282. *U.I.,* 1 June 1889. (Canon Ryan, Aghada, Co. Cork.).
283. *T.L.,* 7 Nov. 1884; *U.I.,* 8 Nov. 1884.
284. *T.A.,* 20 Mar. 1886.
285. *T.A.,* 14 Aug. 1886.
286. *F.J.,* 10 Nov. 1887.
287. See: F.S.L. Lyons, 'Fenianism 1867-1916' in Moody, *Fenian movement,* p.43; Tierney, *Croke.* pp192, 200-204; W.F. Mandle, 'The I.R.B. and the beginnings of the Gaelic Athletic Association', in *I.H.S.,* xx, no. 80 (Sept. 1977), pp418-438.
288. *T.A.,* 18 Apr. 1885, 30 Oct. 1886; *T.P.,* 10 Feb. 1888; *F.J.,* 10 Nov. 1887.
289. See e.g. South eastern divisional report, 4 Oct. 1887 (S.P.O., C.B.S., D.I.C.s 1887-95).
290. Statement of P.N. Fitzgerald at the Thurles Convention *(F.J.,* 10 Nov. 1887).
291. *F.J.,* 14 Nov. 1887 (letter of James Clancy C.C., Feakle, Co. Clare).
292. *F.J.,* 21 Nov. 1887, *T.A.,* 26 Nov. 1887.
293. *F.J.,* 10 Nov. 1887.
294. Letter in *F.J.,* 21 Nov. 1887.
295. Letter in *F.J.,* 15 Nov. 1887.
296. Scanlan's letter in ibid.
297. Report, 5 Dec. 1887 (S.P.O., C.B.S., 1890, 1265 Carton 1).
298. As in n.294.
299. Letter in *T.A.,* 7 Nov. 1885.
300. Report, 17 Nov. 1887 (S.P.O., C.B.S., 1890, 1265 Carton I).
301. Covered by *F.J.,* 10 Nov. 1887, *N.G.,* 12 Nov. 1887, and report as in n300.
302. John Cunningham C.C., Silvermines, John C. Moloney C.C., Toomevara, Patrick Crowe C.C., Burgessbeg.
303. Biographical sketch of Fitzgerald in Report of 11 Aug. 1890 (S.P.O., C.B.S., 1890-1891), See also *Hansard 3,* cclxxxvii, p.49.
304. Reports, 9 Nov. 1887 and 5 Dec. 1887 (S.P.O., C.B.S., 1890, Carton 1, 1265).

305. See Report, 14 Nov. 1887 (Ibid.).
306. Croke to Walsh, 11 Nov. 1887 (D.D.A., W.P.).
307. Their joint letter in *F.J.*, 11 Nov. 1887; see also: *F.J.*, 14 Nov. 1887. (Scanlan) and *F.J.*, 21 Nov. 1887. (Scanlan and John McKenna C.C.); *F.J.*, 29 Nov. 1887 (John Gleeson C.C.).
308. Fenian replies in *F.J.*, 14, 17, 29 Nov. 1887, *T.P.*, 2 Dec. 1887.
309. *F.J.*, 19, 29 Nov. 1887; *T.P.*, 18 Nov. 1887.
310. Letter in *F.J.*, 11 Nov. 1887.
311. *F.J.*, 21 Nov. 1887, *T.A.*, 26 Nov. 1887.
312. Their correspondence in *F.J.*, 22, 29 Nov., 3 Dec. 1887.
313. *F.J.*, 22 Nov. 1887; see *F.J.*, 23 Nov. 1887 for conventions in other counties.
314. Letter in *F.J.*, 26 Nov. 1887.
315. *F.J.*, 24 Nov. 1887.
316. Croke to Walsh, 23 Nov. 1887 (D.D.A., W.P.).
317. See *N.G.*, 3 Dec. 1887, *F.J.*, 1, 2 Dec. 1887.
318. *F.J.*, 14 Dec. 1887.
319. *F.J.*, 5 Jan. 1888, *Gael*, 7 Jan. 1888.
320. *Gael*, 7 Jan. 1888.
321. Report, 20 Oct. 1888 (S.P.O., C.B.S., D.I.Cs. 1887-1895, 523W/8788).
322. *L.R.*, 25 Jan. 1889; *C.E.*, 24 Jan. 1889.
323. Croke's letter in *Gael*, 7 Jan. 1888.
324. Reports 7 Aug. 1888, Sept. 1889, 8 May, 5 Nov. 1890, 23 Feb., 5 May, 5 Sept. 1891 (S.P.O., C.B.S., D.I.Cs., 1887-95, 521W/8199, 10606, 5215/429, 662, 1970, 3596, 4416); report 23 Feb. 1891 (S.P.O., C.B.S., D.I.Cs., 2786/S).
325. Report, 5 May 1890. (S.P.O., C.B.S., D.I.Cs., 1890-91, 501S/122).
326. See: Report 4 Feb. 1891. (S.P.O., C.B.S., D.I.Cs., 1887-95, 521S/2801); *C.C.*, 18 Apr. 1891; *U.I.*, 20 Dec. 1890, *F.J.*, 5 Jan. 1891, 11 20 Mar., 27 Apr., 23, 24 July 1891.
327. E.g., memo of 4 June 1891 on Thurles. (S.P.O., Police and crime reports 1890-94).
328. *T.P.*, 19 Dec. 1890.
329. Report, 5 May 1891. (S.P.O., C.B.S., D.I.Cs. 1887-1895).
330. South eastern divisional report, 5 Mar. 1891, (Ibid.); Fr Horgan, Tralee, to Croke, 14 Jan. 1891 (C.D.A., C.P.); Croke to William O'Brien, 22 Mar. 1891 (N.L.I., T.P. Gill papers, MS 13507.
331. Croke's private circular to his priests, 2 Mar. 1891 (C.D.A., C.P.); Police reports, 5 May 1891 and April 1891 (S.P.O., C.B.S., D.I.Cs., 1887-95, 5235/3612, and 1890-91, carton 9).
332. D.I.Cs. as in n.331.
333. *L.R.*, 19 May 1891; *Nationalist*, 21, 28 Mar., 2 Dec. 1891; *T.P.*, 9 Oct. 1891.
334. Pp220-21.
335. Report, 3 Oct. 1891 (S.P.O., C.B.S., D.I.Cs. 1887-1895, 521S/4557).
336. Entries in minute books of the Young Ireland Society 1881-86, for 7 Oct. 1881, 10 Feb. 1882, Jan. 1883, 1 May, 5, 13 Nov. 1885 (N.L.I., MSS 16601, 19158).
337. *T.A.*, 29 June 1883, 12 Sept. 1885, 2 Jan. 1886.
338. *N.G.*, 9, 16 Dec. 1863.
339. *I.P.*, 24, 31 Dec. 1864, 28 Jan., 16 Sept. 1865.
340. E.g., minute book 1881-1884.
341. *L.R.*, 10 Mar. 1891; minute book entries, 7 Oct. 1881, 30 Oct. 1884, 30 Mar. 1885 and 23 Apr. 1885 (N.L.I., MSS 16601, 19158).
342. *T.A.*, 12 Sept. 1885.
343. *Waterford News and General Advertiser*, 18 Dec. 1885.
344. *F.J.*, 13 Dec. 1890, Ó Broin, *Revolutionary underground*, p.49.
345. Reports, 3 Mar. 1891 (S.P.O., Police and crime records, Police reports, 1890-94) and 5 Mar. 1891 (S.P.O., C.B.S , D.I.Cs., 521S/3058).
346. Memo, 28 Jan. 1891 (S.P.O., Police and crime records, police reports 1890-94).

7. **THE PRIEST AND THE IRISH MEMBERS OF PARLIAMENT 1850-1876**
 1. Pp62-63.
 2. *T.F.P.*, 10, 24 Sept. 1851; *N.G.*, 24 Sept. 1851; *Tablet*, 27 Sept. 1851.
 3. *T.F.P.*, 30 Aug. 1851, 10 Dec. 1851.
 4. *Tablet*, 20 Mar. 1852.
 5. *L.R.*, 16 Apr. 1850.
 6. See J.H. Whyte, *The Independent Irish Party 1850-1859* (Oxford, 1958), pp10, 12.
 7. *F.J.*, 30 Apr. 1851.
 8. Letter in *Tablet*, 7 Dec. 1850.
 9. *T.F.P.*, 19 Feb. 1851; *Tablet*, 1 Mar. 1851.
10. Letter in *T.F.P.*, 26 Nov. 1853.
11. *F.J.*, 7 May 1852; *Tablet*, 8 May 1852.
12. Letter from Archdeacon Fitzgerald, Rathkeale, to John O'Dwyer in *L.R.*, 4 May 1852.
13. Their exchange of letters in *F.J.*, 11 Oct. 1853, *Tablet*, 15, 22 Oct. 1853.
14. *T.F.P.*, 3 July 1852.
15. Letter in *Tablet*, 10 July 1852.
16. *T.F.P.*, 11 Sept. 1852; *F.J.*, 9 Sept. 1852; *N.G.*, 11 Sept. 1852.
17. *T.F.P.*, 1, 19 Jan. 1853.
18. Mackey's letter in *T.F.P.*, 24 Mar. 1853.
19. Letter in *L.R.*, 18 Jan. 1853.
20. Letters in *Tablet*, 8 Jan., 5 Feb. 1853.
21. *Tablet*, 15 Jan. 1853, 5 Feb. 1853.
22. *F.J.*, 12 Jan. 1853, *Tablet*, 15 Jan. 1853.
23. *T.F.P.*, 24 July 1852.
24. Letter in *Tablet*, 26 Mar. 1853; *T.F.P.*, 6 Apr. 1853; *N.G.*, 30 Mar. 1853; *L.R.*, 1 April 1853.
25. *F.J.*, 12 Apr. 1853; *Tablet*, 16 Apr. 1853; *T.F.P.*, 16 Apr. 1853; *N.G.*, 9 Apr. 1853.
26. *Tablet*, 23 Apr 1853.
27. *Tablet*, 9 July 1853.
28. Letters of Pierce Green P.P., Killavullen, Co Cork and T.S. O'Grady P.P., Adare, Co Limerick, in *Tablet*, 2 July 1853, *L.R.*, 31 Oct. 1854.
29. *T.F.P.*, 23 Apr. 1853, *Tablet*, 24 Mar. 1853.
30. Letter in *T.F.P.*, 4 May 1853.
31. *Tablet*, 14, 21 May 1853.
32. P.199.
33. *Tablet*, 7 Dec. 1853.
34. *F.J.*, 8 Oct. 1853, *Tablet*, 15 Oct. 1853.
35. For a detailed account of the campaign see *Tablet*, 12, 26 Nov. 1853.
36. *Tablet*, 26 Nov. 1853; *T.F.P.*, 23 Nov. 1853.
37. See *T.F.P.*, 14 Dec. 1850; *L.R.*, 6, 13 Dec. 1851; C.G. Duffy, *The League of north and south* (London, 1886), p.74.
38. *L.R.*, 29 Jan., 22 Feb. 1850, 23 Apr. 1850; *T.F.P.*, 26 Nov. 1853; Letters of O'Connell and Cornelius Corkran P.P., Carrigaline, Co Cork, and letter of Dr Burke, see also Fogarty, op. cit., p.167.
39. See Denis Gwynn, 'O'Connell, Davis and the Colleagues Bill' in *I.E.R.*, 1948, p.19.
40. *F.J.*, 30 Apr. 1851.
41. *T.F.P.*, 24 Dec. 1853.
42. *Tablet*, 26 Nov. 1853.
43. *L.R.*, 4 Apr. 1854 (written under the pseudonym 'A Priest of the archdiocese of Cashel').
44. *Tablet*, 26 Nov., 10, 17 Dec. 1853.
45. Confidential letter of Slattery to Ryan, 11 Dec. 1853 (C.D.A, S.P.).
46. Ryan's reply, 19 Dec. 1853 (C.D.A., S.P.).
47. *T.F.P.*, 26 Nov. 1853.
48. *T.F.P.*, 24 Dec. 1853; *N.G.*, 24 Dec. 1853.
49. *T.F.P.*, 22 Nov., 6 Dec. 1854, 3 Jan. 1855; *Tablet*, 3 Nov. 1855.

50. Their letters in *L.R.*, 13 Jan. 1854, *Tablet*, 14 Jan. 1854.
51. *Tablet, 25 Feb. 1854.*
52. *T.L.*, 11, 18 Aug., 22, 29 Sept. 1855, 23 Feb. 1856.
53. *T.L.*, 14 Apr. 1855.
54. *Tablet*, 29 Apr. 1854.
55. *Management of Maynooth,* pp12, 36, (1896-1). H.C. 1854-5, xxii.
56. *Tablet*, 3 May 1854.
57. *T.F.P.*, 3 May, 1854.
58. Draft document 'near Lent', 1854 (C.D.A., S.P.).
59. See N.L.I. microfilm P.5524, pp103-105, (MS pp73-74), for letters to Rome by the curates and the text of the letter of suspension. This large file contains all the documents sent to Rome concerning this affair and its later repercussions. The originals are preserved in Propaganda archives Rome, S.C. Irlanda, vol. 158.
60. *Tablet*, 4 Nov. 1854; *L.R.*, 3 Nov. 1854.
61. *Tablet*, 18, 25 Nov. 1854.
62. Copies of the priests memorial (and also that of the M.P.s) are preserved in N.L.I., MS 1587. The priests' memorial is also in Propaganda archives (microfilm P.5524). See O'Shea, op. cit., table 71 for breakdown.
63. P.217.
64. N.L.I. microfilm P.5524 (see n.59).
65. Ibid., p.19. (MS p.27).
66. Ibid., pp12, 18. (MS pp24, 27).
67. Cullen to Slattery, 10 Mar. 1855 (C.D.A., S.P.).
68. Their letters, 14 Feb. 1855, Slattery's reply, 15 Feb. 1855 (C.D.A., S.P.). See also C.D.A., S.P. for two circulars of John O'Dwyer, 6 Dec. 1854 and 12 Dec. 1854, and see Lucas to Duffy, Jan./Feb. 1855 (N.L.I., MS 3738).
69. Leahy to Slattery, 21 Feb. 1855 (C.D.A., S.P.).
70. P.37.
71. Cardinal Fransoni to Slattery, 17 Mar. 1855 (C.D.A., S.P.).
72. Slattery to Fransoni, 7 Apr. 1855 (C.D.A., S.P.), also microfilm P.5524, pp.102-103 (MS p.73).
73. Their letters in *T.F.P.*, 24 Mar. 1855, *T.L.*, 7, 21 Apr. 1855.
74. *T.F.P.*, 23 Sept. 1856.
75. *L.R.*, 3 Mar. 1857 (John Meagher P.P., Toomevara).
76. See *T.F.P.*, 6, 17 Feb. 1857; *L.R.*, 7 Apr. 1857.
77. *T.F.P.*, 21 June 1861.
78. *T.F.P.*, 7 Apr. 1857.
79. *L.R.*, 3 Mar. 1857.
80. Letter in *L.R.*, 24 Mar. 1857.
81. *T.F.P.*, 29 July 1856; *N.G.*, 23 July 1856.
82. *T.F.P.*, 21 Feb. 1857.
83. *T.F.P.*, 27 Feb. 1857; *L.R.*, 27 Feb. 1857.
84. Letter in *L.R.*, 24 Mar. 1857.
85. Letter in *L.R.*, 7 Mar. 1857, see O'Shea, op. cit., tables 74 and 75, pp169-170, for an age breakdown.
86. *T.F.P.*, 3 Mar. 1857, 6 Mar. 1857; *L.R.*, 3 Mar. 1857; *N.G.*, 4 Mar. 1857.
87. *T.F.P.*, 20 Mar. 1857.
88. Whyte, *The Ind. Ir. Party*, p.164.
89. *L.R.*, 24 Mar. 1857; *T.F.P.*, 27 Mar. 1857 (letter of Patrick O'Donnell C.C., Newinn).
90. *T.F.P.*, 27 Feb. 1857, 3 Mar. 1857.
91. *T.F.P.*, 13, 17 Mar. 1857.
92. *T.F.P.*, 17 Mar. 1857.
93. *T.F.P.*, 27 Mar. 1857; *N.G.*, 28 Mar. 1857; *L.R.*, 24 Mar. 1857.
94. *T.F.P.*, 3 Apr. 1857.
95. Leahy's circular to this clergy in *L.R.*, 7 Apr. 1857.
96. See *T.F.P.*, 11, 14 Apr. 1857; *N.G.*, 11, 15 Apr. 1857.

97. *N.G.*, 11 Apr. 1857; *T.F.P.*, 14 Apr. 1857.
98. *T.F.P.*, 4 Feb. 1859.
99. *T.F.P.*, 6 Aug. 1858.
100. *T.F.P.*, 15 Feb. 1859; *N.G.*, 22 Feb. 1859.
101. *T.F.P.*, 22, 25 Feb. 1859; see also letter from a Mr Gordon, Clonmel to Lord Naas, 9 apr. 1859 (N.L.I., Mayo papers MS 11036).
102. *L.R.*, 26 Apr. 1859; *T.F.P.*, 29 Apr. 1859.
103. *T.F.P.*, 29 Apr. 1859; *N.G.*, 30 Apr. 1859.
104. *T.F.P.*, 17, 21 June 1859.
105. *T.F.P.*, 24 June 1859.
106. Norman, *Cath. ch. & Ire.*, pp37-8.
107. See e.g., *T.F.P.*, 28 Feb., 2 Mar., 3 Apr. 1860.
108. *T.F.P.*, 23 Oct. 1860.
109. *T.F.P.*, 19 Oct. 1860.
110. See *T.F.P.*, 6, 13, 23, 30 Dec. 1859, 1 Jan. 1860.
111. *T.P.*, 29 Apr. 1881; *T.A.*, 30 Apr. 1881; Tipperary report, 31 Oct. 1880 (N.L.I., MS 11289).
112. E.g., *T.A.*, 30 Mar. 1861; *T.F.P.*, 26 Apr. 1864.
113. Norman, op. cit., deals with the association in detail.
114. See *T.F.P.*, 17 Nov. 1865 for an awareness of the distinction at local level.
115. P.59.
116. *N.G.*, 25 Feb.1865; *T.F.P.*, 24 Feb. 1865.
117. *T.F.P.*, 20 Oct. 1865.
118. *N.G.*, 18 Feb. 1865.
119. *T.F.P.*, 5 Oct. 1866; *T.A.*, 6 Oct. 1866.
120. Circular, 15 Oct. 1866 (C.D.A., L.P.); *T.F.P.*, 16 Oct. 1866; *F.J.*, 15 Oct. 1866.
121. *T.F.P.*, 16 Oct. 1866.
122. Cullen to Leahy, 30 June 1865. (C.D.A., L.P.).
123. E.g. letter of John Ryan P.P., Newinn in *T.F.P.*, 16 Oct. 1866.
124. *T.F.P.*, 14 July 1865.
125. *T.F.P.*, 18 Sept. 1868.
126. *F.J.*, 27 Oct. 1868.
127. *N.G.*, 11 Nov. 1868.
128. *T.F.P.*, 1 Oct. 1869.
129. Letter to the council of the league in *T.F.P.*, 25 Feb. 1870.

8. THE PRIEST AND THE PARNELLITE PARTY 1877-1891

1. See Thornley, *Butt*, pp235-8, 254-9, 305-7, 323-7, 329-30.
2. *T.F.P.*, 1 May 1877.
3. Letter in *T.F.P.*, 28 Sept. 1877.
4. O'Shea, op. cit., table 76, pp171-173.
5. *T.F.P.*, 8 Feb. 8 Mar. 1878.
6. See telegram, 31 Mar. 1880 from Parnell to Moore (W.D.A., unsorted papers); see also letter from an aggrieved Moore to Parnell, Easter Sunday 1880. (Mooresfort papers).
7. *T.P.*, 1 Apr. 1881.
8. *T.L.*, 12 Jan. 1884.
9. Parnell's letter in *T.L.*, 24 Oct. 1884.
10. *T.P.*, 13 Nov. 1885.
11. *T.F.P.*, 30 Jan. 1879; see pp000 above.
12. *T.F.P.*, 19 Mar. 1880; *C.C.*, 20 Mar. 1880.
13. *T.F.P.*, 26 Mar. 1880.
14. P.214.
15. Croke to Smyth, 18 May 1880 (C.D.A., C.P.).
16. *N.G.*, 22 May 1880.

17. Croke's letters to Smyth, 20, 22 May 1880, Smyth to Croke 21, 28 May 1880; letter May 1880 from the clergy of Cashel and Emly (C.D.A., C.P.); Smyth's letter in *N.G.*, 26 May 1880.
18. Smyth's letter to the party whip in *T.A.*, 22 Jan. 1881.
19. See e.g., *T.P.*, 28 Jan., 29 July 1881; *T.A.*, 5 Feb., 2 Apr. 1881, 2 Feb. 1884; *N.G.*, 5 Feb. 1881; *T.L.*, 17 May 1884; *F.J.*, 10 Feb. 1881; Kiloscully Rept. 22 Aug. 1881 (S.P.O., Spec. Comm., 1888).
20. *T.A.*, 5 Feb. 1881.
21. *F.J.*, 11 Feb. 1881; *N.G.*, 12 Feb. 1881; *T.A.*, 12 Feb. 1881.
22. Letter in *N.G.*, 16 Feb. 1881.
23. For some evidence of this see *T.F.P.*, 23 Sept. 1879, 23 Apr., 19 Nov. 1880; *Tablet*, 28 Aug., 18, 25 Sept. 1880; *C.C.*, 23 Oct. 1880; *T.A.*, 15 Jan. 1881, 18 Mar. 1882; *F.J.*, 13 Mar. 1882.
24. *N.G.*, 12 Feb. 1881; *F.J.*, 16 Feb. 1881.
25. *T.P.*, 14, 21 Apr. 1882; *N.G.*, 18 Apr. 1882. (there were other resolutions on different issues).
26. Letter in *T.P.*, 28 Apr. 1884.
27. See e.g., letter from one of the signatories requesting a favour (N.L.I., P.J. Smyth papers, MS 8215), and a similar letter from Bishop John Power, a staunch oppositionist of the 1850s (N.L.I., MS 8215).
28. Two letters in *N.G.*, 20 May 1882.
29. Letter in *N.G.*, 25 Oct. 1882; see also *N.G.*, 19 Apr. 1884.
30. P.J. Smyth, *The priest in politics* (Dublin, 1885). esp. pp8-9.
31. *N.G.*, 14, 21 Mar. 1883; *T.L.*, 21 Mar. 1883.
32. *U.I.*, 17 Mar. 1883.
33. Croke to Manning 13 Mar. 1884; M. Cecil Donovan to Croke, 19 Dec.1884 (C.D.A., C.P.).
34. *U.I.*, 10 Jan. 1885.
35. *T.P.*, 2 Jan. 1885.
36. *T.L.*, 9 Jan. 1885.
37. *T.L.*, 9, 17 Jan. 1885.
38. Letter in *T.L.*, 22 Jan. 1885.
39. *T.L.*, 30 Jan. 1885.
40. *T.L.*, 14 Mar. 1883.
41. *T.P.*, 9 Jan. 1885; *T.L.*, 9, 17 Jan. 1885. See also Parnell to Bishop John Power, 25 June 884 (W.D.A.).
42. Davitt, *Fall of feudalism*, p.469.
43. Cruise O'Brien, *Parnell*, p.129, Larkin; *R.C. church*, p.335, n.2.
44. O'Shea, op. cit., table 17, p.35 for a synopsis of priestly electioneering for the 60s, 70s, and 80s.
45. *U.I.*, 17 May 1890; Parnell to Croke, 8 May 1890 (C.D.A., C.P.).
46. See N.L.I., Harrington papers MS 5384, pp14, 62, 67, 71.
47. See *T.A.*, 21 Nov., 5 dec. 1885, *T.P.*, 21 Nov. 1885.
48. *T.A.*, 5 Dec. 1885, *N.G.*, 9 Dec. 1885; *F.J.*, 12 Dec. 1885; see also T.W. Rolleston, 'The archbishop in politics' in *Dublin University Review*, Feb. 1886, pp94-95.
49. Croke to Kirby, 15 Dec. 1885 (K.P.).
50. George Errington to Smith, 15 Aug. 1879 (St. Paul's, Rome, Abbot Smith papers).
51. Statements in, *T.A.*, 8 Jan. 1881; *T.L.*, 17 Feb. 1883, 5 Dec. 1884, 30 Jan. 1885.
52. *T.A.*, 30 Apr. 1881; Police report, Bansha, 8 Feb. 1885 (S.P.O., Special Comm., 1888 Carton 1, A-B) (John Tuohy and John Kelly).
53. *T.P.*, 29 July 1881.
54. See Cruise O'Brien, op. cit., pp32-35.
55. O'Shea, op. cit., table 76, pp171-173.
56. Letter in *T.F.P.*, 18 May 1877.
57. Letter in *U.I.*, 4 July 1885.
58. Letter in *F.J.*, 12 Dec. 1885.
59. Letter in *T.A.*, 26 June 1886.

60. *T.P.*, 2 July 1886.
61. *T.F.P.*, 11 Feb. 1850.
62. E.g., *T.F.P.*, 9, 23 Feb., 5 Oct. 1850; *L.R.*, 8, 19 Feb. 1850.
63. *T.F.P.*, 6 Mar. 1850.
64. *T.F.P.*, 12 Mar. 1851.
65. *T.F.P.*, 9 Feb. 1850.
66. *T.F.P.*, 17 July 1852.
67. Statements in *Tablet*, 13 Apr., 4 May, 22 June 1850, 20 Sept. 1854.
68. *F.J.*, 3 Jan. 1868; *Nation*, 4, 25 Jan. 1868.
69. Thornley, op. cit., p.56.
70. *L.R.*, 10, 14 Jan., 14, 18 Feb., 6 Mar. 1868; *T.F.P.*, 6 Mar. 1868, *Nation*, 15 Feb. 1868.
71. *Express* newscutting, 30 Jan. 1868 (N.L.I., Larcom papers, MS 7729); letter in *L.R.*, 17 Mar. 1868.
72. Letter in *L.R.*, 17 Mar. 1868 and his letter in *L.R.*, 10 Jan. 1868.
73. *F.J.*, 9 Jan. 1868.
74. E.g., *Express* newscutting, 23 Jan. 1868, *Mail*, 24 Jan. 1868 (N.L.I., Larcom papers, MS 7729). Fitzgibbon, *Ire. in 1868*, p.253.
75. *T.F.P.*, 24 Nov. 1868.
76. N.L.I., Alfred Webb papers MS 1745.
77. Daunt to Leahy, 8, 20 Dec. 1870 (C.D.A., L.P.).
78. Daunt to Leahy, 29 July 1872 (C.D.A., L.P.).
79. Thornley, op. cit., p.160; Norman, op. cit., p.417 n.6.
80. S.P.O., C.S.O., R.P., 1873/12696.
81. See: *T.F.P.*, 27, 30 Jan. 1874, each edition from 3 Feb. 1874 to 27 Feb. 1874; *N.G.*, 28, 31 Jan. 1874, each edition from 4 Feb. 1874 to 25 Feb. 1874; *Irishman*, 21, 28 Feb. 1874; *Tablet*, 7 Feb. 1874; *L.R.*, 10 Feb. 1874.
82. *T.A.*, 20 Feb. 1875.
83. Leahy to Daunt 7 Dec. 1870 (N.L.I., W. J. O'Neill Daunt papers, MS 8046(7)).
84. Daunt to Leahy, 8 Dec. 1870 (C.D.A., L.P.).
85. Leahy to Daunt, 3 Aug. 1872 (N.L.I., ms 8046).
86. Daunt to Leahy, 20 Dec. 1870 (C.D.A., L.P.).
87. Leahy to Daunt, 14 Feb. and 1 Apr. 1871, see also letters 7 and 28 Dec. 1870 (N.L.I., MS 8046).
88. *T.F.P.*, 9 Jan. 1872.
89. See W. O'Brien, *Recollections*, pp139-141.
90. See *T.F.P.*, 30 Jan., 6, 13, 27 Feb. 1872.
91. Daunt to Leahy, 8 Dec. 1870 (C.D.A., L.P.).
92. *N.G.*, 20 Apr. 1872, 19 July 1873.
93. Letter in *T.A.*, 20 Jan. 1872.
94. *T.F.P.*, 24 Apr. 1877.
95. *T.F.P.*, 30 Jan. 1874.
96. *T.F.P.*, 3 Feb. 1874.
97. Parnell to Bishop John Power, 4 May 1880 (W.D.A.).
98. Names in *T.F.P.*, 9, 23 Feb., 5 Oct. 1850, 17 July 1852; *L.R.*, 8, 19 Feb. 1850; *F.J.*, 9 Jan. 1868 and sources in note 70 above.
99. O'Shea, op. cit., table 78, pp175-176.
100. Ibid.
101. *T.A.*, 27 Mar. 1886.
102. See e.g.: Bishop Keating of Ferns, to Slattery, 22 May 1849; Walsh of Ossory, to Slattery, 24 May 1849; Healy of Kildare to Slattery, 25 Apr. 1849; Archbishop John McHale of Tuam to Slattery, 7 July 1849; Murray to Slattery, 19, 21, 25, 27 July, 1 Aug. 1849. A copy of the address is in C.D.A. S.P. 1849/45.
103. Kirby to Walsh, 17 June 1887 (D.D.A., W.P.).
104. O'Shea, op. cit., table 79, p.177.
105. Blunt, *Land War*, p.100.
106. MS draft 1885 (C.D.A., C.P.); see also his letter in *T.L.*, 15 Apr. 1885.

107. *T.L.*, 15 Apr. 1885.
108. *T.P.*, 15 May 1885.
109. As in note 104.
110. *T.P.*, 2 Dec. 1887, 20 Sept. 1889; *T.N.*, 21 Sept. 1889; *T.A.*, 7 Sept. 1889; Police report, Thurles, 29 Nov. 1887 (S.P.O., Spec. Comm., 1888).
111. *U.I.*, 21 Oct. 1882.
112. See e.g., *T.L.*, 8, 18 Nov., 6, 13 Dec. 1882, 24 Jan. 1883, 7 Mar. 1883, 12 Sept. 1884.
113. See *T.F.P.*, 1 Sept., 17 Oct. 1876, 19 Mar. 1880; *C.C.*, 20 Mar. 1880.
114. *Tablet*, 14 Oct. 1876.
115. *T.L.*, 24 Jan. 1883.
116. *T.L.*, 31 Oct. 1884.
117. *T.L.*, 8 Nov. 1882.
118. O'Shea, op. cit., table 80, p.178.
119. *U.I.*, 27 Sept. 1884.
120. *T.L.*, 6 Dec. 1882 (Michael Hourigan C.C.).
121. O'Shea, op. cit., tables 81 and 82, pp179-182.
122. P.218.
123. *T.A.*, 8 Jan. 1881.
124. *T.L.*, 30 Jan. 1885.
125. *T.A.*, 30 Apr. 1881.
126. Letter in *T.P.*, 25 Mar. 1881.
127. O'Shea, op. cit., table 82, pp81-82.
128. *U.I.*, 21 Apr. 1883; *T.L.*, 14 Apr. 1883.
129. Same as note 121.
130. *T.A.*, 7 Apr. 1883.
131. *T.A.*, 21 Mar. 1883.
132. Letter from Robert Foran P.P. in *T.L.*, 26 May 1883.
133. *T.L.*, 11, 25 Apr. 1883.
134. Letter in *F.J.*, 29 Mar. 1883; *T.L.*, 31 Mar. 1883.
135. See *U.I.*, 5 May 1883; *N.G.*, 12 May 1883; S.C. Irlanda, 1883, vol. 40 ff.75-77, 108-113.
136. Ibid. ff. 131-133, 146-149.
137. *T.A.*, 19, 26 May 1883; *T.L.*, 19 May 1883; *U.I.*, 19, 26, May 1883; Thurles P.L.U. minute book, Feb. 1883-Aug. 1883, 22 May 1883, Cashel P.L.U. minute book no. 73, Dec. 1882-June 1883, p.449.
138. Text in *F.J.*, 15 May 1883 (Latin text in C.D.A., C.P.).
139. *T.L.*, 26 May 1883, 6 June 1883; *T.A.*, 9 June 1883; *T.P.*, 25 May 1883.
140. *T.L.*, 26 May 1883.
141. Burke to Kirby, 17 May 1883 (K.P.).
142. Hasson to Kirby 4 June 1883 (K.P.).
143. *U.I.*, 2 June 1883.
144. *F.J.*, 5 Nov. 1883 (This shows his name as Walsh).
145. *T.L.*, 26 May 1883.
146. Croke to Archbishop McCabe, Dublin, 10 Dec.1883 (C.D.A., C.P.).
147. *F.J.*, 12 Dec. 1883, *T.L.*, 14 Dec. 1883, *T.A.*, 15 Dec. 1883.
148. Diocesan breakdown in S.C. Irlanda, vol. 40, f.461.
149. Davitt, op. cit., p.400.
150. O'Shea, op. cit., table 82, pp181-182.
151. *U.I.*, 5 May 1883.
152. *T.P.*, 24 Apr. 1888, 14 Sept. 1888; *F.J.*, 24 Oct. 1888.
153. *T.N.*, 1 Jan. 1890.
154. *M.T.*, 18 Jan. 1890.
155. *T.P.*, 10 Jan. 1890, *M.T.*, 8 Jan., 25 Oct. 1890; *Nationalist,* 4 Oct., 12, 22, 26, 29 Nov. 1890.
156. *Nationalist,* 3 Jan. 1891.
157. O'Shea, op. cit., table 83, pp183-186.

158. See n.248.
159. *N.G.*, 18 Mar. 1891, *Nationalist*, 25 Mar. 1891.
160. *Nationalist*, 28 Mar., 9 May, 2, 12 Sept. 1891; Police Report, 5 Apr. 1891, 521S/3333 (S.P.O., C.B.S., D.I.Cs., Carton 3).
161. *Nationalist*, 17 Dec. 1890, 15, 18 Apr. 1891; *T.P.*, 17 Apr. 1891, *U.I.*, 18 Apr. 1891; *M.T.*, 13 Dec. 1890; Police report, Nenagh 29 Jan. 1891. (S.P.O., Police and crime records, reports 1890-94).
162. See *U.I.*, 20 Dec. 1890, 10 Jan., 21 Mar., 5 Dec. 1891; *F.J.*, 17, 19 Dec. 1890; 16 Dec. 1890. (S.P.O., C.B.S., D.I.Cs. 1890-1891, 2225/S), (N.L.I., J.F.X. O'Brien papers, MS 15376); E. Larkin. 'Launching the counterattack': in *Review of Politics*, xxviii, (July 1966), pp364-5; F. S. L. Lyons, *Charles Stewart Parnell (Fontana ed. 1978)*, p.582.
163. *Nationalist*, 24 Dec. 1891.
164. For details of this see Lyons, *Parnell*, pp310-16.
165. Humphreys to Dillon, 17 Jan. 1891. (T.C.D., Dillon papers).
166. Humphreys to O'Brien, 20 Jan. 1891 (N.L.I., T. P. Gill papers, MS 13507).
167. *M.T.*, 7 Mar., 9 May 1891 (Denis Sheehan and James Halpin), Keller to J.F.X. O'Brien 17 Dec. 1890, and 19 Dec. 1890 (J.F.X. O'Brien papers, MS 15376) Keller to William O'Brien, 20 Dec. 1890 (N.L.I., MS 13432); Croke to William O'Brien, 16 Dec. 1890, 22 Mar. 29 July 1891 (N.L.I., MS 13507).
168. Croke to Walsh, January 1891 (D.D.A., W.P.).
169. *F.J.*, 15, 22 Dec. 1890, 12 Jan. 1891; *N.G.*, 17 Dec. 1890, 14 Jan. 1891; *T.P.*, 19 Dec. 1890; *Nationalist*, 24 Dec. 1890, 7 Oct. 1891; *Insuppressible*, 12 Jan. 1891; *M.T.*, 17 Jan. 1891.
170. *Nationalist*, 27 May 1891, 3 June 1891; *L.R.*, 22, 26, 29 May, 5 June 1891; police report, Waterford, 22 May 1891 (S.P.O., Police and crime records, reports, 1890-94).
171. Letter in *T.P.*, 27 Feb. 1891; *N.G.*, 26 Feb. 1891; Croke to Walsh, 25 Mar. 1891 (C.D.A., L.P.).
172. Resolutions, 25 June 1891 (C.D.A., C.P.); report, 7 July 1891 (S.P.O., C.B.S. 1891, 255S/4025).
173. Confidential circular to the clergy of Cashel and Emly 'and to them alone', 2 Mar. 1891 (C.D.A., C.P.).
174. Croke to Walsh, 19 Dec. 1890 (C.D.A., C.P.).
175. Croke to Ryan, 9 Nov. 1891 (C.D.A., C.P.).
176. *T.P.*, 20 Nov. 1891, *L.R.*, 20 Nov. 1891.
177. *F.J.*, 15 Dec. 1890; *N.G.*, 17 Dec. 1890; *T.P.*, 19 Dec. 1890.
178. *L.R.*, 5 June 1891.
179. Police reports, Nenagh, 8, 12 Jan. 1891 (S.P.O., Police and crime records, police reports, 1890-94); *N.G.*, 14 Jan. 1891; *M.T.*, 17 Jan. 1891.
180. Police report, Scragg, 9 Jan. 1891. (S.P.O., Police and crime reports, 1890-94).
181. *L.R.*, 28 Mar., 4 Aug. 1891; *Nationalist*, 6, 9 May, 7 Oct. 1891; *Tablet*, 16 May 1891; *U.I.*, 23 May 1891; *N.G.*, 27 May 1891; *F.J.*, 3 Aug. 1891; report, 5 May 1891 (S.P.O., C.B.S., D.I.Cs. 1887-1895, police reports, 523S/3612 Carton 3), police reports, Thurles, 12 Mar., 5 June, 8 Aug. 1891 (S.P.O., Police and crime records, reports, 1890-94 Carton 3).
182. Letter in *L.R.*, 17 Mar. 1891.
183. Statements in *Insuppressible*, 3 Jan. 1891; *M.T.*, 17 Jan., 25 Apr., 9 May 1891; *T.P.*, 9 Oct. 1891; *Tablet*, 13 Dec. 1890.
184. *L.R.*, 5 June 1891; *C.C.*, 3 June 1891, Croke to E. D. Gray, 5 June 1891, 13 June 1891 (C.D.A., C.P.).
185. See *Nationalist*, 3 Jan., 31 Oct. 1891; *C.C.*, 28 Jan., 21 Feb., 4 Apr. 1891; *N.G.*, 6 Dec. 1890, 14 Jan, 14, 17 Feb. 1891; *F.J.*, 11, 12 Mar. 1891; *U.I.*, 14 Mar., 16 May 1891 Nenagh, 9, 31 Jan. 1891, 30 Sept. 1891, Roscrea, 1 Mar. 1891, Newport, 3 Mar. 1891, Thurles, 28 Feb. 1891, 12 Mar. 1891, Waterford 20 Apr. 1891 (Police and Crime, Police Reports, 1890-94, Carton 3). Thurles P.L.U. minute book, Jan.-Aug. 1891 (Tipperary Co Library), pp169, 216, 217.

186. *Nationalist,* 21 Mar. 1891.
187. Police reports, Cloughjordan, 31 Dec. 1890, Templemore, 19 Feb. 1891 (S.P.O., Police and crime reports, 1890-94).
188. Ibid., Templemore, 16 Jan. 1891.
189. See n.157.
190. *Nationalist,* 6 Dec. 1890.
191. His references in *T.P.,* 19 Dec. 1890, 3 Apr. 1891.
192. *M.T.,* 7 Mar. 1891.
193. *Nationalist,* 11 Mar. 1891.
194. See H. Harrison, *Parnell Vindicated* (London, 1931), pp295, 300-301.
195. *U.I.,* 15 Dec. 1890 (Canon John O'Mahony, Cork).
196. *F.J.,* 22 Dec. 1890 (Edmund O'Leary).
197. *Nationalist,* 11 Mar. 1891 (Archdeacon Ryan).
198. *M.T.,* 18 July 1891.
199. *M.T.,* 25 July 1891.
200. Murphy to Harrington, 16 Sept. 1891 (N.L.I., Harrington papers, MS 8576).
201. *Nationalist,* 14 Nov. 1891.
202. *M.T.,* 31 Jan. 1891.
203. *M.T.,* 6 Dec. 1890.
204. *M.T.,* 20 Dec. 1890.
205. E.g., Fr. Horgan, Tralee, to Croke, 14 Jan. 1891 (C.D.A., C.P.).
206. *Tablet,* 13 Dec. 1890.
207. *Nationalist,* 3 Jan. 1891.
208. *C.C.,* 18 Apr. 1891, see also *T.P.,* 12 Dec. 1890, *Nationalist,* 4 Feb. 1891.
209. *M.T.,* 25 Apr. 1891.
210. His letters in *C.C.,* 7 Jan. 1891, 14 Jan. 1891, *T.P.,* 27 Feb. 1891, *L.R.,* 3, 10 Mar. 1891.
211. Letter in *F.J.,* 17 Dec. 1890.
212. *N.G.,* 18 Mar. 1891, *Nationalist,* 25 Mar. 1891, *F.J.,* 18 Dec. 1890 (Robert Power and Nicholas Murphy).
213. Letter in *Nationalist,* 31 Dec. 1890.
214. E.g., *M.T.,* 20 Dec. 1890 (John Tuohy P.P.).
215. *F.J.,* 18 Dec. 1890.
216. *L.R.,* 5 Dec. 1890.
217. *Nationalist,* 20, 24 Dec. 1890; *N.G.,* 17 Dec. 1890; *M.T.,* 6 Dec. 1890; *F.J.,* 22 Dec. 1890.
218. *Nationalist,* 24 Dec. 1890, 3 Jan., 1891; *T.P.,* 2 Jan. 1891.
219. Humphreys to William O'Brien, 20 Jan. 1891 (N.L.I., T.P., Gill papers, MS 13507) also *T.P.,* 19 Dec. 1890.
220. *M.T.,* 6 Dec. 1890.
221. Cardinal Logue to Parnell, 15 Oct. 1890 (N.L.I., T. P. Gill papers, MS 13506).
222. *M.T.,* 13 Dec. 1890.
223. *Insuppressible,* 19 Dec. 1890, 6 Jan. 1891.
224. *M.T.,* 6 Dec. 1890.
225. *M.T.,* 27 Dec. 1890.
226. Police report, Thurles, 6 Mar. 1891 (S.P.O., Police crime reports, 1890-1894).
227. *C.C.,* 18 Mar. 1891, (S.P.O. P.C., Police reports 1890-94, Carton 3, Police report, Waterford, 24 Mar. 1891 (S.P.O., Police and crime reports, 1890-94).
228. *Nationalist,* 24, 31 Oct. 1891.
229. Brownrigg to Croke, 19 Dec. 1890 (C.D.A., C.P.).
230. See, e.g., *Nationalist,* 24 Dec. 1890; R. Barry O'Brien, *The life of Charles Stewart Parnell,* (London, 2 vols. 1898), ii, 300-309. Reports (number 2267) for Dec. 1890 (S.P.O., C.B.S., 1890-1891).
231. *N.G.,* 18 July 1891.
232. Police report, 7 July 1891 (S.P.O., C.B.S, 1891, report. 255S/4025).
233. Ibid.
234. *Insuppressible,* 20 Dec. 1890.

235. *T.P.*, 10 July 1891.
236. *M.T.*, 18 July 1891.
237. See e.g.: *F.J.*, 12 Dec. 1890; *M.T.*, 28 Aug. 1891; *U.I.*, 6 June 1891; Bishop Brownrigg to Croke, 13 Dec. 1890 (C.D.A, C.P.), police report, Thurles, 25 Mar. 1891 (S.P.O., Police and crime, reports, 1890-94).
238. *L.R.*, 5 Dec. 1890; *N.G.*, 28 Jan. 1891; *Nationalist*, 4 Feb. 1891. (David Humphreys and J. J. Crowley C.C.).
239. *M.T.*, 6 June 1891.
240. *Nationalist*, 7 Mar. 1891.
241. Letter in *Nationalist*, 19 Aug. 1891 and statements in *L.R.*, 5 May 1891; *Insuppressible*, 20 Dec. 1890.
242. See Lyons, *Parnell*, pp572, 586.
243. *M.T.*, 2, 23 May 1891; *L.R.*, 5 June 1891; *Nationalist*, 13 June, 21 Nov. 1891; *F.J.*, 9 Nov. 1891.
244. *T.P.*, 23 Jan. 1891; *N.G.*, 9 May 1891; *T.P.*, 22 May 1891.
245. See N.L.I., J.F.X. O'Brien papers, MS 13432(10) for some of his letters, and MS 13438(1) for references of the local T.D.A. secretary, Lewis O'Brien Dalton, to Humphreys; Humphreys to J.F.X. O'Brien, 8 Feb. 1891 (Dillon papers, T.C.D.).
246. MS 13431(2); see also MS 13432.
247. *L.R.*, 5 May 1891.
248. N.L.I., Harrington papers, MS 8576(26).
249. *Nationalist*, 9 Aug. 1890.
250. *M.T.*, 21 Nov., 5 Dec. 1891; South eastern divisional report, 27 Jan. 1891 (S.P.O., C.B.S., D.I.Cs.
251. Letter in *Nationalist*, 1 July 1891.
252. *Nationalist*, 28 Nov. 1891.
253. *Nationalist*, 5 Dec. 1891.
254. Ibid.; *F.J.*, 15 Dec. 1890; report, Roscrea, 1 Mar. 1891. (S.P.O., Police and crime records, reports, 1890-94).
255. *Nationalist*, 18, 21 Nov. 1891; report for Tipperary, 4 Apr. 1891 (S.P.O., Police and crime, reports, 1890-94).
256. Pp106-07.
257. *Nationalist*, 14 Mar., 1 Apr. 1891; report, Newport, 9 Feb. 1891 (S.P.O., Police and crime, reports, 1890-94).
258. See *F.J.*, 17, 31 Mar., 24 July 1891; *M.T.*, 21 Mar. 1891, *C.C.*, 6 May 1891.
259. South eastern divisional report, 30 Sept. 1891 (S.P.O., C.B.S., 4208S).
260. *Nationalist*, 11 Mar. 1891; *F.J.*, 11 Mar. 1891; Davitt, op. cit., pp 660-661.
261. O'Shea, op. cit., table 85, pp 189-192.
262. E.g. *M.T.*, 7 Mar. 1891, *Nationalist*, 10 June 1891.
263. O'Shea, op. cit., table 86, pp193-194.
264. *T.P.*, 7 Aug. 1891 (Thomas O'Dwyer P.P.).
265. *M.T.*, 16 May 1891.
266. *M.T.*, 27 Feb. 1891.
267. *Nationalist*, 6 June 1891.
268. *M.T.*, 14 Mar. 1891.
269. *Nationalist*, 28 May 1890, 16 Aug. 1890, 25 Mar. 1891.
270. *Nationalist*, 28 Mar. 1891.
271. E.g., *T.P.*, 14 Nov. 1884, 18 June 1886; E. Dwyer Gray to Croke undated, but probably Nov. 1884 (C.D.A., C.P.).
272. *N.G.*, 17 Dec. 1890; *M.T.*, 6, 27, Dec. 1890; *T.P.*, 19 Dec. 1890; *F.J.*, 22 Dec. 1890; *Nationalist*, 16 May 1891; 13 June 1891; Police report, Thurles, 12 Mar. 1891. (S.P.O., Police and crime, reports 1890-94).
273. *Nationalist*, 10 Dec. 1890; *Insuppressible*, 14 Jan. 1891. (David Humphreys and Michael B. Corry).
274. *Nationalist*, 11 Mar. 1891.
275. *Nationalist*, 20 Dec. 1890.
276. Croke to William O'Brien, 24 Feb. 1891. (N.L.I., T.P. Gill papers, MS 13507).

277. Letter in *Nationalist*, 24 Jan. 1891.

278. Croke to Walsh, January 1891. (D.D.A., W.P.).

279. Letter in *L.R.*, 31 July 1891.

280. For details of infighting and secret negotiations see Gray to Croke 27 Apr. 1891, 3 Aug. 1891, Croke to Gray 15 May 1891 (C.D.A., C.P.); Police reports, Thurles, 8 May 1891 and 24 May 1891 (S.P.O., Police and crime reports 1890-1894), Larkin, 'Counter attack' pp366-371.

281. Gray to Croke 3 Aug. 1891; 22 Aug. 1891; Mrs Gray (his mother) to Croke, 22 Aug. 1891 (C.D.A., C.P.).

282. *Nationalist*, 22 Aug., 23 Sept. 1891.

283. *M.T.*, 26 Sept. 1891.

284. *M.T.*, 19 Sept. 1891.

285. *M.T.*, 20 Dec. 1890; report, Nenagh, 7 Mar. 1891, Roscrea, 12 Apr. 1891 (S.P.O., Police and crime reports, 1890-1894).

286. Police report, Thurles, 12 Mar. 1891. (S.P.O., Police and crime reports, 1890-94).

287. See Archbishop Walsh to Croke, 13, 14, 20, 22, 23, 24 Mar. 1892 (C.D.A., C.P.).

288. See, e.g., editorial in *U.I.*, 17 Oct. 1891.

289. *Nationalist*, 7 Oct. 1891.

290. *M.T.*, 24 Oct. 1891.

291. Ibid.

292. *F.J.*, 9 Nov. 1891; *Nationalist*, 11 Nov. 1891.

293. *L.R.*, 13 Nov. 1891.

294. James Joyce, *Portrait of the artist as a young man* (London, 1916), pp34, 37-9.

Bibliography

Primary Sources

A. MANUSCRIPT MATERIAL

British Library
Balfour papers, Add. MSS 49821-2 (photostats in Glenstal Abbey)
Gladstone papers, Add. MSS 44434

Cashel Diocesan Archives
Papers of Archbishop Bray
Papers of Archbishop Croke
Papers of Archbishop Laffan
Papers of Archbishop Leahy
Papers of Archbishop Slattery
Notebooks of Canon Fogarty (deposited in St Patrick's College)
The diary of Fr O'Carroll

Dublin Diocesan Archives (Photocopies in Glenstal Abbey)
Papers of Cardinal Cullen
Papers of Cardinal McCabe
Papers of Archbishop Walsh

London (Bayswater)
Papers of Cardinal Manning (transcripts at Glenstal Abbey)

Mooresfort House
Mooresfort Papers (property of Mr Arthur Moore)

National Library of Ireland
Samuel Lee Anderson papers (police reports), MS 11289
F.S. Burke papers, MS 10700
Isaac Butt papers, MS 8706, MS 8698.
Election papers, MS 11037.
T.P. Gill papers, MS 13500, MSS 13506-7.
Timothy Harrington papers, MS 5384, MS 8576.
Timothy Harrington letter books, MS 8933.
I.N.L.L., papers, includes Ladies Land League|, MS 8291, MSS 17761-2.
MSS 17705-6, MS 17709, MS 17712, MS 17715, MS 17693, MS 17699.
Letters of Fr John Kenyon P.P., MS 10518.
Larcom Papers, MS 7590, MS 7594, MS 7636, MS 7729.
Confidential letters from Frederick Lucas at Rome to Charles Gavan Duffy 1885, MS 3738.
Mayo (Naas) papers, MSS 11036-37, MSS 11188-89.
Monsell papers, MS 20673, MS 20677, MS 20683.
Memorials of Irish members of parliament and of a committee of the lower catholic clergy of Ireland to Pope Pius IX concerning clerical connections with politics, MS 1587.
James F.X. O'Brien Papers, MSS 13431-33, MS 13465, MS 13471, MS 15376.
William O'Brien papers, MS 5930.

W.J. O'Neill Daunt Papers, MS 8046.
Otway Papers, MS 13008.
Redmond Papers, MS 15223.
P.J. Smyth Papers, MS 8215.
William Smith O'Brien Papers, MS 446.
Diaries of John Trant, MS 2567.
Trant Papers, unsorted in Box 246.
Alfred Webb Papers, MS 1745.
Minute books of the Young Ireland Society, 1881-86, MS 16095, MS 19158, MS 16601.

Oireachtas Library, Leinster House, Dublin
Transcripts of trial of Charles J. Kickham, 1866 (also in N.L.I., microfilm P.4050).

Rome
Archives of Propaganda, Congregazioni Particolari, vol. 158 (National Library of Ireland, microfilm P.5524).
Archives of Propaganda, Scritture Riferite nei Congressi, Irlanda (Glenstal Abbey transcripts).
Kirby papers (in Irish College).
Register of the Irish College.
Abbot Smith papers (in St. Paul's-outside-the-walls).

State Paper Office — Dublin Castle
Chief Secretary's Office, registered papers.
Irish National League Proceedings 1879-1890.
Crime branch special papers.
Fenian Papers.
Outrage papers — County Tipperary.
Police and crime records.
Crime branch special, D.I.C. reports.

Tipperary County Library, Thurles
Poor Law Union minute books for the unions of Cashel, Clonmel and Thurles.

Trinity College, Dublin
John Dillon papers.

University College, Cork
William O'Brien papers.

Waterford Diocesan Archives
Unsorted collection.
St John's College registers, 1814-22, 1822-26, 1826-54, 1854-73, 1872-88, 1887-1918.

B. WORKS OF REFERENCE
Bassett, G.H., *The book of County Tipperary* (Dublin, 1889).
Blackstone, W., *Commentaries on the laws of England* (London, 1800).
Burke's Peerage (99th ed.) London, 1949).
Catholic Encyclopedia (London, 1908-12).
Dod's Parliamentary Companion, 1852, 1857-1858, 1860, 1864, 1869-1870, 1873-1874.
Hamell, P. J., *Indexes to the Irish Ecclesiastical Record 1864-1962* (Dublin).
Hamell, P. J., *Index of Maynooth students and ordinations, 1795-1895*, A-Mc, Part 1, names beginning A to Mc, in *Irish Ecclesiastical Record* (December 1967-December 1968).
Hamell, P. J., *Index of Maynooth students and ordinations 1795-1895*, Part 2, Mc-Z, unpublished.
Hayes, P. J., *History of Tipperary newspapers* (Thurles 1960; unpublished typescript,

Tipperary County Library, Thurles).
Hayes, R. J., *Manuscript sources for the history of Irish civilisation.*
Index to Townlands, Ordnance Survey of Ireland, 1861.
Index of all articles in the *Irish Monthly* from July 1873 to December 1897 in *Irish Monthly,* xxv (1897).
'Index of surnames in Griffith's *Valuation'* (Typescript in National Library).
Irish Catholic Directory, annual 1836-1946.
Key to catholic ecclesiastical map of Ireland, containing a list of all the chapels, (Dublin, 1859).
Lewis, S., *A Topographical dictionary of Ireland,* (2 Vols. London, 1837).
McLoughney, M., 'A bibliography of Tipperary history and antiquities' (Typescript in County Library Thurles).
Maynooth College Calendarium, annual, 1863-1868, 1869-1870, 1880-1886, 1886-1891.
Nolan, William, *Sources of local studies,* (Dublin, 1977).
Obituaries in *Catholic Record of Waterford and Lismore,* i, (March 1913-February 1914), (March 1917-February 1919), vii (March 1919-February 1920).
Pobal Ailbe: Cashel and Emly, census of population 1841-1971 (Thurles, 1975, with accompanying atlas).

C. NEWSPAPERS

Cashel Gazette	*Clare Journal*	*Clare Champion*
Clonmel Chronicle	*Cork Examiner*	*Express*
Freemans Journal	*Gael*	*Insuppressible*
Irishman	*Irish People*	*Irish Times*
Kilkenny Journal	*Limerick Reporter and Tipperary Vindicator*	*Midland Tribune and Tipperary Sentinel*
Munster Express	*Nation*	*Nationalist*
National Press	*Nenagh Guardian*	*New York Irish People*
Tablet	*Times*	*Tribune*
Tipperary	*Tipperary Advocate*	*Tipperary Free Press*
Tipperary Leader (1850s)	*Tipperary Leader* (1880s)	*Tipperary Nationalist*
Tipperary People	*Tipperary Star*	*United Ireland*
United Irishman	*Waterford News and General Advertiser*	

D. OFFICIAL PUBLICATIONS

1. Richard Griffith, *General valuation of rateable property in Ireland,* 1850-1855.

2. Parliamentary Proceedings
Hansard's parliamentary debates, 3rd Series, Vols 85, 87, 120, 121, 137, 151, 161, 164, 183, 190, 247, 261, 266, 269, 275, 284, 287, 293, 295, 302, 341, (1846-90).

3. Parliamentary Papers
Papers presented to the House of Commons relating to the Royal College of St. Patrick's, Maynooth, 1812-1813(204), vi.
Reports from the Select Committee on the State of Ireland, 1825(129), viii.
Eighth report of the Commissioners of Irish Education, inquiry and appendix to the eighth report, 1826-27(509), xiii.
First report of the Commissioners on Public Instruction, Ireland, 1835(45), (46), xxxiii.
Second report of the Commissioners on Public Instruction, Ireland, 1835(47), xxxiv.
Return of all notices served upon relieving officers of Poor Law districts in Ireland by landowners and others under the act of last session, 11 and 12 Vict. c.47 intituled An Act for the protection and relief of the destitute poor, evicted from their dwellings, 1849(517), xlix.
Census of Ireland 1851.
Report of Her Majesty's Commissioners appointed to inquire into the Management and

government of the College of Maynooth, Part 1, report and appendix, 1854-55 (1896), xxii. *Part II, minutes of evidence and answers to paper (K) etc.* (1896) 1854-55, xxii.

A return of the names, ages and number of students attending the College of Maynooth on the 31st day of August 1844 (being the end of the academic year); the names and numbers, who have entered each year from that time till the 31st day of August 1861, with the age of each student at entering, the names and number, who have left college during that period, who have not completed their course of education, with the date of leaving. 1862(450), xliii.

Minutes of evidence taken before the Select Committee of the Tipperary election petition with the proceedings of the committee, 1867(211), viii.

Index to the minutes of evidence taken before the Select Committee on the Tipperary election petition, 1867. 1867(211-1), viii.

Report from the Select Committee on parliamentary and municipal elections, together with the proceedings of the committee, minutes of evidence and appendix, 1868-69(352), viii.

Copy of minutes of the evidence taken at the trial of the Cashel election petition 1869, 1868-69(65), xlix.

Reports from Poor Law inspectors on the wages of agricultural labourers in Ireland, 1870(C35), 1870, xiv.

Reports of Commissioners appointed under the Act of the 15th and 16th Victoria Cap. 57 for the Purposes of making inquiry into existence of corrupt practices at the last election of Cashel, together with the minutes of evidence, (C9), 1870, xxxii.

Census of Ireland 1871.

©*opy of the shorthand writer's notes of the judgement of Mr. Justice Keogh on the trial of the Galway County election petition,* 1872(241), xlviii.

Copy of minutes of the evidence taken at the trial of the Galway County election petition 1872, with an appendix and index, 1872(241-1); xlviii.

Copy of the shorthand writer's notes of the judgement delivered by the judges of the Court of Common Pleas in Ireland on the 29th Day of April, upon the motion to set aside the petition against the return of John Mitchel for the County of Tipperary on the ground of the death of the sitting member, 1875(241), lx.

Return of owners of land of one acre and upwards in Ireland, (C1492), 1876, lxxx.

Report of Her Majesty's Commissioners of inquiry into the working of the Landlord and Tenant (Ireland) Act 1870 and the acts amending the same, Vol. 2, *Digest of evidence, Minutes of evidence* part 1; Vol. 3, *Minutes of evidence,* Part II, *Appendices,* (C. 7779.1), 1881, xviii, (Bessborough Commission).

Return by provinces and counties, (compiled from returns made to the inspector general, Royal Irish Constabulary), of cases of evictions, which have come to the knowledge of the constabulary in each of the years from 1849 to 1880 inclusive, 1881(185), lxxvii.

Census of Ireland 1881.

Return showing for each month of the years 1879 and 1880 the number of Land League meetings held and agrarian crimes reported to the Inspector General of the Royal Irish Constabulary in each County throughout Ireland, 1881(5), lxxvii.

Return compiled from returns made to the inspector general of the Royal Irish Constabulary of places of eviction, which have come to the knowledge of the constabulary in the quarter ended 31st day of March 1882, showing the number of families evicted in each county in Ireland during the quarter and the number re-admitted as tenants and the number re-admitted as caretakers, 1882(145), lv and 1882(199), lv.

Return of proceedings under the Land Law (Ireland) Act 1881 up to 31st day of July 1883; return showing for each county in Ireland the number of originating notices to have rents fixed lodged with the Irish Land Commissioners during the year ended 21st August 1882, and also the number in each month from 1st September 1882 to 30th April 1883, 1883(352), lviii.

Report from the Select Committee on agricultural labourers (Ireland), together with the proceedings of the committee and minutes of evidence (London, 1884).

Report of the Royal Commission on the Land Law (Ireland) Act 1881 and the Purchase of

Land (Ireland) Act 1885, Vol. 2, *Minutes of evidence and appendices,* (C. 4969), 1887, xxiv.

Return of the number of cases of boycotting and the number of persons wholly and partially boycotted throughout Ireland on 31st July 1887, 1887(280), lxvii.

Return according to provinces and counties of judicial rents fixed by sub-commissioners and civil bill courts as notified to the Irish Land Commission during the months of September and October 1886, specifying dates and amounts respectively of the last increase of rent, where ascertained etc.; similar return for the months of March and April 1887, (C. 5072), 1887, lxviii.

Return showing the working of the Labourers Acts (Ireland), the number of cottages erected and the expenses connected therewith up to 31st March 1887 etc., 1887(202), lxviii.

Return compiled from returns made to the inspector general of the Royal Irish Constabulary of cases of eviction from agricultural holdings, which have come to the knowledge of the constabulary in the quarter ended 30th day of June 1887, showing the number of tenants in each county in Ireland during the quarter and the number re-admitted as tenants or as caretakers on the day the decree was executed, (C. 5095), 1887, lxviii.

Return of the number of evictions from agricultural holdings which have come to the knowledge of the constabulary, and also the number of tenancies determined in the quarter ended 30th day of June 1888. (C. 5498), 1888, lxxxiii.

Return of the number of evictions from agricultural holdings which have come to the knowledge of the constabulary, and also the number of tenancies determined in the quarter ended 31st day of December 1888, (C. 5642), 1889, lxi.

Return of the number of eviction notices filed in the High Court of Justice and the county courts in Ireland under Section 7 of the Land Law Ireland Act 1887 during the quarter ending 31st Day of December 1890, (C. 6248) 1890-91, lxiv.

Return of the number of eviction notices filed in the High Court of Justice and the County Courts in Ireland under Section 7 of the Land Law Ireland Act 1887 during the quarter ending 30th day of June 1891, (C. 6447), 1890-91, lxiv.

Census of Ireland 1891.

The agricultural labourer 1893, iv, Ireland, 1892-3, xxxvii.

E. CONTEMPORARY WORKS

Anson, W. R., *Principles of the English law of contract* (4th Edition, London 1886).

Bagenal, P. H., *The Irish agitation in parliament and on the platform; a complete history of Irish politics for the year 1879* (Dublin, 1880).

Bailly, F., *Theologia Dogmatica et Moralis and usum seminariorum,* vii, (Paris, 1830).

Barry O'Brien, R., *Fifty years of concessions to Ireland 1831-1881* (London, 1883-85).

Barry O'Brien, R., *The parliamentary history of the Irish land question 1829-1869 and the origin and results of the Ulster Custom* (3rd edition, London, 1880).

Barry O'Brien, R., *The life of Charles Stewart Parnell* (2 Vols., London, 1898).

Comerford, M., *Collections relating to the diocese of Kildare and Leighlin* (Dublin and London, 1883).

Cortes, J. D., *Essays in Catholicism, Liberalism and Socialism (Dublin 1874). (Translated by Rev. William McDonald, rector of the Irish College, Salamanca)*

Crolly, George, *Disputationes theologiae de justitia et jure,* iii (Dublin, 1877).

Dillon, M., *The history and development of banking in Ireland* (Dublin, 1889).

Evans, D. M., *Facts, failures and frauds* (London, 1859).

Fitzgibbon, Gerald, *Ireland in 1868: The battlefield for English party strife* (London, 1868).

Fitzgerald, Rev. P., *A narrative of the proceedings of the confederates of '48* (Dublin, 1868).

Gavan Duffy, C., *The league of north and south* (London, 1886).

Gavan Duffy, C., *Young Ireland,* Part II (Dublin, 1883).

Gury, P. J. P., *Compendium theologiae moralis,* (Ratisbon, 1874).
Haverty, M., *History of Ireland* (Dublin, 1860).
Healy, John, *Maynooth College, its centenary history, 1795-1895* (Dublin, 1895).
Lavelle, Rev. Patrick, *The Irish landlord since the revolution* (Dublin, 1870).
Lecky, W. E. H., *Leaders of public opinion in Ireland* (New York, 1889).
Lucas, E., *The Life of Frederick Lucas M.P.* (Dublin, 1887).
O'Connell, M. J., *Charles Bianconi, A biography, 1786-1875* (London, 1878).
Sullivan, A. M., *Chapters from Irish History* (London).
Sullivan, A. M., *New Ireland* (London, 1877).

F. CONTEMPORARY PAMPHLETS

Anonymous, *The land conference, Tuesday, 29 April 1880* (Dublin, 1880).
Bagenal, P. H., *The priest in politics* (London, 1893).
Brady, W. M., *Rome and fenianism — the Pope's anti-Parnellite circular* (London, 1883).
Burke, Rev. M., *Observations on the Queen's Colleges Ireland* (Dublin 1849).
Butt, Isaac, *Fixity of tenure* (Dublin, 1867).
Dawson, Rev. Massy, *The secret history of Romanism* (1853).
Finn, Rev. T., *Notes on the history of two Irish estates* (Dublin, 1881).
Humphreys, Rev. David, *The logic of the land bill* (Dublin, 1881).
Jones, J. L., *Political issues of the nineteenth century, with important statistics* (London, 1886).
Keane, M., *The Irish land question* (Dublin, 1868).
Keller, Rev. D., *The struggle for life on the Ponsonby estate* (London, 1887).
Keller, Rev. D., *The Ponsonby estate and Mr Smith-Barry (London, 1889).*
Lavelle, Rev. P., Patriotism Vindicated (1867).
Leo XIII *Inscrutabili* (21 April, 1878) (contained in *Select letters and addresses on social questions,* London, 1950. All Leo XIII's encyclicals listed here are in this volume).
Leo XIII, *Quod Apostolici Muneris* (12 December 1878).
Leo XIII, *Immortale Dei* (1 November 1885).
Leo XIII, *Libertas Praestantissimum* (20 June 1888).
Leo XIII, *Sapientiae Christianae* (10 January 1890).
Leo XIII, *Rerum Novarum* (15 May 1891).
Liberal Union of Ireland, *The Plan of Campaign on the Smith-Barry Estate, Tipperary* (Dublin, 1890).
Liberal Union of Ireland, *The Plan of Campaign on the Ponsonby Estate* (Dublin, 1890).
Meagher, Rev. Thomas, *The Roman Law of landlord and tenant, with suggestions for its application to Irish tenure* (Dublin, 1854).
Meagher, Rev. T., *Land tenure and the lamentable conditions of the rural poor* (Dublin, 1878).
Mitchel, John, *Ireland revisited* (New York, 1875).
Murray, Rev. Patrick, *Essays, chiefly theological,* iv (Dublin, 1853).
O'Reilly, Rev. E. J., *The relation of the church to society* (London, 1892).
Pastoral address of the Roman Catholic archbishops and bishops to the catholic clergy and people of Ireland (Dublin, 1885).
Queensbury, Charlotte, *Ireland's future.,* (Maidenhead, 1886) (An appreciation of P. J. Smyth).
Report of the committee of the Catholic University and list of subscriptions (Dublin, 1852).
Ryan, Rev. A., *St. Patrick, apostle of Ireland* (Dublin, 1890).
Ryan, Rev. A., *Sermons 1877-1887* (Dublin, 1890).
Smith-Barry, A. H., *A Letter to the Times.*
Smyth, P. J., *The priest in politics* (Dublin, 1885).
Smyth, P. J., *A plea for a peasant proprietary* (Dublin, 1871).
Walsh, Rev. W. J., *A plain exposition of the Irish Land Act of 1881* (Dublin 1881).

G. CONTEMPORARY ARTICLES

Anonymous, 'The Church of Rome and her relations with secular governments' in *D.U.M.*, xxxviii (September 1851).

Anonymous, 'The Irish Elections' in *D.U.M.*, xl (July-December 1852).

Anonymous, 'The Irish College, Paris' in *I.E.R*, ii (1866), pp180-85, 252-62, ii.

Anonymous, 'Catholicity and the spirit of the age' in *Irish Monthly*, i (1873).

Anonymous, 'The Irish College at Rome' in *Irish Monthly*, ii (1874).

Anonymous, 'Ultramontane policy in Ireland', in *D.U.M.*, lxxxiv (1874).

Anonymous, 'The Principles of '89', in *I.E.R.*, 3rd series ii (1881).

Anonymous, 'Obligation of preaching', in *I.E.R.*, 3rd series iii (1882).

Anonymous, 'Divisible dues' in *I.E.R.*, 3rd series, v (1884).

Anonymous, 'Results of the Intermediate Examinations 1883' in *I.E.R.*, 3rd series iv (1883).

Anonymous, 'The obligation of denouncing the heads of secret societies' in *I.E.R.*, 3rd series, vii (1886).

Anonymous, 'Divisible dues' in *I.E.R.*, 3rd series, vii (1887).

Anonymous (C.J.M.), 'Frequent Communion', in *I.E.R.*, 3rd series, vii (1886). (two articles of same title).

Anonymous, 'Secret societies and the confessional' in *I.E.R.*, 3rd series, viii (1887).

Anonymous, 'Offerings given on the occasion of marriage' in *IER*, 3rd series, x, (1889).

Anonymous, 'The history of the devotion to the Sacred Heart of Jesus', in *I.E.R.*, 3rd series, xi (1890).

'Bishops of Dublin province, Mr. Justice Keogh and the clergy,' in *I.E.R.*, new series, viii (1872).

Cantwell, Rev. James, 'Confraternities, their object and use', in *I.E.R.*, 3rd series, iii (1882).

Conroy, George (Bishop of Ardagh), 'The ecclesiastical seminary' in *I.E.R.*, viii (1872).

Finlay, Peter, 'The church and secret societies' in *Irish Monthly*, xxv, (1897).

Gunn, J., 'The foundation of Maynooth College 1795', in *I.E.R.*, iv, (1883).

Gunn, J., 'Reminiscences of Maynooth', in *I.E.R.*, (1883), 3rd series, v (1884).

McD., W., 'Irish College, Salamanca' in *I.E.R.*, ix (1873) and x (1873-4).

Murphy, Rev. A., 'Frequent Communion' in *I.E.R.*, 3rd series, vii (1886).

Neville, Rev. H. F., Theology past and present at Maynooth', in *Dublin Review*, xxxiii (1879).

O'Connor, Rev. M., 'Sogarth Aroon', ("The Irish Priest"), in *I.E.R.*, v (1869).

O'Loan, D., 'The confraternity of the scapular of Our Lady of Mount Carmel', in *I.E.R.*, 3rd series, xi (1890).

O'Loan, D., 'Various confraternities and conditions to be observed in erecting them', in *I.E.R.*, 3rd series, xii (1891).

O'Neill, P., P.P., 'Clerical ministry and civil law in Ireland', in *I.E.R.*, 3rd series, viii (1887).

O'Reilly, E. J., S. J., 'The relation of the church to society', in *Irish Monthly*, iv, (1876).

Roche, J. J., 'Frequent Communion', in *I.E.R.*, 3rd series, viii (1887).

Rolleston, T. W., 'The Archbishop in politics', in *Dublin University Review*, February 1887.

Scannell, T. B., 'The Politics of St. Thomas Aquinas', in *I.E.R.*, 3rd series, viii (1887).

Vaughan, J. S., 'The Priest in Politics', in *I.E.R.*, 3rd series, xii (1891).

Whittle, J. L., 'Irish elections and the influence of the priests', in *Frazer's Magazine*, new series, l, (1870).

Whittle, J. L., 'Ireland and the Irish land questions', in *Frazer's Magazine, new series, i, (1870).*

SECONDARY SOURCES

H. BOOKS AND PAMPHLETS

Abels, J., *The Parnell tragedy* (London, 1966).

Barry, A., *The life of Count Moore* (Dublin, 1905).

Beckett, J. C., *The making of modern Ireland* (London, 1966).

Bew, Paul, *Land and the national question in Ireland, 1858-1882* (Dublin, 1978).

Blunt, W. S., *The Land War in Ireland* (London, 1912).

Bolton, A. D., *The Labourers (Ireland) Acts, 1883-1906* (2 Vols. Dublin, 1908 and 1910).

Bourke, Marcus, *John O'Leary, A study in Irish separatism* (Tralee, 1967).

Boyle, P., The Irish College in Paris, 1578-1901 (Dublin, 1901).

Burke, W. P., *History of Clonmel* (Waterford, 1907).

Carew Hunt, R. N., *The theory and practice of communism,* 5th ed., Harmondsworth, 1973).

Carrigan, Rev. W., *History and antiquities of the diocese of Ossory* (Dublin, 1905).

Comerford, R. V., *Charles J. Kickham: a Study in Irish nationalism and literature,* (Dublin, 1979).

Connolly, S. J., *Priests and People in Pre-Famine Ireland, 1780-1845* (Dublin, 1982).

Connell, K. H., *Irish Peasant Society* (Oxford, 1968).

Cruise O'Brien, C., *Parnell and his party, 1880-1890* (Oxford, 1957).

Cullen, L. M., *An economic history of Ireland since 1660* (London, 1972).

Curtis, L. P., jnr., *Coercion and conciliation in Ireland, 1880-1892; a study in Conservative Unionism* (New Jersey, 1963).

Davitt, Michael, *The fall of Feudalism in Ireland* (London, 1905).

Donnelly, J. S., jnr., *The land and the people of nineteenth century Cork* (London, 1975).

Fogarty, L., *Fr. John Kenyon, A patriot priest of '48* (Dublin, no date).

Gleeson, Rev. J., *History of Ely O'Carroll Territory* (Dublin, 1915).

Guinan, Rev. J., *The Soggarth Aroon* (Dublin, 1925).

Guinan, Rev. J., *Priest and people in Doon* (Dublin and Cork, 1925).

Hales, E. E. Y., *The Catholic church in the modern world* (London, 1958).

Hanham, H. J., *Politics in the time of Disraeli and Gladstone* (London, 1959).

Harrison, H., *Parnell vindicated* (London, 1931).

Healy, T. M., *Letters and leaders of my day* (London, 1928).

Hull, E. R., *A review of Mr McCarthy's book with some personal impressions of Ireland,* (Bombay, 1909).

Inglis, K. S., *Churches and the working classes in Victorian England,* (London, 1963).

Joyce, James, *Portrait of the artist as a Young Man* (London, 1916).

Larkin, Emmet, *The Roman Catholic Church and the creation of the modern Irish state* (Dublin, 1975).

Lee, J. J., *The modernisation of Irish Society,* (Dublin, 1973).

Lee, P. J., *History of the parish of Newport* (Thurles, 1934).

Lyons, F. S. L., *John Dillon* (London, 1968).

Lyons, F. S. L., *Ireland Since the famine* (Glasgow, 1973).

Lyons, F. S. L., *Charles Stewart Parnell* (London, 1977).

McCaffrey, L. J., *Daniel O'Connell and the repeal year* (Kentucky, 1966).

McCarthy, M. J. F., *Priests and people in Ireland* (London and Dublin, 1906).

McDermot, Frank, *Tone and his times* (Tralee, 1969).

McDonald, Walter, *Reminiscences of a Maynooth professor* (London, 1925).

MacSuibhne, Peadar, *Paul Cullen and his contemporaries with their letters from 1920 to 1902* (Naas, 5 vols., 1961-77).

Mansergh, Nicholas, *The Irish question* (London, 1965).

Meehan, Denis, *Window on Maynooth* (Dublin, 1949).

Miller, D. W., *Church, state and nation in Ireland, 1898-1921* (Dublin, 1973).

Norman, E. R., *The catholic church and Ireland in the age of rebellion 1859-1873* (London, 1965).

Norman, E. R., *Anti-Catholicism in Victorian England* (London, 1967).

Nowlan, K. B., *The politics of Repeal: A study in the relations between Great Britain and Ireland 1841-1850* (London, 1965).

O'Brien, William, *Recollections* (London, 1905).

O'Brien, William, *Evening memories* (Dublin, 1920).

O'Broin, Leon, *Fenian fever* (London, 1971).
O'Broin, Leon, *Revolutionary underground: the story of the Irish Republican Brotherhood, 1858-1924* (Dublin, 1976).
O'Connor, T. P., *Memoirs of an old parliamentarian* (London, 1929).
O'Donnell, F. H., *Paraguay on Shannon:— the price of a political priesthood* (London, 1908).
O'Donovan Rossa, Jeremiah, *My years in English jails* ed. by Seán Ó Cearnaigh (Tralee, 1867).
O'Leary, P., *My Story A Translation of Mo Scéal Féin* (London, 1970).
O'Riordan, M., *Catholicity and progress in Ireland* (5th edition, London, 1906).
O'Rourke, Rev. M., *The history of the great Irish famine of 1847* (3rd edition, Dublin, 1902).
O'Sullivan, T. F., *The Young Irelanders* (Tralee, 1944).
Palmer, M. D., *The Irish land league crisis* (London, 1940).
Plunket, Horace, *Ireland in the new century* (London, 1905).
Power, Patrick, *Waterford and Lismore: A compendious history of the united dioceses* (Cork, 1937).
Ryan, Mark, *Fenian memories* (Dublin, 1945).
Sheehan, D., *Nenagh and its neighbourhood* (Nenagh, no date).
Sheehy-Skeffington, *Michael Davitt, revolutionary, agitator and labour leader* (London, 1967).
Solow, B. L., *The land question and the Irish economy, 1870-1903* (Cambridge, Mass., 1971).
Steele, E. D., *Irish land and British politics: tenant right and nationality 1865-1870* (Cambridge, 1974).
Strauss, Emil, *Irish nationalism and British democracy* (London, 1951).
Tierney, Mark, *Murroe and Boher: the history of an Irish country parish* (Dublin, 1965).
Tierney, Mark, *Croke of Cashel* (Dublin, 1976).
Thornely, David, *Isaac Butt and Home Rule* (London, 1964).
de Tocqueville, Alexis, *Journeys to England and Ireland,* ed. by J. P. Mayer (2nd ed., New York, 1968).
Walsh, P. J., *William J. Walsh, archbishop of Dublin* (London, 1928).
Whyte, J. H., *The Independent Irish Party 1850-1859* (Oxford, 1958).
Whyte, J. H., *Church and state in modern Ireland 1923-1970* (Dublin, 1971).
Whyte, J. H., *The tenant league and Irish politics in the 1880s* (Dundalk, 1963).

I. LATER ARTICLES

Anonymous, 'Maynooth one hundred years ago' in *I.E.R.*, 5th series, xvi (July-December 1940).
Ahern, J., 'The plenary synod of Thurles', *I.E.R.*, 5th ser., lxxv (May 1951).
Ahern, J., 'The plenary synod of Thurles' in *I.E.R.*, 5th ser., lxxviii (June 1952).
Barry, D., 'The church and secret societies: the confessor's attitude', in *I.E.R.*, 5th ser., xxxiv (January-June 1932).
Barry, P. C., 'The National Synod of Thurles' in *I.E.R.*, 5th ser., lxxxvi (July-December 1956).
Burns, R. E., 'Parsons, priests and the people: the rise of Irish anti-clericalism 1785-1789' in *Church History*, xxxi, No. 2, (June, 1962).
Canavan, J. E., 'Property and the Church', in *Studies*, xxiv (September 1935).
Clancy, J., 'A Study of Fr Kenyon', in *Molua*, 1946.
Clark, Sam, 'The Social composition of the Land League', in *I.H.S.*, xvii, (September 1971).
Corish, P. J., 'Political problems 1860-1878', in *A history of Irish Catholicism*, v, fasc. 3, (Dublin, 1967).
Corkery, John, 'Ecclesiastical learning', in *A history of Irish catholicism*', v, (Dublin, 1970).

Cronin, T. B., 'The spiritual trenches of Maynooth', in *Catholic Bulletin*, v, (1915).

Culhane, R., 'Does the language of spirituality contradict theology?' in *I.E.R.*, 5th series, lxvii, (January-June 1946).

Cunningham, Terence, 'Church reorganisation' in *A history of Irish catholicism*, v, (Dublin, 1970).

Donnelly, James, jnr., 'The Irish agricultural depression of 1859-64' in *Irish Economic and Social History*, iii, (1976).

Finnegan, F., 'Maurice Lenihan', in *Studies*, xxxv, (September 1946), vol. xxxvi, (March 1947).

Giblin, Cathaldus, 'Irish Exiles', in *A history of Irish catholicism*, iv, (Dublin, 1971).

Gleeson, Dermot, 'Fr John Kenyon and Young Ireland' in *Studies*, xxxv, (March 1946).

Gleeson, Dermot, 'Parish bounds in the Killaloe Diocese', in *North Munster Antiquarian Journal*, vi, no. 1 (1949).

Green, E. R. R., 'The beginnings of fenianism' in *The fenian movement* (Cork, 1968).

Green, E. R. R., 'Charles Joseph Kickham and John O'Leary', in *The fenian movement*, (Cork, 1968).

Gwynn, Denis, 'The priests and Young Ireland in 1948' in *I.E.R.*, lxx (1948).

Gwynn, Denis, 'Fr Kenyon and Young Ireland', part 2 in *I.E.R.*, 5th ser., lxxi (January-June 1949).

Hawkins, Richard, 'Government v. secret societies: The Parnell era' in *Secret societies in Ireland* (Dublin, 1973).

Hayes, Richard, 'Priests in the independence movement of '98' in *I.E.R.*, 5th series, lxvi (1945).

Hegarty, Rev. W. J., 'Gladstone's Attitude to catholicism' in *I.E.R.*, 5th ser., lxxxvi, (July-December 1956).

Kelleher, J., 'The right to rent and the unearned increment', in *Irish Theological Quarterly*, v (1910).

Kennedy, T. P., 'Church Building', in *A history of Irish catholicism*, v (Dublin, 1970).

Larkin, Emmet, 'Church and state in Ireland in the nineteenth century', in *Church History*, (September 1962).

Larkin, E., 'Socialism and catholicism in Ireland', in *Church History*, xxxiii, (December 1964).

Larkin, E., 'Mounting the counter-attack: the Roman Catholic hierarchy and the destruction of Parnellism", in *Review of politics*, xxv (April 1963).

Larkin, E., 'Economic growth, capital investment and the Roman Catholic church', in *American Historical Review*, lxxii (1966-67).

Larkin, E., 'Launching the counter-attack: Part II of the Roman Catholic Hierarchy and the destruction of Parnellism', in *Review of politics*, xxviii (July 1966).

Larkin, E., 'The devotional revolution in Ireland, 1850-75', in *American Historical Review*, lxxvii (June 1972).

Larkin, E., 'Church, state and nation in modern Ireland', in *American Historical Review* (December, 1975).

Lee, J. J., 'The Ribbonman', in T. D. Williams (ed.), *Secret societies in Ireland* (Dublin, 1973).

Lyons, F. S. L., 'Fenianism 1867-1916', in T. W. Moody (ed.), *The fenian movement* (Cork, 1968).

McCaffrey, L. J., 'The Home Rule party and Irish nationalist opinion 1874-1876', in *Catholic Historical Review*, xliii, no. 2 (July 1957).

McCaffrey, L. J., 'Home Rule and the general election of 1874', in *Irish Historical Studies*, ix, no. 34 (September 1954).

McCartney, Donal, 'The Churches and secret societies', in T. D. Williams (ed.) *Secret societies in Ireland*, (Dublin, 1973).

McCartney, Donal, 'The church and the fenians', in *University Review*, iv, no. 3 (Winter 1967).

MacDonagh, Oliver, 'The Irish Catholic clergy and emigration during the great famine', in *I.H.S.*, xx (September 1947).

Mac Donagh, O., 'The politicisation of the Irish catholic bishops, 1800-1850', in *Historical Journal*, xviii (1975).

Mac Donagh, O., 'The Irish famine emigration to the United States' in *Perspectives in American History*, x (1976).

McDonald, Walter, 'The ethical aspects of boycotting', in *Irish Theological Quarterly*, i (1906).

MacSuibhne, Peadar, 'The early history of Carlow College' in *I.E.R.*, 5th ser., lxii (July-December 1943).

Mandle, W. F., 'The I.R.B. and the beginnings of the Gaelic Athletic Association', in *I.H.S.*, xx, no. 80 (September 1977).

Marshall, P., 'The ethical aspect of boycotting', in *Irish Theological Quarterly*, i (1906).

Miller, D. W., 'Irish catholicism and the great famine', in *Journal of Social History*, ix (September 1975).

Moody, T. W., 'Michael Davitt: survey and appreciation' in *Studies*, xxxv (June 1946).

Moody, T. W., 'The fenian movement in Irish history' in *The fenian movement* (Cork, 1968).

Murphy, J. A., 'Priests and people in modern Irish History' in *Christus Rex*, xxiii, no. 4 (1969).

Murphy, J. A., 'The Support of the catholic clergy in Ireland, 1750-1850', in *Historical Studies*, v (London, 1965).

Norman, E. R., *'The Catholic church and Irish politics in the 1860s* (Dundalk, 1965).

Nowlan, K. B., 'The fenian rising of 1867' in T. W. Moody (ed.) *The fenian movement*, (Cork, 1968).

Nowlan, K. B., 'The Fenians at Home' in T. D. Williams (ed.), *Secret Societies in Ireland* (Dublin, 1973).

O'Brien, J. B., 'Sadleirs Bank' in *Journal of the Cork Historical and Archaeological Society*, xxxii, no. 235 (1977).

O'Connell, M. R., 'The political background to the establishment of Maynooth College', part I and part II in *I.E.R.*, 5th ser., lxxxv, (January-June 1956), part III in *I.E.R.*, 5th ser., lxxxvi, (July-December 1956).

O'Dwyer, Rev. C., 'Paying for a cathedral' in *Cuimhneachán Chois tSiúire: Tipperary remembers weekend* (Thurles, 1979).

Ó Fiaich, Tomás, 'The clergy and fenianism 1860-1870' in *I.E.R.*, 5th ser., cix (1968).

O'Rahilly, Alfred, 'Catholic view of state authority' in *Catholic Bulletin*, vi, (1916).

O'Neill, T. P., 'The great famine, 1845-1852' in *I.E.R.*, 5th ser., lxix, (Nov. 1947).

Power, Patrick, 'The bounds and extent of Irish parishes', in *Feilscribhinn Torna* (Cork, 1947).

Senior, Hereward, 'The place of fenianism in the Irish republican tradition' in *University Review*, iv, no. 3 (Winter 1967).

Slater, T. J., 'The ethical aspect of boycotting', in *Irish Theological Quarterly*, ii (1907).

Steele, E. D., 'Cardinal Cullen and Irish nationality' in *I.H.S.*, xix, no. 75 (March 1975).

Thornley, David, 'The Irish Conservatives and Home Rule 1869-1873'', in *I.H.S.*, xi, no. 43 (March 1959).

Walker, Brian, 'The Irish electorate 1868-1915', in *I.H.S.*, xviii, no. 71 (March 1973).

Whyte, J. H., 'Influence of the catholic clergy at elections in nineteenth century Ireland' in *English Historical Review*, lxxv (April 1960).

Whyte, J. H., 'Fresh light on Archbishop Cullen and the Tenant League' in *Irish Ecclesiastical Record*, new ser., xcix (January-June 1963).

Whyte, J. H., 'Political Problems 1850-1860' in *A history of Irish catholicism*, v, fasc. 2, (Dublin 1967).

Williams, T. D., 'John Devoy and Jeremiah O'Donovan Rossa' in T. W. Moody (ed.), *The fenian movement*, (Cork, 1968).

Woods, C. J., 'The Politics of Cardinal McCabe, Archbishop of Dublin, 1879-1885', in *Dublin Historical Record*, xxvi, (June, 1973).

J. THESES AND OTHER UNPUBLISHED WORKS

Connolly, S. J., 'Catholicism and social discipline in pre-famine Ireland' thesis, 2 vols., (D. Phil. New University of Ulster, 1977).

Hanrahan, A. K., 'Irish electioneering 1850-1872' (M.A. thesis, U.C.D., 1965).

Hayes, Rev. W., 'A review of church building in the archdiocese of Cashel and Emly from the penal times'. (Typescript in St Patrick's College, Thurles).

Larkin, Emmet, 'The priest, the land and Home Rule'. (Typescript in Glenstal Abbey).

Marnane, D. G., 'Tipperary town and the Smith Barry estate, 1885-1895'. (M.A. thesis, University College, Dublin, 1975).

O'Dwyer, Rev. C., 'Archbishop Patrick Leahy', (M.A. thesis, Maynooth, 1971).

Ó Riain, P. D., 'Notes on Templemore', (Typescript in National Library Ireland).

Vaughan, W. E., 'A study of landlord and tenant relations in Ireland between the famine and the Land War, 1850-78, (Ph.D. thesis, Trinity College, 1973).

Woods, C. J., 'The catholic church and Irish politics, 1878-91 (Ph.D. thesis, University of Nottingham, 1969).

APPENDIX I : TABLES

NOTE: Some of these Tables, and all of the 'Directory of Secular Priests' (see pp. 326—360 below), have been reproduced directly from the author's typewritten thesis — for reasons of economy and accuracy. In spite of reproduction difficulties (we have obtained the best possible from the originals), these documents are legible and give the reader access to this highly valuable, interesting and original research.

TABLE 1

Republicanism Among the Tipperary Electorate 1869-1877

Election	Registered Electorate	Pop. of County	Electorate as a % of Pop.	Fenian/ Republican Candidate	Fenian/ Repub. Poll	% of Electorate	% of Poll	% + or – on 1869 Poll	Liberal-National Association Home Rule Candidate	Liberal etc. Poll	% of Electorate	% of Pop.	% + or – on 1869 Poll
1869	9507	206726	4.6%	Jer O'Donovan Rossa	1131	11.8%	.5%	–	Denis Caulfield Heron	1028	10.8%	.5%	–
1870	9507	206726	4.6%	Chas. Joseph Kickham	1664	17.2%	.8%	+ 5.4%	D.C. Heron	1668	17.5%	.8%	+6.7%
1874	9572	201687	4.7%	John Mitchel (Peter E. Gill) (George Roe)	1785 (685) (705)	18.6%	.9%	+ 6.8%	Chas. White W.F. O'Callaghan	3623 2735	37.8% 28.5%	1.8% 1.3%	+27% +17.7%
2nd B.E. 1875	9572	201687	4.7%	John Mitchel	3114	32.5%	1.5%	+20.7%	(Conservative Cand.)	(746)	–	–	–
1877	9297	201687	4.5%	J. Sarsfield Casey	1344	14.4%	.7%	+ 2.6%	Ed. Dwyer Gray	3852	41%	1.9%	+30.2%

SOURCES: 1869 *N.G.* 27/11/69 *S.P.O.C.S.O.R.P. 1869 18242*, 27/11/69.
1870 *DOD* MDCCCLXX III P. 148
1874 *DOD* MDCCCLXXIV P. 147
1875 *DOD* MDCCCLXXVII P. 151
1877 *DOD* MDCCCLXXVIII P. 151

DODS PARLIAMENTARY COMPANION (LONDON MDCCCLXX) P. 144
OTHER SOURCES INCORPORATED IN TEXT.

TABLE 2   *Tables* 307

**EXAMPLES OF PRIESTS WITH FARMING BACKGROUND
WHO MINISTERED IN CO. TIPPERARY 1850-1891.**

(Index No. refers to the 'Directory' below, p. 326)

INDEX NO.	NAME	FARM SIZE (STATUTE ACRES)		VALUATION PER ACRE	COUNTY
1.	JOHN BALDWIN		78	10/-	WATERFORD
2.	MICHAEL BANNON		47	14/-	TIPPERARY
3.	MICHAEL BANNON	(A)	37	21/-	TIPPERARY
		(B)	15	21/-	
		(C)	37	22/-	
		TOTAL	89		
19.	JAMES BURKE	(A)	29	20/-	TIPPERARY
		(B)	28	21/-	
		TOTAL	57		
21.	JOHN BURKE	(A)	43	9/-	TIPPERARY
		(B)	36	12/-	
		(C)	7	14/-	
		TOTAL	86		
40.	JAMES CAHER		336	7/-	CLARE
42.	RICHARD CAHILL		97	18/-	TIPPERARY
43.	WILLIAM CAHILL		45	10/-	TIPPERARY
44.	JAMES CALLANAN		60	20/-	TIPPERARY
45.	MICHAEL CALLANAN		BROTHER OF	JAMES	
47.	JAMES CANTWELL		155	16/-	TIPPERARY
51.	WALTER CANTWELL		BROTHER OF	JAMES	
53.	PATRICK CANTY		35	20/-	LIMERICK
65.	MICHAEL CLEARY	(A)	31	16/-	TIPPERARY
		(B)	18	21/-	
		TOTAL	49		
69.	PHILIP CLEARY		102	14/-	TIPPERARY
72.	THOMAS COLLIER	(A)	66	12/-	TIPPERARY
		(B)	56	13/-	
		TOTAL	122		
76.	JOHN CONDON	(A)	28	22/-	LIMERICK
		(B)	26	22/-	
		TOTAL	54		
77.	LAWRENCE CONDON	(A)	62	10/-	WATERFORD
		(B)	62	10/-	
		TOTAL	124		
81.	JOHN COONEY	(A)	96	17/-	TIPPERARY
		(B)	35	18/-	
		TOTAL	131		
85.	WM. CORCORAN	(A)	85	10/-	TIPPERARY
		(B)	39	10/-	
		(C)	46	11/-	
		TOTAL	170		
87.	MICHAEL B. CURRY		32	6/-	CLARE
109.	DAVID DEE	(A)	18	13/-	TIPPERARY
		(B)	6	15/-	
		(C)	24	14/-	
		(D)	26	20/-	
		(E)	8	14/-	
		(F)	19	13/-	
		(G)	23	17/-	
		TOTAL	124		

INDEX NO.	NAME	FARM SIZE (STATUTE ACRES)	VALUATION PER ACRE	COUNTY
111.	JAS. J.DELANEY	90	13/-	TIPPERARY
113.	MICHAEL DEVANE	(A)23	9/-	LIMERICK
		(B)89	9/-	
		TOTAL 112		
114.	EDMUND DOHENY	96	17/-	TIPPERARY
122.	WILLIAM DOWNEY	48	26/-	"
124.	JOHN DUAN	197	~16/-	KILKENNY
126.	NICHOLAS DUGGAN	(A) 85	23/-	TIPPERARY
		(B) 85	23/-	
		TOTAL 170		
127.	THOMAS DUGGAN	74	16/-	TIPPERARY
136.	DENIS ENGLISH	80	17/-	"
137.	THOMAS ENGLISH	27	13/-	"
141.	PATRICK FEEHAN	80	17/-	"
142.	JOHN FENNELLY	169	17/-	"
143.	PATRICK FENNELLY	114	17/-	"
144.	RICHARD FENNELLY	298	10/-	"
145.	THOMAS FENNELLY	213	8/-	"
147.	THOMAS FINN	143	11/-¹	WATERFORD
159.	DANIEL FOGARTY	(A) 17	16/-	TIPPERARY
		(B) 6	19/-	
		TOTAL 23		
166.	JAMES FROST	66	27/-	CLARE
167.	JOHN GARRY	128	6/-	CLARE
177.	PATRICK GLYNN	118	7/-	CLARE
178.	PATRICK GODFREY	(A) 34	27/-	TIPPERARY
		(B) 9	26/-	
		(C) 93	26/-	
		TOTAL 136		
179.	THOMAS GODFREY	BROTHER OF PATRICK		
185.	THOMAS HACKETT	133	14/-	TIPPERARY
188.	EDMUND HANLY	(A) 30	22/-	TIPPERARY
		(B) 73	21/-	
		TOTAL 103		
192.	JAMES HANNIGAN	119	19/-	TIPPERARY
193.	THOMAS HANNIGAN	BROTHER OF JAMES		
194.	MICHAEL HARTY	52	15/-	LIMERICK
195.	JOHN HAYDEN	(A) 151	15/-	TIPPERARY
		(B) 36	17/-	
		TOTAL 187		
206.	WILLIAM HEFFERNAN	62	20/-	TIPPERARY
208.	JAMES HENEBERRY	146 [+ LOTS].	8/-	WATERFORD
214.	JAMES HICKEY	(A) 199	8/-	TIPPERARY
		(B) 57	10/-	
		TOTAL 256		
219.	EDWARD HOGAN	192	15/-	TIPPERARY
220.	JAMES HOGAN	SAME FAMILY		
224.	WILLIAM HOGAN	DO.		
230.	DAVID HUMPHREYS	98	14/-	LIMERICK
241.	PATRICK KENNEDY	(A) 29	13/-	TIPPERARY
		(B) 102	19/-	
		TOTAL 131		

INDEX NO.	NAME	FARM SIZE (STATUTE ACRES)		VALUATION PER ACRE	COUNTY
246.	EDMUND KENRICK	(A)	90.	19/-	TIPPERARY
		(B)	43	16/-	
		TOTAL	133		
249.	T.H.KINNANE		45	19/-	TIPPERARY
255.	MARTIN LAFFAN	(A)	97	7/-	TIPPERARY
		(B)	102	9/-	
		(C)	45	10/-	
		(D)	84	11/-	
		TOTAL	328		
256.	MICHAEL LAFFAN	RELATED TO ABOVE			
257.	PATRICK LAFFAN	RELATED TO ABOVE.			
259.	DANIEL K.LANIGAN	(A)	43	20/-	TIPPERARY
		(B)	43	19/-	
		(C)	69	22/-	
		TOTAL	155		
261.	WILLIAM LANIGAN		40	13/-	TIPPERARY
264.	JOHN LAYNE	(A)	70	9/-	LIMERICK
		(B)	60	8/-	
		(C)	16	9/-	
		(D)	39	7/-	
		(E)	28	8/-	
		(F)	38	8/-	
		(G)	47	6/-	
		(H)	16	9/-	
		(I)	43	5/-	
		(J)	20	5/-	
		TOTAL	377		
270.	PAT.LONERGAN		15	10/-	TIPPERARY
281.	ML.McDONNELL	(A)	28	10/-	TIPPERARY
		(B)	67	10/-	
		(C)	32	14/-	
		TOTAL	127		
289.	JOHN McGRATH	(A)	16	13/-	TIPPERARY
		(B)	61	13/-	
		(C)	48	18/-	
		(D)	102	13/-	
		TOTAL	227		
297.	THOMAS McGRATH		78	13/-	WATERFORD
301.	F.McMAHON		109	12/-	CLARE
308.	THOS.J.MACKEY	(A)	21	17/-	TIPPERARY
		(B)	20	17/-	
		TOTAL	41		
313.	WILLIAM MARINAN		67	8/-	CLARE
318.	EDMUND MEAGHER	(A)	44	18/-	TIPPERARY
		(B)	45	15/-	
		(C)	65	17/-	
		(D)	15	15/-	
		TOTAL	169		
320.	JAMES MEAGHER		54	13/-	TIPPERARY
321.	JAMES MEAGHER (BORN EITHER IN CRANNAGH OR CLONMORE)	(A)	51	14/-	TIPPERARY
		(B)	89	16/-	
		(C)	40	16/-	
		TOTAL (A+B)	140		
		TOTAL C	40		
330.	PATRICK MEAGHER		33	20/-	TIPPERARY
332.	THOMAS MEAGHER		34	21/-	TIPPERARY
334.	THOMAS MEAGHER	(A)	22	15/-	TIPPERARY
		(B)	23	15/-	
		(C)	23	11/-	
		(D)	49	15/-	
		TOTAL	117		

INDEX NO.	NAME	FARM SIZE (STATUTE ACRES)	VALUATION PER ACRE	COUNTY
335.	WILLIAM MEAGHER	120	12/-	TIPPERARY
338.	PATRICK MEANY	44	17/-	WATERFORD
341.	HUGH MOCKLER	140	19/-	TIPPERARY
342.	THOMAS MOLLOY	140	14/-	TIPPERARY
349.	JOHN MOLUMBY	SUBDIVISION— 16 FAMILIES	-	TIPPERARY
353.	JOHN MORAN	118	15/-	TIPPERARY
354.	THOMAS MORAN	BROTHER OF JOHN		
356.	PATRICK J. MORRIS	37	19/-	TIPPERARY
357.	WILLIAM MORRIS	BROTHER OF PATRICK		
363.	PAT. MULCAHY	(A) 37 (B) 18 TOTAL 55	12/- 12/-	TIPPERARY
364.	JAMES MULLALLY	193	15/-	TIPPERARY
365.	WM.F. MULLALLY	BROTHER OF JAMES		
370.	JOHN MURPHY	(A) 10 (B) 31 (C) 46 TOTAL 87	21/- 19/- 20/-	TIPPERARY
379.	CORNELIUS O'BRIEN	143	10/-	TIPPERARY
383.	JAMES O'BRIEN	(A) 71 (B) 51 TOTAL 122	11/- 12/-	TIPPERARY
385.	JOHN O'BRIEN	275	19/-	LIMERICK
386.	MICHAEL O'BRIEN	78	14/-	LIMERICK
387.	RICHARD O'BRIEN	BROTHER OF MICHAEL		
391.	JAMES O'CONNELL	34	17/-	TIPPERARY
392.	MARTIN O'CONNELL	(A) 44 (B) 66 (C) 54 TOTAL 164	13/- 14/- 14/-	TIPPERARY
401.	THOMAS O'CONNOR	33	15/-	TIPPERARY
410.	WILLIAM O'DONNELL	(A) 269 (B) 233 TOTAL 502	19/- 19/-	TIPPERARY
411.	JOHN O'DWYER	(A) 93 (B) 145 TOTAL 238	10/- 13/-	TIPPERARY
412.	THOMAS O'DWYER	104	22/-	TIPPERARY
415.	MALACHY O'GORMAN	79	19/-	CLARE
417.	JOHN O'HALLORAN	167	14/-	CLARE
435.	THEOPHILUS O'MEARA	(A) 34 (B) 33 (C) 13 TOTAL 80	24/- 17/- 23/-	TIPPERARY
438.	MICHAEL O'NEILL	(A) 37 (B) 39 TOTAL 76	24/- 24/-	TIPPERARY
456.	JOHN POWER	128	22/-	TIPPERARY
458.	MAURICE POWER	97	18/-	LIMERICK
465.	PAUL POWER	(A) 161 (B) 58 (C) 57 TOTAL 276	14/- 12/- 16/-	WATERFORD

INDEX NO.	NAME	FARM SIZE (STATUTE ACRES)	VALUATION PER ACRE	COUNTY
478.	ROBERT PROUT	126	14/-	TIPPERARY
483.	CHARLES QUILLINAN	(A) 61 (B) 48 TOTAL 109	22/- 24/-	TIPPERARY
487.	JOHN QUIRKE	(A) 52 (B) 46 TOTAL 98	14/- 15/-	TIPPERARY
488.	WILLIAM QUIRKE	98	15/-	TIPPERARY
489.	NICHOLAS RAFFERTY	(A) 31 (B) 40 TOTAL 71	26/- 27/-	TIPPERARY
493.	EDMUND RYAN	(A) 51 (B) 77 TOTAL 128	11/- 14/-	TIPPERARY
498.	JAMES D. RYAN	39	20/-	LIMERICK
505.	JOHN T. RYAN	250	13/-	TIPPERARY
507.	MATTHEW RYAN	(A) 46 (B) 23 (C) 89 TOTAL 158	14/- 9/- 9/-	LIMERICK
508.	MATTHEW RYAN	29	16/-	LIMERICK
510.	PATRICK RYAN	162	13/-	LIMERICK
513.	PATRICK C. RYAN	(A) 109 (B) 28 TOTAL 137	9/- 9/-	TIPPERARY
514.	PATRICK W. RYAN	(A) 24 (B) 68 (C) 65 TOTAL 157	11/- 9/- 7/-	LIMERICK
520.	JOHN SCANLAN	77	6/-	CLARE
522.	JOHN SCANLAN	(A) 71 (B) 72 (C) 33 (D) 17 TOTAL 193	5/- 7/- 6/- 4/-	CLARE
523.	MICHAEL SCANLAN	299	3/-	CLARE
524.	PHILIP SCANLAN	(A) 119 (B) 21 TOTAL 140	13/- 15/-	TIPPERARY
525.	WILLIAM SCANLAN	(A) 152 (B) 103 TOTAL 255	10/- 10/-	CLARE
536.	JOHN SLATTERY	(A) 21 (B) 63 TOTAL 84	18/- 21/-	TIPPERARY
544.	PATRICK SPRATT	(A) 73 (B) 75 (C) 72 TOTAL 220	18/- 19/- 20/-	WATERFORD
545.	CHARLES STUART	(A) 47 (B) 78 (C) 29 TOTAL 154	5/- 7/- 8/-	CLARE
551.	JOHN TRACY	166	16/-	WATERFORD
554.	JOHN TUOHY	(A) 93 (B) 120 TOTAL 213	14/- 14/-	TIPPERARY

INDEX NO.	NAME	FARM SIZE (STATUTE ACRES)	VALUATION PER ACRE	COUNTY
556.	JAMES VAUGHAN	77	12/-	CLARE
558.	JAMES WALL	82	17/-	WATERFORD
568.	MICHAEL WALSH	(A) 55	20/-	TIPPERARY
		(B) 63	19/-	
		(C) 60	19/-	
		(D) 42	17/-	
		TOTAL 220		

NO. OF PRIESTS: 135 = 23% OF TOTAL TIPPERARY PRIESTHOOD

TOTAL HOLDINGS (INCLUDES SUBDIVISIONS) = 214   VAL. UNDER 10/- = 38 (18%) VAL. OVER 10/- = 176 (82%)

(CLARE ACCOUNTED FOR 14 OF THE UNDER 10/- FARMS AND ONE SUCH CO. LIMERICK FAMILY HAD 10 FARMS UNDER 10/- INDEX NO. 264)

TOTAL UNDIVIDED HOLDINGS 70

BREAKDOWN OF UNDIVIDED HOLDINGS

UNDER 20	20-50	51-80	81-110	111-140	141-170	171-200	OVER 200	OVER 50	OVER 110
1 1%	16 23%	15 21%	10 14%	11 16%	8 12%	3 4%	6 9%	53 76%	28 40%

NOTE: 1 GRIFFITHS VALUATION IS STRUCTURED AS TOWNLAND WITHIN CIVIL PARISH, WITHIN BARONY, WITHIN COUNTY. CO. CLARE IS FILED BY UNION RATHER THAN BARONY, ALTHOUGH THE TOWNLAND INDEX WHICH IS AN ESSENTIAL WORK IN STUDYING GRIFFITHS FOR THE PURPOSE OF THIS STUDY, IS DONE BY BARONY. FORTUNATELY WHERE A TRACT OF LAND IS SHOWN IN GRIFFITHS UNDER A COMMON LEASE THE INDIVIDUAL VALUATIONS OF THE LESSEES ARE ALSO SHOWN. THIS ENABLED THE WRITER, ON A PRO-RATA BASIS, TO COMPUTE THE SIZE OF THE INDIVIDUAL HOLDINGS. SOMETIMES AS THE TABLE INDICATES FARMS WERE SPLIT BETWEEN DIFFERENT CIVIL PARISHES AND LESS FREQUENTLY BETWEEN DIFFERENT BARONIES. OCCASIONALLY THE NAMES OF PRIESTS FATHERS WERE KNOWN TO THE WRITER AND THIS HELPED ACCURACY.

NOTE: 2 REGRETTABLY IT WAS IMPOSSIBLE TO TRACE FARM SIZES FOR ALL TIPPERARY PRIESTS DUE TO THE ABSENCE OF RECORDS. APPENDIX 12 NOTES THE FARMING BACKGROUND OF OTHER PRIESTS NOT LISTED HERE. SUCH INFORMATION WAS OBTAINED FROM THE PRESENT PARISH PRIESTS.

TABLE 3 (Contd. from p 313)

SUMMARY: Total Priests 40

Breakdown of ages on Promotion

AGE	NO.	%
30-40	5	12%
41-50	21	53%
51-60	13	32%
Over 60	1	3%

Breakdown of No. of years in Ministry

No. of Years	No.	%
1-10	4	10%
11-19	9	23%
20-29	27	67%
30 and over	nil	-

(vast majority 20-24)

TABLE 3

PROMOTION OF CURATES TO THE STATUS OF PARISH PRIESTS, 1850-1891

Name	Year Born	Year Ordained	Year Promoted	Age on Promotion	No. of years in ministry when Promoted
Michael Bannon	1797	c1830	1851	54	21
Edmund Burke	c1844	1869	1889	45	20
John Burke	1809	1840	1853	44	13
Michael Burke	1812	1861	1868	56	7
John Butler D.D.	1837	1863	1871	34	18
Nephew of Archbishop Slattery, earlier Dean of St. Patrick's College, Thurles.					
Richard Cahill	1820	1849	1876	56	27
James Callanan	1837	1861	1886	49	25
James Cantwell	1844	1868	1878	34	10
Nephew of the Dean of Cashel. Other relations priests.					
Patrick Canty	c1825	c1850	1871	46	21
John Clancy	1826	1854	1880	54	26
Daniel Cleary	c1818	1843	1862	44	23
Francis Cleary	1811	1834	1860	49	26
William Cooney	1820	1846	1859	39	13
Had a brother a priest.					
Patrick Feehan	1813	1838	1861	48	23
Thomas Fennelly	1845	1870	1887	42	17
Related to Bishop of Limerick.					
Cornelius J. Flavin	1828	1859	1876	48	17
James Howard	1839	1866	1888	49	22
Edmund Kenrick	1826	1869	1889	63	20
T. H. Kinnane	1835	1861	1876	41	15
Relations priests. An intellectual, was Professor of Theology in The Irish College, Paris.					
Patrick Laffan	1802	1827	1850	48	23
Relations priests.					
Patrick Leahy	1806	1833	1855	49	22
Academic career until he became Dean. Later Archbishop of Cashel and Emly.					
Michael McDonnell	1827	1853	1875	48	22
John McGrath	1835	1863	1887	52	24
Relations priests.					
Michael McGrath	1836	1864	1888	52	24
William J. McKeogh	1843	1866	1875	32	9
Interesting case, had many clashes with Archbishop Croke.					
John McMahon	1844	1868	1889	45	21
Edward P. Meagher	1829	1857	1881	52	24
William J. Meagher	1828	1855	1872	44	17
Came from a very wealthy family.					
John Molumby	1825	1855	1876	51	21
Patrick J. Morris	1810	1841	1866	56	25
James O'Connell	1830	1860	1886	56	26
Timothy O'Connell	1831	1856	1885	54	29
Thomas O'Dwyer	1843	1868	1885	42	17
William O'Keane	1821	1854	1875	54	21
Thomas Phelan	1831	1857	1877	46	20
John Power	1809	1832	1852	43	20
Came from a wealthy family. Later Bishop of Waterford.					
Maurice Power	1832	1859	1878	46	19
William Quirke	1808	1844	1868	60	24
Note his age on promotion.					
John Ryan D.D.	1831	1853	1863	32	10
An intellectual, Archbishop Leahy's theologian at the Vatican Council 1870.					
John Slattery	1828	1857	1877	49	20

TABLE 4
Some examples of clerical income 1834—1882

PART 1 - DUES

(A)THURLES PARISH: STATION RETURNS
==============
1834 Easter Station £90.   (£7. 18. 6 Gate Collection included)
Christmas Station £101.11.0. (£5.6.0. "   "   ")
      Total   £191.11.0.

1835 Easter Station £96. (6. 12. 6   "   "   ")
Christmas Station £105.18.0. (£6.13.6." "   "   ")
      Total   £201.18.0. (+5%)

1836 Easter Station £103.8.0. (£3.16.6   "   "   ")
Christmas Station   108.11.6(5. 1.0   "   "   ")
      Total   £211.19.6(+5%)

1837 Easter Station £100. 4.6 (£4.15.4."   "   ")
Christmas Station   110. 9.0 (£7. 7.6."   "   ")
      Total   £210.13.6 (Static)

1838 Easter Station £105.19.0 (£5.10.6 "   "   ")
Christmas Station   117.14.0 (£8. 1.6 "   "   ")
      Total   £223.13.0(+6%)

1839 Easter Station £109.1. 6 (£6. 2.6."   "   ")
Christmas Station £115.7. 6 (£11.4.0."   "   ")
      Total   £224.9. 0 (Static)

1840 Easter Station £106.5. 0 (£9.9. 6 "   "   ")
Christmas Station £107.0. 0 (£4.10.0 "   "   ")
      Total   £213.5. 0(-5%)

1841 Easter Station £112.0. 6 (£9.3. 0 "   "   ")
Christmas Station £113.5. 0 (£8.6. 6 "   "   ")
      Total   £225.5. 6(+6%)

1842 Easter Station £107.19.4 (£9.6. 0 "   "   ")
Christmas Station £100. 6.0 (£10.4.6 "   "   ")
      Total   £208. 5.4(-8%)

1843 Easter Station £100. 2.0 (£12.14.6"   "   ")
 Christmas Station £110. 6.0 (£11. 9.0"   "   ")
      Total   £210. 8.0(+1%)

1844 Easter Station £110. 8.0 (£11.15.6"   "   ")
Christmas Station £114.14.0 (£9.17. 6"   "   ")
      Total   £225. 2.0(+7%)

1845 Easter Station £112.15.6 (£10. 5.6"   "   ")
Christmas Station £111.11.0 (£ 9. 7.6"   "   ")
      Total   £224. 6.6 (Static)

1846 Easter Station £102. 2.0 (£9. 5.6."   "   ")
Christmas Station   93. 8.0 (10.10.0 "   "   ")
      Total   £195.10.0(-13%)

1847 Easter Station £89.10.6 (£10.7.6 "   "   ")
Christmas Station   87.15.6 (£10.10.0"   "   ")
      Total   £177. 6.0(-9%)

1848 Easter Station £83.19.0 (£6.13.6 "   "   ")
 Christmas Station   97.16.0 (£6. 4.6 "   "   ")
      Total   £181.15.0(+3%)(-5% on 1834 dues).

(B)KILCOMMON PARISH:
==================
     FIRST QUARTER OF 1840: £81.5.9 including £66.0.6 for marriages.
Individual marriages £3.2.6, £1, £.6.6.6, £7.18. 0, £3.12.0,
£7.10. 0, £3. £4, £1.13. 0, £2, £1. 5. 0, etc. Total from
certificates of freedom was £4.15. 0 at 10/-,15/- or £1. each.
Station dues £5. 1. 6, Baptisms total £4. "Corpse" Masses total
£1. 8. 9.   Total Expenses = £56. 0. 9 including £30 pension to
the former parish priest (retired): other items were car of turf
2/6, coal £4.13. 0, butter 13/2, fish £1. 0. 6, meat £2. 9. 2,
wine 10/8, Sundries £3.17. 6, a pig £3.4. 0, Quarter of beef
£3. 8. 9, bread £1.10. 0.

(C) BALLINAHINCH PARISH
==================
     Income 29/9/1854 - June 1855   Total Income £141. 13. 6.
     Expenses £145. 10. 3.
Easter Collection was £23. 3. 6, Christmas Collection £25. 13. 0.
Baptism rate 2/6, marriages 10/- and 15/-. Expenses included turf,
turkeys, potatoes, fish, hay, turnips, salt, groceries, housekeeper,
servant.

Income 29/9/1855 - 15/6/1856.   Total Income £136. 1. 6.
Expenses £127. 11. 5, Total Revenue for 12 months £277. 15.0,
Total Expenses £273. 1. 8.

(D) THURLES PARISH
==============
Cathedral Receipts for 1882. (Sunday and holyday collections -
breakdown for each Sunday/holyday given).
January £38.   February £13. 3. 6. (Vincent De Paul and Friars
Collection deducted). March £45. 10. 11, April £26. 2. 4,
May £33. 19. 2, June £43. 19. 11, July £33. 19. 1, Aug. £34.4.9.
Sept. £26. 7. 3, Oct. £26. 17. 10, Nov.£25. 17. 9, Dec. £31.10.0.

Breakdown of the January Collections: Sunday £5. 15. 0.
          Epiphany £7. 3. 6, Sunday £5. 7. 2, Sunday £5. 7. 2.
          Sunday £6. 6. 3, Sunday £6. 19. 5, Sunday £6. 8. 8.

TOTAL RECEIPTS: £379. 12. 2.

(E) KILMOYLER (Prior to amalgamation with Bansha - only one priest
               in the parish). Annual income of £120.

(F) Annual Income of Archbishop Slattery in 1854 was £600.(He
     claimed £564. 4. 6 deductions for income tax purposes).

PART 1 - SOURCES.
(A) Thurles dues book 1834-1848 C.D.A. S.P.(gives a breakdown by
     townland).
(B) C.D.A. S.P. Return of Money received in the parish of
     Kilcommon to 20/3/1840.
(C) Account Book of Ballinahinch and Killoscully 29/9/1854-June
     1855, C.D.A. S.P. 1855(15) and Account Book for do. 29/9/1855
     to 15/6/1856, C.D.A. S.P. 1856(10).
(D) Cathedral Receipts for 1882 C.D.A. C.P. 1882(11).
(E) C.D.A. S.P. James Howley P.P. V.G. to Slattery 8/3/1852.
(F) C.D.A. S.P. 1854(2).

                    Other Sources on Dues:-
Vid.,C.D.A. S.P.   1848(68) 35 pages of accounts for the parish
of Pallasgrean in Co. Limerick (Archdiocese of Cashel and Emly)
from October 1845 to October 1846. The report listed all the
houses where stations were held and gave a monthly breakdown of
all income and expenditure, Vid., C.D.A. S.P. Visitation Report of
Patrick Hickey P.P. Doon, July 19th and 20th 1846 revealing the
adverse impact of the Famine upon the Shrovetide Collection, Vid.,
C.D.A. S.P. Redmond Burke P.P. Newport to Slattery 24/1/1850
showing that he had reaped £20. at a wedding.   On the question of

curates' salaries Vid., Table 5, Vid., C.D.A. S.P. Slattery to
James Howley P.P. V.G. 24/7/1854 ordering that John Hackett C.C.
Donaskeigh should receive 52 guineas a year, and a share in the
"Corpse Masses", Vid., C.D.A. S.P. letter from John Ryan, Cashel
to Slattery, requesting a raise to £52.P.A. Vid., C.D.A. L.P.
Cardinal Barnabo Rome to Leahy 28/5/1867, advising that £20 P.A.
was an insufficient salary for curates. For information on the
issue of "divisible dues", Vid., C.D.A. L.P. Bishop Keane, Cloyne
to Leahy 10/11/1868, answering queries by Leahy. For a schedule
of mulcts for dispensation of banns in the Diocese of Killaloe,
Vid., C.D.A. L.P. Bishop James Ryan to Leahy 1/3/1874. The mulcts
stood at 5/-, 7/6, 10/-, 15/- and £1 for marriage offerings of £2
and under, £2 to £8, £8 - £15,£15 - £20 and over £20 respectively,
also "Divisible Dues",(no author), Irish Ecclesiastical Record,
1884, Vol.V, pp.668-669, pp.801-803, and "Divisible Dues",Irish
Ecclesiastical Record, 1886, Vol.VII, pp. 362-363,365 showing
hay and straw offerings as divisible dues.
Vid., "Offerings given on the Occasion of Marriage",Irish
Ecclesiastical Record, 1889, Vol.X. pp.365-368. Other sources on
clerical dues include P.P. 1825, VIII, op.cit., pp.83,169.
Murphy Historical Studies, 1965, op.cit., pp.108-113.Murphy,
Christus Rex, op.cit., pp.243-244. Larkin A.H.R. 1972 op.cit.,
pp.632,634,635, de Tocqueville op.cit., p.125.

PART 2, SALARY OF WORKHOUSE CHAPLAINS.

For disputes concerning such salaries, Vid., C.D.A. S.P. Matthew
Moore, Chief Clerk, Poor Law Commission to Slattery 6/7/1841
pointing out that the salary was £25 for poorhouses with less
than 600 inmates and £40 for larger ones, Vid., C.D.A. S.P.
Slattery to Moore 12/7/1841, rejecting the salary, Vid.,C.D.A.
S.P. Moore to Slattery 19/7/1841, offering £40 for houses of
1,000 inmates and under £50 for 1000-1500 etc. Vid.,C.D.A. S.P.
Slattery to Poor Law Commissioners1/8/1841, and do. to do.
25/11/1841, refusing to allow the celebration of Mass in the
Thurles workhouse until an agreeable salary was fixed. Dean
Patrick Leahy rejected £70 as chaplain of the Cashel workhouse,
arguing that his predecessor, James McDonnell had received £100 -
C.D.A. L.P. Leahy's reply attached to a letter from William
Stanley, Secretary to the Poor Law Commissioners 28/11/1855 and
C.D.A. L.P. Stanley to Leahy 14/12/1855 and Leahy to Stanely
22/12/1855, refusing £75, also Stanley to Leahy 23/1/1856,Leahy's
reply 21/2/1856, Stanley to Leahy 1/3/1856, Leahy to Stanley
5/3/1856, and Stanley to Leahy 11/3/1856, Vid., Cashel Poor Law
Union Minute Book, July 1847-Jan.1848 p.88: Cashel P.L.U. Minute
Book 1883-1884, p.263, showing salaries of £50 and £90
respectively. The Thurles salary in 1846 was £62.10. 0 which was
increased to £85 in 1853, and stood at this in 1887. Thurles
P.L.U. Minute Book 1846-1847, p.173, Thurles P.L.U. Minute Book
June-Dec.1853,p.135. Thurles P.L.U. Minute Book Dec.1887-June
1888, p.37. (As a point of comparison the workhouse hospital
nurse received £20 P.A. with full board in 1851, wardmasters
received £10 P.A. the Clerk of the Union £80 P.A. the Master of
the workhouse £70 P.A. the Matron £30 P.A. and the Schoolmasturs
salary was £30 P.A. if properly qualified - Thurles P.L. Union
Minute Book 1851, 14/6/1851, 21/6/1851, 19/7/1851, 8/11/1851).

TABLE 5
PARISH PRIESTS WHO LEASED FARMS AT MID-CENTURY
(Source Griffiths Valuations)

INDEX NO.	NAME	FARM SIZE STATUTE ACRES	VAL. (PER ACRE)	TOWN-LAND VAL. (PER ACRE)	BARONY	CIVIL PARISH	TOWN-LAND
1	JOHN BALDWIN	(A) 15	38/-	-	IFFA&UFFA E.	ST.MARYS	(A)BURGAGERY LANDS W.
		(B) 4	59/-	47/-			(B)GORTMALOGE
		TOTAL 19					
5	WM.BARRON	36	20/-	7/-	ELIOGARTY	MOYNE	KILLORAN
37	JOHN BUTLER	(A) 3	12/-	17/-	SLIEVARDAGH	KILCOOLEY	(A)KILCOOLEY ABBEY
		(B) 36	10/-	13/-			(B)CROSSOGUES
		TOTAL 39					
58	JAMES CLANCY	16	19/-	14/-	CLANWILLIAM	CLONBEG	MOORABBEY
84	DANIEL CORCORAN	34	18/-	15/-	SLIEVARDAGH	ISERTKIERAN	BEEVERSTOWN
108	PATRICK DE BURKE	16	20/-	-	IFFA&UFFA W.	TEMPLETENNY	BALLYPOREEN
109	DAVID DEE	(A) 33	16/-	17/-	ELIOGARTY	(A)BALLY-MUREEN	(A)BALLY-MUREEN
		(B) 27	20/-	13/-		(B)LOUGH-MOE EAST	(B)GRAIGUE-FRAHANE
		TOTAL 60					
181	ROBERT GRACE	11	14/-	12/-	ELIOGARTY	MOYCARKEY	BUTLERS FARM
190	JAMES HANLEY	17	28/-	25/-	CLANWILLIAM	LATTIN	BALLYNAD-RUCKILLY
205	WM. HEFFERNAN	30	13/-	15/-	MIDDLETHIRD	COLMAN	MOCKLERSTOWN
210	PAUL HENEY	(A) 12	25/-	24/-	CLANWILLIAM	EMLY	(A)CLASHORUM-SMITH
		(B) 12	25/-	26/-.			(B)FARRAN
		TOTAL 24					
236	JAMES KELLY	46	24/-	-	IFFA&UFFA W.	TULLAGH-ORTON	BALLYBOY
247	JOHN KENYON	7	13/-	10/-	UPPER ORMOND	TEMPLEDERRY	CLOGHONAN
254	WILLIAM KIRWAN	50	25/-	15/-	MIDDLETHIRD	BALLYSHEELAN	BALLINREE
255	MARTIN LAFFAN	21	17/-	11/-	SLIEVARDAGH	GRAYSTOWN	BALLINTOGHER
256	MICHAEL LAFFAN	9	20/-	20/-	MIDDLETHIRD	RATHCOOL	BALLYBOUGH
258	WILLIAM LAFFAN	33	20/-	18/-	ELIOGARTY	HOLYCROSS	BEAKSTOWN
280	JAMES McDONNELL	(A) 11	25/-	-	MIDDLETHIRD	(A)ST.JOHN THE BAPTIST	(A)HUGHES LOT EAST
		(B) 8	20/-			(B)ST.PATS.ROCK	(B)BALLYPA-DEEN
		TOTAL 19					
292	JOSEPH McGRATH	49	14/-	14/-	UPPER ORMOND	KILMORE	SRAGH
296	PATRICK McGRATH	(A) 26	18/-	16/-	IFFA&UFFA WEST	TUBRID	(A)BALLY-GARRANE
		(B) 10	14/-	16/-			(B) DO.
		(C) 13	18/-	16/-			(C) DO.
		(D) 4	15/-	18/-			(D)BALLYHOHAN
		(E) 8	17/-	17/-			(C)DERRAVOHER
		TOTAL 61					
306	JOHN MACKEY	83	21/-	23/-	KILNAMANAGH LR.	CLONOULTY	CLONOULTY HILL
312	EUGENE MALONE	47	10/-	10/-	LOWER ORMOND	KNIGH	BALLYHOGAN
321	JAMES MEAGHER	30	10/-	10/-	ELIOGARTY	MOYALIFF	ROSMULT
325	JOHN MEAGHER	(A) 76	18/-	17/-	UPPER ORMOND	(A)AGHNA-MEADLE	(A)CASTLE-QUARTER
		(B) 39 [=2 LOTS]	14/-	14/-		(B)BALLY-MACKEY	(B)GRENANSTOWN
		TOTAL 115					
346	JOHN MOLONEY	64	4/-	3/-	KILNAMANAGH UPPER	DOON	KNOCKSHAN-BRITTAS
357	WILLIAM MORRIS	(A) 8	20/-	22/-	KILNAMANAGH UPPER	GLENKEEN	(A)COOLATAGGLE
		(B) 18	17/-	18/-			(B)KNUCKBRACKS
		TOTAL 26					

	Name				Barony	Parish	Townland
40	PATRICK MORRISSEY	41	16/-	17/-	IFFA&OFFA E.	KILMURRY	BUTLERSTOWN
41	THOMAS MOYLAN	29	12/-	-	OWNEY&ARRA	CASTLETOWN-ARRA	BALLINGEEK
44	JAMES MULLALLY	42	15/-	16/-	MIDDLETHIRD	KNOCKGRAFFON	LOUGHKENT
45	WILLIAM MULLALLY	(A) 35	11/-	13/-	KILNAMANAGH LR.	(A)AGHACREW	(A)ROSSACROW
		(B) 10	12/-	13/-		(B) DO.	(B) DO.
		(C) 4	14/-	13/-		(C) DO.	(C) DO.
		(D) 2	15/-	10/-		(D)DONOHIL	(D)CLASHNACRONY
		TOTAL 51					
46	THOMAS MULLANEY	(A) 22	21/-	23/-	ELIOGARTY	(A)DROM	(A)DROM
		(B) 29	22/-	22/-		(B)KILFITHMONE	(B)FISHMOYNE
		TOTAL 51					
49	CORNELIUS O'BRIEN	52	10/-	11/-	LR. ORMOND	LORRHA	ABBEYVILLE
3	WILLIAM O'KEANE	26	12/-	6/-	CLANWILLIAM	TEMPLENEIRY	BALLAGH
2	EDMUND O'SHAUGHNESSY	30	17/-	-	MIDDLETHIRD	DRANGAN	NEWTOUNDRANGAN
5	EDMUND PRENDERGAST	(A) 26	16/-	14/-	SLIEVARDAGH	BALLINGARRY	(A)BALLINGARRY LR
		(B) 44	13/-	12/-			(B)GLENGALL
		TOTAL 70					
7	JAMES RYAN	(A) 7	13/-	11/-	OWNEY & ARRA	YOUGHALARRA	(A)CARRIGMADDEN
		(B) 57	14/-	15/-			(B)CURRAGHTEMPLE
		TOTAL 64					
8	ANDREW SCANLAN	33	10/-	10/-	IKERRIN	BOURNEY	CORRIGA
3	MICHAEL SCANLAN	(A) 14	22/-	19/-	LOWER ORMOND	(A)MODREENY	(A)TOWNFIELDS
		(B) 96	10/-	7/-		(B)BALLY-GIBBON	
		TOTAL 110					
9	MICHAEL TOBIN	(A) 9	26/-	24/-	IFFA&OFFA WEST	CAHIR	(A)KILLENLY
		(B) 5	38/-	URBAN			(B)TOWNPARKS
		TOTAL 14					
0	MAURICE WALL	(A) 6	37/-	34/-	IFFA&OFFA EAST	KILGRANT	(A)GURTNAFLEUR
		(B) 34	23/-	23/-			(B)POWERSTOWN
		TOTAL 40					

NO. OF PRIESTS 40.

BREAKDOWN OF FARMS

UNDER 20	20-30	31-40	41-50	51-60	61-70	71-80	81-90	91-100	OVER 100	OVER 40
9	8	6	6	4	4	-	1	-	2	17
22%	20%	15%	15%	10%	10%	-	3%	-	5%	43%

TABLE 6 – Ecclesiastical Statistics for County Tipperary 1835, 1861, 1891. (Area extracted from ailbe census of Cashel and Emly)

PARISH	MASS ATTENDANCE 13% - 30%	NO.OF CHAPELS	TOTAL NO. OF MASSES EACH SUNDAY	NO.OF PRIESTS	R.C.POP. IN 1835	AREA STATUTE ACRES	ONE CHAPEL PER HEAD R.C. POP.	ONE PRIEST PER HEAD OF POP. 1835	TOTAL POP. 1861	NO.OF PRIESTS 1861	ONE PRIEST PER HEAD POP.1861	TOTAL POP. 1891	NO.OF PRIESTS 1891	ONE PRIEST PER HEAD OF POP. 1891
BALLINGARRY	13%	1	1	3	8967	17660	8967	2989	5598	2	2799	3229	2	1614
BANSHA (KILMOYLER OMITTED)	30%	1	1	1	4950	18354	4950	4950	4364	3	1455	2914	3	971
DONASKEIGH	28%	2	2	3	5985	15942	2992	1995	2836	2	1418	2139	2	1069
DOON	25%	2	1	2	5500	15278	5500	2750	3813	2	1906	2954	2	1477
DROM	28%	2	2	2	6127	15408	3063	3063	3017	2	1508	1804	2	902
HOLYCROSS	26%	2	2	2	5728	13459	2864	2864	2963	2	1481	1882	2	941
MOYCARKEY	29%	2	2	3	8199	27716	4099	2733	4385	2	2192	3192	2	1596
NEWINN	25%	2	2	2	4850	14272	2425	2425	2425	2	1212	1664	2	832
SOLOHEAD	27%	2	2	2	6570	14523	3285	3285	4271	3	1424	3414	2	1707
31% - 50%		15	15	20	56876	AVERAGE 16957	3792	2844	33672	20	1684	23192	19	1221
ANACARTY	31%	2	4	2	6364	16087	3182	3182	3263	2	1631	2430	2	1215
BALLINA	48%	2	" (NOT SPECIFIED)	2	7550	12865	3775	3775	2461	2	1230	1978	2	989
BALLINAHINCH	46%	2	3	2	3035	17660	1517	1517	2454	2	1227	1719	2	859
BORRISOLEIGH	41%	2	3	2	6807	14495	3403	3403	3859	3	1929	2710	2	1355
DRANGAN	35%	2	3	2	4487	18944	2243	2243	3494	2	1747	2090	2	1045
EMLY	35%	1	2	2	4307	9764	4307	2153	2747	2	1373	2074	2	1037
GOLDEN	34%	2	2	2	6160	12565	3080	3080	2666	2	1333	1495	2	747
KILLENAULE	45%	2	4	3	7974	25025	3987	2658	5220	3	1740	3307	3	1102
MULLINAHONE	46%	1	2	3	6564	15948	6564	3282	4123	2	2061	2392	2	1196
NEWPORT	35%	3	4	3	9202	22796	3067	3067	5170	3	1723	3646	3	1215
UPPERCHURCH	41%	3	3	2	6315	18513	2105	3157	3999	2	1999	3086	2	1543
51% - 70%		22	27	24	68765	AVERAGE 16787	3126	2865	39456	25	1578	26927	24	1122
CLONOULTY	68%	2	3	3	5893	18029	2946	1964	3484	2	1742	2401	2	1200
GALBALLY	52%	2	2	2	9070	28898	4535	4535	6200	3	2067	4171	3	1390
MOYNE	58%	2	2	3	5200	18734	2600	1733	3008	2	1504	2173	2	1086
TEMPLEMORE	57%	3	4 OR 5	3	9241	21404	3080	3080	7519	4	1880	4542	4	1385
TIPPERARY	54%	1	4	4	13267	14864	13267	3317	9809	3	3270	8493	4	2123
71% - 100%		10	15	15	42671	20386	4267	2845	30020	14	2144	21780	15	1452
CLERIHAN	72%	1	2	2 (DOES NOT INCLUDE FRIARS)	2776	8705	2776	1388	1808	1	1808	1084	1	1084
FETHARD	73%	2 PLUS FRIARY	5 (INCLUDES FRIARY)	3	9522	21973	4761 (DOES NOT INCLUDE FRIARS)	3174 (DOES NOT INCLUDE FRIARS)	5489	3	1830	3533	3	1178
THURLES	90%	3 + ABP	3	3 + A6P	12155	15008	12155	3038	7554	3+A6P	1888	5981	3+A6P	1495
		4+FRIARY	10	8 + ABP	24453	AVERAGE 15229	6113	2717	14851	7+A6P	1856	10598	7+A6P	1325

TABLE 7 — Religion Statistics per Parish in Co. Tipperary 1846–1855 (Cashel only)

Source: Visitations Reports for the parishes in the Cashel Diocesan Archives)

PARISH	POP. IN 1851	YEAR	NO. OF CONFIRMATIONS	% OF POP.	CONFRA-TERNITIES	MONTHLY COMMUNICANTS	% OF POP.	REGULAR SUNDAY INSTRUCTION	SUNDAY CATECHISM IN CHURCH	MASSES	CURATES COLLECTION	PAROCHIAL HOUSE	SOURCES
1.ANACARTY	4105	1847	387	9%	O.L.M.C.	240	6%		1½ HRS.	2(2 CHAPELS) DO.10A.M 10.30A.M	OCT.	NONE	1
		1852	468	11%	B.S. B.V.M. O.L.M.C.	200-240	6%	YES	YES	DO.	DO.	DO.	2
		1855	344	9%	O.L.M.C.	240	6%	YES	YES	DO.	DO.	DO.	3
2.BALLINA	3119	1853	385	12%	B.S. B.V.M.	120	4%	YES	YES	10A.M. AND 11A.M. 2(2 CHAPELS)	NONE		4
3.BALLINA-HINCH	3043	1848	203	7%	NONE	70	2%	YES	YES	2(2 CHAPELS)	-	NONE	5
		1853	382	12%	NONE	30	1%	YES	YES	DO.0,9,30, 11,30	OCT.	DO.	6
4.BALLIN-GARRY	7205	1846	584	8%	B.S. B.V.M. S.F.	100	1%		MAY-OCT.	2(9,11)	NONE	NONE	7
		1851	560	8%	B.S. B.V.M. S.F. S.A.	150	2%	YES	YES	DO.	DO.	DO.	8
		1854	552	8%	B.S. L.R. B.V.M. S.F.	200	3%	AT 2ND MASS	YES	DO.	DO.	DO.	9
5.BANSHA	6222	1846	299	5%	TWO	70	½%		YES	2,9,30, 11,30	OCT.		10
EXCLUDES KILMOYLER		1851	239	4%	TWO	50	¼%	YES	YES	DO.	OCT.		11
INCLUDES KILMOYLER		1854	339	5%	TWO	120	2%	YES	YES	DO.	OCT.		12

Parish	Total	Year	Col A	%	Dedication	Col B	%	Col C	Col D	Chapels	Curate	Last	#
6. BOHER-LAHAN	3994	1846	377	9%	B.S.	200	5%		YES	2(2 CHAPELS)	NONE	NONE	13
		1851	380	9%	B.V.M.	60	2%	YES	YES	DO.	DO.		14
		1854	247	6%	DO.	-		YES	YES	10A.M.	DO.		15
7. BORRISO-LEIGH	4850	1846	560	12%	B.S.	240	5%		YES	3(2 CHAPELS)	SEPT.	NONE	16
		1851	394	8%	B.V.M.	200	4%	YES	YES	DO.9,10,12,	DO.	DO.	17
		1854	335	7%	DO.	180	4%	YES	YES	DO.	DO.	DO.	18
8. CAPPA-WHITE	2735	1847	246	9%	B.V.M. M.H.E.	50-60	2%		YES	1(11A.M.)		NONE	19
		1852	236	9%	M.H.E. L.R.	40-50	2%	YES	YES			DO.	20
		1855	196	7%	B.V.M. B.S.	40	1%	YES	YES	DO.		DO.	21
9. CASHEL	12,521	1846	866	7%	S.H. B.V.M. B.S.	400	3%		YES	4(2 CHAPELS)		-	22
		1851	960	8%	DO.	250-300	2%	YES	YES	3(8,10,12)	MAY ADVENT	-	23
		1854	858	7%	DO.	200	1%	8A.M. 12 NOON	YES	DO.	DO.	-	24
10. CLERIHAN	2201	1847	138	6%	B.S.	100	5%	ENG/IRISH YES	YES	2	NO CURATE	NONE	25
		1852	317	14%	DO.	100	5%		6 MONTHS	2	DO.	DO.	26
		1855	188	9%	DO.	100	5%		YES	2(8,11)	DO.	DO.	27
11. CLONOULTY	4302	1846	375	9%	B.S. B.V.M.	250	6%		EASTER TO MICHELMAS YES	3(2 CHAPELS)	OCT.	NONE	28
		1851	365	8%	DO.	45	1%		YES	3(2 CHAPELS)	DO.	DO.	29
		1854	311	7%	DO.	100	2%		YES BY P.P.	2	DO.	DO.	30
12. DONASKEIGH	3362	1847	217	6%	B.V.M.(150)	250	7%		YES	2(2 CHAPELS)	NONE		31
		1852	250	7%	B.V.M. B.S.	100	3%	YES	YES	2	DO.		32

No.	Parish	Pop.	Year	—	%	Devotions	Attend.	%	Last Mass	6 Summer Months 12–2 P.M.	Masses/Chapels	Month	None
33	13.DOON	4070	1847	227	6%	B.V.M.	150	4%		6 SUMMER MONTHS 12–2 P.M.	2	NONE	NONE
34			1852	430	11%	B.S.	200 MAJORITY ONCE A YEAR	5%	YES	DO.	2	DO.	DO.
35			1855	416	10%	a.V.M. / B.V.M. / L.R. / S.H. / B.S.			YES		2	DO.	DO.
36	14.DRANGAN	4575	1846	418	9%	P.OF F. / B.V.M. / M.H.S. / B.V.M. / B.S. / DO.	400–500	11%		YES	3(2 CHAPELS)	OCT.	NONE
37			1851	308	7%		200–250	5%	YES	YES	DO.	DO.	DO.
38			1854	278	6%		300	7%	YES	YES	DO.	DO.	DO.
39	15.DROM	4299	1848	397	9%	B.V. / M.H.S. / DO.	150	3%	LAST MASS YES / YES	–	3(2 CHAPELS)		
40			1853	440	10%		100	2%	YES	YES	2		
41	16.EMLY	3354	1848	178	5%	B.V.M. / B.S. / B.V.M. / B.S. / S.H.	80	2%	Y	YES	2		NONE
42			1853	280	8%		70–80	2%	YES	YES			DO.
43	17.FETHARD	7056	1847	320	5%	B.S. / B.V.M. / S.H. / DO. / B.S. / B.V.M. / S.H. / L.R.	400	6%	YES	YES	3(2 CHAPELS)	SEPT./OCT.	NONE
44			1852	509	7%		300–400	6%	YES	YES	9,10,12 DO.	DO.	DO.
45			1855				400	6%		YES		DO.	DO.
46	18.GALBALLY	7340	1848	288	4%	B.V.M. / TWO	200	3%	YES	YES	3(2 CHAPELS)	–	NONE
47			1853				200	3%		SUMMER	DO.	NONE	
48	19.GOLDEN	3791	1847	282	7%	B.S. / B.V.M. / B.V.M(350) / B.S.(80) / S.F.(50) / DO.	200	5%	YES	YES	2(2 CHAPELS)	OCT.	NONE
49			1852	397	10%		MOST AT EASTER	–	YES	YES	DO.	DO.	DO.
50			1855	169	4%		APPROX. 400	10%	YES	YES	DO.	DO.	

Parish	Pop.	Year		%	Dedication	"MANY" / No.	%		Time / YES	Chapels	Month		#
20. GURTNAHOE	6654	1846	525	8%	YES	"MANY"	1%	YES	YES	3(2 CHAPELS)	OCT.		51
		1851	503	8%	B.S. B.V.M.	60	1%		10-11A.M.	3(2 CHAPELS)	DO.		52
		1854	431	6%	DO.	60-70			SUMMER	3(2 CHAPELS) DO.	DO.		53
21. HOLYCROSS	4521	1847	233	5%	B.V.M. S.H. B.S.	500	11%		12-2.00P.M.	2(2 CHAPELS)	OCT.		54
		1852	369	8%	B.S.	250-300	7%	YES	YES	DO.	DO.	NONE	55
		1855	269	6%	B.V.M. C.O. B.V.M. B.S.	200	4%	YES	YES	DO.	DO.	DO.	56
22. KILCOMMON	3974	1848	287	7%	B.V.M.(200) B.S.(SMALL) O.L.M.C.	ALL DID EASTER DUTY	4%		YES	2(2 CHAPELS)	NONE	•	57
		1853	478	12%		150		YES	YES	DO.	DO.	YES	58
23. KILLENAULE	6620	1846	646	10%	B.S. B.V.M. PLUS TWO SMALL ONES	400-500 1st AND 3rd SUNDAYS	7%		YES	4(2 CHAPELS)	MICHELMAS		59
		1851	669	10%	B.S.	600	9%	2nd MASS	YES	DO.	DO.		60
		1854	541	8%	B.V.M. DO.	700	11%	YES	1½ HRS.	3	OCT.		61
24. KILMOYLER [SEE BANSHA]	-	1847	175	-	B.V.M.(60) B.E.(60)	130	-		YES				62
25. LATTIN	4026	1846	328	8%	ONE	80(30-40 EVERY SUNDAY)	2%		SUMMER	2(2 CHAPELS)	MICHELMAS	NONE	63
		1854	295	7%		120	3%	YES	YES	DO.	OCT.	DO.	64
26. LOUGHMORE	4625	1846	679	14%	NONE	600	13%		YES	2(2 CHAPELS)	NONE	NONE	65
		1851	368	8%	-	60-70	2%		YES	DO.(10, 11 O.C.)		DO.	66
		1854	245	5%	B.V.M.	200	4%	YES	YES		DO.	DO.	67
27. MOYCARKEY	5335	1847	331	6%	TWO	150	3%	YES	APRIL-OCT. DO.	3(2 CHAPELS) 2	NONE	NONE	68
		1852	494	9%	B.S. B.V.M.	80-100	2%	YES	DO.		DO.	DO.	69
		1855			B.V.M.	150	3%	YES	YES	DO.			70

	Pop.	Year	No.	%	Devotions	No.	%			Chapels	Month		Line
28. MOYNE	4366	1846	430	10%	YES	-			YES	2(2 CHAPELS)	NONE	NONE	71
		1851	477	11%	B.S. / B.V.M.	LOW	2%	YES	YES	2	DO.	DO.	72
		1854			B.V.M. / S.S. / S.H.	100		YES	YES	2	DO.	DO.	73
29. MULLINAHONE	4853	1846	432	9%	B.V.M. / B.V.M.(150)	150	3%		YES	2	NONE		74
		1851	525	11%	B.V.M. / S.H.	200	4%	YES	YES	2	DO.		75
		1854			S.F.	200	4%		YES	2(9,11)	DO.		76
30. NEWINN	2975	1846	329	11%	B.S. / B.V.M. / S.H.	160-180	6%		YES	2	NONE	NONE	77
		1851	172	6%	B.V.M. / B.S. / S.H. / H.R.	50	2%	YES	SUMMER	2(2 CHAPELS)	DO.	DO.	78
		1854	171	6%	L.R.(180) PLUS TWO OTHERS	200	7%	YES	YES	DO.	OCT.	DO.	79
31. NEWPORT	5737	1848	319	6%	NONE	200	3%		YES	4(3 CHAPELS)	OCT.	NONE	80
		1853	711	12%	NONE	100	2%	YES	YES	DO.	DO.		81
32. SOLOHEAD	5640	1847	225	4%	TWO	70	1%		YES	2(2 CHAPELS)	NONE	NONE	82
		1852	620	11%	P.S. / C.R. / L.R.	60	1%	YES	YES	2	DO.		83
		1855	390	7%		80-90	2%	YES	YES				84
33. TEMPLEMORE	9077	1846	562	6%	B.V.M. / B.S.	500	6%		YES	4(3 CHAPELS)	FEB/MAY/OCT.	P.P. LEFT HIS RESIDENCE AS PAROCHIAL HOUSE.	85
		1851	736	8%	DO.	400	4%	YES	YES	DO.	DO.		86
		1854	634	7%	DO.			YES	YES	DO.	DO.		87

34.TIPPERARY	14311	1848	567	4%	B.S.(650) B.V.(500) S.H.(200)	300-400	3%	YES	YES	4	OCT.	NONE	88
		1853	1270	9%	DO.	400	3%	YES	1-2.P.M.	3	DO.	DO.	89
35.UPPERCHURCH	4603	1848	314	7%	TWO	160	3%	YES	YES	1(2 CHAPELS)	NONE OCT.		90
		1853	500	10%	TWO	140	3%	YES	YES	2(2 CHAPELS)			91

* THE HIGHEST FIGURE HAS BEEN TAKEN FOR PERCENTAGE PURPOSES.

CONFRATERNITY CODE
==================
B.E.= BLESSED EUCHARIST, B.S.= BLESSED SACRAMENT, B.V.M.= BLESSED VIRGIN MARY, C.D.= CHRISTIAN DOCTRINE, L.R.= LIVING ROSARY, M.A.S.= MOST ADORABLE SACRAMENT, M.H.E.= MOST HOLY EUCHARIST, M.H.S.= MOST HOLY SACRAMENT, O.L.M.C.= OUR LADY OF MOUNT CARMEL, P.OF F.= PROPAGATION OF THE FAITH, P.S.= PURGATORIAL SOCIETY, S.H.=SACRED HEART, S.A. = ST. AUGUSTINE, S.F.= ST. FRANCIS.

APPENDIX II

Directory of Secular Priests in County Tipperary, 1850 — 1891

Note: The 'Directory of Secular Priests' which begins overleaf has been reproduced directly from the original typewritten version — for reasons of economy and accuracy. In spite of the substantial reductions necessary and the uneven quality, the document is legible and its inclusion serves the author's and publisher's purpose of giving the reader access to a highly valuable and original piece of research.

DIRECTORY OF SECULAR PRIESTS IN
COUNTY TIPPERARY 1850 to 1891

The ministry details are taken from The Irish Catholic Directory 1850-1891. The directory is not noted for its accuracy and so due allowance must be made for errors. Information for the Cashel and Emly priests, however, is taken from the late Canon Walter Skehan's Index of the clergy of those dioceses, a more reliable source. The chief source for the priests' education is P.J. Hamell, Maynooth Students and Ordinations 1795-1895. Each priest in Monsignor Hamell's Index has a special reference or sequence number, and that rather than the page number has been used in sourcing this appendix.

EPISCOPAL SUCCESSION IN CO. TIPPERARY 1850-1891.

ARCHDIOCESE OF CASHEL AND EMLY.

1. MICHAEL SLATTERY 1834-1857.

   Born in Tipperary Town in 1783. Pursued clerical studies in the Abbey school there, and became a lay student in Trinity College in 1798. Took his M.A. in 1803, and entered St. Patrick's College, Carlow, in 1805. He was ordained in 1809, became a Professor in Carlow, and was President of Maynooth College in 1833. Vid. Archbishop Paul Cullen, Vol.11, op.cit., p.16. For further information on Slattery Vid. Introduction to the Slattery archives calender compiled by Dom Mark Tierney.

2. PATRICK LEAHY 1857-1875.

   See Index No.24. See Rev. C. O'Dwyer, 'Archbishop Patrick Leahy', M.A. (U.C.C. 1971).

3. THOMAS W. CROKE 1875-1902.

   Vid. Tierney, Croke of Cashel, pp.1-12.

DIOCESE OF KILLALOE.

1. P. KENNEDY 1836-1850.
2. DANIEL VAUGHAN 1851-1859 (See Index No. 555).
3. MICHAEL FLANNERY 1859-1891.
   Born 17/5/1818, became Dean of the Catholic University, Limerick Reporter 23/6/1891, Limerick Reporter 30/6/1891.
4. NICHOLAS POWER 1865-1871. (Coadjutor).
   Born in the Diocese of Waterford - Limerick Reporter 23/6/1891.
5. JAMES RYAN 1872-1889 (Coadjutor).
6. T.J. McREDMOND 1889-1903.
   Vid. Index No. 305.

DIOCESE OF WATERFORD.

1. NICHOLAS FORAN 1837-1855.
   Born Waterford City, ordained 1808, Educated in Maynooth, and became President of old St. John's College. Vid. Power, Waterford and Lismore,p.38.

2. DOMINICK O'BRIEN 1855-1873.
   Born Waterford City in 1798. Educated in Propaganda University, Rome, became Professor in old St. John's College and President there in 1834. Power, Waterford and Lismore,p.38.

3. JOHN POWER 1873-1887.
   See Index No. 455.
4. PIERSE POWER 1887-1889.
5. JOHN EGAN 1889-1891.
   See Index No. 467.
6. R.A. SHEEHAN 1891-1915.
   Native of Killaloe Diocese - Power, Waterford and Lismore, op. cit., p.40.
   Adm. of St. Peter and Paula Cork - Power, Waterford and Lismore, p.40. Nationalist 23/12/1891.

THE TIPPERARY PRIESTHOOD

1. BALDWIN JOHN
   BORN: 1791, DIED: 27/6/1867, Aged 76, BIRTHPLACE:[2] Parish of Carrick-beg.
   EDUCATION:[3] Maynooth, Theology 1814, Ordained 1816.
   SOCIAL BACKGROUND:[4] Farming.   POLITICAL INVOLVEMENT: Yes.
   DIOCESE: Waterford.   MINISTRY: F.F.St. Mary's Clonmel 1836-1867.

2. BANNON MICHAEL
   BORN 1797   DIED August 8th,1861, Aged 64.   BIRTHPLACE:Tonagha, Thurles Parish.
   EDUCATION:[5] Maynooth, Rhetoric 1825, Ordained C 1830
   SOCIAL BACKGROUND:[6] Farming.   MINISTRY: C.C. Moyne 1834-1851.
   DIOCESE: Cashel.   F.F. Moyne 1851-1861.

3. BANNON MICHAEL
   BORN c.1859   DIED 1926   BIRTHPLACE: Barnacurra, Ballycahill.
   EDUCATION: C.U.S. Thurles, St. Patrick's College, Thurles, Louvain, Ordained Tournoi, Belgium 1884.
   SOCIAL BACKGROUND:[7] Farming.   POLITICAL INVOLVEMENT: No.
   DIOCESE: Cashel.   MINISTRY: C.C. Newlnn 1891-1892.

4. BARRAT PATRICK
   BORN c.1863
   EDUCATION:[8]   Maynooth, Rhetoric 1880, Ordained 1888.
   POLITICAL INVOLVEMENT: Yes.
   DIOCESE: Killaloe.   MINISTRY: C.C. Castletownarra 1888-1891. Dunkerrin and Moneygall 1891-post 1891.

5. BARRON WILLIAM
   BORN 1793   DIED 1857   BIRTHPLACE: Parish of Killenaule
   EDUCATION: Ordained in Carlow 1827.
   POLITICAL INVOLVEMENT: Yes.
   DIOCESE: Cashel   MINISTRY: F.F. Moyne 1841-1851.

6. BARRY GERALD
   BORN 1830   DIED 1872,   BIRTHPLACE: Unknown
   EDUCATION: All Hallows: Left before ordination, taken in by Dr. Slattery, Ordained in Thurles 1855. Professor in St. Patrick's in 1860.
   POLITICAL INVOLVEMENT: Yes.
   DIOCESE: Cashel and Emly.   MINISTRY: C.C. Holycross 1861-1863.
                                          C.C. Clerihan 1867-1868.
                                          C.C. Cappawhite 1868-1872.

7. BARRY JOHN
   BORN: 1841   DIED 1920.   BIRTHPLACE: Bohernore Parish.
   EDUCATION:[9] Maynooth, Physics 1860, Ordained Edinburgh 1866.
   OTHER INFO: Left the Diocese to go to Toronto, admitted as a pauper to the Thurles and Clonmel workhouses.
   DIOCESE: Cashel and Emly.   MINISTRY: C.C. Newinn 1869-1871.

8. BARRY MICHAEL
   BORN: 1846,   DIED 1935   BIRTHPLACE: Knockllong Parish.
   EDUCATION: St. Patrick's, Thurles, Maynooth in 1868, Ordained in Carlow in 1872.
   POLITICAL INVOLVEMENT: Yes.
   DIOCESE: Cashel and Emly.   MINISTRY: C.C. Gurtnahoe 1886-1896.

9. BERGIN LAWRENCE
   BORN: 1812   DIED, 19th October 1855   BIRTHPLACE:[10] Dualla Parish.
   EDUCATION:[10]Maynooth, Logic 1830, Ordained 1837.
   POLITICAL INVOLVEMENT: Yes.
   OTHER INFO: Cousin of Dean James McDonnell.
   DIOCESE: Cashel and Emly.   MINISTRY: C.C. Killuonaule 1850-1851.
                                          C.C. Cashel   1851-1855.

10. BERRINGHAM JAMES
    BORN: c.1792   DIED, 1856
    EDUCATION:[11] Maynooth, Humanity 1812, Ordained No date.
    POLITICAL INVOLVEMENT: Yes.
    DIOCESE: Killaloe   MINISTRY: F.F. Borrisokane pre 1850-1856.

11. BLAKE THOMAS D.D.
    BORN: c.1800   DIED 25/6/1865.
    EDUCATION:[12] Maynooth, Rhetoric 1820, Ordained 1825.
    POLITICAL INVOLVEMENT: Yes.
    DIOCESE: Killaloe.

12. BOWLES JAMES
    BORN[13]10/8/1811   DIED[14]December 1880, BIRTHPLACE,[15]Parish of Tulla.
    EDUCATION: Maynooth Logic 1832, Ordained 1837.
    POLITICAL INVOLVEMENT: Yes.
    OTHER INFO:[7] Uncle of F. McGrath, Solicitor, Roscrea.
    DIOCESE: Killaloe.   MINISTRY: C.C. Nenagh 1850-1852.
                                    C.C. Birr   1852-1856.

13. BREEN MICHAEL
BORN:[18] 1861 BIRTHPLACE:[19] Parish of Kilmacduane.
EDUCATION:[20] Maynooth for 2½ years, Irish College, Rome 1881-1883, Ordained in St. Sulpice, Paris.
POLITICAL INVOLVEMENT: Yes.
DIOCESE: Killaloe. MINISTRY: C.C. Shinrone 1890-post 1891.

14. BRENNAN PATRICK
BORN: c.1843 DIED 29/12/1893.
EDUCATION:[21] Maynooth, Humanity 1860, Ordained 1867/1868.
POLITICAL INVOLVEMENT: Yes.
DIOCESE: Killaloe. MINISTRY: C.C. Kyle and Knock 1867-1868, 1875-1887.

15. BROSNAHAN TIMOTHY D.D.
BORN:[22] c.1844 DIED 11/8/1900.
EDUCATION:[23] Maynooth, Rhetoric 1861. Ordained 1869.
POLITICAL INVOLVEMENT: No.
OTHER INFO:[24] On the Dunboyne Establishment in Maynooth. Had a brother a regular priest.
DIOCESE: Killaloe. MINISTRY: C.C. Shinrone 1869-1870, C.C. Borrisokane 1871-1873, C.C. Burgess and Youghal 1873-1874.

16. BUGLER MICHAEL
BORN:[25] 1808 DIED 14/11/1893. BIRTHPLACE:[26] Whitegate.
EDUCATION:[27] Maynooth, Rhetoric 1829, Ordained 1835.
POLITICAL INVOLVEMENT: Yes.
DIOCESE: Killaloe. MINISTRY: C.C.Borrisokane 1869-1851, P.P.Borrisokane 1856-1859, P.P. Birr 1870-1891.

17. BURKE EDMUND
BORN: c.1844 DIED 1921. BIRTHPLACE: Lisadyhane, Emly Parish.
EDUCATION: St. Patrick's College, Thurles, Irish College, Paris, Ordained in Presentation Convent, Thurles 1869.
SOCIAL BACKGROUND:[28] Farming (40-50 Irish acres).
POLITICAL INVOLVEMENT: Yes.
DIOCESE: Cashel and Emly. MINISTRY: C.C. Newport 1876-1878, C.C. Drangan 1879-1885, C.C. Fethard 1885-1889, P.P. Clerihan 1889-1892.

18. BURKE JAMES
BORN: c.1852 DIED 15/11/1893. BIRTHPLACE: Ardfinan.
EDUCATION: St. John's College, entered 15/?/1872, Ordained 1877.
POLITICAL INVOLVEMENT: Yes.
DIOCESE: Waterford.
OTHER INFO: On mission in Liverpool later.

19. BURKE JAMES
BORN: c.1809 DIED 1858. BIRTHPLACE: Drumcomoge, Emly.
EDUCATION:[29] Maynooth, Physics 1830, Ordained 1834.
SOCIAL BACKGROUND:[30] Farming. POLITICAL INVOLVEMENT: Yes.
DIOCESE: Cashel and Emly. MINISTRY: C.C. Newlon 1841-1850, C.C.Newport 1853-1855.

20. BURKE JOHN
BORN: c.1844. DIED 1898. BIRTHPLACE: Galbally.
EDUCATION:[31] Maynooth, Physics 1864, Ordained (N.D.)in Ursuline Convent, Thurles.
POLITICAL INVOLVEMENT: Yes.
DIOCESE: Cashel and Emly. MINISTRY: C.C. Newport 1870-1875, C.C. Holycross 1879-1884, C.C. Moyne 1884-1891.

21. BURKE JOHN
BORN: 1809, DIED 1891, BIRTHPLACE: Rathnamurkey, Moycarkey.
EDUCATION:[32] Deacon in 1839. Ordained in Thurles 1840.
SOCIAL BACKGROUND:[33] Farming. POLITICAL INVOLVEMENT: Yes.
OTHER INFO: Uncle of Archbishop Thomas Fennelly,(index no.145). Tradition has it that Fr. Burke was one of the few priests to personally welcome Croke when he became Archbishop.
DIOCESE: Cashel and Emly. MINISTRY: C.C. Holycross 1841-1853, F.P. Moycarkey 1853-1891.

22. BURKE MICHAEL
BORN: 1812 DIED 25/8/1875. BIRTHPLACE: Powerstown Parish.
EDUCATION:[34] St. John's College, Ordained 7/4/1861.
POLITICAL INVOLVEMENT: Yes.
DIOCESE: Waterford. MINISTRY: C.C. Clonmel St.Peter and Pauls 1865-1866, P.P. Ballyporeen 1868-1875.

23. BURKE MICHAEL
BORN: c.1822 DIED 5/10/1863.
EDUCATION:[35] St. John's Waterford 24/10/1844-1847, Ordained 1847.
POLITICAL INVOLVEMENT: Yes.
DIOCESE: Waterford. MINISTRY:C.C.Clogheen 1854-1859, C.C.Cammonsfield and Kilcash 1859-1860, C.C.Ardfinan 1860-1872, C.C.Ballyneale 1874-1875.

24. BURKE MICHAEL
BORN:[36] 1763. DIED 11/2/1857, Aged 94.
EDUCATION:[37] Unknown, but ordained in the 1790's.
POLITICAL INVOLVEMENT: Yes.
DIOCESE: Waterford. MINISTRY: P.P. Ardfinan 1851-1857.

25. BURKE MICHAEL D.D.V.G.
BORN:[38] 1789 DIED[39] August 1866 BIRTHPLACE[40] Parish of Kilshealan.
EDUCATION:[41] Maynooth, Physics 1812, Ordained 1816.
SOCIAL BACKGROUND:[42] Farming (size of farm unknown).
POLITICAL INVOLVEMENT: Yes.
OTHER INFO:[43] Began career as Professor in St. John's Waterford, prolonged illness before he died. Uncle of Thomas Burke, index no.30.
DIOCESE: Waterford. MINISTRY: P.F.Clonmel,St.Peter and Pauls 1836-1866.

26. BURKE MICHAEL
POLITICAL INVOLVEMENT: Yes.
DIOCESE: Killaloe MINISTRY: C.C. Birr pre 1850-1851, C.C. Nenagh 1851-1852.

27. BURKE PATRICK
DIED 1863. POLITICAL INVOLVEMENT: No.
DIOCESE: Waterford. MINISTRY: C.C. Four-Mile-Water and Newcastle 1862-1863.

28. BURKE PATRICK
BORN: c.1844 BIRTHPLACE:[45] Powerstown.
EDUCATION:[46]St. John's Waterford 1862-1864, Maynooth 1864-1869, Ordained 1869.
POLITICAL INVOLVEMENT: No.
DIOCESE: Waterford. MINISTRY: C.C. Cloghen 1876-1877.

29. BURKE REDMOND V.F.
BORN: c.1799 DIED November 1875, BIRTHPLACE, Killusty.
EDUCATION:[47] Carlow, Maynooth Logic 1816, Ordained 1824.
POLITICAL INVOLVEMENT: Yes.
DIOCESE: Cashel and Emly. MINISTRY: F.F. Newport 1848-1875.

30. BURKE THOMAS
BORN: c.1830 DIED 5/10/1863. BIRTHPLACE:[48] Powerstown.
EDUCATION:[49]Irish College, Rome 1849-1855.
POLITICAL INVOLVEMENT: Yes.
OTHER INFO:[50] A nephew of Dr. Burke (Index No.25).
DIOCESE: Waterford. MINISTRY: C.C. Cahir 1859-1863.

31. BURKE THOMAS
BORN: c.1816 or c.1820
EDUCATION:[51] St. JohM's College, Waterford 1837-1841.
POLITICAL INVOLVEMENT: Yes.
DIOCESE: Waterford. MINISTRY: C.C. Clonmel, St. Peter and Pauls 1855-1856, C.C. Four-Mile-Water and Newcastle 1858-1868.

32. BURKE TIMOTHY

BORN: c.1852   DIED 1902   BIRTHPLACE: Kilcommon. His people from Anacarty, buried in Kilpatrick.

EDUCATION: St. Patrick's College, Thurles, Ordained there 1877.

POLITICAL INVOLVEMENT: Yes.

DIOCESE: Cashel.   MINISTRY: C.C. Gurtnahoe 1887-1892.

33. BURKE TOBIAS

BORN: c.1842   DIED 28/10/1917. BIRTHPLACE[52] Fowerstown.

EDUCATION[53] St. John's College, Waterford 1862-1867, Ordained 1867.

POLITICAL INVOLVEMENT: No.

OTHER INFO[54] Temporary mission in Kildare after ordination.

DIOCESE: Waterford.   MINISTRY: C.C. Ballyneale 1869-1871.
    C.C. Ballylooby 1871-1872.
    C.C. Clogheen 1873-1875.

34. BURKE WILLIAM

BORN: c.1833   DIED 16/8/1910. BIRTHPLACE[55] "High Road, Ardfinan.

EDUCATION[56] Maynooth, Theology 1855, Ordained N.D.

SOCIAL BACKGROUND[57] A member of "a much respected Tipperary family."

POLITICAL INVOLVEMENT: No.

DIOCESE: Waterford.   MINISTRY: C.C. Ballyporeen 1870-1877.

35. BURKE WILLIAM

BORN[58] 1856.   DIED 21/5/1900. BIRTHPLACE[59] "Clionlara,Doonas Parish.

EDUCATION[60] Diocesan Seminary, Ennis for 2½ years,Irish College, Rome 1875-1881, Ordained 1881.

SOCIAL BACKGROUND[61] Well off, "easy circumstances."

POLITICAL INVOLVEMENT: Yes.

OTHER INFO[62] Brother of P. Burke, President of the Diocesan Seminary, Ennis.

DIOCESE: Killaloe.   MINISTRY[63] C.C. Kilbarron 1883-1886(July).
    C.C. Gorriskeane1886-1890.

36. BUTLER JOHN D.D.

BORN: c.1837   DIED 1876, Aged 39, BIRTHPLACE, Clonmel.

EDUCATION[64] Maynooth, Humanity 1857, Ordained in St. Patrick's Thurles, 1863.

POLITICAL INVOLVEMENT: Yes.

OTHER INFO: Nephew of Archbishop Slattery. Became D.D. after Vatican Council 1870, was Dean of St. Patrick's,Thurles in 1862, before ordination.

DIOCESE: Cashel and Emly. MINISTRY: C.C. Thurles 1864-1871.
    Adm, Thurles 1871-1875.
    P.P. Lattin and Cullen 1875-1876.

37. BUTLER JOHN

BORN: c.1801   DIED 30/9/1877.   BIRTHPLACE: Cahir.

EDUCATION: Irish College, Paris, Ordained there in 1826.

SOCIAL BACKGROUND[65] "Farming, very wealthy "an old and highborn family."

POLITICAL INVOLVEMENT: No.   DIOCESE: Cashel and Emly.

38. BYRNE PATRICK

BORN: c.1847   BIRTHPLACE, 66 Ardfinan.

EDUCATION[67] St. John's College, Waterford, 1864, Ordained 1872.

POLITICAL INVOLVEMENT: Yes.

OTHER INFO: 68 On temporary mission to Dundee.

DIOCESE: Waterford.   MINISTRY: C.C. Powerstown 1876-1884.
    C.C. Clonmel, St. Peter and Pauls 1886-1890.

39. BYRNE PATRICK

BORN: c.1806   BIRTHPLACE, 69 Dungarvan.

EDUCATION[70] St. John's College 1830-1831.

POLITICAL INVOLVEMENT: Yes.

DIOCESE: Waterford.   MINISTRY: C.C. Carrick-On-Suir pre 1850-1857.
    C.C. Ardfinan 1857-1858

40. C?HER JAMES

BORN[71] 30/11/1828. DIED 13/ 2/1915, Aged 87. BIRTHPLACE[72] Runnaleen, Corofin.

EDUCATION[73] Irish College, Paris, 1850's.

SOCIAL BACKGROUND[74] Farming.

POLITICAL INVOLVEMENT[75] "Not in Tipperary, but"an active Land League" in Co. Clare.

DIOCESE: Killaloe.   MINISTRY: C.C. Mounsea 1852-1853.

41. CAHILL JOHN

BORN: 1843   DIED 1891   BIRTHPLACE, Quarry Street, Thurles, son of William Cahill.

EDUCATION: St. Patrick's College, Thurles, Ordained 1869.

POLITICAL INVOLVEMENT: Yes.

OTHER INFO: Chaplain, Presentation Convent Cashel 1883-1884.

DIOCESE: Cashel and Emly. MINISTRY: C.C. Loughmore 1870-1875.
    C.C. Donaskeigh 1880-1882.
    C.C. Mullinahone 1884-1889,
    C.C. Cappawhite 1890-1891.

42. CAHILL RICHARD V.G.

BORN: c.1820.   DIED 1603 BIRTHPLACE, Cloghtanly,Drangan,Son of Philip Cahill.

EDUCATION[76] Maynooth, Rhetoric 1841, was on the Durboyne and lectured in Maynooth for a short time, Ordained 1849.

SOCIAL BACKGROUND[77] Farming.

OTHER INFO[78] One of the ternis after Archbishop Leahy's death.

POLITICAL INVOLVEMENT: Yes.

DIOCESE: Cashel and Emly.   MINISTRY: C.C. Thurles 1850-1856,
    C.C. Tipperary 1856-1863,
    Adm. Tipperary 1857-1863,
    P.P. Donaskeigh 1863-1875,
    P.P. Lattin and Cullen 1876-1884,
    ?.P. Tipperary 1884-1903.

43. CAHILL WILLIAM

BORN: c.1814   DIED 1868 Aged 54, BIRTHPLACE, Ballyboy, Upperchurch.

EDUCATION: 79 Maynooth, Rhetoric 1833, Ordained in Thurles 1840.

SOCIAL BACKGROUND: 80 Farming.

POLITICAL INVOLVEMENT: Yes.

OTHER INFO: 81 Ill between 1858 and 1862. A great orator, known as 'Silver-Tongue.' He wrote poetry for the Nation under the non-de plume alpha, a keen Irish scholar.

DIOCESE: Cashel and Emly.   MINISTRY: C.C. Mullinahone 1847-1855,
    C.C. Killenaule 1855-1858.
    F.P. Cappawhite 1862-1868.

44. CALLANAN JAMES

BORN: 1837   DIED 1889   BIRTHPLACE, Dovea, Oron and Inch.

EDUCATION[82] Maynooth, Physics 1856, Ordained 1861.

SOCIAL BACKGROUND[83] Farming.   POLITICAL INVOLVEMENT: Yes.

OTHER INFO: Brother of Michael (No.45) Chaplain, Presentation Convent, Cashel 1880-1882.

DIOCESE: Cashel and Emly.   MINISTRY: C.C. Holycross   1862-1863.
    C.C. Anacarty   1876-1877.
    C.C. Ballinahinech 1877-1878.
    C.C. Newinn   1882-1886.
    F.P. Donaskeigh   1886-1889.

45. CALLANAN MICHAEL

BORN: c.1819   DIED[84] October 1888   BIRTHPLACE, Dovea.

EDUCATION: Irish College, Rome, Ordained in Thurles 1844.

SOCIAL BACKGROUND 85 Farming.   POLITICAL INVOLVEMENT: No.

OTHER INFO: 86 Brother of James (No.44)"The scion of an old and respectable family, who had suffered eviction."

DIOCESE: Cashel and Emly. MINISTRY: C.C. Galbally 1846-1850.
    C.C. Ballingarry 1858-1868.
    F.P. Cappawhite 1868-1888.

46. FR. CANTWELL

EDUCATION: Unknown, not Maynooth.   POLITICAL INVOLVEMENT: No.

MINISTRY: C.C. Clogheen 1869-1871.

DIOCESE: Waterford.

47. CANTWELL JAMES

BORN: 1844   DIED December 1905   BIRTHPLACE, Loughcapple,Killusty.

EDUCATION: 87 Maynooth, Humanity 1862, Ordained in Ursuline Convent, Thurles 1868.

SOCIAL BACKGROUND: 88 Farming.   POLITICAL INVOLVEMENT: Yes.

OTHER INFO: Nephew of Dean Walter Cantwell (No.50) and brother of Walter No.51.

DIOCESE: Cashel and Emly.   MINISTRY: C.C. Fethard 1868-1876.
    C.C.Thurles 1876-1878.
    Adm.Thurles 1878-1885.
    P.P.Rallingarry 1885-1905.

48. CANTWELL JOHN

BORN: c.1831   DIED 16/7/1903. BIRTHPLACE 89 Kilconsenty,Stradbally.

EDUCATION 90 St. John's College-Waterford 1862-1867,or 1864-1866, Irish College, Rome 1866.

POLITICAL INVOLVEMENT: No.   DIOCESE: Waterford.

49. CANTWELL THOMAS
BORN: c.1845. EDUCATION:[91] St. John's College,Waterford, Ordained c.1870.
POLITICAL INVOLVEMENT: No. DIOCESE: Waterford.
MINISTRY: C.C. Ardfinnan 1875-1876.

50. CANTWELL WALTER D.D. V.G.
BORN: c.1812 DIED 13/1/1878.
EDUCATION: Carlow and Irish College, Paris, Ordained in Thurles 1836.
POLITICAL INVOLVEMENT: Yes.
OTHER INFO:[92] Uncle of James Cantwell (No.47) and Walter (No.51). Tension between him and Archbishop Leahy, cousin of Walter (No.52).
DIOCESE: Cashel and Emly. MINISTRY: Adm. Thurles 1850-1857, Dean of Cashel 1857-1861. Archdeacon of Fechard 1861-1878.

51. CANTWELL WALTER
BORN c.1845. DIED 1917 BIRTHPLACE: Loughcapple, Killusty.
EDUCATION: Irish College, Paris, Ordained there 1870.
SOCIAL BACKGROUND:[93] farming, "an old and respected Irish family. His mother spent £50. annually on the poor of her district."
POLITICAL INVOLVEMENT: Yes.
OTHER INFO: Brother of James Cantwell, No.47 and Nephew of Walter Cantwell, No.50.
DIOCESE: Cashel and Emly. MINISTRY: C.C. Arharlahan 1875-1875.
C.C. Killenaule 1876-1884.
C.C. Tipperary 1884-post 1891.

52. CANTWELL WALTER
BORN: c.1798. DIED 19/3/1883.
EDUCATION:[95] St. John's, Waterford 1830-1832.
OTHER INFO: Cousin of Walter, No.50.
POLITICAL INVOLVEMENT: Yes. MINISTRY: F.F. Ardfinnan 1857-1883.
DIOCESE: Waterford.

53. CANTY PATRICK
BORN: c.1825. DIED 18/10/1877. BIRTHPLACE: Knockling Parish.
EDUCATION: Irish College, Paris, Extern in Maynooth 1849.
SOCIAL BACKGROUND:[96] farming. POLITICAL INVOLVEMENT: Yes.
DIOCESE: Cashel and Emly. MINISTRY: C.C. Moycarkey 1852-1871.
F.P. Kilcommon 1871-1877.

54. CARGOH JOHN
EDUCATION: Unknown, but not Maynooth.
POLITICAL INVOLVEMENT: Yes.
DIOCESE: Killaloe. MINISTRY: C.C. Ardcroney and Ballygibbin, 1865-1867.

55. CASEY DANIEL
BORN: c.1832. EDUCATION:[97] Maynooth, Theology 1852, Deacon 1857.
POLITICAL INVOLVEMENT: No. DIOCESE: Waterford.
MINISTRY:[98] C.C. Ballyneale 1860-1862.

56. CASEY JOHN
BORN:[99] 1852. DIED 6/8/1930. BIRTHPLACE:[100] Mothill, Stradbally.
EDUCATION:[101] St. John's Waterford 17/1/1870-27/5/1875 (Ordained)
MINISTRY: C.C. Clonmel, St. Mary's 1883-1885.
C.C. Carrick-On-Suir 1886-1890.
POLITICAL INVOLVEMENT: Yes DIOCESE: Waterford.

57. CASEY RICHARD 2.
BORN: c.1850 DIED 20/3/1917, BIRTHPLACE:[102] (abbeyside),Cream, Kilmacthomas.
EDUCATION:[103] St. John's Waterford 17/1/1870. Ordained 27/5/1875.
POLITICAL INVOLVEMENT: Yes. DIOCESE: Waterford.
MINISTRY: C.C. Ballyporeen 1882-1884.
C.C. Ardfinan 1884-1885.

58. CLANCY JAMES V.F.
BORN: c.1793. BIRTHPLACE, Knocklong Parish.
EDUCATION: Not Maynooth. POLITICAL INVOLVEMENT: Yes.
DIED 1862 MINISTRY: F.P. Galbally 1847-1862.

59. CLANCY JAMES
BORN:[104] 1858. DIED 4/3/1938, Aged 80, BIRTHPLACE[105] Ennis.
EDUCATION:[106] Irish College, Paris, Ordained 1882.
POLITICAL INVOLVEMENT:[107] Yes.Played an active part in the movement for reconciliation (outside Tipperary) after Parnell's death.
DIOCESE: Killaloe. OTHER INFO:[108] He had a brother a priest.
MINISTRY: C.C. Cloughjordan 1884-1887.

60. CLANCY JOHN
BORN: 1826 DIED 1897.
EDUCATION:[109] Maynooth, Theology 1850, Ordained 1854.
POLITICAL INVOLVEMENT: Yes. DIOCESE: Cashel and Emly.
MINISTRY: C.C. Galbally 1855-1860.
C.C. Newlan 1865-1867.
C.C. Oola and Solohead 1867-1877.
C.C. Donaskeigh 1877-1880.
F.P. Boherlahan 1880-1897.

61. CLEARY DANIEL
BORN c.1818 DIED 1/9/1870.
EDUCATION:[110] Maynooth, Ordained 1843. POLITICAL INVOLVEMENT: Yes.
DIOCESE: Killaloe. MINISTRY: C.C. Roscrea pre 1850-1862.
P.P. Dunkerrin 1862-1870.

62. CLEARY DENIS
BORN: [111] 12/6/1827 DIED 3/2/1911 BIRTHPLACE:[112] Lissenhall,Nonagh.
EDUCATION:[113] Maynooth, Rhetoric 1849, Ordained 1855. Early education at a classical school in Summerhill, Nenagh.
POLITICAL INVOLVEMENT: No. DIOCESE: Killaloe.
MINISTRY: C.C. Nenagh 1854-1856
C.C. Ardcroney 1857-1859
C.C. Castletownarra 1059-1861.

63. CLEARY FRANCIS
BORN:[114] 1811 DIED 31/7/1873.
EDUCATION: Maynooth[115] Humanity 1829, Ordained 1834.
POLITICAL INVOLVEMENT: Yes.
OTHER INFO:[116] had two other brothers priests (possibly No.64 and 67).
DIOCESE: Killaloe. MINISTRY: C.C. Courtagneen 1851-1857.
C.C. Nenagh 1858-1860.
F.F. Courtagneen 1860-1870.
F.F. Dunkerrin 1870-1873.

64. CLEARY MARTIN
BORN: c.1820
EDUCATION:[117]
POLITICAL INVOLVEMENT: Yes. DIOCESE: Killaloe.
MINISTRY:[118] C.C. Lortha pro 1850-1850.
C.C. Birr 1851-1856.
C.C. Kilbirron 1856-1857.
C.C. Nenagh 1857-1861.
Adm. Nenagh 1861-1868.

65. CLEARY RICH. EL
BORN[119] 1267 DIED Feb.1873. BIRTHPLACE, Killaghagen, Drum.
EDUCATION: Irish College, Salamanca 1630's and Irish College, Valladolid. He studied classics at a classical school in Templemore.
SOCIAL BACKGROUND:[120] farming. POLITICAL INVOLVEMENT: Yes.
MINISTRY: C.C. Killnmaule 1848-1855.
C.C. Cashel 1855-1859.

66. CLEARY MICHAEL JOHN
BORN: c.1851. DIED 20/1/1906. BIRTHPLACE, Golden Parish.
EDUCATION: St. Patrick's College, Thurles 1869-1876. Ordained Hamilton, Canada 1876.
POLITICAL INVOLVEMENT: Yes.
OTHER INFO: On mission in Hamilton, Canada after ordination.
DIOCESE: Cashel and Emly. MINISTRY: C.C. Donaskeigh 1886-1887.
C.C. Solohead 1887-1888.
C.C. Newport 1888-1891.
C.C. Templemore 1891-1906.

67. CLEARY F. TRICK
EDUCATION: Unknown, but not Maynooth. POLITICAL INVOLVEMENT: No.
DIOCESE: Killaloe. MINISTRY: C.C. Couragnmeen pro 1850-

68. CLEARY PATRICK
BORN:[121] 1024, DIED 27/2/1863. BIRTHPLACE,[122] Parish of Dungarvan.
EDUCATION:[123] Humanities in St. John's Waterford, Irish College, Rome, 1841-1844.
POLITICAL INVOLVEMENT: Yes.
DIOCESE: Waterford.   MINISTRY: C.C. Ardfinan 1858-1860.
                                 C.C. Commonsfield 1860-1863.

69. CLEARY PHILIP
BORN:[124] 1823,   DIED March 1887 BIRTHPLACE, Cahirvillahow, Knockavolla.
EDUCATION:[125] Maynooth, Theology 1847, Ordained in Limerick 1850.
SOCIAL BACKGROUND:[126] Farming. POLITICAL INVOLVEMENT: Yes.
OTHER INFO: Dean of St. Patrick's College, Thurles 1064-1865.
DIOCESE: Cashel and Emly. MINISTRY: C.C. Gibally 1865-1067.
                                    C.C. Templemore 1867-1869.
                                    C.C. Ballingarry 1870-1873.

70. CLUNE JOHN
BORN:[127] 1814.   DIED 11/7/1890.
EDUCATION: Unknown, but not Maynooth. POLITICAL INVOLVEMENT: No.
DIOCESE: Killaloe.   MINISTRY: C.C. Lorrha 1050-1056.
                                 C.C. Burgessbeg 1056-1858.

71. COFFEY FIERSE
DIED 7/6/1918.
POLITICAL INVOLVEMENT: Yes.
DIOCESE: Waterford.

72. COLLIER THOMAS
BORN: c.1819.   DIED 22/12/1881, BIRTHPLACE, Templetuohy.
EDUCATION: Irish College, Paris 1839-1844, Ordained in Thurles 1844.
SOCIAL BACKGROUND:[120] Farming. POLITICAL INVOLVEMENT: Yes.
DIOCESE: Cashel and Emly. MINISTRY: C.C. Killenaule 1857-1861.
                                    F.F. Billina   1061-1881.

73. COLLINS EDWARD
BORN: c.1819.   DIED   BIRTHPLACE, Bansha or Knockilong Parish.
EDUCATION: St. Patrick's College, Thurles and Carlow, Ordained 1844.
POLITICAL INVOLVEMENT: Yes.
OTHER INFO: Went to Australia in 1859 and died in Melbourne.
DIOCESE: Cashel and Emly. MINISTRY: C.C. Bansha 1844-1050.
                                    C.C. Oola and Solohead 1058-1859.

74. COMERFORD RICHARD
BORN:[129] 1011   DIED 10/6/1809.
EDUCATION: St. John's College, Waterford 1831-1837.
POLITICAL INVOLVEMENT: Yes.
DIOCESE: Waterford.   MINISTRY: C.C. Ballymeale pre 1050-1057.
                                  C.C. Ballydonean 1057-1050.
                                  C.C. Ballyneale 1058-1064.

75. CONDON ANDREW
BORN: c.1048,   DIED 10/5/1921, BIRTHPLACE,[130] Ardfinan.
EDUCATION:[131] St. John's Waterford 1/4/1867, Ordained in Carlow 8/6/1871.
POLITICAL INVOLVEMENT: No.
DIOCESE: Waterford.   MINISTRY: C.C. Powerstown 1865-1890.
                                  C.C. Ardfinan 1890-post 1891.

76. CONDON JOHN
BORN: 1832,   DIED 1099, BIRTHPLACE, Cromwell, Kilteely.
EDUCATION:[132] Theology 1859, Deacon 1862, Ordained in T Thurles 1863.   POLITICAL INVOLVEMENT: Yes.
SOCIAL BACKGROUND:[133] Farming. MINISTRY: C.C. Uppperchurch 1866-1872.
DIOCESE: Cashel and Emly.   C.C. Clerihan   1873-1875.
                                            C.C. Golden   1076-1888.

77. CONDON LAURENCE
BORN: c.1849   DIED   BIRTHPLACE,[134] Coolnabeasoon, Newcastle.
EDUCATION:[135] Maynooth, Rhetoric 1869, Ordained 1874, was in St. John's for a year in 1060.
SOCIAL BACKGROUND:[136] Farming. POLITICAL INVOLVEMENT: Yes.
DIOCESE: Waterford.   MINISTRY:[137] C.C. Cahir 1079-1880
                                     C.C. Cloghean 1060-1081.
                                     C.C. Clonmel, St. Marys 1001-post 1891.

78. CONNELAN ANDREW
BORN:[38] 1822,   DIED 10/6/1974,
EDUCATION:[139] Irish College, Paris. POLITICAL INVOLVEMENT: Yes.
DIOCESE: Killaloe.   MINISTRY: C.C. Nenagh 1051-1852.

79. CONNELAN PETER
BORN: c.1819.
EDUCATION: Unknown, but not Maynooth. POLITICAL INVOLVEMENT: No.
DIOCESE: Killaloe.   MINISTRY: C.C. Nenagh 1050-1051.

80. CONNOLLY GARRET V.G.
BORN: c.1764   DIED 27/5/1662.
EDUCATION:[140] Maynooth, Humanity 1804, Ordained 1809.
POLITICAL INVOLVEMENT: Yes.
OTHER INFO:[141] Voted Dignior for the mitre in 1816.
DIOCESE: Waterford.   MINISTRY: F.F. Carrick-On-Suir 1828-1862.

81. COONEY JOHN
BORN: c.1807,   DIED 1804, aged 76, BIRTHPLACE, Coleman, Clerihan.
EDUCATION:[142] Maynooth Rhotoric 1826, Ordained 1833.
SOCIAL BACKGROUND:[143] Farming.   POLITICAL INVOLVEMENT: Yes.
OTHER INFO: Brother of William (No.82).
DIOCESE: Cashel and Emly. MINISTRY: C.C. Tipperary 1848-1855.
                                    F.F. Loughmore 1855-1861.
                                    P.P. Bansha   1861 1863.

82. COONEY WILLIAM
BORN: 1020   DIED 1892, BIRTHPLACE, Coleman, Clerihan.
EDUCATION: Carlow College, Ordained 1846.
SOCIAL BACKGROUND: See No.81.
OTHER INFO: Brother of John (No.81).
DIOCESE: Cashel and Emly.   MINISTRY: C.C. Moycarkey 1848-1852.
                                      C.C. Holycross 1852-1854.
                                      C.C. Clonoulty 1854-1855.
                                      C.C. Newport   1855-1859.
                                      F.F. Clerihan 1059-1869

83. CORBETT GEORGE
BORN: c.1025   DIED 2/10/1800.
EDUCATION:[144] Maynooth, Humanity 1042, Ordained 1849.
POLITICAL INVOLVEMENT: Yes.
DIOCESE: KILLALOE.

84. CORCORAN DANIEL
BORN: c.1794   DIED 1062, BIRTHPLACE, Graigue, Killenaule.
EDUCATION: Maynooth[145] Physics 1815, Ordained 1819.
SOCIAL BACKGROUND:[146] Farming.   POLITICAL INVOLVEMENT: Yes.
DIOCESE: Cashel and Emly.

MINISTRY: C.C. Birr   1049-1050.
          C.C. Durkeetin 1850-1052.
          C.C. Nenagh   1053-1060.
          Adm. Nenagh   1060-1069
          P.F. Kilbarron 1069-1801.
          P.P. Toomevara 1801-1880.

85. CORCORAN WILLIAM D.D.
BORN: 1837,   DIED 1062, BIRTHPLACE, Tinnock, Ballingarry.
EDUCATION: Irish College, Salamanca, Ordained 1859.
SOCIAL BACKGROUND:[147] Farming.   POLITICAL INVOLVEMENT: Yes.
OTHER INFO:[148] Offered the rectorship of Salamanca, but declined.
DIOCESE: Cashel and Emly.

MINISTRY: C.C. Donaskoigh 1062-1065.
          C.C. Boherlahan 1065-1075.
          C.C. Killenaule 1075-1077.
          C.C. Boherlahan 1877-1081.
          C.C. Knacarty   1881-1804.
          P.P. Upperchurch 1887-1918.

86. CORCORAN WILLIAM
BORN: c.1794   DIED   BIRTHPLACE, Salamanca.
EDUCATION: Unknown, but not Maynooth. POLITICAL INVOLVEMENT: No.
DIOCESE: Killaloe.   MINISTRY: C.C. Courganean 1891-post 1891.

87. CORRY MICHAEL B.
BORN:[149] 1850   DIED 15/5/1915. BIRTHPLACE,[150] Clounwhite, Kilminhil.
EDUCATION: Unknown, but not Maynooth.
SOCIAL BACKGROUND:[151] Farming. POLITICAL INVOLVEMENT: Yes.
OTHER INFO:[152] Collected in America for funds for the Nenagh church.
DIOCESE: Killaloe.   MINISTRY: C.C. Nenagh 1869-post 1891.

88. COSTIGAN JAMES
BORN:[155]1850 DIED 24/11/1935, Aged 85 BIRTHPLACE, Camross, Co. Laois,Diocese of Ossory.
EDUCATION:[155]Maynooth, Humanity 1069, Ordained N.D. Early education in Nenagh C.B.S. then Old Diocesan Seminary, Ennis.
POLITICAL INVOLVEMENT: Yes.
MINISTRY: C.C. Borrisokane 1875-1876.
C.C. Couranganeen 1876-1881.
C.C. Durkertin 1881-1882.
C.C. Birr
DIOCESE: Killaloe.

89. COSTIGAN WILLIAM
DIED 27/2/1896.
POLITICAL INVOLVEMENT: Yes.
EDUCATION: Unknown, but not Maynooth.
MINISTRY: C.C. Kilranave 185.-1060.
C.C. Burgessbeg 186.-1061.
C.C. Mounsea 1061-1063.
C.C. Burgessbeg 1863-1065.
C.C. Burgessbeg 1863-1070.
F.P. Couranganeen 1870-post1891.
DIOCESE: Killaloe.

90. COURTNEY M
BORN:[156] 1852 DIED 23/1/1942, Aged 90. BIRTHPLACE,[157]Killaloe Town.
EDUCATION:[158]Irish College, Paris.
POLITICAL INVOLVEMENT: Yes.
MINISTRY: C.C. Mounsea 1876-1877.
C.C. Castletownarra 1877-1879.
DIOCESE: Killaloe.

91. CROKE MICHEL
BORN: c.1835 DIED 1872, BIRTHPLACE, Ballingarry Parish.
EDUCATION:[159]Maynooth Physics 1855, Ordained 1060.
POLITICAL INVOLVEMENT: Yes.
MINISTRY: C.C. Galbally 186.-1065.
C.C. Tipperary 1069-1070.
C.C. Dromgin 1871-1872.
DIOCESE: Cashel and Emly.

92. CROTTY DAVID
BORN: c.1821, DIED 31/5/1868, BIRTHPLACE[160]Parish of the Holy Trinity.
EDUCATION:[162]Maynooth, Humanity 1837, Ordained 1846.
POLITICAL INVOLVEMENT: Yes.
OTHER INFO: Brother of John Crotty (No.53).
DIOCESE: Waterford.

93. CROTTY JOHN
BORN:[163]1819. DIED 25/12/1866, Aged 67, BIRTHPLACE,[164]Parish of the Holy Trinity.
EDUCATION:[165]Theology in St. John's College, Waterford 1844-1853, and one year in Irish College, Rome.
POLITICAL INVOLVEMENT: Yes.
MINISTRY: F.P.Fowerstown 1856-1881.
DIOCESE: Waterford.

94. CROWE JOHN R.
BORN: c.1843, DIED 1899, BIRTHPLACE, Cappawhite Parish.
EDUCATION:[166]Maynooth, Logic 1863, Ordained St. Patrick's,Thurles, 1868.
POLITICAL INVOLVEMENT: Yes.
MINISTRY: C.C. Cappawhite 1072-1888.
F.P. Cappawhite 1888-1899.
DIOCESE: Cashel and Emly.

95. CROWE PATRICK
BORN:[167]1825, DIED 1/7/1897, BIRTHPLACE[168]Templederry.
POLITICAL INVOLVEMENT: Yes.
EDUCATION:[169]Maynooth, Humanity 1847, Ordained 1853/1854.
OTHER INFO:[170]Related to John (No.94), cousin of Bishop Kelly of Ross.
MINISTRY: C.C. Toomwara 1854-1861.
C.C. Roscrea 1861-1875.
DIOCESE: Killaloe.

96. CROWE PATRICK
BORN:[171]1854 DIED 26/12/1919. BIRTHPLACE[172]The Glen, Killaloe.
EDUCATION:[173]Maynooth, philosophy 1075, Ordained 1080, Early education in the Grammar school, Killaloe and the Diocesan College, Ennis.
MINISTRY: C.C. BURGESSBEG 1880-post 1891.
DIOCESE: Killaloe.

97. CULLEN THOMAS
BORN: 1842 DIED 1896. BIRTHPLACE, The Commons, Ballingarry.
EDUCATION:[174]Maynooth, Humanity 1062, Ordained 1869.
SOCIAL BACKGROUND: His father an Engineer in the Coalmines in the Commons.
POLITICAL INVOLVEMENT: Yes.
MINISTRY: C.C. Ballingarry 1870-1076.
C.C. Clonoulty 1076-1080.
C.C. Galbilly 1880-1889.
DIOCESE: Cashel and Emly.

98. CUMMINS THOMAS
BORN: c.1853
EDUCATION: St. Patrick's, Thurles 1870-1874, Maynooth Philosophy 1874, Ordained 1878.
SOCIAL BACKGROUND:[175] Farmer. POLITICAL INVOLVEMENT: Yes.
MINISTRY: C.C. Drom 1888-1891.
DIOCESE: Cashel and Emly.

99. CUNNINGHAM JOHN
BORN:[176]1855 DIED 7/12/1935, BIRTHPLACE,[177] Kilrush.
EDUCATION:[178]In Kilrush town then Diocesan Seminary, Ennis, then Irish College, Paris. Ordained 1880 in Mount St. Joseph's, Roscrea.
POLITICAL INVOLVEMENT: Yes.
OTHER INFO:[179]Published a volume of poetry at one stage of his career.
MINISTRY: C.C. Castletownarra 1081-1082.
C.C. Silvermines 1882-post 1891.
DIOCESE: Killaloe.

100. CURRAN JOHN B.
BORN: c.1854 DIED 15/3/1909, BIRTHPLACE,[180]Kill.
EDUCATION:[181]St. John's College, Waterford 5/9/1070, Ordained 13/6/1879.
POLITICAL INVOLVEMENT: Yes.
MINISTRY: C.C.Newcastle and Four-Mile-Water 1804-1866.
C.C. Clonmel,St.Peter and Pauls 1866-1886.
C.C. Clonmel,St.Peter and Pauls 1889-post 1891.
DIOCESE: Waterford.

101. CURRAN WALTER
BORN: c.1812 DIED 1/11/1050,
EDUCATION:[182] St. John's College, Waterford 7/9/1833-1837.
POLITICAL INVOLVEMENT: Yes.
MINISTRY: C.C. Ardfinan 1053-1865.
DIOCESE: Waterford.

102. CUTLER HENRY
BORN: c.1846
EDUCATION:[183] Maynooth, Physics 1867. Ordained 1870/1871.
POLITICAL INVOLVEMENT: No.
MINISTRY: C.C. Commonsfield and Kilcash, 1876-1077.
DIOCESE: Waterford.

103. DALY JAMES
BORN: c.1849 DIED 9/7/1923, BIRTHPLACE,[184]Ennis.
EDUCATION:[185] Maynooth, Logic 1867, Ordained 1873/1074.
POLITICAL INVOLVEMENT: Yes.
MINISTRY: C.C. Couranganeen 1884-1885.
C.C. Durkertin and Moneygall 1885-1887.
C.C. Toomwara 1887-post 1891.
DIOCESE: Killaloe.

104. DARCY JOHN
BORN:[186]1861 DIED 4/1/1940, Aged 79, BIRTHPLACE,[187]Ballywilliam, Burgessbeg.
EDUCATION:[188] Maynooth, Rhetoric 1079, Ordained 1885, Emly Early education at C.B.S. Nenagh, then St. Flannans.
POLITICAL INVOLVEMENT: Yes.
MINISTRY: C.C. Kilbarron 1887-1890.
C.C. Mounsea 1890-post 1891.
DIOCESE: Killaloe.

105. DARDDY PATRICK
BORN: c.1842 BIRTHPLACE, Beakstown, Holycross.
EDUCATION: St. Patrick's Thurles 1859-1863, Carlow College 1863-1866, Ordained in Thurles 1066/1867.
SOCIAL BACKGROUND:[189] Farming. POLITICAL INVOLVEMENT: Yes.
MINISTRY: C.C. Clarihon 1075-1079.
C.C. Ballinahinch 1879-1081.
DIOCESE: Cashel and Emly.

106. DAWERN J.MES
BORN: c.1804, DIED 26/9/1850, BIRTHPLACE, Ballyhurst, Tipperary
EDUCATION:[90] Maynooth, Rhetoric 1030. Ordained 1835.
SOCIAL BACKGROUND:[91] Farming. POLITICAL INVOLVEMENT: No.
OTHER INFO: Uncle of Patrick Davern (No.107).
DIOCESE: Cashel and Emly. MINISTRY: C.C. Golden 1849-1850.

107. DAVERN PATRICK
BORN: c.1849 DIED 1911, BIRTHPLACE, Ballyhurst, Tipperary.
EDUCATION: St. Patrick's College, Thurles. Ordained1874.
SOCIAL BACKGROUND:[192] Farming. POLITICAL INVOLVEMENT: No.
DIOCESE: Cashel and Emly. MINISTRY: C.C: Emly 1878-1879.

108. DE BURKE PATRICK
BORN: c.1802, DIED 27/1/1866.
EDUCATION:[193] St. John's College 1821, Maynooth 1822-1827.
POLITICAL INVOLVEMENT: Yes.
OTHER INFO:[194] He disliked the Irish language.
DIOCESE: Waterford. MINISTRY: F.F. Ballyporeen 1847-1860.

109. DEE DAVID
BORN: 1703 DIED 5/3/1855. BIRTHPLACE, Ballyryan, Solohead.
EDUCATION: Carlow College. Educated 1813/1814.
SOCIAL BACKGROUND:[195] Farming. POLITICAL INVOLVEMENT: Yes.
OTHER INFO:[196]. fluent Irish speaker, frequently preached in Irish.
DIOCESE: Cashel and Emly. MINISTRY: P.P. Lourhmore 1832-1855.

110. DEE JOHN
BORN: c.1812 DIED 22/5/1866.
EDUCATION:[197] St. John's College 20/2/1830-1037.
POLITICAL INVOLVEMENT: Yes.
DIOCESE: Waterford. MINISTRY: F.P. Ballyneale 1865-1886.

111. DELANEY JAMES J.
BORN: 1036 DIED 1887, BIRTHPLACE, Forgestown, Moycarkey.
EDUCATION:[198] Maynooth, Theology 1859. Deacon 1863. Ordained in Thurles 1863.
SOCIAL BACKGROUND:[199] Farming. POLITICAL INVOLVEMENT: Yes.
DIOCESE: Cashel and Emly. MINISTRY: C.C. Moyne 1869-1877,
C.C. Gurtnahoe 1879-1883,
C.C. Boherlahan 1883-1887.

112. DELANEY PATRICK D.D.
BORN:[200] 1831 DIED 26/9/1916. BIRTHPLACE,[201] Kilsheelan,
EDUCATION:[202] St. John's, Waterford. Ordained in 1855.
POLITICAL INVOLVEMENT: Yes.
OTHER INFO:[203] Had been President of St. Johns. Had to resign in

113. DEVANE MICHAEL
BORN: c.1856 DIED 1903, BIRTHPLACE, Mongfune, Murroe.
EDUCATION: St. Patrick's College, Thurles 1873-1881. Ordained in Ushaw in 1881.
SOCIAL BACKGROUND:[204] Farming. POLITICAL INVOLVEMENT: Yes.
OTHER INFO: On the English mission 1881-1889.
DIOCESE: Cashel and Emly. MINISTRY: C.C. Holycross 1889-1095.

114. DOHENY EDMOND J.
BORN: c.1842 DIED 1897, BIRTHPLACE, Carrigeen Castle, Fethard.
EDUCATION: St. Patrick's College, Thurles. Ordained 1867.
SOCIAL BACKGROUND:[205] Farming. POLITICAL INVOLVEMENT: Yes.
DIOCESE: Cashel and Emly. MINISTRY: C.C. Clerihan 1868-1872,
C.C. Orangan 1872-1076.
C.C. Galbally 1876-1077.
C.C. Mullinahone 1881-1882.
C.C. Donaskeigh 1082-1883,
C.C. Clonoulty 1885-1889,
P.P. Donaskeigh 1889-1897.

115. DOHERTY JAMES
EDUCATION: Unknown, but not Maynooth.
POLITICAL INVOLVEMENT: No.
DIOCESE: Killaloe. MINISTRY: C.C. Lortha 1075-1076.

116. DOHERTY WILLIAM
BORN: c.1843. DIED 109?, BIRTHPLACE, Tipperary Parish.
EDUCATION:[206] Maynooth, Physics 1063. Ordained in Thurles in 1066.
POLITICAL INVOLVEMENT: Yes.
DIOCESE: Cashel and Emly. MINISTRY: C.C. Cashel 1877-1885,
P.P. Newinn 1891.

117. DONNELLAN JOHN
BORN: c.1855,
EDUCATION:[207] Maynooth, Rhetoric 1874. Ordained 1800.
POLITICAL INVOLVEMENT: Yes.
DIOCESE: Killaloe. MINISTRY: C.C. Ardcroney and Ballygiblin, 1083-1085.

118. DONNELLY JOSEPH
EDUCATION: Unknown, but not Maynooth.
POLITICAL INVOLVEMENT: Yes.
DIOCESE: Killaloe.

119. DONOGHUE MICHAEL
BORN:[208] 1011. DIED 19/11/1886. BIRTHPLACE,[209] Ballintohar, Nenagh.
EDUCATION:[210] Irish College, Paris. Ordained in Nenagh in 1851.
POLITICAL INVOLVEMENT: Yes.

MINISTRY CONTD: C.C. Borrisokane 1855-1871
P.F. Castletownarra 1071-
1080,

120. DONOVAN M
BORN: c.1041 DIED 22/2/1921
EDUCATION:[211] Maynooth, Humanity 1859, Ordained 1865.
POLITICAL INVOLVEMENT: No.
DIOCESE: Killaloe. MINISTRY: C.C. Shinrone 1080-1081.

121. DOOCEY PATRICK
BORN:[212] 1057 DIED 17/6/1919. BIRTHPLACE,[213] Four-Mile-water.
EDUCATION:[214] St. John's, Waterford, Ordained on 10/6/1887.
POLITICAL INVOLVEMENT: Yes.
OTHER INFO:[215] On temporary mission in Liverpool.
DIOCESE: Waterford. MINISTRY: C.C. Clonmel, St. Peter and Pauls,
1090-post 1891.

122. DEVANEY WILLIAM
BORN: 1040 DIED 1900, BIRTHPLACE, Deansgrove, Cashel.
EDUCATION: St. Patrick's, Thurles 1064-1869, Maynooth 1069.
SOCIAL BACKGROUND:[216] Farming. POLITICAL INVOLVEMENT: Yes.
OTHER INFO:[217] His brother owned a public house in Main Street, Cashel. He was rector of a Seminary in Dubuque, where he was on mission 1072-1879.
DIOCESE: Cashel and Emly. MINISTRY: C.C. Killenaule 1079-1801.
C.C. Anncarty 1801-1807.
C.C. Ballingarry 1887-1899.

123. DOYLE JAMES
EDUCATION: Unknown, but not Maynooth.
POLITICAL INVOLVEMENT: No.
DIOCESE: Killaloe. MINISTRY: C.C. Dunkerrin pre 1050-1050.

124. DUAN JOHN J.
BORN: c.1852.
EDUCATION: St. Patrick's Thurles, Maynooth, Humanity 1071, Ordained 1077.
SOCIAL BACKGROUND:[218] Farming. POLITICAL INVOLVEMENT: Yes.
OTHER INFO: Cousin of Archbishop Fennelly. On mission in Westminster 1877-1884.
DIOCESE: Cashel and Emly. MINISTRY: C.C. Killenaule 1884-1891.
C.C. Thurles 1891-1899.

125. DUGGAN MICHAEL
BORN: c.1645 DIED 4/10/1914. BIRTHPLACE, Ballyclerihan.
EDUCATION:[219] Maynooth, Physics 1865, Ordained 1870.
SOCIAL BACKGROUND:[220] Farming. POLITICAL INVOLVEMENT: Yes.
OTHER INFO: Retired 1887, lived at Donegal cottage, Clerihan, where

126. DUGGAN NICHOLAS:

MINISTRY CONTD: C.C. Drom 1878-1881,
C.C. Kilcommon 1881-1882,
C.C. Ballina 1882-1883,
C.C. Gurtnahoe 1883-1887

BORN: 1049. DIED 1926, Aged 77. BIRTHPLACE: Boulick, Gurtnahoe.
EDUCATION: St. Patrick's College, Thurles 1070-1077. Ordained 1077.
SOCIAL BACKGROUND:[221] Farming. POLITICAL INVOLVEMENT: Yes.
OTHER INFO: On mission in Westminster 1077-1903.
DIOCESE: Cashel and Emly. MINISTRY: C.C. Ballina 1083-1005,
C.C. Moycarkey 1005-1901.

127. DUGGAN THOMAS

BORN: c.1030. BIRTHPLACE: Gatryclough, Gurtnahoe.
EDUCATION:[222] Maynooth, Humanity 1057, Deacon 1063. Ordained in Thurles 1063.
SOCIAL BACKGROUND:[223] Farming. POLITICAL INVOLVEMENT: Yes.
OTHER INFO: Died in U.S... on mission there.
DIOCESE: Cashel and Emly.

128. DUNNE THOMAS

BORN: 3/4/1058. DIED 1941. BIRTHPLACE: Curragh House, Killenaule.
EDUCATION:[224] St. Patrick's, Thurles 1076-1601. Maynooth, Theology 1001. Ordained 1004.
POLITICAL INVOLVEMENT: No.
OTHER INFO: On mission in Freston, Liverpool Diocese in 1004.
DIOCESE: Cashel and Emly. MINISTRY: C.C. Emly 1807-1095.

129. DUNPHY EDMUND

BORN: c.1036. DIED 7/3/1915. BIRTHPLACE:[225] Ballycashin.
EDUCATION:[226] St. John's College, Waterford 1057. Ordained 1861.
SOCIAL BACKGROUND:[227] Belonged to one of the oldest families in the County Waterford.
POLITICAL INVOLVEMENT: Yes. OTHER INFO:[228] Brother of Richard (No.131).
DIOCESE: Waterford. MINISTRY: C.C. Ballyportcon 1063-1065,
C.C. Camir 1004-1007.

130. DUNPHY PHILIP

BORN: c.1049. DIED 29/7/1927. BIRTHPLACE:[229] Corbally.
EDUCATION:[230] St. John's Waterford 1066-1069. Maynooth, Rhetoric 1069. Ordained 1074.
POLITICAL INVOLVEMENT: Yes.
DIOCESE: Waterford. MINISTRY: C.C. Commonsfield and Kilcrah 1070-1090, C.C. Clonmel, St. Marys 1090-1091.

131. DUNPHY RICHARD

BORN: c.1031. DIED 9/3/1920. BIRTHPLACE: Ballycashin.
EDUCATION: St. John's, Waterford, Entered 23/1/1056.[231]

132. EGAN CORNELIUS

BORN: c.1030. DIED 1/10/1907.
EDUCATION:[233] Maynooth, Humanity 1355. Ordained 1062/63.
POLITICAL INVOLVEMENT: Yes.
DIOCESE: Killaloe. MINISTRY: C.C. Shintrono 1060-1069,
C.C. Durmcorrin and Moneygall 1869-1870,
C.C. Lortha and Dortha 1070-1075,
C.C. Roscrea 1076-1800,
F.F. Castletownarra 1000-1091,
P.P. Mounsca 1091-post 1091.

133. EGAN JAMES

BORN:[234] 1659. BIRTHPLACE:[235] parish of St. Patrick, Waterford City.
EDUCATION:[236] St. John's, Waterford, 1675-1080, Irish College, Romi, 1081-1002. Ordained 1002.
POLITICAL INVOLVEMENT: Yes.
DIOCESE: Waterford. MINISTRY: C.C. Camir 1691-post 1891.

134. EGAN JOHN

BORN: c.1604. DIED 27/10/107., Aged 66.
EDUCATION: Carlow.
POLITICAL INVOLVEMENT: Yes.
DIOCESE: Killaloe. MINISTRY: F.F. Durkerrin and Moneygall pre 1050-1052, F.F. Birr 1852-1870.

135. EGAN JOHN

BORN: c.1036. DIED 5/4/1090.
EDUCATION: Unknown, but not Maynooth. POLITICAL INVOLVEMENT: Yes.
DIOCESE: Killaloe. MINISTRY: C.C. Nenagh 1050-1051,
C.C. Roscrea 1065-1069,
F.F.Burgussbeg and Youghal 1874-1890.

136. ENGLISH DENIS M.

BORN: 1045. DIED 1910. BIRTHPLACE: Masterstown, Newinn.
EDUCATION: St. Patrick's College, Thurles 1066-1073. Ordained 1073.
SOCIAL BACKGROUND:[237] Farming. POLITICAL INVOLVEMENT: Yes.
OTHER INFO: On mission in Maitland 1873-1882.
DIOCESE: Cashel and Emly. MINISTRY: C.C. Moycarkey 1882-1007.

137. ENGLISH THOMAS

BORN: 1014. DIED 1094. BIRTHPLACE: Cahir.
EDUCATION:[238] St. John's, Waterford 1836-1040.
SOCIAL BACKGROUND:[239] Farming. POLITICAL INVOLVEMENT: Yes.
OTHER INFO:[240] Resigned 1874. Went to Australia, became V.G. of...

138. EVERARD JOHN

BORN:[241] 1050. DIED 26/6/1517. BIRTHPLACE:[242] parish of Ardfinan, Lisheenanool.
EDUCATION:[243] St. John's College, Waterford. Ordained 1073. Early Education in Mount Mellory.
SOCIAL BACKGROUND:[244] "an ancient family".
POLITICAL INVOLVEMENT: Yes.
OTHER INFO:[245] On the English mission after ordination.
MINISTRY: C.C. Clonmel,St.Peter and Pauls
1076-1006,
Adm. Clonmel,St. Peter and Pauls
1006-1000,
C.C. Clonmel, St. Peter and Pauls
1000-post 1091.

139. FAHY JOHN

BORN: 1013. DIED 23/1/1880. BIRTHPLACE: Graystown, Killenaule.
EDUCATION: Unknown, but not Maynooth.
POLITICAL INVOLVEMENT: Yes.
MINISTRY: F.F. Kyle and Knock 1855-1069.
DIOCESE: Killaloe.

140. FANNING JAMES [246]

EDUCATION: Unknown, not Maynooth. MINISTRY: C.C. Burgussbeg and Youghal 1665-1067.
DIOCESE: Killaloe.

141. FEEHAN FATRICK (C.NON)

BORN: 1013. DIED 23/1/1880. BIRTHPLACE: Graystown, Killenaule.
EDUCATION:[247] Maynooth, Logic 1831. Ordained 1830.
SOCIAL BACKGROUND:[240] Farming.
MINISTRY: C.C. Gurtnahoe 1839-1857,
C.C. Cashel 1857-1861,
F.F. Moyne 1861-1068,
F.F. Galbally 1060-1080.
DIOCESE: Cashel and Emly.

142. FENNELLY JOHN

BORN: 1811. DIED 1092. BIRTHPLACE: Ballintaggart, Ballingarry.
EDUCATION:[249] Maynooth, Logic 1036. Ordained 1841.
SOCIAL BACKGROUND:[250] Farming. POLITICAL INVOLVEMENT: Yes.
OTHER INFO: Cousin of Archbishop Fennelly and John Fennelly (No.143).
DIOCESE: Cashel and Emly.

143. FENNELLY FATRICK J.

BORN: c.1033. DIED 1879. BIRTHPLACE: Ballintaggart, Ballingarry.
EDUCATION:[251] Maynooth, Logic 1052. Ordained 1858.
SOCIAL BACKGROUND:[252] Farming. POLITICAL INVOLVEMENT: Yes.
OTHER INFO: Cousin of Archbishop Fennelly and John Fennelly (No.142).
Dean of St. Patrick's College, Thurles 1850-1060.
DIOCESE:Cashel and Emly. MINISTRY:C.C. Killunnagh 1061-1064,
C.C. Kilcommon 1860-1065...

144. **FENNELLY RICHARD**
BORN: 1055   DIED 1920,   BIRTHPLACE, Castletown, Moyne.
EDUCATION:[253] St. Patrick's, Thurles 1070, Maynooth, Rhetoric 1071, Ordained 1070.
SOCIAL BACKGROUND:[254] Farming.   POLITICAL INVOLVEMENT: Yes.
OTHER INFO: Professor St. Patrick's Thurles 1070-1005.
DIOCESE: Cashel and Emly.   MINISTRY: C.C. Killenaule 1086-1092.

145. **FENNELLY THOMAS**
BORN: 1045   DIED 1927   BIRTHPLACE, Coolcony, Moyne
EDUCATION:[255] Maynooth, Logic 1065, Ordained 1070.
SOCIAL BACKGROUND:[256] His family had considerable landed property. His maternal granduncle was Bishop Ryan of Limerick 1825-1064, who had two uncles bishops of Madras and two brothers priests as well as a brother, who was a doctor.
POLITICAL INVOLVEMENT: Yes.
OTHER INFO: Coadjutor Archbishop 1901-1902. Retired to Moycarkey. Nephew of John Bourke, No.21 and was curate under him.
DIOCESE: Cashel and Emly.   MINISTRY: C.C. Moycarkey 1071-1079.
C.C. Thurles 1079-1007.
Adm. Thurles 1007-1009.
Adm. Moycarkey 1090-1091.
P.P. Moycarkey 1091-1901.

146. **FINN MICHAEL**
BORN: 1047   DIED 1926   BIRTHPLACE: Thurles.
EDUCATION: C.B.S. Thurles and Irish College, Louvain. Ordained in Thurles 1072.
POLITICAL INVOLVEMENT: Yes.
DIOCESE: Cashel and Emly.   MINISTRY: C.C. Upperchurch 1072.
C.C. Moycarkey 1074-1076.
C.C. Borrisoleigh 1076-1900.

147. **FINN THOMAS**
BORN: c.1617   BIRTHPLACE,[257] Englishtown, Kilcossenry.
DIED 5/4/1884.
EDUCATION:[258] St. John's College, Waterford 29/6/1038-1842.
SOCIAL BACKGROUND:[260] Farming.   POLITICAL INVOLVEMENT: Yes.
DIOCESE: Waterford.   MINISTRY: C.C. ardfinan 1056-1067.
Adm. Cloghean 1071-1074.
P.P. Newcastle 1074-1884.

148. **FITZGERALD MICHAEL ALOYSIUS**
BORN: c.1035.   DIED 1602.   BIRTHPLACE, Ballingarry Parish.
EDUCATION:[261] Maynooth, Theology 1056, Ordained 1860.
SOCIAL BACKGROUND:[262] Farming.   POLITICAL INVOLVEMENT: Yes.
DIOCESE: Cashel and Emly.   MINISTRY: C.C. Holycross 1863-1064.
C.C. Bohatlahan 1064-1065.
C.C. Doon 1065-1071.
C.C. annacarty 1071-1074.
C.C. Donaskeigh 1074-1077.
C.C. Templemore 1877-1882.

149. **FITZGERALD PHILIP O.D.**
BORN: c.1009   DIED 25/4/1060.   BIRTHPLACE, Lattin Parish.
EDUCATION:[263] Maynooth, Theology 1031, Ordained 1034. Some education in Irish College, Rome it was said.
POLITICAL INVOLVEMENT: Yes.   OTHER INFO: (Uncle of John Murphy(No.360).
DIOCESE: Cashel and Emly.   MINISTRY: C.C. Ballingarry 1042-1052.
P.P. Ballingarry 1052-1060.

150. **FITZGERALD RICHARD V.G.V.F.**
BORN: c.1011.   DIED 27/5/1009.
EDUCATION:[264] Maynooth, Rhetoric 1031, Deacon 1036.
POLITICAL INVOLVEMENT: Yes.
OTHER INFO:[265] Dignissimus for the Mitre in 1073.
DIOCESE: Waterford.   MINISTRY: F.P. Carrick-On-Suir 1062-1809.

151. **FLANNERY DANIEL**
BORN: c.1043   DIED 30/6/1921.   BIRTHPLACE[266] Counsea.
EDUCATION:[267] Maynooth, Humanity 1062, Ordained 1860.
POLITICAL INVOLVEMENT: Yes.
DIOCESE: Killaloe.   MINISTRY: C.C. Castletownarra 1060-1070.
C.C. Claughprior and Mounsea 1870-1872.
C.C. Kilbarron and Tartryglass 1872-1873.
C.C. Toomevara 1873-1078.
C.C. Nenagh 1078-1808.

152. **FLANNERY PATRICK**
BORN: 1047   DIED 30/3/1911.
EDUCATION: Unknown, not Maynooth.
POLITICAL INVOLVEMENT: Yes.
DIOCESE: Killaloe.   MINISTRY: C.C. Toomevara 1069-1873.
C.C. Ritt 1073-1074.
C.C. Nenagh 1074-1078.
F.F. Cloughprior and Mounsea 1070-1891.

153. **FLANNERY WILLIAM**
EDUCATION: Unknown, not Maynooth.   POLITICAL INVOLVEMENT: Yes.
DIOCESE: Killaloe.   MINISTRY: C.C. Toomevara 1059-1060.

154. **FLAVIN CORNELIUS J.**
BORN:[261] 1020   DIED 12/12/1918, Aged 90.   BIRTHPLACE,[269] Cloahmore.
EDUCATION:[270] Maynooth, Ordained 1059.
SOCIAL BACKGROUND:[271] "fine old stock."   POLITICAL INVOLVEMENT: Yes.
DIOCESE: Waterford.   MINISTRY: C.C. Clonmel, St. Marys 1864-1066.
C.C. Ballyvolane 1066-1069.
C.C. Cibhol, St. Peter and Pauls 1069-1076.
Adm. Clonmel, St. Peter and Pauls 1076-1003.
P.P. ardfinan 1884-'91.
Adm. Clonmel, St. Marys 1091-1906.

155. **FLYNN EDWARD**
BORN: c.1044   EDUCATION:[272] Maynooth, Humanity 1862, Ordained N.D.
POLITICAL INVOLVEMENT: Yes.
DIOCESE: Killaloe.   MINISTRY: C.C. Roscrea 1862-post 1891.

156. **FLYNN MAURICE**
BORN:[273] 1041   BIRTHPLACE,[274] nglish near Dungarvan.
DIED 20/7/1911.
EDUCATION: Unknown, but not Maynooth.
POLITICAL INVOLVEMENT: Yes.
OTHER INFO:[275] Spent three years in America collecting for Waterford Cathedral, also on mission in Limerick Diocese at first.
DIOCESE: Waterford.   MINISTRY: C.C. Clonmel, St. Peter and Pauls 1873-1806.

157. **FLYNN PATRICK V.F.**
BORN: c.1034   EDUCATION:[276] Maynooth, Theology 1055, Ordained 1059.
POLITICAL INVOLVEMENT: Yes.
OTHER INFO:[277] Began his mission in the Diocese of Beverley.
DIOCESE: Waterford.   MINISTRY: C.C. Clonmel, St. Marys 1069-1090.

158. **FLYNN PATRICK FRANCIS.**
BORN: c.1034   DIED 16/6/1914.
EDUCATION:[278] St. John's College, Ordained 1859.
POLITICAL INVOLVEMENT: Yes.
DIOCESE: Waterford.   MINISTRY:[279] C.C. Clonmel, St. Peter and Pauls 1073-1076.

159. **FOGARTY DANIEL**
BORN:[200] 1850   DIED 7/1/1903.   BIRTHPLACE:[281] Kilcolemon, Burgessbeg.
EDUCATION:[202] Maynooth, Ordained 1067, Ordained 1072/73. Earlier education in the Diocesan College, Ennis.
SOCIAL BACKGROUND:[203] Farming.   POLITICAL INVOLVEMENT: Yes.
DIOCESE: Killaloe.   MINISTRY: P.P. Toomevara 1088-1903.

160. **FOGARTY MICHAEL**
BORN:[204] 1059   DIED[205] 25/10/1955,   BIRTHPLACE,[206] Kilcolemon.
EDUCATION:[207] Maynooth, Philosophy 1078, Ordained 1085.attended Nenagh C.B.S. as a boy.
POLITICAL INVOLVEMENT: Yes.Became a supporter of Sinn Fein in later years.
OTHER INFO:[208] Professor of Philosophy and Canon Law Carlow 1887, later professor of moral and dogmatic Theology Maynooth, Vice-President Maynooth 1903.
DIOCESE: Killaloe.   MINISTRY: C.C. Toomevara 1886-1887.

161. **FOLEY PETER**
BORN: c.1029.   EDUCATION:[209] Maynooth, Rhetoric 1047, Ordained 1054.
POLITICAL INVOLVEMENT: No.
DIOCESE: Killaloe.   MINISTRY: C.C. Nenagh 1055-1056

MINISTRY CONTD: C.C. Toomevara 1051-1055.
C.C. Castletownarra 1055-1058.
P.P. Castletownarra 1058-1071.

162. FOLEY WILLIAM
BORN: c.1063. EDUCATION:[290] Maynooth, Philosophy 1082,Ordained 1088.
POLITICAL INVOLVEMENT: Yes.
DIOCESE: Killaloe. MINISTRY: C.C. Borrisokane 1090-1091.

163. FORAN ROBERT
BORN:[291] 1031, DIED 24/11/1093. BIRTHPLACE,[292] Windgap.
EDUCATION:[293] Maynooth, Theology 1047, Ordained 1051.
POLITICAL INVOLVEMENT: Yes.
OTHER INFO:[294] Related to Bishop Foran, Waterford.
DIOCESE: Waterford. MINISTRY: P.P. Ballylooby 1076-1093.

164. FRAWLEY PATRICK
BORN: c.1020 DIED 6/6/1094.
EDUCATION:[295] Maynooth, Ordained as an extern 1055.
POLITICAL INVOLVEMENT: No.
DIOCESE: Killaloe. MINISTRY: C.C. Shinrone 1074-1075.

165. FREEHU JOHN
BORN: c.1027 BIRTHPLACE, Sherlow.
EDUCATION: Irish College, Paris 1049. Ordained as an extern in Maynooth 1052.
POLITICAL INVOLVEMENT: Yes. OTHER INFO: Died in Belgium.
DIOCESE: Cashel and Emly. MINISTRY: C.C. Moyne 1053-1057.

166. FROST JAMES K.
BORN:[296] 1052. DIED 0/4/1904. BIRTHPLACE,[297] Knockane, Six-Mile-Bridge, Co. Clare(Rossamagher)(son of John Frost).
EDUCATION:[298] years in Diocesan Seminary, Ennis. Entered Irish College, Rome 1079a, and studied for 2 years at the Propaganda University, then 4 years in St. Sulpice, Paris. Ordained in 1080 at Mount St. Joseph's, Roscrea.
SOCIAL BACKGROUND:[299] Farming. POLITICAL INVOLVEMENT: Yes.
DIOCESE: Killaloe. MINISTRY: C.C. Castletownarra 1080-1081.
C.C. Toomevara 1081-1085.
C.C. Kilnanave and Templederry 1086-1090.

167. GARRY JOHN
BIRTHPLACE, Shankea, Killysart. EDUCATION: Unknown,but not Maynooth.
SOCIAL BACKGROUND:[300] Farming (son of Patrick Garry).
POLITICAL INVOLVEMENT: Yes.
DIOCESE: Killaloe. MINISTRY: C.C. Lorrha 1088-post 1891.

168. GAVAN PATRICK
BORN: c.1819 DIED 12/7/1071.
EDUCATION:[301] Maynooth, Humanity 1036, Ordained 1044.
POLITICAL INVOLVEMENT: Yes.
DIOCESE: Killaloe. MINISTRY: C.C Burgessbeg and Youghal are

169. GILHOOLY THOMAS
BORN: 1819, DIED 1882, BIRTHPLACE, Parish of Kilteely.
EDUCATION:[302] Maynooth, Logic 1842, Ordained 1847.
SOCIAL BACKGROUND:[303] Farming. POLITICAL INVOLVEMENT: Yes.
DIOCESE: Cashel and Emly. MINISTRY: C.C. Oola and Solohead 1848-1858.
C.C. Bansha 1858-1862.
P.P. Clerihan 1869-1882.

170. GLEESON CORNELIUS
BORN: c.1827 EDUCATION:[304] Maynooth, Humanity 1845, Ordained 1852.
POLITICAL INVOLVEMENT: Yes.
DIOCESE: Killaloe. MINISTRY: C.C. Cloughprior and Mounsea 1853-1855.
C.C. Kilbarron and Terryglass 1855-1856.
C.C. Dunkerrin and Moneygall 1860-1861.
C.C. Castletownarra 1861-1867.

171. GLEESON HUGH
EDUCATION: Unknown, but not Maynooth. POLITICAL INVOLVEMENT: Yes.
DIOCESE: Killaloe. MINISTRY: C.C. Kilnanave and Templederry 1865-1875.

172. GLEESON JOHN
EDUCATION: Unknown, not Maynooth. MINISTRY: Yes.
DIOCESE: Killaloe. C.C. Toomevara pre 1850-1851.
C.C. Burgessbeg and Youghal 1861-1862.
C.C. Kilbarron and Terryglass 1865-1866.

173. GLEESON JOHN
BORN:[305] 1055, DIED March 1827. BIRTHPLACE,[306] Old Turnpike, Nenagh.
EDUCATION:[307] Maynooth, Rhetoric 1873, Ordained 1879. Early education in Nenagh c.8.5.
POLITICAL INVOLVEMENT: Yes.
OTHER INFO:[308] He wrote two books: (1) History of Ely O'Carroll, (2) Cashel of the Kings. He had a brother a solicitor and one a coroner. The family owned 76 acres.
DIOCESE: Killaloe. MINISTRY: C.C.Lorrha and Dorrha 1885-1888.
C.C.Kilnanave and Templederry 1888-post 1891.

174. GLEESON MICHAEL
DIED 15/4/1893. EDUCATION: Unknown, not Maynooth.
POLITICAL INVOLVEMENT: Yes.
DIOCESE: Killaloe. MINISTRY:C.C. Kilbarron and Terryglass 1057-1060.
C.C. Nenagh 1060-1069.
P.P. Kilnanave and Templederry 1069-1887.

175. GLEESON TIMOTHY
DIED 0/5/1074. EDUCATION: Unknown, not Maynooth.
POLITICAL INVOLVEMENT: Yes.
DIOCESE: Killaloe. MINISTRY:C.C.Castletownarra pre 1050-1055
F.P. Kilbarron and Terryglass 1055-1069.
P.P. Burgessbeg and Youghal 1069-1074.

176. GLYNN PATRICK
BORN:[312] 1053 DIED 9/6/1921. BIRTHPLACE,[313] Kilmayley.
EDUCATION:[314] Old Seminary, Ennis, Irish College, Paris, Ordained 1077.
SOCIAL BACKGROUND:[315] Farming. POLITICAL INVOLVEMENT: Yes.
DIOCESE: Killaloe. MINISTRY: C.C. Kilnanave and Templederry 1080-1083.
C.C. Birr 1091-post 1091.

177. GODFREY PATRICK
BORN: c. 1049 DIED 7/11/1930. BIRTHPLACE, Greenane, Tipperary
EDUCATION: St. Patrick's College, Thurles 1069-1074. Ordained 1074.
SOCIAL BACKGROUND:[316] Farming. POLITICAL INVOLVEMENT: No.
OTHER INFO:[317] Brother of Thomas (No.178). His relations had a shop in Tipperary town. Paid their rent to Smith-Barry, were dynamited and boycotted. Eventually evicted from both shop and farm.
DIOCESE: Cashel and Emly. MINISTRY: C.C. Moyne 1891-1901.

178. GODFREY THOMAS
BORN: 1057 DIED 1930. BIRTHPLACE, Greenane, Tipperary.
EDUCATION: St. Patrick's College, Thurles 1076-1084. Ordained 1804.
SOCIAL BACKGROUND: (See No.177)
OTHER INFO: (See no. 177) POLITICAL INVOLVEMENT: No.
DIOCESE: Cashel and Emly. MINISTRY: C.C. Cappawhite 1891-1084.

179. GRACE GERALD C.
BORN: c.1048 DIED 1093, BIRTHPLACE, Templebredin Parish.
EDUCATION: St. Patrick's College, Thurles 1071-1073.
POLITICAL INVOLVEMENT: Yes.
OTHER INFO: On mission in Minnesota after ordination.
DIOCESE: Cashel and Emly. MINISTRY: C.C. Donaskeigh 1088.
C.C. Kilcommon 1088-1892.

336 *Directory*

181.
BORN: [318] 1799 DIED 5/10/1052. BIRTHPLACE, Ballingarry.
EDUCATION: [319] Maynooth, Logic 1016, Ordained 1023.
POLITICAL INVOLVEMENT: No.
OTHER INFO: Uncle of Richard Rafter (No.490).
DIOCESE: Cashel and Emly. MINISTRY: P.F. Moycarkey 1040-1052.

182.
GRAHAM PATRICK
BORN: c.1053. DIED 1093. BIRTHPLACE, Ballingarry Parish.
EDUCATION: St. Patrick's College, Thurles 1069, Irish College, Paris, Ordained Thurles 1070.
POLITICAL INVOLVEMENT: Yes.
OTHER INFO: On mission in Glasgow after ordination.
DIOCESE: Cashel and Emly. MINISTRY: C.C. Newport 1808.
C.C. Kilcommon 1000-1093.

183.
GUNNING PATRICK
BORN: c.1064. EDUCATION: [320] Maynooth, Rhetoric 1082, Ordained 1809.
POLITICAL INVOLVEMENT: Yes.
DIOCESE: Killaloe. MINISTRY: C.C. Kilbarron and Terryglass 1090-post 1091.

184.
HACKETT JOHN
BORN: c.1026. DIED 1609. BIRTHPLACE, The Grown, Cashel.
EDUCATION: [321] Maynooth, Theology 1040, Ordained 1051.
SOCIAL BACKGROUND: [322] Extensive Farmers, 100 Irish acres. Owned property around Cashel. Had a brother Manager of the Cashel Loan Office.(type of local bank).
POLITICAL INVOLVEMENT: Yes.
DIOCESE: Cashel and Emly. MINISTRY: C.C. Donaskeigh 1053-1059.
C.C. Newport 1059-1067.
C.C. Golbally 1067-1069.
C.C. Newinn 1071-1074.
C.C. Loughmore 1075-1076

185.
HACKETT THOMAS
BORN: 1047 DIED 1915. BIRTHPLACE: [323] Curragheen,Horse and Jockey, Moycarkey.
EDUCATION: [324] St. Patrick's, Thurles until 1069, Maynooth, Theology 1069. Ordained Thurles 1071.
SOCIAL BACKGROUND: [325] Farming. POLITICAL INVOLVEMENT: Yes.
OTHER INFO: [326] He had a brother a priest, who studied at Mount Mellaray, All Hallows, Bruqhes and Oscott. Had two sisters nuns.
DIOCESE: Cashel and Emly. MINISTRY: C.C. Loughmore 1879-1084.

HALLY JOHN
BORN: c.1800 EDUCATION: [327] St. John's College, Waterford 6/9/1828-1813.
POLITICAL INVOLVEMENT: No.
DIOCESE: Waterford. MINISTRY:C.C. Gammonsfield and Kilcash pro 1050-1050.

186.
HALPIN JAMES
BORN: [320] 1050 DIED 10/2/1925. BIRTHPLACE, [329] Tulla.
EDUCATION: [330] Irish College, Paris. POLITICAL INVOLVEMENT: Yes.
MINISTRY: C.C. Roscrea 1004-post 1091.
DIOCESE: Killaloe.

187.
HANLY EDMUND
BORN: 1053. BIRTHPLACE, Lisobyhane, Emly.
EDUCATION: Mount Molloray, St. Patrick's College, Thurles 1069-75. Ordained 1075.
SOCIAL BACKGROUND: [331] Farming. POLITICAL INVOLVEMENT: Yes.
OTHER INFO: On mission in Wolverhampton 1075-1002.
DIOCESE: Cashel and Emly. MINISTRY: C.C. Sallina 1802.
C.C. Galbally 1002-1902.

188.
HANLEY JAMES
BORN: 1700. DIED 1052. BIRTHPLACE, Ouslla.
EDUCATION: Carlow College. Ordained there 1013.
POLITICAL INVOLVEMENT: No.
DIOCESE: Cashel and Emly. MINISTRY: P.P. Lattin 1027-1652.

189.
HANLY JAMES
BORN: c.1046. DIED 1094. BIRTHPLACE, Templebredin (Scroqy).
EDUCATION: St. Patrick's College, Thurles 1064-1071.
SOCIAL BACKGROUND: [333] Farming. Current farm 60 acres.
POLITICAL INVOLVEMENT: Yes.
OTHER INFO: On mission in Muxham and Newcastle.
DIOCESE: Cashel and Emly. MINISTRY: C.C. Tipperary 1001-1091.
(Really chaplain in the workhouse).

190.
HANLY JOHN B.
BORN: 1035 DIED 3/0/1070. BIRTHPLACE, Cashel town
EDUCATION: [333] Maynooth, Logic 1052, Ordained 1059.
SOCIAL BACKGROUND: [334] His family owned the City Bar The pub is still thoro.Fr. Hanly is buried in the Rock of Cashel.
POLITICAL INVOLVEMENT: Yes.
DIOCESE: Cashel and Emly. MINISTRY: C.C. Newinn 1067-1065.
C.C. Killenmule 1069-1873.
C.C. Cashel 1873-1077.
C.C. Bansha 1077-1079.

191.
HANNIGAN JAMES
BORN: c.1003. BIRTHPLACE, [335] Clashaniaka, Carrick-On-Suir.
EDUCATION: [336] St. John's College, Waterford 31/1/1824-1828.
SOCIAL BACKGROUND: [337] Farming.
OTHER INFO: Brother of Thomas (No.192).
DIOCESE: Waterford. MINISTRY: [32] C.C. Ballyporeen 1050-1058.
C.C. Gammonsfield and Kilcash, 106C-1065.
C.C. Fourstown and Lisronagh, 1865-1875.

192.
HANNIGAN THOMAS
BORN: c.1027. DIED 4/4/1912. BIRTHPLACE, [339] Clashaniaka, Carrick-On-Suir.
EDUCATION: [340] Maynooth, Humanity 1044, Deacon 1652.
SOCIAL BACKGROUND: See No.19?.
OTHER INFO: [341] "His first mission was in Scotland, Brother of James.
(No.194).
DIOCESE: Waterford. MINISTRY: C.C. Cahir 1063-1065.
C.C. Gammonsfield and Kilcash 1069-1070.
P.P. Fourstown and Lisronagh 1001-1912.

193.
HARTY MICHAEL
BORN: c.1026 DIED 1089, BIRTHPLACE, Knocklong Parish.
EDUCATION: Irish College, Paris, Ordained in Fermoy 1857.
SOCIAL BACKGROUND: [342] Farming. POLITICAL INVOLVEMENT: Yes.
DIOCESE: Cashel and Emly.

194.
HAYDEN JOHN
BORN: c.1030 DIED 5/1/1064. BIRTHPLACE, Rathordan, Cashel.
EDUCATION: [343] Maynooth, Logic 1051, Ordained 1057.
SOCIAL BACKGROUND: [344] Farming.The family also had a grocery Shop.
POLITICAL INVOLVEMENT: Yes.
DIOCESE: Cashel and Emly. MINISTRY: C.C. Boherlahan 1857-1063.

195.
HAYES JOHN
BORN: [345] 1036 DIED 5/1/1906. BIRTHPLACE, [346] Co. Tipperary.
EDUCATION: Unknown, not Maynooth.
SOCIAL BACKGROUND: [347] Farmers, "an old and esteemed family."
POLITICAL INVOLVEMENT: Yes.
DIOCESE: Killaloe. MINISTRY: C.C. Nenagh 1069-1076.

196.
HAYES LAURENCE J. D.O.
BORN: 1046 DIED 1905. BIRTHPLACE. Tipperary Parish.
EDUCATION: St. Patrick's,Thurles and Irish College,Rome. Ordained Rome 1069.
SOCIAL BACKGROUND: [340] Member of the Hayes Hotel family, Thurles.
POLITICAL INVOLVEMENT: Yes.
OTHER INFO: [349] Professor of Theology in St. Patrick's,Thurles 1070-1809.
DIOCESE: Cashel and Emly.

197.
HAYES LAURENCE MARY.
BORN: 1035 DIED 1076. BIRTHPLACE, Fallasgreen Parish.
EDUCATION: [350] Maynooth, Theology 1059. Ordained 1065.
SOCIAL BACKGROUND: [351] Farming 30 Irish acres.
POLITICAL INVOLVEMENT: Yes.
OTHER INFO: Chaplain of Presentation Convent, Cashel 1867-1872.
DIOCESE: Cashel and Emly. MINISTRY: C.C. Thurles 1872-1076,

198. HAYES MICHAEL
BORN: c.1052. DIED 3/9/1940.
EDUCATION:[352] Maynooth, Humanity 1871. Ordained 1077.
POLITICAL INVOLVEMENT: Yes.
DIOCESE: Killaloe. MINISTRY: C.C. Shinrone 1834-1866.
C.C. Cloughjordan 1866-1007.

199. HEALY THOMAS
BORN: c.1037 EDUCATION:[353] Maynooth, Humanity 1053. Ordained 1062.
POLITICAL INVOLVEMENT: No.
DIOCESE: Killaloe. MINISTRY: C.C. Shinrone 1067-1060.

200. HEARNE DAVID (AHEARNE)
BORN: c.1037 DIED 13/11/1809. BIRTHPLACE,[354] Stradbally.
EDUCATION:[355] St. John's, Waterford 1056. Ordained 1262 in Maynooth.
POLITICAL INVOLVEMENT: Yes.
DIOCESE: Killaloe. MINISTRY: P.P. Newcastle and Four-Mile-Water 1064-1809.

201. HEELAN EDMOND
BORN: c.1040 DIED 1901. BIRTHPLACE, Knockling or Knocksliny
EDUCATION: St. Patrick's, Thurles 1064-1073. Ordained 1073.
POLITICAL INVOLVEMENT: Yes.
OTHER INFO: On mission to Dubuque after ordination.
DIOCESE: Cashel and Emly. MINISTRY: C.C. Ballinahinch 1805-1809,
C.C. Cappawhite 1809-1990.

202. HEFFERNAN EDMUND.
BORN: 1031 DIED 1860. BIRTHPLACE, Grove, Fethard.
EDUCATION:[356] Maynooth, Physics 1055, Ordained 1051.
POLITICAL INVOLVEMENT: No.
DIOCESE: Cashel and Emly. MINISTRY: C.C. Ballinahinch 1861-1860.

203. HEFFERNAN PIERCE
BORN: c.1013
EDUCATION:[357] St. John's College, Waterford, Feb 2nd 1834-1835.
(Ordained).
POLITICAL INVOLVEMENT: No.
DIOCESE: Waterford. MINISTRY: C.C. Ballylooby 1068-1070.

204. HEFFERNAN TIMOTHY
BORN: 1043 DIED 1901. BIRTHPLACE, Lattin.
EDUCATION:[358] Maynooth, Rhetoric 1863, Ordained 1070.
SOCIAL BACKGROUND:[359] Farming. POLITICAL INVOLVEMENT: Yes.
DIOCESE: Cashel and Emly. MINISTRY: C.C. Upperchurch 1072-1070,
C.C. Bansha 1070-1076,
C.C. Templemore 1076-1090

205. HEFFERNAN WILLIAM
BORN: 1794 DIED 16/6/1058. BIRTHPLACE, Ballydugh, Cashel.
EDUCATION:[360] Maynooth, Humanity 1871, Ordained 1019.
SOCIAL BACKGROUND:[361] Farming. POLITICAL INVOLVEMENT: Yes.
OTHER INFO:[362] He was a fluent Irish speaker.
DIOCESE: Cashel and Emly. MINISTRY: P.P. Clerihan 1040-1050.

206. MEHIR JAMES
EDUCATION: Unknown, not Maynooth. POLITICAL INVOLVEMENT: Yes.
MINISTRY: C.C. Ardcroney and Ballygiblin
1077-1079,
DIOCESE: Killaloe   C.C. Shinrone 1001-1004.

207. HENEBERY JAMES
BORN: c.1045 DIED 23/3/1921. BIRTHPLACE, 36? Kilrossanty.
EDUCATION:[364] St. John's, Waterford. Entered 20/4/1064. Ordained 0/10/107C.
SOCIAL BACKGROUND:[365] Farming. POLITICAL INVOLVEMENT: Yes.
DIOCESE: Waterford. MINISTRY: C.C. Carrick-On-Suir 1091-post rg1.

208. HENEBERRY ROBERT
BORN: c.1806. DIED :2/10/1066.
EDUCATION:[366] Maynooth, Rhetoric 1026. Ordained N.D.
POLITICAL INVOLVEMENT: Yes.
DIOCESE: Waterford. MINISTRY: C.C. Clonmel, St. Peter and Pauls,
pre 1050-1062.

209. HENEY PAUL
BORN: c.1002. DIED 1009. BIRTHPLACE, Killinmule Parish.
EDUCATION: Ordained in Limerick 1031.
POLITICAL INVOLVEMENT: Yes.
DIOCESE: Cashel and Emly. MINISTRY: P.P. Emly 1049-1062.

210. HENNESSY JOHN
BORN: c.1040. DIED 1090. BIRTHPLACE, Anacarty Parish.
EDUCATION: St. Patrick's, Thurles 1066. Ordained 1073.
POLITICAL INVOLVEMENT: Yes.
OTHER INFO: On mission in Dubuque after ordination.
DIOCESE: Cashel and Emly. MINISTRY: C.C. Kilcommon 1082-1086,
C.C. Donaskeigh 1088-1091.

211. HENNESSY PATRICK
BORN: c.1012 DIED 14/11/1805.
EDUCATION:[367] Maynooth, Rhetoric 1031. Ordained 1037.
POLITICAL INVOLVEMENT: No. MINISTRY: C.C. Couraguenaun pre 1050-1050.
DIOCESE: Killaloe.

212. HEWIT THOMAS
BORN: c.1702 DIED 1066. BIRTHPLACE, Tipperary.
EDUCATION:[352] Maynooth, Humanity 1007, Ordained 1019.
POLITICAL INVOLVEMENT: Yes.
DIOCESE: Cashel and Emly. MINISTRY: P.P. Dola and Solohead 1017-1066.

213. HICKEY JAMES
BORN: c.1030 DIED 1901. BIRTHPLACE, Longford Pass, Gortnahoe.
EDUCATION:[369] Maynooth, Physics 1050, Deacon there in 1863. Ordained in Thurles 1065.
SOCIAL BACKGROUND:[370] Farming. POLITICAL INVOLVEMENT: Yes.
OTHER INFO: Cousin of Archbishop Fennelly.
DIOCESE: Cashel and Emly. MINISTRY: C.C. Ballingarry 1066-1069,
C.C. Borrisoleigh 1069-1076,
C.C. Ballingarry 1076-1007,
P.P. Moyne 1007-1901.

214. HICKEY JAMES
BORN: 1050 DIED 1942, Aged 92, BIRTHPLACE, Bishopswood,
Knockavella.
EDUCATION: St. Patrick's Thurles 1071, then Versailles. Ordained
Thurles 1076.
SOCIAL BACKGROUND:[371] Farming 40-50 acres.
POLITICAL INVOLVEMENT: Yes.
OTHER INFO: Professor, St. Patrick's, Thurles 1001-1007.
DIOCESE: Cashel and Emly and Killaloe.
MINISTRY: C.C. Borrisokane 1077-1801.
C.C. Templemore 1807-1091.
C.C. Thurles 1091-1902.

215. HICKEY PATRICK
BORN: Oct.1780. DIED 25/7/1064. BIRTHPLACE, Cassestown, Thurles
EDUCATION:[372] Maynooth, Humanity 1008. Ordained 1014.
SOCIAL BACKGROUND:[373] Farming. POLITICAL INVOLVEMENT: Yes.
OTHER INFO: Related to Archbishop Fennelly, James Hickey(No. 213)
and Thomas Hickey (No. 216).
DIOCESE: Cashel and Emly. MINISTRY: P.P. Doon 1024-1064.

216. HICKEY THOMAS
BORN: c.1874. DIED 12/5/1003. BIRTHPLACE, Cassestown, Thurles
EDUCATION:[374] Maynooth, Rhetoric 1032. Ordained in Thurles 1039.
SOCIAL BACKGROUND:[375] Farming. POLITICAL INVOLVEMENT: Yes.
OTHER INFO:[376] Related to Archbishop Fennelly, Patrick Hickey (No. 215) and James Hickey (No. 213). As parish priest he owned 33 acres.
DIOCESE: Cashel and Emly. MINISTRY: C.C. Lattin and Cullen 1043-1062.
P.P. Mullinahone 1062-1603.

BORN: c.1012, DIED 26/11/1075.
EDUCATION:[377] St. John's Waterford 3/11/1031. Ordained 1040.
POLITICAL INVOLVEMENT: Yes.
DIOCESE: Waterford.   MINISTRY: C.C. Ballylooby 1057-1064.

218. HOGAN EDWARD
BORN: 1041 DIED 1905, BIRTHPLACE, Ballincor, Clerihan.
EDUCATION: Ordained in Thurles 1069.
SOCIAL BACKGROUND:[370] Farming (see 223). POLITICAL INVOLVEMENT: Yes.
OTHER INFO: Nephew of James Hogan (No.219).
DIOCESE: Cashel and Emly. MINISTRY: C.C. Clonoulty 1072-1076.
                                     C.C. Boherlahan 1076-1033.
                                     C.C. Moycarkey 1007-1000.

219. HOGAN JAMES
BORN: c.1022, DIED 1000. BIRTHPLACE, Ballincor,Clerihan.
EDUCATION: St. Patrick's College, Thurles. Ordained 1046.
SOCIAL BACKGROUND: Farming (See 223). POLITICAL INVOLVEMENT: Yes.
OTHER INFO: Uncle of Edward Hogan (No.218).
DIOCESE: Cashel and Emly. MINISTRY: C.C. Holycross 1049-1051
                                     C.C. Lothard and Killusty 1051-
                                     1070,
                           P.P. Boherlahan 1069-1000,

220. HOGAN JAMES
BORN: c.1023   BIRTHPLACE, Tipperary Parish
EDUCATION: St. Patrick's College, Thurles. Ordained 1046. POLITICAL INVOLVEMENT: Yes.
OTHER INFO: He got an excnat in 1007.
DIOCESE: Cashel and Emly. MINISTRY: C.C. Moycarkey 1000-1081,
                                     C.C. Drom   1001-1002.

221. HOGAN MARTIN
BORN:[379] 1059 DIED 10/11/1929. BIRTHPLACE,[360] Ennis.
EDUCATION:[361] Maynooth, Humanity 1076, Ordained N.D. Earlier
          education at St. Flannans, Ennis.
POLITICAL INVOLVEMENT: Yes.
DIOCESE: Killaloe. MINISTRY: C.C. Ardchonry and Ballygibbin
                                     1003-1064.
                             C.C. Dunkerrin and Moneygall 1000-
                                     1091.

222. HOGAN TIMOTHY
BORN:[302] 1037. DIED 2/12/1902. BIRTHPLACE:[303] Corofin(son of T. Hogan).
EDUCATION:[304] Diocesan College, Ennis. Ordained there in 1064.
SOCIAL BACKGROUND:[305] Probably well off. Had a brother a J.P.
POLITICAL INVOLVEMENT: No.
DIOCESE: Killaloe. MINISTRY: C.C. Castleturanta 1070-1072,

BORN: c.1009, DIED 1060, BIRTHPLACE, Ballincor, Clerihan(See
                                     Nos. 218 and 219)
EDUCATION: Irish College, Salamanca. Ordained 1033-34.
SOCIAL BACKGROUND:[306] Farming. POLITICAL INVOLVEMENT: Yes.
DIOCESE: Cashel and Emly. MINISTRY: C.C. Clonoulty 1042-1055.
                                     C.C. Holycross 1055-1050.

223. HORAN PATRICK
DIED 27/7/1097. BIRTHPLACE,[307] Near Scariff.
EDUCATION: Unknown, not Maynooth.
SOCIAL BACKGROUND:[308] Farming 40 acres. POLITICAL INVOLVEMENT: Yes.
DIOCESE: Killaloe. MINISTRY: C.C. Siln rmines 1051-1052,
                             C.C. Kildnorma and Ballysibbin
                                     1352-1053,
                             C.C. Lotrth and Dortha 1056-1057.
                             C.C. Couragbmeen 1057-1061.
                             C.C. Toomvara   1061-1060.

224. HOURIGAN MICHAEL
BORN: c.1846   DIED 1920, BIRTHPLACE, Lattin Parish.
EDUCATION: St. Patrick's, Thurles,1062-1071.
POLITICAL INVOLVEMENT: Yes.
OTHER INFO: Chaplain, Presentation Convent, Cashel 1072-1075,
DIOCESE: Cashel and Emly. MINISTRY: C.C. Newnim 1075-1002,
                                     C.C. Mullinahone 1002-1005,
                                     C.C. Cashel   1005-1009.

225. HOWARD JAMES
BORN:1039   BIRTHPLACE, Ballylanders.
EDUCATION:[309] Maynooth, Physics 1060. Ordained in Edinburgh 1066.
SOCIAL BACKGROUND:[390] Farming 52 Irish acres.
POLITICAL INVOLVEMENT: Yes.
DIOCESE: Cashel and Emly. MINISTRY: C.C. Ballinahinch 1060-1075,
                                     C.C. Ballina   1075-1070,
                                     C.C. Newport   1070-1000.
                                     P.P. Newport   1000-1920,

226. HOWARD JOHN
DIED 22/12/1916.   EDUCATION: Unknown, not Maynooth.
POLITICAL INVOLVEMENT: Yes.
DIOCESE: Killaloe. MINISTRY: C.C. Couragsneen 1060-1076,
                             C.C. Botriskeane 1076-1877.
                             C.C. Kilnahnoud and Templederry
                                     1077-1079.

227. HOWLEY JAMES D.D. V.G.
BORN: c.1796   DIED 11/4/1004. BIRTHPLACE, Ballintoher,
                                     Killenaule.
EDUCATION: St. John's Waterford(old college) Maynooth, Humanity,
          1615. Ordained 1023, was on the Dunbryne Establishment.
SOCIAL BACKGROUND:Farming, wealthy family. He had a brother a
          Lieutenant Colonel in East India. The Howley
          family got land in Ballintoher about the time of
          the Confederation of Kilkenny.
POLITICAL INVOLVEMENT: Yes.

DIOCESE: Cashel and Emly. MINISTRY: P.P. Tipperary 1041-1004.

228. HUMPHREYS DAVID
BORN: 1843, DIED 1930, BIRTHPLACE, Boher, Murroe.
EDUCATION:[392] Maynooth, Theology 1865. Ordained Ursuline Convent,
                                     Thurles 1869.
SOCIAL BACKGROUND:[393] Farming. POLITICAL INVOLVEMENT: Yes.
OTHER INFO: Professor of Logic, St. Patrick's,Thurles 1869-1878.
DIOCESE: Cashel and Emly. MINISTRY: C.C. Galbally 1878-1880,
                                     C.C. Clonoulty 1880-1883,
                                     C.C. Newport   1883-1885.
                                     C.C. Tipperary 1885-1895.

229. HURLEY PATRICK
BORN: c.1826.   EDUCATION:[394] Maynooth, Humanity 1847, Deacon 1853.
POLITICAL INVOLVEMENT: Yes.
DIOCESE: Killaloe.   MINISTRY:C.C. Toomvara 1861-1868.
                              C.C. Birr   1868-1875.

230. HYLAND JOHN
BORN: c.1798.   EDUCATION:[395] St. John's Waterford 27/11/1815-1623.
POLITICAL INVOLVEMENT: Yes.
OTHER INFO:[396] Retired 1869.
DIOCESE: Waterford. MINISTRY: P.P. Gammonsfield and Kilcash
                                     pre 1850-1869.

231. JAMES THOMAS J.
BORN: c.1844   DIED 1689, BIRTHPLACE, Herbertstown.
EDUCATION:[397] Maynooth, Logic 1863. Ordained in Belfast 1869.
SOCIAL BACKGROUND:[398] The family did reside in Herbetstown at one
          time, and were farmers, but Thomas is not on
          the baptismal register there, which would
          indicate that he was not born in the parish.
POLITICAL INVOLVEMENT: Yes.
OTHER INFO: Lived at Springfield House, Boharnacrusha when curate
          in Holycross.
DIOCESE: Cashel and Emly. MINISTRY: C.C. Kilcommon 1876-1881,
                                     C.C. Tamsha and Kilmoyler 1881-
                                     1882,
                             C.C. Holycross 1884-1889.

232. JONES WILLIAM V:
BORN: c.1842, DIED 1907, BIRTHPLACE, Monasterevan, Co. Kildare
EDUCATION: Irish College, Rome. Ordained in Cork in 1867.
SOCIAL BACKGROUND:[399] His father connected with Blanconi's cars.
POLITICAL INVOLVEMENT: Yes.
OTHER INFO: Professor in St. Patrick's, Thurles 1869-79,Vice-
          President 1879, then President to 1887.
DIOCESE: Cashel and Emly. MINISTRY: C.C. Newlim 1867-1869,
                                     F.P. Killenaule 1887-post 1891.

234. **KEATING PATRICK**
DIED: 10/4/1931 ("ripe old age"). BIRTHPLACE:[400] Powerstown Castle.
EDUCATION:[401] St. John's, Waterford 1867-1875.
SOCIAL BACKGROUND:[402] Farming, son of John Keating.
POLITICAL INVOLVEMENT: Yes.
OTHER INFO:[403] Temporary mission in Sheffield.
DIOCESE: Waterford. MINISTRY: C.C. Clogheen 1882-1883.

235. **KELLY JAMES**
BORN: c.1798 DIED [404] July 1852.
EDUCATION:[405] St. John's, Waterford 1818. Ordained N.D.
POLITICAL INVOLVEMENT:[406] "Since the death of O'Connell he withdrew from politics altogether," (was however, occasionally involved from 1850 to 1852).
DIOCESE: Waterford. MINISTRY: P.P. Clogheen 1840-1852.

236. **KELLY JOHN**
BORN: 1846 DIED 1929. BIRTHPLACE:[407] Kylenahore, Killenaule, (Fogarty 'notebook if says the Commons, Ballingarry).
EDUCATION: St. Patrick's, Thurles 1863. Maynooth 1868. Ordained Carlow, 1872.
POLITICAL INVOLVEMENT: Yes.
DIOCESE: Cashel and Emly. MINISTRY: C.C. Jansha 1883-1892.

237. **KELLY WILLIAM B.**
BORN: c.1851. DIED 3/9/1922. BIRTHPLACE:[408] Ballygunner, Waterford.
EDUCATION:[409] St. John's, Waterford 11/9/1865-1869. Maynooth, Humanity 1869. Ordained for Liverpool 1876.
POLITICAL INVOLVEMENT: Yes.
DIOCESE: Waterford. MINISTRY: C.C. Powerstown 1890-post 1891.

238. **KENNEDY JOHN**
DIED 5/11/1900. EDUCATION: Unknown, but not Maynooth.
POLITICAL INVOLVEMENT: Yes.
DIOCESE: Killaloe. MINISTRY: C.C. Dunkettrin and Moneygall 1870-1873.
C.C. Borrisokane 1873-1876.
C.C. Nenagh 1876-1879.
F.P. Kilbarron and Terryglass 1882-1900.

239. **KENNEDY PATRICK**
BORN: c.1855 DIED 9/11/1911.
EDUCATION:[410] Maynooth, Rhetoric 1874. Ordained 1880.
POLITICAL INVOLVEMENT: Yes.
DIOCESE: Killaloe. MINISTRY: C.C. Ardcroney and Ballygiblin 1878-1883.
C.C. Borrisokane 1883-1885.

240. **KENNEDY PATRICK**
BORN: 1826 DIED 1892. BIRTHPLACE:[400] Crohane, Ballingarry.
EDUCATION:[411] Maynooth, Theology 1847, Ordained 1852.
SOCIAL BACKGROUND:[412] Farming.
POLITICAL INVOLVEMENT: Yes.
DIOCESE: Cashel and Emly. MINISTRY: C.C. Ballingarry 1852-1857.
C.C. Orom and Inch 1857-1860.
C.C. Drangan 1860-1861.
C.C. Cashel 1861-1873.
F.P. Drom and Inch 1873-1877.
P.P. Curtnahoe 1877-1892.

241. **KENNEDY PHILIP**
BORN: 1802 DIED [413] 27/10/1381, Aged 79. BIRTHPLACE:[414] Templederry.
EDUCATION:[415] Irish College, Paris. Ordained in 1831, aged 29.
POLITICAL INVOLVEMENT: Yes.
DIOCESE: Killaloe. MINISTRY: F.P. Kilbarron and Terryglass pre 1850-1855.
P.F. Roscrea 1865-1881.

242. **KENNEDY RODERICK**
BORN: c.1828 DIED 6/3/1908.
EDUCATION:[416] Maynooth, Humanity 1847. Ordained 1853.
POLITICAL INVOLVEMENT: Yes.
DIOCESE: Killaloe. MINISTRY: C.C. Nenagh 1866-1874.
P. Kyle and Knock 1874-1880.
Adm. Lorrha and Dorrha 1880-1886.
P.P. Lorrha and Dorrha 1886-1908.

243. **KENNEDY PATRICK**
BORN:[417] 1842, DIED 11/4/1890. BIRTHPLACE: Thurles.
EDUCATION:[418] Maynooth, Humanity 1861. Ordained 1869.
POLITICAL INVOLVEMENT: Yes.
DIOCESE: Cashel and Emly.

244. **KENNY THOMAS**
BORN: c.1805. DIED 17/7/1850. BIRTHPLACE:[419] Co. Clare.
EDUCATION:[419] Maynooth, Rhetoric 1824. Ordained 1830.
SOCIAL BACKGROUND:[420] "A respectable Clare family."
POLITICAL INVOLVEMENT: No.
DIOCESE: Killaloe. MINISTRY: Adm. Nenagh 1849-1850.

245. **KENRICK EDMUND**
BORN: 1826 DIED 1907. BIRTHPLACE:[421] Knockelly, Fethard
EDUCATION:[421] St. Patrick's, Thurles 1857-1861. Maynooth, Logic 1861. Ordained 1869.
SOCIAL BACKGROUND:[422] Farming. POLITICAL INVOLVEMENT: Yes.
DIOCESE: Cashel and Emly. MINISTRY: C.C. Templemore 1873-1883.
C.C. Cashel 1883-1889.
P.P. Borrisoleigh 1889-1900.

246. **KENYON JOHN**[423]
BORN: 1812 DIED 1869. BIRTHPLACE: Thomond Gate, Limerick City, Son of Pat Kenyon and Mary McMahon.
EDUCATION: Maynooth, Logic 1829. Ordained 1835.
SOCIAL BACKGROUND: Father owned a marble works and grocery business.
POLITICAL INVOLVEMENT: Yes.
DIOCESE: Killaloe. MINISTRY: Adm. Templederry 1850-1860.
P.P. Templederry 1860-1869.

247. **KIELY DANIEL**
BORN: 1857. DIED 1925. BIRTHPLACE: Athlacca, Knocklong
EDUCATION: St. Patrick's, Thurles 1871-1877. Maynooth, Theology 1877, then Irish College, Paris. Ordained in Thurles 1881.
POLITICAL INVOLVEMENT: Yes.
OTHER INFO: On mission to Hexham and Newcastle 1881-1888.
DIOCESE: Cashel and Emly. MINISTRY: C.C. Cappawhite 1888-1889.
C.C. Fethard 1889-1895.

248. **KINNANE T.H.**
BORN: 1835. DIED 1913. BIRTHPLACE: Arlomon, Tipperary.
EDUCATION: Irish College, Paris 1857-1861. Ordained there 1861.
SOCIAL BACKGROUND:[424] Farming. POLITICAL INVOLVEMENT: Yes.
OTHER INFO:[425] Professor of Teology Irish College, Paris 1862-1865. Stepbrother of No. 249 and cousin of Matthew Ryan, (No. 50?), wrote a life of St. Joseph.
DIOCESE: Cashel and Emly. MINISTRY: C.C. Templemore 1867-1876.
Adm. Thurles 1876-1878.
Archdeacon Fethard and Killusty, 1878-1887.
Dean Cashel 1887-1913.

249. **KINNANE WILLIAM J.**
BORN: 1858. DIED 1913. BIRTHPLACE: Arlomon, Tipperary.
EDUCATION: St. Patrick's, Thurles 1875-1883.
SOCIAL BACKGROUND: Sec No. 249. POLITICAL INVOLVEMENT: Yes.
OTHER INFO:[426] Stepbrother of Dean Kinnane (No.248) Scent 1883-1890 on the mission in County Carlow.
DIOCESE: Cashel and Emly. MINISTRY: C.C. Donaskeigh 1890-1894.

250. **KINGSTON JOHN B.**
BORN:[427] 1833. DIED 2/8/1912. BIRTHPLACE:[428] Roscrea.
EDUCATION:[429] Maynooth, Humanity 1852. Ordained 1861. Early education in the old Brigidine Convent in Roscrea, then a private school in Birr.
POLITICAL INVOLVEMENT: Yes.
DIOCESE: Killaloe. MINISTRY: C.C. Couraganeen 1861-1864.
C.C. Lorrha and Dorrha 1864-1875.

251. **KIRBY JAMES**
BORN: c.1811. DIED 22/3/1864.
EDUCATION:[430] Maynooth, Humanity 1831. Ordained N.D.

252. KIRWAN JAMES A.
BORN: c.1856 BIRTHPLACE,[431]Fennor, Gurtnahoe.
EDUCATION:[432]St. John's College 13/9/1875-20/8/1381.
POLITICAL INVOLVEMENT: Yes.
OTHER INFO:[433] On mission in Hexham and Newcastle after ordination.
DIOCESE: Waterford. MINISTRY: C.C. Ardfinan 1890-post 1891.

253. KIRWIN WILLIAM
BORN: c.1788 DIED March 1875, BIRTHPLACE, Thurles.
EDUCATION:[434]Maynooth, Humanity 1808, Ordained 1813.
POLITICAL INVOLVEMENT: Yes.
OTHER INFO: Resigned 1869.
DIOCESE: Cashel and Emly. MINISTRY: P.P. Boherlahan 1829-1869.

254. LAFFAN MARTIN
BORN: 1798 DIED 1875, BIRTHPLACE, Kilcurkee, Castleiney.
EDUCATION:[435]Maynooth, Humanity 1817, Ordained 1825.
SOCIAL BACKGROUND:[436]Farming. POLITICAL INVOLVEMENT: Yes.
OTHER INFO: Cousin of Michael (No 255), of Patrick(No.256) and of John Ryan (No.500).
DIOCESE: Cashel and Emly. MINISTRY: P.P. Killenaule 1847-1875.

255. LAFFAN MICHAEL
BORN: 1791. DIED 3/6/1861. BIRTHPLACE, Kilcurkee, Castleiney.
EDUCATION:[437]Maynooth, Theology 1812 Ordained 1814, Carlow College earlier.
SOCIAL BACKGROUND:[438]See No.254. He had a brother a merchant and local director of the National Bank, Thurles.
POLITICAL INVOLVEMENT: Yes.
OTHER INFO:[439]Brother of Patrick (No.256). Cousin of Martin (No. 254) and John Ryan (No.500). He was not on good terms with Archbishop Slattery, having supported a rival candidate for the Mitre. He was however, favoured by Archbishop Leahy.
DIOCESE: Cashel and Emly. MINISTRY: Archdeacon Fethard and Killusty, pre 1850-1861.

256. LAFFAN PATRICK
BORN: 1802 DIED 20/7/1868. BIRTHPLACE, Kilcurkee, Castleiney.
EDUCATION:[440]Maynooth, Rhetoric 1822. Ordained 1827.
SOCIAL BACKGROUND: See No.254. POLITICAL INVOLVEMENT: Yes.
OTHER INFO: Brother of Michael (No.255) cousin of Martin (No.254v) and John Ryan (No.500).
DIOCESE: Cashel and Emly. MINISTRY:C.C. Fethard 1828-1850, F.P. Holycross 1850-1861, Dean Cashel 1861-1868.

257. LAFFAN WILLIAM
BORN: c.1780 DIED 15th March 1850, BIRTHPLACE, Cloverfield, Dromkeen.
EDUCATION:[441]Maynooth, Logic 1803, Ordained 1808.
POLITICAL INVOLVEMENT: No.
DIOCESE: Cashel and Emly. MINISTRY: P.P. Holycross 1827-1850.

258. LANIGAN DANIEL KENNA
BORN: c.1806 DIED 1875. BIRTHPLACE, Ballyheen, Templemore.
EDUCATION:[442]Carlow College. Ordained 1831.
SOCIAL BACKGROUND: Farming. POLITICAL INVOLVEMENT: Yes.
OTHER INFO: Cousin of William (No.260).
DIOCESE: Cashel and Emly. MINISTRY: P.P. Kilcommon 1850-1871.

259. LANIGAN JAMES
BORN: c.1825 DIED 1867. BIRTHPLACE, Templemore Parish.
EDUCATION:[443]Maynooth, Theology 1847. Ordained 1850.
POLITICAL INVOLVEMENT: Yes.
DIOCESE: Cashel and Emly. MINISTRY: C.C. Bansha 1852-1859, C.C. Kilcommon 1859-1864, C.C. Donaskligh 1865-1867.

260. LANIGAN WILLIAM
BORN: 1820 DIED 1900, BIRTHPLACE, Lisdaleon, Moyne.
EDUCATION:[444]Maynooth, Physics 1843. Ordained 1848.
SOCIAL BACKGROUND:[445]Farming. POLITICAL INVOLVEMENT: Yes.
OTHER INFO: Bocame Bishop of Goulbourn, Australia in 1866. Cousin of Daniel (No.258v).
DIOCESE: Cashel and Emly. MINISTRY: C.C. Kilcommon 1849-1859.

261. LANNON JOHN
BORN: c.1856, BIRTHPLACE,[446]Stradbally.
EDUCATION:[447] St. John's College 13/9/1875-19/6/1881.
POLITICAL INVOLVEMENT: Yes.
DIOCESE: Waterford MINISTRY: C.C. Ardfinan 1887-1890.

262. LARKIN EDMUND
BORN: c.1794, DIED 1860
EDUCATION:[448]Maynooth, Humanity 1814, Deacon 1819.
POLITICAL INVOLVEMENT: Yes.
DIOCESE: Waterford. MINISTRY:P.P. Newcastle and Four-Mile-Water 184C-1860.

263. LAYNE JOHN
BORN: c.1854 DIED 1896, BIRTHPLACE, Ballybrion, Ballylanders.
EDUCATION:C.C. St. Patrick's, Thurles 1872-1878. Irish College, Paris, 1879. Ordained there 1879.
SOCIAL BACKGROUND:[449]Farming. POLITICAL INVOLVEMENT: Yes.
OTHER INFO: On mission in Liverpool 1879-1887.
DIOCESE:Cashel and Emly MINISTRY: C.C. Ballylanders 1888-1891.

264. LEAHY PATRICK D.D.
BORN: 1806 DIED 26/1/1875, BIRTHPLACE, Fennor, Gurtnahoe.
EDUCATION:[450]Maynooth, Rhetoric 1826, Ordained 1833. His early education at a classical day school in Thurles, also three months in Clonmel.
SOCIAL BACKGROUND:[451] His father a Civil Engineer and Surveyor.
POLITICAL INVOLVEMENT: Yes.
OTHER INFO: Vice-Rector of the Catholic University and Professor and President of St. Patrick's College, Thurles until 1855. Archbishop of Cashel and Emly 1857-1875.
DIOCESE: Cashel and Emly. MINISTRY: Dean Cashel 1855-1857.

265. LENIHAN DANIEL
EDUCATION: Unknown, not Maynooth.
POLITICAL INVOLVEMENT: No
DIOCESE: Killaloe. MINISTRY: C.C. Mounsea 1872-1871.

266. LENIHAN JOHN
BORN:[452]1825 DIED 30/8/1854, BIRTHPLACE,[453]Newtown.
EDUCATION:[454]St. John's, Waterford 7/9/1840-1844, Maynooth Theology 1845, Deacon 1848.
POLITICAL INVOLVEMENT: Yes.
DIOCESE: Waterford. MINISTRY: Yes.

267. LEYDEN PETER
BORN: c.1806 DIED 31/8/1870.
EDUCATION:[455]Maynooth, Humanity 1826. Ordained N.D.
POLITICAL INVOLVEMENT: No.
DIOCESE: Killaloe. MINISTRY:P.P. Kyle and Knock 1854-1865, 1869.
C.C. Birr 1869-1885.

268. LITTLE ROBERT H.
BORN:[456]1842 DIED 2/1/1910, BIRTHPLACE,[457]Tulla.
EDUCATION:[458]Maynooth, Humanity 1857. Ordained 1865/66.
POLITICAL INVOLVEMENT: Yes.
DIOCESE: Killaloe. MINISTRY:C.C. Burgessbeg and Youghal 1867-1869.

269. LONERGAN PATRICK
BORN: c.1852, DIED 12/5/1931, BIRTHPLACE,[459]Burncourt, Clogheen.
EDUCATION:[460]St. John's, Waterford 1871-1877.
SOCIAL BACKGROUND:[461]Farming. POLITICAL INVOLVEMENT: Yes.
DIOCESE: Waterford. MINISTRY:C.C. Gammonsfield and Kilcash 1879-1884.
C.C. Fowerstown 1884-1885.
C.C. Ballyporeen 1885-post 1891.

270.
LONERGAN STEPHEN M.
BORN: c.1803   DIED 18/6/1873.
EDUCATION:[462] Maynooth, Rhetoric 1823. Ordained N.D.
POLITICAL INVOLVEMENT: Yes.
OTHER INFO:[463] Retired April 1872.
DIOCESE: Waterford.   MINISTRY: C.C. Cahir pre 1850-1852.
                                 P.P. Ballylooby 1852-1873.

271.
LONG GERALD F (GARRETT)
BORN: c.1806   DIED 30/4/1889, BIRTHPLACE, Tallow
EDUCATION:[464] St. John's College; 2/9/1825-1831.
POLITICAL INVOLVEMENT: No.
OTHER INFO: Brother of Jeremiah (No. 272).
DIOCESE: Waterford.   MINISTRY: C.C. Cahir pre 1850-1862.

272.
LONG JEREMIAH (ARCHDEACON)
BORN:[465] 6/5/1815   DIED 6/11/1903. BIRTHPLACE,[466] Tallow.
EDUCATION:[467] St. John's College 1836-1840.
POLITICAL INVOLVEMENT: Yes.
OTHER INFO:[468] Fluent Irish speaker. Gave his sermons in Irish.
DIOCESE: Waterford.   MINISTRY: C.C. Ballylooby 1850-1853.

273.
LUDDY EDWARD W.
BORN: c.1839,   DIED 25/10/1875.
EDUCATION:[469] St. John's 1856-1859, Maynooth, Theology 1859, Ordained 1864.
POLITICAL INVOLVEMENT: Yes.
DIOCESE: Waterford.   MINISTRY: C.C. Ardfinan 1867-1871.
                                 C.C. Ballyneale 1871-1872.
                                 C.C. Ardfinan 1873-1875.

274.
LYNCH MATTHEW
BORN: c.1851   EDUCATION:[470] Maynooth, Philosophy 1871. Ordained 1876.
POLITICAL INVOLVEMENT: No.
OTHER INFO:[471] In conflict with Bishop Ryan 1888, unsure if pertaining to politics.
DIOCESE: Killaloe.   MINISTRY: C.C. Kilbarron and Terryglass 1876-1878.
                                 C.C. Couraganeen   1882-1884.

275.
LYNCH TIMOTHY
BORN: c.1853   DIED 6/9/1934, BIRTHPLACE[472] The Glen, Killaloe.
EDUCATION:[473] Early education at a local Latin school, then Irish College, Paris. Ordained 1878.
POLITICAL INVOLVEMENT: Yes.
DIOCESE: Killaloe.   MINISTRY: C.C. Silvermines 1878-1882,

276.
McCANN JOHN
BORN: c.1844   DIED 12/7/1914, BIRTHPLACE,[474] Kilgobinet,

277.
McCORMACK JOHN
BORN:[476] 1834,   DIED 8/12/.914.
EDUCATION:[477] Maynooth, Humanity 1852. Ordained N.D.
POLITICAL INVOLVEMENT: Yes.
DIOCESE: Killaloe.   MINISTRY:C.C. Lortha and Dortha 1858-1864.
                               C.C. Cloughprior and Mounsea 1864-1872.
                               C.C. Kilnanave and Templederry 1872-1877.
                               C.C. Birr   1877-1879,
                               P.P. Kilnanave and Templederry 187?-1914.

278.
McGRATH JOHN
BORN: 1809,   DIED 7/9/1864 BIRTHPLACE, Tipperary.
EDUCATION:[478] Maynooth, Logic 1830. Ordained 1837.
POLITICAL INVOLVEMENT: Yes.
DIOCESE: Cashel and Emly.   MINISTRY: C.C. Newport 1840-1858
                                       C.C. Tipperary 1858-1864.

279.
McGRATH JAMES V.G.
BORN: 1767,   DIED 12/9/1855. BIRTHPLACE, Gurtnahoe.
EDUCATION: Carlow College 1812-1815. Ordained 1815.
POLITICAL INVOLVEMENT: Yes.
OTHER INFO: Uncle of Michael (No. 281).
DIOCESE: Cashel and Emly.   MINISTRY: Dean Cashel 1831-1855.

280.
McDONNELL MICHAEL
BORN: 1827   DIED 1906, BIRTHPLACE, Inchnrourke, Gurtnahoe.
EDUCATION:[479] Maynooth, Theology 1849. Ordained 1851.   POLITICAL INVOLVEMENT: Yes.
SOCIAL BACKGROUND:[480] Farming.
OTHER INFO: Evicted when P.P. by the Scullys of Golden.
DIOCESE: Cashel and Emly.   MINISTRY: C.C. Mullinahone   1863-1854.
                                       C.C. Orom   1862-1863,
                                       C.C. Moyne   1863-1868,
                                       C.C. Donaskeigh 1868-1874,
                                       C.C. Newlim   1874-1875,
                                       P.P. Golden   1875-1906.

281.
McDONNELL MICHAEL
BORN: 1823,   DIED 30/5/1353 of fever. BIRTHPLACE, Gurtnahoe. Ordained there 1847.
EDUCATION: St. Patrick's College, Thurles.   POLITICAL INVOLVEMENT: Yes.
SOCIAL BACKGROUND: Farming.
OTHER INFO: Nephew of Dean McDonnell (No.279).
DIOCESE: Cashel and Emly.   MINISTRY: C.C. Donaskeigh 1847-1852.
                                       C.C. Cashel   1852-1853.

282.
McDONNELL P.DICK
BORN: c.1842   DIED Sept. 1881.
EDUCATION:[481] Maynooth, Humanity 1859, Ordained 1866/67.
POLITICAL INVOLVEMENT:

MINISTRY CONTD:C.C. Cloughprior and Mounsea 1874-1875.

283.
McDONNELL THOMAS
BORN:[482] 1831,   DIED 1/7/1906, BIRTHPLACE,[483] Tallow.
EDUCATION:[484] Maynooth, Theology 1854, Deacon 1857. Early education at Mount Melleray, then St. John's College.
POLITICAL INVOLVEMENT: Yes.
OTHER INFO: On the Dunboyne establishment in Maynooth. A Professor in St. John's College later.
DIOCESE: Waterford.   MINISTRY: C.C. Clogheen 1871-1875.
                                 C.C. Cahir   1875-1876.
                                 C.C. Clonmel St. Peter and Pauls 1876-1883.
                                 Adm. Clonmel,St. Peter and Pauls 1883-1886.

284.
McENERNEY F.
BORN: 3/5/1919,   EDUCATION: Unknown, not Maynooth.
POLITICAL INVOLVEMENT: No.
DIOCESE: Killaloe.

285.
McGRATH EDWARD
EDUCATION: Unknown, not Maynooth.
POLITICAL INVOLVEMENT: Yes.
DIOCESE: Killaloe.   MINISTRY: C.C. Snirnone 1866-1867.
                               C.C. Ardcroney and Ballygiblin 1867-1876.
                               C.C. Rostrea 1880-1884.

286.
McGRATH JOHN
EDUCATION: Unknown, not Maynooth.   POLITICAL INVOLVEMENT: No.
MINISTRY: Adm.Kilnanave and Templederry pre-1850-1850.
DIOCESE: Killaloe.   MINISTRY: C.C. Silvermines 1849-1874.

287.
McGRATH JOHN
BORN: c.1848   DIED 15/12/1879.
EDUCATION:[485] Maynooth, Humanity 1865. Ordained 1872.
POLITICAL INVOLVEMENT: No.
DIOCESE: Killaloe.   MINISTRY: C.C. Cloughprior and Mounsea 1873-1874.

289.
McGRATH JOHN
BORN: 1835   DIED 25/8/1912, BIRTHPLACE, The Park, Ballingarry.
EDUCATION:[486] Maynooth, Logic 1858. Ordained Presentation Convent, Thurles 1863.
POLITICAL INVOLVEMENT: Yes.
SOCIAL BACKGROUND:[487] Farming.
OTHER INFO: Nephew of John McGrath (No.279), related to John McGrath (No.290) and cousin of W. Power(No.47a) and of Michael Power(No.459).
DIOCESE: Cashel and Emly.   MINISTRY:[488] C.C. Gabbally 1864-1866,
                                          C.C. Newport 1875-1876,
                                          C.C. Golden 1875-1876.

289. McGRATH JOHN

BORN: c.1834, DIED 1876, BIRTHPLACE, Ballingarry.

EDUCATION:[489] Maynooth, Physics 1854. Ordained 1859.

SOCIAL BACKGROUND:[490] Farming. POLITICAL INVOLVEMENT: Yes.

OTHER INFO: Cousin of W. Power(No.474), nephew of John(No.290) and related to John (No.289) and cousin of Michael Power (No.459).

DIOCESE: Cashel and Emly. MINISTRY: C.C. Galbally 1861-1862.
C.C. Lattin and Cullen 1862-1874.
Adm. Thurles 1875-1876.

290. McGRATH JOHN

BORN: 1803, DIED 1874, BIRTHPLACE, Ballingarry.

EDUCATION:[491] Carlow College. Maynooth, Logic 1818. Ordained 1823.

SOCIAL BACKGROUND:[492] Farming. POLITICAL INVOLVEMENT: Yes.

DIOCESE: Cashel and Emly. MINISTRY: P.P. Lattin and Cullen 1853-1874.

291. McGRATH JOSEPH

BORN:[493] 1813, DIED 29/1/1884,

EDUCATION:[494] Unknown, but ordained 1839. POLITICAL INVOLVEMENT: Yes.

OTHER INFO:[495] Complete health breakdown and the parish administered by his brother Patrick (No.294).

DIOCESE: Killaloe. MINISTRY: P.P. Silvermines 1850-1884.

292. McGRATH MICHAEL

BORN: c.1834 EDUCATION:[496] Maynooth, Humanity 1852. Ordained 1859.

POLITICAL INVOLVEMENT: Yes.

DIOCESE: Killaloe. MINISTRY: C.C. Ardcroney and Ballygiblin 1859-1869.
C.C. Dunkerrin and Moneygall 1869-1870.

293. McGRATH MICHAEL

BORN: 1836 DIED 1900, BIRTHPLACE, Castlequarter, Loughmore.

EDUCATION:[497] Maynooth, Physics 1860. Ordained 1864.

SOCIAL BACKGROUND:[498] Farming. POLITICAL INVOLVEMENT: Yes.

DIOCESE: Cashel and Emly. MINISTRY: C.C. Donaskeigh 1867-1868.
C.C. Doon 1868-1873.
C.C. Anacarty 1874-1876.
C.C. Holycross 1876-1879.
C.C. Clerihan 1879-1882.
C.C. Drom 1882-1888.
P.P. Drangan 1888-1900.

294. McGRATH PATRICK

BORN:[499] 1820, DIED 11/6/1890.

EDUCATION:[500] Maynooth. Ordained 1853 (Extern).

POLITICAL INVOLVEMENT: Yes.

OTHER INFO: Brother of Joseph (No.291).

DIOCESE: Killaloe. MINISTRY: P.P. Kounsea 1875-1878.
Adm. Silvermines 1878-1884.
P.P. Silvermines 1884-1890.

295. McGRATH PATRICK

BORN:[501] 1775, DIED 9th November 1865, Aged 90.

EDUCATION: Unknown, but not Maynooth. POLITICAL INVOLVEMENT: Yes.

OTHER INFO:[502] Retired early 1865.

DIOCESE: Waterford. MINISTRY: P.P. Ballylooby 1846-1852.
P.P. Cahir 1852-1865.

296. McGRATH THOMAS

BORN:[503] 17/3/1835, DIED 9/1/1911, BIRTHPLACE,[504] Ballyristeen, Kill.

EDUCATION:[505] Maynooth, Humanity 1862. Ordained N.D. Early education in Mount Melleray, then St. John's College.

SOCIAL BACKGROUND:[506] Farming. POLITICAL INVOLVEMENT: Yes.

DIOCESE: Waterford. MINISTRY: Adm. Clogheen 1877-1896.

297. McGUIRE JOHN F.

BIRTHPLACE,[507] Co. Clare. EDUCATION: Unknown, but not Maynooth.

POLITICAL INVOLVEMENT: Yes.

DIOCESE: Killaloe. MINISTRY: C.C. Dunkerrin and Moneygall 1887-1888.
C.C. Borrisokane 1891-post 1891.

298. JOHN McINERNEY.

EDUCATION: Unknown. POLITICAL INVOLVEMENT: Yes.

DIOCESE: Killaloe. MINISTRY: C.C. Roscrea 1888-post 1891.

299. McKENNA JOHN

BORN:[508] 1847 DIED 2/12/1899.

EDUCATION:[509] Maynooth, Humanity 1866. Ordained 1872. Earlier education in the Diocesan College, Ennis.

POLITICAL INVOLVEMENT: No (was involved in Co. Clare).

OTHER INFO:[510] Killed by a kick from his horse.

DIOCESE: Killaloe. MINISTRY: C.C. Shinrone 1872-1874.
C.C. Silvermines 1874-1878.
C.C. Ardcroney and Ballygiblin 1891-post 1891.

300. McKEOGH WILLIAM JOSEPH.

BORN:[511] 1843, DIED 19/2/1920, BIRTHPLACE, Soloheadbeg.

EDUCATION:[512] St. John's Waterford 27/11/1861-1864. Carlow 1864-1866/67. Ordained there 1866/67.

SOCIAL BACKGROUND:[513] Farming. When he retired he lived on a farm also. He was born on a 30 acre farm, but his father also had an 81 acre farm near Tipperary town.

POLITICAL INVOLVEMENT: Yes.

OTHER INFO:[514] Contrary priest, appointed in 1875 "cum spe" by Croke. Offered to resign 1877. Lived on a farm near Tipperary after retirement to 1911. Collected in U.S. for Thurles Cathedral 1871-1872. The people of Ballinahinch lit bonfires to celebrate his departure.

DIOCESE: Cashel and Emly. MINISTRY:[515] C.C. Borrisoleigh 1868.
C.C. Thurles 1869.
Adm. Ballinahinch 1875-1878.
P.P. Ballinahinch 1878-1887.
P.P. Kilcommon 1887-1911.

BIRTHPLACE, Cannon Island, Kildysart.

EDUCATION:[518] Ennis Diocesan College until 1879, Irish College, Rome 1879-1885.

SOCIAL BACKGROUND:[519] Farming. POLITICAL INVOLVEMENT Yes.

DIOCESE: Killaloe. MINISTRY: C.C. Cloughjordan 1887-1891.

302. McMAHON JOHN

BORN:[520] 1/10/1844, DIED 10/1/1932, BIRTHPLACE,[521] Miltown-Malbay.

EDUCATION:[522] Maynooth, Rhetoric 1862. Ordained 1868. Earlier education at Summerhill College, Sligo.

POLITICAL INVOLVEMENT: Yes.

DIOCESE: Killaloe. MINISTRY: C.C. Nenagh 1878-1889.
P.P. Silvermines 1889-post 1891.

303. McNAMARA DENIS

BORN: c.1860, BIRTHPLACE,[523] Tulla.

EDUCATION:[524] Maynooth, Rhetoric 1879. Ordained 1885.

POLITICAL INVOLVEMENT: Yes.

DIOCESE: Killaloe. MINISTRY: C.C. Castletownarra 1885-1888.
C.C. Toomevara 1888-post 1891.

304. McNAMARA JOHN

BORN:[525] 1853, DIED 3/10/1923, BIRTHPLACE,[526] Kilnasoolagh, Newmarket-on-Fergus.

EDUCATION:[527] Maynooth, Philosophy 1869. Ordained 1873.

SOCIAL BACKGROUND:[528] Farming, "an old and respected family."

POLITICAL INVOLVEMENT: Yes.

DIOCESE: Killaloe. MINISTRY: C.C. Kilbarron and Terryglass 1873-1876.
C.C. Lorrha and Dorrha 1876-1877.
C.C. Birr 1887-1890.

305. McREDMOND T.J.

BORN:[529] 1/7/1836 DIED 5/4/1904, BIRTHPLACE,[530] Near Birr.

EDUCATION:[531] Irish College, Paris 1852-1855, then Maynooth. Ordained 1860.

POLITICAL INVOLVEMENT: Yes.

OTHER INFO: Became President of the New Diocesan College, Ennis which opened in 1866, Bishop of Killaloe 1889-1903.

DIOCESE: Killaloe. MINISTRY:[532] C.C. Couraganeen 1860.
C.C. Toomevara 1860-1861.
C.C. Nenagh 1861-1866.

306. MACKEY JOHN

BORN: 1790, DIED 1855, BIRTHPLACE, Thurles.

EDUCATION:[533] Maynooth, Logic 1810. Ordained 1813.

POLITICAL INVOLVEMENT: Yes.

OTHER INFO: Closely related to James and Thomas O'Carroll (Nos. 389 and 390)

DIOCESE: Cashel and Emly. MINISTRY: P.P. Clonoulty 1839-1855.

307. MACKEY JOHN
BORN: c.1806, BIRTHPLACE: Aughall, Castleiney. POLITICAL INVOLVEMENT: Yes.
EDUCATION: Maynooth. Ordained 1831. MINISTRY: Cashel and Emly.
DIOCESE: Cashel and Emly.

DIOCESE: Killaloe. MINISTRY: C.C. Ardcroney and Ballygiblin 1877-1878.
C.C. Kilbarron and Tetryglass 1878-1883.
C.C. Kilnanave and Templederry 1886-1887.

308. MACKEY THOMAS J.
BORN: c.1847 BIRTHPLACE, College Hill (Ballycahill), "employees.
EDUCATION: St. Patrick's, Thurles. Ordained c.1872.
SOCIAL BACKGROUND 534 Farming. POLITICAL INVOLVEMENT: Yes.
OTHER INFO 535 Spent most of his missionary life in America. Exeat in 1888.
DIOCESE: Cashel and Emly. MINISTRY: C.C. Ballinahinch 1878-1879.
C.C. Curtinhoe 1884-1886.

309. MADDEN JOHN
BORN: c.1837, DIED 1898, BIRTHPLACE, Templebredin.
EDUCATION 536 Maynooth, Logic 1856. Ordained 1862.
POLITICAL INVOLVEMENT: Yes.
DIOCESE: Cashel and Emly. MINISTRY: C.C. Boherlahan and Dualla 1863-1864.
C.C. Emly 1873-1875.
C.C. Kilcommon 1875-1876.
C.C. Loughmore 1875-1879.

310. MAHONY THOMAS
BORN: c.1814, DIED 16/2/1860.
EDUCATION 537 Maynooth, Rhetoric 1833, Deacon 1839.
POLITICAL INVOLVEMENT: Yes.
DIOCESE: Cashel and Emly. MINISTRY: C.C. Nenagh 1852-1853.
Adm. Nenagh 1853-1855.

311. MAHONY THOMAS
BORN: c.1813 DIED 1872 BIRTHPLACE, Knocklong.
EDUCATION 538 Maynooth, Humanity 1831. Ordained 1838.
POLITICAL INVOLVEMENT: Yes.
DIOCESE: Cashel and Emly. MINISTRY: C.C. Knocklong.

312. MALONE EUGENE
BORN: 539 1798 DIED 2/12/1875, BIRTHPLACE 540 Killaloe.
EDUCATION: Carlow College 1825. POLITICAL INVOLVEMENT: Yes.
DIOCESE: Killaloe. MINISTRY: P.P. Cloughprior and Mounsea pre 1850-1875.

313. MARNANE WILLIAM
BORN: 541 1852, DIED 27/31/1932, BIRTHPLACE 542 Freigh,Miltown-Malbay.
EDUCATION 543 Maynooth 1871 Ordained 1875/76

314. MATHEW THEOBALD
BORN: 1834, DIED 1872, BIRTHPLACE, Thomastown, Golden.
EDUCATION 544 Maynooth, Logic 1854. Ordained 1861.
SOCIAL BACKGROUND: Farming. POLITICAL INVOLVEMENT: Yes.
OTHER INFO: He was a candidate for the chair of Humanity of Maynooth in 1859; a nephew of the famous Fr. Theobald Mathew. President in St. Patrick's, Thurles,1860-1872.
DIOCESE: Cashel and Emly. MINISTRY: C.C. Tipperary 1865-1868.

315. MAXEY MICHAEL
BORN: c.1815 EDUCATION 545 St. John's College 1835-1840.
POLITICAL INVOLVEMENT: Yes. MINISTRY: C.C. Cahir 1853-1865.
DIOCESE: Waterford.

316. MAXWELL JOHN
BORN: c.1851. EDUCATION 547 Maynooth, Rhetoric 1879. Ordained 1866.
POLITICAL INVOLVEMENT: Yes. MINISTRY: C.C. Couragancen 1886-1890.
DIOCESE: Killaloe. C.C. Kilnanave and Templederry 1890-post 1891.

317. MEADE JOSEPH
BORN: c.1826 DIED 12/1/1884.
EDUCATION 548 Maynooth, Rhetoric 1841. Ordained in Killaloe 1851.
One year in Irish College, Paris.
POLITICAL INVOLVEMENT: No.
DIOCESE: Killaloe. MINISTRY: P.P.Kyle and Knock 1869-1874.

318. MEAGHER EDWARD P.
BORN: 1829 DIED 1909, BIRTHPLACE, Cormacktown, Holycross.
EDUCATION 549 Maynooth, Logic 1851. Ordained in Dublin 1857.
SOCIAL BACKGROUND 550 Farming. POLITICAL INVOLVEMENT: Yes.
DIOCESE: Cashel and Emly. MINISTRY: C.C. Mullinahone 1859-1862.
C.C. Capnawhite 1862-1865.
C.C. Ballina 1878-1881.
P.P. Ballina 1881-1909.

319. MEAGHER JAMES
BORN: c.1831 DIED 20/8/.880.
EDUCATION 551 Maynooth, Rhetoric 1851. Ordained 1856.
POLITICAL INVOLVEMENT: Yes.
DIOCESE: Killaloe. MINISTRY: C.C. Rosrcea 1862-1876.

320. MEAGHER JAMES
BORN: c.1848, DIED 1915, BIRTHPLACE: Lahy, Castleiney
EDUCATION: St. Patrick's, Thurles 1864-1872. Ordained Kilkenny 1873.
SOCIAL BACKGROUND 552 Farming. POLITICAL INVOLVEMENT: No.
DIOCESE: Cashel and Emly. MINISTRY: C.C. Clerihan 1882-1883.

321. MEAGHER JAMES
BORN: c.1605, DIED 15/7/1066, BIRTHPLACE: (Cronnagh, Templetuohy or Clonmore, Templemore.
EDUCATION: Carlow College. Ordained there 1830.
SOCIAL BACKGROUND 553 Farming. POLITICAL INVOLVEMENT: Yes.
DIOCESE: Cashel and Emly. MINISTRY: P.F. Upperchurch 1849-1066.

322. MEAGHER JEREMIAH
BORN: c.1859, BIRTHPLACE, 554 Tullohea, Ballyneale.
EDUCATION 555 St. John's, Waterford Sept.1877-June 1884 when he was ordained.
SOCIAL BACKGROUND: See No.335. POLITICAL INVOLVEMENT: No.
OTHER INFO: 556 Brother of William Meagher (No.335).Ministered in Scotland.
DIOCESE: Waterford.

323. MEAGHER JOHN
BORN: c.1827 EDUCATION 557 Maynooth, Humanity 1845. Ordained 1852.
POLITICAL INVOLVEMENT: Yes.
DIOCESE: Killaloe. MINISTRY:C.C. Roscrea 1853-1854.
C.C. Nenagh 1854-1855.
C.C. Ardcroney and Ballygiblin 1855-1856.
C.C. Birr 1866-1868.
C.C. Nenagh 1868-1869.
C.C. Kilnanave and Templederry 1869-1872.

324. MEAGHER JOHN
BORN: c.1859 DIED 16/2/1921. EDUCATION: 558 Irish College, Paris.
POLITICAL INVOLVEMENT: Yes.
DIOCESE: Killaloe.

325. MEAGHER JOHN
BORN: c.1792. DIED 6/4/1861.
EDUCATION 559 Maynooth, Logic 1812. Ordained 1817.

OTHER INFO:[578]Collecting for Thurles Cathedral in 1871 in America. He was a cousin of Archbishop Leahy, Archdeacon Jones and the two Fr. O'Carrolls(Nos.389,390).

DIOCESE: Cashel and Emly. MINISTRY: C.C. Templemore 1855-1864.
C.C. Thurles 1864-1871.
P.F. Drangan 1872-1882.
P.P. Templemore 1882-post 1891.

BORN: c.1806, EDUCATION: Maynooth, Rhetoric 1865. Ordained 1870.
POLITICAL INVOLVEMENT: Yes.
DIOCESE: Killaloe. MINISTRY: C.C. Ardcroney and Ballygibblin 1876-1877.

327. MEAGHER MICHAEL
BORN: c.1806, EDUCATION:[561]Maynooth,Humanity 1826,Deacon in 1831.
POLITICAL INVOLVEMENT: Yes.
DIOCESE: Killaloe. MINISTRY:C.C. Ardcroney and Ballygibblin pre 1850-1852.
P.F. Dunkerrin and Moneygall 1852-1862.

328. MEAGHER MICHAEL
BORN: 1831 DIED 29/9/1881, BIRTHPLACE, Laha, Castleiney.
EDUCATION: Irish College, Paris 1853-1857. Ordained 1858.
SOCIAL BACKGROUND:[562]Farming. POLITICAL INVOLVEMENT: Yes.
DIOCESE: Cashel and Emly. MINISTRY: C.C. Holycross 1858-1861.
C.C. Emly 1861-1862.
C.C. Holycross 1863-1875.
P.F. Drom 1877-1881.

329. MEAGHER PATRICK
BORN: 1810 DIED 1852, BIRTHPLACE, Templemore Parish.
EDUCATION: Irish College, Paris. Ordained in Versailles 1836.
POLITICAL INVOLVEMENT: Yes.
DIOCESE: Cashel and Emly. MINISTRY: C.C. Ballingarry 1843-1852.

330. MEAGHER PATRICK
BORN: c.1037 DIED 1906, BIRTHPLACE, Freighduff, Boherlahan.
EDUCATION:[563]Maynooth, Logic 1855. Ordained 1861/62.
SOCIAL BACKGROUND:[564]Farming. POLITICAL INVOLVEMENT: Yes.
OTHER INFO: Related to Thomas (No.332), probably brothers.
DIOCESE: Cashel and Emly. MINISTRY:C.C. Clonoulty (Summer)1861.
C.C. Anacarty 1862-1865.
C.C. Templemore 1866-1867.
C.C. Drangan 1867-1869.
C.C. Drom 1869-1876.
C.C. FETHARD 1876-1881.
P.F. Drom 1881-1906.

331. MEAGHER PATRICK
BORN: 1795, DIED 1852, BIRTHPLACE, Templemore.
EDUCATION:[565]Maynooth, Rhetoric 1824. Ordained 1829.
POLITICAL INVOLVEMENT: Yes. OTHER INFO:Parish united to Bansha 1852.
DIOCESE: Cashel and Emly. MINISTRY: P.P. Kilmoyler 1849-1852.

332. MEAGHER THOMAS
BORN: c.1816, DIED 1888, BIRTHPLACE, Freighduff, Boherlahan.
EDUCATION:[566] Maynooth, Logic 1836. Ordained 1841.
SOCIAL BACKGROUND:[567]Farming. POLITICAL INVOLVEMENT: Yes.
OTHER INFO:Related to Patrick (No.330),probably brothers.

333. MEAGHER THOMAS FRANCIS
BORN: c.1832, DIED 1889, BIRTHPLACE, Friar Street, Thurles.
EDUCATION:[566]Maynooth, Logic 1850. Ordained in Dublin 1857.
SOCIAL BACKGROUND:[569] His parents had a butchers shop in Friar Street.
POLITICAL INVOLVEMENT: Yes.
OTHER INFO: Sent to America in 1867 to collect for Thurles Cathedral.
DIOCESE: Cashel and Emly. MINISTRY: C.C. Mullinahone 1862-1867.
C.C. Tipperary 1868-1877.

334. MEAGHER THOMAS P.
BORN: 1799 DIED 1855, BIRTHPLACE, Gragough, Ballingarry.
EDUCATION: Trinity College, Irish College, Paris. Ordained there 1826.
SOCIAL BACKGROUND:[570]Farming. POLITICAL INVOLVEMENT: Yes.
OTHER INFO:[571] He was on the staff of the Irish College, Paris and had to fly in the 1830 Revolution. Called the Bossuet of Munster because of his oratorical powers.
DIOCESE: Cashel and Emly. MINISTRY: P.P. Ballina 1849-1861.
P.P. Loughmore 1861-1865.

335. MEAGHER WILLIAM.
BORN: c.1847, DIED 14/11/1923, BIRTHPLACE,[572]Tullohea, Ballymeala.
EDUCATION:[573] St. John's College 1864-1872. Ordained by Cardinal Moran in St. Kierans, Kilkenny.
SOCIAL BACKGROUND:[574] Farming. The Meaghers came from Templemore to Tullohea early in the Seventeenth Century.
POLITICAL INVOLVEMENT:[575] Yes. Dublin Castle considered him "outwardly quiet, but troublesome" unlike his brother, Jeremiah (No.322). He was well liked by the Clonmel people, who petitioned the Bishop for his return to Clonmel. The Bishop relented.
DIOCESE: Waterford. MINISTRY:C.C. Clonmel, St. Marys 1873-1890.
C.C. Cahir 1890-1891.
C.C. Clonmel, St. Marys 1891-1902.

336. MEAGHER WILLIAM
DIED 18/3/1892. EDUCATION: Unknown, not Maynooth.
POLITICAL INVOLVEMENT: Yes.
DIOCESE: Killaloe. MINISTRY:C.C. Shinrone pre 1850-1851.
C.C. Burgessbeg and Youghal 1851-1852.
C.C. Dunkerrin and Moneygall 1852-1856.
C.C. BIRR 1856-1866.
C.C. Shinrone 1866-1873.
P.F. Dunkerrin and Moneygall 1873-post 1891.

337. MEAGHER WILLIAM J.
BORN: 1826, DIED 1912, BIRTHPLACE, Templemore.
EDUCATION:[576]Maynooth, Physics 1850. Ordained 1855.
SOCIAL BACKGROUND:[577] Wealthy tenant farmers. He was descended from the Killea branch of the O'Meaghers of Ikerrin,

P.P. Newport 1875-1888,

338. MEANY PATRICK
BORN:[579] 1816, DIED 12/6/1889, BIRTHPLACE,[580] Clonea, Dungarvan.
EDUCATION:[581] St. John's College 1834-1839.
SOCIAL BACKGROUND:[582]Farming. Parents were Pierce and Mary(Nee Redmond) Meany.
POLITICAL INVOLVEMENT: Yes.
OTHER INFO:[583]One of the founders of the Keating Society. Two administrations during his pastoral absences owing periods of illness, 4 uncles and 4 brothers and nephews were priests. Uncle of D. O'Connor (No.395).
DIOCESE: Waterford. MINISTRY: C.C. Clonmel, St. Marys pre 1850-1857.
P.F. Clogheen 1860-1889.

339. MEEHAN PATRICK
BORN: c.1822, DIED 18/5/1893,
EDUCATION:[584] Maynooth, Humanity 1842, Ordained N.D.
POLITICAL INVOLVEMENT: Yes.
DIOCESE: Killaloe. MINISTRY: C.C. Toomvuara 1876-1887.

340. MOCKLER EDMOND
BORN: 1782, DIED 1863.
EDUCATION: Carlow College 1812-1816. Ordained there in 1816.
SOCIAL BACKGROUND:[585]He himself had a farm of 40 acres on a lease for ever at a nominal rent. He willed it to Cardinal Cullen, much to the chagrin of Archbishop Leahy. Mockler had been hostile to Leahy's appointment as Archbishop.
POLITICAL INVOLVEMENT: Yes.
DIOCESE: Cashel and Emly. MINISTRY: P.P. Donaskeigh 1838-1863.

341. MOCKLER HUGH
BORN: 1849, DIED 1910, BIRTHPLACE, The Grange, Thurles.
EDUCATION: St. Patrick's, Thurles 1871-1876. Ordained 1876.
SOCIAL BACKGROUND:[586]Farming. POLITICAL INVOLVEMENT: Yes.
DIOCESE: Cashel and Emly. MINISTRY: C.C. Clerihan 1883-1887.
C.C. Anacarty 1887-1896.

342. MOLLOY THOMAS
BORN: 1811, DIED 12/9/1861, BIRTHPLACE, Ballintoggart, Ballingarry.
EDUCATION:[587] Rhetoric and Physics in Byrnes Hall, Kilkenny, Maynooth, Logic 1836. Ordained 1841.
SOCIAL BACKGROUND:[588]Farming. POLITICAL INVOLVEMENT: Yes.
DIOCESE: Cashel and Emly. MINISTRY: C.C. Drangan 1841-1859.
C.C. Cashel 1859-1861.

343. **MOLONEY DENIS**
BORN: [509] 1814   DIED 3/4/1880.
EDUCATION: [590] Maynooth, Rhetoric 1837. Ordained N.D.
POLITICAL INVOLVEMENT: Yes.
OTHER INFO: [591] As P.P. Ardcroney he had a farm and called himself a "good farmer".
MINISTRY: C.C. Roscrea 1850-1860.
P.P. Ardcroney and Ballygivlin 1869-1880.
DIOCESE: Killaloe.

344. **MOLONEY EUGENE**
DIED 6/12/1905. EDUCATION: unknown, but not Maynooth.
POLITICAL INVOLVEMENT: Yes.
MINISTRY: C.C. Couranganren 1864-1866.
C.C. Roscrea 1876-1881.
DIOCESE: Killaloe.

345. **MOLONEY JOHN**
BORN: c.1849, EDUCATION [592] Maynooth, Rhetoric 1868. Ordained N.D.
POLITICAL INVOLVEMENT: Yes.
MINISTRY: C.C. Ardcroney and Ballygiblin 1878-1883.
C.C. Kilnanave and Templederry 1883-1886.
DIOCESE: Killaloe.

346. **MOLONEY JOHN**
BORN: 1803, DIED 1850(of fever), BIRTHPLACE: Kilmastulla, Ballina.
EDUCATION [593] Maynooth, Humanity 1825. Ordained 1831.
POLITICAL INVOLVEMENT: Yes.
MINISTRY: P.P. Kilcommon 1847-1850.
DIOCESE: Cashel and Emly.

347. **MOLONEY JOHN C.**
BORN: c.1853 EDUCATION: [594] Maynooth, Philosophy 1872. Ordained 1878
POLITICAL INVOLVEMENT: Yes.
MINISTRY: C.C. Lorrha and Dorrha 1878-1885.
C.C. Toomevara 1985-1888.
DIOCESE: Killaloe.

348. **MOLONEY THOMAS**
BORN: c.1815 DIED 1887, BIRTHPLACE: [595] Drumcliff, Ennis.
EDUCATION: [596] Irish College, Rome. Ordained 1840. In the Irish College until 1846. Studied Humanities in private schools.
POLITICAL INVOLVEMENT: No.
MINISTRY: C.C. Birr pre 1850-1853.
DIOCESE: Killaloe.

349. **MOLONY JOHN**
BORN: 1825, DIED 1887, BIRTHPLACE: Moycarkey Village.
EDUCATION: [597] Maynooth, Theology 1850. Ordained 1855.
SOCIAL BACKGROUND: [598] Farming.   POLITICAL INVOLVEMENT: Yes.
DIOCESE: Cashel and Emly.   MINISTRY: C.C. Cashel 1855-1857.
C.C. Fethard 1857-1875

350. **MOONEY EDWARD**   DIED 1891
EDUCATION: [599] St. John's College 5/2/1835-29/8/1835. Maynooth, Humanity 1835. Ordained N.D.
POLITICAL INVOLVEMENT: No.
DIOCESE: Waterford.   MINISTRY: C.C. Ardfinan pre 1850-1851.
C.C. Gammonsfield and Kilcash 1861-1869.
C.C. Ballyneale 1872-1874.

351. **MOONEY MAURICE**
BORN: [600] 1817,   DIED 5/3/1891, BIRTHPLACE: [601] Lacken(between Waterford and Tramore).
EDUCATION: [602] Maynooth, Rhetoric 1834. Ordained N.D.
SOCIAL BACKGROUND: [603] Wealthy, tenant farming, but the family had moved from Lacken prior to Griffiths Valuation.
POLITICAL INVOLVEMENT: Yes.
OTHER INFO: [604] A lazy priest, paralyzed for a year before he died.   MINISTRY: P.P. Cahir 1865-1891.
DIOCESE: Waterford.

352. **MOONEY MICHAEL**
BORN: c. 1832,   EDUCATION [605] Maynooth, Humanity 1852. Deacon 1857.
POLITICAL INVOLVEMENT: No.
MINISTRY: C.C. Cahir 1865-1878.
C.C. Clogheen 1878-1879.
DIOCESE: Waterford.

353. **MORAN JOHN**
BORN: c.1848,   DIED 17/7/1912, BIRTHPLACE: [606] Ballyknockane,Ballylooby.
EDUCATION: [607] St. John's College 1/9/1867-8/6/1873.   POLITICAL INVOLVEMENT: Yes.
SOCIAL BACKGROUND: [608] Farming.
OTHER INFO: [609] Brother of Thomas (No.354). First mission in Scotland.
MINISTRY: C.C. Cahir 1883-1887.
C.C. Ballyneale 1880-post 1881.
DIOCESE: Waterford.

354. **MORAN THOMAS**
BORN: c.1848,   BIRTHPLACE: [610] Ballyknockane, Ballylooby.
EDUCATION: [611] St. John's College 1867-1873.
SOCIAL BACKGROUND: Brother of John, No.353).
OTHER INFO: Brother of John, Nc.353).
DIOCESE: Waterford.   MINISTRY: C.C. Cahir 1876-1877.
C.C. Clogheen 1877-1878.
C.C. Clonmel, S.S. Peter and Paule, 1883-1890.
C.C. Carrick-On-Suir 1890-post 1891.

355. **MORRIS THOMAS**
BORN: c.1846,   DIED 1891.
EDUCATION: Carlow College 1865-1871. Ordained 1871.
POLITICAL INVOLVEMENT: Yes.
DIOCESE: Waterford.
OTHER INFO: [612] Spent some time on mission in England.The people of Killavulla made him a presentation when he arrived

MINISTRY CONTD: C.C. Newport 1885-1886.
C.C. Newport 1888-1889.
C.C. Templemore 1889-1890.
C.C. Newport 1890-1891.

356. **MORRIS PATRICK J.**
BORN: 1810   DIED 1889, BIRTHPLACE, Graigue, Killenaule.
EDUCATION: Carlow College. Ordained there 1841.
SOCIAL BACKGROUND: [614] Farming.   POLITICAL INVOLVEMENT: Yes.
OTHER INFO: Brother of William No.357.
DIOCESE: Cashel and Emly.   MINISTRY: C.C. Borrisoleigh 1842-1860
P.P. Borrisoleigh 1866-1069.

357. **MORRIS WILLIAM**
BORN: 1795,   DIED 4/4/1866, BIRTHPLACE, Graigue, Killenaule.
EDUCATION: Carlow College 1813-1818. Ordained Maynooth 1819.
SOCIAL BACKGROUND: See No.356.   POLITICAL INVOLVEMENT: Yes.
OTHER INFO: Brother of Patrick (No.356).
DIOCESE: Cashel and Emly.   MINISTRY: P.P. Borrisoleigh 1834-1866.

358. **MORRISSEY DAVID**
BORN: [615] 1822,   BIRTHPLACE, [616] Killosera, Dungarvan.
EDUCATION: [617] Rudiments of Grammar at private schools. Irish College Rome, 1842-1849.
POLITICAL INVOLVEMENT: No.
DIOCESE: Waterford.   MINISTRY: C.C. Cahir 1853-1856.

359. **MORRISSEY J.**
BORN: c.1808,   DIED Feb.1069.
EDUCATION: [618] St. John's College 6/4/1825-1033.
POLITICAL INVOLVEMENT: No.
DIOCESE: Waterford.

360. **MORRISSEY PATRICK**
BORN: c.1790,   DIED 1/12/1864.
EDUCATION: [619] Maynooth, Logic 1818. Ordained 1823.
POLITICAL INVOLVEMENT: Yes.
DIOCESE: Waterford.   MINISTRY: P.P. Ballyneale 1824-1864.

361. **MOYLAN THOMAS**
BORN: c.1793,   EDUCATION: [620] Maynooth, Deacon 1818.
POLITICAL INVOLVEMENT: No.
DIOCESE: Killaloe.   MINISTRY: P.P.Castletownarra pre 1850-1058.

362. **MULCAHY JAMES**
BORN: c.1857,   BIRTHPLACE, [621] Clogheen.

363. MULCAHY PATRICK
BORN:[624] 1057, DIED August 1050, BIRTHPLACE, Ballinteenoe, Boher.
EDUCATION: St. Patrick's, Thurles 1873-1881.
SOCIAL BACKGROUND:[625] Farming. POLITICAL INVOLVEMENT: Yes.
OTHER INFO: On mission in London 1882-1009.
DIOCESE: Cashel and Emly. MINISTRY: C.C. Clonoulty 1889-1890.

364. MULLALLY JAMES
BORN:[626] 1864, DIED 4/2/1855, BIRTHPLACE, Ballycullen, Mullinahone.
EDUCATION:[627] Maynooth, Humanity 1022. Ordained1029.
SOCIAL BACKGROUND:[628] Farming. POLITICAL INVOLVEMENT: Yes.
OTHER INFO:[629] Brother of William (No.365). The family produced two priests and four nuns. Related to the Morris Family (Nos.356,357).
DIOCESE: Cashel and Emly. MINISTRY: F.P. Newinn 1649-1855.

365. MULLALLY WILLIAM FRANCIS
BORN: c.1799, DIED 14/11/1864, BIRTHPLACE, Ballycullen, Mullina-hone.
EDUCATION:[630] Maynooth, Logic 1818. Ordained in Thurles 1824.
SOCIAL BACKGROUND: See Index No.364. POLITICAL INVOLVEMENT: Yes.
OTHER INFO: Brother of James (No.364).
DIOCESE: Cashel and Emly. MINISTRY: F.f. Knocanty 1045-1864.

366. MULLANEY THOMAS
BORN: 1791, DIED 1869, BIRTHPLACE, Mullaunbrack, Thurles.
EDUCATION:[631] Maynooth, Humanity 1608. Ordained 1613.
POLITICAL INVOLVEMENT: Yes.
DIOCESE: Cashel and Emly. MINISTRY: F.f. Drom and Inch 1627-1669.

367. MULLINS JOHN
BORN: c.1003, DIED 4/5/1802.
EDUCATION: St. John's College 22/1/1823-1828.
POLITICAL INVOLVEMENT: No.
DIOCESE: Waterford. MINISTRY:C.C. Carrick-On-Suir pre 1050-1050.

368. MURPHY JOHN
BORN: c.1844, DIED 1923, BIRTHPLACE, Emly.
EDUCATION: Irish College, Rome 1864-1869. Ordained there 1869.
POLITICAL INVOLVEMENT: Yes.
OTHER INFO: Nephew of Philip Fitzgerald (No.149).
DIOCESE: Cashel and Emly. MINISTRY: C.C. Mullinahone 1872-1081.
C.C. Moycarkey 1082-1085.
C.C. Lattin and Cullen 1085-1896.

369.
DIOCESE: Killaloc. MINISTRY: C.C.Cloughprior and Mounsea 1851-1052.
C.C.Nenagh 1852-1857.
C.C.Birr 1857-1869.

370. MURPHY JOHN M.
BORN: 1853, DIED 1917, BIRTHPLACE, Duncrumin, Emly.
EDUCATION: St. Patrick's, Thurles 1873-1879. Ordained 1880.
SOCIAL BACKGROUND:[633] Farming. POLITICAL INVOLVEMENT: No.
OTHER INFO: On mission to Scotland to 1880-1889.
DIOCESE: Cashel and Emly. MINISTRY: C.C. Borrisoleigh 1889,
C.C. Moycarkey 1889-1890.

371. MURPHY PATRICK
BORN: c.1056, DIED 1924, BIRTHPLACE, Clonoulty Parish.
EDUCATION:[634]Maynooth, Rhetoric 1874. Ordained 1880/81.
SOCIAL BACKGROUND:[635] Farming. POLITICAL INVOLVEMENT: Yes.
OTHER INFO: On mission to Galloway 1081-1090.
DIOCESE: Cashel and Emly. MINISTRY: C.C. Moycarkey 1090,
C.C. Kilnamule 1890-1891.
C.C. Templemore 1891 - post 1891.

372. MURPHY PETER
BORN:[636] 1826, DIED 2/10/1900, BIRTHPLACE,[637] Lortha.
EDUCATION:[630] Maynooth, Logic 1053. Ordained 1057.
POLITICAL INVOLVEMENT: Yes. (Very heavily involved in the Bodyke evictions dispute, when he was a parish priest of Tuamgraney in which parish Bodyke lies).
DIOCESE: Killaloe. MINISTRY: C.C.Kilnanavo and Templederry 1061-1869.
C.C. Nenagh 1869-1878.

373. MURRAY MICHAEL
BORN:[639] 1863, DIED 30/3/1936, BIRTHPLACE,[640]Toonevara Parish.
EDUCATION:[641] Maynooth, Philosophy 1803. Ordained 1899, early education in Old Diocesan College, Ennis.
SOCIAL BACKGROUND:[642] Farming. POLITICAL INVOLVEMENT: No.
OTHER INFO:[643] Uncle of Dr. Maxwell, Professor, St. Flannans College, Ennis.
DIOCESE: Killaloe. MINISTRY: C.C. Couraganeen 1090-1891.

374. NAGLE PATRICK
BORN: c.1021, DIED 4/6/1886.
EDUCATION:[644] Maynooth, Rhetoric 1839. Ordained 1846.
SOCIAL BACKGROUND:[645] Wealthy brother of Alderman Nagle, Dublin.
POLITICAL INVOLVEMENT: Yes.
OTHER INFO:[646] On the Dunboyne Establishment when in Maynooth. He was chaplain to Lord Bellow for some time.

375. NEWPORT ANDREW
BORN: c.1822, DIED 1080.
EDUCATION:[647] Maynooth, Rhetoric 1841, Deacon 1047, (Retired).
POLITICAL INVOLVEMENT: No.
DIOCESE: Killaloe MINISTRY:C.C. Cloughprior and Mounsea pre 1050-1050.

376. NOLAN JOHN
BORN:[648] 1858, DIED 25/3/1913, BIRTHPLACE,[649] Nenagh Town.
EDUCATION:[650] Maynooth, earlier education at the old Springfield College.
SOCIAL BACKGROUND:[651] "came from a stock of substance and respectability."
POLITICAL INVOLVEMENT: Yes.
DIOCESE: Killaloe. MINISTRY:C.C. Dunkerrin and Moneygall 1882-1885.
C.C. Borrisokane 1885-post 1891.

377. NOLAN PETER
DIED 23/4/1877. EDUCATION: Unknown, but not Maynooth.
POLITICAL INVOLVEMENT: Yes.
DIOCESE: Killaloe. MINISTRY: C.C. Roscrea pre 1850-1854.
C.C. Birr 1854-1859.
F.f. Borrisokane 1859-1877

378. NOONAN JOHN
BORN: 1003, DIED 1068, BIRTHPLACE, Gurtnahoe.
EDUCATION: A seminary in Limerick. Ordained 1026.
SOCIAL BACKGROUND: Farming. POLITICAL INVOLVEMENT: Yes.
DIOCESE: Cashel and Emly. MINISTRY: P.P. Capawhite 1846-1862.
F.f. Galbally 1862-1068.

379. O'BRIEN CORNELIUS
BORN:[652] 1796, DIED 9/10/1086, BIRTHPLACE,[653] Annameadle, Toomevara.
EDUCATION: Unknown, but not Maynooth.
SOCIAL BACKGROUND:[654] Farming. POLITICAL INVOLVEMENT: Yes.
DIOCESE: Killaloe. MINISTRY:F.P. Lortha and Dortha pre 1850-1006.

380. O'BRIEN DANIEL W.
BORN: 1842, DIED 1932, BIRTHPLACE, Bishopswood, Knockavella.
EDUCATION: St. Patrick's, Thurles 1875-1879.
SOCIAL BACKGROUND:[655] Farming. Current farm about 40 Irish acres, came to parish after 1852, not in Griffiths Valuation.
POLITICAL INVOLVEMENT: Yes.
OTHER INFO: On mission in Scotland to 1888.
DIOCESE: Cashel and Emly. MINISTRY: C.C. Galbally 1889-1895.

381. O'BRIEN DENIS
BORN: c.1849. EDUCATION:[656] Maynooth, Humanity 1868. Ordained 1873/74.
POLITICAL INVOLVEMENT: Yes.
DIOCESE: Killaloe. MINISTRY:C.C.Ardcroney and Ballyaiblin 1874-1876. C.C.Kilnanave and Templederry 1876-1880.

382. O'BRIEN FRANCIS
BORN: c.1833, DIED 12/2/1896, BIRTHPLACE:[657] Ring Parish.
EDUCATION:[658] St. John's College. Ordained 1858.
POLITICAL INVOLVEMENT: No.
OTHER INFO:[659] Professor in St. John's College.
DIOCESE: Waterford. MINISTRY:C.C. Ballyneale 1864-1866. C.C. Cahir 1876-1878.

383. O'BRIEN JAMES
BORN: c.1852, DIED 1901, BIRTHPLACE: Glengall,Ballingarry.
EDUCATION: St. Patrick's Thurles 1869-1876. Ordained 1076.
SOCIAL BACKGROUND:[660] Farming. POLITICAL INVOLVEMENT: Yes.
OTHER INFO: On loan to Killaloe Diocese 1877-1081.
DIOCESE: Cashel and Emly. MINISTRY:C.C. Burgessbeg and Youghal, 1077-1081. C.C. Ballinahinch 1081-1885. C.C. Ballina 1885-1901.

384. O'BRIEN JOHN
DIED 22/6/1905, EDUCATION: Unknown, not Maynooth.
POLITICAL INVOLVEMENT: Yes.
DIOCESE: Killaloe.

385. O'BRIEN JOHN
BORN: [661] c.1816, DIED 30/1/1910, BIRTHPLACE: Lissard, Galbally.
EDUCATION:[662] Maynooth, Deacon 1846, also St. Patrick's, Thurles. He was one of the first students to enter St. Patrick's, Thurles when it opened in 1837.
SOCIAL BACKGROUND:[663] Farming. POLITICAL INVOLVEMENT: Yes.
OTHER INFO:[664] The oldest priest in the Archdiocese on his death.
DIOCESE: Cashel and Emly. MINISTRY:C.C. Drom 1847-1857.
C.C. Galbally 1857-1861.
C.C. Doon 1861-1865.
C.C. Kilcommon 1865-1869.
F.F. Holycross 1869-1910.

386. O'BRIEN MICHAEL
BORN: c.1810, DIED 1868, BIRTHPLACE: Loughgur, Knockainy.
EDUCATION:[665] Maynooth, Rhetoric 1026. Ordained 1835.
SOCIAL BACKGROUND:[666] Farming. POLITICAL INVOLVEMENT: Yes.

387. O'BRIEN RICHARD
BORN: 1804, DIED 1877, BIRTHPLACE: Loughgur, Knockainy.
EDUCATION:[667] Maynooth, Physics 1827, Deacon 1831, Ordained 1833.
SOCIAL BACKGROUND: (See No.386). POLITICAL INVOLVEMENT: Yes.
OTHER INFO: Professor in Maynooth for one year prior to ordination. Brother of Michael, No.386.
DIOCESE: Cashel and Emly. MINISTRY:C.C. Tipperary 1849-1853.

388. O'CALLAGHAN DAVID
BORN: c.1848, DIED 1895, BIRTHPLACE:[657] Ballinalacken,Glenbrohane, (Co. Limerick).
EDUCATION: Carlow College 1368-1873. Ordained there 1873.
POLITICAL INVOLVEMENT: Yes.
DIOCESE: Cashel and Emly. MINISTRY:C.C. Moyne 1880-1884.
C.C. Golden 1888-1891.
C.C. Killenaule 1891-1894.

389. O'CARROLL JAMES
BORN: c.1823, DIED 1872, BIRTHPLACE: Templemore town.
EDUCATION: Irish College, Paris 1849-1851. Ordained in Maynooth 1854.
POLITICAL INVOLVEMENT: Yes
OTHER INFO: Brother of Thomas (No.390) and related to John Mackey, (No.306).
DIOCESE: Cashel and Emly. MINISTRY: C.C. Clonoulty 1855-1872.

390. O'CARROLL THOMAS
BORN: 1810, DIED 1865, BIRTHPLACE: Templemore Town.
EDUCATION: Irish College, Paris 1833-1838. Ordained there 1838.
POLITICAL INVOLVEMENT: Yes.
OTHER INFO: Professor St. Patrick's 1052-1055.
DIOCESE: Cashel and Emly.

391. O'CONNELL JAMES
BORN: 1830, DIED 1889, BIRTHPLACE: Cattiganstown, Killenaule.
EDUCATION:[668] Maynooth, Physics 1856. Ordained in Dublin 1860.
SOCIAL BACKGROUND:[669] Farming. POLITICAL INVOLVEMENT: Yes.
DIOCESE: Cashel and Emly. MINISTRY:C.C. Emly 1860
C.C. Galbally 1862-1864.
C.C. Galbally 1864-1875.
C.C. Newport 1875-1883.
C.C. Templemore 1883-1886.
P.P. Clerihan 1886-1889.

392. O'CONNELL MARTIN
BORN: 12/11/1852, DIED 1916, BIRTHPLACE: Clonamuckoge,Loughmore.
EDUCATION: St. Patrick's, Thurles. Ordained 1877.
SOCIAL BACKGROUND:[670] Farming. POLITICAL INVOLVEMENT: Yes.
OTHER INFO: On mission in Westminster 1877-1886.

393. O'CONNELL PATRICK
BORN: c.1826, BIRTHPLACE: Laha, Castleiney.
EDUCATION:[671] Maynooth, Theology 1048. Ordained 1851.
SOCIAL BACKGROUND:[672] Farming. POLITICAL INVOLVEMENT: Yes.
OTHER INFO: Went to Australia in 1861.
DIOCESE: Cashel and Emly. MINISTRY:C.C. Emly 1854-1861.

394. O'CONNELL TIMOTHY
BORN:[673] 1831, DIED 4/4/1891, BIRTHPLACE:[674] Tallow.
EDUCATION:[675] Maynooth, Logic 1849, Deacon 1854, Ordained 1856.
POLITICAL INVOLVEMENT: Yes.
DIOCESE: Waterford. MINISTRY:C.C. Patrick-On-Suir 1857-1885
F.F. Clonmel, St. Marys 1885-1891.

395. O'CONNOR DAVID J.
BORN: 28/10/1903, BIRTHPLACE:[676] Abbeyside Parish.
EDUCATION: Unknown, but not Maynooth.
POLITICAL INVOLVEMENT: Yes.
OTHER INFO: Nephew of Fat Heany (No.338).
DIOCESE: Waterford. MINISTRY: C.C. Ballylooby 1077-post 1891.

396. O'CONNOR JAMES
BORN: c.1797, DIED 21/7/1851,
EDUCATION:[677] Maynooth, Humanity 1817. Ordained N.D.
POLITICAL INVOLVEMENT: No.
DIOCESE: Waterford. MINISTRY: F.P. Ardfinan 1844-1851.

397. O'CONNOR JOHN
BORN: c.1834, DIED 1877, BIRTHPLACE: Fethard.
EDUCATION:[678] Maynooth, Physics 1854. Ordained 1859.
POLITICAL INVOLVEMENT: Yes.
OTHER INFO: Got an exeat from the Diocese in 1870, nephew of Thomas (No.400), and possibly brother of Thomas (No.399).
DIOCESE: Cashel and Emly. MINISTRY: C.C. Donaskeigh 1861-1862.
C.C. Golden 1862-1864.
C.C. Templemore 1864-1867.
C.C. Ballingarry 1868-1869.
C.C. Anacarty 1869-1870.

393. O'CONNOR JOHN
DIED 22/9/1898.
EDUCATION: Unknown, but not Maynooth.
POLITICAL INVOLVEMENT: Yes.
DIOCESE: Waterford. MINISTRY:C.C. Ardfinan 1875-1883.
C.C. Gammonsfield and Kilcash 1083-1887
C.C. Cahir 1887-1890.

369. O'CONNOR PETER
DIED 7/2/1854,
EDUCATION: Unknown, but not Maynooth.

BORN: c.1857, DIED 1920, BIRTHPLACE, Murroe Parish.
EDUCATION:679 St. Patrick's, Thurles 1871-1874, Maynooth, Humanity 1874, Ordained Dehau 1882.
POLITICAL INVOLVEMENT: Yes.
OTHER INFO: On mission in Hexham and Newcastle 1882-1887.
DIOCESE: Cashel and Emly. MINISTRY: C.C. Ballinahinch 1889-1892.

401. O'CONNOR THOMAS
BORN: c.1822, DIED 1882, BIRTHPLACE, Knockelly, Fethard.
EDUCATION: St. Patrick's College, Thurles. Ordained there 1847.
SOCIAL BACKGROUND:680 Farming. POLITICAL INVOLVEMENT: Yes.
OTHER INFO: Nephew of Thomas (No.400) and probably brother of John, (No.397).
MINISTRY:C.C. Templemore 1847-1867.
Adm. Templemore 1867-1871.
F.P. Templemore 1871-1882.
POLITICAL INVOLVEMENT: Yes.
DIOCESE: Cashel and Emly.

402. O'CONNOR THOMAS D.D.
BORN: 1787, DIED 8/2/1867, BIRTHPLACE, Knockelly, Fethard.
EDUCATION:601 Classics and Philosophy in Carlow, Maynooth, Theology 1812 Ordained 1816. Received his early education in Mullinahone and Cashel, spent 3 years on the Dunboyne
POLITICAL INVOLVEMENT: Yes.
OTHER INFO:682 Professor in Maynooth. Uncle of John (No.397) and of Thomas (No.401). He began the building of St. Patricks College, Thurles and was President there for 10 years.
MINISTRY: F.P. Templemore 1847-1867.

403. O'CONNOR WILLIAM
BORN: 1034, DIED 1920, BIRTHPLACE, Bohor, Murroe.
EDUCATION:683 Maynooth, Physics 1854, Ordained 1859.
SOCIAL BACKGROUND:684 Farming.
POLITICAL INVOLVEMENT: Yes.
MINISTRY: C.C. Bansha 1859-1860.
C.C. Ballina 1860-1867.
C.C. Galbally 1867-1882.
F.P. Drangan 1882-1888.
DIOCESE: Cashel and Emly.

404. O'DONNELL EDWARD
BORN: c.1809, DIED 16/6/1881, BIRTHPLACE:685 Carrick-On-Suir.
EDUCATION: St. John's College 11/9/1026-1834.
POLITICAL INVOLVEMENT: No.
DIOCESE: Waterford. MINISTRY: C.C. Ardfinan 1855-1856.

405. O'DONNELL MICHAEL
BORN: c.1821, DIED 10/2/1868.
EDUCATION:687 Maynooth, Humanity 1039, Deacon :046.
POLITICAL INVOLVEMENT: Yes.
MINISTRY:C.C. Gammonsfield and Kilcash pre 1850-1861.
DIOCESE: Waterford.

406. O'DONNELL PATRICK
DIED 30/6/1876, BIRTHPLACE, 688 Fowerstown.
EDUCATION: Unknown, not Maynooth.
DIOCESE: Waterford. MINISTRY:C.C. Fowerstown 1050-1055.
C.C. Ardfinan 1855-1057.
C.C. Catrick-On-Suir 1857-1872,
Adm. Ballylooby 1873-1876.

407. O'DONNELL PATRICK
BORN: c.1826, BIRTHPLACE, Golden Parish.
EDUCATION:689 Maynooth, Theology 1848, Ordained 1054. Was on the Dunboyne. He was educated entirely at private schools in Golden and Cashel and entered St. Patrick's College, Thurles at 16 where he read Humanity, Logic, Metaphysics and Ethics.
POLITICAL INVOLVEMENT: Yes.
OTHER INFO: Went to America in 1861. MINISTRY: C.C. Newinn 1055-1857.
C.C. Galbally 1060-1061.
DIOCESE: Cashel and Emly.

408. O'DONNELL PATRICK
BORN: c.1844, DIED 1908, BIRTHPLACE, Ballingarry Parish.
EDUCATION:690 Maynooth, Rhetoric 1862, Ordained 1869.
POLITICAL INVOLVEMENT: Yes.
OTHER INFO: Nephew of Thomas (No.409).
DIOCESE: Cashel and Emly. MINISTRY: C.C. Killcommon 1869-1873.
C.C. Doon 1873-1892.

409. O'DONNELL THOMAS
BORN: c.1824, DIED 1892, BIRTHPLACE, Ballingarry Parish.
EDUCATION:691 Maynooth 1841-1849.
POLITICAL INVOLVEMENT: Yes.
OTHER INFO: Uncle of Patrick (No.408).
DIOCESE: Cashel and Emly.

410. O'DONNELL WILLIAM B.
BORN:692 1853 DIED 2/2/1933, Aged 80, BIRTHPLACE,693 Seskin, Kilsheelan.
EDUCATION:694 St. John's College 1/9/1871-12/6/1877, Ordained 1877.
SOCIAL BACKGROUND:695 Farming. POLITICAL INVOLVEMENT: Yes.
OTHER INFO:696 On English mission after ordination. Brother of Michael O'Donnell, ex-Secretary of the County Board.
DIOCESE: Waterford. MINISTRY: C.C. Cahir 1881-1882.

411. O'DWYER JOHN
BORN: c.1818, DIED 1872, BIRTHPLACE, Ballintaggart, Ballingarry.
EDUCATION:697 Maynooth, Logic 1838, Ordained 1843. POLITICAL INVOLVEMENT: Yes.
SOCIAL BACKGROUND:698 Farming. POLITICAL INVOLVEMENT: Yes.
OTHER INFO: Ill for a few years before he died.

DIOCESE: Cashel and Emly. MINISTRY: C.C. Doon 1843-1862.
C.C. Cashel 1862-1865,
F.P. Doon 1865-1872.

412. O'DWYER THOMAS
BORN: 1843, DIED 1914, BIRTHPLACE, Clogher, Clonoulty.
EDUCATION:699 St. Johns 1861-1862, Maynooth, Logic 1863. Ordained in Killaloe 1060.
SOCIAL BACKGROUND:700 Farming. POLITICAL INVOLVEMENT: Yes.
OTHER INFO:701 During the strike of 1860 in St. Patrick's Thurles, he went to St. John's, Waterford.
DIOCESE: Cashel and Emly. MINISTRY:C.C. Galbally 1875-1876.
C.C. Drangan 1876-1878.
C.C. Thurles 1878-1885.
Adm. Thurles 1885-1887.
F.P. Solohead 1887-1914.

413. O'GORMAN JOHN (JUNIOR)
BORN: c.1032, EDUCATION:702 Irish College,Paris. Ordained in Waterford in 1857.
POLITICAL INVOLVEMENT: No.
DIOCESE: Waterford. MINISTRY: C.C. Cloghean 1859-1860.
C.C. Clogheen 1865-1869.

414. O'GORMAN JOHN
DIED 28/3/1868, BIRTHPLACE, 703 Cloghean Parish.
EDUCATION: Unknown, not Maynooth.
POLITICAL INVOLVEMENT: Yes.
DIOCESE: Waterford. MINISTRY: P.P. Cloghean Parish 1852-1868.

415. O'GORMAN MALACHY
BORN:704 1038, DIED 7/2/1910, BIRTHPLACE,705 Corofin.
EDUCATION:706 Maynooth, Humanity 1859 Ordained 1865/66. Early education in a classical school, Ennis.
SOCIAL BACKGROUND:707 Farming. POLITICAL INVOLVEMENT: Yes.
OTHER INFO:708 A Professor in Maynooth.
DIOCESE: Killaloe. MINISTRY:C.C.Durketrin and Moneygall 1870-1880.
C.C. Roscrea 1880-1882.

416. O'GORMAN RICHARD
BORN: 709 1031, DIED 11/4/1901.
EDUCATION:710 St. John's College, 1854-1860, Ordained 1860.
POLITICAL INVOLVEMENT: Yes.
DIOCESE: Waterford. MINISTRY:C.C. Clogheen 1860-1868.
C.C.Newcastle and Four-Mile-Water 1868-1884.

417. O'HALLORAN JOHN
BORN: 711 1844, DIED 10/3/1924, Aged 80, BIRTHPLACE:712 Six-Mile-Bridge, Co.Clare,(Iverstown House).
EDUCATION: 713 St. Munchins, Limerick,Irish College, Rome 1866-1873.
SOCIAL BACKGROUND: 714 Farming.

MINISTRY CONTD:P.F.Donaskeigh 1875-1886.

OTHER INFO:[728] Nephew of Bishop Young, Limerick.
DIOCESE: Killaloe.   MINISTRY: F.P. Shinrone pre 1050-1066.
                                F.P. Nenagh   1067-1079.

DIOCESE: Killaloe.   MINISTRY: C.C.Castletownarra 1873-1874.
                                C.C. Burgessbeg and Youghal 1875-1079.
                                C.C. Shinrone 1879-1886.
                                C.C. Birr 1086-1891.
                                F.F. Castletownarra 1891-post 1891.

429. O'MALLEY JOHN
BORN: c.1049,   DIED 17/7/1913,   BIRTHPLACE:[229] Kilmanley, Co. Clare.
EDUCATION:[730] Maynooth, Theology 1871. Ordained N.D.
POLITICAL INVOLVEMENT: Yes.
DIOCESE: Killaloe.   MINISTRY:C.C. Cloughprior and Mounsea 1872-
1090.

418. O'KEANE EDMUND
BORN: c.1812,   DIED 1870,   BIRTHPLACE: Bottomstown, Knockainy.
EDUCATION:[715] Maynooth, Physics 1831, Maynooth 1837.
SOCIAL BACKGROUND:[716] Farming.   POLITICAL INVOLVEMENT: Yes.
OTHER INFO: Related to Edward (No.419) and Timothy (No.421).
DIOCESE: Cashel and Emly.   MINISTRY: C.C. Loughmore 1848-1855.
                                      C.C. Fethard 1855-1857.
                                      C.C. Tipperary 1857-1866.

430. O'MEARA DANIEL
BORN: c.1861,   BIRTHPLACE: Couranganeen (See No.434).
EDUCATION:[731] Maynooth, Rhetoric 1879. Ordained 1086.
POLITICAL INVOLVEMENT: Yes.
OTHER INFO:[732] Brother of Patrick (No.434).Related to Bishop John
Egan, Waterford.
DIOCESE: Killaloe.   MINISTRY:C.C. Kilbarron and Terryglass 1806-
1807.
                               C.C. Ardcroney and Ballygiblin
1807-post 1891.

419. O'KEANE EDWARD
BORN: 1854,   DIED 1941,   BIRTHPLACE: Bottomstown, Knockainy.
EDUCATION:[718] St. Patrick's, Thurles 1872-1880. Ordained 1880.
POLITICAL INVOLVEMENT: Yes.
OTHER INFO: On mission in Edinburgh 1880-1888. Related to Edmund,
(No.418) and Timothy (No.421).
DIOCESE: Cashel and Emly.   MINISTRY: C.C. Moycarkey 1888-1889.
                                      C.C. Newcutt 1889-1900.

431. O'MEARA DANIEL D.D.
BORN: c.1017,   DIED 0/10/1851,
EDUCATION:[733] Earlier studies at the Seminary of Rev.Dr. Cahill,
Seapoint, Maynooth, Rhetoric 1837, Irish College, Rome.
POLITICAL INVOLVEMENT: No.   MINISTRY: C.C. Nenagh pro 1050-1050.
                                       C.C. Kilbarron and Terryglass 1050-
                                       1051.

420. O'KEANE JAMES
BORN: c.1834,   EDUCATION:[717] Maynooth, Rhetoric 1852, Deacon 1059.
POLITICAL INVOLVEMENT: No.
DIOCESE: Killaloe.   MINISTRY:C.C. Kilbarron and Terryglass 1860-
1863.
                              C.C. Cloughprior and Mounsea 10J-
1064.

432. O'MEARA E.
EDUCATION: Unknown, but not Maynooth.   POLITICAL INVOLVEMENT: Yes.
DIOCESE: Waterford.   MINISTRY: C.C. Clonmel,St. Marys 1867-1872.

433. O'MEARA JEREMIAH
BORN: c.1806,   EDUCATION:[734] Maynooth, Physics 1827. Deacon 1831.
POLITICAL INVOLVEMENT: No.   MINISTRY: C.C. Ballylooby pre 1050-1850.
DIOCESE: Waterford.

421. O'KEANE TIMOTHY
BORN: 1810,   DIED 1093,   BIRTHPLACE: Bottomstown, Knockainy.
EDUCATION:[718] Maynooth, Theology 1845, Ordained Limerick 1849/50.
POLITICAL INVOLVEMENT: Yes.
OTHER INFO: Related to Edmund (No.418) and Edward (No.419).
DIOCESE: Cashel and Emly.   MINISTRY: C.C. Drom 1860-1061.
                                      F.P. Loughmore 1874-1893.

434. O'MEARA PATRICK
BORN: c.1053,   DIED 13/3/1927,   BIRTHPLACE:[735] Couranganeen.
EDUCATION:[736] Maynooth, Humanity 1872. Ordained 1878.
POLITICAL INVOLVEMENT: Yes.
OTHER INFO:[737] Brother of Daniel (No.430). Related to Bishop Egan.
DIOCESE: Killaloe.   MINISTRY:C.C. Castletownarra 1860-1881,
                              C.C. Lorrha and Dorrha 1867-1090.

422. O'KEANE WILLIAM
BORN: 1821,   DIED 1093,   BIRTHPLACE: Hospital Parish(Ballinacurra).
EDUCATION:[719] Irish College, Paris. Ordained Maynooth 1854.
SOCIAL BACKGROUND: Not shown in Griffiths Valuation, but William
is shown in the Baptismal Register for Hospital
townland of Ballinacurra as the son of Thomas
Keana and Bridget Ryan 15/5/1821. They were
certainly tenant farmers.
POLITICAL INVOLVEMENT: Yes.

423. O'KEANE WILLIAM
BORN: A769   DIED 16/5/1861.   BIRTHPLACE: Hospital Parish.
EDUCATION: Carlow College. Ordained there 1813.
POLITICAL INVOLVEMENT: Yes.
DIOCESE: Cashel and Emly.   MINISTRY:F.P. Bansha 1827-1861.

424. O'KEEFFE PATRICK
BORN: 1043   DIED 1913, BIRTHPLACE: Kilmore,Knockavilla, then moved
to Camus, Cashel.
EDUCATION:[720] Maynooth, Humanity 1864. Ordained in Tullow 1871.
SOCIAL BACKGROUND:[721] Farming. Current farm 40-50 acres.
POLITICAL INVOLVEMENT: Yes.
OTHER INFO: Half-brother of Thomas O'Keeffe (No.425).
DIOCESE: Cashel and Emly.   MINISTRY: C.C. Cashel 1876-1877(Chaplain
to the Presentation Convent).
                                      C.C. Moyne 1877-1879.
                                      C.C. Fethard 1879-1885.
                                      C.C. Borrisoleigh 1885-1889.
                                      C.C. Templemore 1889-post
1891.

425. O'KEEFFE THOMAS
BORN: c.1864,   DIED 1907,   BIRTHPLACE: Kilmore,Knockavilla, but
family moved to Camus, Cashel.
EDUCATION:[722] St. Patrick's, Thurles 1882-1884, Maynooth 1884-1889.
Ordained 1889.
SOCIAL BACKGROUND: See No. 424.   POLITICAL INVOLVEMENT: Yes.
OTHER INFO: Half-brother o' Patrick (No.424).
DIOCESE: Cashel and Emly.   MINISTRY: C.C. Doon 1090.
                                      C.C. Clonoulty 1890-1907.

426. O'LEARY EDMUND
BORN: c.1819,   DIED 4/10/1894.
EDUCATION:[723] Maynooth, Rhetoric 1838. Ordained 1844.
POLITICAL INVOLVEMENT: Yes.
DIOCESE: Killaloe.   MINISTRY: C.C. Shinrone 1851-1859.
                               C.C. Birr 1859-1860.
                               C.C. Roscrea 1860-1861.
                               F.P. Toomevara 1874-1891.
                               F.P. Roscrea 1891-4/10/1894.

427. O'MAHONY PATRICK VINCENT
BORN: c.1821,   DIED 1870,   BIRTHPLACE: Dualla.
EDUCATION:[724] Maynooth, Logic 1841, Ordained 1846.
SOCIAL BACKGROUND:[725] Farming.   POLITICAL INVOLVEMENT: Yes.
DIOCESE: Cashel and Emly.   MINISTRY:C.C. Loughmore 1849-1870.

428. O'MAILLEY PATRICK V.G.
[726] ...

435. O'MEARA THEOPHILUS
BORN: 1821, DIED 1873, BIRTHPLACE, Rathcannon, Holycross.
EDUCATION:Carlow College 1841-1846. Ordained 1846.
SOCIAL BACKGROUND:[738] Farming. POLITICAL INVOLVEMENT: Yes.
DIOCESE: Cashel and Emly. MINISTRY: C.C. Boherlahan 1846-1855.
          C.C. Cashel 1855-1857.
          C.C. Thurles 1857-1863.
          F.P. Holycross 1863-1869
          P.P. Drom and Inch 1869-1873.

436. O'MEARA THOMAS (JUNIOR).
BORN: c.1032, EDUCATION: [739] St. John's College 20/1/1052-6/6/1057.
POLITICAL INVOLVEMENT: No.
DIOCESE: Waterford. MINISTRY: C.C. Newcastle and Four-Mile-Water,
          1864-1875.

437. O'MEARA THOMAS
BORN: c.1008, DIED 2/11/1874,
EDUCATION:[74C] St. John's College 1026-1033.
POLITICAL INVOLVEMENT: Yes.
DIOCESE: Waterford. MINISTRY:P.P. Newcastle and Four-Mile-Water,
          1860-1874.

438. O'NEILL MICHAEL D.D.
BORN: 1835, DIED 1921, BIRTHPLACE, Barronstown, Tipperary.
EDUCATION: Irish College, Rome, Ordained in Thurles in 1864.
SOCIAL BACKGROUND:[741] Farming. Moorscroft Papers show that he was
related to the O'Neills of Kilross, also had
67 acres of the best land in the Golden Vale.
POLITICAL INVOLVEMENT: Yes.
OTHER INFO:[742] Became Vicar-Capitular after the resignation of
Archbishop Fennelly in 1913.
DIOCESE: Cashel and Emly. MINISTRY:C.C. Tipperary 1869-1884.
          F.P. Littin 1004-post 1891.

439. O'NEILL MICHAEL
BORN: 1816, DIED 21/6/1870, BIRTHPLACE, Gurteen, Emly.
EDUCATION:[743] Maynooth, Logic 1042, Ordained 1847.
SOCIAL BACKGROUND:[744] Farming. POLITICAL INVOLVEMENT: Yes.
DIOCESE: Cashel and Emly. MINISTRY: C.C. Ballina 1840-1060.
          C.C. Newport 1860-1869.

440. O'NEILL PATRICK
BORN: c.1846, DIED 1086, BIRTHPLACE, England.
EDUCATION: St. Patrick's, Thurles 1063-1071, Ordained 1871.
POLITICAL INVOLVEMENT: Yes.
DIOCESE: Cashel and Emly. MINISTRY:C.C. Killenaule 1077-1879.
          C.C. Donaskeigh 1083-1086.

441. ORGAN JOSEPH
BORN: 1000, DIED 12/1/1064, BIRTHPLACE, Turtulla, Thurles.
EDUCATION:[745] Maynooth, Logic 1830. Ordained 1837. Got his earlier
classical education at a grammar school in Cashel.
SOCIAL BACKGROUND:[746] The original name of the family was Horgan.
His grandfather came from Cork to Cashel to
take up an appointment given to him by the
Protestant Archbishop. Later member of the
family is remembered as a steward to Nicholas
V. Maher, the Catholic landlord of Turtulla,
near Thurles.
POLITICAL INVOLVEMENT: Yes.
OTHER INFO:[747] He was employed as an usher in the Erasmus Smith
Endowed Abbey School (Protestant) Tipperary before
entering Maynooth. He became a Professor in
St. Patrick's College, Thurles.

442. O'SHAUGHNESSY EDMUND:
BORN: 1793, DIED 1869, BIRTHPLACE, Ballycahill.
EDUCATION: Carlow College 1813-1819. Ordained 1819.
POLITICAL INVOLVEMENT: Yes.
DIOCESE: Cashel and Emly. MINISTRY: F.P. Drangan 1840-1869.

443. O'SULLIVAN JOHN
BORN: 1033, DIED 1095, BIRTHPLACE, Kiltealy Parish.
EDUCATION:[748] Maynooth, Theology 1059. Ordained in Thurles 1863.
POLITICAL INVOLVEMENT: Yes.
OTHER INFO: Brother of Michael (No.444).
DIOCESE: Cashel and Emly. MINISTRY:C.C. Clerihan 1065-1067.
          C.C. Ballina 1067-1075.
          C.C. Moycarkey 1081-1082.
          C.C. Bansha 1082-1083.
          C.C. Fothard 1083-1084.

444. O'SULLIVAN MICHAEL
BORN: 1856, DIED 1913, BIRTHPLACE, Kiltealy Parish.
EDUCATION: St. Patrick's, Thurles 1870-1877. Ordained 1877.
POLITICAL INVOLVEMENT: Yes.
DIOCESE: Cashel and Emly. MINISTRY: C.C. Uppochurch 1885-1902.

445. PHELAN EDWARD
BORN: c.1816, EDUCATION:[749] Maynooth, Humanity 1836. Ordained N.D.
POLITICAL INVOLVEMENT: Yes.
DIOCESE: Waterford. MINISTRY: C.C. Ballylooby 1050-1052.
          C.C. Newcastle and Four-Mile-Water
          1855-1858.

446. PHELAN JOHN
BORN: c.1829, DIED 1/12/1064.
EDUCATION:[750] Maynooth, Theology 1051, Deacon 1854.
POLITICAL INVOLVEMENT: Yes.
DIOCESE: Waterford. MINISTRY: C.C. Clonmel, St.Peter and Pauls,
          1857-1864.

447. PHELAN JOSEPH AUSTIN
BORN:[751] 1840, DIED 12/10/1891, BIRTHPLACE,[752] High Street,
          Waterford City.
EDUCATION:[753] St. John's College, Carlow College, Maynooth,Rhetoric
1858, Ordained 1866/67.
SOCIAL BACKGROUND:[754] Very wealthy family. His father was one of the
leading merchants in the city and he was
elected to the civic chair succeeding as
chief magistrate of Waterford. His father's
name was Sylvester Phelan.
POLITICAL INVOLVEMENT:[755] Yes. "A quiet and retiring figure in
politics with tendencies rather
conservative,still liberal in the broadest
sense of the word." The first time he
ever spoke at a political meeting was in
November 1889 in Clonmel.
OTHER INFO:[756] Had been President of St. John's College, was 3 years
on the Dunboyne Establishment in Maynooth. Had been
a Professor of Moral Theology in St. Johns prior to
becoming President. Read part of his Philosophy
course under Archbishop Cleary of Kingston,Canada.
He had also been rector of the University school in
Stephen Street. Was at college with Archbishop Logue,
was Vicar-Capitular and was presented with Archbishop
Redmond. He was
elected Dignus for the post of Coadjutor to Bishop
John Power and dignissimus on the death of Bishop
Pierse Power.
DIOCESE: Waterford. MINISTRY: Adm. Clonmel,St. Peter and Pauls,
          1888-1891.

448. PHELAN NICHOLAS
DIED: 1886, BIRTHPLACE,[757] Co. Waterford.
EDUCATION:[758] St. John's College 11/11/1835-1840 and Irish College
Rome,
POLITICAL INVOLVEMENT: No.
DIOCESE: Waterford. MINISTRY: P.P. Cammonsfield and Kilcash,
          1874-1886.

449. PHELAN THOMAS (ARCHDEACON).
BORN:[759] 7/2/1831, DIED 30/5/1903, BIRTHPLACE,[760] Maryborough,
          came to live in Roscrea.
EDUCATION:[761] Maynooth, Logic 1853. Ordained 1857. Earlier
education in St. Patrick's Monastery, Mountrath,
Co. Laois.
POLITICAL INVOLVEMENT: Yes.
DIOCESE: Killaloe. MINISTRY:C.C.Toomvara 1857-1859.
          C.C.Shinrone 1859-1866.
          C.C.Durkerrin and Moneygall 1865-
          1869.
          C.C.Roscrea 1869-1874.
          C.C.Birr 1874-1877.

450. PHELAN WILLIAM J.
BORN:[762] 1832, DIED 22/10/1902, BIRTHPLACE:[763] Barron Strand, Waterford City.
EDUCATION:[764] St. John's College 1855-1859. Sent to Irish College Paris on a burse in 1859
POLITICAL INVOLVEMENT: Yes.
DIOCESE: Waterford. MINISTRY: P.F. Ardfinan 1891-1902.

451. POWER DAVID
BORN: c.1822, EDUCATION:[765] Maynooth, Humanity 1840, Deacon 1847.
POLITICAL INVOLVEMENT: Yes.
DIOCESE: Waterford. MINISTRY:C.C. Carrick-On-Suir pre 1850-1857.

452. POWER JAMES
BORN: c.1810, DIED 22/4/1871.
EDUCATION:[766] Maynooth, Humanity 1830. Deacon 1835.
POLITICAL INVOLVEMENT: Yes.
DIOCESE: Waterford. MINISTRY:C.C. Clogheen pre 1850-1853.
C.C. Ballylooby 1853-1857.
C.C. Ballyneale 1857-1858.

453. POWER JOHN
BORN: c.1847, DIED 1893, BIRTHPLACE, Tipperary Parish.
EDUCATION:[767] St. Patrick's, Thurles 1863-1872. Ordained 1872.
POLITICAL INVOLVEMENT: Yes.
DIOCESE: Cashel and Emly. MINISTRY:C.C. Bansha 1874-1875.
C.C. Gortnahoe 1877-1879,
C.C. Bansha 1879-1881.
C.C. Drangan 1885-1893.

454. POWER JOHN
BORN: c.1819, DIED 1871, BIRTHPLACE, Cleragh, Killeasule or Ballingarry.
EDUCATION:[768] Maynooth, Logic 1839, Ordained 1844. POLITICAL INVOLVEMENT: Yes.
SOCIAL BACKGROUND: Farming. MINISTRY:C.C. Borrisoleigh 1847-1868.
P.P. Ballingarry 1868-1871.
DIOCESE: Cashel and Emly.

455. POWER JOHN D.D.
BORN:[768] 1809, DIED 1887, BIRTHPLACE:[769] Cappoquin (Afane).
EDUCATION:[770] St. John's College. Ordained 1832.
POLITICAL INVOLVEMENT: Yes.
SOCIAL BACKGROUND: "An ancient family (see 470).
OTHER INFO: Brother of Patrick (No.464) and Roger (No.470).
DIOCESE: Waterford. MINISTRY:C.C. Clonmel, St.Peter and Paula pre 1850-1852.
P.P. Powerstown 1852-1866.
P.P. Clonmel, St Peter and Paula...

456. POWER JOHN A.
BORN: c.1841, DIED 1919, BIRTHPLACE, Ballinamarsough, Lattin.
EDUCATION: Carlow College 1861-1866. POLITICAL INVOLVEMENT: Yes.
SOCIAL BACKGROUND:[771] Farming.
DIOCESE: Cashel and Emly. MINISTRY:C.C. Doon 1867-1868.
C.C. Doon 1071-1073.
C.C. Galbally 1873-1875.
C.C. Emly 1875-1877.
C.C. Oola and Solohead 1877-1886.

457. POWER MARTIN
BORN: c.1039, DIED 10/4/1924.
EDUCATION:[772] Maynooth, Humanity 1859. Ordained N.D.
POLITICAL INVOLVEMENT: Yes.
DIOCESE: Waterford. MINISTRY:C.C. Ballylooby 1870-1871.
C.C. Ardfinan 1871-1873.
C.C. Ballyneale 1875-1889.
C.C. Newcastle and Four-Mile-Water, 1889-post 1891.

458. POWER MAURICE
BORN: 1832, DIED 1914, BIRTHPLACE, Cromwell, Kiltealy.
EDUCATION:[773] Maynooth, Phys.cs 1854. Ordained 1859.
SOCIAL BACKGROUND:[774] Farming. Son of John Power.
POLITICAL INVOLVEMENT: Yes.
DIOCESE: Cashel and Emly. MINISTRY:C.C. BallinaHinch 1860
C.C. Anacarty 1661-1669.
C.C. Templemore 1069-1877.
P.F. Emly 1878-1914.

459. POWER MICHAEL
BORN: c.1844, DIED 1099, BIRTHPLACE, Ballingarry. POLITICAL INVOLVEMENT: Yes.
EDUCATION:[775] Maynooth, Logic 1863. Ordained 1869.
SOCIAL BACKGROUND:[776] Farm'ng.
OTHER INFO: Brother of William (No.474) and cousin of John McGrath and John McGrath, nos. 249 and 290).
DIOCESE: Cashel and Emly. MINISTRY:C.C. Lattin and Cullen 1072-1874.
1886-1891.
C.C. Tipperary 1891-1899.
F.P. Newinn

460. POWER MICHAEL
BORN: c.1854, BIRTHPLACE,[777] Ballyneale.
EDUCATION:[778] St. John's College 1668-1879.
POLITICAL INVOLVEMENT: Yes.
DIOCESE: Waterford. MINISTRY:C.C. Gammonsfield and Kilcash 1890-1891.

461. POWER NICHOLAS
BORN:[779] 1056, DIED 29/6/1916, BIRTHPLACE:[780] Pottlaw.
EDUCATION:[781] St. John's College 1/9/1871-15/6/1879.

462. POWER P.
EDUCATION: Unknown, not Maynooth. POLITICAL INVOLVEMENT: No.
DIOCESE: Waterford. MINISTRY:C.C. Clogheen 1875-1076.

463. POWER PATRICK
EDUCATION:[782] Maynooth, Humanity 1841, Ordained N.D.
POLITICAL INVOLVEMENT: Yes.
DIOCESE: Waterford. MINISTRY:C.C. Ardfinan 1055-1056.
C.C. Powerstown 1050-1065.
C.C. Gammonsfield and Kilcash 1866-1870.
C.C. Ardfinan 1873-1074.

464. POWER PATRICK
BORN: c.1815, BIRTHPLACE, Afanc, Cappoquin.
EDUCATION:[783] Maynooth, Humanity 1035, Ordination N.D.
SOCIAL BACKGROUND:[784] Farming. POLITICAL INVOLVEMENT: Yes.
OTHER INFO: Brother of Bishop Power, No. 455 and Roger No.470.
DIOCESE: Waterford. MINISTRY:C.C. Ballyneale pre 1350-1850.
C.C. Carrick-On-Suir 1850-1070.

465. POWER PAUL
BORN:[785] 1846, DIED 16/3/1912, BIRTHPLACE:[786] Ballytennock, Dunhill.
EDUCATION:[787] St. John's College. Ordained 1870.
SOCIAL BACKGROUND:[788] Farming. POLITICAL INVOLVEMENT: Yes.
DIOCESE: Waterford. MINISTRY:Carrick-On-Suir 1870-post 1091.

466. POWER PHILIP
BORN: c.1848, BIRTHPLACE,[789] Clashmore.
EDUCATION:[790] St. John's College 1/9/1867-22/9/1873.
POLITICAL INVOLVEMENT: No.
DIOCESE: Waterford. MINISTRY:C.C. Carrick-On-Suir 1890-1891.

467. POWER FIERSE
BORN: c.1022, DIED May 1089.
EDUCATION:[791] St. John's College. Ordained in Maynooth 1847.
POLITICAL INVOLVEMENT: No.
OTHER INFO:[792] Succeeded John Power as Bishop. After his curacy in Clonmel he became professor and then president of St. John's College.
DIOCESE: Waterford.

468. POWER ROBERT
BORN:[793] 1843, DIED 25/2/1924, Aged 81, BIRTHPLACE:[794] Kilnamuch, Waterford.
EDUCATION:[795] Mount Mellaray and St. John's College.
SOCIAL BACKGROUND:[796] "An old and respected family."

469. POWER ROBERT
DIED 26/9/1895, BIRTHPLACE:[797] Carrick-On-Suir(He went to school there).
EDUCATION:[798] Maynooth, Physics 1057, Ordained N.D. (possibly in Irish College, Rome 1865/66).
POLITICAL INVOLVEMENT: Yes.
MINISTRY: P.P. Ballyneale 1086-1895.
DIOCESE: Cashel and Emly.

470. POWER ROGER V.F.
BORN 11/5/1804, BIRTHPLACE: Affane, Cappoquin.
EDUCATION:[799] St. John's College.
SOCIAL BACKGROUND:[800] Farming, "an ancient family."
POLITICAL INVOLVEMENT: Yes.
OTHER INFO:[801] He had 3 brothers priests, brother of Bishop John Power (No.455).
DIOCESE: Waterford. MINISTRY: P.F. Clonmel,St. Peter and Pauls 1873-1876.

471. POWER THOMAS
BORN: c.1040, BIRTHPLACE:[002] Dungarvan.
EDUCATION:[803] St. John's College 30/8/1067-9/11/1873.
POLITICAL INVOLVEMENT: Yes.
DIOCESE: Waterford. MINISTRY: C.C. Cahir 1079-1801.

472. POWER THOMAS
BORN: c.1051, DIED 31/10/1918, BIRTHPLACE:[804] The Square, Dungarvan.
EDUCATION:[805] St. John's College 1/9/1871-1876.
POLITICAL INVOLVEMENT: Yes.
DIOCESE: Waterford. MINISTRY: C.C. Clogheen 1879-1882.
C.C. Clonmel,St. Peter and Pauls, 1882-1803.

473. POWER WILLIAM
DIED 7/4/1886, EDUCATION: Unknown, not Maynooth.
POLITICAL INVOLVEMENT: Yes.
DIOCESE: Waterford. MINISTRY: C.C. Newcastle and Four-Mile-Water, pre 1850-1055.
C.C. Ballylooby 1055-1056.
C.C. Fowerstown 1056-1067.

474. POWER WILLIAM
BORN: 1830 DIED 1807, BIRTHPLACE: Ballingarry.
EDUCATION:[806] Maynooth, Physics 1054, Ordained 1059.
SOCIAL BACKGROUND:[807] Farming. POLITICAL INVOLVEMENT: Yes.
OTHER INFO: Brother of Michael (No.459) and cousin of the two McGraths (Nos. 199 and 290.
DIOCESE: Cashel and Emly. MINISTRY: C.C. Drom and Inch 1863-1869.
F.P. Orangan 1069-1072
F.P. Moyne 1872-1807.

475. PRENDERGAST EDMUND
BORN:[800] 1780, DIED 15/7/1052.
EDUCATION: Carlow College 1009-1012. Ordained 1012.
POLITICAL INVOLVEMENT: Yes.
DIOCESE: Cashel and Emly. MINISTRY: P.F. Ballingarry 1820-1052.

476. PRENDERGAST JAMES
BORN: c.1011, DIED 12/3/1901.
EDUCATION:[809] Maynooth, Rhetoric 1831. Ordained N.D.
POLITICAL INVOLVEMENT: Yes.
DIOCESE: Waterford. MINISTRY: C.C. Ardfinan pre 1850-1855.

477. PRENDERGAST M.
EDUCATION: Unknown, not Maynooth. POLITICAL INVOLVEMENT: No.
DIOCESE: Waterford. MINISTRY: C.C. Clogheen pre 1850-1850.

478. PROUT ROBERT
BORN: c.1841, DIED November 1885, BIRTHPLACE: Farranrory, Ballingarry.
EDUCATION: St. Patrick's, Thurles, St. John's Waterford. Ordained in Waterford 1066.
SOCIAL BACKGROUND:[810] Farming. POLITICAL INVOLVEMENT: Yes.
OTHER INFO: fell from his horse and was killed.
DIOCESE: Cashel and Emly. MINISTRY: C.C. Killenaule 1873-1876
C.C. Drom and Inch 1876-1878.
C.C. Upparchurch 1878-1085.

479. FYNE MICHAEL D.D.V.G.
BORN:[01] c.1818, DIED 7/1/1892.
EDUCATION:[812] Not Maynooth, but ordained c.1046.
POLITICAL INVOLVEMENT: Yes. OTHER INFO:[813] Ill for a number of years.
DIOCESE: Killaloe. MINISTRY: P.F. Nenagh 1879-1092.

480. QUAIN JOHN J.
BORN: c.1056, BIRTHPLACE:[814] Dungarvan.
EDUCATION:[815] St. John's College 13/9/1075-20/6/1081.
POLITICAL INVOLVEMENT: Yes.
DIOCESE: Waterford. MINISTRY: C.C. Clogheen 1890-post 1891.

481. QUEALLY THOMAS
BORN: c.1006, DIED 1/3/1877.
EDUCATION:[816] St. John's College 24/2/1826-1831.
POLITICAL INVOLVEMENT: No.
DIOCESE: Waterford. MINISTRY: C.C. Ballylooby pre 1850-1850.

482. QUEALLY WILLIAM
BORN: c.1841, BIRTHPLACE:[017] Dungarvan.
EDUCATION:[010] St. John's College 3/9/1060-24/6/1866.
POLITICAL INVOLVEMENT: Yes.
DIOCESE: Waterford. MINISTRY: C.C. Clogheen 1087-1890.

483. QUILLINAN CHARLES
BORN 1817, DIED 16/11/1056, BIRTHPLACE: Carron Tipperary.
EDUCATION:[019] Maynooth, Logic 1839. Ordained 1845.
SOCIAL BACKGROUND:[820] Farming. POLITICAL INVOLVEMENT: Yes.
OTHER INFO: Professor in St. Patrick's, Thurles 1845-1851.
DIOCESE: Cashel and Emly. MINISTRY: C.C. Killenaule 1053-1056.

484. QUINLAN MICHAEL
BORN: c.1032, BIRTHPLACE: Cappawhite Parish.
POLITICAL INVOLVEMENT: No.
EDUCATION: Carlow College 1851-1857. Ordained 1057.
OTHER INFO: Exeat to Australia or U.S.A. 1862.
DIOCESE: Cashel and Emly.

485. QUINN EDMUND
BORN: c.1839, BIRTHPLACE:[021] Dunhill Parish.
EDUCATION:[822] St. Johns 1855-1864. May have been in Irish College, Rome 1859.
POLITICAL INVOLVEMENT: No.
DIOCESE: Waterford. MINISTRY: C.C. Ardfinan 1876-1879.

486. QUINN JAMES
EDUCATION: Unknown, but not Maynooth. POLITICAL INVOLVEMENT: Yes.
DIOCESE: Killaloe. MINISTRY: C.C. Couraganeen 1879-1882.

487. QUIRKE JOHN
BORN: c.1026 DIED 1876, BIRTHPLACE: Toem, Cappawhite.
EDUCATION:[823] Maynooth, Theology 1847. Ordained 1852.
SOCIAL BACKGROUND:[824] Farming. POLITICAL INVOLVEMENT: No.
DIOCESE: Cashel and Emly. MINISTRY: C.C. Galbally 1069-1073.

488. QUIRKE WILLIAM
BORN: 1808, DIED 1887, BIRTHPLACE: Rathsallagh, Fethard,family later moved to Clonman.
EDUCATION:[825] Maynooth, Logic 1839. Ordained 1044.
SOCIAL BACKGROUND:[826] Farming. POLITICAL INVOLVEMENT: Yes.
DIOCESE: Cashel and Emly. MINISTRY: C.C. Anacarty 1846-1861.
C.C. Tipperary 1861-1066.

489. RAFFERTY NICHOLAS
BORN: 1846, DIED 1901, BIRTHPLACE, Oola or Gottakilleen, Cullen.
EDUCATION:[027] Maynooth, Theology 1868, Ordained Thurles 1871.
SOCIAL BACKGROUND:[828] Farming.   POLITICAL INVOLVEMENT: Yes.
DIOCESE: Cashel and Emly.   MINISTRY: C.C. Borrisoleigh 1876-1885,
C.C. Thurles 1885-1890,
Adm. Thurles 1890-post 1891.

490. RAFTER RICHARD
BORN: 1820, DIED 1888, BIRTHPLACE, Farrancroy, Ballingarry.
EDUCATION:[829] Maynooth, Theology 1847. Ordained 1850.
SOCIAL BACKGROUND:[830] Farming.   POLITICAL INVOLVEMENT: Yes.
OTHER INFO: Nephew of Robert Grace (No.101)
DIOCESE: Cashel and Emly.   MINISTRY:P.F. Emly 1852-1806 (Retired 1076).

491. RYAN DANIEL D.D.
BORN: c.1834, DIED 1894, BIRTHPLACE, Emly Parish.
EDUCATION: Irish College, Salamanca 1856-1860. Ordained 1859.
POLITICAL INVOLVEMENT: Yes.
OTHER INFO: Vice-President Salamanca College 1862-1865. Fellow student
of William Corcoran D.D. (No.85) when there.
DIOCESE: Cashel and Emly.   MINISTRY:C.C. Donaskeigh 1862(for 6 months)
C.C. Cashel 1865-1803,
Archdeacon Fethard 1880-1894.

492. RYAN DANIEL M.
BORN: 1839, DIED 1925, BIRTHPLACE, Capercullen, Murroe.
EDUCATION:[831] Maynooth, Theology 1059. Cambrai, France 1861-1862.
Ordained All-Hallows 1863.
SOCIAL BACKGROUND:[832] Farming.   POLITICAL INVOLVEMENT: Yes.
OTHER INFO:[833] Deeply read in the Classics. He established a private
classical school in Cloncuity for aspirants to the
priesthood.
DIOCESE: Cashel and Emly.   MINISTRY: P.P. Cloncuity 1879-1925.

493. RYAN EDMUND
BORN: 1002, DIED 1087, BIRTHPLACE, Sandville (Now Sandylane),Boher,
(Murroe).
EDUCATION: Irish College, Paris. Ordained 1847.
SOCIAL BACKGROUND:[834] Farming.   POLITICAL INVOLVEMENT:
OTHER INFO: President St. Patrick's, Thurles 1855-1866.Responsible
for the student's revolt in Thurles in 1060 by curtailing
students' food to raise finances. Uncle of Patrick Ryan,
No.509.
DIOCESE: Cashel and Emly.   MINISTRY:P.F. Moyne 1066-1872.
P.F. Oola and Solohead 1872-1087.

494. RYAN JAMES
BORN: c.1804, DIED 1875, BIRTHPLACE, Tipperary.
EDUCATION: Not Maynooth. Ordained 1829.   POLITICAL INVOLVEMENT: Yes.
OTHER INFO:[835] Nicknamed "Alt 3" because of his height.

495. RYAN JAMES
BORN: c.1791, DIED 1866, BIRTHPLACE, Kyle or Tonagha, Thurles.
EDUCATION:[036] Carlow College. Ordained c.1026. Studied Classics at
Templemore, was 70 years old when he entered Carlow.
POLITICAL INVOLVEMENT: No.
DIOCESE: Cashel and Emly.   MINISTRY: F.F. Holycross 1061-1863.

496. RYAN JAMES
BORN:1849, DIED 1900, BIRTHPLACE, Templebredin (Tisernanagh).
EDUCATION: St. Patrick's, Thurles 1865-1872. Ordained in Kilkenny,
1872.
SOCIAL BACKGROUND:[037] Farming.   POLITICAL INVOLVEMENT: No.
OTHER INFO: On mission in Baltinoo 1872-1802.
DIOCESE: Cashel and Emly.   MINISTRY: C.C. Tipperary 1891-1900.

497. RYAN JAMES
BORN:[038] 1806 DIED July 1807, BIRTHPLACE,[839] Limerick.
EDUCATION:[040] Early education at a classical school in Limerick.
Irish College, Paris. Ordained in 1830.
POLITICAL INVOLVEMENT: Yes.   OTHER INFO:[041] Became Bishop in 1871.
DIOCESE: Killaloe.   MINISTRY:P.F. Burgessbeg and Youghal 1840-
1869.
Adm. Nenagh 1869-1871.

498. RYAN JAMES D.
BORN:[842] 1841, DIED May 1605, BIRTHPLACE,[843] Killeely Parish in
Scart townland.
EDUCATION:[844] Maynooth, Theology 1864. Deacon 1066. Ordained in
Belfast 1868.Early education in Mount Melleray,then
St. Patrick's, Thurles and Maynooth.
POLITICAL INVOLVEMENT: Yes.
OTHER INFO:[846] On mission in Belfast 1069-1875. He was on the
Dunboyne establishment when in Maynooth. Won first
prize in Mount Melleray in Philosophy in 1860.
DIOCESE: Cashel and Emly.   MINISTRY:C.C. Fethard and Killusty 1o76-
1879,
C.C. Tipperary 1879-1885.

499. RYAN JOHN
BORN: 1093, DIED 15/3/1675, BIRTHPLACE, Ballycamus, Clonoulty.
EDUCATION: Carlow College. Ordained there 1819.
POLITICAL INVOLVEMENT: Yes.
DIOCESE: Cashel and Emly.   MINISTRY:P.F. Golden 1049-1875.

500. RYAN JOHN
BORN: 1809, DIED 1091, BIRTHPLACE, Main Street, Templemore.
EDUCATION:[047] Maynooth, Physics 1828. Ordained 1833.
SOCIAL BACKGROUND: Probably shopkeepers and may have had a farm.
POLITICAL INVOLVEMENT: Yes.
OTHER INFO: Cousin of Archdeacon Laffan (No 255),of Patrick Laffan,

501. RYAN JOHN D.D. V.G.
BORN: 1831, DIED 29/10/1895, BIRTHPLACE, Ballingarry.
EDUCATION:[040] Maynooth, Physics 1849, Deacon 1853.
SOCIAL BACKGROUND:[849] Farming.   POLITICAL INVOLVEMENT: Yes.
OTHER INFO: He was a Professor in Maynooth before ordination, was
Leahy's theologian at the Vatican Council 1870, was
voted dignissimus for the Mitre in 1875. Brother of
Philip Ryan (No.513).
DIOCESE: Cashel and Emly.   MINISTRY: C.C. Moyne 1857-1663,
Adm. Thurles 1663-1871,
P.F. Ballingarry 1871-1885.

502. RYAN JOHN
BORN: c.1843, DIED 15/3/1092, BIRTHPLACE,[850] Abbeyside.
EDUCATION:[851] St. John's College 1861-1862. Maynooth, Rhetoric 1862,
Ordained 1666.
POLITICAL INVOLVEMENT: No.
OTHER INFO:[052] Originally chosen for the Diocese of Dublin.
DIOCESE: Waterford.   MINISTRY: Adm. Clogheen 1874-1877.

503. RYAN JOHN
BORN:[853] 5/6/1852, DIED 21/2/1948, Aged 96, BIRTHPLACE,[354] Glenculloo,
Silvermines,Co. Tipperary.
EDUCATION:[855] Maynooth, Philosophy 1073. Ordained 1070. Early
education in Silvermines N.S, then C.B.S. Nenagh and
Old Diocesan College, Ennis.
POLITICAL INVOLVEMENT: Yes.
DIOCESE: Killaloe.   MINISTRY: C.C. Toomevara 1076-1882,
C.C. Dunkerrin and Moneygall
1882-1608.

504. RYAN JOHN G.
BORN: 1844, BIRTHPLACE, Caherconlish Parish.
EDUCATION:[856] Maynooth, Physics 1063. Ordained 1071/72.
POLITICAL INVOLVEMENT: No.
DIOCESE: Cashel and Emly.   MINISTRY: C.C. Emly 1872-1873.

505. RYAN JOHN T.
BORN: 1040, DIED 1090. BIRTHPLACE, Cooleagh,Ballinure,Killenaule.
EDUCATION: St. Patrick's, Thurles 1066-1069. Louvain 1869-1870.
St. Patricks 1870-1873.
SOCIAL BACKGROUND:[857] Farming.   POLITICAL INVOLVEMENT: Yes.
OTHER INFO:[858] Had been Professor in St. Patrick's, Thurles.
DIOCESE: Cashel and Emly.   MINISTRY:C.C.Templemore 1861-1887.
C.C. Thurles 1887-1890.

506. RYAN MARTIN
BORN: c.1854, DIED 1934, BIRTHPLACE, Fennor, Gurtnahoe.
EDUCATION:[859] St. Patrick's, Thurles 1875-76. Maynooth, Theology
1076. Ordained in Dublin 1879.

RYAN PATRICK
BORN: c.1817, DIED 1865, BIRTHPLACE, Knocknamestra, Murroe.
EDUCATION:[861] Maynooth, Logic 1835, Ordained 1842. POLITICAL INVOLVEMENT: Yes.
SOCIAL BACKGROUND:[862] Farming. MINISTRY:C.C. Golden 1847-1861.
C.C. Tipperary 1861-1865.
DIOCESE: Cashel and Emly.

508. **RYAN MATTHEW**
BORN: 1844, DIED 1937, BIRTHPLACE, Kilduff,Pallasgreen, son of Matthew Ryan. He had a brother a priest in the Ballyluddy).
EDUCATION: Irish College, Paris. Ordained there 1871.
SOCIAL BACKGROUND:[863] Farming. He had a brother a priest in the Limerick Diocese, and a brother a doctor.
POLITICAL INVOLVEMENT: Yes.
OTHER INFO:[864] Spent a year as Professor in the Irish College, Paris. A cousin of Dean Kinnane(No.246). Known as the general. He established a classical school in Latin for aspirants. He was also a keen student of Irish and was Vice-President of the Gaelic League for a number of years. He was on bad terms with Bishop Butler of Limerick.
DIOCESE: Cashel and Emly. MINISTRY: C.C. Lattin and Cullen 1076-1006.
C.C. Oola and Solohead 1890-1897.

509. **RYAN MICHEAL V.F.**
BORN: c.1846, DIED 1902, BIRTHPLACE,[865] Cappanoukee, Murroe.
EDUCATION: St. Patricks, Thurles 1064-1071, Ordained 1871.
POLITICAL INVOLVEMENT: Yes.
OTHER INFO: Dean of St. Patricks, Thurles 1874-1878.
DIOCESE: Cashel and Emly. MINISTRY:C.C. Thurles 1877-1080.

510. **RYAN PATRICK**
BORN: 1030, DIED 1910, BIRTHPLACE, Killinure, Bohar(Murroe).
EDUCATION:[866] Maynooth, Logic 1852. Ordained All Hallows 1857.
SOCIAL BACKGROUND:[867] Farming. POLITICAL INVOLVEMENT: Yes.
OTHER INFO: Nephew of Edmund Ryan (No.493).
DIOCESE: Cashel and Emly. MINISTRY:C.C. Ballingarry 1857-1858.
C.C. Holycross 1864-1876.
P.P. Galbally 1880-1910.

511. **RYAN PATRICK**
BORN: 1015, DIED 1874, BIRTHPLACE, Ballinaglaragh, Killenaule.
EDUCATION:[860] Maynooth, Rhetoric 1836, Ordained 1842.
POLITICAL INVOLVEMENT: Yes.
DIOCESE: Cashel and Emly. MINISTRY:C.C. Galbally 1845-1852.
C.C.Donaskeigh 1852-1853.
P.P.Loughmore 1865-1874.

RYAN PATRICK
BORN: c.1823, DIED 2/4/1867, BIRTHPLACE, Clerihan
EDUCATION:[869] Maynooth 1842. Ordained 1848.
POLITICAL INVOLVEMENT: Yes.
DIOCESE: Ballingarry. MINISTRY:C.C.Ballinahinch 1850-1863(was Adm)
P.P.Ballinahinch 1863-1867.

513. **RYAN PATRICK C.**
BORN: 1859, DIED 1924, BIRTHPLACE, Glenbreeda,Borrisoleigh.
EDUCATION:[870] St. Patricks, Thurles 1875-1880. Maynooth, Theology 1880. Ordained 1883.
SOCIAL BACKGROUND:[871] Farming. POLITICAL INVOLVEMENT:No, but a supporter of Sinn Fein in later years.
OTHER INFO: On mission in Hexham 1883-1891.
DIOCESE: Cashel and Emly. MINISTRY:C.C. Drom and Inch 1891-1897.

514. **RYAN PATRICK W.**
BORN: c.1852, DIED 1930, BIRTHPLACE, Kylegoues, Galbally.
EDUCATION: St. Patricks, Thurles 1870-1877, Ordained 1877.
POLITICAL INVOLVEMENT: Yes.
OTHER INFO: On mission in Westminster 1877-1886.
DIOCESE: Cashel and Emly. MINISTRY:C.C. Newinn 1886-1891.
C.C. Newport 1891-post 1891

515. **RYAN PHILIP**
BORN: 1835, DIED 1895, BIRTHPLACE, Garrynoe, Ballingarry.
EDUCATION:[872] St. Patricks, Thurles, 1852-1854. Maynooth, Physics 1854. Ordained 1859.
SOCIAL BACKGROUND:[873] Farming. POLITICAL INVOLVEMENT: Yes.
OTHER INFO: Brother of John Ryan (No.501).
DIOCESE: Cashel and Emly. MINISTRY:C.C.Ballingarry 1881-1883.
P.P.Mullinahone 1883-1895.

516. **RYAN THOMAS**
BORN: c.1820, DIED 1868, BIRTHPLACE, Killenaule Parish (Kilkennybeg).
EDUCATION:[874] Maynooth, Rhetoric 1839. Ordained 1845.
SOCIAL BACKGROUND:[875] Farming. POLITICAL INVOLVEMENT: Yes.
DIOCESE: Cashel and Emly. MINISTRY:C.C. Upperchurch 1849-1866.
P.P. Upperchurch 1866-1868.

517. **RYAN WILLIAM**
BORN: 1845, DIED 1919, BIRTHPLACE, Emly Parish.
EDUCATION:[876] Maynooth, Rhetoric 1870. Ordained 1876
POLITICAL INVOLVEMENT: Yes.
DIOCESE: Cashel and Emly. MINISTRY:C.C.Boherlahan 1891-1896.

518. **SCANLAN ANDREW JAMES**
BORN:[877] 1780, DIED 28/8/1860, BIRTHPLACE,[878] County Limerick.
EDUCATION: Unknown. POLITICAL INVOLVEMENT: Yes.
DIOCESE: Killaloe. MINISTRY:P.P. Couraganeen pre 1850-1860.

519. **SCANLAN BARTHOLOMEW**
BORN:[879] 1823, DIED 17/5/1903, BIRTHPLACE,[880] Kilrush.
EDUCATION:[881] Maynooth, Rhetoric 1839. Ordained 1846.
POLITICAL INVOLVEMENT: Yes.
DIOCESE: Killaloe. MINISTRY: C.C. Sixr pre 1850-1851
C.C. Nenagh 1852-1853.
C.C. Roscrea 1854-1856.
C.C. Ardcroney and Ballygiblin 1856-1860.
C.C. Sixr 1860-1868.

520. **SCANLAN JOHN (DEAN)**
BORN:[882] 1843, DIED 19/12/1916, BIRTHPLACE,[883] Rosslara, Tulla.
EDUCATION:[884] Maynooth, Humanity 1860. Ordained 1867.Early education at Killaloe and Limerick.
SOCIAL BACKGROUND:[885] His father, Patrick Scanlan, "an extensive farmer".He had a brother a doctor and another brother was the first Chairman of Clare County Council.
POLITICAL INVOLVEMENT: Yes.
OTHER INFO:[886] Archbishop Healy was his class-mate.
DIOCESE: Killaloe. MINISTRY:C.C.Castletounarra 1867-1868.
C.C.Toomevara 1868-1873.
C.C.Dunkerrin and Moneygall 1873-1877.
P.F-Ardcroney and Ballygiblin 1888-post 1891.

521. **SCANLAN JOHN**
BORN: c.1815, DIED 11/8/1871.
EDUCATION:[887] Maynooth. Ordained June 1840.
POLITICAL INVOLVEMENT: Yes.
DIOCESE: Killaloe. MINISTRY:C.C.Ardcroney and Ballygiblin 1851-1852.
C.C.Nenagh 1852-1853.
C.C. Birr 1853-1854.
C.C.Nenagh 1854-1855.
Adm.Nenagh 1855-1861.
P.P.Toomevara 1861-1871.

522. **SCANLAN JOHN**
BORN:[888] 1845, DIED 18/12/1931, BIRTHPLACE,[889] Garranboy,Co. Clare.
EDUCATION: Maynooth, Humanity 1863. Ordained 1870. Early education in Killaloe Seminary.
SOCIAL BACKGROUND: Griffiths Valuation shows 4 families in Garranboy, Civil Parish of Killaloe, Union of Tulla Lower: 71 acres, 72 acres,27 acres,17 acres.
POLITICAL INVOLVEMENT:[891] Yes. "A supporter of the Sinn Fein Movement practically since that party's coming into

DIOCESE: Killaloe.

523. SCANLAN MICHAEL
BORN: c.1803, BIRTHPLACE,[892] Gortmagee, Killaloe.
EDUCATION:[893] Maynooth, Humanity 1822. Ordained 1828.
SOCIAL BACKGROUND:[894] Farming.
OTHER INFO:[895] Brother of Fr. Edward Scanlan, Maynooth.
DIOCESE: Killaloe. MINISTRY: P.P.Ardcroney and Ballygiblin pre 1850-1869.

524. SCANLAN PHILIP
BORN: 1829, DIED 1866, BIRTHPLACE,[896] Gaile, Roycaukey.
EDUCATION:[896] Maynooth, Theology 1850. Deacon 1854.
SOCIAL BACKGROUND:[897] Farming. POLITICAL INVOLVEMENT: Yes.
DIOCESE: Cashel and Emly. MINISTRY:C.C. Killenaule 1856-1867.

525. SCANLAN WILLIAM
DIED 22/1/1917, BIRTHPLACE,[898] Near the town of Quin, Co. Clare.
EDUCATION: Unknown.
SOCIAL BACKGROUND:[899] Farming. POLITICAL INVOLVEMENT: No.
DIOCESE: Killaloe. MINISTRY: C.C. Castletownarra 1891 - post '91.

526. SCOTT EDMUND
BORN: 1849, DIED 1893,
EDUCATION: St. Patricks, Thurles 1866-1874. Ordained 1874.
POLITICAL INVOLVEMENT: Yes.
OTHER INFO: On mission in Liverpool 1874-1881.
DIOCESE: Cashel and Emly. MINISTRY:C.C.Fethard and Killusty 1881-1893.

527. SCULLY ALEXANDER
BORN: February 1836, DIED 1915, BIRTHPLACE, Doobyns Hotel, Tipperary Town.
EDUCATION: Stonyhurst College, Irish College, Rome. Ordained there 1864.
SOCIAL BACKGROUND: Hoteliers.(Owned Dobbyns Hotel,Tipperary Town).
POLITICAL INVOLVEMENT: Yes.
OTHER INFO:[900] Professor St. Patricks Thurles 1864-1868, Vice-President 1868-1872, President 1872-1882. He was a cousin of William Scully of Ballycohey of eviction fame.
DIOCESE: Cashel and Emly. MINISTRY: P.P. Cie-lhan 1882-1886.

528. SHANAHAN JOHN
BORN: c.1819, DIED 10/3/1884,
EDUCATION:[901] St. John's College 1839-1844.
POLITICAL INVOLVEMENT: No.
DIOCESE: Waterford. MINISTRY: C.C. Clogheen 1860-1865.

529. SHANAHAN WILLIAM
BORN: c.1829, DIED 1870.
EDUCATION:[902] Maynooth, Logic 1849, Ordained 1854.
POLITICAL INVOLVEMENT: Yes.
DIOCESE: Waterford. MINISTRY:C.C.Clonmel,St. Peter and Pauls 1854-1857.
C.C. Ballymaule 1860-1861.
C.C. Ballylooby 1865-1868.
C.C. Clogheen 1868-1870.

530. SHANNON PATRICK
BORN: c.1827, DIED 17/2/1886.
EDUCATION:[903] Maynooth, Humanity 1845. Ordained 1852.
POLITICAL INVOLVEMENT: No.
DIOCESE: Killaloe. MINISTRY: C.C. Nenagh 1857-1858.

531. SHEEHAN DENIS
BORN:[904] 1845, DIED 6/10/1938, BIRTHPLACE,[905] Killaloe District.
EDUCATION:[906] Maynooth, Humanity 1862. Ordained 1864.
SOCIAL BACKGROUND: Griffiths Valuation shows only one Sheehan family in Killaloe civil parish, Barony of Tulla Lr. This family had a mill and a marble works.
POLITICAL INVOLVEMENT: Yes.
DIOCESE: Killaloe.

532. SHEEHAN MAURICE
BORN: c.1839, BIRTHPLACE,[907] Bungarvan.
EDUCATION:[908] St. John's College 1862-1863. Maynooth, Logic 1863.
POLITICAL INVOLVEMENT: Yes.
DIOCESE: Waterford.

533. SHEEHAN PATRICK
BORN: c.1846, DIED 17/1/199C, BIRTHPLACE,[909] Town of Carrick-On-Suir.
EDUCATION:[910] Maynooth, Logic 1866. Ordained 1870/71.
POLITICAL INVOLVEMENT: Yes.
OTHER INFO:[911] An intellectual First Class Honours in Theology and Philosophy in Maynooth. His first mission was in Manchester.

534. SHELLEY JOHN
BORN: 1839, DIED 1907, BIRTHPLACE, Graigue, Killenaule.
EDUCATION: Irish College, Paris 1860-1865. Ordained Ursuline Convent, Thurles 1865.
SOCIAL BACKGROUND:[912] Farming. POLITICAL INVOLVEMENT: Yes.
DIOCESE: Cashel and Emly. MINISTRY:C.C.Holycross 1868-1869.
C.C.Drangan 1869-1871.
C.C.Tipperary 1871-1379.
C.C. Emly 1879-1987.

535. SHORT ROBERT
BORN: c.1818, DIED 10/7/1877, BIRTHPLACE, Farranrory,Ballingarry.
EDUCATION: Unknown. Ordained 1842/43.
SOCIAL BACKGROUND: Farming. POLITICAL INVOLVEMENT: Yes.
DIOCESE: Cashel and Emly. MINISTRY:C.C.Oola and Solohead 1859-1867.
P.P.Ballinahinch 1867-1877.

536. SLATTERY JOHN
BORN: 1828, DIED March 1887, BIRTHPLACE, Ballyleithan.
EDUCATION: Irish College, Paris. Ordained 1857
SOCIAL BACKGROUND:[913] Farming.
POLITICAL INVOLVEMENT:[914] "He was no politician and seldom took part in the late agitation,except in his study where he wrote hard for peace and the good of society."
DIOCESE: Cashel and Emly. MINISTRY:C.C.Gurtnahoe 1857-1877.
P.P.Drom and Inch 1877,
F.P.Kilcommon 1877-1887.

537. SLATTERY PATRICK
BORN:[915] 1806, DIED 22/2/1894.
EDUCATION: Unknown, not Maynooth.
POLITICAL INVOLVEMENT: No. OTHER INFO:[916] Spent his youth in Europe.
DIOCESE: Waterford. MINISTRY:C.C.Clonmel, St. Marys 1868-1869.

538. SLATTERY FATRICK
BORN: c.1828, BIRTHPLACE,[917] Nenagh town.
EDUCATION:[918] Maynooth, Rhetoric 1847. Ordained 1853.
POLITICAL INVOLVEMENT: Yes.
DIOCESE: Killaloe.

539. SLATTERY STEPHEN
BORN: c.1857, EDUCATION[919] Maynooth,Rhetoric 1876. Ordained 1882.
POLITICAL INVOLVEMENT: Yes.
DIOCESE: Killaloe. MINISTRY:C.C.Castletownarra 1882-1884.
C.C.Dunkerrin and Moneygall 1886-post 1891

BORN: 1823, DIED 1866, BIRTHPLACE, Culeen, Bansha
EDUCATION:[920] Maynooth, Logic 1842. Ordained 1848.
POLITICAL INVOLVEMENT: Yes.
OTHER INFO: Nephew of Archbishop Slattery.
DIOCESE: Cashel andEmly   MINISTRY:C.C. Thurles 1848-1858.

541. SLEADEN RICHARD
BORN: c.1819,   DIED 31/8/1900.
EDUCATION:[921] St. John's College 1839-1844. Ordained 1844.
POLITICAL INVOLVEMENT: Yes.
DIOCESE: Waterford.   MINISTRY: C.C.Clogheen 1850-1854.
                                 C.C.Cahir   1855-1858.
                                 C.C.Clonmel, St. Marys 1858-1875.

542. SMITH DANIEL
DIED 27/1/1888
POLITICAL INVOLVEMENT: Yes.
DIOCESE: Killaloe.   EDUCATION: Unknown, but not Maynooth.
       MINISTRY: C.C. Roscrea 1874-1880,
                 F.P. Ardcroney and Ballygiblin
                 1880-1888 (Clough Jordan).

543. SEÁN MICHAEL
BORN: c.1821,   EDUCATION:[922] Maynooth, Rhetoric 1839, Ordained 1846.
POLITICAL INVOLVEMENT: Yes.
DIOCESE: Killaloe.   MINISTRY:C.C.Silvermines pre 1850-1850,
                               C.C.Kilnanave and Templederry 1850-
                               1851.
                               C.C.Borrisokane 1851-1855.
                               C.C. Cloughprior and Mounsea 1855-
                               1861.
                               C.C.Dunkerrin and Moneygall 1861-'69.

544. SPRATT PATRICK
BORN: 17/3/1840, DIED 6/12/1919, BIRTHPLACE:[924] Coolcormack,
                                                  Dungarvan.
EDUCATION:[925] St. John's, Waterford 1855-1861. Early education in
             Dungarvan. Irish College, Paris 1861-1865. Ordained
             in Paris 1855.
SOCIAL BACKGROUND:[926] Farming.
DIOCESE: Waterford.   MINISTRY:P.P.Gammonsfield and Kilcash 1887-
                                1906.

545. STUART CHARLES
BORN:[927] 1856,   DIED 8/8/1912, BIRTHPLACE:[928] "Parish of Ogonnelloe,
EDUCATION:[929] Maynooth, Rhetoric 1873. Ordained 1879. Earlier
             education at a Classical school in Killaloe, then the
             Old Seminary, Ennis.
SOCIAL BACKGROUND:[930] Farming."One of the oldest families in the
                        locality.
POLITICAL INVOLVEMENT: Yes.
DIOCESE: Killaloe.   MINISTRY:C.C. Roscrea 1883-1884.
                               C.C. Birr   1884-1886

BORN: 1839, EDUCATION:[931] Maynooth, Humanity 1859, Ordained N.D.
POLITICAL INVOLVEMENT: No.
DIOCESE: Killaloe.   MINISTRY:C.C.Durkerrin and Moneygall 1876-1877.

547. SWEENEY PATRICK
BORN: c.1851,   DIED 20/7/1894, BIRTHPLACE,[932] Birr.
EDUCATION:[933] Maynooth, Rhetoric 1869. Ordained c.1876.
POLITICAL INVOLVEMENT: Yes.
DIOCESE: Killaloe.   MINISTRY:Durkerrin and Moneygall 1877-1882.

548. TERRY J.
BORN: c.1832,   EDUCATION:[934] St. John's College. Ordained 1857.
POLITICAL INVOLVEMENT: No.
DIOCESE: Waterford.   MINISTRY:C.C.Ballyporeen 1858-1865.
                               C.C.Ballyneale 1863-1865.

549. TIERNEY DENIS
BORN: c.1828,   EDUCATION:[935] Maynooth, Humanity 1845. Ordained 1853.
POLITICAL INVOLVEMENT: No.
DIOCESE: Killaloe.   MINISTRY:C.C.Burgensbeg and Youghal 1858-1860.
                               C.C.Ardcroney and Ballygiblin 1860-
                               1862.

550. TOBIN MICHAEL
BORN: c.1787,   DIED 12/3/1852.
EDUCATION:[936] Maynooth Physics 1809. Ordained 1812.
POLITICAL INVOLVEMENT: No.
DIOCESE: Waterford.   MINISTRY: F.P. Cahir 1830-1852.

551. TRACY JOHN
DIED:18/6/1873, BIRTHPLACE:[937] Pilltown.
EDUCATION:[938] Theology in St. Johns College, Irish College, Rome
             1841-1844.
SOCIAL BACKGROUND:[939] Farming.   POLITICAL INVOLVEMENT: Yes.
DIOCESE: Waterford.   MINISTRY:C.C. Cahir 1852-1853.
                               C.C. Ballyneale 1858-1860.

552. TRACY THOMAS
BORN: c.1817,   DIED 30/1/1872.
EDUCATION:[940] Maynooth, Humanity 1837. Ordained N.D.
POLITICAL INVOLVEMENT: Yes.
DIOCESE: Waterford.   MINISTRY:C.C. Cahir 1852-1854.

BORN: c.1827,   DIED 15/12/1907.
EDUCATION:[941] Maynooth, Humanity 1845. Ordained 1852.
POLITICAL INVOLVEMENT: Yes.
DIOCESE: Killaloe.   MINISTRY:C.C. Toomevara 1852-1854,
                               C.C. Birt   1868-1871.
                               P.P. Shinrone 1873-post 1891.

554. TUOHY JOHN
BORN: 1844,   DIED 1908, BIRTHPLACE, Grange, Holycross.
EDUCATION:[942] Maynooth, Physics 1864. Ordained 1869.
SOCIAL BACKGROUND:[943] Farming.   POLITICAL INVOLVEMENT: Yes.
DIOCESE: Cashel and Emly.   MINISTRY: C.C. Drom and inch 1869-1874,
                                       C.C. Kilcommon   1874-1875,
                                       C.C. Bansha   1875-1879,
                                       C.C. Templemore   1882-1889,
                                       C.C. Cashel   1889-1892.

555. VAUGHAN DANIEL
BORN:[944]   DIED 29/7/1859.
EDUCATION:[945] Maynooth, Logic 1812. Ordained 1815.
POLITICAL INVOLVEMENT: Yes.
DIOCESE: Killaloe.   MINISTRY:Adm. Nenagh pre 1850-1851

556. VAUGHAN JAMES
BORN: c.1836,   DIED 12/9/1906, BIRTHPLACE,[946] Kilbane, East Clare.
EDUCATION:[947] Maynooth, Humanity 1853 - Ordained 1861.
SOCIAL BACKGROUND:[948] Farming.   POLITICAL INVOLVEMENT: No.
OTHER INFO:[949] Brother of John Vaughan, Maynooth.
DIOCESE: Killaloe.   MINISTRY:C.C.Ardcroney and Ballygiblin 1862-
                               1865.

557. WALKER JOHN
EDUCATION: Unknown, but not Maynooth.   POLITICAL INVOLVEMENT: No.
DIOCESE: Killaloe.   MINISTRY: C.C. Shinrone 1870-1872.
                               C.C. Cloughprior and Mounsea 1872-
                               1875.
                               C.C. Burgesbeg and Youghal 1875-
                               1876.
                               C.C. Toomevara 1876-1877,
                               C.C. Lortha and Dortha 1877-1878.

558. WALL JAMES P.
BORN: c.1851,   DIED 31/3/1933, BIRTHPLACE:[950] Carrickbeg(Ballyquin).
EDUCATION:[951] St. John's College 1866-1870. Maynooth, Humanity 1870,
             Ordained 1876.
SOCIAL BACKGROUND:[952] Farming.   POLITICAL INVOLVEMENT: Yes.
DIOCESE: Waterford.   MINISTRY:C.C. Ardfinnan 1879-1884,
                               C.C. Ballyporeen 1884-1885,
                               C.C. Ardfinnan   1885-1890,
                               C.C. Clonmel, St. Marys 1890 post
                               1891.

559. WALL JOHN
BORN:[953] 1816, DIED 16/1/1891.
EDUCATION:[954] Maynooth, Humanity 1840, Deacon 1845.
POLITICAL INVOLVEMENT:[955] Not in Tipperary, but he later played a prominent part in the Plan of Campaign struggle on the Vandeleur Estate.
DIOCESE: Killaloe.   MINISTRY: C.C. Roscrea 1868-1865.

560. WALL MAURICE
BORN: c.1780, EDUCATION:[956] Maynooth, Logic 1800. Ordained 1805.
POLITICAL INVOLVEMENT: Yes.
DIOCESE: Waterford.   MINISTRY: P.P. Powerstown and Lisronagh 1815-1852.

561. WALL WILLIAM V.F.
BORN: c.1830, DIED 1890. BIRTHPLACE: Ballynattin, Clerihan.
EDUCATION:[957] Maynooth, Logic 1851. Ordained 1855.
SOCIAL BACKGROUND:[958] Farming. Current farm approx. 200 acres.
POLITICAL INVOLVEMENT:[959] Rare, he had a respect for established order. Through necessity he became involved in the Cloncurty evictions episode in Murroe.
OTHER INFO: Nephew of Archbishop Slattery.
DIOCESE: Cashel and Emly.   MINISTRY: C.C. Thurles 1855-1857, Adm. Thurles 1857-1863, P.P. Doon 1864-1865, F.P. Clonoulty 1865-1879.

562. WALSH ANDREW
BORN: c.1831, DIED 16/8/1877.
EDUCATION:[960] Maynooth, Physics 1851. Ordained N.D.
POLITICAL INVOLVEMENT: Yes.
DIOCESE: Waterford.   MINISTRY: C.C. Clonmel, St. Peter and Pauls, 1856-1872.

563. WALSH EDMUND
EDUCATION: Unknown, but not Maynooth.   POLITICAL INVOLVEMENT: Yes.
DIOCESE: Waterford.   MINISTRY:C.C.Powerstown and Lisronagh pre 1850-1856, C.C.Ballylooby 1856-1866.

564. WALSH EDMUND
BORN: c.1815 EDUCATION:[961] Maynooth, Humanity 1835, Ordained N.D.
POLITICAL INVOLVEMENT: Yes.
DIOCESE: Waterford.   MINISTRY:C.C.Newcastle and Four-Mile-Water pre 1850-1852.

565. WALSH EDMUND P.
BORN:[962] 1816, DIED 22/7/1865, BIRTHPLACE:[963] Waterford.
EDUCATION:[964] Maynooth 1831. Ordained 1840.
POLITICAL INVOLVEMENT: Yes.
DIOCESE: Waterford.   MINISTRY:P.P.Gammonsfield and Kilcash 1869-1874. P.P.Clonmel,St. Marys 1874-1885.

566. WALSH JOHN
DIED 1916, EDUCATION: Unknown, but not Maynooth.
POLITICAL INVOLVEMENT: Yes.
DIOCESE: Waterford.   MINISTRY:C.C. St. Marys, Clonmel 1872-1873,
C.C. Ardfinan 1873-1875,
C.C. Clogheen 1875-1876,
C.C. Ballyporeen 1877-1880,
P.P. Newcastle and Four-Mile-Water 1889-1910.

567. WALSH JOHN
BORN:[965] 1843, DIED 27/1/1911, BIRTHPLACE:[966], Feus, Kilmacthomas.
EDUCATION:[967] St. John's College. Ordained 1866.
POLITICAL INVOLVEMENT: Yes.
OTHER INFO:[968] On mission in Dundee after ordination.
DIOCESE: Waterford.   MINISTRY: C.C. Tubrid 1868-1872,
C.C. Ballyneale 1872-1882,
C.C. Cahir 1882-1884.

568. WALSH MICHAEL F.
BORN:[969] 1858, DIED 11/2/1935, BIRTHPLACE:[970] Ballycadam, Cahir.
EDUCATION:[971] Maynooth, Theology, 1878, Ordained 1881. A year and a half in St. John's College.
SOCIAL BACKGROUND:[972] Farming.   POLITICAL INVOLVEMENT: No.
DIOCESE: Waterford.   MINISTRY:C.C. Clogheen 1883-1887.

569. WALSH NICHOLAS
BORN:[973] 1857, DIED 30/8/1947, Aged 85, BIRTHPLACE:[974] Grange,Youghal.
EDUCATION:[975] Maynooth, Philosophy 1878. Ordained 1883.
POLITICAL INVOLVEMENT: Yes.
OTHER INFO:[976] On mission in Bristol 1883-1886. He was a native Irish speaker.
DIOCESE: Waterford.   MINISTRY:C.C.Newcastle and Four-Mile-Water, 1886-1890.

570. WALSH PATRICK
DIED 13/10/1872, EDUCATION: Unknown, but not Maynooth.
POLITICAL INVOLVEMENT: Yes.
DIOCESE: Waterford.   MINISTRY:C.C.Newcastle and Four-Mile-Water 1856-1862.

571. WALSH PATRICK F.
BORN: c.1846, DIED 8/10/1907.
EDUCATION:[977] Maynooth, Physics 1867. Ordained 1870/71.
POLITICAL INVOLVEMENT: Yes.
DIOCESE: Waterford.   MINISTRY: C.C. Clonmel, St. Marys 1876-1882.

572. WALSH PIERCE
DIED 14/9/1908, EDUCATION: Unknown, but not Maynooth.
POLITICAL INVOLVEMENT: No.
DIOCESE: Waterford.   MINISTRY:C.C. Clogheen 1881-1884.

573. WALSH THOMAS
BORN:[978] DIED 31/10/1903, BIRTHPLACE:[979] Near Cappoquin.
EDUCATION:[980] St. John's College.
POLITICAL INVOLVEMENT: Yes.
DIOCESE: Waterford.   MINISTRY:C.C. Clonmel,St. Marys 1872-1873,
1876-1881,
C.C. Clogheen 1881-1882,
C.C. Ballyporeen 1882-1890,
C.C. Ballyneale 1873.

574. WALSH WILLIAM
BORN: c.1837, EDUCATION:[981] Maynooth. Ordained 1862.
POLITICAL INVOLVEMENT: Yes.
DIOCESE: Waterford.   MINISTRY:C.C.Clonmel,St.Peter and Pauls 1863-1873.

575. WOOD JOHN
BORN: 1825, DIED 1919 Aged 94, BIRTHPLACE: Main Street, Thurles
EDUCATION:[982] Maynooth, Logic 1849. Ordained 1855.
SOCIAL BACKGROUND: Apothecary.   POLITICAL INVOLVEMENT: Yes.
OTHER INFO: Professor in St. Patricks, Thurles 1855-1868. He resigned in April 1887 due to illness and got a pension of £45. F.A.
DIOCESE: Cashel and Emly.   MINISTRY: P.P. Upperchurch 1868-1887.

SOURCES

1. W.P. Burke, History of Clonmel, (Waterford,1907),p.260. 2. Ibid., 3. Hamell, sequence no. 52. 4. Griffiths Valuation, Co. Waterford,Barony of Decies without Drum, Civil Parish of Fews,shows several Baldwin families. 5. Hamell,sequence no.60. 6. Table 11, p.19 above. 7. Table 11, p.19 above. 8. Hamell,sequence no. 83. 9. Ibid., sequence no.112. 10. Hamell, sequence no.161. 11. Ibid., sequence no.161. 12. Ibid., sequence no.188. 13.Tipperary Advocate 8/1/1881. 14. Freemans Journal 30/12/1880. 15.Tipperary Advocate 8/1/1881. 16.Hamell, sequence no.237. 17.Tipperary Advocate 8/1/1881. 18.Register in the Irish College, Rome, Information forwarded by the Archivist to the author. 19. Ibid.,20. Ibid. 21.Hamell, sequence no.407. 22.Clare Journal 20/8/1900. 23.Hamell, sequence no.461. 24.Clare Journal 20/8/1900. 25.Clare Journal 20/11/1893. 26.Kings County Chronicle 16/11/1893. 27.Hamell, sequence no.511. 28.Information given to the author by the parish priest in 1975. 29.

Press 10/8/1866. 40.Burke, History of Clonmel, op.cit.,p.282.41.Hamell, sequence no.525. 42.Tipperary Free Press 23/11/1853 (Burke's speech). 43.Burke, History of Clonmel, op.cit.,p.282. 44.Tipperary Free Press 10/8/1866. 45.W.D.A. St. John's College Register 1854-1873 p.298. 46.Ibid., 47.Hamell, sequence no.527. 48. Register of Irish College Rome as in n18. 49.Register of the Irish College, Rome (Vid.n18). 50.Tipperary Free Press 6/10/1866. 51.W.D.A. St. John's College Register 1826-1854,p.38. 52.W.D.A. St. John's College Register 1854-1873, p.321. 53.Ibid., 54.Ibid., 55.Clonmel Chronicle 20/8/1910. 56.Hamell, sequence no.557. 57.Clonmel Chronicle 20/8/1910. 58.Register of the Irish College, Rome (Vid.n.18). 59.Ibid., 60.Ibid., 61.Kirby Papers, Bishop James Ryan, Killaloe to Kirby 7/10/1875. 62.Clare Journal 24/5/1900. 63. Tipperary Advocate 24/7/1886. 64.Hamell, sequence no.605. 65.C.D.A. Canon Fogarty's Notebook No.10.(not paginated). 66.W.D.A. St. John's College Register 1872-1888, p.377. 67.Ibid., 68.Ibid., 69.W.D.A. St. John's College Register 1826-1854, p.117. 70. Ibid., 71.Clare Journal 17/2/1915. 72. Ibid., 73.Ibid., 74.Table 11, p.19 above. 75.Clare Journal 17/2/1915. 76.Tierney, Murroe and Boher, op.cit.,p.82. Hamell, sequence no.681. 77.Table 11, p. 19 above. 78.C.D.A. Canon Fogarty's Notebook no.10(not paginated). 79.Hamell, sequence no.679. 80.Table 11,p.19 above. 81.Nationalist 22/3/1890. C.D.A. Fogarty's Notebook no.10. 82.Hamell, sequence no.718. 83.Table 11,p.19 above.84.Tipperary People 5/10/1888. 85.Table 11, p.19 above.86.Tipperary People 5/10/1888. 87.Hamell, sequence no.774. 88.Table 11, p. 19 above. 89.W.D.A. St. John's College Register 1854-1873, pp.294,368. 90.Ibid., 91.Ibid.,p.368. 92.C.D.A. C.P.Croke to Cullen 15/7/1875. 93.Table 11,p.19 above. Tipperary People 15/5/1885. 94.Freemans Journal 26/3/1883. 95.W.D.A. St. John's College Register 1826-1854, p.137. 96.Table 11, p. 19 above. 97.Hamell sequence no.885. 98.Tipperary Free Press 19/10/1860. 99.Nationalist 9/8/1930. 100.W.D.A. St. John's College Register 1872-1888,p.650. 101.Ibid., 102.Ibid.,p.652 and Nationalist 21/3/1917. 103.W.D.A. as in n102. 104.Nenagh Guardian 12/3/1938. 105.Ibid., 106.Ibid., 107. Ibid., 108.Ibid., 109. Hamell, sequence no.964. 110.Ibid.,sequence no.1014. 111.Clare Journal 6/2/1911. 112.Ibid., 113.Ibid., and Hamell, sequence no.1021. 114.Tipperary Advocate 2/8/1873. 115.Hamell, sequence no.1011. 116.Limerick Reporter 1/8/1873. 117.Hamell, sequence no.1015. 118.Nenagh Guardian 20/10/1868. 119.Tierney, Murroe and Boher op.cit.,p.82. 120.Table 11, p. 19 above. 121.As in n18. 122.Ibid., 123.Ibid., 124. Tipperary People 25/3/1887. 125.Hamell, sequence no.1020. 126.Table 11, p. 19 above. 127.Midland Tribune 19/7/1890. 128.Table 11, p.19 above. 129.Tipperary Nationalist 15/6/1889. 130.W.D.A. St. John's College Register 1854-1873,p.501. 131.Ibid., 132.Hamell, sequence no.1172. 133.Table 11, p. 19 above. 134.W.D.A. St. John's College Register 1854-1873,p.557,Clonmel Chronicle 20/4/1892. 135.W.D.A. as in n134, Hamell, sequence no.1174. 136.Table 11, p. 19 above. 137.United Ireland 10/9/1881. 138.Clare Journal 17/9/1874. 139.Ibid., 140.Hamell, sequence no.1214. 141. Power,op.cit., p. 122. Connolly's will is preserved in the Waterford Diocesan Archives. 142.Hamell,sequence no.1313. 143.Table 11,p. 19 above. 144.Hamell, sequence no.1331. 145.Ibid.,sequence no.1338. 146.Information to author by the parish priest in 1975. 147.Table 11,p. 19 above. 148.Nationalist 24/6/1890. 149.Clare Journal 15/5/1915. 150.Ibid., 151.Table 11,p. 19 above. 152.Clare Journal 15/5/1915. 153.Tipperary Star 30/11/1935. 154.Ibid., and Clare Champion 30/11/1935. 155.Ibid., and Hamell,sequence no.1384. 156.Clare Champion 31/1/1942. 157.Ibid., 158.Ibid., 159.Hamell, sequence no.1465. 160.Tipperary Free Press 31/1/1868. 161.As in n18. 162.Hamell, sequence no.1483. 163.As in n18. 164.Ibid., 165.Ibid., and W.D.A. St. John's College Register 1854-1873,p.215. 166.Hamell, sequence no.1488. 167.Clare Journal 8/7/1897. 168.Ibid., 169.Hamell,sequence no. 1486. 170.Clare Journal 8/7/1897. 171.Nenagh Guardian 3/1/1920. 172.Ibid., 173.Ibid., and Hamell, sequence no.1490. 174.Hamell, sequence no.1528. 175.Information given to the author by the parish priest in 1975. 176.Nenagh Guardian 7/12/1935.177.Ibid., 178.Ibid.,179. Ibid., 180.W.D.A. St. John's College Register 1854-1873, p.669. 181.Ibid., 182.W.D.A. St. St. John's College Register 1826-1854,p.127. 183.W.D.A. St. John's College Register 1854-1873,p.394, Hamell, sequence no.1624. 184.Clare Champion 14/7/1923. 185.Hamell,sequence no.1657. 186.Nenagh Guardian 6/1/1940. 187.Ibid., 188.Ibid., and Hamell, sequence no.1682. 189.Information supplied to the author by the parish priest in 1975.

above. 196.C.D.A. Canon Fogarty's Notebook no.6(not paginated). 197.W.D.A. St. John's College Register 1826-1854,p.123. 198.Hamell,sequence no.1747. 199.Table 11,p. 20 above. 200.Nationalist 31/5/1916. 201.Ibid., 202. Power p. 92. 203. Ibid., also W.D.A. Delaney's letter of resignation 27/1/1881. 204.Table 11,p. 20 above. 205.Table 11,p. 20 above. 206.Hamell, sequence no.1886. 207.Ibid., sequence no.1935. 208.Tipperary Advocate 20/11/1886. 209.Ibid., 210.Limerick Reporter 28/10/1851. 211.Hamell, sequence no.1983. 212.Nationalist 18/6/1919. 213.W.D.A. St. John's College Register 1872-1888,p.195. 214.Ibid., 215.Ibid., and Nationalist 18/6/1919. 216.Table 11, p. 20 above. 217.The information about the public house supplied to the author by Fr. Bacon C.C. Cashel. (The remainder in Skehan's index). 218.Table 11, p. 20 above. 219.Hamell, sequence no. 2177. 220.Information supplied to the author by the parish priest in 1975. 221.Table 11, p. 20 above. 222. Hamell, sequence no.2176. 223.Table 11, p. 20 above. 224.Hamell, sequence no. 2229. 225.W.D.A. St. John's College Register 1854-1873,p.40. 226.W.D.A. Confidential Register, Bishop's House, Waterford,(not open for inspection). 227.Nationalist 10/3/1915. 228.Ibid., 229.W.D.A. St. John's College Register 1854-1873, p.443. 230.Ibid.,231.Nationalist 10/3/1915. 232.Ibid., 233.Hamell, sequence no.2297. 234.As in n18. 235.Do 236.Do. 237.Table 11,p. 20 above. 238.W.D.A. St. John's College Register 1826-1854,p.95. 239.Table 11, p. 20 above. 240.W.D.A. Letter of resignation 9/1/1874, also Burke, op.cit., p. 281 also Tipperary Free Press 19/12/1876, Tipperary Free Press 26/6/1877. 241.Catholic Record, Vol.V, March 1917-Feb.1918. p.380. 242.W.D.A. Confidential Register, (n226), also Nationalist 29/8/1917. 243.Ibid., 244.Nationalist 29/8/1917. 245. Ibid., 246.Tipperary Free Press 5/10/1866. (Christian name not given in the Catholic Directory). 247.Hamell, sequence no.2454. 248.Table 11, p. 20 above. 249.Hamell, sequence no.2476. 250.Table 11, p. 20 above. 251.Hamell, sequence no.2480.252.Table 11,p. 20 above. 253.Hamell, sequence no.2484. 254.Table 11, p. 20 above. 255.Hamell, sequence no. 2483. 256.Table 11, p. 20 above, C.D.A. Canon Fogarty's Notebook no.3 (not paginated). 257. Freemans Journal 11/4/1884. 258.Tipperary Leader 12/4/1884. 259.Ibid., and W.D.A. St. John's College Register 1826-1854, p.79. 260.Table 11, p. 20 above. 261.Hamell, sequence no.2552. 262.Information supplied to the author in 1975. 263.Hamell, sequence no. 2535. 264.Ibid., sequence no.2536. 265.K.P.Bishop Dominick O'Brien to Kirby 16/12/1872, Power p.122. 266.Clare Champion 14/7/1923. 267.Hamell, sequence no.2656. 268.Nationalist 14/12/1918. 269.Ibid., 270.Hamell, sequence no.2662. 271.Nationalist 14/12/1918. 272.Hamell. sequence no.2701. 273.Clonmel Chronicle 22/7/1911. 274.Ibid., Power, op. cit., p.198. 275.Clonmel Chronicle 22/7/1911. 276.Hamell,sequence no.2700. 277.Catholic Record, Vol.VII, March 1919-Feb.1920,p.34. 278.W.D.A. Confidential Register,(n226). 279.Tipperary Free Press 21/7/1876. 280.Clare Journal 12/1/1903. 281.Ibid., 282.Ibid.,Hamell, sequence no.2718. 283.Table 11, p. 20 above. 284.Irish Catholic Directory 1955, p.220. 285.Ibid., 286.Tipperary Star 29/10/1955. 287.Hamell, sequence no.2719. 288.Irish Catholic Directory 1955,p.220. 289.Hamell, sequence no.2734. 290.Hamell, sequence no.2743. 291.W.D.A. St. John's College Register 1826-1854, p.195. 292.Ibid., 293.Hamell, sequence no.2753. 294. Power, p. 84. 295. Hamell. sequence no.2790. 296.As in n18. 297.do. and Clare Journal 11/4/1904. 298.do. and Ibid., 299.Table 11, p. 20 above. 300.Table 11, p. 20 above. 301.Hamell, sequence no. 2914. 302.Ibid., sequence no.2975. 303.Information supplied to the author by the parish priest in 1975. 304. Hamell, sequence no.3020. 305.Clare Champion 19/3/1927. 306.Ibid., 307.Hamell, sequence no.3021,Gleeson, History of Ely, op.cit.,p.212. 308. Clare Champion 19/3/1927.(309-311 errors). 312.Clare Champion 18/6/1921. 313. Ibid., 314.Ibid., 315.Table 11,p.20 above. 316.Table 11,p.20 above. 317.S.P.O. C.B.S. Reports 1890-91,Carton 9, Div. Report Aug.1890. 318. Limerick Reporter 8/10/1852. 319.Hamell, sequence no.3038. 320. Ibid.,sequence no.3181. 321.Ibid., sequence no.3188. 322.Information given to author by Fr. Bacon C.C. Cashel. 323.Skehan's Index incorrectly shows the birthplace as Piercetown, Thurles. The family moved there in later years. Information given to author by Mr. William Hackett, Thurles. See n325. 324. Hamell,sequence no.319. 325.Table 11,p.20 above. 326. Nationalist 26/8/1891. 327. W.D.A. St. John's College Register 1826-1854,p.97. 328. Clare Champion 14/2/1925.

no.3250. 334.Information supplied to the author by Fr. Bacon C.C.Cashel. 335. Nationalist 6/4/1912. 336.W.D.A. St. John's College Register 1826-1854, p.93. 337.Table 11, p.20 above. 338.Tipperary Free Press 5/3/'75. 339.Nationalist 6/4/1912. 340.Hamell, sequence no.3245. 341.Nationalist 6/4/1912. 342.Table 11, p.20 above. 343.Hamell, sequence no.3364. 344.Table 11, p.20 above,also information from Fr. Bacon C.C. Cashel. 345.Clare Journal 8/1/1906. 346.Ibid., 347.Ibid., 348.Skehan's Index refers to this. Some of Hayes letters in the Mooresfort Papers are on Hayes Hotel notepaper. 349.Tipperary Nationalist 28/12/1889. 350.Hamell, sequence no. 3372. 351.Information supplied to author by parish priest in 1975. 352.Hamell, sequence no.3376. 353.Ibid., sequence nos.3229 and 3410. (Cross referenced between Haly and Healy). 354.C.D.A.St. John's College Register 1854-1873,p.76. 355. Ibid., 356.Hamell, sequence no. 3447. 357.W.D.A. St. John's College Register 1826-1854,p.67. 358.Hamell, sequence no.3449. 359.Tipperary Leader 28/11/1884. 360.Hamell,sequence no.3445. 361.Table 11,p. 20 above. 362.C.D.A. Canon Fogarty's Notebook no.10(not paginated). 363.W.D.A. St. John's College Register 1854-1873, p.358. 364.Ibid., 365.Table 11, p. 20 above. 366.Hamell, sequence no. 3169. 367.Ibid., sequence no.3479. 368.Ibid., sequence no.3510. 369.Ibid., sequence no.3527. 370.Table 11, p.20 above. 371.Information supplied to the author by the parish priest in 1975. 372. Hamell, sequence no. 3513. 373.As in n371. 374.Hamell, sequence no.3518. 375.As in n371. 376.Return of Owners, op.cit.,p.164. 377.W.D.A. St. John's College Register 1826-1854, p.54. 378.Table 11, p. 20 above. 379.Nenagh Guardian 16/11/1929. 380.Ibid., 381.Ibid., and Hamell, sequence no.3588. 382.Clare Journal 4/12/1902. 383.Ibid., 384.Ibid., 385.Ibid., 386.Table 11,p. 20 above. 387.Nation 23/6/1883. 388.Ibid., and Tipperary Advocate 4/8/1883 (His letters). 389.Hamell, sequence no.3648. 390.As in n371. 391. Tipperary Leader 18/4/1884. 392.Hamell, sequence no.3700. 393.Table 11, p.20 above. 394.Hamell, sequence no.3709. 395.W.D.A. St. John's College Register 1814-1822,p.18. 396.W.D.A. His letter of resignation 3/8/1869. 397.Hamell, sequence no.3770. 398.As in n371. 399.C.D.A. Canon Fogarty's Notebook no.10(not paginated). 400.W.D.A. St. John's College Register 1854-1873, p.493, Nationalist 11/4/1931. 401.W.D.A. as in n400. 402. Nationalist 11/4/1931.(Not recorded in Griffiths Valuation). 403.W.D.A. as in n400. 404.Tipperary Free Press 7/7/1852. 405.W.D.A. St. John's College Register 1814-1822,p.47. 406.Tipperary Free Press 7/7/'52. 407.Skehan records as in Index, but Fogarty (Notebook No.10 not paginated records his birthplace as The Commons, Ballingarry). 408.C.D.A. St. John's College Registers 1854-1873, p.413, and 1872-1888,p.62. 409.Ibid.,and Hamell,sequence no.4087. 410.Hamell, sequence no.4160. 411.Ibid.,sequence no.4153. 412.Table 11,p. 20 above. 413.Tipperary Advocate 29/10/1881. 414.Ibid., 415.Ibid., 416.Hamell, sequence no.4154. 417.Nationalist 16/4/1890. 418.Hamell, sequence no.4189. 419.Hamell, sequence no. 4178. 420.Gleeson,History of Ely O'Carroll,op.cit.,p.226. 421.Hamell, sequence no.4198. 422.Table 11, p. 21 above. 423.Biographical details of Kenyon in D.F. Gleeson, "Fr. John Kenyon and Young Ireland", Studies XXXV No.137, March 1946. Vid. also Hamell, sequence no. 4203, and Nenagh Guardian 13/1/1940. 424.Table 11, p. 21 above.425.K.P. James J. Ryan, St. Patrick's College, Thurles to Kirby 28/2/1884. 426.Tipperary People 10/7/1891. 427.Clare Journal 12/8/1912. 428.Ibid., 429.Ibid., also Hamell, sequence no.4306. 430.Hamell, sequence no.4327. 431.W.D.A. St. John's College Register 1872-1888,p.80. 432.Ibid., 433.Ibid., 434.Hamell, sequence no.4333. 435.Ibid., sequence no.4350. 436.Table 11, p. 21 above. 437.Hamell, sequence no.4349. 438.C.D.A. Canon Fogarty's Notebook No.10(Not paginated). 439.Ibid., 440.Hamell, sequence no.4351. 441.Ibid., sequence no.4348. 442.Table 11,p. 21 above. 443.Hamell, sequence no.4391. 444.Ibid., sequence no.4390. 445.Table 11, p. 21 above. 446.W.D.A. St. John's College Register 1872-1888,p.74. 447.Ibid., 448.Hamell, sequence no.4398. 449.Table 11, p. 21 above. 450.P.P. 1826-27(509)XIII, op.cit.,p.424. Hamell, sequence no.4458. 451.Ibid., 452. Tipperary Free Press 2/9/1854. 453.Limerick Reporter 1/9/1854. 454.W.D.A. St. John's College Register 1826-1854,p.135,Hamell, sequence no.4491. 455.Hamell, sequence no.4536. 456.Clare Journal 3/1/1910. 457.Ibid., 458. Hamell, sequence no.4545. 459.W.D.A.St. John's College Register 1872-1888,p.643. 460.Ibid., 461.Table 11,p. 21 above. 462.Hamell,sequence no.4563. 463.W.D.A. Letter of resignation 22/4/1872. 464.W.D.A.St. John's College Register 1822-1826,p.122.

465.Clonmel Chronicle 11/11/1903. 466.Ibid., also W.D.A.St. John's College Register 1826-1854,p.297. 467.Ibid., and Ibid., 468.Clonmel Chronicle 11/11/1903. 469.W.D.A. St. John's College Register 1854-1873, p.20, Hamell, sequence no.4597. 470.Hamell, sequence no.4645. 471.C.D.A. C.F. Letter 17/5/1888. 472.Clare Champion 15/9/1934. 473.Ibid., 474.W.D.A. St. John's College Register 1854-1873,p.353. 475.Ibid., 476.Tipperary Star 12/12/1914. 477.Hamell, sequence no.4925. 478.Ibid.,sequence no. 4956. 479.Ibid., sequence no.5076. 480.Table 11, p.21 above. 481.Hamell, sequence no.5080. 482. Burke, op.cit., p.283. 483.Ibid., 484.Hamell, sequence no.5078. 485.Ibid., sequence no.5301. 486.Ibid., sequence no. 5296. 487.Table 11, p.21 above. 488.Tipperary Free Press 16/10/1866 amends Catholic Directory. 489.Hamell, sequence no. 5295 and 5868 (Cross-ref. with McGrath). 490.Information supplied to author by parish priest in 1975. 491.Hamell, sequence no.5288. 492.As in n490. 493.Tipperary Advocate 2/2/1884. 494.Ibid., 495.Ibid., and K.P.Bishop James Ryan, Killaloe to Kirby 9/12/1878. 496.Hamell, sequence no.5294. 497.Ibid., sequence no.5297. 498.As in n490. 499.Limerick Reporter 13/6/1890. 500.Hamell, sequence no.5293. 501.Tipperary Free Press 17/11/1865. 502.W.D.A. Letter of resignation 10/10/1864. 503.Clonmel Chronicle 11/1/1911. 504.Ibid., 505.Ibid., and Hamell,sequence no.5299. 506.Table 11, p. 21 above. 507.Freemans Journal 21/11/1887. 508. Clare Journal 4/12/1899. 509.Ibid., also Hamell, sequence no.5433. 510.Clare Journal 30/11/1899. 511.Nenagh News 21/2/1920. 512.W.D.A. St. John's College Register 1854-1873, p.292. 513.Tipperary Advocate 1/11/1884, Bessborough Commission, op.cit.,pp.1175-1176. 514.C.D.A.C.P. Notes by Croke June-Oct.1875, also McKeogh to Croke 30/8/1877, also Canon Fogarty's Notebook No.16(Not paginated). 515.Freemans Journal 27/10/1868, Tipperary Advocate 9/10/1869, Nenagh Guardian 6/10/1869.(amends Irish Catholic Directory). 516.As in n18. 517.Clare Champion 17/10/1942. 518.As in n516,517. 519.Table 11, p. 21 above. 520.Nenagh Guardian 16/1/1932. 521.Ibid., 522. Ibid.,also Hamell, sequence no.5565. 523.Clare Journal 8/11/1900. 524.Hamell, sequence no.5649. 525.Clare Champion 13/10/1923. 526.Ibid., 527.Hamell, sequence no.5646. 528.As in n525. 529.Clare Journal 7/4/1904. 530. Ibid., 531.Ibid., and Boyle, op.cit., p.108. 532.As in n529,(amends Catholic Directory). 533.Hamell, sequence no.5475. 534.Table 11, p.21 above. 535.C.D.A. C.P. Note by Croke 6/1/1888. 536.Hamell, sequence no.5783. 537.Ibid., sequence no.5962. 538.Ibid., sequence no.5961. 539.Limerick Reporter 7/12/1885,(Different date in Tipperary Advocate 4/12/1875). 540.Ibid., 541.Nenagh Guardian 30/1/1892. 542.Ibid., 543.Hamell, sequence no.6013. 544.Table 11, p. 21 above. 545.Hamell, sequence no.6056. 546.W.D.A. St. John's College Register 1826-1854,p.98. 547.Hamell, sequence no.6064. 548.Limerick Reporter 28/10/1851, Hamell, sequence no.6067. 549.Hamell, sequence no. 5940 (Maher in Hamell). 550.Table 11,p. 21 above. 551.Tablet 28/8/1880, Hamell, sequence no.5939. 552.Table 11,p. 21 above.553.Table 11,p. 21 above. 554.W.D.A. St. John's College Register 1854-1873,p.362. 555.Letter from Bishop's Secretary to the author 24/11/1976. 556.Clonmel Chronicle 9/9/1893. 557.Hamell, sequence no.6087. 558.Nenagh Guardian 19/12/1921. 559.Hamell, sequence no.6075. 560.Ibid.,sequence no.5944. 561.Ibid., sequence nos.5927,6082(Cross ref. with Maher). 562.Information supplied to the author in 1975. 563.Hamell, sequence no. 5943. 564.Table 11, p. 21 above. 565.Hamell, sequence no.6080. 566.Ibid., sequence no.5930. 567.Table 11, p. 21 above. 568.Hamell, sequence no. 5937. 569.C.D.A. Canon Fogarty's Notebook, No.10 (Not paginated). 570.Table 11, p. 21 above. 571.As in n569. 572.W.D.A. St. John's College Register 1854-1873,p.362. 573.Ibid., and Nationalist 17/11/1923. 574.Nationalist 10/5/1919, also Table 11, p. 22 above. 575.S.P.O. I.N.L. Papers C.B.S. 1890 355 1/4/1890, Nationalist 20/2/1890, Nationalist 8/4/1891. 576.Hamell, sequence no.5936. 577.C.D.A. Canon Fogarty's Notebook No.16(not paginated). 578.Ibid., 579.Tipperary Nationalist 17/8/1889. 580.Ibid., 581.W.D.A. St. John's College Register 1826-1854, p.48. 582.Table 11, p. 22 above. Tipperary Nationalist 17/8/1889. 583. Power op.cit.,p. 135. 584.Hamell,sequence no.6106. 585.C.D.A. Canon Fogarty's Notebook No.16,(Not paginated). 586.Table 11, p. 22 above. 587.Hamell, sequence no.6160. 588. Table 11, p. 22 above. 589.Tipperary Advocate 10/4/1880. 590.Hamell, sequence no.6191. 591.Nenagh Guardian 15/1/1876. 592.Hamell, sequence no.6207. 593.Ibid., sequence no.6168. [illegible]

602.Hamell, sequence no.6326. 603.As in n601. 604.Nationalist 11/3/1891, Power op.cit.,p.96-97. 605.Hamell, sequence no.6336. 606.W.D.A. St. John's College Register 1854-1873,p.490, Nationalist 7/6/1890. 607.Ibid., 608.Table 11, p. 22 above. 609.Nationalist 7/6/1890,Nationalist 20/7/'12. 610.W.D.A. St. John's College Register 1854-1873,p.491, Nationalist 7/6/1890. 611.Ibid., 612.Tipperary Leader 25/7/1884. 613.Tipperary Advocate 23/1/1886(corrects Irish Catholic Directory).614.Table 11,p. 22 above. 615.As in n18. 616.do. 617.do. 618. W.D.A. St. John's College Register 1826-1854,p.113. 619.Hamell, sequence no.6419. 620.Ibid., sequence no.6431. 621.W.D.A.St. John's College Register 1872-1888,p.92. 622.Ibid., 623.Ibid., 624.Nationalist 2/8/1890. 625.Table 11,p. 22 above. 626.Tablet 17/2/1855. 627.Hamell, sequence no.6475. 628.Table 11, p. 22 above. 629.As in n626. 630.Hamell, sequence no.6474. 631.Ibid.,sequence no.6483. 632.Ibid., sequence no.6521A. 633.Table 11,p. 22 above. 634.Hamell, sequence no.6597. 635.Information supplied to author by parish priest in 1975. 636.Clare Journal 8/10/1900. 637.Ibid., 638.Hamell, sequence no.6560. 639.Clare Champion 4/4/1936. 640.Ibid., 641.Ibid.,also Hamell, sequence no.6661. 642.As in n639. 643.do. 644.Hamell, sequence no. 6686. 645.Tipperary Advocate 5/6/1886. 646.Ibid., 647.Hamell, sequence no. 6736. 648.Clare Journal 27/3/1913. 649.Ibid., 650.Ibid.,also Hamell, sequence no.6776. 651.As in n648. 652.Tipperary Advocate 9/10/1886. 653.Tipperary Advocate 6/4/1861. 654.Table 11, p. 22 above. 655. Information supplied by the parish priest in 1975. 656.Hamell, sequence no.6909. 657.W.D.A. St. John's College Register 1854-1873,p.167. 658.Ibid., 659.Clonmel Chronicle 18/2/1896. 660.Table 11,p. 22 above. 661.Tipperary Star 5/12/1910. 662.C.D.A. Fogarty's Notebook,No.6, not paginated, Hamell, sequence no.9259(in Addenda section). 663.Table 11,p. 22 above. 664.As in n661. 665.Hamell, sequence no.6868. 666.Table 11,p. 22 above. 667.Hamell, sequence no.6865. 668.Ibid., sequence no.6988. 669.Table 11, p. 22 above. 670.Table 11, p. 22 above. 671.Hamell, sequence no.6984. 672.Information from parish priest in 1975. 673.Bourke op.cit., p. 282. 674.Ibid., 675.Ibid., and Hamell, sequence no.6985. 676.Power,op.cit., p.80. 677.Hamell, sequence no.7018. 678.Ibid., sequence no.7050. 679.Ibid., sequence no.7067. 680.Table 11,p. 22 above. 681.C.D.A. Fogarty's Notebook 16(not paginated), Hamell, secuence no.7017. 682.Fogarty as in n681. 683.Hamell, sequence no.7053. 684.Information from parish priest in 1975. 685.W.D.A. St. John's College Register 1826-1854,p.144. 686.Ibid., 687.Hamell, sequence no.7138. 688.Tipperary Free Press 6/6/1876. 689.P.P. 1854/55, XXII, op.cit.,p.296, Hamell, sequence no.7146. 690.Hamell, sequence no.7152. 691.Ibid., sequence nos. 5072,7139(Cross-ref. with McDonnell). 692.Tipperary Star 4/2/1933. 693.W.D.A. St. John's College Rctister 1872-1888,p.448 and Tipperary Star 4/2/1933. 694.Ibid., 695.Table 11, p. 22 above. 696.As in n692. 697.Hamell, sequence no.2264. 698.Table 11,p. 22 above. 699.W.D.A. St. John's College Register 1854-1873,p.284, Hamell, sequence no.2265. 700.Table 11,p. 22 above. 701.W.D.A. As in n699. 702.W.D.A. Confidential Register (n226). 703.Power,op.cit., p. 135. 704.Clare Journal 14/2/1910. 705.Ibid., 706.Ibid.,also Hamell, sequence no.7282. 707.Table 11, p. 22 above. 708.As in n704. 709. Clonmel Chronicle 13/4/1901. 710.W.D.A. St. John's College Register 1854-1872,p.10. 711. Clare Champion 22/3/1924. 712.As in n18 and n711. 713.do. and K.P. Bishop James Ryan to Kirby 13/2/1873. 714. Table 11, p. 22 above. 715.Hamell, sequence no.3812. 716.Information supplied by the parish priest in 1975. 717.Hamell, sequence nos.3816,7370(cross-ref. O'Kane/Kane. 718.Ibid., sequence nos.3852,4378(cross-ref.) 719.Ibid., sequence no.3815 (Addenda section). 720. Ibid., sequence no. 721.Information supplied by the parish priest in 1975.Vid. also Nenagh Guardian 2/2/1887 on the Camus farm. 722.Hamell,sequence no.7424. 723.Ibid.,sequence no.7441. 724.Ibid., sequence no.5967. 725.As in n721. 726.Tipperary Free Press 22/4/1879. 727.Tipperary Advocate 19/4/1879. 728.As in n727. 729.Clare Journal 28/7/1913. 730.Hamell, sequence no.7496. 731.Ibid.,sequence no.7518. 732.Midland Tribune 28/11/1891. 733.Irish Catholic Directory 1852,p.219, Hamell, sequence no.7512. 734.Hamell, sequence no.7509. 735.Clare Champion 26/3/1927. 736.Hamell, sequence no. 7517. 737.As in n735. 738.Table 11, p 22 above. 739. W.D.A.St. John's College Register 1854-1873,p.154. 740.W.D.A. St. John's College Register 1826-1854,p.138. 741.Table 11, p. 22 above. 742.C.D.A. Fogarty's Notebook No.3(not paginated).743.Hamell,sequence no.7543. 744.Table 11, p. 22 above. 745.C.D.A. Fogarty's Notebook No.10(not paginated).Hamell.

751.Clonmel Chronicle 14/10/1891. 752.Nationalist 14/10/1891. 753.Hamell, sequence no.7886. 754.As in n751 and 752. 755.As in n751,also Tipperary Nationalist 30/11/1889. 756.As in n751 and 752. 757.K.P. Phelan to Kirby 10/6/1877. 758.W.D.A.St. John's College Register 1826-1854,p.138. K.P. as in n757. 759.Kings County Chronicle 4/6/1903. 760.Ibid., 761.Ibid., and Hamell, sequence no.7883. 762.Clonmel Chronicle 22/10/1902. 763.W.D.A. St. John's College Register 1854-1873,p.35. 764.Ibid., 765.Hamell,sequence no. 7343. 766.Ibid., sequence no.7935. 767.Ibid., sequence no. 7941. 768.Bourke,op.cit., p.283. 769.Bourke,op.cit.,p.283,770.Ibid., 771.Table 11,p. 22 above.772.Hamell,sequence no.7958. 773.Ibid.,sequence no.7952. 774.Table 11, p.22 above. Tipperary People 23/10/1883. 775.Hamell, sequence no.7959. 776.Information supplied by the parish priest. 777.W.D.A. St. John's College Register 1872-1888,p.513. 778.Ibid., 779.Nationalist 1/7/1916. 780.W.D.A. St. John's College Register 1854-1873,p.692. 781.Ibid., 782. Hamell, sequence no.7944. 783.Ibid., sequence no.7937. 784.As in n776. 785.Nationalist 20/3/1912. 786.Ibid., and W.D.A. St. John's College Register 1854-1873, p.543. 787.W.D.A. As in n786. 788. Table 11, p. 22 above. 789.W.D.A. St. John's College Register 1854-1873, p.484. 790.Ibid., 791.Tipperary Free Press 7/9/1858,Tipperary Nationalist 25/5/1889. Power op.cit., p. 40. 792.Power,op.cit.,p.40. 793.Nationalist 5/3/1924. 794.Ibid., 795.Ibid., 796.Ibid., 797.Clonmel Chronicle 28/9/1895. 798.Hamell, sequence no.7957. 799.Tipperary Leader 30/5/1884. 800.Ibid., 801.Ibid., 802.W.D.A. St. John's College Register 1854-1873,p.481. 803.Ibid., 804.W.D.A. St. John's College Register 1872-1888 p.284. 805.Ibid., 806.Hamell, sequence no.7954. 807.Information supplied by the parish priest in 1975. 808.Irish Catholic Directory 1853, p.239. 809.Hamell, sequence no.7976. 810.Table 11,p.23 above. 811. Nenagh Guardian 6/1/1892. 812.Ibid., 813.Ibid., 814.W.D.A. St. John's College Register 1872-1888,p.284. 815.Ibid., 816.W.D.A. St. John's College Register 1826-1854,p.136. 817.W.D.A. St. John's College Register 1854-1873,p.238. 818. Ibid., 819.Hamell, sequence no.8023. 820.Table 11, p. 23 above. 821.W.D.A. St. John's College Register 1854-73, p.47. 822.Ibid., 823.Hamell, sequence no.8101. 824.Table 11,p. 23 above. 825.Hamell, sequence no.8099. 826.Table 11,p. 23 above. 827.Hamell, sequence no.8107. 828.Table 11, p.23 above. 829.Hamell, sequence no. 8109. 830.Information supplied by the parish priest. 831.Hamell,sequence no.8384. 832.Letter of his relation, Archdeacon Ryan to author 14/2/1976. 833.C.D.A. Fogarty's Notebook No.16 (not paginated). 834.Table 11,p. 23 above. 835.C.D.A. Fogarty's Notebook 6(not paginated). 836.Ibid., 837.Information supplied by the Parish priest in 1975. 838.Tipperary Advocate 27/7/1887. 839.Ibid., 840.Ibid., 841.Tablet 9/12/1871. 842.Tipperary People 29/5/1885. 843.Ibid., 844.Ibid.,Hamell, sequence no. 8395. 845.As in n842, Table 11, p.23 above. 846.As in n842. 847.Hamell, sequence no.8356. 848.Ibid., sequence no. 8375. 849.Information supplied by the parish priest in 1975. 850.W.D.A. St. John's College Register 1854-1873,p.280. 851.Ibid., Hamell, sequence no.8391. 852.Ibid., 853.Nenagh Guardian 28/2/1946. 854.Ibid., 855.Ibid., also Hamell,sequence no.8404. 856.Hamell, sequence no.8392. 857.Table 11,p. 23 above. 858.Nationalist 31/12/1890. 859.Hamell, sequence no.8407. 860.Information supplied by the parish priest in 1975. 861.Hamell, sequence no.8364. 862.Table 11, p. 23 above. 863.Table 11, p. 23 above. N.L.I.Monsell Papers,ms.20677(1) Bishop George Butler, Limerick to Monsell 18/3/1873. 864.Nationalist 24/12/1890, C.D.A. Fogarty's Notebook No.16(not paginated). 865.Tierney, Murroe and Boher, op.cit.,p.83. 866.Hamell, sequence no. 8379. 867.Table 11, p.23 above. 868.Hamell, sequence no.8365. 869.Ibid., sequence no.8371. 870.Hamell, sequence no.8414. 871.Table 11,p.23 above. 872.Hamell, sequence no.8382. 873.Information supplied by the parish priest in 1975. 874.Hamell, sequence no.8366. 875.Information supplied by the parish priest in 1975. 876.Hamell, sequence no.8402. 877.Limerick Reporter 4/9/1860. 878.Ibid., 879.Clare Journal 21/5/1903. 880.Ibid., 881.Hamell, sequence no.8471. 882.Freemans Journal 22/12/1916. 883.Ibid., 884.Ibid., also Hamell, sequence no.8462. 885.As in n882,also Table 11, p. 23 above. 886.As in n882. 887.Hamell, sequence no.8459. 888.Clare Champion 26/12/1931. 889.Ibid., 890.Ibid., also Hamell, sequence no.8463. 891.As in n888. 892.Tipperary Advocate 16/2/1889. 893.Hamell,sequence no. 8458. 894.Table 11, p.23 above. 895.As in n892. 896.Hamell, sequence no. 8461. 897.Table 11,p. 23 above. 898.Clare Journal 22/1/1917. 899.Table 11,p.23 above. 900.C.D.A. Fogarty's Notebook,No.10(not paginated).

905.Ibid., 906.Hamell, sequence no.8566. 907.W.D.A. St. John's College
Register 1854-1873,p.313. 908.Ibid., also Hamell, sequence no.8567.
909.Nationalist 4/4/1891. 910.Hamell, sequence no.8570. 911.As in n909.
912.Information from parish priest in 1975. 913.Table 11,p. 23 above.
914.Nemagh Guardian 9/3/1887. 915.Clonmel Chronicle 28/2/1894. 916.Ibid.,
917.Tipperary Free Press 6/3/1857. 918.Hamell, sequence no.8680. 919.Ibid.,
sequence no.8687. 920.Ibid., sequence no.8678. 921.W.D.A. St. John's
College Register 1826-1854,p.126. 922.Hamell, sequence no.8791.
923.Nationalist 10/12/1919. 924.Ibid., 925.Ibid., 926.Table 11,p. 23
above. 927.Clare Journal 12/8/1912. 928.Ibid., 929.Ibid.,also Hamell,
sequence nos.8334,8843 (cross-ref.) 930.As in n927,also Table 11,p. 23
above. 931.Hamell, sequence no.8856. 932.Clare Journal 23/7/1894.933.Ibid.,
also Hamell, sequence no.8868. 934.W.D.A. Confidential Register (n226).
935.Hamell, sequence no.8908. 936.Ibid., sequence no.8925. 937.As in n18.
938.do. 939.Table 11,p. 23 above. 940.Hamell, sequence no.8945.941.Ibid.,
sequence no.8977. 942.Ibid.., sequence nos.8979,8980(cross-ref.) 943.Table
11,p. 23 above. 944.Irish Catholic Directory,1860,p.267. 945.Hamell,
sequence no.9009. 946.Clare Journal 13/9/1906. 947.Hamell,sequence no.
9014. 948.Table 11,p. 24 above. 949.As in n946. 950.W.D.A. St. John's
College Register 1854-1873,p.526. 951.Ibid.,also Hamell, sequence no.
9040A. 952.Table 11, p. 24 above. 953.Midland Tribune 24/1/1891.
954.Hamell, sequence no.9047. 955.As in n953. 956.Hamell, sequence no.
9042. 957.Ibid.,sequence no.9048. 958.Information from the parish priest
in 1975. 959.Tierney, Murroe and Boher,op.cit.,p.82. 960.Hamell,sequence
no.9099. 961.Ibid., sequence no.9081. 962.Waterford News and General
Advertiser 24/7/1885, Bourke,op.cit.,p. 282. 963.Bourke, as in n962.
964.Bourke, as in n 962. 965.Clonmel Chronicle 29/1/1913. 966.Ibid.,
also Catholic Record, Vol.I, March 1913-Feb.1914,p.2. 967.Catholic Record
as in n966. 968.As in n965. 969.Nationalist 13/2/1935. 970.Ibid.,
971.Ibid.,also Hamell, sequence no.9128. 972.Table 11,p. 24 above.
973.Nationalist 2/9/1942. 974.Ibid., 975.Hamell, sequence no.9127.
976.As in n973. 977.Hamell, sequence no.9118. 970.Clonmel Chronicle
4/11/1903. 979.Ibid., 980.W.D.A. Confidential Register (n226). 981.
Hamell, sequence no.9105. 982.Ibid., sequence no.9234. 983.Nationalist
24/6/1890.

Index

361